INTRODUCTORY RUSSIAN GRAMMAR

Galina Stilman and William E. Harkins

both of *Columbia University*

BLAISDELL PUBLISHING COMPANY

A Division of Ginn and Company

New York Toronto London

First Edition, 1964

Library of Congress Catalog Card Number: **63-7428**

PREFACE

This Russian text attempts to combine the advantages of the traditional grammatical approach to the study of a foreign language with certain features of the modern conversational, inductive method. Basic to this combined approach is the use of a great number and variety of pattern sentences: short, typical Russian sentences which can be used in different ways to provide concentrated and appropriate material for language analysis, reading, and drill. In addition to pattern sentences, all units have been provided with dialogues or readings, often with both. A great variety of drill materials has also been supplied. Thus the book can be used as a first-year textbook which is complete in itself, and does not require either a reader or a workbook to accompany it.

The book has been divided into twenty-seven units. Each unit is intended to correspond roughly to one week of a first-year language course on the college level, so that it is possible to finish the book in two semesters of college study, allowing time for review and examinations.

Each unit is divided into sections containing grammar, dialogues and readings, exercises, and vocabulary. The grammar section is in turn divided into topical sub-units, each of which is provided with its own pattern sentences. This division permits maximum flexibility, since most grammar topics in a given unit are followed immediately by drill material which can be assigned as homework.

It is obvious that the actual use of the book depends very much on the teacher's preferences and method of instruction employed. Teachers who prefer a more inductive approach may stress memorization of and reproduction in class of much of the pattern sentence and dialogue material, while those who follow a more grammatical approach may prefer to use these sections only for illustration and analysis. The number and types of drills and exercises covered in class or assigned as homework will also depend on the preference of the teacher and the method followed, as well as on the amount of class time available.

One important feature of the book is the slow, careful, and systematic presentation of the verbal aspects. By breaking aspect formation into several morphological patterns, we have, we believe, greatly simplified the presentation of one of the most difficult subjects in the teaching of Russian.

Another important advantage is the systematic presentation of phonetics and alphabet as part of the lessons themselves, rather than as a separate section, cut off from grammar and vocabulary. Thus the student learns new letters and sounds as he learns the language itself, not as abstract, unrelated material.

A systematic presentation of the script, proceeding from familiar to unfamiliar letters, has been placed between Units 3 and 4, at the conclusion of the presentation of the printed alphabet and phonetics; ample exercises have been provided.

The authors believe that the learning of the pronunciation of Russian is significantly aided by the use of a phonetic transcription, which is employed as an auxiliary used side by side with the orthographic presentation. Phonetic transcription is especially useful as a reminder to the student of certain phonetic features of the language not represented by its spelling, e.g., the reduction of certain vowels by *akanie* and *ikanie*, unvoicing, etc. It has also made the presentation of certain morphological patterns simpler, *e.g.*, the conjugation of verbs, the genitive plural, etc. In devising a system of phonetic transcription we have consciously tried to restrict the use of unfamiliar symbols to a minimum.

The treatment of stress on monosyllabic words requires some comment. The authors were dissatisfied with the general practice of not indicating stress on monosyllables, since in certain contexts many of them are stressed. Furthermore, there is an intermediate stage in which the vowel of a monosyllabic word is not stressed, but still does not undergo reduction by *akanie* or *ikanie*, *e.g.*, the pronouns он and я in certain contexts. Two signs would have been required to indicate these several degrees of reduction. Rather than introduce a system so complicated, we have preferred to follow the practice of indicating as stressed (′) all monosyllabic words which do not undergo vowel reduction.

The vocabulary used is entirely contemporary, and in the choice of words an effort has been made to take into account indications of word-frequency count. Vocabulary reviews have been incorporated, on the average, in every fifth unit. The total vocabulary employed includes approximately 1300 words. A few story-telling words in the later units are marked in vocabularies with an asterisk (*); this indicates that they need not be memorized for active use. A few other such words which are obvious cognates of English are not listed in vocabularies.

The authors acknowledge with sincere gratitude their debt to the many friends and colleagues who have provided helpful advice and criticism. First of all must be mentioned their very great debt to Professor Leon Stilman, who has written a large part of the material on phonetics and grammar, and who has made so many helpful suggestions on all phases of the book that he must be accounted its virtual third author. To Professor Francis J. Whitfield and Dr. Allen R. Taylor of the University of California, and to Professor Edward J. Brown of Brown University, we are also much indebted for helpful advice. To our publishers, and especially to our editor, Mrs. Helen M. LaFleur, we express our thanks for their kind and efficient cooperation and assistance. This work in a preliminary version was used for three years at Columbia University and Barnard College, and at the University of California and Brown University, and to all our colleagues who made suggestions for its improvement on the basis of their experimentation with the book we owe our deep gratitude.

December, 1963
Columbia University

Galina Stilman
William E. Harkins

CONTENTS

Some Suggestions for the Use of This Book

The combination of grammar explanation, pattern sentences, drills, readings, and questions provided in each unit of this book constitutes an integrated whole. Though the amount of time and emphasis devoted to each of these sections may vary, no one of these parts should be sacrificed for another.

1. Every grammar explanation given in class should be followed at once with drills supplied after each grammar topic. This will give an active check and will help the instructor and the student to ascertain if the explanation has been correctly understood or if additional explanation is required. It will also give the student the satisfaction of being able to apply at once and use in practice the knowledge he has freshly acquired.

This functional method will help in the quicker assimilation of the newly presented topic and will make theory more concrete and purposeful.

2. Students should carefully study at home pattern sentences and readings and familiarize themselves with the Russian idioms, speech patterns, and sentence structures embodied in them. They should be prepared to translate quickly and idiomatically from either language into the other. They should be ready to answer in class orally or in writing the questions supplied at the end of each reading. The stories may be also used at the instructor's discretion for reading practice, drill in translation, etc., but they are primarily intended for conversational practice. This can be done first through questions and answers, then, gradually, the students must be able to retell the stories in Russian in their own words. This method will help students to master idioms, vocabulary, and sentence patterns in a more effective and natural, as well as more gratifying way.

3. The transliterated passages provided should be used to remind the student of the principles of Russian phonetics and help him further in mastering pronunciation, which should at no time be neglected.

4. Dialogues may be read or acted out by two or more students.

UNIT I

***Phonetics:* General character of Russian vowels, 2. Accentuation, 2. The vowels [a], [o], [u], 2. The consonant [m], 4. The consonants [p], [k], and [t], 4. The consonants [d], [n], and [l], 5. Pronunciation of consecutive vowels, 5. Other consonants, 6. Unstressed a and o, 7.**

PHONETICS

Introductory. In this and the following units the sounds of the Russian language are presented together with the Russian alphabet as it is used to render these sounds. Russian spelling is far less arbitrary than English, but it is still not a strictly phonetic system. One symbol may have more than one sound value and, conversely, the same sound may be rendered by more than one symbol. This is one of the reasons why it is helpful to use a transcription in which symbols are assigned constant values. Such a transcription is used in this textbook; the value of each symbol will be defined, and transcriptions, whether of separate sounds or of complete words, will always appear in square brackets. The student must remember, for example, that [a] will always be used for the sound "ah," never for *a* as in "at" or in "ate."

There are not many sounds that are exactly alike in English and Russian. In this presentation, Russian sounds are described in terms of their similarities (and dissimilarities) in relation to their closest English equivalents and also in terms of their articulation (position of the tongue, the lips, etc.). With the help of these indications one should be able to approximate correct pronunciation. But it is only through hearing and imitating native speakers that one can advance beyond this "approximate correctness."

1. General character of Russian vowels

Russian, unlike English, does not have "long" and "short" vowels. Most so-called "long" vowels in English are actually diphthongs which combine two sounds; one changing, or "gliding off," into the other (as the vowel sounds in *go out, late hour, poor sight,* etc.). Russian vowels do not have this quality; generally they are not diphthongs, but monophthongs, like Spanish or Italian vowels. Graphically, most English "long" vowels could be compared to curves, Russian vowels to straight lines.

2. Accentuation

Like English, Russian has a strong stress. Only one syllable in a word, however, is accented; secondary accents, such as are often heard in English (*e.g.*, in lábóratòry or sécretàry) must be avoided.[1] In normal connected speech unstressed vowels are somewhat less distinct and only slightly shorter than stressed ones. Some vowels actually change their value when unaccented. The values given below are those of the stressed variant; the unaccented values will be given later.

The stress in Russian falls, in different words, on different syllables, first, last, or any other. Russian texts do not normally use accent marks; in this text, the stress will always be indicated by an accent over the stressed vowel, *e.g.*, **á**—"stressed **a**."

3. The vowels а [a], о [o], and у [u]

А, а—[a]

The Russian letter **а** in stressed syllables stands for the sound heard in *father, palm, car* (in transcriptions [a] will always be used to denote this sound value).

О, о—[o]

A rather close approximation of Russian **о** (stressed) is the vowel sound in words like *war, warm,* and *ward,* pronounced with the initial *w* barely audible. Russian **о** [o] is a back vowel produced with the back portion of the tongue raised toward the soft palate. The lips for this sound protrude somewhat and are rounded (see Illustration 1).

У, у—[u]

This is close to the vowel sound in *woo* or *ooze.* The Russian sound, however, has a deeper, darker quality than the English; this is due to an articulation farther back in the mouth and to more lip rounding. Russian **у** [u] is a back vowel, like [o], but it is produced with the back of the tongue raised more and brought closer to the soft palate than for [o] (see Illustration 2).

[1] A few compound words may have a secondary accent under special conditions; they are an exception.

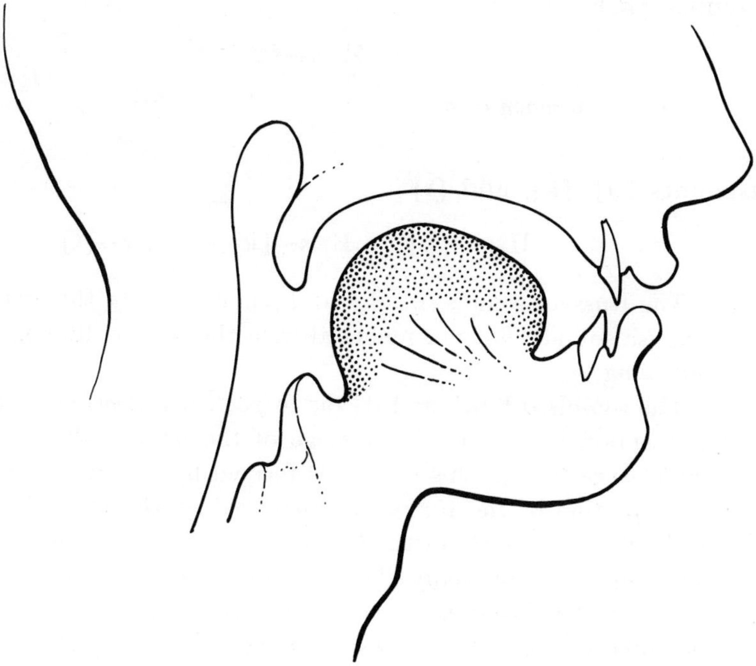

Illustration 1—The Vowel [o]

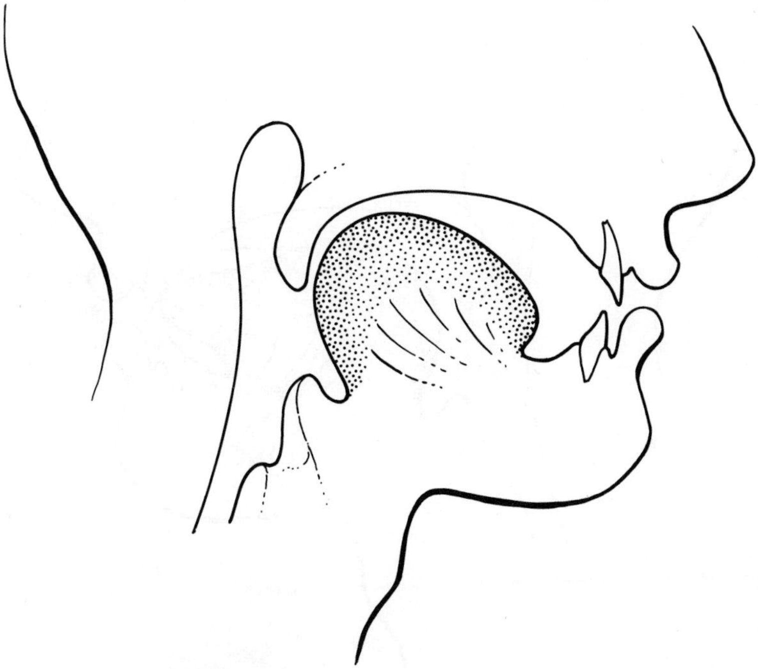

Illustration 2—The Vowel [u]

4. The consonant [m]

М, м—[m]

Like m in *moon* or *swim.*

5. The consonants [p], [k], and [t]

П, п—[p] К, к—[k] Т, т—[t]

The Russian sounds [p], [k], and [t] are close to the corresponding English sounds, but not identical with them; the differences are the following:

The sounds [p], [k], and [t] (as in *pool, cool, tool*) are produced by momentarily blocking the passage of the breath, then "exploding" the closure (for [p] this closure is formed by the lips; for [k] by the back portion of the tongue pressed against the roof of the mouth; and for [t] by the tip of the tongue in the front of the mouth). This mechanism is essentially the same in both languages. In Russian, however, the closure is formed with less tension, and the pressure of the breath, as it "explodes" the closure, is weaker. The result, acoustically, is that in English, aspiration (a short breathing sound)

Illustration 3—The Consonant [t]

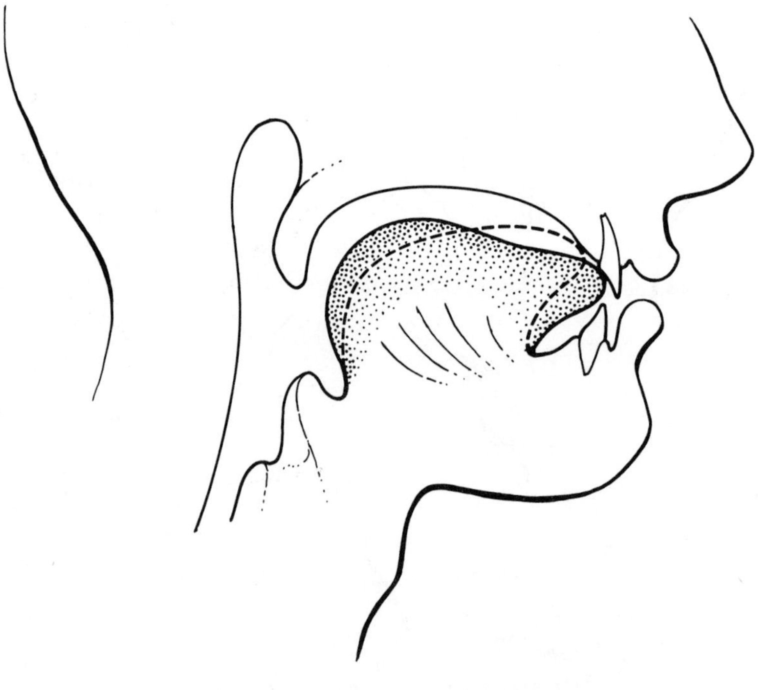

usually accompanies the sounds [p], [k], and [t], especially before stressed vowels. In Russian this aspiration is absent.

For English [t] the tip of the tongue touches the teeth-ridge, just above the inner surface of the upper teeth and gums. For Russian [t] the tip of the tongue contacts the inner surface of the upper teeth themselves. The slight difference in the position of the tongue makes for a perceptibly different quality of the sound (see Illustration 3).

Read the following words, being careful, for [p], [k], and [t], to avoid aspiration, and for [t], to touch the teeth with the tip of the tongue, making the contact lower than in the English articulation.

ТУТ [tút]	here	ТОМ [tóm]	tome	ПАКТ [pákt]	pact
тот	that	там	there	пот	sweat
так	so	ком	lump	па́па	papa
мак	poppy	кум	godfather	пу́ма	puma
как	how	кто	who	ма́ма	mama
кот	tomcat	такт	tact	мука́	flour

6. The consonants [d], [n], and [l]

Д, д—[d] Н, н—[n] Л, л—[l]

As for [t], the tip of the tongue must touch the upper teeth, lower than in the English articulation, for [d], [n], and [l]. Russian [l] in the words listed below, whatever its position in the word, is close to English final *l* as in *bill*.

ДОМ [dóm]	house	НО́ТА [nóta]	note	ЛА́МПА [lámpa]	lamp
да	yes	пол	floor	пла́та	pay
Дон	Don River	па́лка	stick	плато́к	kerchief
ду́ма	thought	он	he	тала́нт	talent
да́ма	lady	по́лка	shelf	кла́пан	valve
Ада́м	Adam	ла́па	paw	тума́н	mist
но	but	план	plan	купо́н	coupon
		ку́кла	doll		

7. Pronunciation of consecutive vowels

Two consecutive vowels do not merge into a one-syllable diphthong in Russian, but are pronounced separately, as in:

кло́ун, clown, pronounced [kló-un], two syllables.
пау́к, spider, pronounced [pa-úk], two syllables.
нау́ка, science, pronounced [na-ú-ka], three syllables.

8. Other consonants

С, с—[s]

Like *s* in *so*, but *not* like *s* in *is*.

сок	juice	стол	table	стака́н	glass (tumbler)
сон	dream	стул	chair	со́да	soda
нос	nose	сукно́	cloth	пост	post
слон	elephant	кусо́к	piece	па́ста	paste

З, з—[z]

Like *z* in *zone* or *s* in *rose*.

за́ла	hall	до́за	dose	мазу́т	heavy oil
замо́к	lock	зонт	umbrella	зано́за	splinter
зо́на	zone	азо́т	nitrogen	каза́к	Cossack
по́за	pose	Му́за	Muse	заку́ска	hors d'oeuvre

В, в—[v]

Like *v* in *velvet*.

вал	wave, billow	ва́нна	bath	сла́ва	glory
вол	ox	ва́кса	shoe polish	ва́за	vase
волк	wolf	воск	wax	звук	sound
ствол	trunk (of tree)	ла́ва	lava	давно́	long ago

Ф, ф—[f]

Like *f* in *fact* or *fun*.

факт	fact	флот	fleet	флако́н	bottle
фа́за	phase	фут	foot (measure)	ко́фта	woman's jacket
фат	dandy	фунт	pound	тафта́	taffeta
фон	background	фо́кус	focus	му́фта	muff

Г, г—[g]

Like *g* in *get* or *good*, never like *g* in *ginger*.

га́га	eider	глаза́	eyes	Во́лга	Volga
ага́т	agate	глаго́л	verb	ваго́н	railroad car
фу́га	fugue	глава́	chapter	лгун	liar
фаго́т	bassoon	га́лка	jackdaw	са́га	saga

Б, б—[b]

Like *b* in *boat* or *bath*.

бал	ball (party)	губа́	lip	суббо́та	Saturday
балко́н	balcony	бума́га	paper	забо́та	worry
ба́за	base	бу́ква	letter (of the alphabet)	заба́ва	fun
каблу́к	heel	таба́к	tobacco	а́збука	alphabet

Р, р—[r]

Russian [r] is "trilled"; it is produced with the tip of the tongue vibrating against the teeth ridge (usually the contact is lateral, slightly to the right or the left of the median line of the tongue and the teeth ridge).

про́за	prose	рот	mouth	порт	port
фра́за	phrase	грот	grotto	спорт	sport
кран	faucet	рука́	hand	форт	fort
крот	mole	ро́за	rose	а́рфа	harp
март	March	пар	steam	ма́рка	stamp

Х, х—[x]

This sound, which has no equivalent in English, will be transcribed as [x] (it must be remembered that [x] in transcription does *not* stand for *ks* or *gz*, the sound value of English *x*, as in *ax* or *exact*). The Russian sound [x] is close to Castilian Spanish *j* (in *Juan*, *jota*), German *ch* (in *Bach* or *doch*), or Scottish *ch* (*loch*). This sound is produced by the breath escaping through a narrow passage between the back of the tongue and the back of the mouth (the soft palate); a complete closure at the same point produces [k]. Russian [x] is not a harsh, scraping sound; to avoid harshness, one must be careful not to make too close a contact between the tongue and the soft palate.

мох	moss	слух	hearing	хвост	tail
му́ха	fly	холм	hill	храп	snoring
Бах	Bach	ха́та	hut	дра́хма	drachma
дух	spirit	хор	chorus	тахта́	divan
за́пах	odor	хлор	chlorine	Па́сха	Easter

9. Unstressed а and о

The sound [o] occurs in Russian only in stressed syllables. Spelling requires **о** in some words and **а** in others in unstressed syllables, but phonetically the two are indistinguishable. The sound value of both symbols in an unstressed syllable varies, depending on the position of this syllable in relation to the syllable under stress.

In the pretonic syllable (the syllable immediately preceding the one on which the stress falls) both **а** and **о** have the value [a] (somewhat less distinct than the stronger articulated stressed [á]):

тала́нт [talánt]	talent	кара́т [karát]	carat
топо́р [tapór]	ax	гора́ [gará]	mountain
бара́н [barán]	ram	доска́ [daská]	board
мото́р [matór]	motor	Москва́ [maskvá]	Moscow

Both **a** and **o** unstressed are also pronounced [a] in initial position, whether pretonic or not:

аромáт [aramát]	aroma	ананáс [ananás]	pineapple
облакá [ablaká]	clouds	остротá [astratá]	sharpness

In all other positions (*i.e.*, neither in pretonic syllables, nor in initial position) both **a** and **o** unstressed have the indistinct, neutral quality of the initial vowel sound in the English words *along*, or *upon*, or of the final vowel in *sofa* or *polka*; this sound is called *schwa* in phonetics and is transcribed [ə]:

молокó [məlakó]	milk	óколо [ókələ]	about
головá [gəlavá]	head	кóлокол [kóləkəl]	bell
таракáн [tərakán]	cockroach	кóмната [kómnətə]	room
потолóк [pətalók]	ceiling	пáтока [pátəkə]	molasses

The following table summarizes the sound value of **a** and **o** in relation to stress (pronunciation in initial position is not included):

		Pretonic Syllable	*Stressed Syllable*		
Spelling:	a o	a o	a o	a o	a o
Value:	[ə]	[a]	[á] [ó]	[ə]	[ə]
молокó, milk	м о [m ə	л о l a	к ó k ó]		
барабáн, drum	б а [b ə	р а r a	б á н b á n]		
контóра, office		к о н [k a n	т ó t ó	р а r ə]	
палáтка, tent		п а [p a	л á т l á t	к а k ə]	
бáрхатка, velvet ribbon			б á р [b á r	х а т x ə t	к а k ə]
кóлокол, bell			к ó [k ó	л о l ə	к о л k ə l]

Pronunciation Drill

онá [aná]	she	осá [asá]	wasp
потóм [patóm]	afterwards	окнó [aknó]	window
контóра [kantórə]	office	дóктор [dóktər]	doctor
докторá [dəktará]	doctors	óблако [óbləkə]	cloud
облакá [ablaká]	clouds	панорáма [pənarámə]	panorama
протокóл [prətakól]	protocol	астронóм [astranóm]	astronomer

онó	it	óрган	organ
парадóкс	paradox	остáток	remnant
городóк	small town	мастодóнт	mastodon
водоворóт	whirlpool	полторá	one and a half
кóротко	short	островá	islands
простотá	simplicity	óкна	windows

UNIT 2

Phonetics: The sound [j] *and its spelling; the letters* й, я, е, ё, *and* ю, **10.** *Palatalization of consonants: the soft sign* ь *and the letters* я, е, ё, *and* ю *after consonants,* **11.** *The vowels* и *and* ы, **15.** *The letter* э, **16.** *Unstressed* е, э, *and* я, **17.** *Open and close variants of* [e], **17.** *Palatalization before soft consonants,* **18.** *Grammar: Absence of articles,* **18.** *Absence of link verb,* **18.** *The indefinite demonstrative* э́то, **19.** *Questions,* **19.** *"Yes" and "no" answers,* **19.** *The word* вот, **20.**

PHONETICS

1. The sound [j] and the letters й, я, е, ё, and ю

The symbol [j] will be used hereafter to transcribe the initial sound heard in *yellow* or *yonder*, or the final sound in *say* or *boy*. In Russian, the sound [j], when it occurs after a vowel (in final position or before a consonant), is denoted by the letter й (called "short i"):

май [máj]	May	Толсто́й [talstój]	Tolstoy
Дуна́й [dunáj]	Danube	га́йка [gájkə]	nut
трамва́й [tramváj]	streetcar	тайга́ [tajgá]	taiga
портно́й [partnój]	tailor	постро́йка [pastrójkə]	building

The sound [j] before a vowel is represented by one of the following letters which stand for the syllable "[j] plus vowel":

Я, я stands for [ja], as *ya* in *yard:*

я́хта [jáxtə]	yacht	я́блоко [jábləkə]	apple
Я́лта [jáltə]	Yalta	мая́к [maják]	lighthouse

Е, е stands for [je], as *ye* in *yes:*

Éва [jévə]	Eve
óн éхал [ón jéxəl]	he was driving
óн уéхал [ón ujéxəl]	he drove away
я́ поéду [já pajédu]	I shall go

Ё, ё stands for [jo], as *yo* in *yore*

ёлка [jólkə]	Christmas tree	óн поёт [ón pajót]	he sings
заём [zajóm]	loan	óн даёт [ón dajót]	he gives

Note: ё occurs only in *stressed* syllables; the accent ['] over ё is therefore omitted.

Ю, ю stands for [ju], as *yu* in *Yukon:*

ю́мор [júmər]	humor	я́ пою́ [já pajú]	I sing
каю́та [kajútə]	cabin	я́ даю́ [já dajú]	I give

2. Palatalization of consonants

Most Russian consonantal sounds occur in two different variants, the "hard" (non-palatalized) and the "soft" (palatalized). The "hard" pronunciation only was described in the preceding unit. Palatalized ("soft") pronunciation will hereafter be indicated in transcriptions by the sign [̧] under the letter: [ţ] = palatalized [t]: [ļ] = palatalized [l], etc.

Palatalized and non-palatalized consonants are opposed in Russian as different sounds, and the "hardness" or "softness" of one consonant may be the only feature distinguishing two words: *e.g.*, [brat] means "brother"; [braţ]—"to take"; [úgəl] means "corner"; [úgəļ]—"coal," etc.

English does not oppose hard and soft consonants as different sounds. More or less distinct palatalization, however, is occasionally heard in English. Thus, the initial [k] sound in *cool* is close to Russian non-palatalized [k]; in *keel,* on the other hand, it is closer to the Russian palatalized variant, [ķ]. Repeating several times *keel-cool,* one will observe that the initial consonant in *keel* is pronounced with the tongue moved forward and upward, its front close to the hard palate; in *cool,* on the other hand, the tongue is drawn back, leaving a space between its surface and the hard palate. This space works as a resonator; when it is narrowed, the sound produced has a higher pitch.

To "palatalize" a consonant means to pronounce it with the tongue brought close to the hard palate with the acoustic effect of higher pitch.

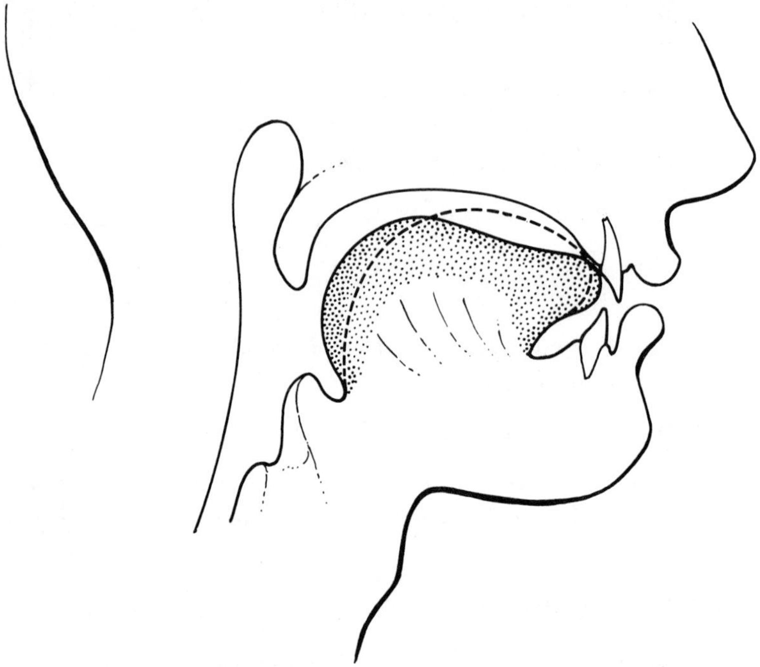

Illustration 4—Palatalized [ț]

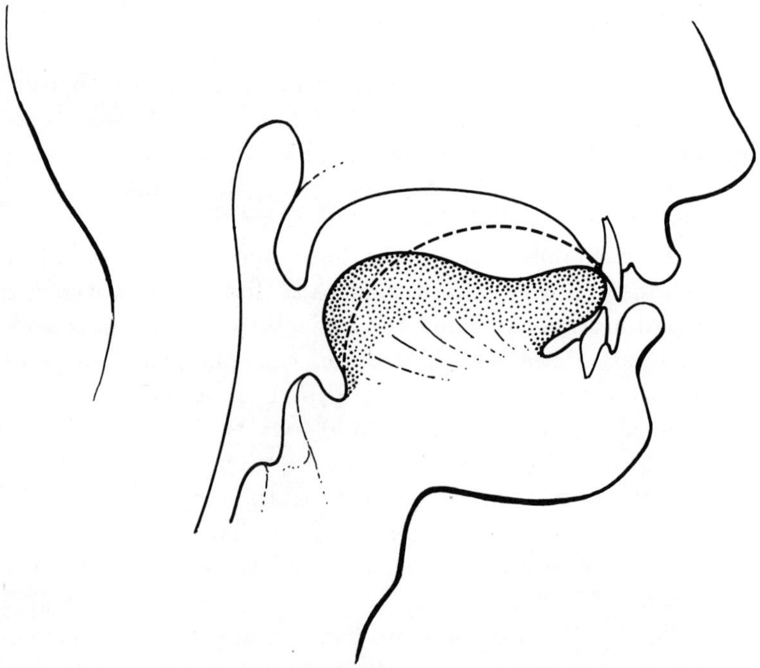

Illustration 5—Palatalized [ņ]

The position of the tongue for palatalized consonants may be described as that of the English "long *e*" vowel. As a first exercise, make a sharp (narrow) "ee . . ." sound, and, trying not to change the position of your tongue, pronounce different consonants:

"ee . . . tee," "ee . . . lee," "ee . . . nee," etc. (see Illustrations 4 and 5).

Spelling of palatalized consonants. Russian spelling has two ways for indicating palatalization:

(1) When a palatalized consonant is in final position in a word, or is followed by a hard consonant, a special letter, **ь** (the "soft sign"), is written after the consonant.

Soft consonant in final position:

брать [bráţ] to take (compare hard: брат [brát] brother)
ýголь [úgəļ] coal (compare hard: ýгол [úgəl] corner)

Soft consonant followed by a hard consonant:

тóлько [tóļkə] only (compare hard: тóлком [tólkəm] sensibly)
гóрько [góŗkə] bitter (compare hard: гóрка [górkə] hill)

(2) When a palatalized consonant is followed by a vowel sound, then the letter representing the vowel also serves to indicate that the consonant is palatalized. The letters used for this double purpose are **я**, **е**, **ё**, and **ю** (and another letter which will be added later in this lesson).

We have seen that initially and after vowels the four letters above mean "j plus vowel." After consonants, however, the same letters mean "palatalized consonant plus vowel." In other words, the sound [a] is written **а** after a hard consonant, but **я** after a palatalized consonant; [o] after a hard consonant is written **о**, after a soft consonant **ё**, etc.

To summarize the meaning of the letters **я**, **е**, **ё**, **ю**:

Initially or after a vowel:	*After a consonant, e.g.* **л***:*
я = [ja]	**ля** = [ļa] (я лягу [já ļágu] I shall lie down)
е = [je]	**ле** = [ļe] (лес [ļés] forest)
ё = [jo]	**лё** = [ļo] (лён [ļón] flax)
ю = [ju]	**лю** = [ļu] (люк [ļúk] hatchway

Pronunciation Drill

Compare the words in the left column with those in the right.

класс [klás]	class	клякса [kļáksə]	ink blot
поклóн [paklón]	bow	клён [kļón]	maple

лук [lúk]	onion	люк [ļúk]	hatchway
ду́ло [dúlə]	muzzle	пу́ля [púļə]	bullet
посо́л [pasól]	ambassador	соль [sóļ]	salt
дал [dál]	gave	даль [dáļ]	distance
то́лком [tólkəm]	sensibly	то́лько [tóļkə]	only
о́н зна́л [ón znál]	he knew	о́н сня́л [ón sņál]	he removed
нос [nós]	nose	нёс [ņós]	carried
рано [ránə]	early	Ва́ня [váņə]	Johnny
внук [vnúk]	grandson	нюх [ņúx]	flair
гран [grán]	grain (measure)	грань [gráņ]	facet
трон [trón]	throne	тронь [tróņ]	touch (imperative)
да́та [dátə]	date	дя́дя [ḑáḑə]	uncle
дом [dóm]	house	дёрн [ḑórn]	turf
ду́ма [dúmə]	thought	дю́на [ḑúnə]	dune
посу́да [pasúdə]	dishes	су́дя [súḑə]	judging (by)
так [ták]	so, thus	пустя́к [puşţák]	trifle
ток [tók]	current	тёк [ţók]	flowed
стук [stúk]	a knock	тюк [ţúk]	bundle
тут [tút]	here	путь [púţ]	way
дра́ма [drámə]	drama	пря́мо [pŗámə]	straight
пра́вда [právdə]	truth	ря́дом [ŗádəm]	beside
ро́за [rózə]	rose	грёза [gŗózə]	daydream
врун [vrún]	liar	рю́мка [ŗúmkə]	wine glass
това́р [tavár]	merchandise	слова́рь [slaváŗ]	dictionary
хор [xór]	chorus	корь [kóŗ]	measles
зал [zál]	hall	взял [vẓal]	took
взор [vzór]	glance	озёра [aẓórə]	lakes
оса́да [asádə]	siege	я́ ся́ду [já şádu]	I shall sit down
ссо́ра [ssórə][1]	quarrel	сёла [şólə]	villages
суда́ [sudá]	vessels	сюда́ [şudá]	here
нос [nós]	nose	ось [óş]	axis, axle
трус [trús]	coward	гусь [gúş]	goose
вол [vól]	ox	вёл [ꝩól]	led
ла́ва [lávə]	lava	ста́вя [stáꝩə]	placing
вал [vál]	wave	вял [ꝩál]	withered
ма́сса [mássə]	mass	мя́со [m̧ásə]	meat
мол [mól]	jetty	мёл [m̧ól]	swept
спал [spál]	slept	спят [sp̧át]	(they) sleep
порт [pórt]	port	Пётр [p̧ótr]	Peter
око́п [akóp]	trench	копь [kóp̧]	mine

[1] Double consonants are pronounced as a long single consonant.

3. The letters и [i] and ы [ɨ]

The letter **и** ([i] in transcription) stands for the vowel sound in *eve, eat,* and *see.* Consonants before **и** are always palatalized;[2] unlike **я**, **е**, **ё**, and **ю**, however, **и** in initial position and after vowels is not usually preceded by [j]:

И initial:

и́скра [ískrə]	spark	Ива́н [iván]	Ivan
и́ли [íļi]	or	Ита́лия [itáļijə]	Italy
я́ иду́ [já idú]	I am going	Ирку́тск [irkútsk]	Irkutsk
иска́ть [iskáţ]	to look for	и́стина [íşţinə]	truth

Post-consonantal:

лимо́н [ļimón]	lemon	ли́ния [ļíņijə]	line
рис [ŗís]	rice	диск [ḑísk]	disk
фи́зика [f̧íz̧ikə]	physics	хи́мия [x̧ím̧ijə]	chemistry
кино́ [ķinó]	movies	кри́тик [kŗíţik]	critic
си́льно [şíļnə]	strongly	фити́ль [f̧iţíļ]	wick

A sound related to [i], but not identical with it, occurs after non-palatalized consonants (never initially or after vowels). The symbol for this sound is **ы**; it will be transliterated [ɨ]. English has no exact equivalent for [ɨ]; as an approximation only, it may be said that [ɨ] is rather close to the English vowel sound in *mill* or *sit,* while the vowel sound in *meal* or *seat* is close to [i]. In English, however, the two sounds differ not only in quality, but also in length, the vowel in *seat* or *meal* being longer, in *sit* or *mill* shorter. In Russian there is no difference in length, but only in the quality of the sound. Moreover, Russian **ы** [ɨ] is pronounced with the tongue a little farther back than the sound in *sit* or *mill* (but not quite as far back as for **у** [u]).

Exercise: Pronounce the English word, then the Russian word, drawing the tongue a little farther back; also, be careful, in pronouncing the Russian dentals, to place the tip of your tongue against the inner surface of the upper teeth, not the teeth-ridge above the gums as in English (see page 5).

English	*Russian*	*English translation*
dim	дым [dɨ́m]	smoke
till	тыл [tɨ́l]	rear
click	клык [klɨ́k]	tusk
nil	ныл [nɨ́l]	moaned

[2] Three consonantal sounds, which will be given later, are an exception.

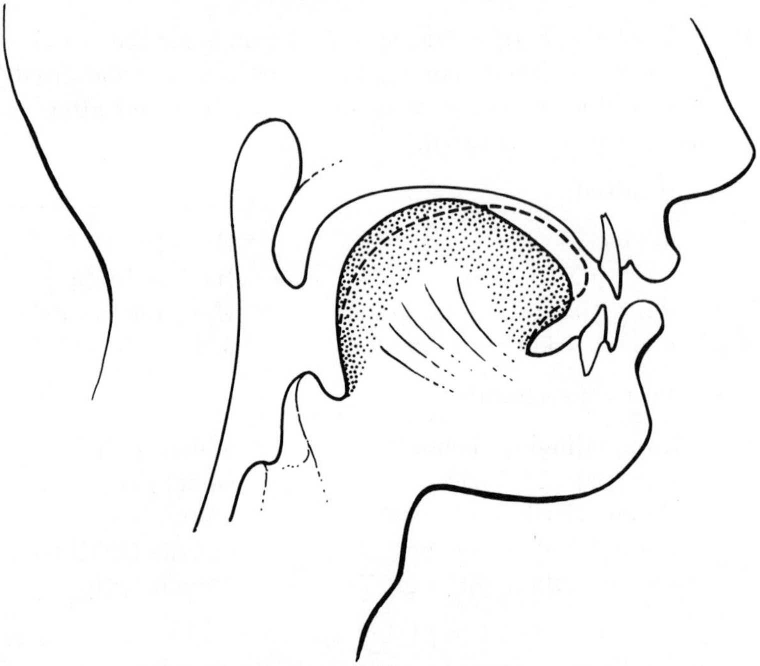

Illustration 6—The Vowel [ɨ]

Pronunciation Drill

Compare the words in the left column with those in the right:

стиль [ş̦ţíļ]	style	осты́л [astɨ́l]	grew cold
суди́ть [suḑíţ]	to judge	суды́ [sudɨ́]	courts
ми́ли [m̦íļi]	miles	мы́ли [mɨ́ļi]	(they) washed
си́то [şítə]	sieve	сы́ты [sɨ́tɨ]	sated
висо́к [v̦isók]	temple (of head)	высо́ко [vɨsókə]	high
кри́зис [ķŗíẓis]	crisis	кры́са [krɨ́sə]	rat
Рим [ŗím]	Rome	Крым [krɨ́m]	Crimea
бить [b̦íţ]	to beat	быть [bɨ́ţ]	to be
заби́ть [zab̦íţ]	to kill	забы́ть [zabɨ́ţ]	to forget
усни́ [uşņí]	fall asleep (imperative)	сны [snɨ́]	dreams

4. The letter э ("e reversed")

One more letter must be added to the vowels given above: the "reversed е," written э. This letter forms a pair with the letter е; as we know, е means [je] in initial position or after a vowel; after a consonant it means that this consonant is palatalized, *e.g.*, те [ţe].

The letter э, written initially or after a vowel, stands for the sound [e] without a [j]:

ел [jél]	ate	эл [él]	name of the letter л
я́ поéду [já pajédu]	I shall go	поэ́т [poét]	poet

The letter э thus belongs to the series **а**, **о**, **у**, and **ы**. "Reversed **е**" is not written after consonants (except for a few transliterations of foreign names), however, so that there are no hard counterparts for syllables like **те** [ţe], **де** [d̡e], **ле** [l̡e], etc.

The letter э is written initially; it occurs, however, only in the different forms of the Russian demonstrative э́тот (this), э́ти (these), etc., and in a number of words of foreign origin, *e.g.*:

э́пос [épəs]	epos	э́хо [éxə]	echo
э́тика [éţikə]	ethics	Э́мма [émmə]	Emma
э́ра [érə]	era	Э́тна [étnə]	Mount Etna

5. Unstressed е, э, and я

In unstressed syllables (with the exception of certain grammatical endings), **е**, **э**, and **я** are pronounced close to [i], and will be transcribed as [i]:

тепéрь [ţipéŗ]	now	телефóн [ţil̡ifón]	telephone
тянýть [ţinúţ]	to pull	прямóй [pŗimój]	straight
эпóха [ipóxə]	epoch	элемéнт [il̡im̡ént]	element

The [j] is preserved if unstressed **е** or **я** are initial or follow vowels:

едá [jidá]	food	мы́ знáем [mí znájim]	we know
язы́к [jizík]	language	пóяс [pójis]	belt

Depending on the position in the word and on the tempo of delivery, the sound of unstressed **я** and **е** may be further weakened, becoming [ə].

6. Open and close (narrow) variants of [e]

The sound [e] (**е** or **э** stressed) varies somewhat depending on the following sound: [e] is *open* if followed by a non-palatalized consonant (also in final position); *close* (or narrow) if followed by a palatalized consonant. The range of [e] sounds may be said to occupy a place between [a] and [i], with open [e] being nearer to [a] and close [e] nearer to [i]. Open [e] resembles the *e* of English *met;* close [e] the *a* of English *mate,* but without the "y" element of the long English "a" sound.

Close [e] will be transcribed [ẹ].

Compare words in the left column with those in the right:

[e]		[ẹ]	
вес [ṿés]	weight	весь [ṿẹ́ṣ]	the whole
плен [pḷén]	captivity	лень [ḷẹ́ṇ]	laziness
э́то [étə]	this	э́ти [ẹ́ṭi]	these
те [ṭé]	those	тень [ṭẹ́ṇ]	shadow
где [gḍé]	where	день [ḍẹ́ṇ]	day

Other vowels too have a somewhat higher quality, due to a narrower articulation, before palatalized consonants, and especially between two palatalized sounds; compare:

[a] in лопа́та [lapátə]	spade, and in пять [p̣ạ́ṭ]	five
[o] in тот [tót]	that, and in тётя [ṭọ́ṭə]	aunt
[u] in Ту́ла [túlə]	Tula (town), and in тюль [ṭụ́ḷ]	tulle

7. Palatalization before soft consonants

In certain combinations, consonants are palatalized when followed by other palatalized consonants, *e.g.*:

гость [góṣṭ]	guest	[ṣ] before [ṭ]
здесь [ẓḍẹ́ṣ]	here	[ẓ] before [ḍ]
зо́нтик [zóṇṭik]	umbrella	[ṇ] before [ṭ]
индюк [iṇḍúk]	turkey cock	[ṇ] before [ḍ]

The consonant [l] is pronounced hard before palatalized consonants. All consonants remain hard before [g̣], [ḳ], [x̣], and [ṛ].

GRAMMAR

1. Absence of articles

Russian has no articles, definite or indefinite (such as "the" and "a" in English).

2. Absence of link verbs in present tense

A sentence present in meaning is formed in Russian without a link verb ("am," "is," "are" serve as link verbs in English). Words other than verbs may be used as predicates, *e.g.*, adverbs:

О́н **ту́т.**	He is here.
Газе́та **та́м.**	The newspaper is there.

or nouns:

Ива́н **до́ктор.**	Ivan is a doctor.
Ло́ндон **по́рт.**	London is a port.
Во́лга **река́.**	The Volga is a river.

3. The indefinite demonstrative э́то

The word **э́то** points out (or "introduces") something of which the sentence supplies the name or definition:

Э́то университе́т.	This (or that) is a university.
Э́то профе́ссор Бра́ун.	This (or that) is Professor Brown.
Э́то Во́лга.	This (or that) is the Volga.

4. Questions

The word order in an interrogative sentence is usually the same as in a declarative sentence. The key word in a question (often but not always the last word in a "yes-or-no" question) is marked by a rising intonation, especially on its stressed syllable:

О́н ту́т?	Is he here?
Газе́та та́м?	Is the newspaper there?
Ива́н до́ктор?	Is Ivan a doctor?
Во́лга река́?	Is the Volga a river?
Э́то университе́т?	Is that the university?
Э́то профе́ссор Бра́ун?	Is this Professor Brown?

5. "Yes" and "no" answers

"Yes" in Russian is **да**. In a "yes" answer, the question, or the key word alone, is often repeated after the introductory **да**:

Question	*"Yes" answer*
О́н ту́т? Is he here?	Да́, о́н ту́т. (or: Да́, ту́т.)
Газе́та та́м? Is the newspaper there?	Да́, газе́та та́м. (or: Да́, та́м.)
Бра́ун профе́ссор? Is Brown a professor?	Да́, о́н профе́ссор. (or: Да́, профе́ссор.)

"No" in Russian is **нет**; like **да** it is an independent word-phrase. The negative particle, English "not," is **не**; it is pronounced jointly with the word negated:

не ту́т [ṇitút]	not here
не студе́нт [ṇistuḍént]	not a student
не до́ма [ṇidómə]	not at home
не та́м [ṇitám]	not there

Question	*"No" answer*
Бра́ун профе́ссор? Is Brown a professor?	Не́т, о́н не профе́ссор.
Э́то музе́й? Is this the museum?	Не́т, э́то не музе́й.
Библиоте́ка ту́т? Is the library here?	Не́т, библиоте́ка не ту́т. Ту́т музе́й.

6. The word вот

The word **вот** points out something or someone present or coming into sight, usually with a gesture in the direction of this object or person:

Во́т перо́.	Here's a pen.
Во́т Ива́н!	Here's Ivan! (Here comes Ivan!)
Во́т газе́та.	There's the newspaper.

The different uses of тут, э́то, and вот may be illustrated as follows:

Газе́та ту́т.	The newspaper *is here.*
До́ктор Бра́ун ту́т.	Doctor Brown *is here.*

The above are statements about location in which тут, "here" may mean "somewhere" in this house, apartment, or room, but not necessarily in sight.

Э́то газе́та.	*This is* a newspaper.
Э́то до́ктор Бра́ун.	*This is* Doctor Brown.

These sentences identify an object or a person present, the assumption being that the listener does not know what the object or who the person is.

Во́т газе́та.	*Here's* the (or a) newspaper.
Во́т до́ктор Бра́ун!	*Here's* Doctor Brown!

The first sentence may be uttered while pointing at the paper (the listener was looking for it), or handing it to the listener. The second sentence may signal the arrival of Doctor Brown, a person known to the listener.

The word вот is never used in interrogative or negative sentences; its function is limited to asserting the presence of a person or object.

Pattern Sentences

1. Э́то кла́сс.[3]	1. This is a classroom.
2. Э́то стена́; та́м окно́ и по́лка.	2. That's a wall; over there are a window and a bookcase.
3. Во́т сто́л; во́т бума́га и перо́.	3. Here's a table; here's some paper and a pen.
4. Во́т А́нна и О́льга!	4. Here are Anna and Olga!
5. —Э́то до́м? —Да́, э́то до́м.	5. —Is that a house? —Yes, that's a house.
6. —Та́м окно́? —Да́, э́то окно́.	6. —Is that a window there? —Yes, that's a window.
7. —Э́то потоло́к? —Не́т, э́то не потоло́к! Э́то по́л!	7. —Is that the ceiling? —No, that isn't the ceiling! It's the floor!
8. —Где́ кни́га? —Во́т кни́га.	8. —Where is the book? —Here is the book.
9. —Где́ ла́мпа?— Ла́мпа та́м.	9. —Where is the lamp? —The lamp is there.
10. —Э́то доска́ и́ли по́лка? —Э́то доска́.	10. —Is this a blackboard or a bookcase? —It's a blackboard.
11. —Где́ музе́й? —Во́т музе́й.	11. —Where is the museum? —There is the museum.
12. —Э́то сту́л и́ли сто́л? —Э́то сту́л! Сто́л та́м.	12. —Is this a chair or a table? —It's a chair! The table is over there.
13. —Вы́ Ю́рий и́ли Ива́н? —Я́ Ю́рий.	13. —Are you Yuri or Ivan? —I am Yuri.
14. —Где́ тепе́рь Ива́н? —О́н до́ма.	14. —Where is Ivan now? —He's at home.
15. —Зо́я и О́льга ту́т? —Не́т, они́ тепе́рь до́ма.	15. —Are Zoya and Olga here? —No, they're at home now.
16. Ива́н студе́нт и А́нна студе́нтка.	16. Ivan is a student and Anna is a (girl) student.

[3] Declarative sentences in Russian have a pronounced falling intonation at the end of the sentence, more so than in English. Questions formed with question words (*e.g.*, где) have *rising* intonation on the question word, *falling* intonation at the end. "Yes-or-no" questions (*e.g*, Э́то до́м?) have rising intonation on the key word of the question, usually the last word in short sentences, in this case, дом.

Drills

A. *Translate into Russian.*

1. The museum is here.
   The museum is not there.
   This is not the museum.
   The museum's (over) there.
2. This is a newspaper.
   Here's the newspaper.
   The newspaper is here.
3. Anna is not here; she is at home.
   This is not Anna; this is Olga.
   Here are Anna and Olga.
4. Here is a lamp.
   The lamp is there.
   This is not a lamp; this is a window.

B. *Translate into Russian the answers to the questions below.*

1. Э́то музе́й?	Yes, this is a museum.
	No, this is not a museum.
2. Ива́н студе́нт?	Yes, he is a student.
	No, he is not a student.
3. До́ктор ту́т?	Yes, he is here.
	No, he is not here.
4. О́льга ту́т?	Yes, she is here.
	No, she is at home.

UNIT 3

Phonetics: the letters ж, ш, ц, ч, *and* щ, 23. *Consonant-vowel incompatibilities,* 25. *Palatalization of* г, к, *and* х, 26. *Voiced and voiceless consonants,* 27. *The separative signs,* 28. *The Russian script,* 32.

PHONETICS

1. The letters Ж, ж [ž], and Ш, ш [š]

The letter **ж** (transcribed ž) stands for a sound close to that of *s* in *pleasure* or *z* in *azure*; the letter **ш** (transcribed š) for a sound close to *sh* in *ship*.

The Russian sounds [ž] and [š] are "harder" (they have a lower pitch) than the corresponding English sounds. English [ž] (*s* in *pleasure*) and [š] (*sh* in *ship*) are articulated with the tongue brought close to the frontal part of the roof of the mouth (the hard palate), in a position much like the one for Russian palatalization. The tip of the tongue is on the level of the teeth-ridge. For the Russian articulation the tongue is drawn farther back and its tip (slightly curved upward) is just above the teeth-ridge.

The sounds denoted in Russian by the letters **ж** (*s* in *pleasure,* but harder) and **ш** (*sh* in *ship,* but harder) are peculiar in that they are never palatalized. The two sounds are hard even when followed by a "soft sign" (ь). This "soft sign" is purely orthographic and does not affect pronunciation.

The spelling of vowel sounds after **ж** [ž] and **ш** [š] is governed by tradition, and does not always reflect the phonetic reality.

Vowels after **ж** [ž] and **ш** [š] are written and pronounced as follows: [a] is written **a**: жар [žar] fever; шар [šar] ball, sphere. [o] is written **o** in some words (but only in stressed syllables), **ё** in others, with no difference in pronunciation: прыжóк [prižók] jump; жёлтый [žóltij] yellow; шóпот [šópət] whisper; шёлк [šolk] silk. [u] is written **у**: жук [žuk] beetle; шум [šum] noise. [e] is written **е**, but without palatalization of the consonant: жест [žest] gesture; шест [šest] pole, staff. Unstressed **е**, normally pronounced [i], sounds like [ɨ] after **ж** and **ш**: желéзо [žiļézə] iron; шестóй [šistój] sixth. The letter **ы** is never written after **ж** and **ш**, but **и** is pronounced [ɨ] without palatalization: óн жúл [ón žíl] he lived; óн шúл [ón šíl] he sewed.

Pronunciation Drill

пожáр [pažár]	fire	шáпка [šápkə]	cap
обжóра [abžórə]	glutton	мешóк [ɱišók]	bag
жокéй [žaķéj]	jockey	шофёр [šaf̧ór]	chauffeur
абажýр [abažúr]	lampshade	шýтка [šútkə]	joke
жир [žír]	fat	широтá [širatá]	breadth
жесть [žéşţ]	tin plate	шесть [šéşţ]	six
женá [žiná]	wife	решетó [ŗišitó]	sieve
жёны [žóni]	wives	решётка [ŗišótkə]	lattice

2. The letter Ц, ц [c]

The letter **ц** (transcribed [c]) stands for the sound *ts* as in *its* or *tz* in *Switzerland*. Like **ж** [ž] and **ш** [š], **ц** [c] is always hard. Both the vowels **и** and **ы** are written after **ц** (**и** in words of foreign origin, **ы** in native words and in grammatical endings); both **и** and **ы** after **ц** sound like [ɨ]. Unstressed **е** also has the [ɪ] sound:

цирк [círk]	circus	цилúндр [ciļíndr]	cylinder
цúник [cíņik]	cynic	цинк [cínk]	zinc
цензýра [cinzúrə]	censorship	цемéнт [ciɱént]	cement
ценá [ciná]	price	поцелýй [pacilúj]	kiss
цыплёнок [cípļónək]	chick	цынгá [cingá]	scurvy
птúца [pţícə]	bird	птúцы [pţíci]	birds
конéц [kaņéc]	end	концы́ [kancí]	ends (pl.)

3. The letters Ч, ч [ç̌] and Щ, щ [ş̌ç̌]

The letter **ч** [ç̌] represents the sound of *ch* in *cheese* or *cheap*; it is always soft and is quite close to the English sound.

The letter **щ** stands for a combination of a soft [ş̌] and a soft [ç̌], as in *Danish cheese* pronounced as one word: "*Danishcheese.*" The [ç̌] element tends to be rather weak, and in a pronunciation which is perfectly correct and prevalent in Central Russia, the [ç̌] in **щ** is replaced by a second soft [ș], the letter **щ** sounding like *Danish sheep* pronounced as one word: "*Danishsheep.*"

Both [ç̌] and [șç̌] ([șș]) are always palatalized. Just as **ж** and **ш** remain hard even when followed by a soft sign, so **ч** and **щ** are soft whether followed or not by a soft sign in final position; this soft sign is purely orthographic:

ночь [nóç̌] night	врач [vráç̌] physician
вещь [y̧ẹ́șç̌] thing	товáрищ [taváŗișç̌] comrade

The spelling of vowels after **ч** [ç̌] and **щ** [șç̌] is also rather arbitrary. Vowels after **ч** [ç̌] and **щ** [șç̌] are written and pronounced as follows:

[a] is written **a** (never **я**!):

час [ç̌ás] hour	пощáда [pașç̌ádə] mercy

[o] is written **ё** and in some words, in stressed syllables, **o**:

чёрный [ç̌órnɨj] black	щётка [șç̌ótkə] brush
крючóк [kŗuç̌ók] hook	борщóк [baŗșç̌ók] a soup

[u] is written **y** (never **ю**!):

чýдо [ç̌údə] miracle	щýка [șç̌úkə] pike (fish)
я хочý [já xaç̌ú] I want	я тащý [já tașç̌ú] I drag

[e] is written **e** (stressed):

честь [ç̌ẹ́șţ] honor	щель [șç̌ẹ́ļ] crack

[i] is written **и**:

читáть [ç̌itáţ] to read	щи [șç̌í] cabbage soup
чи́стый [ç̌ístɨj] clean	щипцы́ [șç̌ipcí] pliers

[i] is also the sound of unstressed **a** and **e**:

часы́ [ç̌isí] hours, clock	щади́ть [șç̌iḑíţ] to show mercy, spare
чемодáн [ç̌imadán] suitcase	щекá [șç̌iká] cheek
черни́ла [ç̌iŗņílə] ink	щенóк [șç̌inók] puppy

4. Consonant-vowel incompatibilities

With the three sounds that are always hard: **ж** [ž], **ш** [š], and **ц** [c], and the two that are always soft: **ч** [ç̌] and **щ** [șç̌], Russian spelling does not make a consistent use of the devices normally showing palatalization. Thus the soft sign is written in certain words after **ж**, **ш**, **ч**, and **щ** in final position, though **ж** and **ш** remain hard despite the soft sign, and **ч** and **щ** are soft even when no soft sign is written after them.

It has been seen also that not all vowels are written after the three "always hard" consonants, **ж**, **ш**, and **ц**, and the two "always soft" ones, **ч** and **щ**, nor are those that are written used consistently in terms of palatalization. The combinations of the five consonants with different vowels are given below; **т** [t] has been added as an example of any consonant with a normal range of hard-soft oppositions.

	with [a]		with [ó][1]		with [u]		with [i]/[ɨ]		with [e]	
	hard	soft	hard	soft	hard	soft	hard	soft	hard	soft
т [t]·	**та** [ta]	**тя** [ţa]	**тó** [tó]	**тё** [ţó]	**ту** [tu]	**тю** [ţu]	**ты** [tɨ]	**ти** [ţi]		**те** [ţe]
ж [ž]:	**жа** [ža]		**жó**, **жё** [žó]		**жу** [žu]		**жи** [žɨ]		**же** [že]	
ш [š]:	**ша** [ša]		**шó**, **шё** [šó]		**шу** [šu]		**ши** [šɨ]		**ше** [še]	
ц [c]:	**ца** [ca]		**цó** [có]		**цу** [cu]		**цы**, **ци** [cɨ]		**це** [ce]	
ч [ç̌]:		**ча** [ç̌a]		**чё**, **чо** [ç̌ó]		**чу** [ç̌u]		**чи** [ç̌i]		**че** [ç̌e]
щ [ş̌ç̌]:		**ща** [ş̌ç̌a]		**щё**, **що** [ş̌ç̌ó]		**щу** [ş̌ç̌u]		**щи** [ş̌ç̌i]		**ще** [ş̌ç̌e]

5. Palatalization of г, к, and х

Another group of consonants, known as velars, **г** [g], **к** [k], and **х** [x], can be both palatalized and non-palatalized. They are palatalized, however, only before the vowel sounds [e] and [i], indeed they are *always* palatalized before these vowels. In other words, non-palatalized [g], [k], [x] *never* occur before [i]. Hence the velars **г** [g], **к** [k], and **х** [x] do not appear in the hard-soft oppositions possible with most consonants:

before [a]:	га [ga],	ка [ka],	ха [xa]	—hard only
before [o]:	го [go],	ко [ko],	хо [xo]	—hard only
before [u]:	гу [gu],	ку [ku],	ху [xu]	—hard only
before [i/ɨ]:	ги [ģi],	ки [ķi],	хи [x̧i]	—*soft* only
before [e]:	ге [ģe],	ке [ķe],	хе [x̧e]	—*soft* only
final:	г[2]	к [k],	х [x]	—hard only

[1] It will be recalled that the vowel sound [o] occurs only under stress. Unstressed, the letter **o** sounds like **a** ([a] or [ə]—see page 7).

[2] The pronunciation of **г** in final position is treated in Section 6 below.

Summary of consonant-vowel incompatibilities. Some of the incompatibilities between consonants and vowels mentioned above are phonetic, *e.g.*, the sound [ɨ] is never heard after the sound [ç̌], nor is the letter **ы** written after the letter **ч**. The sound [ɨ], however, is heard after [ž], but a rule of spelling, which is arbitrary, requires it to be written **и**. The following is a summary of consonant-vowel incompatibilities considered from the viewpoint of *spelling*:

о	*only if stressed* after	ж	ш	ц	ч	щ			
ы	*never* after	ж	ш		ч	щ	г	к	х
я	*never* after	ж	ш	ц	ч	щ	г	к	х
ё	*never* after			ц			г	к[3]	х
ю	*never* after	ж	ш	ц	ч	щ	г	к	х

6. Voiced and voiceless consonants

The sound we call "voice" is produced by the breath when, as it passes through the larynx, it makes the vocal cords vibrate. All vowel sounds are "voiced." As for consonants, some (like [z], [v], [d], [g]) are produced with the sound of the voice, as if, when articulating them, we were also uttering an indefinite vowel sound. Other consonants (like [s], [f], [t], [k]) are "voiceless"; they are produced with the breath alone, with no vibration of the vocal cords. The difference becomes clear if one compares two consonants articulated in exactly the same manner except that one is voiced and the other voiceless, *e.g.*, "zzz. . ." (voiced) and "sss. . ." (voiceless).

Most Russian consonants fall into pairs in which two sounds (like [z] and [s]) are identical in articulation and differ only in the voice being present in one and absent in the other:

Voiced:	б [b]	в [v]	д [d]	з [z]	ж [ž]	г [g][4]	–	–	–
	| |	| |	| |	| |	| |	| |			
Voiceless:	п [p]	ф [f]	т [t]	с [s]	ш [š]	к [k]	ц [c]	ч [ž]	щ [§ç̌]

Voiced consonants (both hard and soft) are "unvoiced," that is, they sound like their voiceless counterparts: [b] like [p], [v] like [f], etc., in: (1) final position, and (2) before voiceless consonants.

[3] The syllable **кё** [ķó] occurs in one verb.

[4] But **г** is pronounced as [x] before [k], *e.g.*, лёгкий [ļóxķij], "easy"; мягкий [máxķij], "soft"; also in **Бог** [bóx], "God."

(1) Unvoicing in final position:

[b]>[p]:	зуб [zúp]	tooth	дробь [drópˌ]	fraction
[v]>[f]:	ров [róf]	ditch	кровь [krófˌ]	blood
[d]>[t]:	сад [sát]	garden	сядь [şáţ]	sit down (imperative)
[z]>[s]:	туз [tús]	ace	мазь [máş]	ointment
[ž]>[š]:	нож [nóš]	knife	рожь [róš]	rye
[g]>[k]:	снег [şņék]	snow	луг [lúk]	meadow

(2) Unvoicing before voiceless consonants:

[bk]>[pk]:	скобка [skópkə]	bracket
[vč̦]>[fč̦]:	вчера́ [fč̦irá]	yesterday
[gk]>[xk]:	легко́ [ļixkó]	easy
[dp]>[tp]:	по́дпись [pótpˌiş]	signature
[žk]>[šk]:	ло́жка [lóškə]	spoon
[zk]>[sk]:	у́зко [úskə]	narrow
[bs]>[ps]:	обсуди́ть [apsuḑíţ]	to discuss
[vt]>[ft]:	автомоби́ль [aftəmabˌíļ]	automobile
[gt]>[kt]:	ля́гте [ļákţi]	lie down (imperative)
[dk]>[tk]:	ло́дка [lótkə]	boat
[žk]>[šk]:	кру́жка [krúškə]	mug
[zk]>[sk]:	бли́зко [bļískə]	near

On the other hand, voiceless consonants are voiced before **б** [b], **д** [d], **з** [z], **ж** [ž], and **г** [g]:

[sb]>[zb]:	сбор [zbór]	collection, gathering
[td]>[dd]:	отде́л [aḑḑél]	division, department
[tz]>[dz]:	о́тзвук [ódzvuk]	echo
[kž]>[gž]:	та́кже [tágžə]	equally
[sg]>[zg]:	сгиба́ть [zgˌibáţ]	to bend

7. The separative signs

In certain Russian words the sound [j] is heard between a consonant and a vowel, *e.g.*, [şiṃjá], "family," or [staţjá], "article"; a sound close to [ţja] is heard in rapid speech in an English phrase such as "we*t y*ard."

In spelling the combination of sounds "consonant + [j] + vowel" is rendered by writing a soft sign **ь** (or a special separative sign **ъ**—see next paragraph) after the consonant, followed by the letter **я** for [ja], **е** for [je], **ё** for [jo], or **ю** for [ju]. The sign "separates" the consonant from the vowel, the latter preserving its initial [j]. Compare:

хотя́ [xaţá]	although	—no [j];	but	статья́ [staţjá]	article—[j] before [a]
Пётр [pˌótr]	Peter	—no [j];	but	пьёт [pˌjót]	drinks—[j] before [o]
ключ [kļúč̦]	key	—no [j];	but	я лью [já ļjú]	I pour—[j] before [u]

In a number of words another sign, the "separative sign" **ъ** is used rather than the soft sign in the words above; phonetically there is no difference between the two:

объявле́ние [aḇjivḽẹ́ṋijə]	advertisement
отъе́зд [aţjést]	departure
объя́тие [aḇjáţijə]	embrace
съесть (şjẹşţ)	to eat up
съезд (şjest)	congress
въе́хать (ɣ̦jéxəţ)	to drive in

Pronunciation Drill

(*Read across.*)

сча́стье [şç̌áşţjə]	luck, happiness	ча́сти [ç̌áşţi]	parts
пья́ница [p̦jáṋicə]	drunkard	пя́тница [p̦áţṋicə]	Friday
Татья́на [taţjánə]	Tatiana	тя́нет [ţáṋit]	pulls
съёмка [şjómkə]	filming	сёмга [şómgə]	smoked salmon
шитьё [šɨţjó]	sewing	тёмный [ţóмnɨj]	dark
пла́тье [pláţjə]	dress	Ка́тя [káţə]	Katia
съесть [şjẹ́şţ]	to eat up	сесть [şẹ́şţ]	to sit down
судья́ [suḑjá]	judge	идя́ [iḑá]	walking

Pattern Sentences

1. —Что́[5] э́то? —Э́то лицо́.	1. —What is this? —That is a face.
2. —Что́ э́то? —Э́то гла́з, э́то но́с.	2. —What is this? —That's an eye, that's a nose.
3. —Э́то то́же но́с? —Не́т, э́то не но́с, э́то ро́т.	3. —Is this a nose too? —No, it's not a nose; it's a mouth.
4. —Кто́ э́то? —Э́то Бори́с.	4. —Who is that? —That's Boris.
5. —Кто́ о́н? —О́н студе́нт.	5. —Who is he? —He's a student.
6. —Кто́ вы́? Вы́ то́же студе́нт? —Не́т, я́ учи́тель.	6. —Who are you? Are you a student too? —No, I am a teacher.
7. —Э́то Ю́рий? —Да́, э́то о́н.	7. —Is that Yuri? —Yes, it's he.
8. —Что́ э́то? —Э́то каранда́ш.	8. —What's that? —It's a pencil.
9. —Э́то то́же каранда́ш? —Не́т, э́то не каранда́ш. Э́то журна́л.	9. —Is that a pencil too? —No, that's not a pencil. That's a magazine.
10. Жу́ков не студе́нт; о́н тепе́рь уже́ учи́тель.	10. Zhukov is not a student; he is already (now) a teacher.
11. —Вы́ уже́ ту́т? —Да́, мы́ уже́ ту́т.	11. —You are here already? —Yes, we are here already.
12. —Где́ А́нна и Ива́н? —Они́ уже́ до́ма.	12. —Where are Anna and Ivan? —They are at home already.

[5] The word **что** is pronounced [što].

CONVERSATION

Учи́тель и кла́сс

Учи́тель. —До́брый де́нь! Ка́к вы́ пожива́ете?	—Good day! How are you?
Класс. —О́чень хорошо́, спаси́бо. Вы́ ка́к?	—Very well, thank you. How are you?
У. —Спаси́бо, то́же хорошо́. Джо́н, покажи́те, где́ по́л и потоло́к.	—I'm well too, thank you. John, show where the floor and the ceiling are.
Джон. —Во́т по́л, во́т потоло́к.	—There is the floor, there is the ceiling.
У. —Пра́вильно. Тепе́рь вы́, Мэ́ри, покажи́те, где́ доска́.	—Correct (right). Now you, Mary, show (us) where the blackboard is.
Мэ́ри. —Во́т доска́.	—There is the blackboard.
У. —Не́т, э́то не доска́; э́то стена́!	—No, that isn't the blackboard; that's the wall!
М. —А́х, да́! Э́то стена́. Доска́ та́м.	—Oh yes! That's the wall. The blackboard is over there.
У. —Пра́вильно. Повтори́те, пожа́луйста.[6]	—Correct (right). Please repeat.
М. —Э́то стена́. Доска́ та́м.	—That is the wall. The blackboard is over there.
У. —То́м, что́ э́то?	—Tom, what is that?
Том. —Э́то лицо́.	—That is a face.
У. —А что́ э́то?	—And what is that?
Т. —Э́то гла́з.	—That's an eye.
У. —Хорошо́. Э́то то́же гла́з?	—All right. Is this an eye too?
Т. —Не́т, э́то не гла́з; э́то ро́т.	—No, that's not an eye; that's a mouth.
У. —Покажи́те, где́ голова́ и где́ рука́.	—Show me where the head is and where the hand is.
Том. —Во́т голова́, во́т рука́.	—Here is the head, and here is the hand.
У. —Хорошо́. О́льга, тепе́рь чита́йте, пожа́луйста.	—Fine. Olga, read now, please.
О́льга. —«Во́т ка́рта. Э́то Сове́тский Сою́з. Во́т го́род. Э́то Москва́.»	—"Here is a map. This is the Soviet Union. Here is a city. It is Moscow."
У. —Повтори́те.	—Repeat.
О. —«Во́т ка́рта. Э́то Сове́тский Сою́з. Во́т го́род. Э́то Москва́.»	—"Here is a map. This is the Soviet Union. Here is a city. It is Moscow."
У. —Хорошо́. Тепе́рь пиши́те: «Во́т Ленингра́д, Ки́ев и Ха́рьков. Во́т река́. Э́то Во́лга. Во́т Сиби́рь и во́т Кавка́з.» О́чень хорошо́. Э́то всё; уже́ звоно́к. До свида́ния.	—Fine. Now write: "Here are Leningrad, Kiev, and Kharkov. Here is a river. It's the Volga. Here is Siberia and here is the Caucasus." Very good. That's all; there's the bell already. Good-bye.

[6] Пожа́луйста (please), pronounce [pažálustə].

РОССИ́Я
0 375
Масштаб
Ледови́тый океа́н
НОРВЕ́ГИЯ
ШВЕ́ЦИЯ
ФИНЛЯ́НДИЯ
Балти́йское мо́ре
Ленингра́д
Нева́
Москва́
Во́лга
УРАЛ
СИБИ́РЬ
Свердло́вск
ПО́ЛЬША
Р О С С И́ Я
ЧЕХОСЛОВА́КИЯ
ВЕ́НГРИЯ
Днепр
Ки́ев
УКРАИ́НА
Ха́рьков
Дон
Волгогра́д
Оде́сса
РУМЫ́НИЯ
КРЫМ
Я́лта
БОЛГА́РИЯ
Чёрное мо́ре
Со́чи
КАВКА́З
Эльбру́с
ГРЕ́ЦИЯ
Каспи́йское мо́ре
Баку́
ТУ́РЦИЯ
ИРА́Н

EXERCISE

Translate into Russian.

1. —Is Olga already at home? —Yes, she is at home. 2. —Is the pencil also here? —Yes, the pencil is also here. 3. That is the teacher. 4. —Here is the book. —Thank you. 5. —How are you? —Thank you, not very well. 6. The window is (over) there. 7. —Where is the paper? —Here it is. 8. —Is this the floor or the ceiling? —It's the floor. 9. —Who are you? —I'm a student. 10. —What is this? —It's a pen. —Correct. 11. —Good day! How are you? —Fine, thank you! 12. —Where is the wall and where is the window? —The window and the wall are there. 13. —What is that? Is it the bell already? —Yes, it's the bell already. 14. That's all. Good-bye!

THE RUSSIAN SCRIPT

The letters а, о, е, и, у

А, а 

И, и 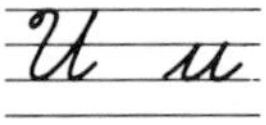

О, о 

У, у 

Е, е 

The letters с, р, в, х

С, с 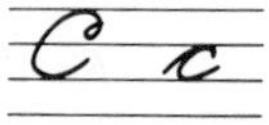

В, в 

Р, р 

Х, х 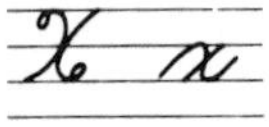

Copy the following words:

Рис, Rice 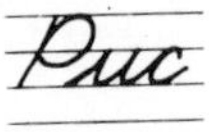

Уха́, Fish soup

Хе́рес, Sherry (Jerez)

Ве́ра, Е́ва и Варва́ра. Vera, Eva, and Barbara.

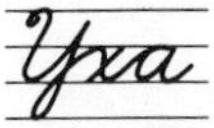

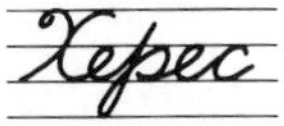

В Саха́ре су́хо. In the Sahara it is dry.

The letters д, п, т

Д, д

Note that capital **Д** is written like the English capital D, while the small letter is written like English small g.

П, п

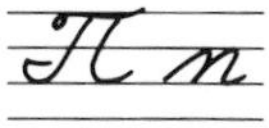

Note that small Russian **п** is written like English n.

Т, т

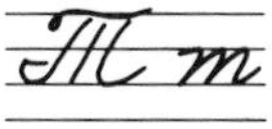

Note that small Russian **т** is written like English m.
Copy the following words:

Дави́д, David

Пётр, Peter

О́пера, Opera

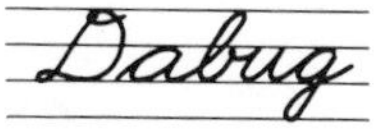

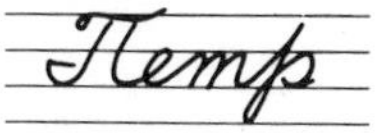

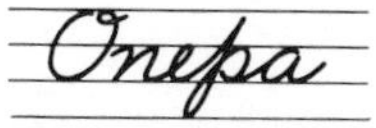

Спорт, Sport

Теа́тр, Theater *Театр*

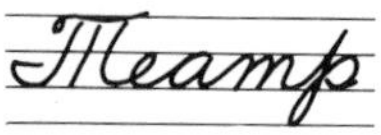

Write in Russian script:

Ве́ра и Пётр в теа́тре.
Vera and Peter are at the theater.

Варва́ра сестра́ Дави́да.
Barbara is David's sister.

А́йда о́пера Ве́рди.
Aida is an opera by Verdi.

Ту́т в теа́тре поёт хо́р.
Here in the theater a chorus is singing.

The letters к, н, ш

К, к *К к* (not *к*)

Н, н *Н н*

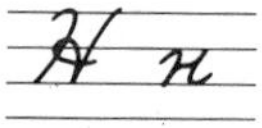

One should be careful not to write small **н** like English n which is
the small Russian **п**; the capital letter is like English capital H.

Ш, ш *Ш ш*

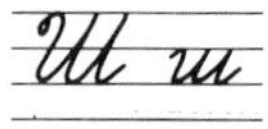

Note that this letter is written like English u with a third vertical
stroke.
Copy the following words:

Ко́рсика, Corsica *Корсика*

Кра́ков, Cracow *Краков*

Ни́на, Nina *Нина*

А́нна, Anna *Анна*

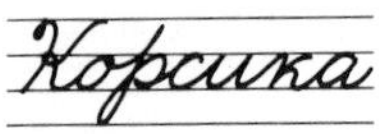

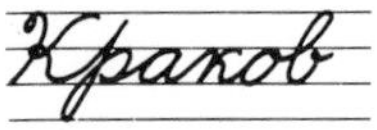

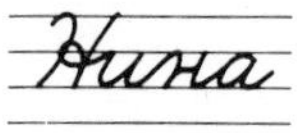

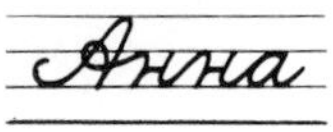

Нанки́н, Nanking *Нанкин*

Шах, the Shah *Шах*

Ша́шки, Checkers *Шашки*

Write in Russian script:

О́н шве́д.	He is a Swede.
Она́ хорошо́ поёт.	She sings well.
Нанки́н в Кита́е.	Nanking is in China.
Шу́ра сестра́ Константи́на.	Shura is Konstantin's sister.

The letters г, з, б

Г, г *Г г*

The capital is like English T; the small letter is like the second element of a small English n: *г*

З, з *З з* Б, б *Б б*

Begin the small letter like an o, then continue upward and to the right: *с б*

Copy the following words:

Григо́рий, Gregory *Григорий*

(Note the sign of brevity on the final **й**.)

Бсг, God *Бог*

За́греб, Zagreb *Загреб*

Занзиба́р, Zanzibar *Занзибар*

Write the following words in Russian script:

Ро́за и хризанте́ма.	A rose and a chrysanthemum.
Ива́н Гро́зный.	Ivan the Terrible.
Го́род Босто́н.	The city of Boston.
И́х ребёнок хорошо́ хо́дит.	Their child can walk well.
Его́ сестру́ зову́т Зи́ной.	His sister is called Zina.

The letters л, м, я

Л, л 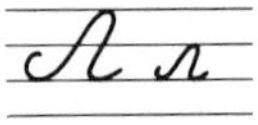

М, м 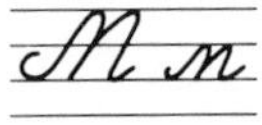

Я, я 

Note that small **л**, **м**, and **я** begin with a little hook above the lower line, at about one third of the height of the letters: 

The letter **я** continues with a loop to the left, then with a vertical stroke: 

Copy the following words, being careful to retain the initial hooks:

Ли́ма, Lima 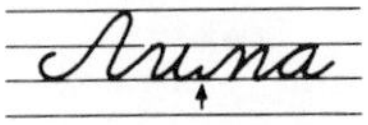

Мари́я, Maria 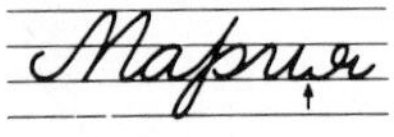

Япо́ния, Japan 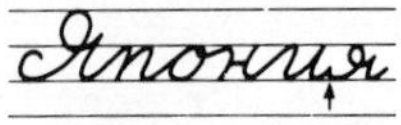

Ита́лия, Italy 

Ленингра́д, Ло́ндон, Москва́, Я́лта, Я́ва, Мила́н, Влади́мир, Маяко́вский, Ле́в Толсто́й, Я́сная Поля́на, Илиа́да Гоме́ра.

The letters ц and щ

Ц, ц 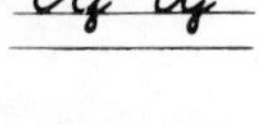

Щ, щ 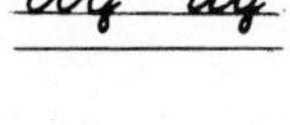

Note that these two letters are written respectively like **и** and **ш**, but with a small loop at the bottom of the last vertical stroke; this loop is much shorter than the "long" letters, such as **р** or **у**:

Цирк, Circus *цирк* Щу́ка, Pike *щука*

Copy the following words:

Цита́та из Цицеро́на, A quotation from Cicero

Цитата из Цицерона

Ще́бет пти́ц, The twitter of birds

Щебет птиц

Цена́ щётки, The price of the brush

Цена щетки

Write out the following words and phrases:

Це́лый ме́сяц.
A whole month.

Цена́ веще́й.
The price of things.

Щека́ ещё распу́хла.
The cheek is still swollen.

Л. В. Ще́рба специали́ст по ру́сской грамма́тике.
L. V. Shcherba is a specialist in Russian grammar.

The letter ч

Ч, ч *Ч ч*

Copy the following words:

Анто́н Па́влович Че́хов. Anton Pavlovich Chekhov.

Антон Павлович Чехов

Чёрная шля́па. A black hat. 

О́н вра́ч. He is a physician. 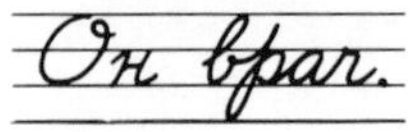

Write out the following words and phrases:

Си́ние черни́ла.
Blue ink.

О́н говори́т по-че́шски.
He speaks Czech.

Пра́га столи́ца Чехослова́кии.
Prague is the capital of Czechoslovakia.

Я́йца ку́рицу не у́чат.
Eggs don't teach the hen (*i.e.*, elders know better).

The letter ж

Ж, ж 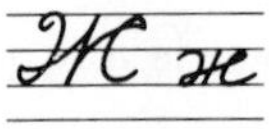

The tracing of capital Ж can be presented in several stages, as follows:

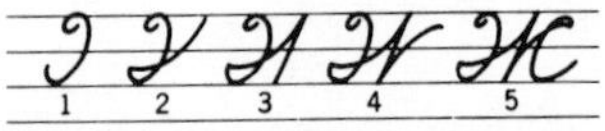

The small letter is ordinarily written like the capital, but smaller in size; a somewhat simplified way for writing it, like the one above, may, however, be suggested.

Copy the following words or phrases:

Жо́рж живёт в Пари́же. George lives in Paris.

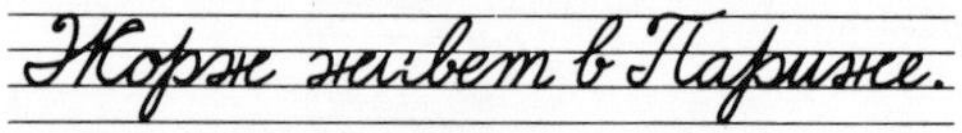

Жёлтая ко́жа. Yellow leather.

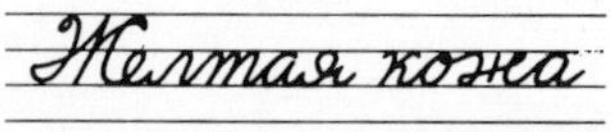

Положи́ ножи́ и ло́жки на сто́л.
Put the knives and the spoons on the table.

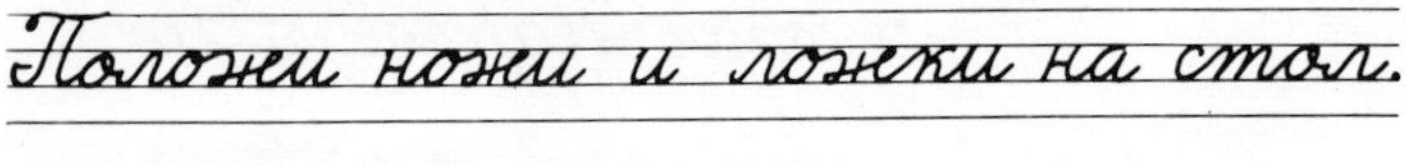

Write out the following words:

Её му́ж живёт в Жене́ве.
Her husband is living in Geneva.

Журна́л «Сове́тская же́нщина».
The journal "Soviet Woman."

Сего́дня ужа́сно жа́рко.
It's terribly hot today.

The letter ф

Ф, ф 

The tracing of capital **Ф** may be presented in several stages, as follows: 

The small letter is, approximately, an о combined with a р:

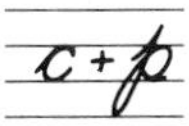

Copy the following words:

Фотогра́фия, Photograph 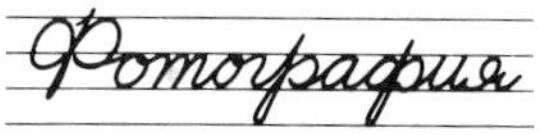

Фарфо́р, Porcelain 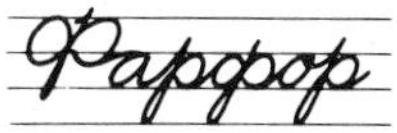

Филосо́фия, Philosophy 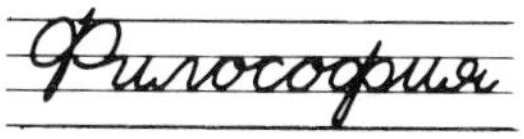

Фу́нт фи́ников, A pound of dates 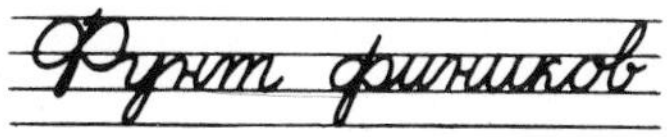

Write out the following words:

Флот, Fleet Симфо́ния, Symphony Фи́зика, Physics
Фами́лия, Family name.

The letter э

Э, э 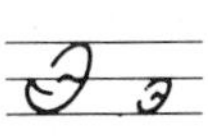

Copy the words below:

Эконо́мика, Economics — *Экономика*

Эпо́ха, Epoch — *Эпоха*

Э́хо, Echo — *Эхо*

Этногра́фия, Ethnography — *Этнография*

Электри́ческая эне́ргия, Electrical energy

Электрическая энергия

Поэ́зия, Poetry — *Поэзия*

Аэропо́рт, Airport — *Аэропорт*

Write out the following words:

О́н поэ́т.	He is a poet.
О́н экономи́ст.	He is an economist.
Э́то э́хо.	This is the echo.
Энциклопе́дия.	Encyclopedia.

The letter ю

Ю, ю — *Ю ю*

This letter may be described as a vertical stroke attached to an o.

Copy the words below:

Ю́рий юри́ст. Yuri (George) is a jurist.

Юрий юрист.

О́н лю́бит юриспруде́нцию. He loves jurisprudence.

Он любит юриспруденцию.

Я люблю южную приро́ду. I love southern nature.

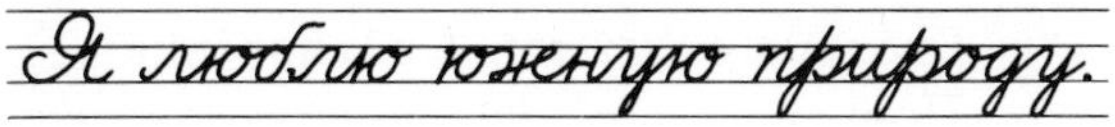

Я люблю южную природу.

Они́ приезжа́ют сюда́ ка́ждую зи́му. They come here every winter.

Они приезжают сюда каждую зиму.

Юката́н, Yukatan Каю́та, Cabin Рю́мка, Wineglass
Юг, South Индю́к, Turkey cock

The letters ь, ы, ъ

These three letters are never written initially and are never capitalized.

ь *ь* ы *ы* ъ *ъ*

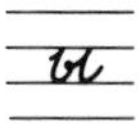

Note that the small loop, the common feature of the three letters above, comes up to only half the height of the letter:

ь ы ъ

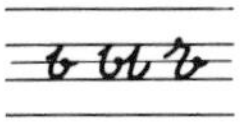

The letter ы is a ь with another vertical stroke; the ъ is like a ч with the little loop of the ь.

Copy the words below:

Мы́ бы́ли до́ма весь де́нь. We were at home all day.

Мы были дома весь день.

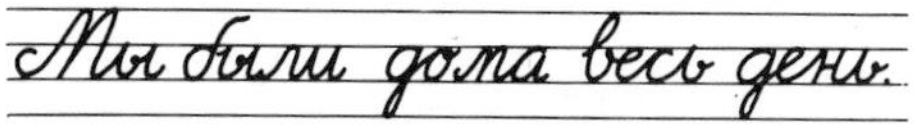

Кто́ съе́л всё конфе́ты? Who ate all the candies?

Кто съел все конфеты?

Я пью́ то́лько во́ду. I drink only water.

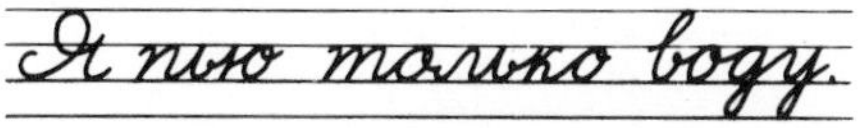

Я пью только воду.

То́лько ию́ль бы́л о́чень жа́ркий. Only July was very hot.

Только июль был очень жаркий.

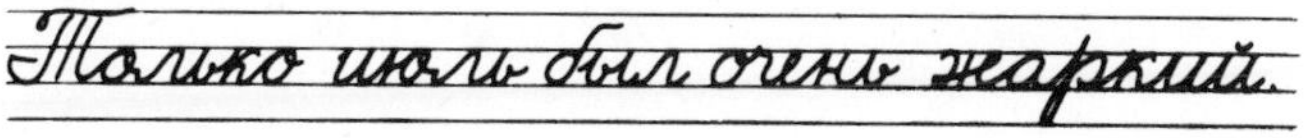

Write out the words below:

Ско́лько сто́ит тако́е объявле́ние?
How much does such an advertisement cost?

Э́тот ковёр о́чень пы́льный.
This rug is very dusty.

То́лько вы́ по́няли его́ объясне́ния.
Only you understood his explanations.

THE RUSSIAN ALPHABET

Printed Letters	*Script*	*Phonetic Transcription*	*Name of Letter*
А а	*А а*	a	a
Б б	*Б б*	b	be
В в	*В в*	v	ve
Г г	*Г г*	g	ge
Д д	*Д д*	d	de
Е е	*Е е*	e, je	je
Е ё	*Ё ё*	o, jo	jo
Ж ж	*Ж ж*	ž	že
З з	*З з*	z	ze
И и	*И и*	i	i
Й й	*Й й*	j	í krátkəjə
К к	*К к*	k	ka
Л л	*Л л*	l	el
М м	*М м*	m	em

Н	н	*Н*	*н*	n	en
О	о	*О*	*о*	o	o
П	п	*П*	*п*	p	pe
Р	р	*Р*	*р*	r	er
С	с	*С*	*с*	s	es
Т	т	*Т*	*т*	t	te
У	у	*У*	*у*	u	u
Ф	ф	*Ф*	*ф*	f	ef
Х	х	*Х*	*х*	x	xa
Ц	ц	*Ц*	*ц*	c	ce
Ч	ч	*Ч*	*ч*	ç̌	ç̌a
Ш	ш	*Ш*	*ш*	š	ša
Щ	щ	*Щ*	*щ*	ş̌ç̌	ş̌ç̌a
	ъ[1]		*ъ*	—	tṿórdɨj znák (hard sign)
	ы[1]		*ы*	ɨ	ɨ
	ь[1]		*ь*	.[2]	ṃáxkəj znák (soft sign)
Э	э	*Э*	*э*	e	e
Ю	ю	*Ю*	*ю*	u, ju	ju
Я	я	*Я*	*я*	a, ja	ja

The student is reminded that the pronunciation of certain of the vowels changes when unstressed. The values given in the table above are for stressed vowels only.

[1] Capital forms are not given for these letters since they never begin words.
[2] This sign is subscribed beneath consonants, and indicates their palatalization, *e.g.*, день [ḍéṇ].

UNIT 4

GRAMMAR

1. Gender in Russian (introductory)

Russian has three genders: masculine, feminine, and neuter. Generally, the gender of a Russian noun depends on its form and has no relation to meaning. This is obviously so with names of inanimate objects, or with abstract nouns, some of which are masculine, others feminine, and still others neuter:

Both стол, table, and ум, mind, are masculine.
Both ко́мната, room, and нау́ка, science, are feminine.
Both окно́, window, and иску́сство, art, are neuter.

In the case of names of male and female beings, the meaning is for the most part reflected in the form: most nouns denoting male and female beings have endings indicative of the corresponding grammatical gender.

2. Personal pronoun, third person

The gender of a noun determines the form of the third person pronoun (English "he," "she," "it") that may be used to replace it. The three gender forms of the pronoun in singular are:

for masculine nouns:	ОН [ón]
for neuter nouns:	ОНО́ [anó]
for feminine nouns:	ОНА́ [aná]

The pronouns он and она́ replace not only nouns denoting male and female beings (like "he" and "she" in English), *e.g.*:

—Где́ до́ктор? —Он ту́т.
—Where is the doctor? —*He* is here.

—Где́ сестра́? —Она́ та́м.
—Where is Sister? —*She* is there.

but also inanimate nouns of the masculine or feminine gender:

—Где́ университе́т? —Он та́м.
—Where is the university? —It is there.

—Где́ кни́га? —Она́ ту́т.
—Where is the book? —It is here.

3. Gender endings of nouns

The pattern of the third person pronouns, masculine **он**, neuter **оно́**, feminine **она́**, is followed by very many nouns:

nouns ending in a consonant (like the pronoun **он**), are masculine, *e.g.*, до**м**, house;
nouns ending in the vowel **-о** (like the pronoun **оно́**), are neuter, *e.g.*, окн**о́**, window;
nouns ending in the vowel **-а** (like the pronoun **она́**), are feminine, *e.g.*, ко́мнат**а**, room.

Drill

Form questions and answers on the pattern of —**«Где́ кни́га?»** —**«Она́ та́м,»** *substituting for* **кни́га** *the nouns given below and using the proper form of the personal pronoun* (**он, оно́, она́**) *in the answer:*

каранда́ш	pencil	стул	chair	ма́сло	butter
письмо́	letter	Ива́н	Ivan	река́	river
таре́лка	plate	сестра́	sister	О́льга	Olga
вино́	wine	окно́	window	молоко́	milk
хлеб	bread	телефо́н	telephone	по́лка	shelf
шко́ла	school	кни́га	book	журна́л	magazine

4. Gender endings continued: the stem and the suffix; hard and soft endings

The three gender forms of the third person pronoun, он, оно́, and она́ all have the element **он**; it is also present in the plural for all genders, **они́**, "they." The element **он** stands alone in the masculine singular, but adds different endings in the other forms. Thus, if the ending **-о** means neuter, the ending **-а** feminine, and **-и** plural, then the absence of any addition to the stem means masculine. A form with no additions to the stem is said to have a "zero ending" when it belongs to a series of related forms which take different endings:

	Masc.	он	suffix *zero*
Sing.	*Neut.*	оно́	suffix **-о**
	Fem.	она́	suffix **-а**
Pl. all genders		они́	suffix **-и**

Like **он**, the masculine nouns listed in the table above are stems with zero suffixes, while the neuter and feminine nouns have the suffixes **-о** and **-а** respectively.

The vowel suffixes in neuter and feminine nouns are stressed in some words and unstressed in others. Since both **о** and **а** unstressed are [ə], the suffixes, described phonetically, for neuter are [ó] or [ə]; for feminine [á] or [ə]:

Neut.	окно́ [akn.ó]	window,	but	кре́сло [kr̦ésl.ə]	armchair
Fem.	стена́ [șțin.á]	wall,	but	шко́ла [škól.ə]	school

Stems of all nouns end in consonantal sounds. In the examples given up to now these final stem consonants are *hard:*

телефо́н [țil̦ifón.]	stem ending [n] + suffix zero
письмо́ [p̦ișm.ó]	stem ending [m] + suffix [ó]
шко́ла [škól.ə]	stem ending [l] + suffix [ə]

Other nouns have *soft* stem endings: palatalized consonants, or the sound [j]. In terms of sound rather than spelling, nouns with soft stem endings have the same gender suffixes as nouns of the hard type: masculine zero, neuter [ó] or [e], feminine [á] or [e]:

Masc.	учи́тель [uč̦íțil̦.]	teacher, stem ending [l̦] + suffix zero
	слова́рь [slavár̦.]	dictionary, stem ending [r̦] + suffix zero
	музе́й [muz̦ẹ́j.]	museum, stem ending [j] + suffix zero
Neut.	бельё [b̦il̦j.ó]	linen, stem ending [j] + suffix [ó]
	по́ле [pól̦.ə]	field, stem ending [l̦] + suffix [ə]
	зда́ние [zdán̦ij.ə]	building, stem ending [j] + suffix [ə]
Fem.	туфля́ [tufl̦.á]	slipper, stem ending [l̦] + suffix [á]
	статья́ [stațj.á]	article, stem ending [j] + suffix [á]
	ку́хня [kúxn̦.ə]	kitchen, stem ending [n̦] + suffix [ə]
	иде́я [id̦ẹ́j.ə]	idea, stem ending [j] + suffix [ə]

One group of nouns of the feminine gender does not conform to the general pattern described above. Nouns of this type, which will be referred to as "Fem. II," end in soft consonants (or in [ž] and [š], which cannot be palatalized). They are written with a soft sign at the end:

соль salt дверь door тень shade, etc.

The following sums up the endings of nouns of the three genders:

GENDER ENDINGS OF NOUNS

Masculine: Zero Ending

Spelling: Hard: **any consonant**		*Soft:* **ь** or **й**	
стол [stól.]	table	слова́рь [slaváŗ.]	dictionary
брат [brát.]	brother	учи́тель [uçíţiļ.]	teacher
		чай [çáj.]	tea
		музе́й [muẓéj]	museum

Neuter: [o] (if unstressed [ə])

Spelling: Hard: **о**		*Soft stressed:* **ё (ьё)**	
окно́ [akn.ó]	window	бельё [ḅiļj.ó]	linen
кре́сло [kŗésl.ə]	armchair	*Soft unstressed:* **е**	
		по́ле [póļ.ə]	field
		мо́ре [móŗ.ə]	sea
		зда́ние [zdáņij.ə]	building

Fem. I: [a] (if unstressed [ə])

Spelling: Hard: **а**		*Soft:* **я**	
сестра́ [şistr.á]	sister	туфля́ [tufļ.á]	slipper
ко́мната [kómnət.ə]	room	ку́хня [kúxņ.ə]	kitchen
		иде́я [iḍéj.ə]	idea

Fem. II: Zero Ending; the stem ends in a soft consonant

		Spelling: Soft: **ь**[1]	
		соль [sóļ.]	salt
		ночь [nóç.]	night
		мышь [míš.]	mouse

[1] Fem. II nouns can generally not be distinguished from masculine nouns ending in a soft consonant, and the gender of these two types must be memorized. It should be noted, however, that *all* nouns ending in **-жь**, **-шь**, **-чь**, and **-щь** are Fem. II; the consonants **ж** and **ш** are, of course, always hard, while **ч** and **щ** are always soft, so that the **-ь** here serves solely as an indication of gender. Nouns ending in **-ж**, **-ш**, **-ч**, and **-щ**, *without* a soft sign, are always masculine, *e.g.* врач, "physician"; това́рищ, "comrade".

Pattern Sentences

1. —Где́ Ива́н? —**О́н** здéсь.	1. —Where is Ivan? —He's here.
2. —Где́ сто́л? —**О́н** ту́т.	2. —Where is the table? —It's here.
3. —Э́то О́льга? —Да́, э́то **она́.**	3. —Is that Olga? —Yes, it's she.
4. —Где́ кни́га? —Во́т **она́.**	4. —Where is the book? —There it is.
5. —Где́ письмо́? —Во́т **оно́.**	5. —Where is the letter? —Here it is.
6. —Где́ газе́та? —Во́т **она́.**	6. —Where is the newspaper? —Here it is.
7. —Кто́ Ю́рий? О́н студе́нт? —Не́т, о́н учи́тель.	7. —Who is Yuri? Is he a student? —No, he is a teacher.
8. —Кто́ Ни́на? Она́ студе́нтка? —Не́т, она́ учи́тельница.	8. —Who is Nina? Is she a student? —No, she is a teacher.
9. —Бори́с учи́тель и́ли журнали́ст? —О́н журнали́ст.	9. —Is Boris a teacher or a journalist? —He is a journalist.
10. —О́льга учи́тельница и́ли журнали́стка? —Она́ журнали́стка.	10. —Is Olga a teacher or a journalist? —She is a journalist.

Drill

Replace the dash with **он, оно́,** *or* **она́** *as required.*

1. —Э́то Ива́н? —Да́, э́то ....
2. —Музе́й зде́сь? —Не́т, ... та́м.
3. —Ни́на до́ма? —Да́, ... до́ма.
4. —Где́ ла́мпа? —Во́т ....
5. —О́льга студе́нтка? —Да́, ... студе́нтка.
6. —Где́ перо́? —Во́т ....
7. —Бори́с студе́нт? —Не́т, ... профе́ссор.
8. —Где́ по́лка? —...... ту́т.
9. —Окно́ та́м? —Да́, ... та́м.
10. —Где́ газе́та? —...... ту́т.
11. —Письмо́ ту́т? —Да́, ... ту́т,
12. —Где́ журна́л? —Во́т ....

5. Personal pronouns

Following is a table of Russian personal pronouns:

		Singular		Plural	
1st Pers.		я	I	мы	we
2nd Pers.		ты	you (thou)	вы	you
	Masc.	он			
3rd Pers.	*Neut.*	оно́	he, she, it (see Sect. 2)	они́	they
	Fem.	она́			

Like French, German, and other languages (but unlike English), Russian has preserved the second person singular pronoun. This pronoun, **ты**, is used in familiar address between close friends, members of a family, very young people, between and in addressing children, etc. Otherwise the pronoun **вы** is used. **Вы**, the second person plural, serves both for one person in formal address, and also as the actual plural, when more than one person is addressed.

Unlike "I" in English, the Russian first person pronoun **я** is not capitalized unless it is at the beginning of a sentence.

Pattern Sentences

1. —Кто́ **вы́?** —**Я́** студе́нт.	1. —Who are you? —I'm a student.
2. —Кто́ **о́н?** —**О́н** то́же студе́нт.	2. —Who is he? —He's a student too.
3. —Кто́ О́льга? —**Она́** студе́нтка.	3. —Who is Olga? —She's a student.
4. —Э́то **ты́,** Ива́н? —Да́, э́то **я́.**	4. —Is that you, Ivan? —Yes, it's I.
5. —Где́ Бори́с и А́нна? —**Они́** до́ма.	5. —Where are Boris and Anna? —They're at home.
6. —**Вы́** профе́ссор Па́влов? —Да́, **я́** Па́влов.	6. —Are you Professor Pavlov? —Yes, I am Pavlov.
7. **Я́** до́ма и Ива́н то́же. **Мы́** до́ма.	7. I'm at home and Ivan is too. We are at home.
8. **Я́** ту́т и **ты́** ту́т. **Мы́** ту́т.	8. I'm here and you're here. We are here.
9. **Ты́** ту́т и О́льга ту́т. **Вы́** ту́т.	9. You are here and Olga is here. You (both) are here.
10. **О́н** до́ма и **она́** до́ма. **Они́** до́ма.	10. He's at home and she's at home. They are at home.

6. Possessive pronoun-adjectives ("my," "your," "our")

The Russian possessive pronoun-adjectives agree in gender with the noun denoting the object owned. The distinction between "my" and "mine," "your" and "yours," etc. is not made in Russian, and the forms listed below correspond in use to both English forms.

"My" and "mine"	with *masc.*:	**мо́й** до́м.
	with *neut.*:	**моё** письмо́
	with *fem.*:	**моя́** ко́мната
"Your" and "yours" (correspond to informal **ты**)	with *masc.*:	**тво́й** до́м
	with *neut.*:	**твоё** письмо́
	with *fem.*:	**твоя́** ко́мната

"Our" and "ours"	with *masc.*:	**на́ш** до́м
	with *neut.*:	**на́ше** письмо́
	with *fem.*:	**на́ша** ко́мната
"Your" and "yours" (correspond to pl. or formal **вы**)	with *masc.*:	**ва́ш** до́м
	with *neut.*:	**ва́ше** письмо́
	with *fem.*:	**ва́ша** ко́мната

The interrogative "whose," also has three gender forms; questions of the type "Whose . . . . . . is this?" are usually formed with the word **это** unstressed:

"Whose"	with *masc.*:	**Че́й** это до́м?
	with *neut.*:	**Чьё** это письмо́?
	with *fem.*:	**Чья́** это ко́мната?

One will note that the gender forms of the possessive pronoun follow the general pattern described above. In masculine, the different forms are stems with a zero ending. To these stems, neuter adds [ó] and feminine [á] (or, if unstressed, [ə] for both). In the stems [mój] and [tvój] the usual phonetic change [ó] to [a] takes place when the stress shifts to the ending (see page 7):

Masculine: zero		*Neuter:* [ó—ə]		*Feminine:* [á—ə]	
мой	[mój.]	моё	[maj.ó]	моя́	[maj.á]
твой	[tvój.]	твоё	[tvaj.ó]	твоя́	[tvaj.á]
наш	[náš.]	на́ше	[náš.ə]	на́ша	[náš.ə]
ваш	[váš.]	ва́ше	[váš.ə]	ва́ша	[váš.ə]

The stem of the interrogative has an [é] in the masculine which does not appear in the other forms:

чей	[č̦ẹ́j.]	чьё	[č̦j.ó]	чья	[č̦j.á]

Pattern Sentences

1. —**Че́й** это каранда́ш? —Э́то **мо́й** каранда́ш.	1. —Whose pencil is this? —It's my pencil.
2. —**Чьё** это перо́? —Оно́ **моё.**	2. —Whose pen is this? —It's mine.
3. —**Чья́** это ко́мната? —Э́то **моя́** ко́мната.	3. —Whose room is this? —It's my room.
4. —**Че́й** это сту́л? —Э́то **ва́ш** сту́л.	4. —Whose chair is this? —It's your chair.
5. —Где́ **тво́й** до́м? —О́н та́м.	5. —Where is your house? —It's over there.
6. —Где́ **на́ше** письмо́? —Во́т оно́.	6. —Where is our letter? —Here it is.

7. —Кто́ это? —Э́то **моя́** до́чь.	7. —Who is that? —That's my daughter.
8. —**Чья́** это по́лка? **Ва́ша?** —Не́т, не **моя́**.	8. —Whose shelf is this? Yours? —No, it is not mine.
9. —Э́то **тво́й** журна́л? —Да́, **мо́й**.	9. —Is this your magazine? —Yes, it is mine.
10. —**Чьё** это письмо́? —**На́ше**.	10. —Whose letter is this? —Ours.

Drill

Fill in the blanks under (A) with the proper form of the interrogative **чей** *and those under (B) with the proper Russian form of the possessive pronoun given in English.*

Model: —**Че́й** это сто́л? —**Мо́й.**

	(A)	(B)	
1.	...... это кни́га?	....	(Mine)
2.	...... это до́м?	....	
3.	...... это окно́?	....	
4.	...... это журна́л?	....	(Yours, *sing.*)
5.	...... это газе́та?	....	
6.	...... это письмо́?	....	
7.	...... это перо́?	....	(Ours)
8.	...... это каранда́ш?	....	
9.	...... это по́лка?	....	
10.	...... это окно́?	....	(Yours, *pl.*)
11.	...... это сту́л?	....	
12.	...... это грамма́тика?	....	

7. Demonstrative pronoun-adjectives

Like English, Russian has two kinds of demonstratives: one used in pointing out objects or persons that are near to the speaker (English *this*); the other, those that are more remote (*that*). In Russian each of the two kinds of demonstratives has three gender forms:

This (*near*)		*That* (*remote*)	
Masc.			
э́тот [étət] до́м	this house	то́т [tót] до́м	that house
Neut.			
э́то [étə] окно́	this window	то́ [tó] окно́	that window
Fem.			
э́та [étə] ко́мната	this room	та́ [tá] ко́мната	that room

The form "that," in English usage, tends to be the more general one, used when nearness or remoteness are not specified or contrasted; in Russian, on the other hand, "this" forms, **э́тот**, **э́то**, **э́та**, are more general. The forms **тот**, **то**, **та** are used mainly when nearness and remoteness are contrasted, *e.g.*, **Э́та** ко́мната моя́, а **та́** (ко́мната may be omitted) ва́ша, This room is mine, and that one is yours.

The use of the neuter form **э́то** as an indefinite pronoun has been discussed in Unit 2 (page 19). It has been seen that a complete sentence can be formed with the word **э́то** (without gender agreement) and a noun.

Э́то сто́л.	This is a table.
Э́то кни́га.	This is a book.

Such sentences state, about something which is pointed out ("э́то") that "*it*" is a table, a book, etc. On the other hand, in э́тот сто́л or э́та кни́га, a particular table, or book, is pointed out by the demonstrative, but no statement is made about it. The word groups э́тот сто́л or э́та кни́га are therefore not sentences. To form a sentence a statement must be made, *e.g.*, that the table or the book "is mine":

Э́тот сто́л **мо́й.**	This table *is mine.*
Э́та кни́га **моя́.**	This book *is mine.*

With neuter nouns, the form **э́то** is ambiguous: **э́то** перо́ may mean both "This is a pen" and "This pen":

Что́ э́то? **Э́то перо́.**
What is this? *This is a pen.*

Э́то перо́ не моё. То́ перо́ моё.
This pen is not mine. That pen is mine.

Pattern Sentences

1. **Э́тот** студе́нт мо́й сы́н.	1. This student is my son.
2. **Э́та** студе́нтка моя́ до́чь.	2. This student is my daughter.
3. —**Э́тот** журна́л ва́ш? —Не́т, о́н ва́ш.	3. —Is this magazine yours? —No, it's yours.
4. —**Э́то** перо́ моё. —Не́т, оно́ моё.	4. —This pen is mine. —No, it's mine.
5. —Кто́ э́т**а** же́нщина? —**Э́то** моя́ ма́ть.	5. —Who is that woman? —It's my mother.
6. **Э́то** газе́та «Пра́вда».	6. This is the newspaper *Pravda.*
7. —**Э́та** газе́та ва́ша? —Не́т, она́ ва́ша. **Та́** моя́.	7. —Is this newspaper yours? —No, it's yours. That one is mine.
8. **Э́тот** сту́л не ва́ш. **То́т** ва́ш.	8. This chair isn't yours. That one is yours.

9. —**Э́то** перó моё? —Нéт, **э́то** моё. **Тó** вáше.

9. —Is this pen mine? —No, this one is mine. That one is yours.

Drill

Fill in the blanks, using the proper form of the words in boldface in the model sentences.

Model: **Э́тот** дóм **мóй.** *This* house is *mine.*

1. ...... письмó ....
2. ...... кни́га ....
3. ...... сту́л ....
4. ...... перó ....
5. ...... лáмпа ....
6. ...... крéсло ....
7. ...... ку́хня ....
8. ...... кóмната ....

Model: **Э́то** журнáл. **Э́тот** журнáл **вáш.** This is a magazine. This magazine is yours.

1. ...... кни́га. ...... кни́га ....
2. ...... перó. ...... перó ....
3. ...... кóмната. ...... кóмната ....
4. ...... письмó. ...... письмó ....
5. ...... стóл. ...... стóл ....
6. ...... газéта. ...... газéта ....

Table of Gender Endings:
Nouns, Third Person Pronouns, Possessive and Demonstrative Pronoun-Adjectives

	Masculine: zero		*Neuter:* [ó]—[ə]		*Feminine:* [á]—[ə]	
Nouns	стол учи́тель музéй	[stól.] [uç̌íţiļ.] [muz̧ẹ́j.]	окнó бельё крéсло здáние	[akn.*ó*] [b̧iļj.*ó*] [kŗésl.*ə*] [zdáņij.*ə*]	стенá земля́ шкóла идéя	[şţin.*á*] [z̧im̧ļ.*á*] [škól.*ə*] [iḑẹ́j.*ə*]
3rd Pers. Pron.	он	[ón]	онó	[an.*ó*]	онá	[an.*á*]
Poss.	мой, твой наш, ваш	[mój.], [tvój.] [náš.], [váš.]	моё, твоё нáше, вáше	[maj.*ó*], [tvaj.*ó*] [náš.*ə*], [váš.*ə*]	моя́ твоя́ нáша вáша	[maj.*á*] [tvaj.*á*] [náš.*ə*] [váš.*ə*]
Dem.	э́тот, тот	[ét.ət], [tót.]	э́то, то	[ét.*ə*] [t.*ó*]	э́та, та	[ét.*ə*], [t.*á*]

8. Conjunctions **и** and **а**

The conjunction **и** connects several members of a sentence to which the statement made is equally applicable:

Ива́н и О́льга до́ма.	Ivan and Olga are at home.

Ива́н \
⋮
и 〉 до́ма.
⋮
О́льга /

Ivan \
⋮
and 〉 are at home.
⋮
Olga /

Another conjunction, the separative conjunction **а** (always with a comma before it), is used in Russian when two different statements are made about two members of a sentence:

Ива́н ту́т, а О́льга до́ма.	Ivan is here, and (but) Olga is at home.
Ива́н——**ту́т,**	*Ivan*——is *here,*
. . . . . **а**	. . . . and (or but) . . . .
О́льга——**до́ма.**	*Olga*——is *at home.*

The separative **а** must be used in Russian with statements that are merely different, even when, as in the example above, they are not felt to be conflicting or contrasted; its use is not optional as is the use of *but* in English in this example.

The conjunction **а** is also used in sentences of the type "This is not A, but B" (or "This is B, and not A"):

Она́ не ту́т, а до́ма. (or: Она́ до́ма, а не ту́т.)
She is not here, but at home. (or: She is at home, and not here.)

О́н не студе́нт, а журнали́ст. (or: О́н журнали́ст, а не студе́нт.)
He is not a student, but a journalist. (or: He is a journalist, and not a student.)

Questions are often introduced by **а**, especially following a statement:

Ива́н ту́т. А где́ О́льга?
Ivan is here. And where is Olga?

И . . . и means "both . . . and":

О́н **и** профе́ссор **и** до́ктор.
He is both a professor and a doctor.

Pattern Sentences

1. О́льга студе́нтка **и** Ли́дия то́же студе́нтка.	1. Olga is a student, and Lydia is a student too.
2. Бори́с учи́тель, **а** Вади́м студе́нт.	2. Boris is a teacher, and Vadim is a student.
3. Я́ студе́нт **и** о́н студе́нт.	3. I am a student, and he is a student.
4. Я́ учи́тель, **а** о́н студе́нт.	4. I am a teacher, and he is a student.
5. Я́ не учи́тель, **а** студе́нт.	5. I am not a teacher, but a student.
6. Я́ студе́нт, **а** не учи́тель.	6. I am a student, and not a teacher.
7. —Я́ учи́тель. **А** кто́ вы́? —Я́ студе́нт.	7. —I am a teacher. And who are you? —I'm a student.
8. —Мы́ ту́т. **А** где́ они́? —Они́ до́ма.	8. —We are here. And where are they? —They are at home.
9. Андре́й Ко́лосов **и** журнали́ст **и** до́ктор.	9. Andrey Kolosov is both a journalist and a doctor.
10. Э́тот до́м на́ш, **а** то́т ва́ш.	10. This house is ours, and that one is yours.

Drill

A. *Insert* **и** *and* **а** *in the blanks as required.*

1. Она́ не секрета́рша, .. учи́тельница.	1. She is not a secretary, but a teacher.
2. Сестра́ .. бра́т до́ма.	2. The sister and the brother are at home.
3. Ива́н не до́ктор, .. журнали́ст.	3. Ivan is not a doctor, but a journalist.
4. О́льга .. Ива́н бра́т .. сестра́.	4. Olga and Ivan are brother and sister.
5. Я́ учи́тель, .. она́ секрета́рша.	5. I am a teacher, and she is a secretary.
6. О́н .. журнали́ст .. профе́ссор.	6. He is both a journalist and a professor.
7. Вы́ ту́т до́ма, .. я́ ту́т то́лько го́сть.	7. You are at home here, and I'm only a guest here.
8. А́нна .. учи́тельница .. студе́нтка.	8. Anna is both a teacher and a student.
9. Сы́н .. до́чь ту́т, .. оте́ц .. ма́ть до́ма.	9. The son and daughter are here, and the father and mother are at home.
10. Ва́ш оте́ц до́ктор .. на́ш то́же.	10. Your father is a doctor, and ours is too.
11. Э́то письмо́ моё, .. то́ твоё.	11. This letter is mine, and that one is yours.
12. Э́та газе́та моя́, .. та́ ва́ша.	12. This newspaper is mine, and that one is yours.
13. Э́тот журна́л мо́й, .. то́т ва́ш.	13. This magazine is mine, and that one is yours.
14. Э́то по́ле на́ше .. то́ то́же на́ше.	14. This field is ours, and that one is also ours.

15. Э́то по́ле на́ше, .. то́ не́т.[2] — 15. This field is ours, and that one is not.
16. —Ва́ш сы́н учи́тель, как вы́? —Не́т, о́н не учи́тель, .. до́ктор. — 16. —Is your son a teacher like yourself? —No, he is not a teacher, but a doctor.

B. *Transpose the following sentences according to the model.*

Model: Я́ не до́ктор, а профе́ссор.
Я́ профе́ссор, а не до́ктор.

1. Я́ не профе́ссор, а студе́нт.
2. Они́ не ту́т, а до́ма.
3. Бори́с не журнали́ст, а учи́тель.
4. О́льга не учи́тельница, а секрета́рша.

CONVERSATION

Па́влов. —Прости́те, ка́к ва́ша фами́лия?
Орло́в. Моя́ фами́лия Орло́в. А ка́к ва́ша?
П. —Я́ Па́влов.
О. —О́чень прия́тно. Вы́ профе́ссор Па́влов?
П. —Да́. Вы́ то́же профе́ссор?
О. —Не́т, я́ не профе́ссор, а журнали́ст. А э́то моя́ до́чь Со́ня. Она́ то́же журнали́стка, как я́. А э́то моя́ до́чь Ли́дия. Она́ учи́тельница. А э́то моя́ жена́. Ни́на, э́то профе́ссор Па́влов.
Ни́на. —Здра́вствуйте.[3] О́чень прия́тно.
П. —О́чень прия́тно. А вы́ то́же журнали́стка, как ва́ш му́ж?
Н. Не́т, я́ не журнали́стка и я́ не учи́тельница. Я́ то́лько жена́ и ма́ть.
П. Э́то о́чень хорошо́!
Н. Почему́ э́то так хорошо́?
П. Потому́ что хорошо́, когда́ же́нщина до́ма.

EXERCISES

A. *Answer the following questions.*

1. Па́влов журнали́ст? 2. Орло́в то́же профе́ссор, как Па́влов? 3. Кто́ Со́ня? Она́ учи́тельница? 4. Почему́ э́то хорошо́, что Ни́на не журнали́стка? 5. А кто́ вы́? Вы́ журнали́ст? 6. Ва́ша ма́ть то́же учи́тельница, как Ли́дия?

[2] The Russian word **не** may not end a sentence; **нет** is used in this position.
[3] The two в's of здра́вствуйте are usually not pronounced: [zdrástujţi].

B. *Translate into Russian.*

1. —Hello. How are you? 2. —Very well, thank you. And how are you? 3. —Also very well. 4. —This is our apartment; here is the kitchen, and here is my room. 5. —Whose dictionary is this? 6. —It's my dictionary. 7. —And whose letter is this? Is it yours? —It's not mine, but yours. 8. —Whose field is this? —It's our field. 9. This magazine is mine, and that one is yours. 10. —Why are you here? —Because this is my house. 11. This magazine is yours and that (one) is also yours. 12. This is my room, and that (one) is yours. 13. —What is your (last) name? —My name is Orlov. And what is yours? 14. His daughter is both a journalist and a teacher. 15. —Whose guest is he? —Ours.

VOCABULARY[4]

а and; but
брат brother
газе́та newspaper
гость (*masc.*) guest
до́ктор doctor
дочь (*fem.*) daughter
жена́ wife
же́нщина woman
журнали́ст journalist
журнали́стка woman journalist
здесь here
и́ли or
как how; like, as
когда́ when
ко́мната room
ку́хня kitchen
мать (*fem.*) mother
муж husband
оте́ц father
письмо́ letter
по́ле field
почему́ why
потому́ что because
секрета́рша secretary
сестра́ sister
слова́рь (*masc.*) dictionary, vocabulary
сын son
так so, thus
то́же also, too
то́лько only
хорошо́ well, good
учи́тель (*masc.*) teacher
учи́тельница woman teacher

Expressions

Здра́вствуйте! Hello! (How are you?)
Ка́к ва́ша фами́лия? What is your (last) name?
О́чень прия́тно Glad to know you (*lit.*: very pleasant)
Прости́те Excuse me
Э́то хорошо́ That's fine (good)
не . . . . а not . . . but
и . . . и both . . . and

[4] Consult the vocabularies at the end of the book for words used in the first three lessons.

UNIT 5

GRAMMAR

1. Declension (introductory)

In English the relations between words in a sentence are expressed mostly by word order ("John saw Peter," "Peter saw John") or by prepositions ("a letter sent *to* Peter," "a letter sent *by* John," etc.). With nouns, one type of relation may be expressed by using a special form of the word itself: in "John's room" the form "John's" indicates that the relation of "John" to "room" is that of possessor to object possessed. Personal pronouns in English have a wider range of forms denoting different types of relations: he, his, him; they, their, them, etc.

Russian, unlike English, has an extensive system of inflection, that is, nouns, adjectives, and other classes of words take different endings depending on their function in the sentence. These functions, or types of relations, are grouped into cases, and each case has its own endings. To *decline* a noun (or another declinable word) is to combine its stem with the endings of the different cases. Some types of relations are expressed in Russian by a case form alone, while others require both a case form (the adding of the proper suffix to the noun) and a preposition.

There are in all six cases in Russian, including the nominative. The nominative may be regarded as the basic form; it is in this form that nouns and other words appear when they are isolated from a context, as in dictionaries or vocabularies. The most important function of the nominative in a sentence is that of the subject.

The other five cases are traditionally listed after the nominative in the following order: genitive, dative, accusative, instrumental, and locative.

Paradigms (sets of case forms) are given below of two masculine and two feminine nouns representing the hard and soft stem ending types of these genders. Both feminines are of class I; the declension of Fem. II will be given later. A neuter noun has not been included since the neuter declension is like the masculine.

It is not necessary to memorize the declensions at this point.

Masculine

	Ending	*Hard:* стол, table		*Soft:* словáрь, dictionary	
Nom.	[zero]	стол	[stól.]	словáрь	[slaváŗ.]
Gen.	[a]	столá	[stal.á]	словарń	[sləvaŗ.á]
Dat.	[u]	столý	[stal.ú]	словарю́	[sləvaŗ.ú]
Acc.	[zero]	стол	[stól.]	словáрь	[slaváŗ.]
Instr.	[om]	столóм	[stal.óm]	словарём	[sləvaŗ.óm]
Loc.	[e]	столé	[staļ.é]	словарé	[sləvaŗ.é]

Feminine

		Hard: сестрá, sister		*Soft:* туфля́, slipper	
Nom.	[a]	сестрá	[şistr.á]	туфля́	[tufļ.á]
Gen.	[i/ɨ]	сестры́	[şistr.ɨ́]	туфли́	[tufļ.í]
Dat.	[e]	сестрé	[şistŗ.é]	туфлé	[tufļ.é]
Acc.	[u]	сестрý	[şistr.ú]	туфлю́	[tufļ.ú]
Instr.	[oj]	сестрóй	[şistr.ój]	туфлёй	[tufļ.ój]
Loc.	[e]	сестрé	[şistŗ.é]	туфлé	[tufļ.é]

It will be observed that:

(1) In most case forms the hardness or softness of the stem ending is preserved and is shown by spelling. Thus, in the masculine declension, the genitive ending [-a] is spelled **-а** in the hard variant, **-я** in the soft; similarly, dative [-u] is spelled **-у** and **-ю**; instrumental [-om], **-ом** and **-ём**. In the feminine declension we find **-ы**, **-у**, **-ой** in the hard variant corresponding to **-и**, **-ю**, **-ёй** in the soft. (Unstressed endings, which are slightly different, are not considered here.)

(2) An exception to the above is the suffix **-е**, as in masculine locative and feminine dative and locative. Before the vowel **е** all consonants are palatalized,[1] and the usual hard-soft opposition is

[1] Except, of course, those consonants which are always hard: **ж**, **ш**, and **ч**.

lacking in those cases which have **-e** as their ending; thus, the locative case forms столе́ [staļ.é] and сестре́ [şistŗ.é] have soft stem endings even though both nouns are of the hard variant.

(3) Certain changes may occur in the pronunciation of the stem of a noun as it is declined. Thus, in the declension of стол [stól], there is a change [ó > a] in the vowel of the stem when the stress shifts to the ending; also, the hard stem ending [l] becomes soft [ļ] in the locative. These and similar changes, however, are secondary; they are side effects of shifts of stress, of the addition of certain case endings in declension, etc. Except for certain automatic phonetic changes, the stem remains fixed.

2. The locative case of nouns

A. Forms of the locative. Most nouns of the three genders take in the locative case the ending **-e** ([-é]; if unstressed [-i]).

		Nominative		*Locative*	
	hard stem end.	стол	[stól.]	столе́	[staļ.é][2]
	,,	стул	[stúl.]	сту́ле	[stúļ.i]
Masc.	soft stem end.	слова́рь	[slaváŗ.]	словаре́	[sləvaŗ.é][2]
	,,	гость	[góşţ.]	го́сте	[góşţ.i]
	,, [j]	музе́й	[muẓéj.]	музе́е	[muẓéj.i]
	hard stem end.	окно́	[akn.ó]	окне́	[akņé]
Neut.	,,	о́зеро	[óẓir.ə]	о́зере	[óẓiŗ.i]
	soft stem end. [j]	бельё	[ḅiļj.ó]	белье́	[ḅiļj.é]
	,,	по́ле	[póļ.ə]	по́ле	[póļ.i]
	hard stem end.	сестра́	[şistr.á]	сестре́	[şistŗ.é]
	,,	ко́мната	[kómnət.ə]	ко́мнате	[kómnəţ.i]
Fem.	soft stem end.	туфля́	[tufļ.á]	туфле́	[tufļ.é]
	,,	ку́хня	[kúxņ.ə]	ку́хне	[kúxņ.i]
	,, [j]	иде́я	[iḑéj.ə]	иде́е	[iḑéj.i]

Note: The word по́ле and other words of this type are spelled alike in the nominative and locative; the final unstressed **-e**, however, tends to be pronounced as a neutral sound [ə] in the nominative but with an [i] quality in the locative.

B. Uses of the locative. As stated earlier, different cases are used with prepositions in some instances and without prepositions in others. The locative case is never used alone, but only with certain

[2] A number of masculine nouns which have the stress on the stem in the nominative shift the stress to the ending in other cases.

prepositions. There are in all five prepositions that require the use of (or "govern") this case; two of these, **в** and **на**, will be introduced now (a third will be added later in this lesson):

The basic meaning of **в** is *in:*	in the house—в до́ме
The basic meaning of **на** is *on:*	on the table—на столе́

Like the adverbs тут, там, до́ма, etc., phrases with **в** or **на** and a noun in the locative answer the question "where?"—"**где?**"

Где́?	В теа́тре [fţiátŗi]	in (at) the theater
	В шко́ле [fškóļi]	in (at) the school
	В воде́ [vvaḑé]	(pronounce with a single long [v]) in the water
	На стене́ [nəşţiņé]	on the wall
	На столе́ [nəstaļé]	on the table

Observe in the examples above that a prepositional phrase (preposition plus noun in the proper case form) is pronounced as a single word.

The preposition **на**, in addition to its primary meaning, is also used with nouns denoting activities or events one attends rather than actual places (in this use **на** often corresponds to English "at"):

на конце́рте	at a concert
на уро́ке	at a lesson
на рабо́те	at work, at one's place of work
на о́пере	at an opera
на футбо́ле	at a football game

But **в**, *at* or *in* a building, enclosed place:

в теа́тре	at (in) the theater
в шко́ле	at (in the) school
в библиоте́ке	at (in) the library
в музе́е	at (in) the museum

Pattern Sentences

1. Во́т го́род. **В го́роде** у́лица. **На у́лице** до́м.	1. Here is a city. In the city is a street. On the street there is a house.
2. **В до́ме** кварти́ра. **В кварти́ре** ко́мната.	2. In the house there's an apartment. In the apartment there's a room.
3. Э́та ко́мната—мо́й кабине́т.[3] Я́ **в кабине́те.**	3. That room is my study. I am in the study.
4. Э́то мо́й сто́л; **на столе́** мо́й слова́рь.	4. This is my table (desk); on the table is my dictionary.

[3] In sentences of this type, in which one noun is the subject and a second noun the predicate, a dash is sometimes written to separate the two nouns.

5. Отéц **на рабóте,** а мáть **в теáтре.**	5. Father is at work and Mother is at (has gone to) the theater.
6. —Гдé мóй карандáш? —Óн **на столé.**	6. —Where is my pencil? —It's on the table.
7. —Гдé письмó? —Онó тáм **на стýле.**	7. —Where is the letter? —It's there, on the chair.
8. —Твоя́ сестрá дóма? —Нéт, моя́ сестрá **на концéрте.**	8. —Is your sister at home? —No, my sister is at (has gone to) a concert.
9. —Гдé вáш брáт? —Мóй брáт **в библиотéке** и́ли **в музéе.**	9. —Where is your brother? —My brother is at the library or at the museum.
10. Ивáн **на футбóле,** а Óльга **в шкóле на экзáмене.**	10. Ivan is at a football game, and Olga is at school at an exam.
11. —«Карти́на»—э́то picture? —Дá, вóт мóй словáрь, а вóт **в словарé** слóво «карти́на».	11. —Is карти́на "picture"? Yes, here's my dictionary, and here in the dictionary is the word карти́на.
12. Карти́на тáм **на стенé**—кóпия; оригинáл **в Москвé,** в музéе.	12. The picture on the wall there is a copy; the original is in Moscow, in a museum.
13. Моя́ сестрá тепéрь **в Нью-Йóрке.**	13. My sister is in New York now.
14. —Пётр тепéрь **в Еврóпе?** —Дá, óн **в Пари́же.**	14. —Is Peter in Europe now? —Yes, he is in Paris.

Drills

A. *Fill in the blanks in each of the numbered sentences below, using the locative case form of the noun that occurs in the preceding sentence in the nominative.*

a. Вóт гóрод.	b. Вóт шкóла.	c. Вóт стенá.
1. В ...... ýлица.	1. В ...... клáсс.	1. На ...... кáрта.
2. На ...... дóм.	2. В ...... экзáмен.	2. На ...... Еврóпа.
3. В ...... кварти́ра.	3. На ...... моя́ сестрá.	3. В ...... Пари́ж.
4. В ...... кóмната.		4. В ...... мóй брáт.
5. В ...... стóл.		
6. На ...... бумáга.		
7. На ...... перó.		

B. *Translate into Russian the answers to the following questions; the Russian noun to be used in the answer is given in parentheses in the nominative case after the English phrase.* (*Be careful to use proper forms in translating "it".*)

1. Гдé вáш карандáш?	It is on the table. (стол)
2. Гдé музéй?	It is in the city. (гóрод)
3. Гдé кáрта?	It is on the wall. (стенá)

4. Где́ на́ша учи́тельница? She is at school. (шко́ла)
5. Где́ ма́ма? She is in the kitchen. (ку́хня)
6. Где́ ва́ша до́чь? She is at work. (рабо́та)
7. Где́ тво́й бра́т? He is in Europe. (Евро́па)
8. Где́ мо́й слова́рь? It is over there, on the armchair. (кре́сло)
9. Где́ бума́га? It is on the chair. (стул)
10. Где́ моё перо́? It is in the study. (кабине́т)

C. *Supply the proper preposition* (**в** *or* **на**) *in each question and answer it, using a suitable word from the vocabulary you have learned; follow this model.*

Model: —Кто́ в кабине́те? —**В кабине́те мо́й оте́ц.**

1. —Кто́ ...... у́лице? —......
2. —Кто́ ...... теа́тре? —......
3. —Кто́ ...... Москве́? —......
4. —Кто́ ...... экза́мене? —......
5. —Что́ ...... ко́мнате? —......
6. —Кто́ ...... библиоте́ке? —......
7. —Кто́ ...... конце́рте? —......
8. —Кто́ ...... кла́ссе? —......
9. —Кто́ ...... футбо́ле? —......
10. —Что́ ...... ка́рте? —......
11. —Что́ ...... музе́е? —......
12. —Кто́ ...... Пари́же? —......

3. Locative case of third person pronouns

		Nominative	*Locative*
Sing.	*Masc.*	он	(в, на) нём [ņóm]
	Neut.	оно́	
	Fem.	она́	(в, на) не́й [ņẹ́j]
Pl. all gend.		они́	(в, на) ни́х [ņíx]

4. Locative case of possessive and demonstrative pronouns

The locative and other case forms of the possessive and demonstrative pronouns are closely related to those of the third personal pronouns. The possessives and demonstratives take the following endings in the locative:

Masc., *Neut.* } **-ом, -ём, -ем** pronounced [óm] ([əm] unstressed)

Fem. **-ей, -ой** pronounced [ẹ́j] or [ój] ([əj] unstressed)

The locative forms of the different pronouns are given below together with the corresponding nominative forms:

	NOMINATIVE *Masculine*	*Neuter*	LOCATIVE *Masculine and Neuter*
3rd Pers. Pron.	он [ón.-]	онó [an.ó]	нём [n̦.*óm*]
Possessives	мóй [mój.-] твóй [tvój.-] нáш [náš.-] вáш [váš.-]	моё [maj.ó] твоё [tvaj.ó] нáше [náš.ə] вáше [váš.ə]	моём [maj.*óm*] твоём [tvaj.*óm*] нáшем [náš.*əm*] вáшем [váš.*əm*]
Demonstratives	э́тот [ét.ət] тот [t.ót]	э́то [ét.ə] то [t.ó]	э́том [ét.*əm*] том [t.*óm*]

Feminine

3rd Pers. Pron.	онá [an.á]	ней [n̦.*ẹ́j*]
Possessives	моя́ [maj.á] твоя́ [tvaj.á] нáша [náš.ə] вáша [váš.ə]	моéй [maj.*ẹ́j*] твоéй [tvaj.*ẹ́j*] нáшей [náš.*əj*] вáшей [váš.*əj*]
Demonstratives	э́та [ét.ə] та [t.á]	э́той [ét.*əj*] той [t.*ój*]

Pattern Sentences

1. Э́то мóй кабинéт. В **моём** кабинéте стóл и крéсло.
2. —Чтó на **вáшем** столé? —На **нём** лáмпа, бумáга, словáрь.
3. —Э́то нáш дóм; в **нём** нáша квартíра. —Ктó тепéрь в **вáшей** квартíре? —В **нéй** тепéрь мóй отéц и мáть.
4. Тепéрь в **нáшей** шкóле экзáмен. На **нём** моя́ сестрá.
5. На **э́той** у́лице нáш теáтр; тепéрь в **нём** концéрт.

1. This is my study. In my study there is a table (desk) and an armchair.
2. —What is on your table? —On it are a lamp, paper, a dictionary.
3. —That is our house; in it is our apartment. —Who is in your apartment now? —My father and my mother are in it now.
4. There is an exam now in our school. My sister is at it.
5. On this street is our theater; now there is a concert in it.

Drills

A. *Substitute the proper pronoun for the noun used, according to the model.*

Model: Вóт стóл; на **нём** лáмпа.

1. Вóт нáш дóм; в ...... мóй кабинéт.
2. Вóт кни́га; в ...... кáрта.
3. Вóт крéсло; на ...... газéта.
4. Вóт стýл; на ...... мóй словáрь.
5. Вóт нáш клáсс; в ...... доскá.
6. Вóт кýхня; в ...... стóл.

B. *Complete the sentences below by adding the words in parentheses in the locative case.*

1. Словáрь на ...... (мóй стóл).
2. Газéта в ...... (твóй кабинéт).
3. Нáша кварти́ра в ...... (э́тот дóм).
4. Шкóла на ...... (э́та ýлица).
5. Ивáн в ...... (твоя́ кóмната).
6. Пётр тепéрь в ...... (нáша шкóла).

5. Past tense of verbs

The Russian verb has only one past tense. In the past tense the verb is not conjugated (does not change according to person—first, second, or third), but agrees in gender and number with its subject; it has three gender forms in the singular and one form for all genders in the plural.

The past tense is formed with a stem which is the same as that of the infinitive. With very few exceptions the infinitive ending of Russian verbs is **-ть** [-ţ]:

рабóтать,	to work,	stem:	рабóта-
читáть,	to read,	stem:	читá-
говори́ть,	to speak,	stem:	говори́-
стоя́ть,	to stand,	stem:	стоя́-

Instead of the infinitive ending **-ть** [-ţ], the past tense in all its forms adds to the stem the element **-л** [-l]. No further suffix is added for the masculine; for the neuter **-о** is added after л; for the feminine **-а**; and for the plural, all genders **-и** (compare the third person pronoun он, он**ó**, он**á**, он**и́**).

Masculine	*Neuter*	*Feminine*	*Plural, All Genders*
рабóта**л**	рабóта**ло**	рабóта**ла**	рабóта**ли**
читá**л**	читá**ло**	читá**ла**	читá**ли**
говори́**л**	говори́**ло**	говори́**ла**	говори́**ли**
стоя́**л**	стоя́**ло**	стоя́**ла**	стоя́**ли**

The following table illustrates the use of the different past forms according to the gender and number of the subject:

Masc. Sing.	Ива́н сто́л я́ (man speaking) ты́ (to a man) о́н	стоя́л [stajá.l.]
Neut. Sing.	кре́сло оно́	стоя́**ло** [stajá.l.ə]
Fem. Sing.	А́нна ла́мпа я́ (woman speaking) ты́ (to a woman) она́	стоя́**ла** [stajá.l.ə]
Pl., All Genders	Ива́н и А́нна кре́сло и ла́мпа мы́ вы́ они́	стоя́**ли** [stajá.l̦.i]

The Russian forms **стоя́л** or **рабо́тал** may be translated, according to context, as "stood," "was standing," "did stand," "has (or had) stood"; or: "worked," "was working," "has (or had) worked," etc.

Note that the plural forms (**стоя́ли**, **рабо́тали**) are always used with **вы**, whether it is the actual plural or the "formal."

The verb "to be"; past tense.

Infinitive: быть, "to be":

Past tense:

	Masc.	**был:**	Зде́сь **бы́л** сто́л. There was a table here.
Sing.	*Neut.*	**бы́ло:**	Кре́сло **бы́ло** в кабине́те. The armchair was in the study.
	Fem.	**была́:**	Кни́га **была́** на столе́. The book was on the table.
Pl., all genders		**бы́ли:**	Ива́н и О́льга **бы́ли** до́ма. Ivan and Olga were at home.

Note the use of был, бы́ли в . . . , or на . . . , in Russian (literally, "was-were at"), often corresponding to English "went to" (*i.e.*, "attended"), as in:

Мы́ **бы́ли** в теа́тре.	We *went to* the theater.
Я́ вчера́ **бы́л** на конце́рте.	I *went to* a concert yesterday.

The negative, "was not," "were not," is formed with the **не** particle which is pronounced jointly with the verb; observe accentuation (stress shifting to **не**) in the masculine and neuter singular and the plural:

не́ был	[n̥ébɨl]
не́ было	[n̥ébɨlə]
не была́	[n̥ibɨlá]
не́ были	[n̥ébɨl̥i]

Note: the negative particle **не** affects the word which immediately follows it:

Positive statement:

Я́ бы́л в теа́тре вчера́.
I went to (was at) the theater yesterday.

Different elements negated:

Я́ **не́ был** в теа́тре вчера́.
I *did not go* to the theater yesterday.

Не я́ бы́л в теа́тре вчера́, а мо́й бра́т.
It wasn't I who went to the theater yesterday (but my brother).

Я́ бы́л **не в теа́тре** вчера́, а на конце́рте.
It was *not to the theater* that I went yesterday (but to a concert).

Я́ бы́л в теа́тре **не вчера́**, а сего́дня.
It was *not yesterday* that I went to the theater (but today).

Verb List

быть	to be	говори́ть	to say, tell; speak, talk
стоя́ть	to stand	чита́ть	to read
жить[4]	to live	писа́ть	to write
знать	to know	переводи́ть	to translate
ду́мать	to think	слу́шать	to listen (to)
де́лать	to make, do	рабо́тать	to work

[4] The verb **жить** has a shifting stress in the past tense: жил, жи́ло, жила́, жи́ли.

Pattern Sentences

1. В ко́мнате **бы́л** сто́л.[5] На столе́ **бы́л** каранда́ш и **была́** бума́га. А на бума́ге **была́** му́ха!
2. Ту́т **стоя́л** телефо́н. Где́ о́н?
3. Ту́т **стоя́ла** ла́мпа. Где́ она́?
4. О́льга и Вади́м **бы́ли** зде́сь. Они́ зде́сь вме́сте **рабо́тали.**
5. —Что́ они́ **де́лали?** —О́н **чита́л,** а она́ **переводи́ла.**
6. —А что́ ты́ **де́лал?** —Я́ **писа́л** письмо́ и коне́чно **слу́шал,** что́ они́ **говори́ли.**
7. —Ка́к они́ **говори́ли**: по-англи́йски и́ли по-ру́сски? —По-ру́сски, коне́чно!
8. Я́ **жи́л** в Ло́ндоне, когда́ ва́ш бра́т то́же та́м **жи́л.**
9. Мы́ не **зна́ли,** что[6] вы́ вчера́ **бы́ли** в теа́тре.
10. Вчера́ **бы́л** конце́рт. Ю́рий **бы́л** на конце́рте, а Ни́на **была́** в теа́тре.
11. —Где́ Анна? —Она́ **была́** на уро́ке, а тепе́рь она́ в библиоте́ке.
12. —Я́ не́ **был** в библиоте́ке. Э́то далеко́ и́ли бли́зко? —О́чень бли́зко.

1. In the room there was a desk (or: there was a desk in the room).[5] On the desk there was a pencil and there was some paper. And on the paper there was a fly!
2. Here there used to be a telephone (standing). Where is it?
3. There was a lamp standing here. Where is it?
4. Olga and Vadim were here. They were working here together.
5. —What were they doing? —He was reading, and she was translating.
6. —And what were you doing? —I was writing a letter, and of course I was listening to what they were saying.
7. —What were they speaking: (in) English or Russian? (In) Russian, of course!
8. I was living in London when your brother was living there too.
9. We didn't know that[6] you had been to the theater yesterday.
10. Yesterday there was a concert. Yuri was at the concert, and Nina was at the theater.
11. —Where is Anna? —She was at class and now she is at the library.
12. —I haven't been to the library. Is it far or near? —Very near.

[5] Note in this and the following sentences that the inverted order of the Russian sentence corresponds to English sentences in which the subject is used with an *indefinite* article ("*a* desk"). A comparable Russian sentence with normal order would correspond to the *definite* article in English: Сто́л бы́л в ко́мнате. *The table was in the room.*

[6] The word **что** is used as an interrogative pronoun and as a relative pronoun. In both cases it is translated as "what" and is stressed (see Sentence 6). **Что** is also used as a conjunction (see Sentence 9), introducing a clause after "to know, say, think," etc., corresponding to "that." As a conjunction it is unstressed. Note that colloquial English frequently omits the conjunction "that"; in Russian, however, it must not be omitted.

Interrog.:	**Что́** о́н чита́л?	*What* was he reading?
Relative:	Я́ не зна́л, **что́** о́н чита́л.	I did not know *what* he was reading.
Conjunct.:	Я́ зна́л, **что** о́н чита́л по-ру́сски.	I knew (*that*) he was reading in Russian.

13. —Вы́ **бы́ли** в Евро́пе? —Да́, мы́ та́м **бы́ли.** —Где́ вы́ та́м **жи́ли**? —Мы́ **жи́ли** в Ло́ндоне и в[7] Пари́же.	13. —Have you been to Europe? —Yes, we've been there. —Where did you live there? —We lived in London and Paris.
14. —Что́ вы́ та́м **де́лали?** —Мы́ **рабо́тали.** Я́ писа́тель и жена́ моя́ писа́тельница. Мы́ вме́сте **писа́ли** рома́н. —Как интере́сно!	14. —What were you doing there? —We were working. I am a writer and my wife is a writer (too). We were writing a novel together. —How interesting!

Drills

A. *Supply the correct past tense form of the verb indicated for each of the following three groups:*

(1) **быть**

a. Мы́ вчера́ ...... на конце́рте.
b. В ку́хне ...... сто́л.
c. На столе́ ...... кни́га.
d. На кни́ге ...... письмо́.
e. О́льга сего́дня ...... на уро́ке.

(2) **жить**

a. —Вы́ ...... в Пари́же? —Да́, я́ та́м ....
b. —Кто́ ...... в Ло́ндоне? —Бори́с ...... та́м.
c. —Они́ ...... в Нью-Йо́рке? —Не́т, они́ та́м не ....
d. —Ни́на ...... в Москве́? —Да́, она́ та́м ....
e. —Ты́ ...... в Ленингра́де? —Не́т, я́ ...... в Москве́.

(3) **стоя́ть**

a. На столе́ ...... ла́мпа.
b. На столе́ ...... телефо́н.
c. На по́лке ...... кни́га.
d. На по́лке ...... слова́рь.
e. В ко́мнате ...... кре́сло (armchair).
f. В ку́хне ...... ма́ма.

B. *Supply the correct past tense form of* **де́лать** *in the questions and translate the answers into Russian.*

1. Что́ О́льга вчера́ ......?	She read.
2. Что́ Ива́н вчера́ ......?	He wrote.
3. Что́ э́та студе́нтка вчера́ ......?	She worked.
4. Что́ ты́ вчера́ ......?	I translated.[8]
5. Что́ ты́ и тво́й бра́т вчера́ ......?	We talked.

[7] Unlike English, Russian usually repeats a preposition before a second object.
[8] In this and later drills with the word "I," always use the gender appropriate to yourself.

6. The preposition о, об

Another preposition which, like **в** and **на**, governs the locative case (though it does not show location), is the preposition **о** (**об** before words beginning with a vowel sound).[9] A prepositional phrase with **о** denotes content or topic:

Я́ ду́мал об э́той пробле́ме.	I thought of that problem.
Мы́ говори́ли о ва́шем бра́те.	We talked about your brother.
О́н писа́л о спо́рте в Евро́пе.	He wrote about sports in Europe.
Во́т статья́ о ва́шей кни́ге.	Here is an article about your book.
Я́ чита́л об э́том в газе́те.	I read about it in the paper.

The questions "about what?" or "about whom?" are formed in Russian with the preposition **о** and the word **что** (what) or **что** (who), in the locative case. "About what" is **о чём**?, and "about whom" is **о ко́м**? Like all prepositions, **о** is pronounced together with the word it governs: о чём [aç̌óm], о ко́м [akóm], о спо́рте [aspórţi], об э́том [abétəm].

Pattern Sentences

1. —О ко́м они́ говори́ли? —Они́ говори́ли о писа́теле Шо́лохове.[10]
2. —О чём[11] вы́ говори́ли? —Мы́ говори́ли о ва́шей кни́ге.
3. —О чём э́та статья́? —О теа́тре в Аме́рике.

1. —Whom were they talking about? —About the writer Sholokhov.
2. —What were you talking about? —We were talking about your book.
3. —What is this article about? —About theater in America.

Drills

A. *Complete the answers below using the correct form of the preposition* **о/об** *and the locative form for each noun and pronoun:*

1. —О чём вы́ говори́ли? —Я́ говори́л(а) о/об: он, оно́, она́, они́, Че́хов, Москва́, на́ша рабо́та, э́тот уро́к, твоё письмо́, э́та газе́та.
2. —О ко́м вы́ ду́мали? —Я́ ду́мал(а) о/об: Ива́н, О́льга, мо́й учи́тель, моя́ жена́, твоя́ учи́тельница, на́ш студе́нт, ва́ша студе́нтка, ва́ш сы́н, э́тот журнали́ст, э́та писа́тельница, до́ктор Ива́нов, профе́ссор Ро́бинсон.
3. —О чём ва́ша статья́? Моя́ статья́ о/об: спо́рт, о́пера, на́ш го́род, э́та пробле́ма, ва́ш профе́ссор, на́ш теа́тр, на́ша шко́ла.

[9] But not before initial [j], written **я, е, ё**, or **ю**.

[10] Two words in apposition in Russian (as писа́тель and Шо́лохов here) are both declined; both take the locative ending in the example above.

[11] Observe that prepositions and their objects may not be separated in Russian; a Russian sentence may not end with a preposition.

B. *Supply the correct form of the third person pronoun.*

1. —Вы́ писа́ли о Че́хове? —Да́, я́ о . . . . . . писа́л(а).
2. —Вы́ писа́ли об э́той о́пере? —Не́т, я́ о . . . . . . не писа́л(а).
3. —Вы́ говори́ли об Ива́не и об О́льге? Да́, мы́ о . . . . . . говори́ли.
4. —Вы́ говори́ли об э́том письме́? —Не́т, мы́ о . . . . . . не говори́ли.
5. —Вы́ слы́шали об э́той кни́ге? —Да́, я́ о . . . . . . слы́шал(а).
6. —Ты́ слы́шал(а) о на́шем экза́мене? —Да́, я́ о . . . . . . слы́шал(а).

CONVERSATION

А. В кла́ссе

А. Бори́с, вы́ сего́дня бы́ли **в** шко́ле?
Б. —Коне́чно бы́л![12]
А. —Что́ вы́ де́лали **на** уро́ке?
Б. Мы́ как всегда́ чита́ли, писа́ли **на** доске́, переводи́ли и, коне́чно, говори́ли.
А. —Ка́к сего́дня чита́ла Со́ня?
Б. —Она́ чита́ла ма́ло, но́ хорошо́ и хорошо́ переводи́ла.
А. —А ка́к говори́ла Ни́на?
Б. —Я́ не слу́шал, но́ вероя́тно она́, как всегда́, говори́ла мно́го и пло́хо.
А. —А ка́к переводи́л Андре́й?
Б. —О́чень хорошо́. О́н о́чень хорошо́ зна́л уро́к.
А. —Э́то стра́нно, потому́ что вчера́ о́н о́чень пло́хо чита́л, пло́хо писа́л на доске́ и да́же не слу́шал, о чём говори́л учи́тель.
Б. —Э́то коне́чно пло́хо, но́ э́то быва́ет.

В. В библиоте́ке

О́льга сего́дня мно́го рабо́тала и до́ма и в шко́ле: она́ чита́ла, переводи́ла, слу́шала, что́ говори́л учи́тель и писа́ла сочине́ние. Тепе́рь она́ в библиоте́ке. А Вади́м не́ был в шко́ле, но́ тепе́рь о́н то́же в библиоте́ке.

Вади́м. Здра́вствуй, О́льга.
О́льга. Здра́вствуй, Вади́м. Ка́к ты́ пожива́ешь?
В. Спаси́бо, о́чень хорошо́. А ты́ ка́к?

[12] Pronoun subjects are sometimes omitted when they are obvious. Their omission is especially frequent in replies to questions in which the verb used in the question is repeated in the reply.

О. —Плóхо. Рабóта, рабóта, и тóлько рабóта! Скóро экзáмен и я́ тепéрь всегдá и́ли в клáссе, и́ли в библиотéке. А чтó ты́ дéлал? Почемý ты́ нé был в шкóле?

В. Я́ бы́л на футбóле. Бы́ло óчень интерéсно.

О. Скóро экзáмен, а ты́ бы́л на футбóле?!

В. —Нý, так чтó? А тепéрь я́ здéсь в библиотéке тóлько потомý что я́ знáл, что ты́ здéсь.

О. —Вади́м!

В. —Чтó «Вади́м»? Э́то прáвда. Я́ так рáд, что мы́ здéсь вмéсте!

О. —Ты́ рáд, а я́ не рáда. Когдá Ни́на былá здéсь—онá былá твоя́ герои́ня. А тепéрь, когдá Ни́на в Нью-Йóрке—герои́ня я́! Э́то тóлько потомý, что онá далекó, а я́ бли́зко.

В. —О́льга, э́то непрáвда! Э́то не тáк!

О. —Конéчно э́то тáк! Нéт, Вади́м. Ты́ не мóй герóй. До свидáния!

Answer the following questions.

1. Почемý О́льга тепéрь всегдá и́ли в клáссе, и́ли в библиотéке? 2. Почемý Вади́м в библиотéке? 3. Кáк бы́ло на футбóле? 4. Почемý Вади́м рáд? 5. Чтó бы́ло, когдá Ни́на былá здéсь? 6. Гдé онá тепéрь?

EXERCISES

Translate into Russian.

1. —Where is Mama? —She is in the kitchen. 2. We stood on the street and, as usual, talked about our work. 3. In Boston they probably lived in an apartment. 4. —Is the museum far away? —No, it's very close. 5. My brother lived in Moscow, but my sister lived in Leningrad. 6. He, as usual, knew very little about that. 7. I am very glad that you are here. 8. We talked a lot about my article. 9. —Tom wasn't in class yesterday. He was at (a) football (game). —No, that isn't true! 10. —What were you speaking about? —We were speaking about our exam. 11. —About whom was he talking? —He talked, as usual, about Chekhov. 12. She is either at the concert or at the theater. 13. Yesterday she read poorly, but that can happen. 14. —Olga, did you speak about Chekhov in Russian or in English? —In Russian, of course.

VOCABULARY

библиоте́ка library
бли́зко near, close
вероя́тно probably
вме́сте together
всегда́ always
вчера́ yesterday
геро́й hero
герои́ня heroine
го́род city, town
да́же even
далеко́ far (away)
интере́сно interesting
кабине́т study
карти́на picture
кварти́ра apartment
коне́чно (*pronounce* [kaņéšnə]) of course, certainly
конце́рт concert
ма́ло little, few
ма́ма mama
мно́го much, many
но but
писа́тель (*masc.*) writer
писа́тельница woman writer
пло́хо bad, badly; poorly
пра́вда truth, true, right
рабо́та work
рад (*masc.*) **ра́да** (*fem.*) glad
сего́дня (*pronounce* [şivóḑņə]) today
ско́ро soon
сочине́ние composition
статья́ article
стра́нно strange
теа́тр theater
у́лица street
уро́к lesson
футбо́л football (soccer)
что that (*conj.*)
шко́ла school
экза́мен examination

Expressions

и́ли . . . и́ли either . . . or
по-англи́йски (in) English
по-ру́сски (in) Russian
говори́ть, чита́ть, писа́ть по-ру́сски to speak, read, write (in) Russian
как всегда́ as always; as usual
Э́то пра́вда That's right; that's true
Э́то непра́вда That's not so; not true
Э́то быва́ет That happens; that can happen
Здра́вствуй! Hello! (*familiar*)
Ка́к ты́ пожива́ешь? How are you? (*familiar*)
Ну́, так что́? Well, what of it?

Places

Аме́рика	**Евро́па**	**Сове́тский Сою́з**
Босто́н	Ло́ндон	Москва́
Нью-Йо́рк[13]	Пари́ж	Ленингра́д

[13] Only the last part of a hyphenated word is declined: в Нью-Йо́рке, "in New York."

Vocabulary Review

The Family

муж
жена́
оте́ц
мать
сын
дочь
брат
сестра́

Professions

студе́нт, -ка
учи́тель, -ница
писа́тель, -ница
журнали́ст, -ка
секрета́рь, секрета́рша
профе́ссор[14]
до́ктор[14]

Buildings

дом
шко́ла
музе́й
теа́тр
библиоте́ка

School

шко́ла
класс
уро́к
доска́

At Home

дом
кварти́ра
ко́мната
кабине́т
ку́хня
стол
стена́
пол
потоло́к
окно́
карти́на
ла́мпа
по́лка

Activities[15]

уро́к
рабо́та
конце́рт

Parts of the Body

голова́
лицо́
рот
нос
глаз
рука́

Adverbs of Place

где?
тут, здесь
там
до́ма
бли́зко
далеко́

Reading Matter

кни́га
журна́л
газе́та
статья́
письмо́
слова́рь (*masc.*)
грамма́тика

Adverbs of Time

когда́?
всегда́
вчера́
сего́дня

[14] These two words are used in the masculine form for feminine members of the profession as well.
[15] These take **на** with the locative: *e.g.*, на уро́ке, at the lesson.

UNIT 6

***Adjectives, nominative and locative cases,* 75. *Relative* кото́рый, 81.**

GRAMMAR

1. Adjectives

Like the possessives and the demonstratives studied in the preceding lesson, Russian adjectives agree in gender, number, and case with the noun they modify. In the examples below, adjectives in boldface are given in the three gender forms of the nominative singular.

Ва́ш **но́вый** до́м	Your *new* house	*Masc.*
Мо́й **си́ний** каранда́ш	My *blue* pencil	
На́ш **большо́й** го́род	Our *big* city	
То́ **но́вое** перо́	That *new* pen	*Neut.*
Ва́ше **си́нее** пла́тье	Your *blue* dress	
Э́то **большо́е** по́ле	This *big* field	
Ва́ша **но́вая** кварти́ра	Your *new* apartment	*Fem.*
Моя́ **си́няя** шля́па	My *blue* hat	
Твоя́ **больша́я** ко́мната	Your *big* room	

As may be seen from the above examples, the endings of adjectives present certain variations in each of the gender forms.

The most common type is illustrated by **но́вый**, "new"; adjectives of this type are stressed on the stem (in this case [nóv.]), with the final stem consonant *hard:*

		Ending
Masc.:	но́вый	-ЫЙ
Neut.:	но́вое	-ОЕ
Fem.:	но́вая	-АЯ

In a relatively small group of adjectives the stem ends in a *soft* consonant: *e.g.*, **си́ний**, "blue" (stem [şíņ.]); in writing, the softness of the stem ending is shown by the first vowel of the ending:

		Ending
Masc.:	си́ний	**-ИЙ**
Neut.:	си́нее	**-ЕЕ**
Fem.:	си́няя	**-ЯЯ**

A third group has hard stem endings, but with the stress falling on the ending; the masculine ending in this group is **-о́й**, as in больш**о́й**, "big":

		Ending
Masc.:	большо́й	**-О́Й**
Neut.:	большо́е	-О́Е
Fem.:	больша́я	-А́Я

Summary

	Masculine	*Neuter*	*Feminine*
Stress on stem: *hard*	но́вый -ЫЙ	но́вое -ОЕ	но́вая -АЯ
Stress on stem: *soft*	си́ний -ИЙ	си́нее -ЕЕ	си́няя -ЯЯ
Stress on ending: *hard only*	большо́й -О́Й	большо́е-О́Е	больша́я-А́Я

Drill

Fill in the correct endings of the following adjectives:

но́вый, new
си́ний, blue

но́в.... ко́мната
но́в.... студе́нт
но́в.... перо́
но́в.... кре́сло
но́в.... ку́хня
си́н.... пла́тье (dress)
си́н.... костю́м (suit)
си́н.... шля́па (hat)
си́н.... кре́сло

большо́й, big
молодо́й, young

больш′.... го́род
больш′.... по́ле
больш′.... кварти́ра
молод′.... до́ктор
молод′.... секрета́рша
молод′.... лицо́

после́дний, last
пе́рвый, first

после́дн.... письмо́
после́дн.... статья́
после́дн.... до́ллар
после́дн.... сло́во (word)
пе́рв.... сло́во
пе́рв.... уро́к
пе́рв.... статья́
пе́рв.... кни́га

Spelling rules and adjectives endings. The rules given in Unit 3, page 25, on consonant-vowel incompatibilities have several applications to the spelling of adjective endings. These are formulated as Spelling Rules A and B.

Spelling Rule A. The vowel **ы** is *never* written after the velar consonants **г**, **к** and **х**, nor after the hushing consonants **ж**, **ч**, **ш** and **щ**. In grammatical endings the letter **и** is written after these consonants, never **ы**.

Spelling Rule B. An unstressed **о** is *never* written after the consonants **ж**, **ч**, **ш**, **щ** and **ц**. The letter **е** is written after these consonants if this vowel is unstressed; if the vowel is stressed, **о** is written.

Application of spelling rules. Adjectives with stressed stems replace in spelling the **ы** in the masculine ending **-ый** with an **и** if the stem ends in one of the following consonants:

	Masculine			*Neuter*	*Feminine*
Г	стро́гий	strict	*but no change in*	стро́гое	стро́гая
К	ру́сский	Russian		ру́сское	ру́сская
Х	ти́хий	quiet		ти́хое	ти́хая

In addition to the substitution of **и** for **ы** in the masculine, the substitution of **е** for unstressed **о** in the neuter is required after the following final stem consonants:

	Masculine	*Neuter*	*Feminine*
Ж	све́ж**ий** fresh	све́ж**ее**	све́ж**ая**
Ш	хоро́ш**ий** good, nice	хоро́ш**ее**	хоро́ш**ая**
Ч	горя́ч**ий** hot	горя́ч**ее**	горя́ч**ая**
Щ	бу́дущ**ий** future	бу́дущ**ее**	бу́дущ**ая**

Adjectives with stems ending in the consonants listed above, but with the stress on the *ending* have normal endings of the stressed type, *e.g.*, дорог**о́й**, дорого́е, дорога́я; плох**о́й**, плохо́е, плоха́я; больш**о́й**, больш**о́е**, больша́я; чуж**о́й**, чуж**о́е**, чужа́я.

Summary

Stems ending in Г, К, Х:		
Masc.:	ру́сский ←———	-ИЙ (not -ЫЙ!)
Neut.:	ру́сское	
Fem.:	ру́сская	

Stems ending in Ж, Ш, Ч, Щ:		
Masc.:	хоро́ший ←———	-ИЙ (not -ЫЙ!)
Neut.:	хоро́шее ←———	-ЕЕ (not -ОЕ!)
Fem.:	хоро́шая	

Note on pronunciation. The vowel **ы** [ɨ] in unstressed masculine endings is pronounced [ə]: [nóvəj], [trúdnəj], etc.; the **и** required by spelling after **г**, **к**, **х**, **ж**, and **ш**, does *not* produce palatalization, and also sounds like [ə]: хоро́ший [xaróšəj], све́жий [şy̧éžəj], ру́сский [rúskəj], ти́хий [ţíxəj], etc.

Thus, the correlation between the unstressed masculine ending written **-ый** and the stressed written **-óй** is phonetically the normal correlation [ó]—[ə]: молодóй [məladój]—нóвый [nóvəj].

There is, however, an increasing tendency among native speakers to pronounce most endings as spelled, in particular **-ый** as [ɨj] rather than [əj], and **-ий** after **г**, **к**, **х** as [ij] with palatalization: рýсский [rúsķij], тúхий [ţiχ̧ij], etc. Final **-жий** and **-ший** are then pronounced [žɨj] and [šɨj]. This alternate pronunciation is now also regarded as correct.

Drill

Fill in the correct endings of the following adjectives:

рýсский, Russian	**хорóший,** good
лёгкий, easy, light	**свéжий,** fresh, cool
рýсск.... слóво	хорóш.... автомобúль
рýсск.... словáрь	хорóш.... письмó
рýсск.... жéнщина	хорóш.... журналúстка
рýсск.... граммáтика	хорóш.... дóм
рýсск.... гóрод	хорóш.... крéсло
лёгк.... плáтье	свéж.... дéнь (day, *masc.*)
лёгк.... урóк	свéж.... мя́со
лёгк.... кнúга	свéж.... лицó

Adjective List

какóй	what kind of, which, what (a)	лёгкий[1]	easy, light
такóй	such (a), so	тёплый	warm
нóвый	new	холóдный	cold
стáрый	old	бéлый	white
молодóй	young	чёрный	black
мáленький	little, small	красúвый	beautiful, handsome
большóй	big, large	интерéсный	interesting
хорóший	good, fine, nice	приятный	pleasant
плохóй	bad, poor	серьёзный	serious
трýдный	hard, difficult	стрáнный	strange
рýсский	Russian	сúний	blue
америкáнский	American	зúмний	winter (*adj.*)[2]
свéжий	fresh, cool	лéтний	summer (*adj.*)[2]
цéлый	whole	сегóдняшний	today's
пéрвый	first	вчерáшний	yesterday's
послéдний	last, latest		

[1] Pronounce [ļóxķij].

[2] Observe that in contrast to English, Russian does not use nouns adjectivally, *e.g.*, "a *winter* day," **зúмний** дéнь. In such cases adjectives are derived from nouns by the addition of one of several suffixes.

Pattern Sentences

Note that the adjective **ка́ко́й** *may mean "what," "which," or "what kind of," depending on the context:*

1. —**Како́й** студе́нт Вади́м? —Вади́м **хоро́ший** студе́нт.
2. —**Кака́я** это газе́та, «Пра́вда» и́ли «Та́ймз»? —Э́то «Пра́вда».
3. —**Кака́я** газе́та «Та́ймз»? —«Та́ймз» **хоро́шая** и **серьёзная** газе́та.
4. —**Како́й** это рома́н? —Э́то «А́нна Каре́нина».
5. —**Кака́я** ва́ша ко́мната, э́та и́ли та́? —Э́та.
6. **Како́й тру́дный** вопро́с!
7. **Како́й лёгкий** уро́к!
8. О́н **тако́й плохо́й** студе́нт!
9. Она́ **така́я краси́вая**!

1. —What sort of a student is Vadim? —Vadim is a good student.
2. —Which paper is that, *Pravda* or the *Times*? —It's *Pravda.*
3. —What sort of paper is the *Times*? —The *Times* is a good, serious paper.
4. —What novel is that? —It's *Anna Karenina.*
5. —Which is your room, this one or that one? —This one.
6. What a difficult question!
7. What an easy lesson!
8. He is such a poor student!
9. She is so beautiful!

Drills

Fill in the blanks with the correct form of the word above in the same column.

A. 1. —Како́й костю́м ва́ш, э́тот и́ли то́т? —Э́тот мо́й.
2. —. . . . . . ко́мната . . . ., ... и́ли . . .? —. . . . .
3. —. . . . . . по́ле . . . ., ... и́ли . . .? —. . . . .
4. —. . . . . . слова́рь . . . ., ... и́ли . . .? —. . . . .

B. 1. —Кака́я она́ студе́нтка? —Она́ хоро́шая студе́нтка.
2. —. . . . . . о́н писа́тель? —О́н . . . . писа́тель.
3. —. . . . . . это перо́? —Э́то . . . . перо́.
4. —. . . . . . это пла́тье? —Э́то си́нее пла́тье.
5. —. . . . . . это костю́м? —Э́то . . . . . костю́м.
6. —. . . . . . это шля́па? —Э́то . . . . . шля́па.

C. 1. Кака́я плоха́я журнали́стка!
2. . . . . ле́то (summer)!
3. . . . . зима́ (winter)!
4. . . . . рома́н (novel)!
5. . . . . пого́да (weather)!

D. 1. Ва́ш сы́н тако́й краси́вый!
2. . . . . жена́ . . . .!
3. . . . . пла́тье . . . .!
4. . . . . го́род . . . .!
5. . . . . шля́па . . . .!

2. Locative case of adjectives

Adjectives take the following endings in the locative case:

Masc.
Neut. [-óm], [-əm] written: **-ом** (**-ем** in some instances)

Fem. [-ój], [-əj] written: **-ой** (**-ей** in some instances)

The spelling is generally **-ом** for masculine and neuter and **-ой** for feminine; **е** replaces **о** (**-ем**, **-ей** instead of -ом, -ой) in adjectives with stems ending in a soft consonant (си́н**ем**, си́н**ей**) or in **ж**, **ш**, **ч**, **щ** if the stress is on the stem (хоро́ш**ем**, хоро́ш**ей**, but больш**о́м**, больш**о́й**).

NOMINATIVE		LOCATIVE	
Masculine	*Neuter*	*Masculine and Neuter*	
он	оно́	н**ём** [n̥.óm]	
мой	моё	мо**ём** [maj.óm]	
но́вый	но́вое	но́в**ом** [nóv.əm]	
большо́й	большо́е	больш**о́м** [bal̥š.óm]	
си́ний	си́нее	си́н**ем** [sín̥.əm]	spelled with **е**
хоро́ший	хоро́шее	хоро́ш**ем** [xaróš.əm]	spelled with **е**
Feminine		*Feminine*	
она́		н**ей** [n̥.ẹ́j]	
моя́		мо**е́й** [maj.ẹ́j]	
но́вая		но́в**ой** [nóv.əj]	
больша́я		больш**о́й** [bal̥š.ój]	
си́няя		си́н**ей** [s̥ín̥.əj]	spelled with **е**
хоро́шая		хоро́ш**ей** [xaróš.əj]	spelled with **е**

Pattern Sentences

1. Мо́й сы́н рабо́тал **в** ма́леньк**ом** го́роде.
2. —**О чём** они́ говори́ли? —**О** после́дн**ем** рома́не.
3. —**О ко́м** писа́ла О́льга? —**О** хоро́ш**ем** молод**о́м** писа́теле.
4. Моя́ до́чь жила́ **в** э́т**ой** ма́леньк**ой** дере́вне.
5. Она́ говори́ла **о** хоро́ш**ей** но́в**ой** кни́ге.
6. О́льга вчера́ была́ **в** краси́в**ой** си́н**ей** шля́пе.

1. My son worked in a small town.
2. —What were they talking about? —About the latest novel.
3. —Whom was Olga writing about? —About a good young writer.
4. My daughter lived in that small village.
5. She was talking about a good new book.
6. Yesterday Olga was wearing a pretty blue hat.

Drills

A. *Translate into English.*

1. В Босто́не мы́ жи́ли в большо́м но́вом до́ме.
2. А́нна была́ вчера́ в краси́вом си́нем пла́тье.
3. Кто́ жи́л в э́той ма́ленькой кварти́ре?
4. Мы́ говори́ли о ва́шем после́днем письме́.
5. Моя́ до́чь мно́го говори́ла о чёрной шля́пе и о бе́лом пла́тье.
6. Кто́ та́м в э́том краси́вом си́нем автомоби́ле?
7. Мы́ ду́мали о пе́рвом ле́тнем дне́.

B. *Fill in the blanks with the correct endings.*

1. Мы́ бы́ли на э́т.... хоро́ш.... конце́рте.
2. Мы́ бы́ли в э́т.... ру́сск.... дере́вне.
3. Мы́ бы́ли в на́ш.... ма́леньк.... ко́мнате.
4. Мы́ бы́ли в ва́ш.... больш.... кабине́те.
5. Они́ говори́ли об э́т.... ру́сск.... же́нщине.
6. Они́ говори́ли об э́т.... ру́сск.... словаре́.
7. Они́ говори́ли о тру́дн.... ру́сск.... сло́ве.
8. Они́ говори́ли о но́в.... си́н.... шля́пе.

C. *Fill in the blanks with correct forms of* **како́й** *and translate the words in parentheses.*

1. В како́м го́роде о́н рабо́тал? (In our big one).[3]
2. В ...... ко́мнате о́н рабо́тал? (In my pleasant one).
3. В ...... ку́хне о́н рабо́тал? (In our small one).
4. В ...... по́ле о́н рабо́тал? (In your big one).
5. В ...... кабине́те о́н рабо́тал? (In my small one).

D. *Translate the words in parentheses.*

1. Мы́ говори́ли о (your last letter).
2. Мы́ говори́ли о (cold winter weather).
3. Мы́ говори́ли о (my black dress).
4. Мы́ говори́ли о (first [girl] student).
5. Мы́ говори́ли о (your white hat).
6. Мы́ говори́ли о (my blue suit and blue hat).
7. Мы́ говори́ли о (your last car).

3. Relative кото́рый, "who," "which," "that"

Russian, unlike English, uses only one relative to mean "who," "which," or "that."

Кото́рый is declined as an adjective. It agrees in gender and number with the noun it replaces. But its *case* depends on its use in

[3] The English word "one" ("big one," "new one," etc.) in these sentences has no correspondent in Russian and must not be translated.

its own clause. Note that clauses with **кото́рый** are always set off by commas.

1. Где́ э́та интере́сная но́вая кни́га, **кото́рая** была́ ту́т на столе́?
   Where is that interesting new book which was here on the table?

2. Во́т мо́й бра́т, **кото́рый** жи́л в Нью-Йо́рке.
   Here is my brother who lived in New York.

3. Перо́, **кото́рое** бы́ло на столе́, не моё.
   The pen which was on the table is not mine.

4. До́м, **в кото́ром** о́н жи́л в Ло́ндоне, бы́л о́чень ста́рый.
   The house in which he lived in London was very old.

5. Кварти́ра, **в кото́рой** мы́ жи́ли, была́ о́чень больша́я.
   The apartment we lived in[4] was very large.

6. Э́то **та́** краси́вая молода́я студе́нтка, **о кото́рой** говори́л ста́рый профе́ссор.
   That is the pretty young student the old professor was talking about.

То́т, кото́рый means "he who," "the one who" ("which") ("that"). Та́ студе́нтка, кото́рая . . . —the (girl) student who . . . . Observe in Sentence 6 above that in Russian, unlike English, the preposition always precedes the relative **кото́рый**: **та́** студе́нтка, о **кото́рой** . . . ; in other words, the preposition must not stand at the end of a Russian sentence.[5]

Drills

A. *Transform the two sentences into one by using relative clauses with* **кото́рый,** *according to the models.*

Model: Где́ мо́й сто́л? О́н стоя́л ту́т.
—Где́ мо́й сто́л, кото́рый стоя́л ту́т?

1. Где́ ва́ша ла́мпа? Она́ стоя́ла ту́т.
2. Где́ ва́ш телефо́н? О́н стоя́л ту́т.
3. Где́ твоё кре́сло? Оно́ стоя́ло ту́т.

[4] In such sentences as this and the following one, the relative must not be omitted in Russian, although it frequently is omitted in colloquial English.

[5] **Кото́рый** also means "which," "which one." It is used to point out or select from a limited number of alternatives, *e.g.*, **Кото́рый** ва́ш сы́н? Which one is your son? Otherwise **како́й** is used, *e.g.*, В **како́м** го́роде вы́ жи́ли? In which town did you live? В **како́й** кни́ге вы́ э́то ви́дели? In which book did you see that?

Model: Вóт дóм. Мы́ в нём жи́ли.
—Вóт дóм, в котóром мы́ жи́ли.

1. Вóт гóрод. Мы́ в нём жи́ли.
2. Вóт у́лица. Мы́ на нéй жи́ли.
3. Вóт кварти́ра. Мы́ о нéй говори́ли.
4. Вóт автомоби́ль. Мы́ о нём говори́ли.

B. *Fill in the blanks with the correct form of* **котóрый.** *Change the words in parentheses to the correct case.*

1. Стóл, ... стоя́л в (твóй) кабинéте, тепéрь в (моя́) кóмнате.
2. Письмó, ... бы́ло на (мóй) столé, тепéрь на (ваш).
3. Кни́га, ... былá в (твоя́) кóмнате, тепéрь в (твóй) кабинéте.
4. Автомоби́ль, ... бы́л в (ваш) гаражé, тепéрь на (нáша) у́лице.

CONVERSATION

Óн и компози́тор и пиани́ст

Семёнов. —Чтó вы́ вчерá дéлали, Андрéй?
Мáслов. —Я́ бы́л вчерá на óчень интерéсном концéрте.
С. —Гдé был э́тот концéрт?
М. —Óчень бли́зко; в нóвой шкóле на нáшей у́лице.
С. —А я́ дáже не знáл, что тáм вчерá бы́л концéрт. А ктó игрáл вчерá?
М. —Вóльский,[6] молодóй и óчень тала́нтливый (talented) музыкáнт (musician).
С. —На чём óн игрáл?
М. —На роя́ле.
С. —Э́то тóт пиани́ст, о котóром говори́ла вáша женá, когдá мы́ бы́ли в Большóм теáтре?
М. —Я́ не слу́шал, о кóм и о чём говори́ла Óльга. Онá так мнóго говори́ла!
С. —А я́ слу́шал. Прáвда—я́ не му́ж.
М. —Дá, конéчно. Вероя́тно онá говори́ла о Вóльском.[6] Óн óчень интерéсный музыкáнт: óн как Рахмáнинов и компози́тор (composer) и пиани́ст.
С. —Как жáль, что я́ не знáл об э́том концéрте!
М. —Дá, óчень жáль. Э́то бы́л послéдний концéрт в э́том сезóне.

[6] Some Russian last names have the form of adjectives and are so declined.

Pronunciation Drill

štó ví fčirá ḑéləḷi, andṛéj?

já bíl fčirá naóčiṇ iṇṭiṛésnəm kancérṭi.

gḑé bil étət kancért?

óčiṇ bḷískə; vnóvəj škóḷi, katórəjə nanášij úḷici.

a já dáži ṇiznál, štə tám fčirá bíl kancért.

Answer the following questions in Russian.

1. Какóй бы́л концéрт, на котóром бы́л Мáслов? 2. Гдé бы́л э́тот концéрт? 3. Почемý Семёнов тáм нé был? 4. Гдé Óльга говори́ла об э́том талáнтливом музыкáнте? 5. Почемý Мáслов не знáл, о кóм и о чём говори́ла женá? 6. А почемý Семёнов слýшал, о чём онá говори́ла? 7. Почемý жáль, что Семёнов нé был на э́том концéрте?

READING

И тáк всегдá!

Как жáль, что сегóдня такáя плохáя и холóдная погóда! Это, конéчно, нормáльно: тепéрь ещё зимá. Нó вчерá бы́л такóй хорóший, тёплый дéнь! Я дýмал, что ужé лéто.

Вчерá, вероя́тно, бы́ло óчень хорошó в дерéвне, а я цéлый дéнь бы́л дóма и рабóтал! Я переводи́л нóвый америкáнский ромáн. Ромáн э́тот óчень интерéсный. Это ромáн о молодóй краси́вой жéнщине, котóрая жилá однá (alone) в большóм дóме. Дóм э́тот стоя́л в большóм краси́вом пáрке. Бы́ло лéто. Погóда былá хорóшая и тёплая.

Недалекó, в мáленьком бéлом дóме, жил молодóй талáнтливый музыкáнт. Óн игрáл на гитáре, а жéнщина в большóм дóме слýшала, когдá óн игрáл. Музыкáнт жил оди́н (alone).

Это тóлько начáло (beginning). Ромáн óчень интерéсный. Нó как жáль, что вчерá, когдá я цéлый дéнь бы́л дóма и рабóтал, погóда былá хорóшая, а сегóдня погóда такáя плохáя! И тáк всегдá!

Answer the following questions in Russian.

1. Какáя сегóдня погóда? 2. Почемý э́то нормáльно, что сегóдня хóлодно? 3. Почемý я дýмал вчерá, что ужé лéто? 4. Гдé, вероя́тно, бы́ло хорошó вчерá? 5. Чтó я вчерá дéлал?

6. О ко́м э́тот рома́н? 7. В како́м до́ме жила́ герои́ня? 8. Где́ стоя́л э́тот до́м? 9. В како́м до́ме жи́л молодо́й музыка́нт? 10. Что́ де́лал музыка́нт? 11. Како́й э́то рома́н? 12. Кака́я пого́да была́ вчера́ и кака́я пого́да сего́дня?

EXERCISES

A. *Translate into English.*

1. Сего́дня тёплый ле́тний де́нь. 2. Кака́я холо́дная зи́мняя но́чь! 3. Она́ така́я краси́вая же́нщина! 4. Э́тот уро́к о́чень тру́дный, а то́т бы́л о́чень лёгкий. 5. На́ша кварти́ра така́я ма́ленькая, а ва́ша така́я больша́я! 6. Зима́ была́ холо́дная, а ле́то тёплое и прия́тное. 7. Э́то мя́со ещё све́жее и хоро́шее. 8. Она́ ещё така́я молода́я! 9. —Како́й автомоби́ль ва́ш, чёрный и́ли бе́лый? —Чёрный. 10. —Чьё си́нее пла́тье та́м на сту́ле? —Моё. 11. —О како́м музыка́нте о́н писа́л в ва́шем журна́ле? —О Рахма́нинове. 12. —На чём она́ игра́ла, на роя́ле и́ли на гита́ре? —На роя́ле. 13. Э́то то́т интере́сный но́вый рома́н, о кото́ром я́ чита́л, когда́ я́ бы́л в Москве́. 14. Сми́т о́чень серьёзный, но́ стра́нный студе́нт. 15. Писа́тельница, кото́рая жила́ ту́т, тепе́рь в Вашингто́не. 16. Но́чь была́ не о́чень холо́дная. 17. Где́ кре́сло, кото́рое зде́сь всегда́ стоя́ло? 18. —О ко́м вы́ говори́ли? —Мы́ говори́ли о профе́ссоре Семёнове, кото́рый жи́л в Ло́ндоне, когда́ мы́ то́же та́м жи́ли. 19. —О чём э́та кни́га? —О молодо́м до́кторе, кото́рый жи́л и рабо́тал в А́фрике. 20. Студе́нтка, кото́рая говори́ла вчера́ о Че́хове, говори́ла ма́ло, но́ хорошо́. 21. Како́й стра́нный вопро́с! 22. Кака́я она́ стра́нная же́нщина!

B. *Translate into Russian.*

1. She is such a serious student! 2. When she lived in this small apartment, she worked day and night. 3. What a strange woman she is! 4. This new lesson is very easy. 5. My sister, about whom we were speaking, lived in Leningrad. 6. I read that old novel about which you were speaking; it is very difficult. 7. The house in which we lived in Moscow was large and pleasant. 8. My mother was very beautiful when she was young, and she played the piano well. 9. Where is the white armchair which was in this room? 10. This meat is still good and fresh. 11. Yesterday was a warm, pleasant summer day. 12. —Have you thought about that difficult question? —Not

yet. 13. My sister was thinking about a new black hat. 14. My mother was wearing a blue summer dress. 15. What a strange word! It's very difficult. 16. About which novel were you speaking? About my first novel or my last (one)? 17. Yesterday we went to (were in) the country.

VOCABULARY

(For adjectives introduced in this lesson, see Section 1).

автомоби́ль (*masc.*) automobile, car
вопро́с question
гара́ж garage
день (*masc.*) day
дере́вня village; country
ещё still
ещё не not yet[7]
зима́ winter
костю́м suit
кре́сло armchair
ле́то summer
мя́со meat
недалеко́ not far (away)
норма́льно normal(ly)
ночь (*fem.*) night
парк park
пла́тье dress
пого́да weather
рома́н novel
роя́ль (*masc.*) piano
сло́во word
шля́па hat

Expressions

Жа́ль, что . . . It's too bad that . . .
Как жа́ль! What a pity!
игра́ть на (+ *loc.*) to play (an instrument)
быть в (+ *loc.*) to be wearing
И та́к всегда́! And so it goes! It's always that way!

[7] Without a verb or other predicate, this becomes ещё не́т or не́т ещё, *e.g.*, —Вы́ чита́ли э́тот рома́н? —**Не́т ещё.** But with a verb: О́н об э́том **ещё не** зна́л.

UNIT 7

***Genitive case of nouns, pronouns, and modifiers,* 87. *Genitive with expressions of quantity,* 94. Есть *and* нет, 95. *Nouns with fleeting* о *or* е, 97. *The adverb,* 98. *Vocabulary review,* 103.**

GRAMMAR

1. Genitive case of nouns

The main function of the genitive case in Russian is similar to that of the English possessive form of nouns (Mary's, teacher's etc.), as well as to prepositional phrases with *of*, such as *a glass of milk*, *the color of the car*, etc.

In the examples below, nouns in the genitive are in boldface.

а́дрес **до́ктора** (nom. до́ктор)	the doctor's address
ко́мната **сестры́** (nom. сестра́)	Sister's room
фами́лия **го́стя** (nom. гость)	the guest's last name
нача́ло **уро́ка** (nom. уро́к)	the beginning of the lesson
фу́нт **мя́са** (nom. мя́со)	a pound of meat
стака́н **воды́** (nom. вода́)	a glass of water

Forms of nouns in the genitive. Nouns take the following endings in the genitive case:

		Spelling: Hard	Spelling: Soft
Masc. and Neut.	stressed: [á]; unstressed: [ə]	**-а**	**-я**
Fem.	[i/ɨ]	**-ы**	**-и**

		Nominative	*Genitive*
Masc.	Hard	стол [stól.] брат [brát.]	стол**а́** [stal.á] бра́т**а** [brát.ə]
	Soft	слова́рь [slaváŗ.] гость [góşţ.] музе́й [muz̧ẹ́j.]	словар**я́** [sləvaŗ.á] го́ст**я** [góşţ.ə] музе́**я** [muz̧ẹ́j.ə]
Neut.	Hard	окно́ [akn.ó] кре́сло [kŗésl.ə]	окн**а́** [akn.á] кре́сл**а** [kŗésl.ə]
	Soft	бельё [b̧iļj.ó] по́ле [póļ.ə]	бель**я́** [b̧iļj.á] по́л**я** [póļ.ə]
Fem. I	Hard	сестра́ [şistr.á] ко́мната [kómnət.ə]	сестр**ы́** [şistr.ɨ́] ко́мнат**ы** [kómnət.ɨ]
	Soft	земля́ [z̧im̧ļ.á] (earth) ку́хня [kúxņ.ə] иде́я [iḑẹ́j.ə]	земл**и́** [z̧im̧ļ.í] ку́хн**и** [kúxņ.i] иде́**и** [iḑẹ́j.i]
Fem. II		дверь [ḑv̧ẹ́ŗ.]	две́р**и** [ḑv̧ẹ́ŗ.i]

In accordance with Spelling Rule A (see Unit 6, page 77), feminine nouns with stems ending in **г**, **к**, **х**, **ж**, **ш**, **ч**, and **щ** take **-и**, not **ы**, in the genitive:

кни́га	кни́г**и**	[kņíg̡.i]
студе́нтка	студе́нтк**и**	[stuḑéntķ.i]
Ма́ша[1]	Ма́ш**и**	[máš.ɨ]
ко́жа (skin, leather)	ко́ж**и**	[kóž.ɨ]

Pattern Sentences

1. —Чья́ э́та ко́мната? —Э́то ко́мната профе́ссор**а** Па́влов**а**.
2. —А чья́ та́ ко́мната? —Та́ ко́мната жен**ы́** Па́влов**а**.
3. Во́т две́рь ко́мнат**ы** го́ст**я**. А э́то две́рь ку́хн**и**.

1. —Whose is this room? —It's Professor Pavlov's room.
2. —And whose is that room? —It's the room of Pavlov's wife.
3. Here is the door of our guest's room. And this is the door of the kitchen.

[1] Nickname of Мари́я, "Mary."

4. Цвéт крéсла óчень краси́вый.	4. The color of the armchair is very pretty.
5. Вóт конéц пóля.	5. Here is the end of the field.
6. Начáло кни́ги интерéсное.	6. The beginning of the book is interesting.

Drills

A. *Supply correct case forms of the nouns given in parentheses.*

1. —Чéй это дóм? —Э́то дóм (брат).
2. —Чьё это перó? —Э́то перó (сестрá).
3. —Чья́ это кáрта? —Э́то кáрта (учи́тель).
4. —Чéй это автомоби́ль? —(Дóктор Смирнóв).
5. —Чья́ это кварти́ра? —Э́то кварти́ра (Ивáн и А́нна).
6. —Чéй это áдрес? —Э́то áдрес (профéссор Пáвлов).

B. *Translate the following into Russian.*

1. This is the beginning of the lesson.
2. —Where is the guest's room? —It's (over) there.
3. —Whose book is this? —This is Olga's and Vadim's book.
4. —Whose armchair is this? —It's Father's armchair.
5. —Whose wife is she? —She is Doctor Smirnov's wife.
6. —Who is he? —He is Anna's husband.
7. —Whose house is this? —This is the house of Doctor Robinson.

2. Third person pronouns in the genitive

The forms of the third person pronouns in the genitive are as follows:

	Nominative	*Genitive*
Masc.	он [ón.]	**егó** [j.ivó]
Neut.	онó [an.ó]	
Fem.	онá [an.á]	**её** [j.ijó]
Pl.	они́ [an̦.í]	**их** [íx]

Note the pronunciation of г as [v] in **егó**; this pronunciation is also found in the genitive endings of modifiers, **-его** [evo] and **-ого** [ovo], which are related to the third person pronoun (see below).

As has been seen earlier (Unit 4, page 49), possession is expressed by possessive pronoun-adjectives for the first and second persons ("I" and "you"). The genitive case, on the other hand, is used when the possessor is referred to by a third person pronoun ("he," "she," "it," "they") or a noun:

Possessor: 1st and 2nd Person Possessive Pronouns	3rd Person Pronoun in Genitive Case	Nouns in Genitive Case
я ты мы вы ↓ ↓ ↓ ↓ мóй, твóй, нáш, вáш —стóл моё, твоё, нáше, вáше —перó моя́, твоя́, нáша, вáша —кни́га	он/онó онá ↓ ↓ ⎧стóл егó, её ⎨перó ⎩кни́га	брат сестрá ↓ ↓ стóл перó ⎫ брáта, сестры́ кни́га⎭

E.g.:

егó крéсло	his armchair
её кóмната	her room
и́х дóм	their house
в егó крéсле	in his armchair
в её кóмнате	in her room
об и́х сы́не	about their son
крéсло егó брáта	his brother's armchair
дóм её сестры́	her sister's house

Observe that nouns in the genitive usually *follow* the noun to which they refer, *e.g.*, кабинéт **профéссора**, while pronouns *precede*, *e.g.*, **егó** кабинéт.

3. Genitive case of modifiers

It has been pointed out earlier (Unit 5, page 63) that the case endings of possessives and demonstratives, adjectives, and certain other classes of words are closely related to the corresponding case forms of the third person pronouns. Thus, in the prepositional case, masculine and neuter: нём—моём, э́том, си́нем, большóм.

The declensional pattern followed by most declinable words other than nouns is called the pronominal declension.

Modifiers (possessives, demonstratives, and adjectives) take the following endings in the genitive case:

Masc.⎫ *Neut.*⎭	**-ого, -его**	*Pronunciation:* the consonant г is pronounced [v]; the vowels of the endings vary according to the position of the stress.
Fem.	**-ой, -ей**	

(The feminine ending **-ой/-ей** is not apparently related to the corresponding form of the third person pronoun её; the feminine modifiers deviate from the third person pronoun pattern in the genitive and the accusative cases.)

The genitive forms of different classes of modifiers are given below together with the nominative forms.

| | NOMINATIVE | | GENITIVE |
	Masculine	*Neuter*	*Masculine and Neuter*
3rd Pers. Pron.	он	оно́	его́ [j.ivó]
Adjectives	но́вый	но́вое	но́вого [nóv.əvə]
	молодо́й	молодо́е	молодо́го [məlad.óvə]
	си́ний	си́нее	си́него [şíɲ.əvə]
	большо́й	большо́е	большо́го [baɭš.óvə]
	ру́сский	ру́сское	ру́сского [rúsk.əvə]
	хоро́ший	хоро́шее	хоро́шего [xaróš.əvə]
Possessives	мой	моё	моего́ [məj.ivó]
	твой	твоё	твоего́ [tvəj.ivó]
	наш	на́ше	на́шего [náš.əvə]
	ваш	ва́ше	ва́шего [váš.əvə]
Demonstratives	э́тот	э́то	э́того [ét.əvə]
	тот	то	того́ [t.avó]
Interrogatives	кто		кого́ [k.avó]
		что	чего́ [č̦.ivó]

Feminine

	Feminine		
3rd Pers. Pron.	она́		её [j.ijó]
Adjectives	но́вая		но́вой [nóv.əj]
	молода́я		молодо́й [məlad.ój]
	си́няя		си́ней [şíɲ.əj]
	больша́я		большо́й [baɭš.ój]
	ру́сская		ру́сской [rúsk.əj]
	хоро́шая		хоро́шей [xaróš.əj]
Possessives	моя́		мое́й [maj.éj]
	твоя́		твое́й [tvaj.éj]
	на́ша		на́шей [náš.əj]
	ва́ша		ва́шей [váš.əj]
Demonstratives	э́та		э́той [ét.əj]
	та		той [t.ój]

Spelling. The endings are spelled **-ого** for masculine and neuter and **-ой** for feminine after hard final stem consonants: э́того, э́той; но́вого, но́вой; after **ш** and **ж** the endings **-ого**, **-ой** are written only if the ending is stressed: больш**о́го**, больш**о́й**.

The endings **-его** for masculine and neuter and **-ей** for feminine are written after soft final stem consonants, *e.g.*, си́н**его**, си́н**ей**, and also after the sound [j]: мо**его́**, мо**е́й**; тво**его́**, тво**е́й**. In accordance with Spelling Rule B (Unit 6, p. 77), **-его**, **-ей** are also written after **ш** and **ж** if the ending is unstressed: на́ш**его**, на́ш**ей**; ва́ш**его**, ва́ш**ей**; хоро́ш**его**, хоро́ш**ей**.

Pattern Sentences

1. Э́то кварти́ра до́ктор**а** Смирно́в**а** и **его́** жен**ы́**.	1. This is the apartment of Dr. Smirnov and his wife.
2. Во́т две́рь **его́** кабине́т**а**, а во́т две́рь **её** ко́мнат**ы**.	2. Here is the door of his study, and here is the door of her room.
3. Та́м ко́мната **и́х** сы́н**а** Анто́н**а**.	3. Over there is their son Anton's room.
4. Во́т чёрный автомоби́ль **и́х** гост**я́**. Кры́ша **его́** автомоби́л**я** бе́лая.	4. Here is their guest's black car. The roof of his car is white.
5. Э́то коне́ц на́ш**его** ру́сск**ого** уро́к**а**.	5. This is the end of our Russian lesson.
6. —Вы́ давно́ зде́сь? —Не о́чень.	6. —Have you been here long? —Not very.
7. Я́ давно́ не́ был в столи́це ва́ш**ей** стран**ы́**.	7. I haven't been in the capital of your country for a long time.
8. Они́ неда́вно бы́ли в но́вом до́ме мо**его́** прия́тел**я**.	8. Recently they were in my friend's new house.
9. —Нача́ло э́т**ой** ру́сск**ой** кни́г**и** о́чень интере́сное. —Как**о́й** кни́г**и**?[2] —**То́й**,[2] кото́рая на моём столе́.	9. —The beginning of this Russian book is very interesting. —Of which book? —The one which is on my table.
10. Они́ уже́ бы́ли в Москве́, в столи́це Сове́тск**ого** Сою́з**а**, а вы́ ещё не́ были та́м!	10. They have already been to Moscow, the capital of the Soviet Union, and you haven't been there yet!
11. Ка́к назва́ние э́т**ой** кни́г**и**? «Нача́ло ле́т**а**»? —Не́т, «Коне́ц зим**ы́**».	11. What is the title of that book? "The Beginning of Summer?" —No, "The End of Winter."
12. —Ка́к и́мя ва́ш**его** бра́т**а**? —Его́ и́мя И́горь.	12. —What is your brother's name? —His name is Igor.
13. —Ка́к а́дрес тво**е́й** учи́тельниц**ы**? —**Её** а́дрес в но́вой телефо́нной кни́ге.	13. —What is your teacher's address? —Her address is in the new telephone book.

[2] In Russian elliptical (incomplete) sentences continue the grammatical pattern already established. Hence, **како́й кни́ги** and **то́й** are in the genitive case, although the word which governs the genitive occurs only in the first sentence. Remember that **тот** serves as a pronoun with **кото́рый** to mean "he who," "the one who," "the one which," etc.

14. —Кака́я цена́ э́т**ой** бе́л**ой** шля́п**ы**? Она́ дорога́я и́ли дешёвая? —Она́ не о́чень дорога́я.	14. —What is the price of this white hat? Is it expensive or cheap? —It's not very expensive.
15. —Как**о́го** цве́т**а** но́вое пла́тье э́т**ой** молод**о́й** же́нщин**ы**? —Си́н**его**.[3]	15. —What color is that young woman's new dress? —It's blue.
16. Учи́тель, в кварти́ре кото́р**ого** мы́ жи́ли, тепе́рь в Ло́ндоне.	16. The teacher in whose apartment we lived is now in London.
17. Писа́тельница, рома́н кото́р**ой** вы́ чита́ли, сестра́ на́ш**его** профе́ссор**а**.	17. The (woman) writer whose novel you've read is our professor's sister.

Drills

A. *Supply the correct case forms of the words given in parentheses. Then reword the sentence by substituting a pronoun in the genitive, as in the model.*

Model: —Че́й это до́м? —Э́то до́м **моего́ бра́та.** Э́то **его́** до́м.

1. —Че́й это автомоби́ль? —Э́то автомоби́ль (мо́й сы́н).
2. —Чьё это перо́? —Э́то перо́ (моя́ жена́).
3. —Чья́ это ко́мната? —Э́то ко́мната (на́ш сы́н).
4. —Че́й это костю́м? —Э́то костю́м (мо́й му́ж).
5. Э́то кварти́ра (ва́ш учи́тель и его́ жена́).
6. Э́то газе́та (до́ктор Петро́в).
7. Э́то кре́сло (тво́й ста́рый го́сть).
8. Э́то кни́га (на́ш хоро́ший учи́тель).
9. Э́то но́вое пла́тье (моя́ ма́ленькая сестра́).
10. Э́то журна́л (на́ша но́вая учи́тельница).
11. Э́то автомоби́ль (на́ш ру́сский го́сть и его́ жена́).

B. *Change the words in the right-hand column to the genitive.*

1. Кака́я цена́ . . .	What is the price of . . .	э́тот си́ний автомоби́ль? э́то хоро́шее перо́? э́та ста́рая кни́га? э́то большо́е по́ле?
2. Ка́к и́мя[4] . . .	What is the name of . . .	ва́ша краси́вая сестра́? то́т молодо́й писа́тель? тво́й ма́ленький бра́т?
3. Ка́к назва́ние[4] . . .	What is the name of . . .	ва́ш но́вый рома́н? э́та хоро́шая кни́га? её но́вая статья́? (article)

[3] See footnote 2. Observe that this Russian idiom reverses English practice: "Of what color. . . .?" rather than "What is the color of. . .?"

[4] **И́мя** means "name," and is used only of persons. **Назва́ние** is used for objects.

4. Ка́к а́дрес . . . What is the address of . . . ва́ша молода́я прия́тельница? на́ш но́вый учи́тель? его́ ста́рый до́ктор? та́ больша́я гости́ница?

4. Genitive with expressions of quantity

The genitive is used with expressions of quantity, in particular with **мно́го** (much, many), **ма́ло** (little, few), and **ско́лько** (how many?, how much?). Note that in sentences like those below the verb when in the past tense is *neuter singular*:

Ско́лько хле́ба **бы́ло** на столе́?
How much bread was on the table?

На столе́ **бы́ло ма́ло** хле́ба.
There was little bread on the table.

Words like **кусо́к,** "piece," **фунт,** "pound," **стака́н,** "glass," etc., also govern the genitive; the verb agrees with **кусо́к, фунт,** etc.:

На столе́ **бы́л стака́н** воды́.
There was a glass of water on the table.

Pattern Sentences

1. —**Ско́лько** ту́т мя́са? —Ту́т фу́нт мя́са.
2. —**Ско́лько** та́м бы́ло вина́? —Та́м была́ одна́ буты́лка.
3. Я́ ви́дел на по́лке **кусо́к** сы́ра и **стака́н** молока́.
4. О́льга е́ла **ма́ло** ма́сла.
5. В буты́лке бы́ло о́чень **ма́ло** вина́.
6. Ива́н всегда́ пи́л **мно́го** воды́ и е́л **мно́го** хле́ба.

1. —How much meat is here? —Here is a pound of meat.
2. —How much wine was there? —There was one bottle.
3. I saw on the shelf a piece of cheese and a glass of milk.
4. Olga ate little butter.
5. There was very little wine in the bottle.
6. Ivan always drank much water and ate much bread.

Drill

Fill in the correct case forms of the nouns given in parentheses.

1. В стака́не бы́ло ма́ло (вода́).
2. —Ско́лько (мя́со) вы́ купи́ли? Я́ купи́л ма́ло (мя́со), но́ мно́го (хле́б).
3. —Ско́лько ту́т (молоко́)? —Ту́т то́лько стака́н (молоко́).
4. —Ско́лько (сы́р) в (ку́хня)? —В (ку́хня) фу́нт (сы́р).

5. На (по́лка) то́лько одна́ буты́лка (вино́).
6. Назва́ние (э́тот рома́н) «Нача́ло и коне́ц.»
7. Э́то нача́ло (уро́к).
8. Э́то коне́ц (конце́рт).
9. Я́ ви́дел то́лько ма́ленький кусо́к (хлеб) на (стол).

5. Есть and нет

The Russian word **есть** ("there is," "there are") is used to express the existence or availability of something or someone:

—Что́ **е́сть** в э́том ма́леньком го́роде? —В э́том го́роде **е́сть** музе́й, **е́сть** теа́тр, и да́же **е́сть** стадио́н!
—What is there in this small town? —In this town there is a museum, there is a theater, and there is even a stadium!

На на́шей у́лице **е́сть** гости́ница.
On our street there is a hotel.

—Зде́сь **е́сть** хоро́шая библиоте́ка? —Да́, **е́сть**.
—Is there a good library here? —Yes, there is.

Note that Russian declarative sentences of this type usually open with an adverb (*e.g.*, **здесь**) or a prepositional phrase (*e.g.*, **в на́шем го́роде**), though the equivalent English sentences often start with "there is," "there are."

The *negative* of **есть** is **нет** (colloq. **не́ту**), "there is no," "there are no." Nouns (or pronouns) governed by **нет** take the *genitive case*:

—**Чего́ не́т** в на́шем го́роде? —В на́шем го́роде **не́т** теа́тр**а**.
—What is there not (what is lacking) in our town? —There is no theater in our town.

На на́шей у́лице **не́т** гости́ниц**ы**.
There is no hotel on our street.

Зде́сь **не́т** библиоте́к**и**.
There is no library here.

На столе́ **не́т** си́н**его** пер**а́**.
There is no blue pen on the desk.

—На столе́ е́сть мя́со? —Не́т, **не́ту** (colloq.).
—Is there meat on the table? —No, there isn't.

Есть is generally used when English employs the *indefinite* article, and is generally omitted when English employs the *definite* article:

На э́той у́лице **е́сть** библиоте́ка.
There is *a* library on our street.

But: Библиоте́ка на э́той у́лице.
The library is on this street.

The past tense of **есть** is **был**, **бы́ло**, **была́**, **бы́ли**. The verb agrees with the subject in gender and number:

На столе́ **бы́л** каранда́ш. (There was a pencil on the table.)
На столе́ **бы́ло** перо́.
На столе́ **была́** кни́га.
На столе́ **бы́ли** кни́ги. (books—nom. pl.)

The past tense of **нет** is **не́ было** ("there was/were no"). The verb is always neuter singular, regardless of the gender and number of person(s) or thing(s) concerned. Like **нет**, **не́ было** requires the genitive case:

Зде́сь **не́ было** карандаша́. (There was *no* pencil here.)
На столе́ **не́ было** пера́.
На э́той у́лице **не́ было** шко́лы.
На по́лке **не́ было** кни́г. (books—gen. pl.)

Нет also serves often to denote the absence of a *particular* person or thing, though the comparable English construction does not use "there is/are no":

Ива́на **не́т** до́ма. **Его́ не́т** до́ма.
Ivan is not at home. He isn't at home.

Вчера́ Ива́на **не́ было** до́ма. **Его́ не́ было** до́ма.
Ivan was not at home yesterday. He wasn't at home.

Моего́ си́него пера́ **не́ было** на столе́. **Его́** та́м **не́ было.**
My blue pen wasn't on the desk. It wasn't there.

Кни́ги **не́ было** в моей ко́мнате. **Её** та́м **не́ было.**
The book was not in my room. It wasn't there.

Note that in contrast to this use of the genitive, the *nominative* case used with the negative of "to be" often has the sense of "go," "come," "visit," or "attend" in English:

О́н давно́ **не́ был** в Нью-Йо́рке.
He hasn't been (gone) to New York for a long time (he lives outside it).

But: Тогда́ **его́ не́ было** в Нью-Йо́рке.
At that time he wasn't (didn't happen to be) in New York (perhaps he lives in it).

—**Он** сегóдня **нé был** в шкóле? —**Нéт**, нé был.
—Wasn't he at school today (didn't he attend)? —No, he wasn't (didn't).

Drills

A. *Translate the phrases in the left column and combine each of them with each of the words in the right column.*

On the table there is no On the table there was On the table there was no	книга. перó. рýсский словáрь. рýсская граммáтика. нóвый ромáн. свéжее мя́со. бéлая бумáга.

B. *Supply the correct form of the words in parentheses.*

1. На твоём столé (there was no pencil).
2. Сегóдня, когдá я́ былá в кýхне, (Olga was not there).
3. Как стрáнно, что вчерá (Ivan was not at home).
4. На э́той ýлице (there is) францýзский ресторáн.
5. Э́тот францýзский ресторáн (is on this street).
6. (Boris was not in Moscow), когдá я́ тáм бы́л.
7. В кабинéте моегó брáта (there is) телефóн, а в моём кабинéте (there is no telephone).
8. На егó столé (there is) лáмпа. На моём столé (there was a lamp), нó тепéрь на нём (there is no lamp).
9. В нáшем мáленьком гóроде (there was a doctor), а в вáшем гóроде (there was no doctor).
10. В начáле урóка (Ivan was not in class).

6. Nouns with fleeting о or е

In declension some masculine nouns drop the vowel **о** or **е** which precedes the final consonant in the nominative:

Nominative		*Genitive*	*Locative*
отéц	(father)	отцá	об отцé
конéц	(end)	концá	в концé (at the end)
потолóк	(ceiling)	потолкá	на потолкé
кусóк	(piece)	кускá	в кускé
день	(day)	дня	о днé

Drill

Translate the words in parentheses.

1. Кóмната и́х гóстя (at the end) коридóра.
2. В кабинéте (of Father) большóй стóл.
3. В дóме нéт (a piece) хлéба.
4. (On the ceiling) мýха (a fly).
5. Э́то бы́ло в (end of the day).
6. Мы́ говори́ли (about his father).

7. The adverb

Adverbs formed from adjectives normally end in **-о**; the ending is added to the stem of the adjective:

прия́тн.ый	pleasant	прия́тн**о**	pleasantly
серьёзн.ый	serious	серьёзн**о**	seriously
стрáнн.ый	strange	стрáнн**о**	strangely
удóбный	comfortable, convenient	удóбн**о**	comfortably, conveniently

Бори́с óчень **серьёзный** студéнт; óн всегдá óчень **серьёзно** рабóтал.
Boris is a very serious student; he has always worked very seriously.

In many cases there occurs a shift of accent:

хор**ó**ший	good	хорош**ó**	well
плох**ó**й	bad	пл**ó**хо	badly
л**ё**гкий	easy, light	легк**ó**	easily, lightly
св**é**тлый	light, bright	светл**ó**	brightly
т**ё**мный	dark	темн**ó**	darkly

E.g.: Онá хор**ó**шая студéнтка; онá всегдá хорош**ó** рабóтала.
She is a good student; she has always worked well.

In Russian, adverbs are used in impersonal expressions, while English uses adjectives for such expressions. Note that impersonal expressions in Russian have no subject; English "it" must not be translated:

Здéсь **прия́тно.**
It's pleasant here.

На ýлице **хóлодно.**
It's cold on the street (=outside).

Хорошó, что вы́ бы́ли тáм.
It's good that you were there.

In the past tense these impersonals take a neuter verb:

Вчера́ было **хо́лодно.**
It was cold yesterday.

Note from the examples above that in Russian such impersonal expressions often open with an adverb or adverbial phrase of place or time (здесь, вчера́, на у́лице, etc.).

Another type of impersonal construction is used with infinitives:

По-ру́сски **легко́ чита́ть,** но́ **говори́ть тру́дно.**
It's easy to read Russian but hard to speak it.

Жи́ть в го́роде о́чень **прия́тно.**
It's very pleasant to live in the city.

Pattern Sentences

1. Вчера́ бы́ло **тепло́,** да́же **жа́рко,** а сего́дня **хо́лодно.**
2. Она́ плоха́я студе́нтка. Она́ всегда́ **ма́ло** рабо́тала, и всё, что[5] она́ де́лала, она́ де́лала **пло́хо.**
3. По-англи́йски о́чень **тру́дно** писа́ть, но́ **легко́** говори́ть.
4. Э́то бы́л о́чень хоро́ший кла́сс. В на́шем хоро́шем ру́сском кла́ссе мы́ всегда́ **хорошо́** рабо́тали.

1. Yesterday it was warm, even hot, but today it's cold.
2. She is a poor student. She always worked little, and everything that she did she did poorly.
3. It's very hard to write English, but easy to speak it.
4. That was a very good class. In our good Russian class we always worked well.

Drill

Translate the following adjectives and adverbs given in parentheses.

1. Э́то бы́л (serious) вопро́с, и мы́ (seriously) о нём ду́мали.
2. Бори́с бы́л (good) студе́нт. О́н всегда́ рабо́тал (well).
3. Ни́на (poor) студе́нтка. Она́ всегда́ рабо́тала (little and poorly).
4. Она́ была́ о́чень (strange) же́нщина; она́ всё де́лала о́чень (strangely).
5. Зде́сь (it is pleasant) жи́ть. Э́то (a pleasant) го́род.
6. На у́лице (it is cold), а ту́т в моём кабине́те (warm and pleasant).
7. (It was interesting) чита́ть в газе́те о (new) рома́не э́того (interesting) писа́теля.
8. Вчера́ (it was warm), а сего́дня о́чень (cold).
9. Како́й (cold) де́нь!
10. На́ша гости́ница о́чень (comfortable).
11. Так (convenient) жи́ть в це́нтре го́рода!
12. Как зде́сь (dark)! Э́то о́чень (dark) кварти́ра.
13. Кака́я (bright) ко́мната!
14. Как (pleasant) в ва́шей (bright) ко́мнате.

[5] Всё, что, everything that, all that.

CONVERSATION

Ро́бертс. —До́брый ве́чер. Моё и́мя Пи́тер Ро́бертс. Я́ корреспонде́нт америка́нск**ого** журна́л**а** «Вре́мя.»

Мати́сс. —О́чень прия́тно. Я́ . . .

Р. —Вы́ Пье́р Мати́сс, корреспонде́нт францу́зск**ой** газе́т**ы** «Ве́чер.»

М. —Я́ Мати́сс, но́ моё и́мя не Пье́р, а Жа́к; и я́ корреспонде́нт не «Ве́чер**а**,» а «У́тр**а**.»

Р. —А́х да́! Коне́чно! Пожа́луйста прости́те! О́чень прия́тно. Вы́ давно́ в Аме́рике?

М. —Не́т, неда́вно.

Р. —Вы́ ви́дели то́лько Нью-Йо́рк?

М. —Не́т, не то́лько Нью-Йо́рк. Я́ бы́л в столи́це ва́ш**ей** прекра́сн**ой** стран**ы́**. Вашингто́н европе́йский го́род! Ма́ленький Пари́ж.

Р. —Э́то коне́чно большо́й комплиме́нт. Что́ же[6] вы́ ви́дели в Вашингто́не?

М. —Я́ всё ви́дел. Я́ жи́л в гости́нице в це́нтре го́род**а**. Э́то бы́ло о́чень **удо́бно**: всё бы́ло бли́зко. Я́ коне́чно бы́л в Бе́лом до́ме—в до́ме ва́ш**его** президе́нт**а**; в Библиоте́ке Конгре́сс**а**; я́ ви́дел па́мятник Ли́нкольн**а**; я́ бы́л в Национа́льном музе́е. Прекра́сный музе́й! Я́ бы́л в о́чень хоро́шем францу́зском рестора́не на кры́ше больш**о́й** гости́ниц**ы**, и на о́чень прия́тном и интере́сном ве́чере, в до́ме мо**его́** прия́тел**я** писа́тел**я** Жира́р**а**. На э́том ве́чере бы́л реда́ктор (editor) сове́тск**ой** газе́ты «Пра́вда.»[7] Мы́ вме́сте пи́ли и мно́го говори́ли о поли́тике **его́** стран**ы́**. Бы́ло о́чень **интере́сно.**

Р. —Реда́ктор «Пра́вд**ы**»?[7] О́н мо́й прия́тель, Кузнецо́в. Кузнецо́в . . . Не́т. Кузнецо́в реда́ктор журна́л**а** «Де́нь сове́тск**ой** же́нщин**ы**.» Так ка́к же и́мя мо**его́** прия́тел**я**? Уфф! . . . Я́ ма́ло спа́л, мно́го рабо́тал и весь де́нь пи́л мно́го и вод**ы́** и ви́ски (whiskey): бы́ло так **жа́рко**!

М. —Да́, де́нь бы́л **жа́ркий**, и я́ то́же мно́го пи́л. Но́ как **уже́ по́здно**!

Р. —По́здно? Почему́ по́здно? **Ещё** о́чень **ра́но**: на у́лице **ещё светло́.**

[6] The unstressed particle **же** has many functions. When used after question words (ка́к **же**? что́ **же**? где́ **же**?), it adds a tone of emphasis or interest (sometimes of impatience or perplexity). Что́ **же**, "what then?" "just what?" etc.

[7] Observe that the titles of books, organizations, etc. are declined, unless they are used with a classifying noun (рома́н, о́пера, газе́та, etc.), *e.g.* —Вы́ бы́ли на о́пере «Аида»?—Да́, мы́ бы́ли на «Аиде».

М. —Не **ещё** светло́, а **уже́** светло́, потому́ что **уже́** у́тро.
Р. —**Уже́** у́тро? Ну́, тогда́ до свида́ния, Пье́р, до свида́ния. Но́, ка́к а́дрес мо**е́й** гости́ниц**ы**?

Pronunciation Drill

dóbrəj y̧ę̧çir. majó ím̧ə P̧íţir Rób̧erc. já kəŗŗispanḑént am̧iŗikánskəvə žurnálə vŗę̧m̧ə.
óçiņ pŗijátnə. já . . .
vɨ p̧jér Maţíss, kəŗŗispanḑént francúskəj gaẓéţɨ y̧ę̧çir.
majó ím̧ə ņip̧jér, a žák; i já kəŗŗispanḑént ņiy̧ę̧çirə, a útrə.
áx dá! kaņéšnə! pažálustə, praşţíţi. óçiņ pŗijátnə.

Answer the following questions in Russian.

1. Что́ ду́мал Ро́бертс о Мати́ссе? 2. Что́ говори́л Мати́сс о Вашингто́не? 3. В како́м рестора́не о́н е́л, и где́ бы́л э́тот рестора́н? 4. Кто́ бы́л на ве́чере в Вашингто́не? 5. О поли́тике како́й страны́ они́ говори́ли? 6. Кузнецо́в реда́ктор «Пра́вды»? 7. Почему́ Ро́бертс ду́мал, что ещё ра́но? 8. Почему́ о́н не зна́л, ка́к а́дрес его́ гости́ницы?

EXERCISES

A. *Translate into English the words in parentheses.*

1. Мы́ жи́ли в гости́нице (in the center of Moscow). 2. Э́то окно́ (of my father's study), а то́ окно́—окно́ (of our bright kitchen). 3. —Ка́к и́мя (of your girl student)? —(Of which student)? —(The one), кото́рая жила́ (in Olga's apartment). —Её и́мя Ни́на. 4. —Ка́к назва́ние (of that magazine)? —(Of which magazine)? —(The one about which) мы́ сего́дня говори́ли. 5. На столе́ стоя́л стака́н (of water). 6. Где́ коне́ц (of this street)? 7. Ка́к фами́лия (of your good friend)? 8. Она́ жила́ в кварти́ре (of our dear son). 9. Э́то до́м (of Ivan Ivanovich and his sister). 10. Нача́ло (of her new novel) о́чень интере́сное. 11. Э́то автомоби́ль (of our dear guest). 12. Ка́к и́мя (of that American girl student)? 13. Э́тот па́мятник стоя́л (in the center of their little town). 14. Я́ бы́л (at my good friend's party). 15. Ка́к назва́ние (of your Soviet book)? 16. Ка́к а́дрес (of your sister Anna)?

B. *Translate into Russian.*

1. What is his name? 2. What is his brother's name? 3. What is your sister's name? 4. What is the name of this town? 5. What is the name of this street? 6. —Have you been here long? —All day. 7. —What is the color of their house? —Their house is white. 8. This is the beginning of the book. 9. At the end of the summer his son will be in Moscow, the capital of the Soviet Union. 10. We have not yet been in his sister's apartment. 11. He has already written about the capital of your small country. 12. About whom were you talking? 13. About the friend (*fem.*) of your father. 14. It was dark on the street; it was already night. 15. It was so hot yesterday that I drank a great deal of water. 16. —What is the price of her white dress? Is it expensive? —Yes, very. 17. —What is the title of his book about the Soviet Union? —"The New Policy (**поли́тика**) of the Soviet Union." 18. At the end of the street stood his brother's house. 19. We drank much water, but ate little bread and meat. 20. What a strange study! There is no window here. 21. In our classroom there was always a blackboard, but in this one there is no blackboard. 22. —Boris wasn't in town yesterday, but today he was at the lesson. 23. It was very cold outside, but in the house it was warm and pleasant. 24. We thought very seriously about our new lesson. 25. It's hard to speak English, but easy to read (it). 26. At the end of the day we were still in the city.

VOCABULARY

а́дрес address
ах! Ah! Oh!
ве́чер evening; evening party
вода́ water
вре́мя[8] time
всё (*nom. sing.*) everything, all
гости́ница hotel
давно́ long ago, long since
дверь (*fem.*) door
дешёвый cheap, inexpensive
дорого́й dear, expensive
европе́йский European
жа́ркий (*adv.* **жа́рко**) hot (of weather)
и also, too, even
и́мя[8] (first) name
коне́ц (*gen.* **конца́**) end, finish
кры́ша roof
кусо́к (*gen.* **куска́**) piece, bit
молоко́ milk
назва́ние name, title (of objects)
нача́ло beginning
неда́вно recently, not long ago
па́мятник monument, memorial
по́здно[9] late, it's late

[8] A few nouns which end in **-мя** are neuter in gender.
[9] The д of по́здно is only slightly pronounced.

прекра́сный fine, wonderful, excellent
прия́тель, *fem.* **-ница** friend
ра́но early, it's early
рестора́н restaurant
све́тлый (*adv.* **светло́**) bright, light
ско́лько (+ *gen.*) how much? how many?
сове́тский Soviet (*adj.*)
Сове́тский Сою́з Soviet Union
стака́н glass, tumbler
столи́ца capital
страна́ country, land
сыр cheese
тёмный (*adv.* **темно́**) dark
удо́бный comfortable, convenient
уже́ already
у́тро morning
францу́зский French (*adj.*)
фунт pound
хлеб bread
цвет color
цена́ price
центр center

Verbs

ви́деть to see
ел, е́ло, е́ла, е́ли (*verb in past tense*) ate
пить to drink
спать to sleep

Expressions

До́брый ве́чер! Good evening!
До́брое у́тро! Good morning!
Ка́к ва́ше и́мя? What is your (first) name?
Ка́к назва́ние (+ *gen.*)? What is the name (title) of . . . (an object, book, etc.)?
Ка́к а́дрес (+ *gen.*)? What is the address of . . .?
Кака́я цена́ (+ *gen.*)? What is the price of . . .?
Како́го цве́та (+ *nom.*)? What is the color of . . .? What color is . . .?
в нача́ле (+ *gen.*) at the beginning of . . .
в конце́ (+ *gen.*) at the end of . . .
весь де́нь all day long
Вы́ давно́ зде́сь? Have you been here long?
Я́ давно́ не́ был . . . I haven't been for a long time . . .

Vocabulary Review

Give opposites for the following words:

день	ве́чер	хорошо́	зи́мний
пе́рвый	тру́дный	коне́ц	бе́лый
большо́й	молодо́й	холо́дный	дорого́й
но́вый	зима́	по́здно	давно́
	ма́ло	плохо́й	

UNIT 8

***Accusative singular of nouns and modifiers,* 104. *Accusative singular of pronouns,* 106. *Accusative of time,* 109. *Present tense of verbs,* 109. *Negative expressions,* 112. *Declension of* оди́н, 113. До́лжен, 114.**

GRAMMAR

1. Accusative singular of nouns and modifiers

The accusative case is the case of the direct object. The direct object is the person or thing which is directly affected by the action of a verb (verbs which may take a direct object are called *transitive*). In the following examples the words in italics are direct objects: he bought a *book;* we know *John;* she loves her *mother;* he drinks *tea;* we saw *him;* they liked *her.*

The direct object in Russian takes the *accusative case.*

A. Masculine. Russian distinguishes between *animate* nouns (persons and animals) and *inanimate* nouns (things and abstract concepts). *Animate* nouns of *masculine* gender have the same forms in the accusative as in the *genitive. Inanimate* masculine nouns have the same forms as in the *nominative:*

	Animate	*Inanimate*
Nom.	брат	стол ←
Gen.	бра́та ←	стола́
Acc.	бра́та ←	стол ←

The same rule applies to all modifiers of animate masculine nouns (modifiers include adjectives, possessives, and demonstratives):

	Animate	*Inanimate*
Nom.	мóй дорогóй брáт	э́тот большóй стóл ←
Gen.	моегó дорогóго брáта ←	э́того большóго столá
Acc.	моегó дорогóго брáта ←	э́тот большóй стóл

E.g.: Вóт кóмната моегó дорогóго брáта. (*Gen.*)
О́н ви́дел моегó дорогóго брáта. (*Acc.*)
But: О́н ви́дел мóй автомоби́ль. (*Acc.*)

B. Neuter. All *neuter* nouns and modifiers have in the accusative the same form as in the nominative.

C. Feminine. *Feminine nouns ending in* **-а** *and* **-я**. This is the only class of nouns having a distinct ending in the accusative singular: this ending is [-u], spelled **-у** after hard consonants (сестрá-сестру́), and **-ю** after soft consonants (ку́хня-ку́хню).[1] *There is no difference between animate and inanimate feminines in the singular.*

Modifiers of feminine nouns. Hard adjectives end in **-ую**; soft adjectives in **-юю**:

Nom.	нóв**ая**	си́н**яя**
Acc.	нóв**ую**	си́н**юю**

Feminine demonstratives and possessives in the accusative end in **-у**/**-ю**:

Nom.	э́т**а**	т**а**	нáш**а**	вáш**а**	мо**я́**	тво**я́**
Acc.	э́т**у**	т**у**	нáш**у**	вáш**у**	мо**ю́**	тво**ю́**

E.g.: Онá знáла мо**ю́** молод**у́ю** секретáрш**у**.
Я́ читáл э́т**у** интерéсн**ую** кни́г**у**.
Я́ ви́дел тво**ю́** си́н**юю** шля́п**у**.

Feminine nouns ending in **-ь** (*Fem. II*). These nouns, both animate and inanimate, have the same form in the accusative as in the nominative:

Nom. and *Acc.* мать дочь дверь ночь, etc.

E.g.: Я́ ви́дел вáшу дóчь.

[1] Some feminine nouns shift the stress to the first syllable in the accusative: рукá—ру́ку; головá—гóлову; рекá—рéку; зимá—зи́му, etc.

To summarize for nouns in the accusative:

Я ви́дел	**бра́та.**	Masc., anim.: like *gen.*	
	сто́л.	Masc., inan.: like *nom.*	
	окно́.	Neut., (*all*): like *nom.*	
	сестру́.	Fem. I, anim.:	special *acc.* ending **-у**
	ко́мнату.	Fem. I, inan.:	(or **-ю**, *e.g.*, дере́вню)
	ма́ть.	Fem. II, anim.:	like *nom.*
	две́рь.	Fem. II, inan.:	like *nom.*

2. Accusative singular of pronouns

A. Personal pronouns. All personal pronouns have an accusative identical in form with the genitive. The forms of the third person pronouns have already been given in Unit 7.

Nom.	я	ты	мы	вы	он оно́	она́	они́
Gen. and *Acc.*	меня́	тебя́	нас	вас	его́	её	их

E.g., О́н ви́дел **меня́.** Я́ зна́л **её.** Мы́ зна́ли **и́х.** Я́ ви́дел **ва́с** и **его́.**

B. Interrogative pronouns. Что? "what?" is inanimate in meaning and is used in both nominative and accusative.

Кто? "who?" has in the genitive and accusative the form **кого́?** (pronounce [kavó]).

E.g.:

Что́ вы́ чита́ли? What were you reading?
Кого́ вы́ ви́дели? Whom did you see?

Pattern Sentences

1. —**Что́** вы́ чита́ли в библиоте́ке? —Я́ чита́л интере́сный рома́н Фо́лькнера.
2. —**Что́** вы́ вчера́ ви́дели в теа́тре? —Мы́ ви́дели интере́сн**ую** пье́с**у** Ми́ллера. —Я́ то́же **её** ви́дел.
3. —**Кого́** вы́ вчера́ ви́дели в теа́тре? —Я́ ви́дел ваш**его** бра́т**а** и его́ жен**у́**. А́нна то́же ви́дела **и́х,** но́ они́ не ви́дели **на́с.**

1. —What were you reading at the library? —I was reading an interesting novel by Faulkner.
2. —What did you see yesterday at the theater? —We saw an interesting play by Miller. —I've seen it too.
3. —Whom did you see at the theater yesterday? —I saw your brother and his wife. Anna saw them too, but they didn't see us.

4. —Мы́ ви́дели Бори́са и его́ до́чь О́льгу. —Где́ вы́ **и́х** ви́дели? —Мы́ ви́дели **его́** на у́лице, а **её** в па́рке.

4. —We saw Boris and his daughter Olga. —Where did you see them? —We saw him in the street, and her in the park.

5. —Кто́ чита́л рома́н Толсто́го[2] «Война́ и Ми́р»? —Мы́ все́ чита́ли «Войну́ и Ми́р».

5. —Who has read Tolstoy's novel *War and Peace*? —We have all read *War and Peace*.

6. Ты́ ви́дел, что она́ слу́шала то́лько **меня́**, а не **тебя́**!

6. You saw that she was listening only to me, and not to you!

7. Вчера́ на конце́рте мы́ ви́дели **ва́с**, но́ вы́ не ви́дели **на́с**.

7. Yesterday at the concert we saw you, but you didn't see us.

8. Её оте́ц зна́л Че́хова.

8. Her father knew Chekhov.

9. Э́тот журнали́ст зна́л президе́нта Тру́мана и его́ жену́.

9. That journalist knew President Truman and his wife.

10. Они́ ви́дели балери́ну А́нну Па́влову в Большо́м теа́тре. Э́то бы́ло о́чень давно́!

10. They saw the ballerina Anna Pavlova at the Bolshoi Theater. That was very long ago!

Drills

A. *Translate into English.*

1. Когда́ ру́сский бале́т бы́л зде́сь, мы́ ви́дели балери́ну Гали́ну Ула́нову.
2. Бори́с то́же ви́дел её.
3. Мы́ вчера́ ви́дели интере́сную истори́ческую пье́су. Ива́н то́же ви́дел её.
4. Я́ так давно́ ва́с не ви́дел!
5. —Вы́ чита́ли вчера́шнюю газе́ту? —Да́, я́ чита́л её.
6. О́н не слу́шал на́с.
7. —Где́ журна́л «Но́вое вре́мя»? —Я́ не ви́дел его́.
8. —Э́то пра́вда, что ты́ давно́ не ви́дел А́нну? —Не́т, э́то непра́вда, я́ ви́дел её вчера́.
9. —Когда́ вы́ ви́дели О́льгу и Ива́на? —Я́ ви́дел и́х сего́дня.

B. *Fill in the form of the direct object of the pronoun which corresponds to the subject of the first sentence.*

Model: О́н бы́л в Нью-Йо́рке. Я́ **его́** та́м ви́дел.

1. Кни́га была́ в кабине́те. Я́ . . . . . . та́м ви́дел.
2. Журна́л бы́л на столе́. Я́ . . . . . . та́м ви́дел.
3. Они́ бы́ли в Аме́рике. Я́ . . . . . . та́м ви́дел.
4. Бори́с бы́л в Москве́. Я́ . . . . . . та́м ви́дел.
5. И́х ма́ть была́ на конце́рте. Я́ . . . . . . та́м ви́дел.
6. О́льга и Ива́н бы́ли в па́рке. Я́ . . . . . . та́м ви́дел.

[2] Russian family names ending in **-ий** and **-ой** are declined as adjectives, *e.g.*, Мы́ говори́ли о Достое́вском. Women members of the same family use the same name, declined as a feminine adjective, *e.g.*, Толст**а́я**, Достое́вск**ая**.

C. *Fill in the direct object pronouns.*

Model: Почему́, когда́ **она́** говори́ла, ты́ **её** не слу́шал?

1. Почему́, когда́ **мы́** говори́ли, ты́ ...... не слу́шал?
2. Почему́, когда́ **я́** говори́л, ты́ ...... не слу́шал?
3. Почему́, когда́ **вы́** говори́ли, о́н ...... не слу́шал?
4. Почему́, когда́ **ты́** говори́л, о́н ...... не слу́шал?
5. Почему́, когда́ **они́** говори́ли, ты́ ...... не слу́шал?
6. Почему́, когда́ А́нна говори́ла, ты́ ...... не слу́шал?
7. Почему́, когда́ Бори́с говори́л, ты́ ...... не слу́шал?

D. *Put the words in parentheses in the correct case form and translate.*

1. Я́ уже́ чита́л (э́та кни́га).
2. Андре́й писа́л (но́вая пьє́са).
3. Мы́ вчера́ ви́дели (О́льга Смирно́ва).
4. Я́ ви́дела (она́) на уро́ке.
5. Мы́ не зна́ли (он).
6. Профе́ссор Па́влов зна́л (они́).
7. Они́ зна́ли (профе́ссор Па́влов). Они́ хорошо́ зна́ли (он).
8. Мы́ чита́ли (А́нна Каре́нина).
9. Моя́ ма́ть зна́ла (э́тот тала́нтливый писа́тель). Она́ ви́дела (он) в Москве́.
10. —Где́ газе́та? —Я́ ви́дел (она́) в кабине́те.
11. —Где́ журна́л? —Я́ не ви́дел (он).
12. —Где́ Андре́й? —Я́ не ви́дел (он).
13. —Где́ ты́ ви́дел (я)? —Я́ ви́дел (ты) на у́лице.
14. О́н не слу́шал (ни вы́ ни мы́).
15. Я́ хорошо́ зна́л (ва́ша до́чь О́льга) и (ва́ш ста́рший сы́н Бори́с).
16. Никто́ не зна́л (на́ш но́вый инжене́р).
17. Мы́ вчера́ ви́дели (тво́й ста́рый дру́г).

E. *Translate into Russian.*

1. Did you see the president of our country when he was in your city?
2. No, but I saw him when I was in the capital.
3. Where did Tolstoy write *War and Peace*?
4. He probably wrote that novel in the country.
5. Have you read *Boris Godunov* by (= of) Pushkin?
6. Yes, I have read that play.
7. Where did you see us?
8. I saw you in a store, but you didn't see me.
9. —Whom did you know there? —I knew only their sister.
10. —Did you see our brother? —Yes, I saw him.
11. —Have you seen my book? —Yes, I saw it.
12. —Have you seen my dictionary? —No, I haven't seen it.

3. Accusative of time

Besides serving as direct object, the accusative case is used to designate the *period of time* in which an action is carried out:

Они́ рабо́тали **де́нь и но́чь.**
They worked day and night.

Мы́ рабо́тали **це́лую неде́лю.**
We worked a whole week.

Сего́дня я́ **весь де́нь** чита́л.
Today I read all day long.

Ка́ждую неде́лю я́ чита́л но́вый рома́н.
Every week I read a new novel.

4. Present tense of verbs

Russian has two conjugations, a first, or **-е-**, conjugation, and a second, or **-и-**, conjugation. The basic endings of the two conjugations in the *present tense* are spelled as follows:

	1st Conjugation	2nd Conjugation
	Singular	*Singular*
1st pers.:	**-ю**	**-ю**
2nd pers.:	**-е**шь	**-и**шь
3rd pers.:	**-е**т	**-и**т
	Plural	*Plural*
1st pers.:	**-е**м	**-и**м
2nd pers.:	**-е**те	**-и**те
3rd pers.:	**-ю**т	**-я**т

Note that these two sets of endings are the same, except for the vowels (**е** or **и**) in the second and third persons singular and the first and second persons plural; the vowel of the third plural ending of the first conjugation (**-ют**) must also be distinguished from that of the second conjugation (**-ят**).

The majority of verbs with infinitives ending in **-ать** or **-ять** belong to the first conjugation. The final **-ть** of the infinitive is dropped, and the present endings of the first conjugation are added:

Conjugation of **чита́ть,** *"to read"*

1st pers.:	я́ чита́**ю**	мы́ чита́**ем**
2nd pers.:	ты́ чита́**ешь**	вы́ чита́**ете**
3rd pers.:	о́н (она́, оно́) чита́**ет**	они́ чита́**ют**

Russian has only one present tense form corresponding to the various forms of the English present: simple, progressive, and emphatic ("I read," "am reading," "do read").

TABLE OF FIRST CONJUGATION VERBS
(conjugated like чита́ть)

Verbs Used in Earlier Lessons		*New Verbs*	
де́лать	to make, do	начина́ть	to begin, start
ду́мать	to think	конча́ть	to end, finish
знать	to know	закрыва́ть	to close, shut
рабо́тать	to work	открыва́ть	to open
слу́шать	to listen (to)	понима́ть	to understand
игра́ть	to play	спра́шивать	to ask, inquire
		отдыха́ть	to rest, relax
		покупа́ть	to buy
		объясня́ть	to explain

Most verbs with infinitives ending in **-ить** belong to the *second* conjugation. The final **-ить** of the infinitive is dropped, and the present endings of the second conjugation are added:

SECOND CONJUGATION

Conjugation of **говор.и́ть,** *"to speak, say, talk"*

1st pers.:	я́ говор**ю́**	мы́ говор**и́м**
2nd pers.:	ты́ говор**и́шь**	вы́ говор**и́те**
3rd pers.:	о́н (она́, оно́) говор**и́т**	они́ говор**я́т**

Other second conjugation verbs will be treated in Unit 11.

Pattern Sentences

1. Я́ хорошо́ **зна́ю** э́ту библиоте́ку. Я́ **рабо́таю** та́м ка́ждый ве́чер.
2. Они́ **говоря́т,** что **зна́ют** ва́шу до́чь Ле́ну и ва́шего сы́на Ива́на. Они́ хорошо́ и́х **зна́ют.**
3. —Вы́ **зна́ете** на́шу молоду́ю секре-та́ршу и её ску́чную подру́гу? —Да́, **зна́ю.**
4. —Мы́ тепе́рь **чита́ем** Шекспи́ра. —Каку́ю пье́су вы́ **чита́ете?** —Мы́ **чита́ем** «Га́млета», моноло́г «Бы́ть и́ли не бы́ть».

1. I know that library well. I work there every evening.
2. They say that they know your daughter Lena and your son Ivan. They know them well.
3. —Do you know our young secretary and her boring (girl) friend? —Yes, I do.
4. —We are reading Shakespeare now. —Which play are you reading? —We're reading *Hamlet*—the monologue "To be or not to be."

5. Я́ не всегда́ **понима́ю,** о чём вы́ **говори́те.**
5. I don't always understand what you are talking about.

6. Вы́ меня́ не **понима́ете,** потому́ что вы́ меня́ не **слу́шаете.**
6. You don't understand me, because you don't listen to me.

7. —Вы́ **зна́ете** у́зкую, тёмную у́лицу, где́ жи́л на́ш дру́г Смирно́в? —Не́т, не **зна́ю.**
7. —Do you know the narrow dark street where our friend Smirnov lived? —No, I don't.

8. Я́ ви́дел в Москве́ широ́кую у́лицу, где́ жи́л поэ́т Пу́шкин.
8. In Moscow I saw the broad street where the poet Pushkin lived.

9. В на́шем кла́ссе все́ **говоря́т** то́лько по-ру́сски. Все́ **говоря́т** хорошо́, но́ иногда́ не о́чень бы́стро.
9. In our class everyone speaks only Russian. Everyone speaks well, but at times not very fast.

10. Мы́ всё **понима́ем,** когда́ вы́ говори́те ме́дленно.
10. We understand everything when you speak slowly.

11. —Почему́ ты́ **закрыва́ешь** окно́? —Я́ **закрыва́ю** его́, потому́ что хо́лодно.
11. —Why are you closing the window? —I am closing it because it's cold.

12. —Почему́ вы́ **открыва́ете** окно́? —Потому́ что ту́т о́чень жа́рко.
12. —Why are you opening the window? —Because it's very hot here.

13. Я́ жи́л в Ки́еве **це́лый ме́сяц** и почти́ **це́лую неде́лю** в Сталингра́де.
13. I stayed in Kiev a whole month and almost a whole week in Stalingrad.

14. **Ка́ждую неде́лю** учи́тель **объясня́ет** в кла́ссе но́вый уро́к, а мы́ **слу́шаем.**
14. Every week in class the teacher explains a new lesson, and we listen.

15. Ты́ то́лько **начина́ешь** чита́ть э́ту кни́гу, а я́ уже́ **конча́ю** её.
15. You are only beginning to read that book, and I am already finishing it.

16. —Ле́на, как хорошо́ ты́ сего́дня **игра́ешь**! —Спаси́бо за комплиме́нт! —Э́то не комплиме́нт, э́то пра́вда.
16. —Lena, how well you are playing today! —Thank you for the compliment! —It's not a compliment, it's the truth.

Drills

A. *Translate into English.*

1. Я́ начина́ю понима́ть, о чём вы́ говори́те.
2. Я́ отдыха́ю, когда́ я́ слу́шаю му́зыку.
3. Все́ всё понима́ют, когда́ вы́ не сли́шком бы́стро говори́те.
4. Когда́ я́ не понима́ю, я́ спра́шиваю учи́теля.
5. —Где́ вы́ покупа́ете сы́р? —Я́ покупа́ю его́ в ма́леньком магази́не на мое́й у́лице.
6. Мы́ конча́ем но́вый уро́к.
7. Они́ конча́ют чита́ть э́ту ску́чную кни́гу, а я́ то́лько начина́ю её.
8. Мо́й мла́дший бра́т покупа́ет но́вую пласти́нку ка́ждую неде́лю.
9. Его́ ста́ршая сестра́ ка́ждый ве́чер слу́шает серьёзную му́зыку.
10. Я́ говорю́ то́лько по-ру́сски.

B. *Fill in the correct endings of the verbs.*

1. Я́ мно́го рабо́та.....
2. Что́ ты́ спра́шива....?
3. О чём они́ говор....?
4. Мы́ ва́с слу́ша.....
5. Они́ отдыха́.....
6. О́н говор.... по-англи́йски.
7. Почему́ ты́ не конча́....... письмо́?
8. Я́ не понима́...., что́ ты́ говор.....
9. Вы́ хорошо́ объясня́.... грамма́тику.
10. Что́ они́ де́ла....?
11. Они́ говор.... по-ру́сски.
12. Мы́ начина́.... понима́.....

C. *Change the infinitives in parentheses to the correct forms of the present.*

1. Они́ мно́го (рабо́тать).
2. Я́ его́ (спра́шивать), где́ о́н (рабо́тать).
3. Где́ вы́ (покупа́ть) газе́ту?
4. Они́ (говори́ть) о́чень ме́дленно.
5. Я́ (понима́ть) всё, что ты́ (говори́ть).
6. Почему́ ты́ не (слу́шать), когда́ я́ (говори́ть)?
7. Я́ всегда́ (слу́шать), когда́ вы́ (говори́ть).
8. Ива́н (закрыва́ть) две́рь, а вы́ (открыва́ть) её!
9. —Что́ вы́ (де́лать)? —Я́ (закрыва́ть) окно́.
10. Мы́ (начина́ть) (чита́ть) но́вую пье́су.
11. Они́ (конча́ть) (писа́ть) перево́д.
12. Ты́ (объясня́ть) пра́вило, но́ я́ не (понима́ть) его́.
13. Они́ (отдыха́ть) в дере́вне.
14. Я́ никогда́ не (отдыха́ть); я́ всегда́ (рабо́тать).
15. Вы́ не (рабо́тать), а (говори́ть).
16. —О ко́м ты́ (ду́мать)? —Я́ не (зна́ть).
17. Вы́ не (слу́шать), когда́ они́ (говори́ть).

5. Negative expressions

Many negative expressions are formed in Russian by prefixing **ни-** to an interrogative:

Interrogative	*Negative*	*English Translation*
когда́?	никогда́	never, not . . . ever
кто́?	никто́ (nom.) никого́ (gen. and acc.; pronounced [n̦ikavó])	no one, not . . . anyone
что?	ничего́ (derived from genitive of что; pronounced [n̦ičivó])	nothing, not . . . anything
где?	нигде́	nowhere, not . . . anywhere
	ни . . . ни	neither . . . nor (or), no . . . or

When one of these negative expressions is used in a sentence, the negative particle **не** is placed before the verb or other predicate (adverb, adjective, etc.).

> Óн **никогдá не** рабóтает.
> He never works.
>
> Онá **ничегó не** знáет.
> She knows nothing (or: She doesn't know anything).
>
> Мы́ **никогó не** ви́дели.
> We didn't see anyone.
>
> Я́ **не** знáю **ни** Петрá **ни** егó брáта.
> I know neither Peter nor his brother (or: I don't know either . . . or . . .).

When used alone, without a verb, the **не** is, of course, omitted:

> —Чтó э́тот студéнт знáет? —Ничегó!
> —What does that student know? —Nothing!
>
> —Когó óн знáет? —Никогó.
> —Whom does he know? —No one.

6. Declension of **оди́н** "one"

Оди́н, "one," is declined like **э́тот** (pronominal declension). The **и** of the masculine nominative drops out in other cases:

	Masculine	*Neuter*	*Feminine*
Nom.	оди́н	однó	однá
Gen.	одногó[3]	Same as masc.	однóй
Acc.	одногó[3] *an.* оди́н *inan.*	однó	однý
Loc.	в/на/об однóм	Same as masc.	в/на/об однóй

E.g., На моём столé **оди́н** журнáл, **однá** кни́га и **однó** перó.

Оди́н sometimes has the meaning of English "a," "a certain":

> В вáшем клáссе я́ знáю **однý** óчень краси́вую дéвушку.
> In your class I know a very pretty girl.

[3] Pronounced [adnavó].

Оди́н also means "alone."

Я́ бы́л та́м **оди́н.**	I was there alone.
Она́ жила́ **одна́.**	She lived alone (by herself).

In this sense the word may also be used in the plural:

Они́ жи́ли **одни́.**	They lived alone.

7. До́лжен, "must"

До́лжен agrees in gender and number with the subject and is used with infinitives. Note that the masculine has a fleeting **е** which drops out in the other forms; note also stress shift to the ending in the feminine singular and plural:

Pres. masc. sing.:	О́н тепе́рь до́лжен мно́го рабо́тать. He must (has to) work a lot now.
Past fem. sing.:	Она́ должна́ была рабо́тать. She had to work.
Pres. pl.:	Вы́ не должны́ так мно́го рабо́тать. You should not work so much.
Past pl.:	Они́ не должны́ были рабо́тать вчера́. They didn't have to work (or: weren't supposed to work) yesterday.

Note that **не** is placed before **до́лжен**, and that **до́лжен** comes before **был**. Both the present and past may frequently be translated as "to be supposed to":

О́н **до́лжен был** игра́ть вчера́ на конце́рте, но́ не игра́л.
He was supposed to play at the concert yesterday, but didn't.

Pattern Sentences

1. Э́тот студе́нт **ничего́ не** понима́ет!	1. That student understands nothing!
2. Почему́ вы́ **ничего́ не** де́лаете? Вы́ **должны́** рабо́тать!	2. Why don't you do anything? You must work!
3. —Где́ ты́ тепе́рь рабо́таешь? —Я́ тепе́рь **нигде́ не** рабо́таю.	3. —Where are you working now? —I'm not working anywhere now.
4. —Ни́на, почему́ ты́ **никогда́ не** говори́шь по-ру́сски? Ты́ **должна́** всегда́ говори́ть по-ру́сски. —Я́ иногда́ говорю́.	4. —Nina, why don't you ever speak Russian? You must always speak Russian. —I do speak it sometimes.
5. Почти́ ка́ждую неде́лю моя́ жена́ покупа́ет но́вое пла́тье. А я́ **никогда́ ничего́ не** покупа́ю!	5. Almost every week my wife buys a new dress. But I never buy anything!

6. —Ива́н, почему́ ты́ **никогда́ не** игра́ешь на роя́ле? Ты́ **до́лжен** игра́ть ка́ждый де́нь. —Я́ иногда́ игра́ю.
7. Когда́ мо́й ста́рший бра́т жи́л далеко́, о́н **до́лжен был** всё покупа́ть в э́том магази́не. Та́м, где́ о́н жи́л, **ничего́ не́ было.**
8. **Оди́н** до́ктор говори́т, что все́ **должны́** бо́льше спа́ть и ме́ньше е́сть.[4]
9. Я́ зна́ю **одного́** челове́ка, кото́рый **никогда́ не** отдыха́ет.
10. Мо́й мла́дший бра́т ви́дел на **одно́й** вечери́нке **одну́** о́чень краси́вую де́вушку, кото́рая ва́с зна́ет.
11. Почти́ **никто́** его́ **не** понима́ет, да́же когда́ о́н говори́т ме́дленно.

6. —Ivan, why don't you ever play the piano? You should play every day. —I do play sometimes.
7. When my elder brother lived far away, he had to buy everything in this store. There was nothing there where he lived.
8. A (certain) doctor says that everyone should sleep more and eat less.
9. I know a man who never rests.
10. My younger brother saw at a party a very beautiful girl who knows you.
11. Hardly anyone understands him, even when he speaks slowly.

Drills

A. *Translate into English.*

1. Я́ ничего́ не понима́ю, когда́ вы́ так бы́стро говори́те.
2. Почему́ вы́ никогда́ ничего́ не спра́шиваете?
3. Вы́ должны́ меня́ спра́шивать, когда́ вы́ не понима́ете, что́ я́ говорю́.
4. Никто́ не говори́т зде́сь по-ру́сски.
5. Мы́ вчера́ нигде́ не́ были.
6. Они́ говори́ли об одно́й де́вушке, кото́рую и вы́ хорошо́ зна́ете, но́ кото́рую я́ никогда́ не ви́дел.
7. Мы́ жи́ли в Ленингра́де почти́ це́лую неде́лю. Мы́ та́м никого́ не зна́ли.
8. Когда́ я́ жи́л оди́н, я́ до́лжен был ка́ждое у́тро покупа́ть молоко́, све́жий хле́б и ру́сскую газе́ту. Тепе́рь всё покупа́ет моя́ жена́.
9. Ле́на, ты́ должна́ ка́ждый де́нь игра́ть на гита́ре. Я́ не понима́ю, почему́ ты́ не игра́ешь.
10. Я́ ещё никого́ зде́сь не зна́ю.
11. О́н ду́мает, что о́н уже всё зна́ет, но́ все́ зна́ют, что о́н почти́ ничего́ не зна́ет.
12. И́горь до́лжен бо́льше чита́ть, писа́ть и переводи́ть и ме́ньше игра́ть в футбо́л. О́н сли́шком ма́ло рабо́тает.

B. *Fill in correct forms of* **оди́н.**

1. Анна́ была́ на конце́рте ....
2. Ива́н бы́л до́ма ....

[4] Есть is the infinitive of the verb "to eat" (past ел, etc.). It must be distinguished from есть, "there is."

3. Я́ зна́ю ...... хоро́шего журнали́ста и ...... хоро́шую журнали́стку.
4. Мы́ говори́ли об ...... хоро́шем до́кторе.
5. Мы́ жи́ли в ...... ко́мнате.
6. Они́ жи́ли ....

C. *Translate into Russian.*

1. She had to live alone.
2. You never work. You ought to work more.
3. Why don't you do anything?
4. Why do you never listen when I speak? You must listen!
5. We don't have to work today; we are resting.
6. She was supposed to speak in class today.
7. We don't know anything.
8. They never speak Russian.
9. He doesn't do anything.
10. Nowhere did I see her.
11. They don't understand anything.
12. Today he was neither in class nor at home.

READING

Сестра́ и бра́т

Я́ ти́хий челове́к. Я́ ма́ло говорю́ и мно́го рабо́таю. Когда́ я́ не рабо́таю, я́ почти́ всегда́ до́ма и почти́ всегда́ оди́н. До́ма я́ чита́ю серьёзный журна́л и́ли хоро́шую кни́гу, и́ли слу́шаю класси́ческую му́зыку, как наприме́р, Бетхо́вена, Чайко́вского, Шопе́на. Чте́ние и му́зыка—э́то мо́й о́тдых. Я́ так хорошо́ отдыха́ю, когда́ я́ оди́н!

Но́ моя́ ста́ршая сестра́ Ле́на[5] меня́ не понима́ет. Вы́ зна́ете мою́ ста́ршую сестру́ Ле́ну? Она́ хоро́шая де́вушка, но́ она́ ду́мает, что она́ всё зна́ет и всё понима́ет. Она́ говори́т, что я́, её мла́дший бра́т, до́лжен её слу́шать!

Ле́на почти́ всегда́ та́к начина́ет неприя́тный разгово́р: «Ты́, Алёша,[5] сли́шком мно́го чита́ешь и ду́маешь. Э́то потому́ что ты́ сли́шком мно́го оди́н. Я́, коне́чно, не зна́ю о чём ты́ ду́маешь, потому́ что ты́ никогда́ ничего́ не говори́шь, но́ я́ зна́ю, что э́то пло́хо. Почему́ ты́ не как все́? Почему́ ты́ тако́й ску́чный челове́к?»

[5] Ле́на, diminutive form (nickname) of Еле́на. Алёша, diminutive of Алексе́й. Diminutive forms of men's names ending in **-а** and **-я** are declined like feminine nouns, *e.g.*, Я́ зна́ю Алёшу.

Я́ слу́шаю сестру́, но́ ничего́ не говорю́. Я́ ду́маю, что она́ не должна́ та́к говори́ть. Почему́ я́ ску́чный? И почему́ я́ до́лжен бы́ть как все́? И кто́ э́то—«все́»? И почему́ всё, что я́ де́лаю—пло́хо, а всё, что она́ де́лает—хорошо́? Наприме́р: ка́ждую неде́лю Ле́на покупа́ет но́вое пла́тье—э́то хорошо́. Я́ покупа́ю ка́ждую неде́лю но́вую кни́гу—э́то пло́хо. Ле́на покупа́ет ка́ждый ме́сяц но́вую дорогу́ю шля́пу—э́то хорошо́. Я́ покупа́ю пласти́нку—э́то пло́хо! Я́ ничего́ не понима́ю!

А вы́ зна́ете подру́гу Ле́ны, краси́вую брюне́тку Ни́ну Ла́пину? Вы́ зна́ете о чём они́ говоря́т, когда́ они́ вме́сте? Я́ иногда́ слу́шаю и́х разгово́р. Сего́дня, наприме́р, они́ говори́ли об о́чень дорого́й бе́лой шля́пе, кото́рую Ни́на ви́дела в одно́м магази́не; и об одно́м прия́тном и краси́вом молодо́м челове́ке, кото́рого они́ ви́дели на одно́й вечери́нке; и о то́лстой блонди́нке, кото́рая была́ в о́чень у́зком кра́сном пла́тье. Я́ не зна́ю, о ко́м и о чём они́ ещё говори́ли—я́ не слу́шал.

Ну́, кто́ ску́чный, я́ ва́с спра́шиваю!

Не́т, я́ не понима́ю сестру́, а она́ не понима́ет меня́.

Pronunciation Drill

já ţíx̧ij çilaγék. já málə gəvaŗú i mnógə rabótəju. kagdá já ņirabótəju, já paçţí fşigdá dómə i paçţí fşigdá aḑín. dómə já çitáju şiŗjóznij žurnál, íļi xaróšuju kņígu, íļi slúšəju klaşşíçiskuju múzɨku.

Answer the following questions in Russian.

1. Ка́к отдыха́ет геро́й на́шего расска́за? 2. Почему́ Ле́на говори́т о бра́те, что о́н ску́чный челове́к? 3. Почему́ она́ не зна́ет, о чём Алёша ду́мает? 4. Что́, по мне́нию (according to) Ле́ны, хорошо́ и что́ пло́хо? 5. Каку́ю шля́пу ви́дела Ле́на? 6. Кого́ она́ ви́дела на вечери́нке? 7. Кто́ бы́л в у́зком кра́сном пла́тье? 8. Алёша всегда́ слу́шает, когда́ Ле́на и Ни́на говоря́т? 9. Почему́ Алёша не зна́л, о чём ещё они́ говори́ли?

EXERCISES

A. *Change the words in parentheses to the accusative case, and fill in the blanks with appropriate pronouns.*

1. —Вы́ ви́дели (но́вая гости́ница)? —Да́, я́ ви́дел .... Во́т .... 2. —Ты́ зна́ешь (мо́й бра́т)? —Да́, я́ хорошо́ зна́ю ......; ...... мо́й прия́тель. 3. —Мы́ начина́ем чита́ть (э́та интере́сная кни́га). А они́ конча́ют .... —Чья́ ......? —...... моя́.

4. —Ктó всегдá открывáет (э́то окнó)? —Андрéй открывáет .... 5. Я́ закрывáю (э́та двéрь). Я́ кáждый вéчер закрывáю .... 6. Я́ спрáшиваю (вáша сестрá и вы́) о вáшем брáте. 7. Бори́с говори́т, что óн знáет (оди́н талáнтливый инженéр). Андрéй тóже знáет .... 8. Онá покупáет (чёрное плáтье и крáсная шля́па). 9. Я́ знáю (э́тот ресторáн и ти́хий человéк), котóрый тáм рабóтает. 10. Я́ не понимáю (вáш хорóший дрýг). Я́ не понимáю ......, а ...... не понимáет .... 11. Вчéра мы́ ви́дели (нáш учи́тель и нáша учи́тельница); мы́ ви́дели ...... в теáтре.

B. *Translate into Russian.*

1. When my elder brother is alone at home, he reads the paper. 2. —What paper does he read? —I think that sometimes he reads a Russian paper. 3. You rest too much. That isn't good. 4. She buys meat every day. 5. I know a very pretty brunette, whom I think you also know. 6. He doesn't understand anything, because he never listens. 7. You must not ask Olga what she does. 8. Every morning he opens the store. He opens it very early. 9. I know that young American writer and his pretty wife. I saw them in London at a party. 10. He is very dull and never reads anything. 11. Whom do you know in this town? 12. I know only one old doctor and his eldest son. 13. —Do you know her mother? —No, I never saw her. 14. They are not doing anything; they say that they are resting. 15. Sometimes she asks me, "Whom are you (ты) thinking about? Why don't you ever listen? Why do you close your door?" What a dull conversation! 16. The hat (that) we saw in the store is too expensive. 17. She is buying a cheap hat. 18. Every evening he closes the store late. 19. Olga knows Ivan and Ivan knows Olga. 20. In my room there is only one small narrow table, and in my sister's room there is a large wide one.

VOCABULARY

блонди́н, *fem.* **-ка** blond(e) (*noun*)
брюнéт, *fem.* **-ка** brunet(te) (*noun*)
бóльше more
бы́стро fast, quick
вечери́нка (informal) evening party
все (*pl.*) everyone, all[6]
всё (*neut. sing.*) everything[6]
дéвушка girl

[6] Все (everyone, all) is always plural in Russian, *e.g.*, Они́ **всé** бы́ли там. **Всé** знá**ют**, что э́то непрáвда. Всё (everything) is always neuter singular, *e.g.*, **Всё** бы́ло на столé. **Всё, что** óн говори́л, бы́ло óчень интерéсно.

друг friend
иногда́ sometimes
ка́ждый every, each
кра́сный red
магази́н store, shop
ме́дленно slowly
ме́ньше less
ме́сяц month; moon
мла́дший younger, youngest
му́зыка music
наприме́р for example
неде́ля week
неприя́тный unpleasant
о́тдых rest, relaxation
пласти́нка phonograph record
подру́га girl friend
почти́ almost
пье́са play, drama
ску́чный [skúšnij] dull, boring, tedious
сли́шком too, excessively
ста́рший elder, eldest; older, oldest
ти́хий quiet, soft (of voice)
то́лстый fat, stout
у́зкий narrow
челове́к man, person, human being
чте́ние reading
широ́кий wide, broad

Expressions

Спаси́бо за комплиме́нт! Thanks for the compliment!
почти́ ничего́ hardly anything
почти́ никого́ hardly anyone, etc.

UNIT 9

***Dative case of nouns, pronouns, and adjectives,* 120. *Dative of state or condition,* 126. *The adjective* нужный, 126. Нужно *or* надо, 126. *First conjugation verbs (continued),* 128. *Conjugation of* давать, 129. *Reflexive possessive* свой, 131.**

GRAMMAR

1. Dative of nouns

The dative case denotes the recipient or addressee of something that is given, sent, transmitted, or communicated.

A sentence with a *direct object* (the thing given, sent, communicated, etc.) and an *indirect object* (the recipient) may be represented as follows:

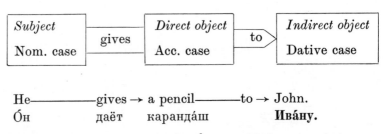

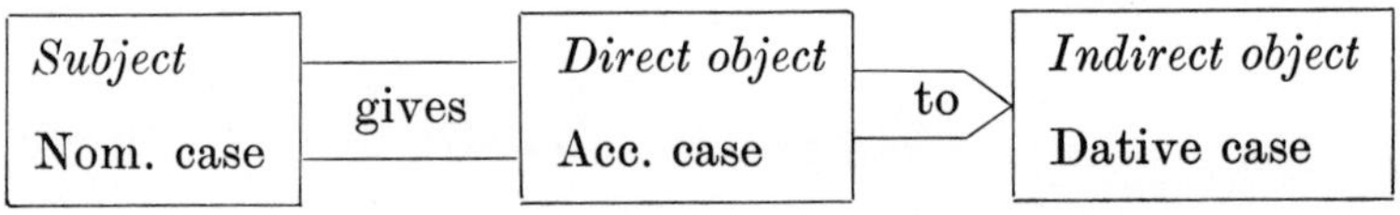

He————gives → a pencil————to → John.
Óн даёт карандáш **Ивáну.**

Or: He gives John a pencil: Óн даёт **Ивáну** карандáш.

An indirect object in the dative may also occur in a sentence without a direct object expressed:

She wrote to John every day.
Онá писáла **Ивáну** кáждый дéнь.

Ending of Nouns in the Dative Case

		Spelling: *Hard*	Spelling: *Soft*
Masc. / *Neut.*	[-u]	**-у**	**-ю**
Fem.	[-e] stressed / [-i] unstressed	**-е**	

	Nominative	*Dative*
Masc.	стол [stól.] гость [góşţ.] музе́й [muẓéj.]	столу́ [stal.ú] го́стю [góşţ.u] музе́ю [muẓéj.u]
Neut.	окно́ [akn.ó] по́ле [pól̦.ə]	окну́ [akn.ú] по́лю [pól̦.u]
Fem.	жена́ [žɨn.á] ку́хня [kúxņ.ə]	жене́ [žiņ.é] ку́хне [kúxņ.i]

(Feminines of Class II will be treated in Unit 12.)

Verbs Used with the Dative
(not a complete list)

"Giving"

дава́ть (I) to give (to)
продава́ть (I) to sell (to)
посыла́ть (I) to send (to)
помога́ть (I) to help (give help to)
покупа́ть (I) to buy (for)

"Communicating"

говори́ть (II) to tell, say (to)
писа́ть (I) to write (to)
чита́ть (I) to read (to)
объясня́ть (I) to explain (to)
звони́ть (II) to phone (to)
пока́зывать (I) to show (to)
отвеча́ть (I) to answer (to)

The verbs посыла́ть, помога́ть, объясня́ть, пока́зывать, and отвеча́ть are conjugated in the present like чита́ть. Говори́ть and звони́ть belong to the second conjugation (see Unit 8). The conjugation of дава́ть, продава́ть, and писа́ть will be presented later in this unit.

Спра́шивать (to ask), unlike отвеча́ть (to answer), takes the *accusative* of the person asked.

Pattern Sentences

Observe in the following sentences that the dative of **кто** *is* **комý.**

1. А́нна говори́т Ивáну, что óн дóлжен чáсто писáть отцý.
2. —**Комý** вы́ посылáете э́ту кни́гу? —Я́ посылáю её дрýгу.
3. О́н никогдá ничегó не посылáет сестрé!
4. Они́ посылáют привéт профéссору Пáвлову.
5. Я́ объясня́ю А́нне, кáк писáть э́то упражнéние.
6. Отéц объясня́ет сы́ну, чтó óн дóлжен дéлать.
7. Я́ покáзываю секретáрше нáшу нóвую контóру.
8. Мýж дóлжен помогáть женé, а женá должнá помогáть мýжу.
9. —**Комý** вы́ звони́те? —Я́ звоню́ дóктору.
10. Молодóй инженéр чáсто звони́т по телефóну О́льге.

1. Anna is telling Ivan that he must write to his father often.
2. —To whom are you sending this book? —I am sending it to a friend.
3. He never sends anything to his sister!
4. They are sending their regards to Professor Pavlov.
5. I am explaining to Anna how to write this exercise.
6. The father is explaining to his son what he ought to do.
7. I am showing the secretary our new office.
8. A husband must help his wife, and a wife must help her husband.
9. —Whom are you calling (telephoning)? —I am calling the doctor.
10. The young engineer often calls Olga on the phone.

Drills

A. *Translate into English.*

1. Кáждое ýтро Ивáн Ивáнович объясня́ет секретáрше, чтó онá должнá дéлать весь дéнь.
2. Мáть кáждую недéлю покупáет пласти́нку и посылáет её сы́ну.
3. Сы́н нáшего дóктора, котóрый тепéрь живёт в Вашингтóне, чáсто звони́т Вéре.
4. Я́ покáзываю прия́телю мою́ нóвую кварти́ру.
5. Я́ посылáю телегрáмму Бори́су.
6. О́н никогдá не помогáет отцý.

B. *Put the words in parentheses into the correct case and translate.*

1. Я́ помогáю (брат).
2. Я́ слýшаю (брат).
3. О́н вчерá ви́дел (профéссор Пáвлов).
4. О́н помогáет (профéссор Пáвлов).
5. Я́ спрáшиваю (друг), чтó óн дéлает.
6. Я́ посылáю телегрáмму (друг).
7. Почемý вы́ не звони́те (дóктор)?
8. Когдá вы́ ви́дели (дóктор)?

9. Чтó ты́ объясня́ешь (Ни́на)?
10. Когдá ты́ ви́дел (Ни́на)?
11. Студéнт отвечáет (профéссор).
12. Óн спрáшивает (профéссор), чтó óн дóлжен тепéрь читáть.

C. *Translate into Russian.*

1. —Whom are you helping? —I am helping my brother.
2. —Whom is the student answering? —He is answering the teacher, who is questioning him.
3. —To whom is the teacher explaining the new rule? —To a girl student.
4. —To whom are you showing your new suit? —To Olga.
5. —Whom are you calling on the phone? —I am calling the secretary.
6. —To whom are you sending this letter? —I am sending it to a friend.
7. I don't understand to whom you are giving this advice.
8. Who was explaining this rule in class?
9. He is showing our apartment to Galina.
10. I am sending my regards to Doctor Semënov.

2. Dative of pronouns and adjectives

The dative masculine-neuter ending of these forms is spelled **-ому** (hard); or **-ему** (soft). The dative feminine ending is spelled **-ой** (hard); or **-ей** (soft).

MASCULINE AND NEUTER

	NOMINATIVE		DATIVE
	Masculine	*Neuter*	*Masculine and Neuter*
3rd pers. pron.	он	онó	емý [j.imú]
Adjectives	нóвый си́ний хорóший	нóвое си́нее хорóшее	нóвому [nóv.əmu] си́нему [ʂíŋ.əmu] хорóшему [xaróš.əmu]
Possessives	мой наш	моё нáше	моемý [məj.imú] нáшему [náš.əmu]
Demonstratives	э́тот тот	э́то то	э́тому [ét.əmu] томý [t.amú]
Interrogatives	кто	 что	комý [k.amú] чемý [ç̌.imú]
	оди́н	однó	одномý [adn.amú]

FEMININE

	NOMINATIVE	DATIVE
3rd pers. pron.	она́	ей [j.ẹj]
Adjectives	но́вая си́няя хоро́шая	но́вой [nóv.əj] си́ней [ş͡íņ.əj] хоро́шей [xaróš.əj]
Possessives	моя́ на́ша	мое́й [maj.ẹ́j] на́шей [náš.əj]
Demonstratives	э́та та	э́той [ét.əj] той [t.ój]
	одна́	одно́й [adn.ój]

The datives of the other personal pronouns have forms distinct from those given above:

Nom.	я	ты	мы	вы	они́
Gen.-Acc.	меня́	тебя́	нас	вас	их
Dat.	мне	тебе́	нам	вам	им

Pattern Sentences

1. Дире́ктор пока́зывает го́род но́**вому** инжене́ру и всё **ему́** объясня́ет.
2. На́ш нача́льник пока́зывает конто́ру но́**вой** секрета́рше и всё **е́й** объясня́ет.
3. Моя́ ма́ть объясня́ла э́т**ой** молод**о́й** хозя́йк**е**, где́ она́ обы́чно покупа́ет све́жую ры́бу.
4. Почему́ я́ до́лжен отвеча́ть э́т**ому** глу́п**ому** челове́ку?
5. Мы́ должны́ помога́ть на́ш**ему** ста́р**ому** отцу́. О́н всегда́ помога́л **на́м**.
6. Я́ иногда́ звоню́ ва́ш**ей** ми́л**ой** сестр**е́**.

1. The director is showing the city to the new engineer and is explaining everything to him.
2. Our director is showing the office to the new secretary and is explaining everything to her.
3. My mother was explaining to this young housewife where she usually buys fresh fish.
4. Why do I have to answer that stupid man?
5. We must help our old father. He has always helped us.
6. I sometimes call up your charming sister.

7. Вчера́ я́ звони́л **ва́м,** но́ ва́с не́ было.
8. Я́ посыла́ю приве́т **ва́м,** **ва́шей** ми́**лой** жене́ и ва́ш**ему** у́мн**ому** ма́леньк**ому** сы́ну.
9. Она́ ча́сто говори́т **мне́,** что её му́ж настоя́щий ге́ний! Я́ ничего́ **е́й** не отвеча́ю.

7. I called you yesterday, but you were not there.
8. I am sending regards to you, to your charming wife, and to your intelligent little son.
9. She often tells me that her husband is a real genius! I don't answer her anything.

Drills

A. *Translate into English.*

1. Ка́ждый ве́чер ма́ма чита́ет интере́сную исто́рию мне́ и моей ма́ленькой сестре́.
2. —Андре́й, кому́ вы́ пока́зывали на́шу но́вую библиоте́ку? —Я́ пока́зывал её моему́ хоро́шему дру́гу, реда́ктору журна́ла «Но́вый ми́р».
3. Моя́ ма́ть посыла́ет приве́т то́й ми́лой ти́хой де́вушке, кото́рую она́ ви́дела в ва́шей конто́ре.
4. —Како́й подру́ге звони́т Ле́на почти́ ка́ждый де́нь? —Она́ звони́т краси́вой брюне́тке Ни́не.
5. Вы́ не должны́ объясня́ть хоро́шей хозя́йке, где́ и что́ она́ должна́ покупа́ть!
6. Как легко́ объясня́ть грамма́тику у́мному студе́нту!
7. —Како́му дире́ктору вы́ посыла́ете письмо́? —На́шему.

B. *Put the words in parentheses into the correct case.*

1. Андре́й говори́т (молода́я блонди́нка), что она́ о́чень краси́вая.
2. Профе́ссор объясня́ет (молодо́й музыка́нт), ка́к игра́ть на гита́ре.
3. Вы́ не должны́ говори́ть (настоя́щий писа́тель), ка́к писа́ть рома́н!
4. Ве́ра звони́т (хоро́шая подру́га).
5. Я́ посыла́ю приве́т (твоя́ ми́лая жена́).
6. Мы́ пока́зываем го́род (сове́тская журнали́стка и сове́тский журнали́ст).
7. Мы́ мно́го говори́м о (сове́тская журнали́стка).
8. О́н ча́сто ду́мает о (краси́вая брюне́тка).
9. Мы́ посыла́ем пода́рок (ты́ и твоя́ ма́ленькая сестра́).

C. *Translate into Russian.*

1. He is sending the magazine to a talented young man.
2. He was telling that to your older brother.
3. We are showing our school to our new teacher.
4. —Whom is he helping? —He is helping me today.
5. We always help him and his wife, but they never help us.
6. Every day I explain to my dear husband why he must write to my sister every week.

3. Dative of state or condition

Impersonal expressions have already been discussed in Unit 7 (page 98).

E.g.:
Здéсь жáрко.
It is hot here.

Вчерá бы́ло хóлодно.
It was cold yesterday.

На концéрте бы́ло скýчно.
It was boring at the concert.

When such states or conditions are referred to as experienced by a person, that person is denoted by a noun or pronoun in the *dative* case:

Мнé хóлодно.
I am cold.

Áнне здéсь жáрко.
Anna feels hot here.

Ивáну бы́ло скýчно.
Ivan was bored. (Contrast: Ивáн скýчный, Ivan is dull.)

Сми́ту трýдно говори́ть по-рýсски.
It is difficult for Smith to speak Russian.

Note that with these expressions the verb "to be" in the past is *always* neuter.

4. The adjective нýжный, нýжное, нýжная, нýжные, "necessary"

Э́то **нýжная** вéщь.	This is a necessary thing.
Вóт **нýжные** докумéнты.	Here are the necessary documents.

5. Нýжно or нáдо (interchangeable)

The words **нýжно** or **нáдо**, followed by an infinitive, both express that "it is necessary" to do something, that something "must"/ "should"/"has to" be done. Нýжно and нáдо are used in impersonal constructions (*i.e.*, in constructions which do not have a subject in the nominative case). The statement may be general ("it is necessary . . . ," "one should . . . ," etc.) or it may refer to a particular person ("it is necessary for someone . . . ," "someone should . . . ," etc.). In the latter case the noun or pronoun denoting the person is in the *dative*. To express the past tense the neuter verb form **бы́ло** is added.

A. General statements.

Ну́жно всегда́ говори́ть пра́вду.
One must always tell the truth.

Ну́жно было всё ему́ рассказа́ть.
It was necessary to tell him everything.

Э́то **на́до** было сде́лать ра́ньше.
This should have been done earlier.

B. Statement with reference to a particular person (with dative).

Мне́ ну́жно купи́ть аспири́н.
I must buy aspirin.

Отцу́ ну́жно купи́ть друго́й автомоби́ль.
Father has to buy another car.

Ва́м ну́жно бо́льше спа́ть.
You need to sleep more.

The ну́жно/на́до construction with the dative is often used in a meaning very close to that of до́лжен used with a nominative (see Unit 8, page 114). But with impersonals only ну́жно or на́до may be used.

Pattern Sentences

1. Бори́су ску́чно в кла́ссе.	1. Boris is bored in class.
2. Бори́с ску́чный.	2. Boris is boring.
3. Мо**ему́** бра́ту всегда́ хо́лодно.	3. My brother always feels cold.
4. Мо́й бра́т тако́й холо́дный челове́к.	4. My brother is such a cold person.
5. Вчера́ бы́л пра́здник. Я́ была́ до́ма одна́. **Мне́** бы́ло ску́чно.	5. Yesterday was a holiday. I was at home alone. I was bored.
6. —Ва́**шей** сестр**е́** бы́ло интере́сно в Москве́? —**Е́й** бы́ло та́м о́чень интере́сно.	6. —Did your sister have an interesting time in Moscow? (Was it interesting for her there?) —It was very interesting for her there.
7. Ва́ша сестра́ о́чень интере́сная де́вушка.	7. Your sister is a very interesting girl.
8. **На́м** всегда́ прия́тно ва́с ви́деть!	8. We are always pleased to see you!
9. **Мне́** ещё тру́дно говори́ть по-ру́сски; **мне́** ну́жно бо́льше говори́ть.	9. It's still hard for me to speak Russian; I must speak it more.

Drill

Translate into Russian.

1. I am closing the window because my sister feels cold.
2. She was alone and she was bored.
3. You need to read more.
4. Boris must work less.
5. He was pleased to see me.
6. Are you cold?
7. It was interesting for us to listen to her.
8. It was very interesting for my son to listen to you.
9. My son is so interesting!
10. She is bored.
11. She is boring.
12. You don't need to work so much now.

6. First conjugation verbs (continued)

First conjugation verbs of the type studied in the preceding unit all have a vowel (**а**, **я**, sometimes **е** or **у**) before the endings, *e.g.*, чита́ю, чита́ешь; объясня́ю, объясня́ешь, etc.

A large group of verbs have stems which end in a consonant. Their endings in the present are spelled somewhat differently from those of the type чита́ть: instead of **-ю** (first singular) and **-ют** (third plural), they take **-у** and **-ут** respectively.

Present Tense, First Conjugation

	писа́ть, *"to write"* (*present stem:* **пиш-**)	*Compare* **ду́мать**, *"to think"*
	Singular	
1st pers.	пишу́	ду́маю
2nd pers.	пи́шешь	ду́маешь
3rd pers.	пи́шет	ду́мает
	Plural	
1st pers.	пи́шем	ду́маем
2nd pers.	пи́шете	ду́маете
3rd pers.	пи́шут	ду́мают

Present Tense of **жить**, *"to live"*

	Singular	*Plural*
1st pers.	живу́	живём
2nd pers.	живёшь	живёте
3rd pers.	живёт	живу́т

With this group of "consonant stems," the last consonant of the stem frequently differs from that of the infinitive (infinitive писа́ть: present пишу́), or may disappear entirely in the infinitive, as is the case with the verb жить, conjugated живу́, живёшь, etc.

Every Russian verb follows one of three patterns of stress in the present tense: (1) the stress is on the stem throughout: ду́маю, ду́маешь, etc.; (2) the stress is on the ending throughout: живу́, живёшь, etc. (in this case the **е** of the ending becomes **ё** under stress); (3) the stress is on the ending in the first person singular, but shifts to the stem in all other persons: пишу́, пи́шешь, пи́шет, etc.

It is essential, therefore, to memorize three forms of the verb: the *infinitive*, *first person singular present*, and *second person singular present*. These three forms will be given in the vocabularies for all first conjugation verbs with present stems ending in a consonant, and for all second conjugation verbs.

7. Present tense of дава́ть, "to give"

The suffix **-ва** disappears in the present tense of the verb. The stress is on the ending (**е** becomes **ё**):

	Singular	*Plural*
1st pers.	даю́	даём
2nd pers.	даёшь	даёте
3rd pers.	даёт	даю́т

Продава́ть, "to sell" (продаю́, продаёшь, etc.), is conjugated like дава́ть.

Pattern Sentences

1. Андре́й ре́дко **пи́шет** жене́.
2. —Кому́ ты́ **пи́шешь?** —Я́ **пишу́** до́ктору Смирно́ву.
3. О́н никому́ не пока́зывает, что́ о́н **пи́шет.**
4. —Како́му бра́ту вы́ **пи́шете?** —Я́ **пишу́** моему́ ста́ршему бра́ту. Я́ **пишу́** ему́ почти́ ка́ждую неде́лю.
5. —Где́ вы́ тепе́рь **живёте?** —Я́ **живу́** в Нью-Йо́рке.
6. Они́ говоря́т, что они́ **живу́т** в э́той гости́нице.
7. Бори́с никому́ не говори́т, где́ о́н **живёт.**

1. Andrey rarely writes to his wife.
2. —Whom are you writing to? —I am writing to Dr. Smirnov.
3. He doesn't show anyone what he writes.
4. —To which brother are you writing? —I am writing to my elder brother. I write to him almost every week.
5. —Where are you living now? —I am living in New York.
6. They say they live in this hotel.
7. Boris doesn't tell anyone where he lives.

8. Ка́ждый ве́чер я́ **даю́** Вади́му и О́льге уро́к му́зыки.
9. Они́ **продаю́т** до́м инжене́ру Андре́еву.
10. Что́ **продаю́т**[1] в э́том магази́не?

8. Every evening I give Vadim and Olga a music lesson.
9. They are selling their house to Engineer Andreyev.
10. What do they sell in this store?

Drills

A. *Put the words in parentheses into the correct case and translate.*

1. О́н даёт кни́гу (профе́ссор Па́влов).
2. Я́ пишу́ письмо́ (сестра́).
3. Ве́ра хоро́шая до́чь, она́ обы́чно помога́ет (оте́ц).
4. Вади́м обы́чно не слу́шает (учи́тель), но́ ча́сто даёт (учи́тель) сове́т, ка́к объясня́ть грамма́тику.
5. Я́ спра́шиваю (сестра́), почему́ она́ так ре́дко пи́шет.
6. Я́ спра́шиваю (Ива́н), где́ о́н живёт.
7. Я́ говорю́ (Ива́н), где́ я́ живу́.
8. До́ктор даёт сове́т (на́ш молодо́й дру́г).

B. *Fill in the blanks with the suitable form of the verbs.*

1. Кому́ вы́ пи́ш......?
2. Я́ пиш...... Ива́ну.
3. Они́ ча́сто пи́ш...... отцу́.
4. А́нна и О́льга жив...... в э́том до́ме.
5. Я́ тепе́рь жив...... зде́сь. Вы́ то́же зде́сь жив......?
6. Мы́ ка́ждый ме́сяц пи́ш...... на́шему дру́гу Константи́ну Ряби́нину, кото́рый жив...... в Оде́ссе.

C. *Translate into Russian.*

1. I often lend (give) my dictionary to Vadim and (to) his wife.
2. I am selling my pen to Boris.
3. They are writing to Engineer Andreyev.
4. Why are you selling your library to Anna and not to Boris?
5. To whom are you writing?
6. I am writing to Olga and her sister.
7. He is writing to the young Soviet (woman) writer.
8. He sometimes gives us good advice.
9. In the classroom there was no dictionary.
10. Ivan is giving Anna the teacher's dictionary.
11. I write every month to my sister.
12. My friend Andrey is writing a play!

[1] The third person plural without a subject is often used in the indefinite sense of "people," "one," "they," etc., *e.g.*, Что́ о нём говоря́т? What do people say about him? Sometimes the translation may be passive, as in the sentence above: What *is sold* in this store?

8. Reflexive possessive свой

Russian has a reflexive possessive, **свой**, "one's own," which refers back to the subject of the same sentence or clause. **Свой** is declined like **мой**:

> Я́ даю́ **свою́** кни́гу сестре́.
> I am giving *my* book to my sister.

> О́н объясня́ет уро́к **своему́** дру́гу.
> He is explaining the lesson to *his* (*own*) friend.

With subjects in the first two persons, мой, твой, наш, and ваш may be used instead of свой, especially in colloquial style:

> Я́ говори́л о **мое́й** (**свое́й**) рабо́те.
> I spoke about *my* work.

> Вы́ хорошо́ зна́ете **ва́шего** (**своего́**) учи́теля?
> Do you know *your* teacher well?

When the subject is in the third person, however, **свой** *must always be distinguished* from **его́**, **её**, or **их**:

> О́н хорошо́ зна́ет **сво́й** го́род.
> He knows *his* (*own*) city well.

But:

> О́н хорошо́ зна́ет **его́** го́род.
> He knows his (someone else's) city well.

Remember that **свой** can refer back only to the subject of *its own clause:*

> О́н говори́т, что **его́** ма́ть до́ма.
> He says that his mother is at home.

Here **свой** may not be used, even though the mother is his own, since **он**, to which the possessive **его́** refers, is the subject of a different clause.

Drills

Translate into Russian.

1. Ivan helps his father.
2. I help Ivan and his father.
3. He is buying a present for his wife.
4. Boris is buying a present for his (Ivan's) wife.
5. She is a good sister; she helps her sister.
6. He is a good husband; he is buying a dress for his wife.
7. He was in his wife's room.

8. He was in his (Ivan's) room.
9. She is buying a present for her husband, and Boris is also buying a present for her husband.
10. They say that their father is now living in New York.
11. Ivan saw his friend and says that his friend is now working here.
12. He is a bad man; he never helps either his family or his brother's family.

CONVERSATION

Кому́ ты́ пи́шешь?

Бра́т. —Кому́ ты́ пи́шешь, Ле́на?
Сестра́. —Я́ пишу́ одно́й мое́й но́вой подру́ге, кото́рую ты́ ещё не зна́ешь.
Б. —Ка́к её и́мя?
С. —Почему́ ты́ спра́шиваешь? Я́ говорю́ тебе́, что ты́ её не зна́ешь!
Б. —А почему́ ты́ мне́ не отвеча́ешь? Мне́ интере́сно зна́ть, кому́ ты́ пи́шешь.
С. —Го́споди, Алёша! Како́й ты́ ску́чный челове́к! Ну́, хорошо́. Я́ пишу́ Ни́не Ла́пиной.[2]
Б. —Ни́не Ла́пиной? Как ску́чно!
С. —Почему́ э́то ску́чно?
Б. —Потому́ что Ни́на о́чень глу́пая. Но́ я́ ду́маю, что ты́, как всегда́, говори́шь мне́ непра́вду и пи́шешь не е́й.
С. —А что́ пра́вда? Что́ ты́ ду́маешь, кому́ я́ пишу́?
Б. —Я́ ду́маю, что ты́ пи́шешь Бори́су, молодо́му челове́ку, кото́рого ты́ неда́вно ви́дела на вечери́нке, и о кото́ром ты́ так мно́го говори́шь.
С. —Ну́ хорошо́. Я́ пишу́ э́тому молодо́му челове́ку. Тепе́рь ты́ ра́д?
Б. —Ра́д, что ты́ ему́ пи́шешь? Не зна́ю. Я́ никогда́ не ви́дел э́того геро́я, но́ я́ ра́д, что ты́ не пи́шешь твое́й ску́чной Ни́не.

Pronunciation Drill

—kamú tɨ p̡išɨš, ļénə?
—já p̡išú adnój padrúg̡i, katóruju tɨ ņiznáiš.
—kák jijó ím̡ə?
—já gəvaŗú ţib̡é, štə tɨ jijó ņiznáiš! Pəçimú tɨ sprášɨvəiš?
—mņé iņţirésnə znáţ, kamú tɨ p̡išɨš.

[2] Last names ending in **-ов** and **-ин** (fem. **-ова** and **-ина**) have a mixed declension; some cases are declined like nouns, others like adjectives. See Appendix A.

READING

Письмó стáрому дрýгу

Сегóдня прáздник, и поэ́тому я́ не рабóтаю. Я́ весь дéнь дóма и пишý письмó моемý хорóшему стáрому дрýгу Константи́ну Антóновичу Ряби́нину.

Я́ так давнó éму не писáл, что я́ дáже не знáю, о чём емý писáть. Э́то трýдный вопрóс. Я́ начинáю письмó тáк:

«Дорогóй Кóстя![3]

Кáк ты́ поживáешь? Я́ рéдко тебé пишý, нó чáсто о тебé дýмаю.» (Э́то не óчень оригинáльное начáло, нó э́то ничегó—тáк всé пи́шут). «Нó ты́ знáешь, как мнóго я́ рабóтаю. Я́ весь дéнь в контóре. Контóра моя́ в цéнтре гóрода, а живý я́ óчень далекó.

Нó э́то ещё не всё. Кáтя, моя́ женá, как ты́ знáешь, óчень ми́лая и ýмная жéнщина, нó плохáя хозя́йка. И, поэ́тому, дóма я́ дóлжен éй помогáть. Мнé óчень трýдно рабóтать и в контóре и дóма. Конéчно, э́то нормáльно, что я́ помогáю женé, нó почемý тóлько я́ дóлжен э́то дéлать?

Нáша дóчь Вéра нáм никогдá не помогáет. Онá почти́ весь дéнь в шкóле, гдé, по-мóему, онá ничегó не дéлает, а дóма—телеви́зор, рáдио (онá слýшает тóлько джáз и глýпую мýзыку) и телефóн. Кáждый вéчер онá звони́т своемý дрýгу Пáвлу, и́ли своéй подрýге Óльге, и́ли они́ звоня́т éй, и они́ говоря́т и говоря́т весь вéчер. Когдá я́ объясня́ю женé, что э́то нехорошó, онá говори́т мнé, что я́ не понимáю Вéру, и что я́ ничегó не дóлжен éй говори́ть. Вéра ещё молодáя, всé тáк живýт и всё э́то нормáльно. Я́ ничегó не говорю́ Вéре.

Нáш сы́н Серёжа[4] нáм тóже не помогáет: óн пи́шет! Óн дýмает, что óн писáтель! Я́ не знáю ни чтó óн пи́шет, ни о чём, —óн никогдá ничегó не покáзывает ни мнé, ни Кáте, ни дáже своéй сестрé. Кáтя дýмает, что Серёжа настоя́щий писáтель и гéний. И я́, конéчно, ничегó не говорю́ сы́ну.

Тепéрь ты́ всё знáешь о моéй семьé и понимáешь, почемý мнé трýдно тебé чáсто писáть. Нó почемý ты́ так рéдко пи́шешь мнé, твоемý стáрому дрýгу? Мнé óчень интерéсно знáть, кáк ты́ живёшь, кáк твоя́ семья́.

Привéт тебé и твоéй семьé.

Твóй Волóдя[5]

[3] Кóстя, nickname of Константи́н.
[4] Серёжа, nickname of Сергéй.
[5] Волóдя, nickname of Влади́мир.

Answer the following questions in Russian.

1. Почему́ Воло́дя (а́втор письма́) не зна́ет, о чём писа́ть своему́ дру́гу? 2. Воло́дя сего́дня рабо́тает в конто́ре? 3. О́н мно́го отдыха́ет? 4. Почему́ Воло́дя до́лжен помога́ть свое́й жене́? 5. Почему́ и́м ма́ло помога́ет до́чь Ве́ра? 6. Что́ об э́том ду́мает ма́ть? 7. Серёжа то́же рабо́тает в конто́ре, как оте́ц? 8. Почему́ ма́ть не говори́т сы́ну, что о́н то́же до́лжен рабо́тать и помога́ть отцу́? 9. Почему́ оте́ц не зна́ет, что́ и о чём пи́шет его́ сы́н? 10. Почему́ Воло́дя так ре́дко пи́шет своему́ дру́гу? 11. Что́ ему́ интере́сно зна́ть? 12. Кому́ о́н посыла́ет приве́т?

EXERCISES

A. *Replace the English in parentheses by the Russian interrogative in its proper form.*

1. (Who) объясня́ет грамма́тику? 2. (Whom) о́н зна́ет? 3. (To whom) они́ даю́т э́тот слова́рь? 4. (What) студе́нтку вы́ ви́дели? 5. (To what) прия́телю вы́ даёте сове́т? 6. (Who) бы́л та́м? 7. (What) журна́л вы́ чита́ете? 8. (What) реда́ктора она́ ви́дела? 9. (What) журнали́стка была́ на вечери́нке? 10. (To what) журнали́стке вы́ даёте сего́дня уро́к? 11. (To whom) ты́ продаёшь твоё перо́? 12. (To what) студе́нту ты́ объясня́ешь пра́вило? 13. (What) ва́ше и́мя? 14. (What) вы́ де́лаете? 15. (What) ва́ша фами́лия?

B. *Translate into Russian.*

1. He seldom writes to his old teacher (*feminine*). 2. Why do they never write to their father? 3. We live in my brother's house and they live in their sister's house. 4. To whom do you explain the grammar every day? 5. Why don't you say anything to your wife? 6. What does he buy for you? 7. I know his sister very well and I often write to her. 8. —What are you sending to Nina? —I am sending her a new Russian novel. 9. They never answer us and we never answer them. 10. We know that they give us good advice. 11. What are they selling you? 12. —To whom are you sending this book? —I am sending it to an English newspaperman. 13. It is hard for him always to speak Russian, and therefore he often speaks English. 14. For Ivan, of course, that is easy: he is Russian. 15. It is boring for us to listen to her. 16. I am selling her my old hat cheap.

17. Why don't you explain to me what I must do? 18. He often calls up that old writer. 19. What are people saying about her? 20. What is sold in this store?

VOCABULARY

а́втор author
ге́ний genius
глу́пый foolish, silly
джаз jazz
дире́ктор director
инжене́р engineer
исто́рия history; story
конто́ра office
ми́лый nice, sweet, kind, likable, charming
настоя́щий real
нача́льник chief, superior, boss
нехорошо́ not good, bad
обы́чно usually, ordinarily
оригина́льный original
отве́т answer, reply
пода́рок (*gen.* **пода́рка**) present, gift
поэ́тому therefore, so
пра́вило rule
пра́здник holiday
приве́т (+ *dat.*) greeting(s), regards
ра́дио (*neuter indecl.*)[6] radio
ре́дко rarely, seldom
ры́ба fish
семья́ family
сове́т advice, counsel; council
тала́нтливый talented
телеви́зор television set
телегра́мма telegram
телефо́н telephone
у́мный intelligent
упражне́ние exercise
хозя́йка housewife; hostess; landlady
ча́сто often

Expressions

посыла́ть приве́т (+ *dat.*) to send greetings (regards)
звони́ть по телефо́ну (+ *dat.*) to call on the telephone
Я так давно́ не писа́л. I haven't written for so long.
Го́споди! Heavens! Goodness!
по-мо́ему in my opinion

[6] Certain nouns of foreign origin ending in **-о**, **-е**, and **-и** are indeclinable, that is, they never change in form.

UNIT 10

***Future tense of* быть, 136. *Prepositions* до, по́сле, без, кро́ме *with the genitive,* 138. *Possession expressed by the preposition* у *with the genitive,* 140. У *with genitive—"at the house of,"* 143. Ну́жен, 144. *Numerals 2, 3, 4,* 146. *Modal verbs:* хоте́ть, мочь, 147. *Vocabulary review,* 153.**

GRAMMAR

1. Future tense of быть, "to be"

	Singular	*Plural*
1st pers.	бу́ду	бу́дем
2nd pers.	бу́дешь	бу́дете
3rd pers.	бу́дет	бу́дут

—Где́ вы́ **бу́дете** за́втра? —Я́ **бу́ду** до́ма.
—Where will you be tomorrow? —I'll be at home.

The third person forms **бу́дет, бу́дут** serve as the future tense of **есть** ("there will be . . . ," "there is going to be . . .").

Зде́сь **бу́дет** теа́тр.	There will be a theater here.
Зде́сь не **бу́дет** теа́тра (genitive).	There will be no theater here.

Pattern Sentences

1. —Е́сли за́втра **бу́дет** хо́лодно,[1] где́ вы́ **бу́дете?** —Мы́ **бу́дем** до́ма.
2. —Экза́мен **бу́дет** за́втра? —Не́т, за́втра **не бу́дет** экза́мена, экза́мен бы́л вчера́.

1. —If it's cold tomorrow,[1] where will you be? —We'll be at home.
2. —Will the exam be tomorrow? —No, there will be no exam tomorrow; the exam was yesterday.

[1] Е́сли always takes the future in Russian if the meaning is future, although the corresponding English is usually present.

3. За́втра в магази́не **бу́дет** францу́зский сы́р.
4. За́втра **не бу́дет** францу́зского сы́ра.
5. —Е́сли Вади́м и О́льга **бу́дут** в библиоте́ке за́втра, я́ мо́жет быть то́же та́м **бу́ду**; я́ ещё не зна́ю.
6. Мы́ **бу́дем** о́чень ра́ды ва́с ви́деть.
7. За́втра Ива́на **не бу́дет** до́ма; о́н **бу́дет** весь де́нь в дере́вне.
8. Ива́н за́втра **не бу́дет** в кла́ссе.

3. Tomorrow there will be French cheese at the store.
4. Tomorrow there will be no French cheese.
5. —If Vadim and Olga will be at the library tomorrow, perhaps I will be there too; I don't know yet.
6. We will be very glad to see you.
7. Ivan won't be at home tomorrow; he is going to be in the country all day.
8. Ivan won't come to class tomorrow.

Drills

A. *Translate into English.*

1. О́н ещё не зна́ет, где́ о́н бу́дет за́втра.
2. За́втра на́с весь де́нь не бу́дет до́ма.
3. Ива́н вчера́ не́ был в библиоте́ке.
4. Когда́ я́ бы́л в библиоте́ке, Ива́на та́м не́ было.
5. Е́сли за́втра бу́дет жа́рко, я́ бу́ду весь де́нь до́ма.
6. Вы́ ду́маете, что та́м никого́ не бу́дет?
7. В кабине́те звони́л телефо́н, но́ та́м никого́ не́ было.
8. Моя́ жена́ бу́дет о́чень ра́да ва́с ви́деть.

B. *Fill in the blanks with proper forms of the future tense of the verb "to be."*

1. Где́ вы́ ...... за́втра?
2. За́втра я́ ...... до́ма.
3. Где́ сего́дня ...... Ива́н?
4. О́н ...... в библиоте́ке.
5. Мы́ ...... в шко́ле. Вы́ то́же та́м ......?
6. Да́, мы́ то́же ...... та́м.
7. Кто́ ещё та́м ......?
8. Та́м ...... Ива́н и А́нна.
9. —Где́ вы́ ...... за́втра? —Я́ ещё не зна́ю, где́ я́ ......

C. *Translate into Russian.*

1. There is a library here.
2. There is no library here.
3. There was a library here.
4. There will be a library here.
5. There will be no library here.
6. There is a town there.
7. There is no town there.
8. There was a town there.
9. There will be a town there.
10. —Who will not be at home tonight? —We won't be.

2. Prepositions до, по́сле, без, кро́ме with genitive

The following prepositions govern the *genitive* case:

до	before, till, until, up to
по́сле	after
без	without
кро́ме	except, besides

До войны́ они́ жи́ли в Москве́, а **по́сле** войны́ в Оде́ссе.
Before the war they lived in Moscow, and after the war in Odessa.

Петро́в бы́л в Евро́пе **без** жены́.
Petrov was in Europe without his wife.

О́н е́л всё **кро́ме** мя́са.
He ate everything except meat.

The accusative forms of the personal pronouns given in Unit 8 are also the genitives: меня́, тебя́, нас, and вас; без меня́, кро́ме ва́с, etc.

Pronouns of the third person prefix an **н-** after prepositions: без **н**его́, without him; без **н**её, without her; кро́ме **н**и́х, besides them.

But when его́, её, их are used as possessives and modify a noun in the genitive which is governed by a preposition, the prefix **н-** is not added:

без **его́** сы́на	without his son
без **её** отца́	without her father
кро́ме **и́х** бра́та	besides their brother

Pattern Sentences

До, по́сле

1. **По́сле** теа́тра о́н бу́дет до́ма.
2. —Где́ вы́ бу́дете **по́сле** уро́ка? —Я́ бу́ду в рестора́не.
3. **По́сле** рабо́ты я́ ничего́ не де́лаю; я́ отдыха́ю.
4. —Где́ вы́ бы́ли **до** обе́да? —Я́ бы́л в музе́е, а **до э́того** я́ бы́л до́ма.

1. After the theater he will be at home.
2. —Where will you be after class? —I'll be at the restaurant.
3. After work I do nothing; I relax.
4. —Where were you before dinner? —I was at the museum, and before that I was at home.

Drill

Translate into English.

1. Я́ не ви́дел его́ по́сле войны́.
2. Что́ вы́ де́лали до конце́рта?
3. Где́ ты́ бу́дешь по́сле рабо́ты?
4. Что́ она́ де́лала по́сле обе́да?
5. Я́ не ви́дел его́ по́сле э́того.
6. До́ войны́ мы́ никогда́ зде́сь не́ были.

Pattern Sentences

без, кро́ме

1. О́льга была́ в библиоте́ке **без** Вади́ма. — 1. Olga was at the library without Vadim.
2. Вади́м бы́л в теа́тре **без** О́льги. — 2. Vadim was at the theater without Olga.
3. Она́ была́ зде́сь **без** му́жа. — 3. She was here without her husband.
4. Все́ бы́ли на конце́рте **кро́ме** А́нны. — 4. Everyone was at the concert except Anna.
5. **Кро́ме** А́нны все́ бы́ли на конце́рте. — 5. Besides (except for) Anna, everyone was at the concert.
6. На столе́ е́сть всё **кро́ме** хле́ба. — 6. On the table there's everything except bread.
7. О́н ничего́ не е́л **кро́ме** мя́са. — 7. He ate nothing but meat.

Drills

A. *Translate.*

1. Кто́ бы́л та́м кро́ме ва́с?
2. Что́ вы́ е́ли кро́ме мя́са?
3. На́м тру́дно жи́ть без неё.
4. Я́ сего́дня ничего́ не е́л кро́ме сы́ра и хле́ба.
5. Мы́ бы́ли в рестора́не без А́нны.
6. Оте́ц тепе́рь живёт без ни́х.

B. *Translate the words in parentheses.*

1. Что́ вы́ де́лали (before the lesson)?
2. Я́ ви́дел Андре́я (after the concert).
3. Они́ жи́ли в Аме́рике (before the war).
4. (After the theater) мы́ бу́дем до́ма.
5. Она́ была́ та́м (without Ivan and without Anna).
6. (After work) я́ бу́ду зде́сь.
7. Мы́ тепе́рь живём (without Olga).
8. —Кто́ бу́дет до́ма (besides Father and Zina)? —(Except for them) та́м никого́ не бу́дет.
9. На́м тру́дно жи́ть (without him and without her).
10. Мы́ бы́ли в Евро́пе (before them).
11. Она́ бу́дет та́м (without Brother).
12. Э́тот журнали́ст ничего́ не ви́дел (besides Moscow and Leningrad).
13. (After dinner) мы́ говори́ли о поли́тике.
14. Мы́ никогда́ та́м не́ были (before that).
15. На столе́ ничего́ не́ было (except meat), и мы́ должны́ бы́ли е́сть мя́со (without bread).
16. (After dinner) мы́ рабо́тали.

C. *Translate into Russian.*

1. He never drank anything but (except) water.
2. They never relax after work.
3. My husband was at the theater without me.
4. We will all be there after dinner.
5. Everyone was there except him.
6. Everybody was there except his son.
7. Will you be at home after the theater?
8. Where did you live before the war?

3. Possession expressed by the preposition у with the genitive

Russian uses the preposition **у** with the *genitive* case to express possession, where English employs the verb "have." The object or objects possessed are in the *nominative* case; the possessor is in the *genitive* after **у**. The word **есть** is often used in this construction:

У до́ктор**а** е́сть до́м.	The doctor has a house.
У бра́т**а** е́сть автомоби́ль.	My brother has a car.

A. У with pronouns.

У кого́ е́сть автомоби́ль?	Who has a car?
У меня́ е́сть бра́т.	I have a brother.
У тебя́ е́сть перо́?	Do you have a pen?

Third person pronouns governed by **у** (and other prepositions) prefix **н-**:

У него́ е́сть сы́н.	He has a son.
У неё е́сть до́чь.	She has a daughter.
У ни́х е́сть до́м.	They have a house.

But when его́, её, and их modify a noun in the genitive which itself is governed by **у**, the prefix **н-** is not added:

	У **н**его́ е́сть до́м.	He has a house.
But:	У **его́** бра́та е́сть до́м.	His brother has a house.
	У **н**её е́сть сы́н.	She has a son.
But:	У **её** сестры́ е́сть сы́н.	Her sister has a son.
	У **н**и́х е́сть автомоби́ль.	They have a car.
But:	У **и́х** дру́га е́сть автомоби́ль.	Their friend has a car.

B. Use of есть. The word **есть** is generally used with **у** phrases when the object is referred to as merely any one of a kind or category (in English this is expressed by the indefinite article):

У кого́ **е́сть** слова́рь?
Who has *a* dictionary?

—У ва́с **е́сть** слова́рь? —Да́, **е́сть.**
—Do you have *a* dictionary? —Yes, I have one.

У моего́ бра́та **е́сть** автомоби́ль.
My brother has *a* car.

When a particular object is referred to—one previously mentioned, known to be owned by someone, etc.—then **есть** is generally omitted (in English this definiteness may be expressed by the article *the, my, the doctor's*, etc.):

У кого́ слова́рь?
Who has *the* dictionary? (The one just mentioned or seen, etc.)

—У ва́с слова́рь? —Да́, о́н у меня́.
—Do you have *the* dictionary? —Yes, I have it.

C. Negative. In the negative, **нет** is used. The thing *not* possessed is in the *genitive:*

	У меня́ е́сть рабо́та.	I have work.
But:	У меня́ **не́т** рабо́т**ы**.	I have no work.
	У бра́та е́сть до́м.	My brother has a house.
But:	У бра́та **не́т** до́м**а**.	My brother has no house.

D. Past tense. The past tense, affirmative, of the **у** construction uses бы́л, была́, бы́ло, бы́ли. The verb agrees in gender and number with the thing (or things) possessed:

У меня́ **бы́л** до́м.	I had a house.
У меня́ **была́** кварти́р**а**.	I had an apartment.
У меня́ **бы́ло** пер**о́**.	I had a pen.

The past tense, negative, of the **у** construction employs **не́ было** and the *genitive*, regardless of the gender and number of the object:

У меня́ **не́ было** до́м**а**.	I had no house.
У меня́ **не́ было** кварти́р**ы**.	I had no apartment.
У меня́ **не́ было** пер**а́**.	I had no pen.

E. Future tense.

У меня́ **бу́дет** кварти́ра.	I shall have an apartment.
У меня́ **не бу́дет** кварти́р**ы**.	I shall not have an apartment.

Pattern Sentences

1. **У** профе́ссор**а** е́сть сы́н.
2. **У** сестр**ы́** е́сть э́та пласти́нка.
3. **У** А́нн**ы** е́сть оте́ц, а **у** Ива́н**а** **не́т** отц**а́**.

1. The professor has a son.
2. My sister has that record.
3. Anna has a father, but Ivan has no father.

4. **У** Ни́ны е́сть бра́т, а **у** Бори́са **не́т** бра́та. **У него́** никогда́ **не́ было** бра́та.
5. —**У тебя́** е́сть сестра́? —Да́, е́сть.
6. **У** А́нны **не́т** сестры́.
7. **У неё** никогда́ **не́ было** сестры́.
8. —**У ва́с** е́сть э́тот уче́бник? —У на́с бы́л э́тот уче́бник, но́ тепе́рь **у на́с его́** не́т.
9. **У ва́шего** учи́теля о́н е́сть.
10. Я́ ду́маю, что **у на́с** ско́ро бу́дет э́тот уче́бник.
11. —**У кого́ е́сть** слова́рь? —Ни у кого́[2] не́т словаря́.
12. —У кого́ мо́й словарь? —О́н **у** Бори́са.

4. Nina has a brother, but Boris has no brother. He never had a brother.
5. —Do you have a sister? —Yes, I do.
6. Anna has no sister.
7. She never had a sister.
8. —Do you have that textbook? —We did have that textbook (in stock), but now we don't have it.
9. Your teacher has it.
10. I think that we'll soon get (have) that textbook.
11. —Who has a dictionary? —No one has a dictionary.
12. —Who's got my dictionary? —Boris has it.

Drills

A. *Translate into English.*

1. У Вади́ма и у О́льги ничего́ не́т!
2. У ни́х никогда́ ничего́ не́ было.
3. У ни́х никогда́ ничего́ не бу́дет.
4. Бори́с говори́т, что у него́ е́сть хоро́ший францу́зский слова́рь, но́ о́н тепе́рь у Андре́я.
5. —Андре́й, у тебя́ слова́рь Бори́са? —Да́, о́н у меня́.
6. Ско́ро у ни́х всё бу́дет.
7. —У кого́ моя́ газе́та? —У О́льги.
8. У кого́ е́сть интере́сная кни́га?
9. Ни у кого́ не́т интере́сной кни́ги.
10. У ни́х бы́л о́чень хоро́ший учи́тель.
11. —У Ива́на никогда́ не́ было автомоби́ля?
12. Не́т, у него́ бы́л автомоби́ль, но́ тепе́рь у него́ не́т автомоби́ля.
13. У него́ ско́ро бу́дет автомоби́ль.
14. У него́ никогда́ не бу́дет автомоби́ля.

B. *Questions and answers.*

Be prepared to answer, on the basis of actual fact, questions of the type: У ва́с е́сть бра́т? Same for: автомоби́ль, сестра́, сын, жена́, слова́рь, перо́.

C. *Translate into Russian.*

1. Vadim has a little sister.
2. He had a little sister.
3. They had no little sister.
4. I have no little sister.

[2] Prepositions with никто́ (no one) and ничто́ (ничего́, "nothing") are placed *between* the ни and the declined form of кто or что, *e.g.*, ни у кого́ (no one has), ни о ко́м (about no one), ни в чём (in nothing), etc.

5. She had a new house.
6. We will soon have a new house.
7. Who had a new house?
8. Her friend has a blue car.
9. His doctor has no car.
10. Anna had a good doctor.
11. Do you have a good doctor?
12. Who has a good doctor?
13. I don't have a good doctor.
14. We will have a big summer house.
15. Father doesn't have a big summer house.
16. His brother has a summer house.
17. They had a small summer house.

4. У + genitive— "at the house of"

Phrases with the preposition **у** perform another important function: with nouns or pronouns designating persons, these phrases are used to express "visiting—, being with—, seeing someone, being at someone's place or house" (compare French *chez*, German *bei*).

Сего́дня я́ обе́даю **у сестры́.**
Today I'm having dinner at my sister's.

Кто́ **у ва́с** вчера́ бы́л?
Who was at your place yesterday?

Кто́ **у ва́с** за́втра бу́дет?
Who will be at your place tomorrow?

The possessive pronoun **свой** (see Unit 9, page 131) may be used in the nominative case in conjunction with phrases of the «у меня́» type:

У моего́ бра́та е́сть **сво́й** до́м.
My brother has *his own* house.

У на́с тепе́рь е́сть **своя́** библиоте́ка.
We have a library *of our own* now.

Prepositional phrases with **у** (у меня́, у отца́, etc.) may be combined with other prepositional phrases to indicate location:

У меня́ в ко́мнате е́сть дива́н.
There is a sofa in my room.

Телефо́н **у отца́ в кабине́те.**
The telephone is in Father's study.

Pattern Sentences

1. —**У кого́** вы́ живёте? —Я́ живу́ **у Бори́са.**
2. Мы́ тепе́рь живём **у** отца́, а Ни́на живёт **у** А́нны.
3. Твоя́ кни́га **у меня́** на столе́.

1. —At whose house do you live? —I live at Boris's.
2. We're living at Father's now, and Nina is living at Anna's.
3. Your book is on my desk.

4. Э́та же́нщина рабо́тает **у на́с** и **у на́шего бра́та.**	4. That woman works at our place and at our brother's.
5. **У** отц**а́** в кабине́те большо́й пи́сьменный сто́л.	5. In Father's study there is a large desk.
6. Мы́ вчера́ бы́ли **у ва́шего** учи́теля.	6. Yesterday we were at your teacher's.
7. —**У** как**о́го** до́ктор**а** о́н вчера́ бы́л? —О́н бы́л **у** сво**его́** ста́р**ого** до́ктор**а**.	7. —At which doctor's was he yesterday (which doctor did he go to see yesterday)? —He was at his old doctor's (he went to see his old doctor).
8. О́н вчера́ рабо́тал **у меня́.**	8. Yesterday he was working at my place.
9. Андре́й не бу́дет за́втра **у на́с**; у него́ о́чень мно́го рабо́ты.	9. Andrey will not come to our place tomorrow; he has a lot of work (to do).

Drills

A. *Translate into English.*

1. У А́нны е́сть до́м в дере́вне. Вчера́ все́ кро́ме О́льги и Вади́ма бы́ли у неё.
2. —У кого́ живёт его́ ма́ть? —Она́ живёт у свое́й мла́дшей сестры́.
3. —У кого́ рабо́тает ва́ш ста́рший бра́т? —О́н рабо́тает у до́ктора Смирно́ва.
4. Вчера́ все́ бы́ли у на́с.
5. За́втра все́ бу́дут у но́вого учи́теля.
6. У на́шего ста́рого профе́ссора молода́я жена́.
7. У кого́ вы́ ви́дели э́ту кни́гу?

B. *Translate into Russian.*

1. I shall be at your place tomorrow.
2. They lived at our place.
3. He will soon be at the doctor's.
4. She will be at my brother's.
5. At whose house are they living now?
6. She is working at Professor Robinson's.
7. All except the secretary were at his place.
8. We lived at his son's.
9. He has no son.

5. Ну́жен

This word corresponds literally to the English word "necessary." As we have seen in the preceding lesson, the neuter form **ну́жно** is used with infinitives to express necessity or obligation: Мне́ **ну́жно** рабо́тать; Ва́м **ну́жно** э́то зна́ть, etc.

The declined forms **ну́жен, ну́жно, нужна́, нужны́** are used to express the idea rendered in English by the word "need." Ну́жен agrees in gender and number with the object needed, which is in the *nominative* case; the person who needs it is in the *dative:*

Pres.	**Мне́ ну́жен** автомоби́ль.	I need a car.
	Ему́ нужна́ рабо́та.	He needs work.
	Бра́ту ну́жно перо́.	Brother needs a pen.
	Они́ на́м нужны́.	We need them.

Observe in the last sentence above that when the object or person needed is designated by a pronoun, that pronoun comes first in the sentence.

Past	**Мне́ ну́жен** был автомоби́ль.	I needed a car.
	Ему́ нужна́ была́ рабо́та.	He needed work.
	Бра́ту ну́жно было перо́.	Brother needed a pen.
	Они́ **на́м** были нужны́.	We needed them.

Fut.	**Мне́** ну́жен бу́дет автомоби́ль.	I will need a car.
	Ему́ нужна́ бу́дет рабо́та.	He will need work.
	Бра́ту ну́жно бу́дет перо́.	Brother will need a pen.
	Они́ **на́м** бу́дут нужны́.	We will need them.

Negative:

Мне́ не ну́жен до́м.	I don't need a house.
Ему́ не нужна́ была́ рабо́та.	He didn't need work.

Pattern Sentences

1. **Мне́ ну́жен** сове́т.	1. I need advice.
2. **Мне́** нужна́ э́та кни́га.	2. I need that book.
3. **Вы́ на́м** бу́дете нужны́ за́втра.	3. We will need you tomorrow.
4. **Вы́ на́м** бы́ли нужны́ вчера́.	4. We needed you yesterday.
5. **Кому́ я́ ну́жен?**	5. Who needs me?
6. **И́м ну́жно** бо́льше чита́ть и писа́ть.	6. They need to read and write more.
7. У неё е́сть **всё, что е́й** ну́жно.	7. She has everything that she needs.
8. **На́м** нужна́ была́ ва́ша по́мощь.	8. We needed your help.
9. **Ва́м на́до** ме́ньше рабо́тать.	9. You should work less.
10. Где́ Андре́й и Зо́я? **Они́ мне́ нужны́.**	10. Where are Andrey and Zoya? I need them.
11. **Они́ никому́** не нужны́.	11. No one needs them.
12. Э́тот уче́бник **мне́** бо́льше не **ну́жен.**	12. I don't need this textbook any more.

Drills

A. *Translate.*

1. Бори́с ну́жен Ива́ну.
2. Ива́н ну́жен Бори́су.
3. Вчера́шняя газе́та никому́ не нужна́.

4. Где́ Бори́с и Ива́н? Они́ на́м нужны́.
5. —Кому́ ну́жен сту́л? —О́н ну́жен А́нне.
6. Мне́ о́н бо́льше не ну́жен.
7. У кого́ журна́л Бори́са? О́н ну́жен учи́телю.
8. Мы́ за́втра бу́дем нужны́ Ива́ну.
9. Я́ ду́маю, что вы́ ему́ бы́ли нужны́ вчера́. Сего́дня вы́ ему́ бо́льше не нужны́.
10. Она́ никому́ не нужна́.
11. Кому́ нужна́ сего́дняшняя газе́та? Она́ мне́ бо́льше не нужна́.
12. —Когда́ я́ ва́м бу́ду ну́жен? —Вы́ мне́ бу́дете нужны́ за́втра.
13. Бори́с, ты́ бы́л мне́ ну́жен вчера́. Где́ ты́ бы́л? Тепе́рь ты́ мне́ бо́льше не ну́жен.
14. А́нна, отцу́ нужна́ твоя́ по́мощь.
15. За́втра мне́ бу́дет ну́жен тво́й слова́рь.

B. *Form sentences with the following words according to the models.*

Model: У меня́ не́т ко́мнаты. Мне́ нужна́ ко́мната.
Same for: кварти́ра, учи́тель, перо́, секрета́рша.

Model: У ва́с не́ было кре́сла. Ва́м ну́жно бы́ло кре́сло.
Same for: по́лка, прия́тель, мя́со.

Model: У бра́та не́т хле́ба. Ему́ ну́жен хле́б.
Same for: шля́па, костю́м, кре́сло.

Model: У сестры́ не бу́дет автомоби́ля. Е́й ну́жен бу́дет автомоби́ль.
Same for: пла́тье, до́ктор, слова́рь.

6. Numerals 2, 3, 4

два (masc. and neut.) две (fem.)	two
три	three
четы́ре	four

The numeral "two" has two gender forms: **два** for the masculine and neuter, and **две** for the feminine.

Nouns with these numerals take the genitive singular.

два́ до́ма (masc.)
два́ окна́ (neut.)
But: две́ ла́мпы (fem.)
три́ / четы́ре } до́ма, окна́, ла́мпы

With numerals and other expressions of quantity the word **есть** is generally omitted from the "have" and "there are" constructions:

На столе́ два́ карандаша́. На столе́ мно́го хле́ба.
У него́ три́ сы́на. У него́ мно́го хле́ба.

Pattern Sentences

1. В кабинéте **трú** лáмпы. — 1. In the study there are three lamps.
2. В моéй кóмнате **двá** стýла. — 2. In my room there are two chairs.
3. На столé **двé** чáшки. — 3. On the table there are two cups.
4. На пóлке **четы́ре** кнúги. — 4. On the shelf are four books.
5. У нáшей сосéдки **двá** сы́на. — 5. The woman next door to us has two sons.
6. У меня́ **двé** собáки. — 6. I have two dogs.
7. Мы́ вúдели пьéсу Чéхова «**Трú** сестры́.» — 7. We saw Chekhov's play, "The Three Sisters."
8. У кáждого человéка **двé** нóги, **двé** рýки, **двá** глáза, **двá** ýха, нó тóлько однá головá. — 8. Each person has two legs, two arms, two eyes, two ears, but only one head.

Drills

Fill in the correct form of the numerals and change the nouns in parentheses to the proper case form.

1. У Нúны 2 (сестрá).
2. У меня́ 2 (брат).
3. У вáс 4 (лáмпа).
4. Тýт 3 (крéсло).
5. У дирéктора 3 (секретáрша).
6. На пúсьменном столé 2 (телефóн).
7. У собáки 4 (ногá).
8. У Борúса 2 (перó).

7. Modal verbs хотéть and мочь

Хотéть means "to want," "wish," "desire." In the singular it is conjugated as a first conjugation consonant stem (with the stem **хоч-**), but the plural is second conjugation (with the stem **хот-**). The past tense is regular: хотéл, о, -а, -и.

Singular (*1st conjugation*)	*Plural* (*2nd conjugation*)
я́ хочý	мы́ хотúм
ты́ хóчешь	вы́ хотúте
óн хóчет	онú хотя́т

Хотéть is used with a noun, in the accusative case,[3] or with an infinitive.

Я́ хочý э́ту кнúгу. — I want that book.
Мы́ хотúм **рабóтать.** — We want to work.

[3] But the genitive case is regularly employed with хотéть with abstractions ("fame," "happiness," etc), or when one desires only *a part* of the total amount present: Вы́ хотúте **хлéба**? Do you want (some) bread? This is the so-called partitive genitive.

Мочь, "to be able," is conjugated as a first conjugation consonant stem. The first singular and the third plural have a stem ending in **-г-**; the other forms have a stem in **-ж-**:

я́ могу́	мы́ мо́жем
ты́ мо́жешь	вы́ мо́жете
о́н мо́жет	они́ мо́гут

Past tense: мог, могло́, могла́, могли́.

Мочь is used with the infinitive to mean "can:"

Вы́ **мо́жете бы́ть** та́м за́втра?	Can you be there tomorrow?
О́н не **мо́г рабо́тать.**	He couldn't work.

Pattern Sentences

Хоте́ть

1. —Что́ вы́ тепе́рь **хоти́те** чита́ть? —Ива́н и я́, мы́ **хоти́м** чита́ть Пу́шкина.	1. —What do you want to read now? —Ivan and I want to read Pushkin.
2. О́н ничего́ не **хо́чет** де́лать.	2. He doesn't want to do anything.
3. Андре́й, что́ ты́ **хо́чешь?** —Ничего́.	3. —Andrey, what do you want? —Nothing.
4. —Ты́ **хо́чешь** хле́ба? —Да́, **хочу́.**	4. —Would you like some bread? —Yes, I would.
5. Вчера́ на уро́ке я́ **хоте́л** спа́ть.	5. Yesterday in class I felt like sleeping (got sleepy).
6. —Кто́ **хо́чет** е́сть? Ни́на, ты́ хо́чешь? —Да́, **хочу́.**	6. —Who's hungry (who wants to eat)? Nina, are you? —Yes, I am.

Мочь

1. —Я́ хочу́ писа́ть, но́ не **могу́.** —Ты́ не **мо́жешь** и́ли не хо́чешь? —Я́ не **могу́,** потому́ что у меня́ не́т бума́ги.	1. —I want to write, but I can't. —You can't, or you won't? —I can't, because I have no paper.
2. Вы́ **мо́жете** да́ть мне́ ту́ кни́гу?	2. Could you give me that book?
3. Вчера́ Ива́н не **мо́г** спа́ть. Мы́ то́же не **могли́.**	3. Yesterday Ivan couldn't sleep. We couldn't either.

Drills

A. *Fill in the proper forms of the verbs indicated.*

хоте́ть (*present*)

1. О́н всегда́ ...... спа́ть.
2. Почему́ вы́ не ...... отвеча́ть?
3. —Что́ ты́ ......? —Я́ ...... говори́ть.
4. —Кто́ ...... два́ до́ллара? —Все́ ....

5. —Что́ вы́ . . . . . . ? —Я́ ничего́ не . . . .
6. —Мы́ . . . . . . зна́ть пра́вду. Вы́ то́же . . . . . . ? —Коне́чно! Все́ . . . .

Мочь (*present*)

1. Сего́дня я́ не . . . . . . чита́ть.
2. Почему́ ты́ не . . . . . . ?
3. Мы́ не . . . . . . бы́ть до́ма весь де́нь.
4. Все́ . . . . . . э́то де́лать и вы́ то́же . . . .
5. Ива́н не . . . . . . бы́ть зде́сь за́втра.

Мочь (*past*)

1. Ива́н не . . . . . . бы́ть в кла́ссе.
2. А́нна не . . . . . . бы́ть в кла́ссе.
3. Мы́ не . . . . . . бы́ть в кла́ссе.
4. Она́ не . . . . . . бы́ть в кла́ссе.

B. *Translate into Russian.*

1. I cannot eat.
2. He couldn't play the piano; it was very late.
3. She wanted to work, but she couldn't.
4. They want to sleep, but they cannot.
5. Nobody knows what she wants.
6. —What do you want? —I don't want anything.
7. We want to work.
8. They don't want anything.
9. Why can't they work?
10. They couldn't work; it was dark.

CONVERSATION

А́нна. —Мо́жет бы́ть вы́ зна́ете, у кого́ е́сть ру́сско-англи́йский слова́рь? Мне́ о́н о́чень ну́жен. Я́ про́сто не зна́ю, что́ мне́ де́лать!

Боб. —Вы́ спра́шивали в на́шем кни́жном магази́не? Мо́жет быть у ни́х е́сть слова́рь?

А́. —Коне́чно, спра́шивала. Вчера́ у ни́х не́ было словаря́, и они́ не зна́ют, когда́ о́н у ни́х бу́дет.

Б. —А заче́м о́н ва́м так ну́жен?

А́. —Я́ хочу́ чита́ть Че́хова в оригина́ле. Мне́ ску́чно чита́ть Че́хова в перево́де. Но́ я́, коне́чно, ещё не могу́ чита́ть без словаря́.

Б. —А мо́жет быть вы́ мо́жете?

А́. —Я́ говорю́ ва́м, что не могу́: когда́ я́ чита́ю без словаря́, я не всё понима́ю.

Б. —Хоти́те мо́й? О́н мне́ бо́льше не ну́жен.

А́. —Е́сли о́н ва́м не ну́жен, о́чень хочу́,[4] коне́чно. Большо́е спаси́бо!

Б. —Не́ за что.

Pronunciation Drill

móžɨt bɨţ, ví znáiţi, ukavó jéşţ rúskə-angļískəj slaváŗ? mņé on óçiņ núžən. já próstə ņiznáju, štó mņe ḑéləţ!

Ví spráŝɨvəļi vnáŝəm kņížnəm məgaẓíņi? móžɨt bɨţ uņíx jéşţ slaváŗ?

Kaņéšnə, spráŝɨvəl. Fçirá uņíx ņébɨlə sləvaŗá, i aņí ņiznájut, kagdá ón uņíx búḑit.

Answer the following questions in Russian.

1. Что́ А́нне ну́жно? 2. В кни́жном магази́не е́сть слова́рь? 3. Что́ она́ тепе́рь хо́чет чита́ть? 4. Почему́ она́ не хо́чет чита́ть Че́хова в перево́де? 5. Бо́б то́же ду́мает, что е́й ну́жен слова́рь? 6. А что́ она́ говори́т? 7. Почему́ Бо́б мо́жет да́ть е́й сво́й слова́рь?

READING

Что́ Ко́ле[5] ну́жно?

Кали́нины[6] живу́т в дово́льно хоро́шей кварти́ре. У ни́х четы́ре ко́мнаты: спа́льня, столо́вая, гости́ная, и ко́мната и́х сы́на Ко́ли.

Ко́ля хоро́ший, приле́жный учени́к, но́ у него́ плохо́й хара́ктер. О́н большо́й эгои́ст. У Ко́ли прекра́сная све́тлая ко́мната. Ме́бель в его́ ко́мнате о́чень хоро́шая. У него́ е́сть всё, что ему́ ну́жно: у него́ е́сть крова́ть, пи́сьменный сто́л, две́ по́лки (одна́ ни́зкая и одна́ высо́кая). У него́ е́сть сту́л, два́ кре́сла и две́ ла́мпы. На одно́й стене́—карти́на, а на друго́й—ка́рта ми́ра.

И вы́ вероя́тно ду́маете, что Ко́ля дово́лен? Не́т, Ко́ля всегда́ недово́лен. Что́ же ему́ ещё ну́жно? О́н говори́т отцу́, что ему́ ну́жен ещё оди́н сту́л. Оте́ц Ко́ли хоро́ший челове́к, и о́н покупа́ет сы́ну ещё сту́л. Тогда́ Ко́ля говори́т, что, хотя́ у него́ уже́ е́сть две́ ла́мпы, о́н хо́чет ещё одну́.

Оте́ц Ко́ли не о́чень бога́тый челове́к и ему́ не легко́ покупа́ть

[4] О́чень (and not о́чень мно́го) is used with verbs of wanting, liking, etc., where English uses "very much." *E.g.*, Я́ о́чень хочу́ чита́ть, I very much want to read. But: Я́ о́чень мно́го чита́ю, I read a great deal.

[5] Ко́ля, nickname of Никола́й (Nicholas). Masculine nicknames, diminutives, and other masculine nouns which end in **-а** or **-я** are declined like feminines.

[6] The Kalinins.

всё, что Ко́ля хо́чет. Но́ Ко́ле э́то всё равно́: о́н говори́т, что ему́ нужна́ ла́мпа, и оте́ц покупа́ет ему́ ла́мпу (как мы́ уже́ зна́ем, Кали́нин о́чень хоро́ший челове́к).

И вы́ ду́маете, что тепе́рь Ко́ля дово́лен? Совсе́м не́т! Тепе́рь о́н говори́т, что у него́ не́т ковра́ и что ему́ ну́жен ковёр!

Как хорошо́, что ни у ва́с, ни у меня́ не́т тако́го сы́на!

Answer the following questions in Russian.

A. *On the reading above:*

1. В како́й кварти́ре живёт Ко́ля Кали́нин? 2. У Ко́ли тёмная ко́мната? 3. Что́ е́сть в его́ ко́мнате? 4. Како́й челове́к Ко́ля? 5. Почему́ я́ ду́маю, что Ко́ле не нужна́ ещё одна́ ла́мпа? 6. Почему́ его́ отцу́ дово́льно тру́дно покупа́ть всё, что Ко́ля хо́чет? 7. Почему́ оте́ц ему́ всё э́то покупа́ет? 8. Почему́ мы́ должны́ бы́ть ра́ды? 9. Что́ тако́е (what is) лени́вый студе́нт, и что́ тако́е приле́жный?

B. *From your own experience:*

1. У ва́с то́лько ко́мната и́ли це́лая кварти́ра? 2. Что́ у ва́с та́м е́сть? 3. У ва́с хоро́шая ме́бель? 4. Како́й у ва́с хара́ктер? 5. У ва́с е́сть всё, что ва́м ну́жно? 6. Что́ ва́м ещё ну́жно?

EXERCISES

Translate into Russian.

1. —Who has Nina's pencil? —I have it. 2. Do you have a pen? I cannot write without a pen. 3. My brother has a pen. 4. Boris has two pens, and says that he needs one more. 5. We will not be at home tomorrow. We will be at Nina's. 6. They now live at Ivan's. 7. He cannot work without me. 8. We all worked after dinner. 9. I will soon need your help. 10. Our neighbor needed our advice. 11. He needs a mother. 12. I want to sleep, but I cannot! 13. —Who wants to eat? —They all want (to). All except Boris. 14. —I don't understand why she doesn't want to help us. —She wants to, but she cannot. 15. We cannot write without paper. We need paper. 16. My son needs me, and I need my son. I need him very much. 17. We spoke about you before dinner. 18. Everyone was[7] at the concert, except Anna, of course. 19. We will be at their house before the concert. 20. She saw Chekhov's play "The Three Sisters."

[7] Remember that все (everyone) is always plural in Russian.

VOCABULARY

англи́йский English
бога́тый rich, wealthy
ва́нная[8] bathroom
война́ war
высо́кий high, tall
голова́ head
гости́ная[8] living room
дере́вня village, country
дово́лен (*masc.*), **дово́льна** (*fem.*), **дово́льны** (*pl.*) satisfied, content
дово́льно rather, fairly, enough
е́сли if
за́втра tomorrow
заче́м what for, why
кни́жный магази́н bookstore
ковёр (*gen.* **ковра́**) rug, carpet
крова́ть (*fem.*) bed
лени́вый lazy
ме́бель (*fem.*, *no pl.*) furniture
мир world; peace
недово́лен, *etc.* (like **дово́лен**) dissatisfied
ни́зкий low
нога́ leg, foot
обе́д dinner
перево́д translation
пи́сьменный сто́л writing table, desk
по́мощь (*fem.*) help
приле́жный diligent, industrious
про́сто simply
расска́з (short) story
ру́сско-англи́йский Russian-English
соба́ка dog
сосе́д neighbor
сосе́дка neighbor woman
спа́льня bedroom
столо́вая[8] dining room
тогда́ then, at that time
у́хо ear
уче́бник textbook
учени́к pupil[9]
учени́ца girl pupil[9]
хара́ктер disposition, character
хотя́ although, though
ча́шка cup

Expressions

мо́жет быть maybe, perhaps
Не мо́жет бы́ть! It can't be! I can't believe it!
бо́льше не no more, no longer
ещё оди́н (одна́, одно́, *etc.*) one more, another, an additional
большо́е спаси́бо many thanks
Не́ за что. Don't mention it (in reply to thanks).
Мне́ всё равно́. I don't mind, I don't care.
Ему́ это всё равно́. He doesn't care about that.
Я про́сто не зна́ю. I simply don't know.
Что́ мне́ де́лать? What am I to do?
Совсе́м не́т. Not at all.

[8] These words are declined as adjectives, though they function as nouns; with them the noun ко́мната is understood, *e.g.*, Мы́ бы́ли в гости́**ной**, We were in the living room.
[9] The word студе́нт/-ка is used only for university students; for elementary and secondary students учени́к/учени́ца is used.

Vocabulary Review

Parts of the body	Clothing	Furnishings	
голова́	пла́тье	ме́бель	ковёр
глаз	костю́м	стол	карти́на
рот	шля́па	пи́сьменный сто́л	по́лка
у́хо		стул	ра́дио
рука́		кре́сло	телефо́н
нога́		крова́ть	телеви́зор
		ла́мпа	

Rooms	Occupations	Food and Drink	Buildings
гости́ная	учи́тель/-ница	хлеб	дом
столо́вая	профе́ссор	мя́со	шко́ла
ва́нная	студе́нт/-ка	сыр	теа́тр
ку́хня	учени́к/учени́ца	ры́ба	музе́й
спа́льня	до́ктор	молоко́	библиоте́ка
кабине́т	инжене́р	вода́	магази́н
	писа́тель/-ница		кни́жный магази́н
	журнали́ст/-ка		гости́ница
			рестора́н

Adverbs of Time	Geography (adjectives)	For reading
всегда́	ру́сский	рома́н
ча́сто	сове́тский	пе́ьса
иногда́	англи́йский	расска́з
ре́дко	европе́йский	статья́
никогда́	францу́зский	газе́та
	америка́нский	журна́л

Give opposites of the following:

све́тлый	блонди́н/-ка	молодо́й	продава́ть
ни́зкий	ме́ньше	ску́чный	рабо́тать
лени́вый	бы́стро	хоро́ший	но́вый
прия́тный	бе́лый	лёгкий	ма́ленький
у́мный	мла́дший	ночь	у́тро
пло́хо	о́тдых	после́дний	ле́то
нача́ло	ле́тний	конча́ть	мно́го
жа́ркий	дешёвый	закрыва́ть	широ́кий
ра́но	неда́вно	отвеча́ть	

UNIT 11

GRAMMAR

1. Second conjugation, continued.

A. Stress patterns of the second conjugation. Second conjugation verbs have the same rule for stress as first conjugation verbs (see Unit 9, page 129). They have three possible stress patterns for the present tense: (1) stress on the stem throughout; (2) stress on the ending throughout; and (3) stress on the ending in the infinitive and first person singular; this stress shifts back to the stem one syllable in all other forms of the present.

	(1) Stress on Stem	*(2) Stress on Ending*	*(3) Shifting Stress*
	по́мнить (to remember)	**стоя́ть** (to stand)	**кури́ть** (to smoke)
1st sing.	я́ по́мню	я́ стою́	я́ курю́
2nd sing.	ты́ по́мнишь	ты́ стои́шь	ты́ ку́ришь (← stress)
3rd sing.	о́н по́мнит	о́н стои́т	о́н ку́рит
1st pl.	мы́ по́мним	мы́ стои́м	мы́ ку́рим
2nd pl.	вы́ по́мните	вы́ стои́те	вы́ ку́рите
3rd pl.	они́ по́мнят	они́ стоя́т	они́ ку́рят

B. Л after labial consonants. Second conjugation verbs with stems ending in the labial consonants **б, в, м, п,** and **ф** have an **л** inserted after the labial consonant in the first person singular, *e.g.*, спать, to sleep: сплю, спишь, спит, etc.; люби́ть, to love: люблю́, лю́бишь, лю́бит, etc. (note also the shift of stress in this verb).

C. Spelling rule C. The vowel letters **а** and **у** are written after the consonants **ж, ц, ч, ш,** and **щ**. The vowel letters **я** and **ю** must not be written after these consonants (see Unit 3, page 25).

Verbs with stems ending in **ж, ц, ч, ш,** and **щ** have in the first person singular the ending **-у** (not **-ю**), and in the third plural **-ат** (not **-ят**).

Conjugation of **держа́ть** (*to hold, keep*)	*Compare* **говори́ть**
я́ держ**у́**	я́ говор**ю́**
ты́ де́ржишь	ты́ говори́шь
о́н де́ржит	о́н говори́т
мы́ де́ржим	мы́ говори́м
вы́ де́ржите	вы́ говори́те
они́ де́рж**ат**	они́ говор**я́т**
(Note shift in stress.)	

Similarly: лежа́ть (to lie, be lying): я́ лежу́, ты́ лежи́шь . . . они́ леж**а́т**; слы́шать (to hear): я́ слы́ш**у**, ты́ слы́шишь . . . они́ слы́ш**ат**. Remember that лежа́ть, слы́шать, держа́ть (like *most* verbs ending in **-жать** or **-шать**) are *second conjugation*, not first (*but* слу́шать, I: слу́шаю, слу́шаешь, "to listen").

D. Consonant changes. In the second conjugation mutations of the final consonant of the stem affect *the first person only*. For example, final **д** of the stem becomes **ж** in the first person singular.

Conjugation of **сиде́ть** (*to sit*)

я́ си**жу́**	мы́ сиди́м
ты́ сиди́шь	вы́ сиди́те
о́н сиди́т	они́ сидя́т

Also ви́деть (to see): **ви́жу**, ви́дишь, etc.

Pattern Sentences

1. —Я́ не **ви́жу,** где́ они́ **стоя́т,** а вы́ **ви́дите?** —Да́, я́ **ви́жу.**
2. —Вы́ **ви́дите,** где́ **лежи́т** мо́й слова́рь? —Не́т, не **ви́жу.** —О́н **лежи́т** на сту́ле.
3. Две́ газе́ты и два́ журна́ла **лежа́т** на дива́не.
4. Когда́ я́ слу́шаю ра́дио, я́ всегда́ **сижу́** на э́том дива́не.
5. Почему́ они́ **сидя́т** так далеко́?

1. —I don't see where they are standing. Do you see? —Yes, I do.
2. —Can you see where my dictionary is lying? —No, I can't. —It's lying on the chair.
3. Two newspapers and two magazines are lying on the sofa.
4. When I listen to the radio, I always sit on this couch.
5. Why do they sit so far away?

6. —Что́ вы́ **де́ржите** в руке́? —Я́ **держу́** два́ до́ллара.	6. —What are you holding in your hand? —I am holding $2.
7. —Вы́ **ку́рите?** —Да́, я́ **курю́,** но́ ма́ло. До́ктор говори́т, что я́ совсе́м не до́лжен **кури́ть,** но́ э́то тру́дно, когда́ все́ **ку́рят.**	7. —Do you smoke? —Yes, I smoke, but (only a) little. The doctor says that I shouldn't smoke at all, but that's hard (to do) when everyone smokes.
8. —Вы́ хорошо́ **спи́те?** —Не́т, я́ пло́хо **сплю́.** Когда́ жа́рко, почти́ все́ пло́хо **спя́т.**	8. —Do you sleep well? —No, I sleep badly. When it's hot almost everyone sleeps badly.
9. —Алло́! Алло́! Я́ ва́с не **слы́шу.** А вы́ меня́ **слы́шите?** —Да́, я́ ва́с хорошо́ **слы́шу.**	9. —Hello, hello! I can't hear you. Can you hear me? —Yes, I can hear you (very) well.
10. —Вы́ **лю́бите** Толсто́го? —Да́, о́чень **люблю́.**[1] —Почти́ все́ его́ **лю́бят.**	10. —Do you like Tolstoy? —Yes, very much. —Almost everyone likes him
11. У А́нны Ива́новны о́чень плоха́я па́мять. Она́ сего́дня не **по́мнит,** что́ бы́ло вчера́!	11. Anna Ivanovna has a very bad memory. She doesn't remember today what happened yesterday!

Drills

A. *Supply the correct forms of the verb in parentheses in the present tense for questions and answers.*

Вопро́с	**Отве́т**
1. Кого́ вы́ (ви́деть)?	Мы́ ...... ва́с.
2. Кого́ Ива́н ......?	О́н ...... на́с.
3. Кого́ я́ ......?	Вы́ ...... учи́теля.
4. Кого́ они́ ......?	Они́ ...... бра́та.
5. Кого́ мы́ ......?	Вы́ ...... сестру́.
6. На чём вы́ (сиде́ть)?	Мы́ ...... на кре́сле.
7. На чём о́н ......?	О́н ...... на кре́сле.
8. На чём ты́ ......?	Я́ ...... на сту́ле.
9. На чём она́ ......?	Она́ ...... на дива́не.
10. На чём они́ ......?	Они́ ...... на кре́сле.
11. На чём я́ ......?	Ты́ ...... на сту́ле.
12. Почему́ ты́ не (спать)?	—Потому́ что я́ не (хоте́ть).
13. Почему́ Ива́н не ......?	—Потому́ что о́н не ....
14. Почему́ вы́ не ......?	—Потому́ что я́ не ....
15. Почему́ О́льга не ......?	—Потому́ что она́ не ....

[1] Intensity with verbs of wishing, liking, etc. (люби́ть, хоте́ть) is expressed in Russian by о́чень (compare English "very much").

16. Почему́ они́ не . . . . . . ? —Потому́ что они́ не . . . .
17. Почему́ мы́ не . . . . . . ? —Потому́ что вы́ не . . . .
18. Почему́ я́ не . . . . . . ? —Потому́ что ты́ не . . . . . .

B. *Supply the correct present tense form of* **люби́ть** *and translate the infinitives in parentheses.*

1. Что́ о́н (люби́ть)? —О́н . . . . . . (to smoke).
2. Что́ я́ . . . . . . ? —Вы́ . . . . . . (to sleep).
3. Что́ они́ . . . . . . ? —Они́ . . . . . . (to listen).
4. Что́ она́ . . . . . . ? —Она́ . . . . . . (to play).
5. Что́ Ива́н . . . . . . ? —О́н . . . . . . (to eat).
6. Что́ вы́ . . . . . . ? —Я́ . . . . . . (to sit).

C. *Supply the correct present tense form of the verbs in parentheses.*

1. Я́ ничего́ не (по́мнить).
2. Они́ ничего́ не . . . .
3. Ты́ ничего́ не . . . .
4. Мы́ ничего́ не . . . .
5. Она́ ничего́ не . . . .
6. Что́ они́ (держа́ть)?
7. Что́ ты́ . . . . . . ?
8. Что́ вы́ . . . . . . ?
9. Что́ я́ . . . . . . ?
10. Что́ О́льга . . . . . . ?
11. Что́ мы́ . . . . . . ?

D. *Translate into English.*

1. Мо́й оте́ц всегда́ де́ржит э́тот докуме́нт в своём пи́сьменном столе́.
2. До́ктор держа́л Серге́я две́ неде́ли до́ма.
3. —Вы́ по́мните исто́рию, кото́рую Вади́м расска́зывал на после́дней вечери́нке? —Не́т, не по́мню. Я́ его́ не слу́шал.
4. Я́ не понима́ю, о чём вы́ говори́те.
5. Как стра́нно, что они́ на́с ещё по́мнят!
6. —Почему́ ты́ так мно́го ку́ришь? —Я́ не могу́ не кури́ть.
7. Я́ не понима́ю, почему́ мы́ ва́с тепе́рь так ре́дко ви́дим.
8. Ты́ ви́дишь, та́м на по́лке стоя́т две́ кни́ги, а учебник лежи́т на столе́.
9. По́сле обе́да оте́ц лю́бит лежа́ть на дива́не, кото́рый стои́т в моей ко́мнате.
10. —Что́ ва́м пи́шет Ива́н? —О́н на́м совсе́м не пи́шет.

E. *Replace the infinitives in parentheses with the correct form of the present tense and translate.*

1. Я́ не (по́мнить), где́ вы́ (жить).
2. Я́ не (понима́ть), что́ вы́ (говори́ть).
3. Я́ не (хоте́ть) слы́шать, что́ они́ (говори́ть)!
4. Ты́ (слы́шать), что́ я́ (говори́ть)?
5. Они́ не (понима́ть), почему́ мы́ и́х не (слы́шать).
6. —Кто́ (спать) в э́той ко́мнате? —Зде́сь я́ (спать), а они́ (спать) в кабине́те.

7. —Почему́ вы́ (стоя́ть)? —Потому́ что все́ (стоя́ть).
8. Я́ не (люби́ть) стоя́ть.
9. —А что́ вы́ (люби́ть)? —Я́ (люби́ть) лежа́ть.
10. Мы́ не (ви́деть), что́ о́н (держа́ть) в руке́.
11. Я́ то́же не (ви́деть).
12. —Я́ не (по́мнить), ва́ш бра́т (кури́ть) и́ли не́т? —В моей семье́ все́ (кури́ть). Как стра́нно, что вы́ не (по́мнить)!
13. —Что́ ты́ (де́лать)? —Я́ (сиде́ть) и (писа́ть) письмо́ сестре́.
14. Они́ почти́ всегда́ (сиде́ть) до́ма и (писа́ть).

F. *Translate into Russian.*

1. —What are you writing? —I am writing a translation.
2. —Do you see him often? —We don't see him at all.
3. I don't remember where he lives.
4. He lives at Anna's, and I live there too.
5. I see him almost every day.
6. We never see him.
7. I hear very well what you are saying.
8. They say that they remember us well.
9. They have a good memory.
10. I don't understand why you smoke!
11. Everybody smokes.
12. Why am I sitting when you are standing?
13. He is holding two dictionaries.
14. I have a good memory, but I don't remember the monument you are talking about.
15. I write often to my family.
16. They live far (away) and see their son rather seldom.

2. Instrumental case of nouns

The instrumental case is used to express the means, instrument, manner, or agent by which an action is performed. Thus it generally corresponds to the English preposition "with" in the sense of "by means of":

Я́ пишу́ **перо́м.**
I write *with* (by means of) a pen (*instrument*).

Я́ посыла́ю письмо́ **по́чтой.**
I am sending the letter *by* mail (*means*).

О́н говори́т **гро́мким го́лосом.**
He speaks in a loud voice (*manner*).

Endings of Nouns in the Instrumental Case

		Spelling Hard	Spelling Soft
Masc. / *Neut.*	[-óm]([-əm] if unstr.)	**-ом**	**-ём** (unstr. **-ем**)
Fem.	[-ój]([-əj] if unstr.)	**-ой**	**-ёй** (unstr. **-ей**)[2]

	Nominative	*Instrumental*
Masc.	стол [stól.] гость [gós̡t̡.] музéй [muz̡ẹ́j.]	стол**óм** [stal.óm] гóст**ем** [gós̡t̡.əm] музé**ем** [muz̡ẹ́j.əm]
Neut.	окнó [akn.ó] пóле [pól̡.ə]	окн**óм** [akn.óm] пóл**ем** [pól̡.əm]
Fem.	женá [žɨn.á] кýхня [kúxn̡.ə]	жен**óй** [žɨn.ój] кýхн**ей** [kúxn̡.əj]

The unstressed instrumental endings, masculine and neuter [-əm] and feminine [-əj], are always written **-ем** and **-ей** respectively in nouns with stems ending in **ж**, **ш**, **ц**, **ч**, and **щ** (according to Spelling Rule B, unstressed **о** cannot be written after these letters):

Masc.	мý**ж**—мý**жем** мéся**ц**—мéся**цем** товáри**щ**—товáри**щем**	(but: нó**ж**—но**жóм**) (but: отé**ц**—от**цóм**) (but: бóр**щ**—бор**щóм**) (a soup)
Neut.	сóлн**це**—сóлн**цем** (sun)	(but: ли**цó**—ли**цóм**)
Fem.	кры**ша**—кры**шей** (roof) дá**ча**—дá**чей** (summer cottage)	(but: ду**шá**—ду**шóй**) (soul) (but: све**чá**—све**чóй**) (candle)

[2] The feminine instrumental has the alternate ending **-ою/-ею**, which is used mostly in poetry.

Pattern Sentences

(Note that the instrumental of что is **чем**).

1. —**Чéм** вы́ пи́шете, пер**óм** и́ли каран-даш**óм**? —Я́ всегдá пишý пер**óм**. — 1. —What do you write with, a pen or a pencil? —I always write with a pen.
2. Óн дéлает жéст рук**óй**. — 2. He is making a gesture with his hand.
3. —**Чéм** Ни́на пи́шет на доскé? —Онá пи́шет мéл**ом**, как всé. — 3. —What does Nina write with on the blackboard? —She writes with chalk, like everybody.
4. Óн дéржит шля́пу рук**óй**, потомý что вéтер. — 4. He is holding his hat with his hand because it's windy.
5. Андрéй пáльц**ем** покáзывает на кáрте, гдé óн жи́л. — 5. Andrey is pointing out on the map with his finger where he used to live.
6. Отéц óчень довóлен Óльг**ой** и Кáт**ей**. — 6. Father is very pleased with Olga and Katya.
7. Учи́тельница довóльна Ивáн**ом** и Андр**éем**. — 7. The teacher is pleased with Ivan and Andrey.

Drill

Put the words in parentheses into the correct case and translate.

1. Я́ держý бумáгу (рукá).
2. Мы́ дýмаем (головá).
3. Профéссор довóлен (Áнна).
4. Мы́ довóльны (дóктор).
5. Студéнтка недовóльна (профéссор).
6. Мáть недовóльна (Ивáн).
7. Я́ никогдá не пишý (карандáш).
8. Чтó óн дéлает (ногá)?
9. Чтó ты́ дéлаешь (головá)?
10. Мы́ довóльны (гость).
11. Они́ бы́ли óчень довóльны (дерéвня).
12. Учи́тель довóлен (Кáтя), нó недовóлен (Óльга).

3. Instrumental of pronouns and adjectives

The basic endings of the instrumental case, pronominal declension, are spelled as follows:

	Hard	*Soft*
Masc. *Neut.*	**-ым**	**-им**
Fem.	**-ой**[3]	**-ей**[3]

[3] The feminine forms have the alternate endings **-ою** (hard) and **-ею** (soft) throughout this declension, but these forms are largely poetic.

Masculine and Neuter

	NOMINATIVE *Masculine*	*Neuter*	INSTRUMENTAL *Masculine and Neuter*
3rd pers. pron.	он	онó	**им** [ím]
Adjectives	нóвый си́ний хорóший рýсский	нóвое си́нее хорóшее рýсское	нóв**ым** [nóv.ɨm] си́н**им** [şíņ.im] хорóш**им** [xaróš.ɨm] рýсск**им** [rúsķ.im][4]
Possessives	мой наш	моё нáше	мо**и́м** [maj.ím] нáш**им** [náš.ɨm]
Demonstratives	э́тот тот	э́то то	э́т**им** [ẹ́ţ.im][5] т**ем** [ţ.ém][5]
Interrogatives	кто	что	к**ем** [ķ.ém][5] ч**ем** [č̦.ém][5]
	оди́н	однó	одн**и́м** [aḑņ.ím][5]

Feminine

3rd pers. pron.	онá	ей [j.ẹ́j]
Adjectives	нóвая си́няя хорóшая	нóв**ой** [nóv.əj] си́н**ей** [şíņ.əj] хорóш**ей** [xaróš.əj]
Possessives	моя́ нáша	мо**е́й** [maj.ẹ́j] нáш**ей** [náš.əj]
Demonstratives	э́та та	э́т**ой** [ét.əj] т**ой** [t.ój]
	однá	одн**óй** [adn.ój]

[4] Adjectives with stems ending in **г, к, х** have the ending **-им** in the masculine-neuter instrumental (Spelling Rule A).

[5] The stems of э́тот, тот, кто, and оди́н are soft in the instrumental, masculine-neuter: э́тот has э́тим, and оди́н has одни́м, while тот and кто have the ending **-ем**, as does что.

The Instrumental Case of Other Personal Pronouns

Nominative:	я	ты	мы	вы	они́
Instrumental:	мной	тобо́й	на́ми	ва́ми	и́ми

Pattern Sentences

1. —Каки́м карандашо́м ты́ пи́шешь, кра́сным и́ли чёрным? —Чёрным.
2. —Каки́м ме́лом вы́ лю́бите писа́ть? —Коне́чно, бе́лым! —А я́ люблю́ писа́ть жёлтым.
3. —Како́й руко́й пи́шет Бори́с? —О́н пи́шет ле́вой.
4. Вы́ зна́ете, что в Евро́пе все́ должны́ писа́ть пра́вой руко́й?
5. Ле́на о́чень дово́льна свое́й но́вой си́ней шля́пой.
6. Мы́ о́чень дово́льны на́шим но́вым профе́ссором, и о́н дово́лен на́ми.
7. Они́ недово́льны свои́м ста́ршим сы́ном.
8. Профе́ссор о́чень дово́лен мно́й, и я́ дово́льна и́м.
9. Почему́ вы́ говори́те таки́м ти́хим го́лосом?

1. What sort of pencil do you write with, a red or a black one? —With a black one.
2. —What kind of chalk do you like to write with? —With white chalk, of course! —But I like to write with yellow chalk.
3. —Which hand does Boris write with? —He writes with his left hand.
4. Do you know that in Europe everyone must write with his right hand?
5. Lena is very pleased with her new blue hat.
6. We are very pleased with our new professor, and he is pleased with us.
7. They are displeased with their eldest son.
8. The professor is very pleased with me, and I am pleased with him.
9. Why do you speak in such a low voice?

Drill

Put the words in parentheses into the correct case and translate.

1. Я́ пишу́ (жёлтый ме́л).
2. Ни́на пи́шет (чёрный каранда́ш).
3. Мы́ дово́льны (но́вый до́ктор).
4. Я́ не люблю́ писа́ть (но́вое перо́).
5. Бори́с пока́зывает (то́лстый па́лец) на ка́рте, где́ о́н жи́л.
6. Ка́к ты́ мо́жешь писа́ть (ле́вая рука́)?
7. Я́ не могу́ рабо́тать (одна́ рука́).
8. До́ктор дово́лен (но́вая секрета́рша).
9. Мы́ дово́льны (но́вый слова́рь).
10. А́нна дово́льна (си́нее пла́тье).

11. О́льга дово́льна (молодо́й го́сть).
12. Реда́ктор дово́лен (мо́й пе́рвый рома́н).
13. О́н недово́лен (ва́ша после́дняя кни́га).
14. Актёр говори́л (прия́тный, ти́хий го́лос).

4. The preposition **с** with the instrumental

With the instrumental case, the preposition **с** means "with," "along with," "together with":

Во́т ма́ть **с ребёнком.**
Here is a mother with her child.

Я́ пью́ ча́й **с лимо́ном.**
I drink tea with lemon.

Вчера́ я́ рабо́тал **с бра́том** (pronounce [zbrátəm]).
I worked with my brother yesterday.

Remember that when "with" does not mean "along with" or "together with," the instrumental is used without any preposition:

Я́ пишу́ **перо́м.**
I write *with a pen* (by means of a pen).

Он дово́лен **на́ми.**
He is pleased *with us.*

But: Я́ чита́ю **с сестро́й.**
I am reading *with my sister* (*together with my sister*).

With a double object **с** (like other Russian prepositions) is usually repeated:

Я́ бы́л та́м **с** бра́том и **с** его́ прия́телем.
I was there with my brother and (with) his friend.

The form **со** is used before some words beginning with a double consonant, *e.g.*, **со мно́й** (with me); **со все́й** семьёй (with the whole family), etc.[6]

The preposition **с** is used with the instrumental of abstract nouns to form phrases of the type:

с удово́льств**ием**	with pleasure
с аппети́т**ом**	with an appetite
с труд**о́м**	with difficulty

But: О́н говори́т гро́мким го́лосом (without **с**).
He speaks in a loud voice.

[6] The form **со** is also used before certain consonant clusters, the first member of which is **с** or **з**, *e.g.*, **со** стол**о́м**.

The following idiomatic expressions are extremely typical in Russian and are used frequently:

Мы́ с . . . (+ instr.)	someone and I
Вы́ с . . . (+ instr.)	someone and you

Сего́дня **мы́ с бра́том** не́ были в шко́ле.
Today my brother and I didn't go to school.

Вы́ с жено́й давно́ в Аме́рике?
Have you and your wife been in America long?

After the preposition **с** (as after other prepositions), the declined forms of the third person pronouns have a prefixed **н-**.

с ним	with him, it
с ней	with her, it
с ни́ми	with them
Я́ ча́сто говори́л **с ни́ми.**	I often spoke with them.

Pattern Sentences

1. —**С ке́м** ты́ была́ в теа́тре? —Я́ была́ **с** дру́г**ом**.
2. Вади́м живёт тепе́рь **с** отц**о́м**. О́н живёт **с ни́м** уже́ два́ ме́сяца.[7]
3. О́льга была́ **с** А́нн**ой** в рестора́не, а пото́м она́ была́ **с не́й** у до́ктора.
4. Мы́ хоти́м переводи́ть э́тот рома́н **с ва́ми.** Вы́ хоти́те рабо́тать **с на́ми?**
5. Вади́м не разгова́ривает **со мно́й,** и я́ не разгова́риваю ни **с ни́м,** ни **с** его́ глу́п**ым** дру́г**ом**.
6. —**С ке́м** бы́л Бори́с вчера́ на вечери́нке? —О́н бы́л **со мно́й и с** мо**е́й** мла́дш**ей** сестр**о́й**.
7. —**С че́м** Ива́н Ива́нович обы́чно пьёт ча́й, **с** лимо́н**ом** и́ли **с** молок**о́м**? —О́н пьёт ча́й то́лько **с** са́хар**ом**.
8. О́льга Ива́новна лю́бит пи́ть ча́й без са́хара, но́ **с** варе́нь**ем**.

1. —With whom were you at the theater? —With a friend.
2. Vadim now lives with his father. He has been living[7] with him for two months now.
3. Olga was at the restaurant with Anna, and then she was with her at the doctor's.
4. We want to translate that novel with you. Do you want to work with us?
5. Vadim isn't speaking to me, and I'm not speaking either to him or to his stupid friend.
6. —With whom was Boris at the party yesterday? —He was with me and my younger sister.
7. —With what does Ivan Ivanovich usually take his tea, with lemon or milk? —He drinks tea only with sugar.
8. Olga Ivanovna likes to drink tea without sugar, but with jam.

[7] When a period of time is given, Russian verbs in the present tense correspond to English verbs in the *present perfect* tense, *e.g.*, Мы́ ту́т **живём** две́ неде́ли. We *have been living* here for two weeks. Compare also: Мы́ ту́т давно́ живём. We *have been living* here for a long time.

9. В францу́зском ресторáне мы́ éли óчень вкýсное мя́со **с** картóфел**ем** и **с** салáт**ом**.	9. At the French restaurant we ate very delicious meat with potatoes and with salad.
10. Нóвый инженéр говори́т по-англи́йски прáвильно, нó **с** рýсск**им** акцéнт**ом**, и я́ **с** труд**óм** егó понимáю.	10. The new engineer speaks English correctly, but with a Russian accent, and I have difficulty understanding him (understand him with difficulty).
11. Смирнóв, как всегдá, éл **с** больш**и́м** удовóльстви**ем** и **с** аппети́т**ом**.	11. Smirnov, as always, ate with great enjoyment and appetite.
12. Вы́ говори́те прáвильно, нó **с** акцéнт**ом**.	12. You speak correctly, but with an accent.

Drills

A. *Translate into English.*

1. Я́ вáс спрáшиваю, почемý вы́ не хоти́те говори́ть со мнóй?
2. Ивáн хóчет писáть со мнóй кни́гу о рýсской мýзыке.
3. Я́ не люблю́ Óльгу и не могý рабóтать с нéй.
4. Я́ ви́дела Ивáна, и мы́ с ни́м говори́ли об э́той пьéсе.
5. Я́ давнó не говори́л с ни́м.
6. Я́ давнó не рабóтал с нéй.
7. Я́ хочý переводи́ть э́ту кни́гу с вáми.
8. Мы́ с женóй ви́дели вчерá прекрáсную пьéсу.

B. *Give answers to the questions asked, supplying the correct case form of the words in the right-hand column.*

	Вопрóс		**Отвéт**
С чём	вы́ éли хлéб?	С	(сыр)
	вы́ пи́ли чáй?		(сáхар) и с (варéнье)
	вы́ пи́ли кóфе?		(молокó)
	вы́ éли мя́со?		(картóфель) и с (салáт).
С кéм	Бори́с бы́л в Бостóне?		Óн бы́л с (брат).
	Áнна былá в Москвé?		...... с (друг).
	вы́ бы́ли на концéрте?		...... с (дóктор).
	отéц говори́л пóсле обéда?		...... с (гость).
	Рóберт говори́т по-рýсски?		...... с (учи́тель).

C. *Put the nouns and pronouns in parentheses into the correct form.*

1. —Кéм отéц недовóлен? —Óн недовóлен (я́ и ты́).
2. Óн хóчет серьёзно говори́ть с (ты́ и я́).
3. —Кéм учи́тель довóлен? —Óн довóлен (óн и онá).
4. —С кéм вы́ хоти́те рабóтать? —Я́ хочý рабóтать с (он) и с (онá).
5. —С кéм Áнна ви́дела Бори́са? —Онá ви́дела егó с (вы) и с (онá).
6. Óн хóчет говори́ть с (они́) и с (вы).

7. Кто́ хо́чет рабо́тать с (они́) и с (мы)?
8. Почему́ вы́ не говори́те с (она́)?

D. *Translate into Russian.*

1. —What did you eat the bread with? —I ate it with cheese.
2. —With whom did you work? —I worked with her and (with) her silly brother.
3. —What do you write with in class? —I write with the new pen.
4. —Why don't you want to speak with me? —I don't want to speak with you because I am displeased with you.
5. I never drink coffee with sugar.
6. —With whom does he talk? —He talks with his young secretary and with my sister.
7. He is very pleased with this secretary.
8. She cannot live with her sister, and therefore she lives with mine.

5. Predicate instrumental

In "John was a student" the words "was a student" form the predicate, and "student" is said to be the *predicate noun*. Predicate nouns in Russian usually take the instrumental case when the link verb быть is in the past or in the future tense:

Её ма́ть была́ актри́с**ой**.
Her mother was an actress.

Её му́ж бы́л хоро́ш**им** инжене́р**ом**.
Her husband was a good engineer.

Она́ бу́дет актри́с**ой**.
She will be an actress.

Я́ ду́маю, что о́н бу́дет хоро́ш**им** инжене́р**ом**.
I think he will be a good engineer.

Я́ тогда́ бы́л ещё студе́нт**ом**.
At that time I was still a student.

Ра́ньше Петербу́рг бы́л столи́ц**ей**, а тепе́рь столи́ца Москва́.
Saint Petersburg was formerly the capital, but now the capital is Moscow.

Э́та пло́щадь ра́ньше была́ це́нтр**ом** го́рода.
This square used to be the center of the city.

But in the present tense: Её ма́ть актри́с**а**. Её му́ж хоро́ш**ий** инжене́р.

Adjectives in the predicate are also sometimes in the instrumental:

Когда́ Толсто́й бы́л молод**ы́м**, о́н бы́л офице́р**ом**.
When Tolstoy was young, he was an officer.

Nouns and adjectives always take the instrumental case with **быть** in the infinitive, as in:

> Тру́дно **бы́ть** хоро́шим инжене́ром.
> Бра́т моей подру́ги хо́чет (or хоте́л) **бы́ть** диплома́том.
> —**Ке́м** хо́чет **бы́ть** А́нна? —А́нна хо́чет **бы́ть** учи́тельницей.
> Я́ ду́маю, что она́ бу́дет хоро́шей учи́тельницей.
> Когда́ мо́й сы́н бы́л ма́леньким, о́н хоте́л **бы́ть** диплома́том или адмира́лом.

6. Instrumental of time

Adverbs denoting seasons of the year or parts of the day are instrumental in form:

Nominative		*Instrumental*	
весна́	spring	весно́й	in spring
ле́то	summer	ле́том	in summer
о́сень (*fem.*)	fall, autumn	о́сенью[8]	in fall
зима́	winter	зимо́й	in winter
у́тро	morning	у́тром	in the morning
день (*masc.*)	day, afternoon	днём	in the daytime; in the afternoon
ве́чер	evening	ве́чером	in the evening
ночь (*fem.*)	night	но́чью[8]	at night

Note the expressions:

сего́дня у́тром	this morning
вчера́ ве́чером	last evening
сего́дня ве́чером	tonight (this evening)

Russian is more consistent than English in using ве́чер (ве́чером) for the period between 6:00 and about 10:00 p.m.

> Вчера́ ве́чером мы́ бы́ли в теа́тре.
> Last night we went to the theater.

Pattern Sentences

1. Зима́ была́ холо́дная. Ту́т всегда́ хо́лодно **зимо́й.**
2. Ле́то бы́ло жа́ркое. В го́роде обы́чно жа́рко **ле́том.**

1. Winter was cold. It is always cold here in winter.
2. Summer was hot. In the city it's usually hot in summer.

[8] Fem. II nouns end in **-ью** in the instrumental.

3. Весна́ зде́сь о́чень хоро́шая. Как хорошо́ **весно́й** в дере́вне!
4. О́сень зде́сь о́чень прия́тная. **О́сенью** прия́тно и в го́роде и в дере́вне.
5. Како́й прия́тный ве́чер! Что́ вы́ де́лаете сего́дня **ве́чером**?
6. Сего́дня бы́ло настоя́щее весе́ннее у́тро. Что́ вы́ де́лали сего́дня **у́тром**?
7. —Вы́ уже́ за́втракали? —Да́, я́ люблю́ за́втракать ра́но **у́тром.**
8. Кака́я тёмная но́чь!
9. Я́ люблю́ рабо́тать **но́чью,** когда́ все́ спя́т.
10. Я́ никогда́ не сплю **днём.**

3. Spring here is very nice. How nice it is in the country in spring!
4. Fall here is very pleasant. In fall it is nice both in the city and in the country.
5. What a pleasant evening! What are you doing this evening (tonight)?
6. Today it was a real spring morning. What were you doing this morning?
7. —Have you eaten breakfast already? —Yes, I like to have breakfast early in the morning.
8. What a dark night!
9. I like to work at night when everybody is asleep.
10. I never sleep in the daytime.

Drill

Translate into English.

1. Вчера́ ве́чером мы́ с Ле́ной обе́дали у Бори́са.
2. Я́ хочу́ ка́ждое у́тро за́втракать с ва́ми.
3. Сего́дня у́тром Смирно́в за́втракал с на́ми.
4. Ле́том А́нна жила́ у своего́ ста́ршего бра́та.
5. О́льга лю́бит жи́ть в дере́вне зимо́й.
6. Вчера́ у́тром Андре́я не́ было в кла́ссе.
7. Весно́й мы́ бу́дем в Москве́.
8. Я́ люблю́ ру́сскую весну́.
9. Пу́шкин люби́л о́сень. О́н всегда́ мно́го писа́л о́сенью.
10. Вчера́ ве́чером мы́ с бра́том обе́дали в италья́нском рестора́не.
11. У́тром Андре́й рабо́тает в библиоте́ке, а днём—до́ма.

7. Russian names

«Ива́н Ива́нович Ива́нов.» In addition to the first name (и́мя) and the family name (фами́лия), Russians also use the patronymic (о́тчество), a form derived from the father's name by adding the suffix **-ович** (or **-евич** or **-ич**) in the *masculine,* and **-овна** (**-евна**) in the *feminine*, thus:

Ива́н Ива́нович (Ivan, Ivan's son); А́нна Ива́новна (Anna, Ivan's daughter)

Бори́с Петро́вич (Boris, Peter's son); Мари́я Петро́вна (Marie, Peter's daughter)

Серге́й Андре́евич (Sergey, Andrew's son); Еле́на Андре́евна (Helen, Andrew's daughter), etc.

The first name followed by the patronymic is a very commonly used form of address. In rapid speech, the patronymic suffix is often slurred or contracted, *e.g.*, Ива́нович is pronounced [ivániç̌]; Андре́евна is pronounced [andr̦évnə], etc.

The first name alone (or, quite frequently, a diminutive, such as Ва́ня for Ива́н, Пе́тя for Пётр, Ко́ля for Никола́й, О́ля for О́льга, Та́ня for Татья́на, etc.) is used between friends and relatives, or in addressing young people and children.

The Russian equivalents of "Mr." and "Mrs." are господи́н and госпожа́; they are not in use in the Soviet Union (except when addressing foreigners); the terms used instead are това́рищ, "comrade," for both sexes, and граждани́н, "citizen," feminine, гражда́нка (with the last name).

CONVERSATION

В рестора́не «Росси́я»

А. —Я́ звони́л ва́м вчера́, Серге́й Петро́вич. Я́ звони́л у́тром, днём и ве́чером, но́ никто́ не отвеча́л.

Б. —Что́ было вчера́? Да́, по́мню! У́тром я́ рабо́тал в конто́ре, а днём мы́ с жено́й покупа́ли ме́бель. У на́с но́вая кварти́ра, и у на́с о́чень ма́ло ме́бели.

А. —Но́ я́ звони́л ва́м дово́льно по́здно ве́чером. Ва́с не́ было.

Б. —Вчера́ ве́чером мы́ обе́дали с господи́ном Джо́нсоном и с его́ жено́й. Вы́, мо́жет бы́ть, слы́шали: Ро́берт Джо́нсон, исто́рик.

А. —Да́, я́ слы́шал о нём. Говоря́т, что о́н интере́сный челове́к. Вы́ обе́дали у ни́х?

Б. —Не́т, мы́ обе́дали в рестора́не «Росси́я».

А. —«Росси́я?» Я́ никогда́ не слы́шал об э́том рестора́не.

Б. —Ну́ что́ вы́ говори́те, Ю́рий Бори́сович! Мы́ с ва́ми та́м вме́сте обе́дали. Пра́вда, э́то было давно́, ещё до войны́. Э́то ма́ленький рестора́н ря́дом с Но́вым теа́тром. По́мните?

А. —Не по́мню. Ну́, расскажи́те, что́ вы́ та́м е́ли. Я́ люблю́ слу́шать, когда́ говоря́т о еде́ (food). Расскажи́те мне́, како́е было меню́.

Б. —С удово́льствием. Снача́ла мы́ пи́ли. Госпожа́ Джо́нсон пила́ кокте́йль, мы́ с Ро́бертом пи́ли во́дку, а моя́ жена́ ничего́ не пила́—она́ никогда́ не пьёт. Я́ пью, но́ ма́ло.

А. —Ну́, хорошо́, а что́ по́сле кокте́йля и во́дки?

Б. —Мы́ е́ли настоя́щий украи́нский (Ukrainian) бо́рщ, а по́сле борща́ мы́ е́ли о́чень вку́сное мя́со с карто́фелем и с о́чень вку́сным сала́том.

А. —А пото́м десе́рт?

Б. —Коне́чно! По́сле десе́рта Джо́нсоны[9] пи́ли чёрный ко́фе, а мы́ с жено́й пи́ли ча́й с варе́ньем (jam). Непло́хо, пра́вда?

А. —Совсе́м непло́хо!

Pronunciation Drill

—já zvaņíl vam f̧ç̌irá, şiŗģéj p̧itróɣ̧iç̌. já zvaņíl útrəm, ḑņóm i ɣ̧ẹ́ç̌irəm, no ņiktó ņiatɣ̧iç̌ál.

—štó bɨ́lə f̧ç̌irá? dá, pómņu! útrəm já rabótəl fkantóŗi, a ḑņóm mɨ zžɨnój pəkupáļi m̧ẹ́b̧iļ. unás nóvəjə kvarţírə i unás óç̌iņ málə m̧ẹ́b̧iļi.

—no ja zvaņíl vám davóļnə póz*d*nə ɣ̧ẹ́ç̌irəm. vás ņébɨlə.

Answer the following questions in Russian.

1. Расскажи́те, что́ вчера́ де́лал Серге́й Петро́вич у́тром и днём. 2. Что́ о́н де́лал ве́чером? 3. Кто́ Ро́берт Джо́нсон? 4. Где́ рестора́н «Росси́я?» 5. Почему́ Ю́рий Бори́сович спра́шивает своего́ дру́га, како́е бы́ло меню́? 6. Что́ они́ снача́ла де́лали в рестора́не? 7. Что́ они́ е́ли? С че́м они́ е́ли мя́со? 8. Они́ по́сле мя́са ничего́ не е́ли? 9. С че́м они́ пи́ли ча́й? 10. Како́й ко́фе пи́ли Джо́нсоны? 11. Что́ вы́ ду́маете об э́том обе́де?

READING

Всё э́то бы́ло давно́

Я́ о́чень люблю́ разгова́ривать с мои́м хоро́шим ста́рым дру́гом Лунёвым.

Лунёв о́чень у́мный и интере́сный челове́к, и мне́ всегда́ интере́сно разгова́ривать с ни́м. Вы́ вероя́тно то́же лю́бите разгова́ривать с у́мным челове́ком?

У Лунёва была́ о́чень интере́сная жи́знь. О́н бы́л исто́риком, и

[9] The Johnsons.

однó врéмя óн бы́л диплома́том. О́н бы́л вездé, óн мнóго ви́дел, мнóго знáет и всё пóмнит.

Зимóй мы́ чáсто сиди́м вéчером в егó кабинéте, пьём чáй с рóмом (rum) и́ли турéцкий (Turkish) кóфе; кýрим и разговáриваем. Я́ сижý ти́хо, пью чáй, мнóго курю́, мáло говорю́ и слýшаю моегó дрýга.

Лунёв говори́т ти́хим и прия́тным гóлосом. О́н обы́чно кýрит свою́ турéцкую трýбку, пьёт чёрный кóфе и расскáзывает о своéй жи́зни. С каки́м интерéсом я́ егó слýшаю! У негó прекрáсная пáмять; óн всё пóмнит. О́н ви́дел вéсь ми́р. О́н знáет А́зию, А́фрику, Амéрику. О́н дóлго жи́л в Китáе, в Аргенти́не. О́н знáл рýсского царя́ и разговáривал с ни́м. О́н разговáривал с америкáнским президéнтом Вильсóном, и с турéцким султáном. Нó всё э́то бы́ло давнó . . . .

Тепéрь Лунёв живёт в э́том мáленьком гóроде со своéй сестрóй Елизавéтой. Ли́за[10] чáсто сиди́т с нáми и с интерéсом слýшает своегó брáта. Ря́дом с Лунёвым на жёлтом крéсле лежи́т и́ли сиди́т егó собáка Мáшка и тóже с больши́м удовóльствием слýшает своегó хозя́ина. Онá óчень довóльна свои́м хозя́ином. Мéсто на жёлтом крéсле—её, и онá всегдá óчень недовóльна мнóй, когдá я́ сижý на её мéсте.

На столé стои́т лáмпа с си́ним абажýром (shade), стои́т буты́лка с рóмом и лежи́т кáрта ми́ра. Лунёв пáльцем покáзывает мнé на кáрте Росси́ю, Аргенти́ну, Китáй . . . . Я́ курю́ и слýшаю. Ужé пóздно. Ли́за спи́т на своём крéсле, а Мáшка на своём. А мы́ с Лунёвым иногдá сиди́м тáк всю нóчь и разговáриваем до утрá.

Answer the following questions in Russian.

1. Почемý интерéсно слýшать Ю́рия Бори́совича? 2. Кéм бы́л Лунёв? О́н бы́л учи́телем? 3. Какóй óн человéк? 4. Когдá вы́ обы́чно разговáриваете с Лунёвым? 5. Вы́ обы́чно сиди́те с ни́м в вáшей комнáте? 6. Чтó вы́ дéлаете, когдá óн говори́т? 7. Каки́м гóлосом вы́ говори́те? 8. Вы́ тóже ви́дели вéсь ми́р? Чтó вы́ ви́дели? 9. Кáк Лизавéта слýшает своегó брáта? 10. Ктó ещё сиди́т в кабинéте? 11. Когó слýшает Мáшка, вáс и́ли Ли́зу? 12. Гдé стои́т крéсло, на котóром сиди́т Мáшка? 13. Почемý вы́ не сиди́те нá её мéсте? 14. Какóго цвéта крéсло Мáшки? 15. Чтó в буты́лке, котóрая стои́т на столé? 16. С чéм вы́ лю́бите пи́ть чáй? 17. Чéм Лунёв покáзывает на кáрте, гдé óн бы́л? 18. Ли́за и Мáшка слýшают Лунёва всю нóчь?

[10] Nickname for Елизавéта.

EXERCISE

Translate into Russian.

1. —With whom were you there last evening? —With her and with her sister. 2. I am very pleased with her. 3. —Did you speak with him this morning? —Yes, and I am very pleased with him. 4. I want to work with you. 5. I am very pleased with you and with them. 6. In the spring we always live at Olga's. 7. Spring in Europe is usually nice. 8. I don't know where he was in the summer, but I know that the summer was very hot. 9. —Where will you be in the fall? —If the fall is nice, we will be in the country. 10. Tonight the Russian historian will be at the theater with his pretty wife. 11. —Where were you last night? —I was at the concert with my old friend. 12. She works with Anna in the morning, but in the afternoon she works alone 13. They will be here in winter with their son. 14. I don't like winter; I don't like (it) when it is cold and I don't like the cold wind. 15. When I work late in the evening, I don't sleep at night. 16. What a cold night! 17. Her son thinks that he will be a writer! 18. That good student always listens to the professor with great interest. 19. When he was a young man, he lived with his family in China. 20. —Who was he? —He was an engineer. 21. My father was a teacher, and I want to be a teacher. 22. —Why do you smoke? —I can't help smoking. 23. We have been living in America three years.

VOCABULARY

Áзия Asia
алло́! hello! (on the telephone)
аппети́т appetite
А́фрика Africa
борщ borsch (soup)
буты́лка bottle
везде́ everywhere
весна́ spring
ве́тер (*gen.* **ве́тра**) wind; it's windy
вку́сный delicious, tasty (**вкус**, taste)
во́дка vodka
го́лос voice
господи́н Mr.
госпожа́ Mrs.
дива́н sofa, couch
до́лго[11] long, for a long time

[11] До́лго is used to denote the length of time it takes to perform an action. Давно́ (literally, "long ago") is used with the present tense in Russian to correspond to the English present perfect tense, to describe an action begun in the past and still continuing in the present, *e.g.*:

	О́н **до́лго жи́л** в Аме́рике.	He *lived* in America for a long time.
But:	О́н **давно́ живёт** в Аме́рике.	He *has been living* in America for a long time.

жёлтый yellow
жизнь (*fem.*; *loc.* **жи́зни**) life
жест gesture
за́втрак breakfast, lunch
интере́с interest
исто́рик historian
карто́фель (*masc., no pl.*) potato(es)
Кита́й China
ко́фе (*masc. indeclinable*) coffee
ле́вый left
лимо́н lemon
мел chalk
ме́сто place, space; seat
непло́хо not bad(ly)
о́сень (*fem.*) autumn, fall
па́лец (*gen.* **па́льца**) finger; toe
па́мять (*fem.*) memory
пото́м[12] then, next; later, afterwards
пра́вый right
президе́нт president
Росси́я Russia
ря́дом nearby, next door
ря́дом с (+*instr.*) beside, side by side, next to
сала́т salad
са́хар sugar
снача́ла at first, first
совсе́м quite, entirely
совсе́м не (**не́т**) not at all
тру́бка pipe
труд labor
удово́льствие pleasure
хозя́ин master; host; landlord
царь (*masc.*) tsar
чай tea

Verbs

(See also Section 1).
за́втракать (I)[13] to have breakfast (lunch)
обе́дать (I)[13] to have dinner
пить (I: **пью, пьёшь**, etc.) to drink
разгова́ривать (I)[13] to converse, have a conversation, talk
расска́зывать (I)[13] to narrate, tell (a story); **р. о** (+ *loc.*) tell about (someone or something)

Expressions

расскажи́те tell (*imperative*)
одно́ вре́мя at one time
всю но́чь all night
Ну что́ вы́ говори́те! You don't mean it! What are you talking about!
Не могу́ не (+ *inf.*) I can't help (doing something)
с трудо́м with difficulty

[12] Пото́м is used for the next of a series of actions. Тогда́ (then) means "at that time," *e.g.*, Э́то бы́ло до войны́; я **тогда́** бы́л ещё совсе́м молоды́м. That was before the war; *then* I was still quite young. *But:* Я́ снача́ла бы́л в шко́ле, а **пото́м** в университе́те. First I was in school, and *then* at the university.

[13] From now on, first conjugation verbs conjugated like чита́ть will be designated by the symbol (I) without forms of the present tense. First conjugation "consonant stems" (like писа́ть) will be designated by the same symbol plus the first and second persons singular, *e.g.*, писа́ть (I: пишу́, пи́шешь).

UNIT 12

Declension of nouns in singular, review, **174.** *Locative masculine in* **-ý/-ю́,** **175.** *Dative and locative ending* **-ии,** **176.** *Declension of Fem. II nouns in singular,* **177.** *Declension of neuter nouns in* **-мя,** *singular,* **178.** *Indeclinable nouns,* **179.** *The preposition* **на** *and the locative (supplement),* **181.** *Locative of personal pronouns,* **182.** *Adjective and pronoun-adjective declension in the singular, review,* **183.**

GRAMMAR

1. Declension of nouns in singular, review

In Unit 5, page 58, a preliminary survey was given of the three classes of Russian noun declensions. All the regular case forms in the singular of the first two classes of nouns have been presented, and will be reviewed and supplemented in this unit. Feminine nouns ending in **-ь** (Fem. II) will be introduced in Section 4 below.

Masculine, Neuter, and Fem. I Nouns

	Masculine		*Neuter*		*Fem. I*	
	Hard	Soft	Hard	Soft	Hard	Soft
Nom.	дом	автомоби́ль	окно́	по́ле	ко́мната	ку́хня
Gen.	до́ма[1]	автомоби́ля[1]	окна́	по́ля	ко́мнаты[5]	ку́хни
Dat.	до́му	автомоби́лю	окну́	по́лю	ко́мнате	ку́хне
Acc.	дом[2]	автомоби́ль[2]	окно́	по́ле	ко́мнату	ку́хню
Instr.	до́мом[3]	автомоби́лем	окно́м	по́лем	ко́мнатой[6] (-ою)	ку́хней (-ею)
Loc.	до́ме[4]	автомоби́ле[4]	окне́	по́ле	ко́мнате	ку́хне

[1] Some masculine nouns may take an alternative genitive ending **-у/-ю**. Most of these nouns denote divisible matter (like foodstuffs, tobacco, etc.), and the **-у/-ю** ending is used in a *partitive* meaning, when a quantity is referred to: *e.g.*, ско́лько/немно́го/фу́нт ри́су (rice), са́хару, ча́ю, таба́ку́ (tobacco), сы́ру, шокола́ду (chocolate), and a few others.

[2–6] See next page.

2. Locative masculine in -ý/-ю́

Some hard masculine nouns (mostly of one syllable) end in **-ý** in the locative singular after the prepositions **в** and **на**. This ending is always stressed:

пол	на полу́	on the floor
сад	в саду́	in the garden
лес	в лесу́	in the woods
у́гол	в углу́	in the corner
бе́рег	на берегу́	on the shore, bank
мост	на мосту́	on the bridge
Крым	в Крыму́	in the Crimea
Дон	на Дону́	on the Don, in the Don region
год	в про́шлом году́	(in the) last year
	в э́том году́	(in) this year

Similarly, a few soft masculine nouns of one syllable ending in **-й** have a locative singular in **-ю́** with **в** and **на**:

рай	в раю́	in paradise
край	на краю́	on the edge

With the preposition **о**, these nouns end in **-е** (usually unstressed): о са́д**е**, о ле́с**е**, о ра́**е**, etc.

Pattern Sentences

1. Во́т у́гол мое́й у́лицы. Я́ живу́ в до́ме на пра́вом углу́, а на ле́вом углу́ апте́ка.
2. У на́с е́сть ма́ленькая да́ча на берегу́ реки́.
3. У на́с та́м большо́й са́д. Я́ люблю́ рабо́тать в на́шем саду́.
4. Во́т на́ша да́ча. Напра́во по́ле, а нале́во ле́с. Как прохла́дно ле́том в лесу́!
5. Во́т река́ и мо́ст. Чья́ маши́на стои́т на мосту́? Где́ милиционе́р? Маши́на не должна́ стоя́ть на мосту́!

1. Here is the corner of my street. I live in the house on the right corner; on the left corner there's a drugstore.
2. We have a small summer cottage on the bank of a river.
3. We have a large garden there. I like to work in our garden.
4. Here is our summer cottage. On the right is a field, and on the left a wood. How cool it is in the summer in the woods!
5. Here is the river and the bridge. Whose car is parked on the bridge? Where is a policeman? A car should not be parked on a bridge!

[2] Masculine animate nouns have the accusative like the genitive: сы́н**а**, го́ст**я**, etc.
[3] Spelling Rule B (page 77) applies: това́рищ**ем**.
[4] The locative masculine ending **-ý/-ю́** is given in Section 2 below.
[5] Spelling Rule A (page 77) applies: кни́г**и**, да́ч**и**, etc.
[6] Spelling Rule B (page 77) applies: у́лиц**ей**, да́ч**ей**, etc.

Drill

Answer in complete sentences, using the word given in the right-hand column in your answer.

	Вопро́с	Отве́т
Model:	Где́ прия́тно бы́ть, когда́ жа́рко?	(лес)—Прия́тно бы́ть **в лесу́.**
1.	Где́ Шо́лохов писа́л «Ти́хий До́н?»	(Дон)
2.	Где́ вы́ лю́бите рабо́тать ле́том?	(сад)
3.	На чём лежи́т ковёр?	(пол)
4.	На чём стои́т ла́мпа?	(стол)
5.	Где́ стои́т на́ша да́ча?	(бе́рег)
6.	Где́ стои́т милиционе́р?	(у́гол)
7.	Где́ я́ ви́жу челове́ка?	(мост)
8.	Где́ вы́ ви́дели А́нну?	(шко́ла)
9.	Где́ Я́лта?	(Крым)
10.	Где́ вы́ бы́ли вчера́ днём?	(го́род)
11.	Где́ вы́ рабо́тали сего́дня у́тром?	(библиоте́ка)
12.	Когда́ вы́ бы́ли в Крыму́?	(про́шлый го́д)

3. The dative and locative ending -ии

Nouns of all three genders with the following nominative endings:

Masc. **-ий** [-ij]
Neut. **-ие** [-ijə]
Fem. **-ия** [-ijə]

have in the prepositional case the ending **-ии** [-ii].

Thus:

Nominative	*Locative*
ге́н**ий**	ге́н**ии** (о ге́нии)
зда́н**ие**	зда́н**ии** (о зда́нии)
Росс**и́я**	Росс**и́и** (в Росси́и)

The ending **-ии** is pronounced as two distinct **и**'s [-ii], without slurring.

Likewise, *feminine* nouns ending in the nominative in **-ия** take the ending **-ии** in the dative: Росс**и́я** (Russia), dative: Росс**и́и**.

Pattern Sentences

1. Росс**и́я** огро́мная страна́.
2. В Росс**и́и** была́ револю́ц**ия**.
3. Ку́к бы́л в Росс**и́и** по́сле револю́ц**ии**.

1. Russia is an immense country.
2. There was a revolution in Russia.
3. Cook was in Russia after the revolution.

4. Ра́ньше Смирно́в жи́л во Фра́нц**ии**.[7] О́н говори́т, что Фра́нц**ия** замеча́тельная страна́.	4. Formerly, Smirnov lived in France. He says that France is a wonderful country.
5. Я́ бо́льше люблю́ Ита́л**ию**. Мы́ ра́ньше жи́ли в Ита́л**ии**.	5. I like Italy more. We used to live in Italy.
6. Ле́том А́нна была́ с бра́том в А́нгл**ии**. Они́ о́чень лю́бят А́нгл**ию**.	6. In the summer Anna was in England with her brother. They like England very much.
7. Вы́ ви́дите то́ высо́кое зда́н**ие**? Моя́ конто́ра в э́том зда́н**ии**.	7. Do you see that tall building? My office is in that building.
8. За́втра бу́дет интере́сная ле́кц**ия** о ру́сской исто́р**ии**. Я́ бу́ду на э́той ле́кц**ии**.	8. Tomorrow there will be an interesting lecture on Russian history. I will be at that lecture.
9. Вчера́ ве́чером на собра́н**ии** я́ ви́дел Лунёва.	9. Last night I saw Lunyov at the meeting.

Drill

Translate into Russian.

1. My father loves Russia.
2. He lived in Russia for a whole year.
3. Tell (*imperative*) Maria about our work at the university.
4. We spoke a great deal about Russian history and about the Russian revolution.
5. Yesterday there was a lecture about England. I was at that lecture.
6. Yesterday we were all in the country. We love the country!
7. I have never been in Italy.
8. The concert was in this tall building.
9. In the morning I was at a meeting.

4. Declension of Fem. II nouns

These end in a soft consonant. They are declined as follows:

	жизнь "*life*"
Nom.	жизнь
Gen.	жи́зни
Dat.	жи́зни
Acc.	жизнь
Instr.	жи́знью
Loc.	жи́зни

[7] The form **во** is used in place of **в** before certain words beginning with a consonant cluster, especially when the first consonant is **в** or **ф**.

Two words, **мать** (mother) and **дочь** (daughter), add the suffix [**-ер-**] before the ending in all cases other than the nominative and accusative singular:

Nom.	мать	дочь
Gen.	ма́тери	до́чери
Dat.	ма́тери	до́чери
Acc.	мать	дочь
Instr.	ма́терью	до́черью
Loc.	ма́тери	до́чери

Note that all Fem. II nouns have an accusative like their nominative.

5. Declension of neuter nouns in -мя (singular)

A few neuter nouns end in **-мя** in the nominative singular (they must not be confused with feminines!). They add the suffix [**-ен-**] before the endings of all cases in the singular other than nominative and accusative:

	и́мя "*first name*"	**вре́мя** "*time*"
Nom.	и́мя	вре́мя
Gen.	и́мени	вре́мени
Dat.	и́мени	вре́мени
Acc.	и́мя	вре́мя
Instr.	и́менем	вре́менем
Loc.	и́мени	вре́мени

Pattern Sentences

1. О́сен**ью** О́льга была́ с ма́т**ерью** в А́нглии.
2. Я́ зна́ю одного́ англи́йского писа́теля, кото́рый всю́ жи́знь жи́л в Ита́лии. О́н бы́л о́чень дово́лен своей жи́зн**ью** та́м.
3. Во́т на ка́рте Сиби́р**ь**. В Сиби́р**и** зима́ дли́нная и холо́дная, а ле́то коро́ткое.
4. Ива́н Бори́сович лю́бит говори́ть о свое́й жи́зн**и**. О́н ду́мает, что его́ жи́зн**ь** о́чень интере́сная.
5. Те́ма но́вой пье́сы Уи́льямса любо́в**ь** и сме́рт**ь**.
6. Я́ ду́маю, что э́то не о́чень оригина́льная те́ма; все́ пи́шут о любв**и́** и о сме́рт**и**.

1. In the fall Olga was with her mother in England.
2. I know an English writer who lived in Italy all his life. He was very pleased with his life there.
3. Here on the map is Siberia. Siberia has (in Siberia there is) a long, cold winter, and a short summer.
4. Ivan Borisovich likes to talk about his life. He thinks his life is very interesting.
5. The theme of Williams' new play is love and death.
6. I don't think that's a very original theme; everyone is writing about love and death.

7. —Вы́ ви́дите ту́ зелёную две́р**ь**? —Да́, ви́жу. —Вы́ ви́дите, како́й но́мер на две́р**и**? —Не́т, не ви́жу.	7. —Do you see that green door? —Yes, I see it. —Can you see what number is on the door? —No, I can't.
8. —У ва́с е́сть вре́м**я** сего́дня ве́чером рабо́тать со мно́й? —Не́т, сего́дня ве́чером у меня́ не́т вре́м**ени**.	8. —Do you have time this evening to work with me? —No, this evening I have no time.

Drill

Put the nouns in parentheses in the proper case.

1. Андре́й лю́бит лежа́ть на (крова́ть).
2. Я́ ви́жу но́мер на (дверь).
3. Она́ всегда́ ду́мает о (смерть).
4. Ма́ть расска́зывает о свое́й (жизнь).
5. Она́ дово́льна свое́й (жизнь).
6. Э́тот писа́тель всегда́ пи́шет о (любо́вь).
7. Ма́ть дово́льна но́вой (крова́ть).
8. Я́ люблю́ её (дочь).
9. Я́ люблю́ говори́ть с её (дочь).
10. Я́ мно́го говорю́ о её (дочь).
11. У него́ не́т (мать).
12. Она́ живёт с (мать).
13. У кого́ е́сть (вре́мя)?
14. У меня́ не́т (вре́мя).
15. У э́той соба́ки не́т (и́мя).
16. Я́ пока́зываю письмо́ (мать).
17. Я́ посыла́ю пода́рок (сестра́).

6. Indeclinable nouns

Nouns of foreign origin are declined in Russian only if they end in a consonant (like телефо́н or автомоби́ль) or in **-а**/**-я** (like дра́ма or револю́ция). Nouns ending in the vowels **-е**, **-и**, **-о**, and **-у** are not declined; most of them are of neuter gender (all listed below except two):

желе́	jelly	метро́	subway
кафе́	cafe	пальто́	topcoat, overcoat
ко́фе (*masc.*)	coffee	ра́дио	radio
ви́ски	whisky	фо́то	photo
такси́	taxi	кенгуру́ (*masc.*)	kangaroo
кино́	movies	рагу́	ragout, stew

Also indeclinable are foreign geographical or personal names ending in the vowels listed above, *e.g.*, Миссу́ри, Ве́рди, Чика́го,

Пикассó, Кéннеди, etc. Similarly, place names in the Soviet Union, but of non-Russian origin, like Бакý[8] (Baku) or Сóчи[9] (Sochi) are indeclinable.

Pattern Sentences

1. Вóт стои́т **такси́.** Я́ никогó не ви́жу в **такси́.**
2. Мы́ ви́дели профéссора Пáвлова на стáнции **метрó.**
3. Москóвское **метрó** óчень удóбное и довóльно бы́строе.
4. Прóшлым лéтом мы́ жи́ли в Я́лте, а Кали́нины жи́ли в **Сóчи.** Мы́ почемý-то не óчень лю́бим **Сóчи.**
5. Мы́ вчерá бы́ли в **кинó** и ви́дели замечáтельный францýзский фи́льм.
6. Сегóдня прохлáдно; почемý ты́ без шля́пы и без **пальтó?** Гдé твоё **пальтó?**
7. Мóй сы́н живёт в Хáрькове, а дóчь в **Бакý.** (**Бакý** на берегý Каспи́йского мóря).
8. Я́ бы́л в И́таке, нó я́ почемý-то нé был в **Бýффало.**

1. There is a taxi standing. I don't see anyone in it.
2. We saw Professor Pavlov at the subway station (station of the subway).
3. The Moscow subway is very convenient and rather fast.
4. Last summer we lived in Yalta, and the Kalinins lived in Sochi. For some reason we don't like Sochi very much.
5. Yesterday we went to the movies and saw a wonderful French film.
6. Today it's cool; why aren't you wearing a hat and coat? Where is your coat?
7. My son is living in Kharkov, and my daughter in Baku. (Baku is on the shore of the Caspian Sea).
8. I have been in Ithaca, but for some reason I haven't been in Buffalo.

Drill

Answer in complete sentences, using the nouns in the right-hand column with a suitable preposition, or the word **нет.**

	Вопрóс	**Отвéт**
1.	Гдé ты́ бы́л, Ивáн?	(теáтр)
2.	Гдé А́нна?	(кинó)
3.	Гдé вы́ бы́ли вчерá?	(концéрт)
4.	Гдé вы́ ви́дели Андрéя?	(такси́)
5.	Чегó у вáс нéт?	(костю́м)
6.	Чегó нéт у Алёши?	(пальтó)
7.	Чегó нéт у Ни́ны?	(шля́па)
8.	Гдé вы́ бы́ли веснóй?	(Бýффало)
9.	Гдé слýжит вáш брáт?	(Вашингтóн)
10.	Чегó нéт у сестры́?	(рáдио)
11.	О чём вы́ дýмаете?	(Я́лта и Сóчи)

[8] An important center of oil industry on the Caspian Sea.
[9] A resort city on the Black Sea.

12. Где́ река́ Ле́на?	(Сиби́рь)
13. Где́ вы́ обыкнове́нно живёте?	(Аргенти́на)
14. Где́ живёт господи́н Карбу́чио?	(Перу́)

7. The preposition на and the locative (supplement).

The preposition **на** and not **в** (with the locative case) is used to express location with some nouns, including certain geographical nouns:

по́чта	на по́чте	at the post office
заво́д	на заво́де	at the plant
фа́брика	на фа́брике	at the factory
вокза́л	на вокза́ле	at the terminal
ста́нция	на ста́нции	at the station
Кавка́з	на Кавка́зе	in the Caucasus
Дон	на Дону́	in the Don region
Ура́л	на Ура́ле	in the Urals
Украи́на	на Украи́не	in the Ukraine

(See Unit 5, page 61, for the use of **на** with nouns denoting activities or events.)

Pattern Sentences

1. Ни́на слу́жит **на** по́чте, а Ива́н слу́жит в ба́нке.	1. Nina works at the post office, and Ivan works at the bank.
2. Сы́н А́нны Ива́новны рабо́тает **на** большо́м заво́де, а до́чь слу́жит в апте́ке.	2. Anna Ivanovna's son works at the big factory, and the daughter works in a drugstore.
3. Когда́ мы́ бы́ли в Сове́тском Сою́зе, мы́ бы́ли в Крыму́, но́ не́ были **на** Кавка́зе. У на́с бы́ло ма́ло вре́мени.	3. When we were in the Soviet Union, we visited the Crimea, but didn't go to the Caucasus. We had little time.
4. И́х до́чь живёт **на** Украи́не.	4. Their daughter lives in the Ukraine.
5. Она́ хорошо́ зна́ет Украи́ну: она́ жила́ **на** Украи́не це́лый го́д.	5. She knows the Ukraine well: she lived in the Ukraine a whole year.
6. Джо́нсон бы́л везде́: о́н бы́л в Сиби́ри, **на** Ура́ле и **на** Кавка́зе, но́ о́н почему́-то не́ был в Крыму́.	6. Johnson has been everywhere: he has been in Siberia, in the Urals, and in the Caucasus, but for some reason he hasn't been in the Crimea.
7. Писа́тель Шо́лохов жи́л **на** Дону́ и та́м о́н писа́л сво́й рома́н «Ти́хий До́н.»	7. The writer Sholokhov lived on the Don and there he wrote his novel *The Silent Don*.
8. Я́ всегда́ покупа́ю газе́ту **на** ста́нции.	8. I always buy my newspaper at the station.

Drill

Answer in complete sentences, using the word given in the right-hand column in your answer.

	Вопрóс	**Отвéт**
Model:	Гдé вы́ живёте?	(Бостóн)—Я́ живу́ в Бостóне.
1.	Гдé рабóтает Ивáн?	(завóд)
2.	Гдé вы́ слу́жите?	(пóчта)
3.	Гдé живёт Ивáн Петрóвич?	(Москвá)
4.	Гдé вы́ покупáете плáтье?	(магази́н)
5.	Гдé вы́ обыкновéнно ви́дите Áнну?	(стáнция)
6.	Гдé Ки́ев?	(Украи́на)
7.	Гдé чáсто жи́л Чéхов?	(Я́лта)
8.	Гдé ты́ живёшь лéтом?	(Кавкáз)
9.	Гдé Зи́мний дворéц (Winter Palace)?	(Ленингрáд)
10.	Гдé ты́ бу́дешь сегóдня вéчером?	(теáтр)
11.	Гдé Бори́с?	(концéрт)
12.	Гдé ты́ обыкновéнно рабóтаешь днём?	(библиотéка)
13.	Гдé зимá дли́нная?	(Сиби́рь)
14.	Гдé вáжный металлурги́ческий цéнтр?	(Урáл)

8. Locative of personal pronouns

Sing.	*Nom.*	я	ты	он ↘ онó ↙	онá
	Loc.	обо мнé	о тебé	о нём	о нéй
Pl.	*Nom.*	мы	вы	они́	
	Loc.	о нáс	о вáс	о ни́х	

Note the special forms of the preposition used with the first person singular pronoun мне: **обо** мнé; **во** мнé.

Pattern Sentences

1. Если ты́ **обо мнé** ду́маешь, я́ прóсто не понимáю, почему́ ты́ мнé не пи́шешь!
2. Я́ чáсто ду́маю **о вáс,** а вы́ **обо мнé** не ду́маете.
3. Моя́ мáть говори́т, что онá всегдá ду́мает **о нáс,** а что мы́ **о нéй** никогдá не ду́маем.

1. If you do think of me, I simply don't understand why you don't write me!
2. I often think of you, but you don't think of me.
3. My mother says that she is always thinking about us, but that we never think of her.

4. —Ка́к пожива́ет тво́й нача́льник? —Я́ не хочу́ говори́ть ни **о нём** ни о его́ жене́.

4. —How is your boss? —I don't want to talk about him or about his wife.

5. —Вы́ чита́ли э́ту пье́су? —Да́, чита́л. Но́ я́ не хочу́ говори́ть **о не́й.**

5. —Have you read that play? —Yes, I have. But I don't want to talk about it.

Drill

Translate the English in parentheses into Russian.

	Вопро́с		**Отве́т**	
1.	Что́ ты́ зна́ешь	(about me)?	Я́ ничего́ не зна́ю	(about you).
2.	Что́ вы́ зна́ете	(about us)?	Мы́ всё зна́ем	(about you).
3.	Что́ ты́ ду́маешь	(about Boris)?	Я́ ничего́ не ду́маю	(about him).
4.	Ты́ иногда́ ду́маешь	(about Maria)?	Да́, я́ ча́сто ду́маю	(about her).
5.	Что́ ты́ зна́ешь	(about Katya and Vera)?	Я́ ма́ло зна́ю	(about them).

9. Adjective and pronoun-adjective declensions in the singular, review

Most adjectives belong to the hard type and have the stress on the stem; some, however, have the accent on the ending which, for masculine nominative, is **-о́й** instead of **-ый** of the unstressed variant. A relatively small group of adjectives follows the soft pattern.

"Hard" type, or pattern, means that the final consonant of the stem is hard, and "soft" means that this consonant is soft (it is most often a soft **н** [ņ]). The vowels appearing after the final consonant in the different case and gender forms follow the usual pattern (the soft endings are never accented):

Hard:	**-а-**	**-о-**	**-у-**	**-ы-**
Soft:	**-я-**	**-е-**	**-ю-**	**-и-**

The endings of masculine and neuter adjectives in cases other than the nominative closely resemble the corresponding case forms of **он** and **оно́** (in the feminine, the similarity with the declension of **она́** is not consistent).

	Masculine-Neuter			*Feminine*		
		Hard	Soft		Hard	Soft
Nom.	[он/оно́]	но́вый/но́вое	си́ний/си́нее	[она́]	но́в**ая**	си́н**яя**
Gen.	**его́**	но́в**ого**	си́н**его**	**её**	но́в**ой**	си́н**ей**
Dat.	**ему́**	но́в**ому**	си́н**ему**	**ей**	но́в**ой**	си́н**ей**
Acc.	**его́**	[Like Nom. or Acc.]		**её**	но́в**ую**	си́н**юю**
Instr.	**им**	но́в**ым**	си́н**им**	**ей**	но́в**ой**	си́н**ей**
Loc.	**нём**	но́в**ом**	си́н**ем**	**ней**	но́в**ой**	си́н**ей**

Hard type with stress on the ending:

	Nom.	*Gen.*	*Dat.*	*Acc.*	*Instr.*	*Loc.*
Masc. *Neut.*	молод**о́й** молод**о́е**	молод**о́го**	молод**о́му**	—	молод**ы́м**	молод**о́м**
Fem.	молод**а́я**	молод**о́й**	молод**о́й**	молод**у́ю**	молод**о́й**	молод**о́й**

The spelling of the endings differs from the patterns given above in adjectives with stems ending in **г**, **к**, and **х** and in **ж**, **ч**, **ш**, and **щ**. In terms of spelling, the first group may be regarded as basically hard and the second (if the stress is *not* on the ending) as basically soft. In both groups there are a few deviations from the regular patterns in accordance with the spelling rules (see Unit 6, page 77).

Stems in г, к, and х, basically *hard* pattern. The masculine declension presents two deviations:

	Normal hard endings	Stems in **г**, **к**, **х**, e.g., ру́сский
Nom.	**-ый**	ру́сск**ий** (no **ы** after **г**, **к**, **х**!)
Gen.	-ого	normal
Dat.	-ому	normal
Acc.	[Like Nom. or Gen.]	
Instr.	**-ым**	ру́сск**им** (no **ы** after **г**, **к**, **х**!)
Loc.	-ом	normal

Neuter has the normal hard ending **-ое** in the nominative and accusative, and is like masculine in the other cases. Feminine follows the normal pattern.

Stems in ж, ч, ш, and щ (stress on the stem), basically *soft* pattern. Masculine and neuter, *e.g.*, хоро́ший, хоро́шее, follow the normal soft pattern (see above). Feminine presents two deviations:

	Normal soft endings	Stems in **ж**, **ч**, **ш**, **щ**, e.g., хоро́шая
Nom.	**-яя**	хоро́ш**ая** (no **я** after **ж**, **ч**, **ш**, **щ**!)
Gen.	-ей	normal
Dat.	-ей	normal
Acc.	**-юю**	хоро́ш**ую** (no **ю** after **ж**, **ч**, **ш**, **щ**!)
Instr.	-ей	normal
Loc.	-ей	normal

Some adjectives with stems in **г**, **к**, **х** and **ж**, **ч**, **ш**, **щ** have stressed endings, e.g., плохóй, плохóе, плохáя; большóй, большóе, большáя. They follow the regular hard pattern with only one exception: the instrumental ending in masculine and neuter is **-им**, not **-ым**.

It must be understood that the rules given above concern spelling, not pronunciation. Thus, the sounds [š] and [ž] remain hard even when the vowels **и** and **е** are written after them; and the sounds [ç̌] and [ş̌ç̌] remain soft even when followed by **а** or **у**.

Pronoun-adjective declension. Pronoun-adjectives have a declension which is similar to, but not entirely identical with, the adjective declension. The forms of the nominative and some forms of the accusative are distinct.

(1) *Declension of demonstratives.*

Declension of **э́тот**, *"this"*

	Masculine	*Neuter*	*Feminine*
Nom.	э́тот	э́то	э́та
Gen.	э́того	like masc.	э́той
Dat.	э́тому	like masc.	э́той
Acc.	like Nom. or Gen.	э́то	э́ту
Instr.	э́тим[10]	like masc.	э́той
Loc.	э́том	like masc.	э́той

Оди́н, "one," is declined like **э́тот**, but has final stress (одногó, одномý, etc.). The vowel **и** drops out in all cases other than the masculine singular nominative.

Declension of **тот**, *"that"*

	Masculine	*Neuter*	*Feminine*
Nom.	тот	то	та
Gen.	тогó	like masc.	той
Dat.	томý	like masc.	той
Acc.	like Nom. or Gen.	то	ту
Instr.	тем[10]	like masc.	той
Loc.	том	like masc.	той

(2) *Declension of possessives.*

Declension of **мой**, *"my," "mine"*

	Masculine	*Neuter*	*Feminine*
Nom.	мой	моё	моя́
Gen.	моегó	like masc.	моéй

[10] These stems become soft in the instrumental: [éţ] and [ţ].

Dat.	моему́	like masc.	мое́й
Acc.	like Nom. or Gen.	моё	мою́
Instr.	мои́м	like masc.	мое́й
Loc.	моём	like masc.	мое́й

Твой, "your," "yours," and **свой**, "one's own" are declined like **мой**.

Declension of **наш,** *"our," "ours"*

	Masculine	*Neuter*	*Feminine*
Nom.	наш	на́ше	на́ша
Gen.	на́шего	like masc.	на́шей
Dat.	на́шему	like masc.	на́шей
Acc.	like Nom. or Gen.	на́ше	на́шу
Instr.	на́шим	like masc.	на́шей
Loc.	на́шем	like masc.	на́шей

Ваш, "yours," "yours", is declined like **наш**.

(3) *Declension of* **весь**, *"all."*

	Masculine	*Neuter*	*Feminine*
Nom.	весь	всё	вся
Gen.	всего́	like masc.	всей
Dat.	всему́	like masc.	всей
Acc.	like Nom. or Gen.	всё	всю
Instr.	всем	like masc.	всей
Loc.	всём	like masc.	всей

(4) *Declension of interrogative pronouns.*

	кто, *"who"*	**что,** *"what"*
Nom.	кто	что
Gen.	кого́	чего́
Dat.	кому́	чему́
Acc.	кого́	что
Instr.	[кем]	[чем]
Loc.	ком	чём

Pattern Sentences

1. **Вся́** на́ша семья́ живёт тепе́рь вме́сте.	1. All our family is living together now.
2. Ма́ть должна́ ду́мать **обо все́й** семье́.	2. The mother has to think about the whole family.
3. Хоро́шая хозя́йка должна́ **всё** по́мнить и должна́ **обо всём** ду́мать.	3. A good housewife must remember everything and must think about everything.

4. Учи́тель недово́лен **всё́м** кла́ссом. О́н ка́ждый де́нь говори́т э́то **всему́** кла́ссу.
5. Ива́н Ива́нович люби́мый учи́тель **всего́** кла́сса.

4. The teacher is dissatisfied with the whole class. Every day he tells the whole class that.
5. Ivan Ivanovich is the favorite teacher of the whole class.

Drill

Put the words in parentheses in the correct case and translate.

1. У меня́ не́т (ве́сь те́кст).
2. У меня́ не́т (ве́сь перево́д).
3. Я́ до́лжен ду́мать обо (всё).
4. Я́ ви́дел (вся́ семья́).
5. Я́ ви́дел (вся́ пье́са).
6. Я́ дово́лен (вся́ семья́).
7. Я́ до́лжен ду́мать обо (вся́ семья́).

READING

В Сове́тском Сою́зе

1. Пе́рвая ча́сть

Вы́ вероя́тно ви́дели высо́кое зда́ние ря́дом с университе́том на углу́ э́той у́лицы? В э́том зда́нии на́ш студе́нческий клу́б.

Вчера́ в на́шем клу́бе бы́ло собра́ние. На э́том собра́нии Бо́б Ку́к чита́л докла́д о Сове́тском Сою́зе, где́ о́н бы́л в про́шлом году́ о́сенью. О́н бы́л та́м це́лый ме́сяц.

Мне́ бы́ло о́чень интере́сно слу́шать Ку́ка. Я́ не о́чень мно́го зна́ю об э́той стране́. Во́т всё, что я́ зна́ю: в Росси́и была́ револю́ция. До револю́ции та́м бы́л ца́рь, а по́сле револю́ции у ни́х бы́л во́ждь Ле́нин. По́сле Ле́нина вождём бы́л Ста́лин; по́сле Ста́лина, Хрущёв. Во вре́мя войны́ Сове́тский Сою́з бы́л на́шим сою́зником (ally). Сове́тский гражда́нин Ю́рий Гага́рин—пе́рвый астрона́вт. Сове́тский Сою́з огро́мная страна́. Та́м коммуни́зм, и та́м о́чень хо́лодно.

Э́то почти́ всё, что я́ зна́ю, и поэ́тому я́ слу́шал Ку́ка с больши́м интере́сом.

Ку́к говори́т, что Ленингра́д, бы́вшая (former) столи́ца Росси́и, замеча́тельно краси́вый го́род. Та́м е́сть одно́ осо́бенно краси́вое зда́ние—Зи́мний дворе́ц (palace), где́ до револю́ции жи́л ца́рь со свое́й семье́й. В Зи́мнем дворце́—музе́й Эрмита́ж.

На берегу́ Невы́ (Neva River)—поэти́ческий Ле́тний са́д. В э́том саду́ стои́т краси́вый, но́ просто́й ле́тний дворе́ц Петра́

Вели́кого.[11] Пётр Вели́кий люби́л простýю жи́знь и чáсто жи́л в э́том дворцé.

Бо́б не о́чень мно́го ви́дел в Ленингрáде, тáк кэк бы́л тáм то́лько три́ дня́. О́н жи́л в гости́нице «Асто́рия,» кото́рая стои́т на углý большо́й пло́щади и ýлицы Гéрцена. В Асто́рии у Кýка былá удо́бная ко́мната с вáнной. Мéбель в ко́мнате былá дово́льно богáтая и дово́льно старомо́дная (old-fashioned). На пи́сьменном столé стоя́ла огро́мная бро́нзовая (bronze) лáмпа—фáвн (faun), кото́рый игрáет на флéйте (flute). В Асто́рии éсть ресторáн, и Кýк обыкновéнно зáвтракал и обéдал тáм. Всё бы́ло дово́льно удо́бно, но́ о́чень до́рого.

Answer the following questions in Russian.

1. Гдé бы́ло собрáние? 2. О чём Кýк читáл доклáд? 3. Когдá о́н бы́л в Совéтском Сою́зе, и ско́лько врéмени о́н тáм бы́л? 4. Почемý мнé бы́ло интерéсно его́ слýшать? 5. Росси́я мáленькая странá? 6. Что́ я́ знáю о Росси́и? 7. Како́й го́род Ленингрáд? 8. Что́ о́н говори́л о Зи́мнем дворцé? 9. Гдé Кýк ви́дел Лéтний дворéц Петрá Вели́кого, и что́ о́н рассказывал о Петрé? 10. На берегý како́й реки́ Лéтний сáд? 11. В како́й гости́нице жи́л Кýк и что́ о́н о нéй дýмает?

2. Вторáя чáсть. (Second Part)

В Москвé, столи́це Совéтского Сою́за, Кýк жи́л двé недéли. Москвá о́чень большо́й и интерéсный го́род. Э́то полити́ческий и культýрный цéнтр страны́. Кýку тáм бы́ло о́чень интерéсно.

В цéнтре Москвы́ стои́т Крéмль.[12] Э́та истори́ческая чáсть го́рода—люби́мое мéсто Кýка в Москвé. Ря́дом с Кремлём, на Крáсной пло́щади, стои́т мавзолéй Лéнина. Кýк бы́л в мавзолéе и ви́дел Лéнина и Стáлина, кото́рые тáм лежáли (тепéрь в мавзолéе лежи́т то́лько Лéнин).

О́н расскáзывал, что бы́л в Большо́м теáтре на балéте «Лебеди́ное о́зеро»[13] Чайко́вского и на о́пере «Ти́хий До́н.» О́н о́чень лю́бит балéт и о́перу и бы́л о́чень дово́лен и балéтом и о́перой.

О́н бы́л конéчно и в моско́вском метро́, гдé «во́здух всегдá свéжий, как в дерéвне», как говори́л его́ ги́д-перево́дчик.

Кýк бы́л в огро́мном здáнии но́вого Моско́вского университéта, гдé о́н слы́шал лéкцию об англи́йской литератýре (по-рýсски, конéчно). По́сле лéкции оди́н совéтский студéнт (его́ и́мя бы́ло Бори́с) покáзывал Кýку университéт и всё емý объясня́л.

[11] Пётр Вели́кий, Peter the Great (1672–1725).

[12] The Kremlin is the walled center of the city, containing palaces, churches, government buildings, etc.

[13] Swan Lake.

Бори́с дово́льно хорошо́ зна́ет англи́йский язы́к, кото́рый о́н изуча́ет уже́ три́ го́да. Люби́мый писа́тель Бори́са—Хэ́мингуэй, кото́рого о́н чита́л в оригина́ле. Ма́рка Твэ́йна о́н то́же о́чень лю́бит. Ку́к изуча́л ру́сский язы́к то́лько два́ го́да, но́ та́к как о́н всегда́ бы́л хоро́шим студе́нтом, ему́ бы́ло не сли́шком тру́дно говори́ть с Бори́сом по-ру́сски. Снача́ла они́ говори́ли об университе́те, пото́м об астрона́вте Гага́рине, пото́м немно́го о поли́тике, исто́рии и эконо́мике, пото́м о литерату́ре. Ку́к хорошо́ зна́ет ру́сскую литерату́ру, котору́ю о́н чита́ет и в оригина́ле и в перево́де. Они́ говори́ли и по-ру́сски и по-англи́йски и бы́ли о́чень дово́льны свои́м разгово́ром.

Answer the following questions in Russian.

1. Ско́лько вре́мени Ку́к жи́л в Москве́? 2. Почему́ Ку́ку бы́ло так интере́сно та́м? 3. В како́м теа́тре о́н бы́л и что́ о́н ви́дел? 4. Что́ о́н говори́л о Кремле́? 5. Где́ мавзоле́й Ле́нина? 6. Что́ о́н ви́дел в мавзоле́е? 7. Что́ говори́л о метро́ его́ ги́д-перево́дчик? 8. Где́ ещё бы́л Ку́к? 9. О чём профе́ссор чита́л ле́кцию? 10. Что́ бы́ло по́сле ле́кции? 11. Что́ о́н расска́зывал о Бори́се? 12. О чём они́ говори́ли? 13. Ка́к Ку́к чита́ет ру́сскую литерату́ру?

3. Тре́тья ча́сть. (Third Part)

По́сле Москвы́ Ку́к бы́л неде́лю на Украи́не. Снача́ла о́н бы́л в Ки́еве, столи́це Украи́ны. Ки́ев краси́вый го́род на берегу́ Днепра́. Ки́ев и Дне́пр игра́ли ва́жную ро́ль в исто́рии Росси́и. В Ха́рькове (то́же на Украи́не) Ку́к бы́л на огро́мном автомоби́льном и тра́кторном заво́де. Ха́рьков тепе́рь большо́й индустриа́льный це́нтр.

О кли́мате Сове́тского Сою́за Ку́к расска́зывает, что, когда́ о́н бы́л в Ленингра́де, та́м уже́ бы́ло дово́льно хо́лодно, в Москве́ бы́ло прохла́дно, а на Ура́ле о́н да́же ви́дел сне́г (snow). А на берегу́ Чёрного мо́ря, наприме́р в Я́лте в Крыму́, и в Со́чи на Кавка́зе, бы́ло ещё тепло́, как ле́том.

Ни в Сиби́ри, ни в центра́льной А́зии Ку́к не́ был: у него́ бы́ло сли́шком ма́ло вре́мени.

Я́ бы́л о́чень дово́лен всём э́тим докла́дом. Я́ тепе́рь ещё бо́льше хочу́ изуча́ть ру́сский язы́к. Я́ ду́маю, что э́то о́чень ва́жно.

Answer the following questions in Russian.

1. Ско́лько вре́мени Ку́к бы́л на Украи́не? 2. Что́ о́н говори́л о Ки́еве? 3. Где́ о́н бы́л в Ха́рькове? 4. Что́ о́н говори́т о Ха́рькове? 5. Кака́я пого́да была́ в Ленингра́де? 6. Что́ о́н ви́дел на Ура́ле? 7. Ка́к бы́ло на Кавка́зе и в Крыму́? 8. Где́ Ку́к не́ был? Почему́? 9. Что́ я́ тепе́рь хочу́ де́лать и почему́?

EXERCISE

Translate into Russian.

1. About me. 2. About you (*sing.*). 3. About you (*pl.*). 4. About us. 5. About everything. 6. About him. 7. About his sister. 8. About her. 9. About her father. 10. With me. 11. With him. 12. With his mother and sister. 13. We are having dinner with her. 14. I saw Olga at the theater and her mother at the movie. 15. He lives in Leningrad and works in a drugstore. 16. His daughter lives in the Crimea and works in a post office. 17. Yalta is on the shore of the Black Sea. 18. Their son lives in California (Калифо́рния), and they seldom talk about him. 19. I have never been in Siberia, but I have been in the Ukraine. 20. Our school is in this big building. 21. I heard his lecture at a meeting yesterday in our club. 22. I seldom write to my mother, because I have no time, but I always think about her. 23. Do you know his mother? 24. I know only his daughter and his sister. 25. She often talks about them and about their friend. 26. They were at my lecture. 27. I've heard so much about Italy! 28. When Tolstoy was young, he lived in the Caucasus. He was then an officer. 29. My old dog always lies on the floor next to the chair on which I am sitting. 30. He remembers everything and talks about everything. 31. My friend seldom talks about his daughter. 32. What did you hear about me? 33. They are writing a book together with me. I help them and they help me. 34. Today is a fine fall day. 35. It is difficult for him to work at this plant. 36. He always writes at night. 37. I am very pleased with my life. 38. Our teacher knows a great deal about Russia and especially about the Russian revolution.

VOCABULARY

апте́ка drugstore
банк bank
бе́рег shore, coast, bank (of a river)
ва́жный important
вождь (*masc.*) leader
во́здух air
гид guide
год year
граждани́н citizen
гражда́нка citizeness
да́ча summer cottage
дли́нный long
докла́д report, talk, speech
заво́д plant, factory
замеча́тельный remarkable, wonderful
зда́ние building

зелёный green
кино́ (*neut. indecl.*) movies, movie theater
кли́мат climate
клуб club
коро́ткий short
ле́кция lecture
лес woods, forest
люби́мый favorite, beloved
любо́вь (*gen.* **любви́**; *instr.* **любо́вью**) love
маши́на machine; car
метро́ (*neut. indecl.*) subway
мо́ре sea
мост bridge
нале́во on (to) the left
напра́во on (to) the right
но́мер number; room number; hotel room
обыкнове́нно usually, ordinarily
огро́мный huge, enormous, immense
осо́бенно especially
пальто́ (*neut. indecl.*) coat, overcoat
перево́дчик (*fem.* **-ица**) translator, interpreter
пло́щадь (*fem.*) square
по́чта post office; mail
просто́й simple, plain
прохла́дно cool
про́шлый past, last
ра́ньше earlier, formerly, before (*adv.*)
револю́ция revolution
роль (*fem.*) role, part
сад garden; orchard
смерть (*fem.*) death
собра́ние meeting; collection
ста́нция station
такси́ (*neut. indecl.*) taxi
те́ма theme, subject
у́гол (*gen.* **угла́**) corner; angle
университе́т university
фильм film
часть (*fem.*) part
язы́к language; tongue

Verbs

изуча́ть (I) to learn, study (*trans.*)
служи́ть (II: **служу́, слу́жишь**) to serve, work, be employed

Expressions

ско́лько вре́мени? how long?
во вре́мя (+ *gen.*) during
та́к как since, as, because
почему́-то for some reason
чита́ть докла́д to give a talk
игра́ть ро́ль to play a part
ещё бо́льше even more
в про́шлом году́ last year
в э́том году́ this year

Geographical Terms

А́нглия England
англи́йский English (*adj.*)
Дон Don (river)
Ита́лия Italy
Кавка́з Caucasus (mountains)
моско́вский of Moscow (*adj.*)
Сиби́рь (*fem.*) Siberia
Украи́на Ukraine
Ура́л Urals (mountains)
Фра́нция France

UNIT 13

GRAMMAR

1. Nominative plural of nouns

The great majority of nouns take one of two types of ending in the nominative plural:

		Spelling Hard	Soft
1. Most *masc.*, all *fem.*	[ɨ/i]	**-ы**	**-и**
2. Some *masc.*, all *neut.*	[a]	**-а**	**-я**

Examples:

		Singular	*Plural*
Type 1 [ɨ] or [i]	*Masc.*	сто́л [stól.] гость [góşţ.] музе́й [muẓẹ́j.] оте́ц (aţéc)	стол**ы́** [stal.ɨ́] го́ст**и** [góşţ.i] музе́**и** [muẓẹ́j.i] отц**ы́** (atcɨ́)
	Fem. I	стена́ [şţin.á] кни́га [kņíg.ə] ку́хня [kúxņ.ə]	сте́н**ы** [şţén.ɨ] кни́г**и**[1] [kņíg̡.i] ку́хн**и** [kúxņ.i]
	Fem. II	дверь [ḑʏ̡ẹ́ŗ.]	две́р**и** [ḑʏ̡ẹ́ŗ.ɨ]

[1] Spelling Rule A (page 77) applies.

Type 2 [a]	*Masc.*	hard: дом [dóm.] soft: учи́тель [uçíţiļ.]	дома́ [dam.á] учителя́ [uçiţiļ.á]
	Neut.	hard: окно́ [akn.ó] soft: по́ле [póļ.ə]	о́кна [ókn.ə] поля́ [paļ.á]

Feminine and neuter nouns frequently undergo a shift of stress in the plural; this distinguishes the nominative plural from the genitive singular, *e.g.*:

Nominative Singular	*Genitive Singular*	*Nominative Plural*
страна́	страны́	стра́ны
окно́	окна́	о́кна
по́ле	по́ля	поля́

In some words the vowel **е** of the stem becomes **ё** under stress:

жена́	жены́	жёны
сестра́	сестры́	сёстры
о́зеро (lake)	о́зера	озёра

Drill

Change the following nouns from nominative singular to nominative plural. The exercise below does *not* include masculine nouns with plurals in **-а**/**-я**; a list of these will follow in Section 4. [In the exercise below masculines (as well as feminines) end only in **-ы**/**-и** (neuters of course end in **-а**/**-я**).] Nouns with a shift of stress in the plural are marked with an asterisk (*).

*стол	гость	исто́рик	*вода́	*страна́
*сад	ку́хня	инжене́р	*рука́	*ме́сто
оте́ц	геро́й	прия́тель	*нога́	*сло́во
уро́к	ле́кция	учи́тельница	*река́	*по́ле
това́рищ	дверь	*вождь	*гора́	*мо́ре (sea)
ко́мната	да́ча	пло́щадь	*цена́	*окно́
*каранда́ш	кре́сло	де́вушка	*сестра́	*письмо́
карти́на	зда́ние	кварти́ра	*жена́	*о́зеро

2. Nominative plural of pronoun-adjectives

It has been seen that the third person pronoun **они́** is used for *all three genders* in the plural. The same is true of the plural of pronouns and adjectives; none of these have distinct gender forms in the plural.

Like **они́**, the possessives, the demonstrative **э́тот**, and the numeral **оди́н** take the ending **-и** in the plural:

Singular	*Plural*
мой [mój.]	мои́ [maj.í]
твой [tvój.]	твои́ [tvaj.í]
свой [svój.]	свои́ [svaj.í]
наш [náš.]	на́ши [náš.ɨ]
ваш [váš.]	ва́ши [váš.ɨ]
чей, чья, чьё [stem ç̌j.]	чьи [ç̌j.í]
э́тот [ét.ət]	э́ти [éţ.i][2]
оди́н [aḑín]	одни́ [aḑņí][2]

The demonstrative **тот** has the plural **те.**[2] **Весь** (all) has the plural **все,** all genders.

3. Nominative plural of adjectives

In the nominative plural, hard adjectives take the ending **-ые** (но́в**ые**). Soft adjectives take the ending **-ие** (си́н**ие**). With adjectives with stems ending in the consonants **г, к, х, ж, ч, ш,** and **щ** the ending is spelled **-ие** (ру́сск**ие**, хоро́ш**ие**):

Masculine Singular	*Plural All Genders*
но́вый [nóv.əj]	но́вые [nóv.ɨji]
молодо́й [məlad.ój]	молоды́е [məlad.íji]
си́ний [şíņ.əj]	си́ние [şíņ.iji]
ти́хий [ţíx.əj]	ти́хие [ţíx̧.iji]
хоро́ший [xaróš.əj]	хоро́шие [xaróš.ɨji]

Drills

A. *Form plurals of the following.*

э́тот у́мный студе́нт	э́тот сове́тский писа́тель	э́то тру́дное пра́вило
то́ высо́кое зда́ние	ва́ш но́вый уче́бник	ру́сский ца́рь
твоя́ приле́жная учени́ца	твоё дли́нное пальто́	чьё окно́?
мо́й у́зкий боти́нок	на́ш си́ний автомоби́ль	э́та америка́нская семья́
на́ш глу́пый ма́льчик	э́та удо́бная крова́ть	вся́ кни́га

B. *Read and translate.*

1. В э́том го́роде е́сть дли́нн**ые** у́лицы.
2. Э́тот писа́тель пи́шет ску́чн**ые** рома́н**ы**.[3]

[2] Note that the final stem consonant of these words softens in the plural.
[3] The accusative plural of *inanimate* nouns, all genders, is the same as the nominative plural.

3. Э́то на́ши но́вые студе́нты.
4. —Кто́ э́ти молоды́е писа́тели? —Они́ ру́сские.
5. —Чьи́ э́ти ма́ленькие ма́льчики? Они́ ва́ши? —Да́, мои́.
6. В э́той шко́ле хоро́шие ученики́.
7. Я́ чита́ю рома́н «Дни́ и но́чи» Си́монова.
8. На́м нужны́ удо́бные кре́сла.
9. Мои́ сёстры пи́шут мне́ коро́ткие пи́сьма.
10. В э́той ко́мнате больши́е о́кна.
11. Каки́е огро́мные поля́!
12. В на́шей кварти́ре больши́е све́тлые ко́мнаты.
13. У неё краси́вые то́нкие ру́ки.
14. У него́ хоро́шие секрета́рши.
15. —Де́вочки! Чьи́ э́ти но́вые тетра́ди? Они́ ва́ши? —Не́т, они́ то́й де́вочки.
16. Я́ люблю́ ни́зкие крова́ти.

C. *Translate into Russian.*

1. What long novels!
2. Where are your pretty secretaries?
3. Everyone likes comfortable apartments.
4. In Italy we saw narrow old streets.
5. These little boys are my pupils.
6. Who are these little girls? They are my sister's pupils.
7. I love green fields.
8. My sister has slender legs.
9. Whose are these blue notebooks?
10. Where do you buy your armchairs?
11. These were his last words.
12. My students are very good. They are intelligent and diligent.

4. Masculine nouns with nominative plurals in -á/-я́

Following are some of the more important nouns taking **-á/-я́** in the masculine plural. This ending is stressed throughout the plural in the masculine (in contrast to the genitive singular of these words, which has stress on the stem):

Nominative Singular	*Nominative Plural*	
дом	дома́	houses
по́езд	поезда́	trains
го́род	города́	cities
лес	леса́	forests
ве́чер	вечера́	evenings
бе́рег	берега́	shores
го́лос	голоса́	voices

цвет	цвета́	colors
но́мер	номера́	numbers
а́дрес	адреса́	addresses
глаз	глаза́	eyes
до́ктор	доктора́	doctors
профе́ссор	профессора́	professors
дире́ктор	директора́	directors
учи́тель	учителя́	teachers

Drills

A. *Change the words in parentheses to plural and translate.*

1. На э́той у́лице то́лько (ни́зкий до́м).
2. В э́том го́роде (дли́нная у́лица).
3. В Сиби́ри (огро́мный ле́с).
4. Я́ люблю́ (ста́рый истори́ческий го́род).
5. В на́шей кварти́ре (больша́я ко́мната).
6. (Э́тот по́езд тако́й ме́дленный).
7. (Бе́рег) Во́лги о́чень (краси́вый).
8. У на́с вчера́ бы́ли (францу́зский профе́ссор).
9. У меня́ е́сть (хоро́ший студе́нт).
10. В э́той шко́ле (серьёзный учи́тель).
11. В э́том го́роде е́сть (хоро́ший до́ктор).
12. (Чья́ э́та ру́сская газе́та)?
13. (Како́й дли́нный ве́чер!).
14. На полу́ лежа́т (ста́рый журна́л).

B. *Translate into Russian.*

1. Where are those old forests?
2. These good students are mine.
3. I love big cities.
4. Whose are these new cars?
5. The trains here are very fast.
6. Do you have good teachers?
7. Do you see those red walls?
8. The shores of the Black Sea are very beautiful.
9. These doctors are very expensive.
10. Who are these professors?
11. We need new tables.
12. Whose teachers are they?
13. What nice homes!
14. They buy expensive lamps.
15. Our professors are very serious.
16. She has blue eyes.

5. Nominative plurals in -ья

A few masculine and neuter nouns form plurals in **-ья** [-já] or [-jə]. Some of these undergo change of final stem consonant, insertion of a suffix, shift of stress, etc.:

Nominative Singular	*Nominative Plural*	
муж	мужья́	husbands
друг	друзья́	friends
сын	сыновья́	sons
брат	бра́тья	brothers
стул	сту́лья	chairs
лист	ли́стья[4]	leaves[4]
перо́	пе́рья	pens
де́рево	дере́вья	trees

Drills

A. *Translate into English.*

1. Бори́с дру́г Ва́ди́ма. Бори́с и Вади́м друз**ья́**.
2. Мои́ сыно**вья́** живу́т в А́нглии; оди́н сы́н живёт в Ло́ндоне, а друго́й в Ливерпу́ле.
3. Мои́ бра́**тья** мно́го рабо́тают; оди́н бра́т слу́жит в ба́нке, а друго́й в апте́ке.
4. —Чьи́ э́ти пе́**рья**? —Чёрное перо́ моё, а чьё зелёное—я́ не зна́ю.
5. Все́ э́ти сту́**лья** о́чень дороги́е; то́лько э́тот ма́ленький сту́л дешёвый.
6. В на́шем саду́ ста́рые и то́лстые дере́**вья**, и то́лько одно́ де́рево та́м молодо́е и то́нкое.
7. Все́ ли́ст**ья** на э́том де́реве жёлтые, но́ оди́н ли́ст ещё зелёный.

B. *Translate into Russian.*

1. They say that they are our friends.
2. Where are all the new pens?
3. Whose brothers are they?
4. In what store do (they) sell cheap chairs?
5. My sons seldom write to me.
6. In our forest there are thick, tall trees.
7. These chairs are not comfortable.
8. Does she have friends?
9. Their sons work in this factory.
10. Nina's brothers live in Italy.
11. The leaves on this old tree are red.
12. She always buys expensive pens.
13. Our friends were then in Europe.
14. Here are our husbands.

[4] But листы́, "sheets (of paper)."

6. Miscellaneous categories of nominative plurals

The following words are not irregular in the nominative plural, but require special attention:

Nominative Singular	*Nominative Plural*	
мать	ма́тери	mothers
дочь	до́чери	daughters
вре́мя	времена́	times
и́мя	имена́	names
(челове́к, "person")	лю́ди	people
(ребёнок, "child")[5]	де́ти	children

Live Сосе́д ("neighbor") has the irregular nominative plural сосе́ди (soft throughout the plural).

Drills

A. *Read and translate.*

1. Во́т её до́ч**ери** и её сын**овья́**.
2. У неё две́ до́чери и два́ сы́на.
3. Смирно́вы дру**зья́** моей ма́тери.
4. У меня́ зде́сь два́ дру́га.
5. Все́ ма́т**ери** ду́мают, что и́х **де́ти** замеча́тельные.
6. Мо́й му́ж всегда́ говори́т, что на́ш **ребёнок** глу́пый, а все́ други́е **де́ти** у́мные.
7. Андре́й и И́горь дру**зья́** мое́й до́чери. Э́то краси́вые име**на́**, пра́вда?[6]
8. Ма́ма говори́т, что Ива́н Петро́вич о́чень ми́лый челове́к. Пра́вда,[7] ма́ма ду́мает, что все́ **лю́ди** ми́лые.
9. Во́т сосе́**ди** мое́й ста́ршей до́чери. Я́ не зна́ю и́х име**на́**.
10. —Ка́к и́мя э́той соба́ки? —У неё не́т и́мени.
11. —Ско́лько вре́мени вы́ жи́ли в А́фрике? —Два́ го́да.
12. Ма́ленький Ко́ля зна́ет все́ време**на́** го́да: о́сень, зи́му, весну́ и ле́то.
13. О́н зна́ет, что е́сть четы́ре вре́мени го́да.
14. —Вы́ бу́дете за́втра на конце́рте? —Не́т, у меня́ не́т ни биле́та ни вре́мени.
15. —У ни́х е́сть **де́ти?** —Да́, е́сть. У ни́х оди́н **ребёнок.**

B. *Translate into Russian.*

1. This is my mother's room.
2. Here are our mothers.
3. Her daughters are very beautiful.
4. This is our daughter's friend.
5. She has nice friends.
6. We have friends in Moscow.
7. They never have time!
8. We don't remember their names.
9. —How long did your neighbors live in Europe? —A whole year.
10. —Where are your sons? —They are at my mother's.

[5] There is a word дитя́ (neuter singular), "child," which is now archaic and poetic.
[6] Isn't it? aren't they?, etc.
[7] True.

11. Their children are very nice.
12. —Whose child is this? —This is my neighbor's child.
13. We have good neighbors.
14. I like Russian names.

C. *Translate the words in parentheses and mark the stress. Remember that the numerals* 2, 3, *and* 4 *take the genitive singular.*

Вопро́с	Отве́т
1. У ва́с е́сть сёстры?	Да́, у меня́ (two sisters).
2. В коридо́ре е́сть о́кна?	Да́, та́м (three windows).
3. В ва́шей ко́мнате е́сть кре́сла?	Да́, в мое́й ко́мнате (four armchairs).
4. У неё е́сть до́чери?	Да́, у неё (two daughters).
5. Зде́сь е́сть озёра?	Да́, зде́сь (two lakes).
6. Все́ мужья́ на собра́нии?	Не́т, то́лько (two husbands).
7. Где́ на́ши жёны?	Не́ зна́ю. Зде́сь то́лько (two wives).
8. Все́ доктора́ живу́т зде́сь?	Не́т, то́лько (two doctors).
9. Все́ э́ти поля́ ва́ши?	Не́т, то́лько (two fields).
10. Все́ э́ти дома́ но́вые?	Не́т, то́лько (four homes).

7. The reciprocal pronoun дру́г дру́га

The reciprocal pronoun **дру́г дру́га** corresponds to English "one another," "each other." The first word never changes; the second is declined:

Gen.	дру́г дру́га
Dat.	дру́г дру́гу
Acc.	дру́г дру́га
Instr.	дру́г дру́гом
Loc.	дру́г о дру́ге

E.g.: Они́ лю́бят **дру́г дру́га.** They like each other.
Мы́ помога́ем **дру́г дру́гу.** We help one another.

Prepositions are inserted between the two words:

Мы́ мно́го разгова́риваем **дру́г с дру́гом.**
Вади́м и О́льга ча́сто ду́мают **дру́г о дру́ге.**

Drill

Translate into Russian.

1. We love each other.
2. Boris and Anna often talk with one another.
3. Do they send each other letters?
4. They do not like one another.
5. We do not understand one another.
6. They seldom talk about one another.

READING

Уро́к геогра́фии

На уро́ке геогра́фии учи́тель обыкнове́нно пока́зывает на́м на ка́рте ра́зные стра́ны и расска́зывает на́м о ни́х.

Но́ не все́ ученики́ слу́шают учи́теля. Хоро́шие и приле́жные ученики́ всегда́ слу́шают со внима́нием и задаю́т у́мные вопро́сы. Но́ вы́, мо́жет бы́ть, хоти́те зна́ть, что́ де́лают во вре́мя уро́ка те́ лени́вые ученики́, кото́рые не слу́шают учи́теля? Одни́ спя́т, други́е разгова́ривают дру́г с дру́гом и расска́зывают дру́г дру́гу ра́зные глу́пые исто́рии.

Сего́дня, на уро́ке геогра́фии, учи́тель говори́т о Сове́тском Сою́зе. На стене́ в кла́ссе больша́я ка́рта СССР. Учи́тель пока́зывает на́м на ка́рте моря́ и ре́ки э́той огро́мной страны́. О́н пока́зывает на́м где́ леса́, где́ сте́пи, где́ го́ры. Во́т высо́кие Кавка́зские го́ры. Эльбру́с са́мая высо́кая гора́ Кавка́за. На э́той горе́ всегда́ лежи́т сне́г. Во́т озёра. Са́мое большо́е и глубо́кое о́зеро— Байка́л. Во́т Во́лга. Э́то о́чень дли́нная река́, но́ са́мые дли́нные ре́ки Сове́тского Сою́за в Сиби́ри. Учи́тель пока́зывает на́м сове́тские города́ и грани́цы СССР.

Но́ во́т, оди́н учени́к, кото́рый не слу́шал о чём це́лый ча́с говори́л учи́тель и кото́рый расска́зывал своему́ сосе́ду, каки́е интере́сные детекти́вные фи́льмы о́н ви́дел и говори́л с ни́м о футбо́ле, на кото́ром о́н неда́вно бы́л, вдру́г задаёт учи́телю вопро́с: —А почему́ я́ не ви́жу на ка́рте реку́ Миссиси́пи? Ну́, что́ де́лать с таки́м ученико́м?

Answer the following questions in Russian.

1. Что́ сего́дня пока́зывает учи́тель на ка́рте? 2. Кто́ его́ слу́шает со внима́нием? 3. Кто́ его́ не слу́шает? 4. Что́ е́сть в Сове́тском Сою́зе? 5. О чём оди́н учени́к расска́зывает своему́ сосе́ду? 6. О чём э́тот учени́к вдру́г спроси́л учи́теля?

CONVERSATION

Бе́дная продавщи́ца!

В магази́не. **Покупа́тельница.** (Же́нщина с неприя́тным лицо́м и неприя́тным го́лосом). **Продавщи́ца.** (О́чень молода́я де́вушка с приятным лицо́м и приятным го́лосом.)

Покуп.—У ва́с е́сть ле́тние костю́мы и пла́тья?

Прод.—Коне́чно, е́сть. У на́с о́чень большо́й вы́бор. Како́го цве́та вы́ хоти́те костю́м и како́го цве́та пла́тье?

Покуп.—Я́ ещё не зна́ю. Покажи́те мне́, что́ у ва́с е́сть.

Прод.—Како́й ва́ш разме́р? Во́т, пожа́луйста. Зде́сь костю́мы, а зде́сь блу́зки и пла́тья. Ви́дите: ю́бки тепе́рь у́зкие, а жаке́ты коро́ткие и широ́кие. Э́то са́мая после́дняя мо́да! О́чень краси́во.

Покуп.—Да́, ви́жу. Ужа́сная мо́да! И каки́е высо́кие це́ны! Э́то сли́шком до́рого! У ва́с е́сть други́е костю́мы?

Прод.—У на́с е́сть и дешёвые. Во́т э́ти костю́мы то́лько два́ дня́ как у[8] на́с в магази́не. Чёрные, наприме́р, о́чень краси́вые. Ви́дите: ю́бки широ́кие, а жаке́ты у́зкие. После́дняя мо́да!

Покуп.—Э́то то́же после́дняя мо́да? И то́лько два́ дня́ как вы́ и́х продаёте?[8] По-мо́ему, я́ ви́дела э́ти костю́мы в про́шлом году́. А ско́лько вре́мени вы́ зде́сь слу́жите?

Прод.—Кто́, я́?

Покуп.—Да́, вы́.

Прод.—Я́? . . . два́ дня́.

Answer the following questions in Russian.

1. Что́ ну́жно покупа́тельнице? 2. Кака́я после́дняя мо́да? 3. Почему́ да́ма не покупа́ет пе́рвый костю́м, кото́рый е́й пока́зывает продавщи́ца? 4. Како́й вопро́с да́ма задаёт продавщи́це? 5. Почему́ она́ его́ задаёт?

READING FOR VOCABULARY REVIEW

Го́род

Что́ е́сть в ка́ждом большо́м го́роде?

В ка́ждом большо́м го́роде е́сть больши́е и ма́ленькие дома́ и зда́ния; е́сть дли́нные и коро́ткие у́лицы. Е́сть у́лицы широ́кие и у́зкие. В ка́ждом го́роде е́сть гла́вная у́лица: в Москве́, наприме́р, э́то у́лица Го́рького (Gorky Street), в Ленингра́де знамени́тый Не́вский проспе́кт (Nevsky Prospect).

В ка́ждом большо́м го́роде е́сть теа́тры, музе́и, па́рки, пло́щади, па́мятники; е́сть дешёвые и дороги́е рестора́ны и гости́ницы; е́сть шко́лы, институ́ты, библиоте́ки и университе́т; е́сть обыкнове́нные магази́ны и е́сть универма́ги.

[8] . . . то́лько два́ дня́ как . . . only two days that (since); . . . как вы́ и́х продаёте, that (since) you have been selling them.

В ка́ждом го́роде—большо́м и́ли ма́леньком—е́сть лю́ди бога́тые и е́сть бе́дные, е́сть лю́ди счастли́вые и е́сть несча́стные.

Answer the following questions in Russian.

1. Каки́е больши́е города́ вы́ зна́ете? 2. В большо́м го́роде все́ дома́ больши́е? 3. Что́ вы́ зна́ете о Не́вском проспе́кте? 4. Что́ е́сть в ка́ждом большо́м го́роде? 5. Каки́е та́м живу́т лю́ди?

Шко́ла

В ка́ждой шко́ле е́сть кла́ссные ко́мнаты, е́сть ученики́ и учени́цы, е́сть учителя́ и учи́тельницы. Учителя́ объясня́ют уро́ки в кла́ссе. Они́ объясня́ют пра́вила и задаю́т уро́ки (зада́ния), кото́рые ученики́ должны́ гото́вить до́ма.

Приле́жные, у́мные ученики́ слу́шают, что́ говори́т учи́тель, хорошо́ де́лают зада́ния и обыкнове́нно получа́ют хоро́шие отме́тки.

Лени́вые ученики́ ничего́ не де́лают. Они́ не слу́шают объясне́ния учи́теля и иногда́ да́же не зна́ют, где́ и́х уче́бники и где́ и́х тетра́ди. Они́ и́ли ничего́ не чита́ют и́ли чита́ют то́лько глу́пые кни́ги, пою́т глу́пые пе́сни и говоря́т то́лько о футбо́ле. Таки́е ученики́ получа́ют плохи́е отме́тки, но́ э́то и́м всё равно́.

Answer the following questions in Russian.

1. Что́ де́лают учителя́ в кла́ссе? 2. Каки́е ученики́ слу́шают учи́теля? 3. Что́ ученики́ должны́ де́лать до́ма? 4. Что́ ча́сто де́лают лени́вые ученики́?

Университе́т

В ка́ждом университе́те е́сть аудито́рии и библиоте́ки, е́сть студе́нты, студе́нтки и профессора́.

Профессора́ чита́ют ле́кции. Студе́нты запи́сывают то́, что ва́жно и пото́м, до́ма, чита́ют свои́ запи́ски. Иногда́ по́сле ле́кции они́ задаю́т вопро́сы профе́ссору.

В конце́ го́да все́ студе́нты де́ржат экза́мены. Хоро́шие студе́нты выде́рживают экза́мены, а плохи́е не́т. Те́ студе́нты, кото́рые выде́рживают экза́мены, получа́ют дипло́мы.

Answer the following questions in Russian.

1. Что́ де́лают профессора́? 2. Что́ запи́сывают студе́нты во вре́мя ле́кции? 3. Что́ они́ иногда́ де́лают по́сле ле́кции? 4. Что́ все́ студе́нты де́лают в конце́ го́да?

Универма́г

В универма́ге продавцы́ и продавщи́цы продаю́т ра́зные ве́щи, как наприме́р: пла́тья, ю́бки и блу́зки, гото́вые костю́мы, пиджаки́, брю́ки, руба́шки, шля́пы, боти́нки. Покупа́тели покупа́ют э́ти ве́щи.

Во́т э́тому высо́кому господи́ну нужны́ руба́шки. Продавщи́ца спра́шивает, како́й его́ разме́р и пока́зывает ему́ руба́шки, но́ высо́кий господи́н говори́т, что э́ти руба́шки сли́шком дороги́е. Тогда́ она́ пока́зывает ему́ други́е, дешёвые, и о́н и́х покупа́ет. (Вы́бор в магази́не дово́льно ма́ленький.)

Нале́во—отде́л ме́бели. Та́м продаю́т столы́, сту́лья, буфе́ты, ра́зные кре́сла, крова́ти, кни́жные по́лки и ковры́. Во́т молода́я па́ра покупа́ет ме́бель. Она́ хо́чет э́ти сту́лья, а му́ж хо́чет те́. Жена́ хо́чет си́ние кре́сла, а о́н хо́чет зелёные. Они́ спо́рят. Продавщи́ца ду́мает: мо́жет быть э́то и́х пе́рвый спо́р, но́, коне́чно, не после́дний.

Напра́во отде́л посу́ды. Та́м продаю́т стака́ны, ча́шки, таре́лки, ва́зы. Во́т э́той то́лстой же́нщине в жёлтом пла́тье нужны́ бе́лые ча́шки. Продавщи́ца говори́т е́й, что сего́дня в магази́не е́сть то́лько си́ние и зелёные, но́ за́втра бу́дут и бе́лые и кра́сные. Но́ же́нщина в жёлтом пла́тье о́чень недово́льна: е́й нужны́ ча́шки сего́дня, а не за́втра!

Answer the following questions in Russian.

1. Кто́ продаёт в универма́ге? 2. Кто́ покупа́ет та́м ра́зные ве́щи? 3. Каки́е, наприме́р, ве́щи покупа́ют в магази́не? 4. Что́ ну́жно высо́кому господи́ну? 5. Како́й вопро́с задаёт ему́ продавщи́ца? 6. Почему́ о́н не покупа́ет те́ руба́шки, кото́рые она́ ему́ снача́ла пока́зывает? 7. Каки́е о́н покупа́ет? 8. Како́й вы́бор в э́том отде́ле? 9. Что́ мы́ ви́дим в отде́ле ме́бели? 10. Что́ покупа́ет молода́я па́ра и о чём они́ спо́рят? 11. Что́ ду́мает продавщи́ца, когда́ слы́шит э́тот спо́р? 12. Что́ мы́ ви́дим в отде́ле посу́ды? 13. Что́ ну́жно то́лстой же́нщине в жёлтом пла́тье? 14. Что́ е́й говори́т продавщи́ца? 15. Почему́ покупа́тельница так недово́льна?

EXERCISES

Translate into Russian.

1. We need good historians. 2. In summer the trees are green, but in fall their leaves are yellow or red. 3. These students write down all that their professors say. 4. I think that that is unnecessary. They must write down only what (that which) is important. 5. Boris needs new suits. He says that all his expensive suits are already old.

6. Her daughters are journalists. 7. The saleswomen in this department store are very good, but they say that they have too much work. 8. I think they need one more saleswoman. 9. The old cities which we saw in Italy were very interesting. 10. Her sons write letters to me every week. Sometimes I answer, and sometimes I don't (answer). But they don't care. 11. Sergey has friends who live in our house. 12. In our capital there are beautiful parks, monuments, museums, long streets, and comfortable and expensive hotels. 13. Yesterday we had company (guests); we drank and sang old songs. 14. She has beautiful eyes. 15. —Do you have any brothers? —Yes, I have two brothers: one is an engineer and the other is a writer. 16. My brothers and their wives live in the center of Boston. 17. He (gives) lectures well and his lectures are almost always interesting. 18. He likes to buy shirts, suits, and overcoats. 19. All schoolboys and schoolgirls must prepare their lessons every day. That is very important. 20. These are very difficult rules. 21. Some students get good grades; other students get poor grades. 22. They like one another very much. 23. We often talk with each other. 24. We need white plates and blue cups. 25. We always buy furniture and china in this department store.

VOCABULARY

бéдный poor
аудитóрия auditorium, lecture room
блýзка blouse
боти́н.ок (*gen.* **-ка**) shoe
брю́ки (*pl. only*) trousers
вдруг suddenly
вещь (*fem.*) thing
внимáние attention
вы́бор choice
глáвный main, chief
глубóкий deep
горá mountain
готóвый ready
грани́ца boundary, frontier
дéвочка (little) girl
дéрево tree
дéти (*pl.*) children
другóй other; another
задáние task, assignment
запи́ска note
знамени́тый famous, celebrated
лист leaf (*pl.* **ли́стья**) sheet (*pl.* **листы́**)
лю́ди (*pl. only*) people
мáльчик boy
мóда fashion, style
несчáстный unhappy, unfortunate
объяснéние explanation
обыкновéнный ordinary, customary
óзеро lake
отмéтка grade, mark
пáра couple, pair
пéсня song
пиджáк jacket, coat
пóезд train
покупáтель (*fem.* **-ница**) customer
посýда (*collective*) dishes, china

продав.е́ц (*gen.* **-ца́**) salesman
продавщи́ца saleswoman
разме́р size, measure
ра́зный (*mostly pl.*) various[9]
ребён.ок (*gen.* **-ка**) child (*sing. only*)
руба́шка shirt
са́мый most (*with adjectives*)
снег (*loc.* **в/ на снегу́**) snow
спор argument
СССР (pronounce [esesesér], *indecl.*) U.S.S.R.
степь (*fem.*) steppe, prairie
счастли́вый happy, fortunate
таре́лка plate
тетра́дь (*fem.*) copybook, school notebook
то́нкий thin, fine
ужа́сный terrible, horrible
универма́г (**универса́льный магази́н**) department store
ю́бка skirt

Verbs

гото́вить (II: **гото́влю, гото́вишь**) to prepare; to cook
задава́ть (I: **задаю́, задаёшь**) to assign; **задава́ть вопро́с** to ask a question
запи́сывать (I) to note down
получа́ть (I) to receive, get
спо́рить (II: **спо́рю, спо́ришь**) to argue

Expressions

одни́ . . . други́е some . . . others
то́, что what; that which
Что́ де́лать? What can one do? What is to be done?
чита́ть ле́кцию to give a lecture, to lecture
держа́ть экза́мен to take an exam
выде́рживать экза́мен to pass an exam
вре́мя го́да season
гото́вый костю́м ready-made suit
са́мый после́дний very latest

[9] Observe that други́е means "different" in the sense of "other," while ра́зные means "different" in the sense of "various."

UNIT 14

Verbal Aspects, 206.

GRAMMAR

1. The category of aspect in the Russian verb

We have seen that the Russian verb has only three tense forms: a present, a past, and a future. There is in addition to tense, however, another category in the Russian verb system, that of *aspect*.

Nearly all Russian verbs are of either the *imperfective* or the *perfective* aspect. All verbs given until now have been *imperfective*.

Imperfective verbs are used to describe:

(1) actions in progress over a period of time without any reference to completion or termination (*He was*, or *is*, *writing letters*); (2) actions performed repeatedly (*He writes*, or *wrote*, *home every week—often*); and (3) actions spoken of in general terms, without reference to an actual performance at any particular time (*My father spoke five languages; she buys her hats in Paris.*)

Perfective verbs are used to describe actions that have been or will be brought to completion or termination (She bought a hat; I will write you tomorrow).

In very general terms, then, an imperfective verb means: an action is (was or will be) in progress (continuously or as a series of repeated acts). A perfective verb means: an action has been (or will be) performed, something has been or will be done.

In most cases imperfective and perfective verbs fall into pairs in which the two verbs are identical (or very close) in meaning but different in aspect. One such pair is писáть and написáть; both verbs mean *to write*, the first being *imperfective* and the second *perfective*.

The English and the Russian verb systems are based on different kinds of distinctions and no precise equivalence between the two sets of forms can be established; the correlations, however, are as follows (considering the past tense only):

Yesterday he *was writing* all day.
Вчера́ о́н **писа́л** весь де́нь. (imperf.)

He *wrote* (*used to write*) every day.
О́н **писа́л** ка́ждый де́нь. (imperf.)

He *wrote* Russian and English very well.
О́н о́чень хорошо́ **писа́л** по-ру́сски и по-англи́йски. (imperf.)

He *wrote* (*has written*) this letter this morning.
О́н **написа́л** э́то письмо́ сего́дня у́тром. (perf.)

He *wrote* to Olga yesterday.
О́н вчера́ **написа́л** О́льге. (perf.)

2. Aspect and tense

Perfective verbs speak of actions that have reached (or will reach) a terminal point, not of actions as processes unfolding in time; they have, therefore, no present tense, since "present" means that an action is currently in progress, or that a state or condition is present "now," at the time when the statement is made. Perfective verbs have only two tenses: a past (meaning that something has been done) and a future (meaning that something will be done).

Imperfective verbs have all three tenses: present, past, and future.

Formation of tenses. Perfective verbs do not have any special endings different from those of imperfective verbs. The past tense forms are similar for both aspects; thus:

Imperfective: писа́л, писа́ло, писа́ла, писа́ли.
Perfective: написа́л, написа́ло, написа́ла, написа́ли.

In the future tense perfective verbs are conjugated with the same types of endings as imperfective verbs in the present: thus написа́ть is conjugated exactly like писа́ть, but with *future* meaning:

я́ напишу́, ты́ напи́шешь, etc.
I *shall* write, *shall* have written, etc.

The future of imperfective verbs is formed with the future of the auxiliary verb быть and the infinitive: я́ бу́ду писа́ть, ты́ бу́дешь писа́ть, etc.: I shall write, shall be writing, etc.

The difference in meaning of the two aspect forms in the future parallels the difference between them in the past tense:

Imperfective Future

За́втра я́ **бу́ду писа́ть** весь де́нь. I'll write (be writing) all day tomorrow.	(action in progress)
О́н **бу́дет** на́м ча́сто **писа́ть.** (or: ка́ждую неде́лю, etc.) He will write to us often, every week, etc.	(repeated action)
Я́ **бу́ду** ва́м **писа́ть** то́лько по-ру́сски. I will write to you only in Russian.	(action in general, not one specific performance)

Perfective Future

Я́ ему́ **напишу́** за́втра. I will write to him tomorrow.	(future completed action)

The same distinction applies to the use of the infinitive:

В кла́ссе мы́ должны́ **писа́ть** по-ру́сски. In class we must write in Russian.	(imperf.) (action in general)
Я́ хочу́ за́втра ему́ **написа́ть.** I want to write to him tomorrow.	(perf.) (action to be completed)

To sum up the aspect and tense system:

IMPERFECTIVE ASPECT		
Past an action *was* in progress: о́н писа́л	*Present* an action *is* in progress: о́н пи́шет	*Future* an action *will be* in progress: о́н бу́дет писа́ть

PERFECTIVE ASPECT	
Past an action *has been* completed: о́н написа́л	*Future* an action *will be* completed: о́н напи́шет

3. Forms of the aspects

Perfective verbs differ from corresponding imperfective verbs in several ways; there is no one definite pattern in this type of correlation.

In the case of the verbs писа́ть—написа́ть, the difference between the two aspect forms is that the perfective has a prefix, **на-**, while the imperfective has none. Many other verbs have non-prefixed imperfectives with perfectives formed by adding one of several prefixes *e.g.*:

Imperfective	*Perfective*
чита́ть (чита́ю—pres.)	прочита́ть (прочита́ю—future)
де́лать (де́лаю—pres.)	сде́лать[1] (сде́лаю—future)
игра́ть (игра́ю—pres.)	сыгра́ть[2] (сыгра́ю—future)
звони́ть (звоню́—pres.)	позвони́ть (позвоню́—future)
гото́вить (гото́влю—pres.)	пригото́вить (пригото́влю—future)

In these examples the prefixes change only the aspect of the verbs; their meaning remains unchanged. (In other combinations, prefixes may affect not only the aspect of a verb, but its meaning as well.)

A small number of pairs consist of two verbs derived from different roots; two such pairs are given below:

Imperfective: **говори́ть**		*Perfective:* **сказа́ть** (to say, tell)[3]	
Present	*Past*	*Future*	*Past*
говорю́	говори́л	скажу́	сказа́л
говори́шь	говори́ло	ска́жешь	сказа́ло
говори́т	говори́ла	ска́жет	сказа́ла
говори́м	говори́ли	ска́жем	сказа́ли
говори́те		ска́жете	
говоря́т		ска́жут	

Imperfective: **брать**		*Perfective:* **взять** (to take)	
Present	*Past*	*Future*	*Past*
беру́	брал	возьму́	взял
берёшь	бра́ло	возьмёшь	взя́ло
берёт	брала́	возьмёт	взяла́
берём	бра́ли	возьмём	взя́ли
берёте		возьмёте	
беру́т		возьму́т	

Pattern Sentences

Писа́ть (*imperfective*), **написа́ть** (*perfective*).

1. Моя́ сестра́ уже́ два́ го́да **пи́шет** кни́гу, но́ пока́ она́ **написа́ла** то́лько пе́рвую главу́.

1. My sister has been working on (writing) a book now for two years, but so far she has written (finished writing) only the first chapter.

[1] A voiceless consonant before a voiced consonant sounds voiced (see Unit 3, page 28); thus сде́лать is pronounced [zd̨élət].

[2] When a prefix consisting of a consonant like **с-** (or ending in a consonant like **под-** or **от-**) is combined with a verb beginning with **и** the consonant is not softened, but instead **и** becomes **ы**: **с** + игра́ть = сыгра́ть. The same is true phonetically when **с**, **от**, or **под** as prepositions precede a noun beginning in **и-**, *e.g.*, с Ива́ном, [sɨvánəm].

[3] Сказа́ть is the perfective of говори́ть only in the sense of "to say," "tell." In the sense of "to speak," "talk," говори́ть has another perfective, which will be given in Unit 25.

2. Она́ вероя́тно **бу́дет писа́ть** её ещё го́д и́ли два́. — 2. She will probably be writing it for another year or two.
3. Ко́ля **прочита́л** мне́ письмо́, кото́рое о́н то́лько что **написа́л** свое́й сестре́. — 3. Kolya has read me the letter which he has just written to his sister.
4. Вы́ зна́ете, что э́та писа́тельница **написа́ла** уже́ два́ рома́на? — 4. Do you know that this writer has written two novels already?
5. Когда́ я́ наконе́ц **напишу́** мою́ статью́, я́ ва́м её **прочита́ю.** — 5. When I finally get my article written, I shall read it to you.
6. —Мы́ за́втра обо всём **напи́шем** отцу́. —Вы́ ка́ждый де́нь говори́те, что **напи́шете** ему́ за́втра. — 6. —Tomorrow we will write to Father about everything. —Every day you say that you'll write to him tomorrow.
7. Я́ **писа́л** четы́ре часа́ и **написа́л** то́лько э́то письмо́! — 7. I've been writing for four hours, and I've written only this letter!

Drills

A. *Choose the correct form of the verb and translate.*

1. Вчера́ Ве́ра (писа́ла/написа́ла) два́ часа́.
2. О́н говори́т, что (о́н напи́шет/бу́дет писа́ть) на́м ка́ждый де́нь.
3. Я́ должна́ за́втра (писа́ть/написа́ть) Бори́су.
4. Когда́ вы́ (бу́дете писа́ть/напи́шете) Ни́не?
5. Я́ вчера́ (написа́л/писа́л) весь де́нь.
6. Я́ е́й ско́ро (бу́ду писа́ть/напишу́).

B. *Translate into Russian.*

1. He wrote Father a long letter.
2. The children say that they will write to us often.
3. I wrote to Nina yesterday and will write her again tomorrow.
4. Lena wrote for three hours.
5. She wrote two letters.

Pattern Sentences

Чита́ть (*imperfective*), **прочита́ть** (*perfective*).

1. Алёша **чита́л** вчера́ весь де́нь и **прочита́л** ве́сь э́тот дли́нный рома́н. — 1. Alyosha was reading all day yesterday and read that whole long novel.
2. Ле́на **прочита́ла** то́лько полови́ну э́того рома́на. — 2. Lena has read only half of that novel.
3. За́втра, е́сли у неё бу́дет вре́мя, она́ **прочита́ет** ещё две́ главы́. — 3. If she has time tomorrow, she will read two more chapters.
4. Мы́ **бу́дем** ка́ждый де́нь **чита́ть** ру́сскую газе́ту; на́м нужна́ пра́ктика. — 4. We shall read a Russian newspaper every day; we need practice.
5. А́нна то́лько что **прочита́ла** ва́шу интере́сную статью́. — 5. Anna has just read your interesting article.

6. Ле́том я́ **чита́л** Достое́вского. Я́ **прочита́л** рома́ны «Идио́т» и «Бра́тья Карама́зовы».

6. In the summer I was reading Dostoyevsky. I read the novels *The Idiot* and *The Brothers Karamazov*.

Drills

A. *Choose the correct form of the verb and translate.*

1. Я́ (бу́ду чита́ть/прочита́ю) ва́м своё письмо́.
2. Тепе́рь вы́ должны́ (чита́ть/прочита́ть) то́лько по-ру́сски.
3. Ле́на (чита́ла/прочита́ла) вчера́ пе́рвую главу́, и тепе́рь бу́дет чита́ть втору́ю.
4. Снача́ла я́ (бу́ду чита́ть/прочита́ю) письмо́, а пото́м мы́ бу́дем разгова́ривать.
5. Я́ до́лжен (чита́ть/прочита́ть) его́ письмо́, тогда́ я́ бу́ду зна́ть, о чём (о́н пи́шет/напи́шет).
6. Когда́ я́ бу́ду во Фра́нции, я́ (бу́ду чита́ть/прочита́ю) то́лько францу́зские газе́ты.

B. *Translate into Russian.*

1. I have read only half of his letter.
2. We shall read a lot in the summer.
3. He will read us her letter.
4. I shall read you what Father writes.
5. I've read only two words, but I already know what he wants.
6. I shall read less in the winter.

Pattern Sentences

Де́лать (*imperfective*), **сде́лать** (*perfective*).

1. —Что́ вы́ **де́лали** вчера́? —Я́ ничего́ не **де́лал.** Я́ отдыха́л.
2. Мы́ ещё не зна́ем, что́ мы́ **бу́дем де́лать** ле́том.
3. Мо́й му́ж всё лю́бит **де́лать** са́м. О́н, наприме́р, са́м **сде́лал** э́ти по́лки.
4. —Почему́ ты́ ещё не **сде́лал** э́то упражне́ние? —У меня́ не́ было вре́мени. Я́ **сде́лаю** его́ ве́чером.
5. Я́ не зна́ю, что́ мне́ **де́лать** с Ко́лей. О́н тако́й эгои́ст!
6. Где́ моё перо́? Что́ ты́ с ни́м **сде́лал?**
7. Мэ́ри хорошо́ говори́т по-францу́зски, но́ она́ ещё **де́лает** оши́бки.
8. Вчера́ в кла́ссе она́ **сде́лала** две́ оши́бки.

1. —What did you do yesterday? —I didn't do anything. I relaxed.
2. We don't know yet what we shall be doing in the summer.
3. My husband likes to make everything himself. For instance, he made these shelves himself.
4. —Why haven't you done that exercise yet? —I had no time. I'll do it this evening.
5. I don't know what to do with Kolya. He is so selfish!
6. Where is my pen? What have you done with it?
7. Mary speaks French well, but she still makes mistakes.
8. In class yesterday she made two mistakes.

Drills

A. *Choose the correct form of the verb and translate.*

1. Я́ ещё не зна́ю, что́ я́ (бу́ду де́лать/сде́лаю) за́втра.
2. Что́ ты́ (де́лал/сде́лал)!
3. О́н хорошо́ перево́дит Шекспи́ра, но́ э́тот перево́д о́н (де́лал/сде́лал) пло́хо.
4. Я́ должна́ (де́лать/сде́лать) э́то упражне́ние! Сего́дня у меня́ не́т вре́мени, но́ за́втра я́ его́ (сде́лаю/бу́ду де́лать).

B. *Translate into Russian.*

1. Why did you make this mistake?
2. I know that she will make this mistake again in her translation.
3. He doesn't know yet what he will do in the winter.
4. I did it every day.
5. Yesterday we did all that we had to do.
6. What did you do with the letter?
7. —What did you do yesterday? —We read.

Pattern Sentences

Игра́ть (*imperfective*), **сыгра́ть** (*perfective*).

1. Пиани́ст Во́льский вчера́ прекра́сно **игра́л.** О́н осо́бенно хорошо́ **сыгра́л** ва́льс Шопе́на.
1. The pianist Volski played marvellously yesterday. He played a waltz by Chopin especially well.
2. Мы́ вчера́ **игра́ли** в те́ннис с Ива́ном. Мы́ **сыгра́ли** четы́ре па́ртии.
2. I played tennis yesterday with Ivan. We played four games.
3. Я́ **сыгра́ю** ва́м мело́дию, кото́рую я́ то́лько что слы́шал.
3. I shall play you a tune which I have just heard.
4. По́сле конца́ семе́стра я́ **бу́ду** ка́ждый де́нь **игра́ть** на роя́ле.
4. After the end of the semester, I shall play the piano every day.
5. Во́льский наконе́ц **сыгра́л** сона́ту, кото́рую я́ та́к люблю́!
5. Volski at last played the sonata which I like so much.
6. Как то́лько хозя́йка **сыгра́ет**[4] мазу́рку, мы́ бу́дем обе́дать.
6. As soon as the hostess plays[4] the mazurka we are going to have dinner.

Drills

A. *Choose the correct form of the verb and translate.*

1. Вчера́ мо́й му́ж (игра́л/сыгра́л) весь ве́чер в ка́рты.
2. А я́ (игра́ла/сыгра́ла) то́лько две́ па́ртии и бо́льше я́ не хоте́ла (игра́ть/сыгра́ть).
3. Е́сли хоти́те, я́ по́сле обе́да (бу́ду игра́ть/сыгра́ю) но́вое танго́.
4. Е́сли хоти́те, я́ ча́сто (бу́ду игра́ть/сыгра́ю) ва́м.

[4] Как то́лько + perfective future—corresponds to English present.

B. *Translate into Russian.*

1. They never play cards.
2. My son played tennis with Anna.
3. They played three games, and she didn't want to play any more.
4. I shall play only one game and then I shall work.
5. He will play with us in winter.
6. Who will play with him?
7. We often played cards in winter.

Pattern Sentences

Говори́ть (*imperfective*), **сказа́ть** (*perfective*).

1. На́ш нача́льник опя́ть мно́го **говори́л** на собра́нии и, как обы́чно, не **сказа́л** ничего́ интере́сного.[5]	1. Our boss again talked a great deal at the meeting and, as usual, said nothing interesting.
2. Оте́ц то́лько что мне́ **сказа́л,** что учи́тель **говори́л** с ни́м[6] обо мне́.	2. Father just told me that the teacher talked to him[6] about me.
3. Я́ **скажу́** е́й, что она́ не должна́ та́к **говори́ть** с ма́терью.[6]	3. I shall tell her that she should not talk that way to her mother.[6]
4. Андре́й то́лько что **сказа́л** О́льге, что о́н её лю́бит. Наконе́ц!	4. Andrey has just told Olga that he loves her. At last!
5. На́ш ма́ленький Ко́ля ещё не **говори́т.** О́н мо́жет то́лько **сказа́ть** «па́па», «ма́ма» и «Ко́ко» (Ко́ля).	5. Our little Kolya doesn't talk yet. He can only say "papa," "mama," and "Koko" (Kolya).
6. Когда́ жена́ мне́ **ска́жет,**[7] что́ она́ хо́чет де́лать за́втра, я́ ва́м сейча́с же позвоню́.	6. When my wife tells me what she wants to do tomorrow, I will call you up at once.
7. Е́сли вы́ ему́ э́то **ска́жете,**[7] вы́ бу́дете непра́вы. Э́то бу́дет большо́й оши́бкой.	7. If you tell him that, you will be wrong. It will be a great mistake.

Drills

A. *Choose the correct form of the verb and translate.*

1. Кто́ вчера́ (говори́л/сказа́л) на собра́нии?
2. Кто́ за́втра (бу́дет говори́ть/ска́жет) на собра́нии?
3. Когда́ вы́ (бу́дете говори́ть/ска́жете) Серге́ю, что экза́мен бу́дет за́втра?
4. За́втра профе́ссор (бу́дет говори́ть/ска́жет) о сме́рти Пу́шкина.
5. Ива́н на́м за́втра (бу́дет говори́ть/ска́жет), где́ о́н живёт.

[5] Ничего́ (nothing) takes the genitive case of adjectives.

[6] Говори́ть/сказа́ть (in the sense of "to say," "tell") takes the *dative* of the person told. But говори́ть (in the sense of "to speak," "talk") takes **с** and the *instrumental* only.

[7] Observe again that Russian uses the future (usually perfective) with когда́, е́сли, как то́лько to refer to a future action, though English generally employs the present.

B. *Translate into Russian.*

1. Does her little daughter talk already?
2. Who said that the concert was dull?
3. I shall tell him that his article is very good.
4. She always talks a great deal.
5. They will not tell him what the professor said of him.
6. Zoya told me that she speaks English well.
7. He did not want to talk to me.

Pattern Sentences

Брать (*imperfective*), **взять** (*perfective*).

1. Ле́на всегда́ **берёт** все́ мои́ ве́щи!	1. Lena always takes all my things!
2. Зимо́й она́ ча́сто **брала́** мои́ кни́ги!	2. In the winter she often took my books!
3. Вчера́ она́ **взяла́** мо́й уче́бник.	3. Yesterday she took my school book.
4. Е́сли она́ за́втра опя́ть его́ **возьмёт,** я́ скажу́ ма́ме.	4. If she takes it again tomorrow, I'll tell Mama.
5. О́сенью Алёша **бу́дет бра́ть** уро́ки англи́йского языка́.	5. In the fall Alyosha will take English lessons.
6. Пока́ о́н **взя́л** то́лько четы́ре уро́ка.	6. So far he has taken only four lessons.
7. Я́ **взя́л** э́ту пласти́нку у Ни́ны.[8] Я́ ча́сто **беру́** у неё[8] пласти́нки.	7. I took (borrowed) that record from Nina. I often borrow records from her.

Drills

A. *Choose the correct form of the verb and translate.*

1. В про́шлом году́ я́ ка́ждый де́нь (бра́л/взя́л) кни́ги в библиоте́ке.
2. Где́ мо́й слова́рь? Кто́ (бра́л/взя́л) его́?
3. Ле́том я́ (возьму́/бу́ду бра́ть) уро́ки те́нниса.
4. Они́ за́втра (возьму́т/бу́дут бра́ть) на́ш автомоби́ль.
5. Мы́ иногда́ (бра́ли/взя́ли) и́х автомоби́ль.
6. Вчера́ Ива́н (бра́л/взя́л) у меня́ после́дний до́ллар.
7. Каку́ю шля́пу вы́ (бу́дете бра́ть/возьмёте) в дере́вню, бе́лую и́ли чёрную?

B. *Translate into Russian.*

1. Zoya took my hat; I will take yours.
2. Who took the letter which was lying on my desk?
3. He always used to take my textbooks.
4. I know that you have no dictionary, but you can always take mine.
5. They will take your records tomorrow night.
6. Will you take meat or fish?
7. I am going to take French lessons in the spring.

[8] Брать/взять takes у (+ genitive), "to take from."

CONVERSATION

Серёжа написа́л рома́н!

Бори́с. —Вади́м, ты́ зна́ешь Серёжу Козло́ва?

Вади́м. —Я́ его́ ма́ло зна́ю, но́ я́ мно́го о нём слы́шал.

Б. —Что́ ты́ о нём слы́шал?

В. —Ра́зные ве́щи.

Б. —Как наприме́р?

В. —Наприме́р, говоря́т, что о́н большо́й эгоист.

Б. —Почему́ о́н эгоист?

В. —Говоря́т, что оте́ц Серёжи совсе́м не бога́тый челове́к и о́чень мно́го рабо́тает и на слу́жбе и до́ма, а Серёжа, кро́ме писа́ния, ничего́ не хо́чет де́лать. О́н не хо́чет помога́ть отцу́. О́н почему́-то ду́мает, что бу́дет знамени́тым писа́телем. Но́ я́ слы́шал, что пока́ о́н ничего́ хоро́шего не написа́л и, вероя́тно, ничего́ хоро́шего не напи́шет. Оте́ц, коне́чно, недово́лен сы́ном, но́ ма́ть (как все́ ма́тери) ду́мает, что её сы́н ге́ний. Во́т, что о нём говоря́т.

Б. —А что́ ты́ о нём ду́маешь? Мне́ говори́ли, что ты́ его́ не лю́бишь. Э́то пра́вда?

В. —Не́т, э́то совсе́м не та́к, но́, сказа́ть пра́вду, о́н меня́ про́сто ма́ло интересу́ет (interests). Как я́ тебе́ уже́ сказа́л ра́ньше, я́ его́ ма́ло зна́ю. Я́ ду́маю, что о́н про́сто лени́вый па́рень.

Б. —А я́ до́лжен тебе́ сказа́ть, Вади́м, что ты́ непра́в, и лю́ди, кото́рые ду́мают как ты́, то́же непра́вы, а права́ его́ ма́ть.

В. —Ты́ хо́чешь сказа́ть, что о́н ге́ний? Я́ зна́ю, Бори́с, что ты́ его́ почему́-то лю́бишь.

Б. —Де́ло совсе́м не в э́том, а де́ло в то́м, что о́н настоя́щий писа́тель.

В. —Э́то но́вость! Но́ почему́ ты́ э́то говори́шь?

Б. —Слу́шай (listen). Вчера́ ве́чером я́ бы́л в на́шем студе́нческом клу́бе. Бы́ло ещё дово́льно ра́но и кро́ме меня́ и Серёжи та́м никого́ не́ было. Серёжа сиде́л в углу́ и ду́мал.

В. —Вероя́тно у него́ в голове́ бы́л пла́н бу́дущего рома́на.

Б. —Не́т, не пла́н в голове́, а рома́н на бума́ге.

В. —Я́ не ве́рю.

Б. —Я́ зна́ю, что ты́ ске́птик. Ты́ мо́жешь мне́ не ве́рить, но́ э́то фа́кт. Серёжа уже́ написа́л четы́ре главы́. Две́ о́н мне́ вчера́ прочита́л. По-мо́ему, о́н пи́шет замеча́тельную ве́щь.[9]

В. —Э́то действи́тельно но́вость. О чём же э́тот рома́н?

Б. —Э́то рома́н о молодо́м тала́нтливом хи́мике, кото́рый слу́жит

[9] Вещь is also used in the sense of work of literature, music, art.

на заво́де на Ура́ле. Васю́шкин (э́то фами́лия хи́мика) сде́лал одно́ о́чень ва́жное откры́тие. Э́то откры́тие не́которое вре́мя должно́ бы́ть секре́том. Э́то о́чень ва́жно. Об э́том секре́те, кро́ме Васю́шкина, зна́ет то́лько машини́стка Ната́ша. Она́ рабо́тает в заводско́й конто́ре. Васю́шкин и Ната́ша лю́бят дру́г дру́га.

В. —Ну́, коне́чно! Что́ да́льше?

Б. —Слу́шай. В лаборато́рии, кро́ме Васю́шкина, е́сть ещё друго́й хи́мик, Кири́ллов. Кири́ллов не тако́й тала́нтливый, как Васю́шкин, и о́н э́то зна́ет. О́н большо́й интрига́н (intriguer). О́н ненави́дит Васю́шкина. Кири́ллов зна́ет, что Васю́шкин всю зи́му по́здно ве́чером рабо́тал оди́н в лаборато́рии. Кири́ллову о́чень ва́жно узна́ть (to find out, perf.), каки́е откры́тия сде́лал Васю́шкин.

В. —Ну́, что́ да́льше?

Б. —Не зна́ю. Я́ тебе́ сказа́л, что Серёжа прочита́л мне́ вчера́ то́лько две́ главы́. Но́ о́н сказа́л мне́, что е́сли геро́и его́ рома́на на́с интересу́ют (interest), о́н прочита́ет на́м ещё две́ главы́ сего́дня ве́чером. О́н сде́лает э́то с удово́льствием. И́ли, е́сли хо́чешь, я́ возьму́ у него́ э́ти гла́вы, и ты́ са́м и́х прочита́ешь.

В. —Где́ о́н бу́дет чита́ть?

Б. —В клу́бе.

В. —Я́ бу́ду та́м. Я́ хочу́ слы́шать, ка́к о́н чита́ет и меня́ интересу́ет, что́ бу́дет с Васю́шкиным и с его́ откры́тием.

Чита́йте э́ти вопро́сы и отвеча́йте на ни́х (*read these questions and answer them*).

1. Ке́м Серёжа хо́чет бы́ть? 2. Почему́ говоря́т, что о́н эгои́ст? 3. Почему́ Бори́с ду́мает, что Вади́м не лю́бит Серёжу? 4. Вади́м действи́тельно его́ не лю́бит? 5. Что́ бы́ло вчера́ ве́чером? 6. Кто́ Васю́шкин? 7. Где́ о́н рабо́тает? 8. Что́ о́н сде́лал? 9. Кто́ Ната́ша и где́ она́ рабо́тает? 10. О чём она́ зна́ет? 11. Расска-жи́те, что́ вы́ зна́ете о Кири́ллове. 12. Почему́ Бори́с не зна́ет, что́ бу́дет да́льше? 13. Что́ Серёжа сде́лает с удово́льствием? 14. Почему́ Вади́м бу́дет ве́чером в клу́бе?

EXERCISES

A. *Read the following sentences and be ready to explain the use of the aspects.*

1. Она́ сказа́ла, что бу́дет ча́сто на́м писа́ть. Но́ она́ написа́ла на́м то́лько одно́ коро́ткое письмо́. 2. До войны́, когда́ Серге́й

жи́л с ма́терью в Крыму́, о́н иногда́ писа́л Зи́не. 3. По́сле войны́ о́н написа́л е́й то́лько два́ письма́. 4. —Что́ тебе́ пи́шет Та́ня? —Когда́ я́ прочита́ю её письмо́, я́ тебе́ скажу́. 5. Я́ не зна́ю, что́ де́лать: я́ сего́дня должна́ прочита́ть э́ту кни́гу, но́ у меня́ так ма́ло вре́мени! 6. Все́ э́ти дни́ Андре́й ничего́ не де́лал, но́ вчера́ о́н наконе́ц сде́лал все́ упражне́ния и да́же сде́лал дли́нный и тру́дный перево́д. 7. —В и́х кварти́ре никогда́ не звони́л телефо́н; но́ вчера́, когда́ я́ бы́л у ни́х, телефо́н вдру́г позвони́л. —Кто́ э́то бы́л? —Э́то была́ оши́бка! 8. Я́ позвоню́ О́льге по́сле уро́ка. 9. Я́ бу́ду ча́сто е́й звони́ть: она́ така́я ми́лая де́вушка! 10. —Кто́ взя́л мо́й учёбник? —Я́ взя́л его́: о́н мне́ бы́л о́чень ну́жен. —А у тебя́ не́т учёбника? Стра́нно! —Коне́чно е́сть, но́ Зо́я всегда́ его́ берёт.

B. *Choose the correct form of the two forms given in parentheses.*

1. О чём профе́ссор вчера́ (говори́л/сказа́л)? 2. Когда́ вы́ (бу́дете говори́ть/ска́жете) на́м, когда́ бу́дет экза́мен? 3. Что́ она́ (бу́дет де́лать/сде́лает) всё ле́то? 4. Мы́ (бу́дем писа́ть/напи́шем) ва́м ча́сто. 5. Когда́ вы́ (бу́дете бра́ть/возьмёте) ва́шу ла́мпу? 6. О́н уже́ (де́лал/сде́лал) всё, что бы́ло ну́жно. 7. Вчера́ по́сле конце́рта о́н мне́ (говори́л/сказа́л), что о́н меня́ лю́бит! 8. Я́ (бу́ду звони́ть/позвоню́) ва́м за́втра у́тром. 9. Сего́дня ве́чером она́ (бу́дет бра́ть/возьмёт) моё чёрное пла́тье. 10. Ле́том я́ (бу́ду бра́ть/возьму́) кни́ги в библиоте́ке ка́ждую неде́лю. 11. Я́ (бу́ду чита́ть/прочита́ю) тебе́ мою́ статью́, как то́лько я́ её (бу́ду писа́ть/напишу́). 12. О чём профе́ссор Сми́т (бу́дет говори́ть/ска́жет) за́втра на свое́й ле́кции? 13. О́н бы́стро (гото́вил/пригото́вил) уро́к и написа́л письмо́. 14. Когда́ я́ (бу́ду гото́вить/пригото́влю) уро́к, я́ ва́м (бу́ду звони́ть/позвоню́).

C. *Translate into Russian.*

1. —When did you write this letter? —I wrote it last night. 2. I'll tell you what I think about it when I read (will have read) it. 3. —What are you going to (will) do tomorrow? —I am going to work. 4. He is going to take my car tonight. 5. I am going to tell him that in the spring I shall often take his car. 6. Who is going to speak about Shakespeare at the meeting? 7. She talked a great deal, but didn't say with whom she had been at the movies. 8. I did everything yesterday, and today I will rest. 9. He read three articles before dinner. 10. I will be at home after class and will read Chekhov all evening. 11. —Whose dictionary did you take? —I always take Boris's dictionary. 12. —When and where did he write this wonderful novel? —He wrote it in Italy before the war. He was working on it (was writing it) for four years. 13. I must write at once to my mother! 14. He made three mistakes in his translation.

VOCABULARY

бу́дущий future, next
выраже́ние expression
глава́ chapter; head, chief
глаго́л verb
действи́тельно indeed, in fact, really, actually
де́ло matter, affair, business
заводско́й factory (*adj.*)
машини́ст (*fem.* **-ка**) machinist; typist
наконе́ц finally, at last
непра́в, неправа́, непра́вы wrong (*in predicate only*)
но́вость (*fem.*) (piece of) news
но́вости (*pl.*) news
опя́ть again
откры́тие discovery
оши́бка mistake
па́р.ень (*gen.* **-ня**: *colloq.*) fellow
па́ртия game; (political) party
писа́ние writing
план plan
пока́ so far, to now; as long as
полови́на (+ *gen.*) half
прав, права́, пра́вы right (in predicate only)
пра́ктика practice
сам, само́, сама́, са́ми oneself: myself, yourself, himself, themselves, etc.
сейча́с now; right away, soon
сейча́с же at once, immediately
секре́т secret
слу́жба job, work; service
студе́нческий student (*adj.*)
хи́мик chemist
час hour
эгои́ст (*fem.* **-ка**) selfish person, egoist

Verbs

ве́рить (imperf., II: **ве́р.ю, -ишь**), **пове́рить** (perf., II) to believe (+ *dat.*)
ненави́деть (imperf. only, II: **ненави́.жу, -дишь**) to hate

Expressions

то́лько что (+ *past*) (have) just
как то́лько as soon as
игра́ть в ка́рты to play cards
хоте́ть сказа́ть to mean, mean to say
Де́ло в то́м, что . . . The thing is that . . .
Не в э́том де́ло. That's beside the point, that's not the point
не́которое вре́мя for some time
Что́ да́льше? What next?
Что́ бу́дет с . . . (+ *instr.*)? What will happen to . . .? What will become of . . .?

UNIT 15

***Aspects, continued,* 219. *Prepositions* из *and* от *with the genitive,* 226. *Tenses in reported speech,* 227.**

GRAMMAR

1. Aspects, continued

In the preceding lesson we have seen that perfective verbs can be formed from imperfectives through the addition of one of a number of prefixes, *e.g.*, imperfective **писа́ть**, perfective **написа́ть**. We have also seen that in exceptional cases a pair of verbs with different roots can be related, *e.g.*, imperfective **говори́ть**, perfective **сказа́ть**; or imperfective **брать**, perfective **взять**.

In other cases, the two verbs have identical stems, but differ in the elements that follow the stem (suffixes) both in the infinitive and the personal forms of the conjugation, thus:

Imperf. конча́ть (I: конч.а́ю, -а́ешь)
Perf. ко́нчить (II: ко́нчу, ко́нчишь)

Imperf. объясня́ть (I: объясн.я́ю, -я́ешь)
Perf. объясни́ть (II: объясню́, объясни́шь)

Sometimes there are also differences in the stem vowel (often **а** alternates with **о**), or differences in the final stem consonant:

Imperf. спр**а́ш**ивать (I: спр**а́ш**ив.аю, -аешь)
Perf. спр**ос**и́ть (II: спр**ош**у́, спр**о́с**ишь)

Imperf. отве**ч**а́ть (I: отве**ч**.а́ю, -а́ешь)
Perf. отве́**т**ить (II: отве́**ч**у, отве́**т**ишь)

In the preceding lesson it has been indicated that a prefix added to a verb may change its aspect, *e.g.*, imperfective писа́ть, perfective **на**писа́ть. But the same verb писа́ть may take other prefixes as well, *e.g.*, **за-**, **пере-**, **под-**; the resulting verbs, записа́ть, переписа́ть, подписа́ть, are perfective; besides changing the aspect to perfective, these prefixes also add new meanings to **писа́ть**: thus **записа́ть** means "to note down"; **переписа́ть**, means "to rewrite," "transcribe"; **подписа́ть** means "to underwrite," "subscribe," "sign."

Obviously, such perfective verbs as записа́ть, переписа́ть, подписа́ть, formed with "meaningful" prefixes, must have corresponding imperfectives that would mean not simply "to write," but "to note down," "to rewrite," or "to sign." Perfective verbs thus formed with "meaningful" prefixes are "de-perfectivized" by the insertion of a suffix; in the case of the prefixed forms of писа́ть (and of many other verbs), the suffix **-ыва-** (or **-ива-**) is used. Thus are formed the imperfective verbs запи́**сывать**, перепи́**сывать**, подпи́**сывать**.

To sum up:

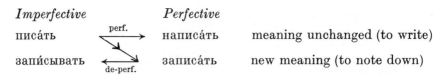

Imperfective		*Perfective*	
писа́ть	perf. →	написа́ть	meaning unchanged (to write)
запи́сывать	← de-perf.	записа́ть	new meaning (to note down)

The procedure described above is used to form imperfective-perfective pairs of prefixed verbs identical in meaning, and differentiated as to aspect by their suffixes.

All imperfective prefixed verbs with an inserted **-ыва-** or **-ива-** are conjugated like чита́ть, regardless of the original perfective form. Thus:

запи́сываю
запи́сываешь, etc.

Learn the verbs in the table at the top of the next page and their conjugation. Most of these verbs have already been presented in their imperfective aspect forms.

The imperfective дава́ть (даю́, даёшь) has as its corresponding perfective the verb дать. This verb follows a distinct conjugation pattern:

я́ да́м	(I will give)	мы́ дади́м
ты́ да́шь	etc.	вы́ дади́те
о́н да́ст		они́ даду́т

The compound verb продава́ть—прода́ть (to sell) is conjugated

Imperfective (*Infinitive and Present Tense*)	*Perfective* (*Infinitive and Future Tense*)
кончáть (I: конч.áю, -áешь) to end, finish	кóнчить (II: кóнчу, кóнчишь . . . кóнчат)
получáть (I: получ.áю, -áешь) to receive, obtain, get	получи́ть (II: получý, полýчишь . . . полýчат)
объясня́ть (I: объясн.я́ю, -я́ешь) to explain	объясни́ть (II: объясню́, объясни́шь . . . объясня́т)
отвечáть (I: отвеч.áю, -áешь) to answer	отвéтить (II: отвéчу, отвéтишь . . . отвéтят)
запи́сывать (I: запи́сыв.аю, -аешь) to note down	записáть (I: запишý, запи́шешь . . . запи́шут)
перепи́сывать (I: перепи́сыв.аю, -аешь) to copy, rewrite	переписáть (I: перепишý, перепи́шешь . . . перепи́шут)
покáзывать (I: покáзыв.аю, -аешь) to show	показáть (I: покажý, покáжешь . . . покáжут)
рассkáзывать (I: рассkáзыв.аю, -аешь) to narrate, tell	рассказáть (I: расскажý, расскáжешь . . . расскáжут)
спрáшивать (I: спрáшив.аю, -аешь) to narrate, tell	спроси́ть (II: спрошý, спрóсишь . . . спрóсят)
начинáть (I: начин.áю, -áешь) to begin, start	начáть (I: начнý, начнёшь . . . начнýт) *Past:* нáчал, нáчало, началá, нáчали.
давáть (I: даю́, даёшь) to give	дать (see page 220)
продавáть (I: прод.аю́, -аёшь) to sell	продáть (see page 220)

exactly like давáть—дать. (But note that the stress in the past tense of продáть is on the prefix **про-** in all forms except the feminine: прóдал, продалá, прóдали. (As a rule, the prefixes of verb compounds are not stressed, but there are some exceptions.)

The verb начáть inserts an **н** throughout the future tense: нач**н**ý, нач**н**ёшь, etc. (This **н** is also found in all forms of the imperfective начи**н**áть.)

The perfective verbs показáть and рассказáть are conjugated in the future exactly like сказáть: покажý, покáжешь; расскажý, расскáжешь, etc.

There is a tendency for the stress to shift to the ending of the past tense in the feminine: был**á**, жил**á**, дал**á**, продал**á**, начал**á**, брал**á**, взял**á**, etc.

Pattern Sentences

Объясня́ть (*imperfective*), **объясни́ть** (*perfective*).

1. И́х ста́рый учи́тель всегда́ хорошо́ **объясня́л** и́м пра́вила грамма́тики.
2. Па́вел **объясни́л** мне́, почему́ ему́ бы́ло так ску́чно на ле́кции.
3. Мне́ бы́ло тру́дно **объясни́ть** учи́телю, почему́ я́ сде́лал э́ту глу́пую оши́бку.
4. Я́ **объясню́** Ни́не, ка́к сде́лать э́тот перево́д.
5. Её роди́тели **объясня́т** е́й, что́ она́ должна́ бу́дет де́лать в дере́вне.
6. На ка́ждом уро́ке я́ **бу́ду объясня́ть** ва́м грамма́тику.

1. Their old teacher always explained rules of grammar to them well.
2. Paul explained to me why he was so bored at the lecture.
3. I had trouble explaining to the teacher why I made that stupid mistake.
4. I shall explain to Nina how to do that translation.
5. Her parents will explain to her what she will have to do in the country.
6. At every class session I shall explain the grammar to you.

Drills

A. *Choose the correct form of the verb and translate.*

1. Я́ (бу́ду объясня́ть/объясню́) ва́м, где́ я́ покупа́ю ры́бу.
2. Я́ зна́ю тепе́рь э́то пра́вило; учи́тель хорошо́ (объясня́л/объясни́л) мне́ его́.
3. Как ску́чно ка́ждый де́нь (объясня́ть/объясни́ть) секрета́рше, что́ она́ должна́ де́лать!
4. Моя́ жена́ не слу́шала, когда́ сы́н (объясня́л/объясни́л) на́м сво́й но́вый пла́н.
5. Мо́й нача́льник (бу́дет объясня́ть/объясни́т), что́ я́ до́лжен бу́ду де́лать за́втра.

B. *Translate into Russian.*

1. Who will explain this rule to you?
2. She explained to me why she doesn't want to work here.
3. The teacher was explaining grammar, but I didn't listen.
4. If you want, I'll explain my plan to you.
5. Every day he will explain a new rule to us.

Pattern Sentences

Отвеча́ть (*imperfective*), **отве́тить** (*perfective*).

1. Мне́ бы́ло легко́ **отве́тить** учи́телю; его́ вопро́с бы́л о́чень лёгкий.
2. Лунёв ре́дко **отвеча́л** своему́ бра́ту на его́ пи́сьма,[1] но́ вчера́ о́н вдру́г **отве́тил** ему́ дли́нным письмо́м.

1. I had no trouble answering the teacher; his question was very easy.
2. Lunyov rarely answered his brother's letters, but yesterday he suddenly replied with a long letter.

[1] Отвеча́ть/отве́тить takes the dative of persons, but **на** + accusative with things (questions, letters, etc.).

3. Я́ **отве́чу** Ива́ну, когда́[2] у меня́ бу́дет вре́мя. — 3. I shall answer Ivan when I have time.
4. Когда́ же они́ наконе́ц **отве́тят** на все́ э́ти вопро́сы? — 4. When will they finally answer all these questions?
5. Е́сли о́н бу́дет задава́ть мне́ глу́пые вопро́сы, я́ не **бу́ду** ему́ **отвеча́ть.** — 5. If he is going to ask me silly questions, I am not going to answer him.
6. А́нна сейча́с же мне́ **отве́тила.** — 6. Anna answered me at once.

Drills

A. *Choose the correct form of the verb and translate.*

1. Почему́ вы́ не (отвеча́ли/отве́тили) на его́ письмо́?
2. Я́ (бу́ду отвеча́ть/отве́чу) сего́дня ве́чером.
3. Когда́ вы́ (отвеча́ли/отве́тили) на э́то письмо́?
4. Я́ (отвеча́л/отве́тил) вчера́ у́тром.
5. Е́сли ты́ бу́дешь писа́ть мне́, я́ коне́чно (бу́ду отвеча́ть/отве́чу) тебе́.

B. *Translate into Russian.*

1. He never answers my letters.
2. He usually answered the teacher quickly and well.
3. He didn't answer your question.
4. —Have you answered him? —Not yet. I'll answer soon.
5. They will answer the letter tomorrow.
6. Why don't you answer Ann's letters?
7. I couldn't answer that question.

Pattern Sentences

Спра́шивать (*imperfective*), **спроси́ть** (*perfective*).

1. Что́ ты́ **отве́тишь** учи́телю, е́сли о́н тебя́ **спро́сит,** почему́ тебя́ вчера́ не́ было в кла́ссе? — 1. What will you answer the teacher if he asks you why you weren't in class yesterday?
2. О́н никогда́ об э́том не **спра́шивает.** — 2. He never asks about that.
3. Вчера́ Ка́тя меня́ **спроси́ла** о ва́с. — 3. Yesterday Katya asked me about you.
4. —Е́сли они́ тебя́ **спро́сят** что́ ты́ де́лал всё лето, что́ ты́ и́м **отве́тишь**? —Я́ **отве́чу** пра́вду. — 4. —If they ask you what you were doing all summer, what will you answer them? —I shall answer the truth.
5. Я́ **спрошу́** отца́, с ке́м о́н хо́чет сего́дня рабо́тать в саду́. — 5. I shall ask Father with whom he wants to work today in the garden.

[2] Remember that the *future* tense must be used in Russian subordinate clauses beginning with е́сли and когда́, although the present tense is used in English with future meaning, *e.g.*: Когда́ я́ получу́ отве́т, я́ ва́м позвоню́. When I *get* the answer, I will call you up.

Drills

A. *Choose the correct form of the verb and translate.*

1. Ты́ (спра́шивал/спроси́л) Бори́са, где́ о́н бы́л вчера́?
2. Не́т ещё, но́ я́ (бу́ду спра́шивать/спрошу́) его́.
3. Ле́на (спра́шивала/спроси́ла) меня́, почему́ я́ не была́ на вечери́нке.
4. Я́ никогда́ не (спра́шивала/спроси́ла) Ле́ну, почему́ она́ ничего́ не чита́ет.
5. Вы́ (бу́дете спра́шивать/спро́сите) Ле́ну, где́ она́ покупа́ет пласти́нки?

B. *Translate into Russian.*

1. I asked Nina who was at her party.
2. I shall ask my sister what she is going to do tomorrow.
3. I never ask to whom she writes, and she never tells me about it.
4. We often asked Boris about you.
5. Why didn't you ask Ivan Ivanovich where he had been last night?
6. Perhaps they will ask us what we think of them.
7. If they ask, what will you tell them?

Pattern Sentences

Начина́ть (*imperfective*), **нача́ть** (*perfective*).
Конча́ть (*imperfective*), **ко́нчить** (*perfective*).

These verbs are followed by the accusative case, or, if by a verb, the *imperfective* infinitive.

1. Зо́я неда́вно **начала́** рабо́тать на по́чте. На заво́де она́ **начина́ла** рабо́тать о́чень ра́но, а тепе́рь она́ **начина́ет** по́зже.	1. Recently Zoya began to work at the post office. At the plant she used to start work very early, but now she starts later.
2. Андре́й вдру́г **на́чал** писа́ть ле́вой руко́й, а Ка́тя вдру́г **начала́** кури́ть!	2. Andrey has suddenly begun to write with his left hand, and Katya has suddenly begun to smoke!
3. Вы́ должны́ **нача́ть** говори́ть по-ру́сски!	3. You must start speaking Russian!
4. Я́ **ко́нчил** чита́ть пе́рвую главу́.	4. I have finished reading the first chapter.
5. Зимо́й я́ **конча́л** рабо́тать дово́льно по́здно.	5. In the winter I used to finish working rather late.
6. Когда́ ты́ **ко́нчишь** э́ту ску́чную рабо́ту?	6. When will you finish that boring work?
7. Я́ ещё не зна́ю, когда́ я́ её **ко́нчу**; я́ то́лько неда́вно **на́чал.**	7. I don't know yet when I'll finish it; I only started recently.
8. В бу́дущем году́ мы́ **начнём** но́вую жи́знь!	8. Next year we shall begin a new life!

Drills

A. *Choose the correct form of the verb and translate.*

1. За́втра я́ (бу́ду начина́ть/начну́) чита́ть но́вую главу́.
2. Тепе́рь Ива́н ка́ждое у́тро (бу́дет начина́ть/начнёт) рабо́тать ра́ньше.
3. Ле́том я́ о́чень ра́но (начина́ла/начала́) сво́й де́нь.
4. Когда́ вы́ (бу́дете начина́ть/начнёте) писа́ть статью́?
5. Я́ давно́ (конча́л/ко́нчил) её.
6. Как то́лько я́ (бу́ду конча́ть/ко́нчу) писа́ть э́то письмо́, я́ сейча́с же (бу́ду начина́ть/начну́) друго́е.
7. Ни́на то́лько что (конча́ла/ко́нчила) гото́вить уро́ки.

B. *Translate into Russian.*

1. We must begin a new life!
2. I will start reading the second chapter at once.
3. My brothers finished their work.
4. In the fall they used to finish working quite late.
5. First I will finish writing the letter, and then I will read it to you.
6. —When will you finish reading this play? —I haven't started it yet.
7. —Have you finished reading that novel yet? —Not yet.
8. I started writing a letter to my mother, but I haven't finished it yet.
9. I always begin working early and finish late.

Pattern Sentences

Дава́ть (*imperfective*), **дать** (*perfective*).

1. —Кто́ **да́ст** мне́ папиро́су? —Я́ **да́м** тебе́, е́сли у меня́ е́сть.	1. —Who will give me a cigarette? —I shall give you one if I have any.
2. —Что́ ты́ мне́ **да́шь?** —Я́ могу́ **да́ть** тебе́ четы́ре рубля́.	2. —What will you give me? —I can give you four roubles.
3. А́нна лю́бит **дава́ть** сове́ты.	3. Anna likes to give advice.
4. —О́ля, что́ ты́ **сде́лала** с мое́й газе́той? —Я́ её **прочита́ла** и **дала́** ма́ме, а ма́ма, когда́ **прочита́ет, да́ст** её тебе́.	4. —Olya, what have you done with my paper? —I read it and gave it to Mama, and Mama, when she finishes reading it, will give it to you.
5. Э́та ми́лая да́ма **дава́ла** на́м уро́ки два́ го́да.	5. That nice lady has given us lessons for two years.
6. Вчера́ она́ **дала́** на́м после́дний уро́к. О́сенью она́ опя́ть бу́дет **дава́ть** на́м уро́ки.	6. Yesterday she gave us the last lesson. In the fall she will be giving us lessons again.
7. —Е́сли ва́м нужны́ бу́дут де́ньги, мы́ **дади́м** ва́м всё, что у на́с е́сть. —Большо́е спаси́бо!	7. —If you need money, we shall give you all we have. —Many thanks!

Drills

A. *Choose the correct form of the verb and translate.*

1. Я́ не люблю́ (дава́ть/да́ть) уро́ки.
2. Кто́ (дава́л/да́л) тебе́ уро́ки зимо́й?
3. Зи́на (дава́ла/дала́) мне́ три́ уро́ка те́нниса.
4. Оте́ц (бу́дет дава́ть/да́ст) мне́ де́ньги ка́ждый ме́сяц.
5. Кто́ (дава́л/да́л) тебе́ э́тот до́ллар?
6. Я́ (бу́ду дава́ть/да́м) тебе́ моё пальто́ за́втра ве́чером.
7. Кому́ вы́ (бу́дете дава́ть/дади́те) э́ту кни́гу?

B. *Translate into Russian.*

1. I just gave Ivan $2.
2. I often gave him money.
3. Zoya will give you her textbook.
4. I'll give mine to Vadim.
5. What will you give me?
6. They will give this money to Father.
7. Who gave Anna this dictionary?
8. Mother gave her good advice.
9. I will give my brother lessons every morning.

2. Prepositions из and от with the genitive

The prepositions **из,** meaning "out of," "from," and **от,** meaning "from," "away from," both take the *genitive* case.

Из is used with most places, while **от** is used with persons:

—**Отку́да** э́то письмо́? —Письмо́ **из** Москв**ы́**.
—Where is that letter from? —The letter is from Moscow.

—**От кого́** э́то письмо́? —Письмо́ **от** бра́т**а**.
—Whom is that letter from? —The letter is from Brother.

Я́ получи́л телегра́мму **от** сестр**ы́** **из** А́нгли**и**.
I got a telegram from my sister in (from) England.

Pattern Sentences

Получа́ть (*imperfective*), **получи́ть** (*perfective*).

1. Серёжа наконе́ц **получи́л** отве́т **из** Москв**ы́**. — Seryozha finally got an answer from Moscow.
2. Я́ ду́маю, что они́ за́втра **полу́чат** телегра́мму **из** Оде́ссы. — I think that tomorrow they will get a telegram from Odessa.
3. До войны́ о́н ча́сто **получа́л** пи́сьма **от** свое**го́** дру́г**а**. — Before the war he often got letters from his friend.
4. —**От кого́** вы́ **получи́ли** э́тот замеча́тельный пода́рок? —Я́ **получи́ла** его́ **от** мое́й ста́рш**ей** до́чер**и**. — —From whom did you get that wonderful present? —I got it from my elder daughter.

5. Когдá я́ **получу́** отве́т **от** дире́ктора, я́ ва́м сейча́с же позвоню́.
6. Я́ ду́маю, что ты́ тепе́рь ча́сто **бу́дешь получа́ть** пи́сьма **от** Бори́са.
7. —**Отку́да** э́то письмо́? —Оно́ **из** Я́лты. **Я́ получи́ла** его́ вчера́.

5. When I get an answer from the director, I'll phone you at once.
6. I think that now you will be getting letters from Boris often.
7. —Where does this letter come from? —It comes from Yalta. I got it yesterday.

Drills

A. *Choose the correct form of the verb and translate.*

1. Зи́на, от кого́ вы́ (получа́ли/получи́ли) э́тот пода́рок?
2. Я́ (получа́ла/получи́ла) его́ от Андре́я.
3. Ра́ньше Ива́н ча́сто (получа́л/получи́л) пода́рки из Аме́рики.
4. Как то́лько я́ (бу́ду получа́ть/получу́) отве́т от Ни́ны, я́ ва́м сейча́с же позвоню́.
5. Оте́ц ду́мает, что мы́ ре́дко (бу́дем получа́ть/полу́чим) пи́сьма от Серёжи.

B. *Translate into Russian.*

1. I often receive letters from my mother.
2. I used to receive a letter from her every week.
3. Yesterday our friend received this letter from Leningrad.
4. Nina thinks that tomorrow she will receive an answer from Moscow.
5. When I get an answer from Boris, I will tell you.
6. From where is that telegram?

3. Tenses in reported speech

In Russian the tense used in reported discourse (indirect quotation) is the same as that used in the original statement. *E.g.*:

Original statement in the present tense:

(Ivan speaking) «Я́ **пишу́** письмо́ бра́ту.»

Reported by another as an indirect quotation:

Ива́н сказа́л, что о́н **пи́шет** письмо́ бра́ту.

(Contrast English: He said that he *was writing* a letter to his brother.)

Original statement in the past tense:

(Ivan speaking) «Я́ **написа́л** письмо́ бра́ту.»

Reported by another:

Ива́н сказа́л, что о́н **написа́л** письмо́ бра́ту.

(Compare English: He said that he *had written* a letter to his brother.)

Original statement in the future:

(Ivan speaking) «**Я́ напишу́** письмо́ бра́ту.»

Reported by another:

Ива́н сказа́л, что о́н **напи́шет** письмо́ бра́ту.

(Contrast English: He said that he *would write* a letter to his brother.)

In colloquial English the conjunction "that" is often omitted in indirect quotation, *e.g.*, "He said he would answer you soon." In Russian, however, the conjunction **что** must *never* be omitted: О́н сказа́л, **что** о́н ско́ро ва́м отве́тит.

Drill

A. *Translate into English.*

1. Я́ спроси́л Ива́на, ско́лько вре́мени о́н живёт в э́том го́роде.
2. О́н отве́тил, что живёт зде́сь три́ го́да.
3. Сего́дня у́тром я́ писа́л письмо́.
4. Бори́с спроси́л меня́, кому́ я́ пишу́.
5. Я́ отве́тил, что пишу́ ма́ме.
6. Вчера́ о́н мне́ сказа́л, что о́н пи́шет но́вый рома́н.
7. Вчера́ о́н мне́ сказа́л, что о́н написа́л но́вый рома́н.
8. Вчера́ о́н мне́ сказа́л, что о́н ско́ро напи́шет но́вый рома́н.
9. О́н отве́тил в письме́, что у него́ не́т вре́мени на́м помога́ть.
10. Он рассказа́л на́м, где́ о́н бы́л, и что́ о́н де́лал.
11. О́н сказа́л на́м, что за́втра о́н бу́дет до́ма весь де́нь.
12. Когда́ я́ ви́дел Ве́ру, она́ мне́ сказа́ла, что она́ чита́ет Че́хова.

EXERCISES

A. *Read and translate.*

1. В бу́дущем году́ мы́ **продади́м** на́ш до́м и бу́дем жи́ть у сы́на. 2. —Кому́ ты́ **прода́шь** твои́ францу́зские кни́ги? —Я́ **прода́м** и́х одному́ францу́зскому журнали́сту. 3. Лунёв лю́бит **расска́зывать** о свое́й жи́зни в Кита́е. 4. О́н **рассказа́л** на́м вчера́ о́чень интере́сную исто́рию, кото́рую я́ **расскажу́** ва́м по́сле уро́ка. 5. Она́ должна́ была́ **переписа́ть** э́тот дли́нный перево́д, потому́ что бума́га, на кото́рой она́ его́ **написа́ла,** была́ гря́зная. Она́ взяла́ чи́стую бума́гу и всё **переписа́ла.** 6. Я́ бы́л вчера́ на́ о́чень интере́сной ле́кции и **записа́л** ка́ждое сло́во, кото́рое я́ слы́шал.

7. Я́ зна́ю одного́ студе́нта, кото́рый никогда́ ничего́ не **запи́сывает,** но́ кото́рый лю́бит задава́ть вопро́сы. 8. —Вы́ зна́ете но́вость? Смирно́вы **про́дали** сво́й до́м. И́м нужны́ были де́ньги. —Кто́ ва́м э́то **рассказа́л?** —Мы́ **получи́ли** от ни́х коро́ткое письмо́, в кото́ром они́ на́м об э́том **пи́шут.** —Как жа́ль! Э́то бы́л замеча́тельный ста́рый до́м и, как все́ говори́ли, настоя́щий истори́ческий па́мятник. 9. Воло́дя показа́л мне́ своё но́вое перо́, кото́рое ему́ **про́дал** оди́н его́ дру́г.[3] 10. —Э́тому дру́гу нужны́ были де́ньги. —А я́ ду́мал, что э́то бы́л пода́рок от его́ жены́. 11. Я́ возьму́ чи́стый ли́ст бума́ги и **перепишу́** письмо́, кото́рое я́ **написа́л** дире́ктору. 12. Снача́ла я́ **покажу́** его́ моей́ жене́, а пото́м я́ да́м его́ ва́м. 13. —Что́ вы́ **отве́тите** э́тому глу́пому ма́льчику, е́сли о́н вас **спро́сит,** о чём вы́ говори́ли с его́ ма́терью? —Я́ **отве́чу** ему́, что э́то секре́т, и что о́н не до́лжен меня́ об э́том **спра́шивать,** потому́ что я́ всё равно́ ему́ ничего́ не **скажу́.**

B. *Underline the correct form and translate the whole sentence into English.*

1. За́втра о́н (бу́дет дава́ть/да́ст) мне́ после́дний уро́к. 2. Моя́ учени́ца (спра́шивала/спроси́ла) Андре́я Петро́вича, где́ живёт его́ до́чь, но́ о́н почему́-то е́й не (отвеча́л/отве́тил). 3. Кто́ (дава́л/да́л) ва́м уро́ки весь го́д? 4. Когда́ я́ (бу́ду получа́ть/получу́) от него́ письмо́, я́ ему́ сейча́с же (бу́ду отвеча́ть/отве́чу). 5. За́втра по́сле уро́ка я́ (бу́ду спра́шивать/спрошу́) учи́теля, когда́ у на́с бу́дет экза́мен. 6. Вы́ всегда́ должны́ (перепи́сывать/переписа́ть) ва́ши упражне́ния. 7. —О́н ва́м (пока́зывал/показа́л) сво́й но́вый ковёр, кото́рый о́н (получа́л/получи́л) из Ту́ниса? —Не́т ещё. О́н (бу́дет пока́зывать/пока́жет) мне́ его́ за́втра. 8. Когда́ ты́ (бу́дешь пока́зывать/пока́жешь) мне́ твою́ статью́? 9. Я́ (бу́ду пока́зывать/покажу́) её тебе́, как то́лько я́ её (бу́ду конча́ть/ко́нчу). 10. Я́ ду́маю, что они́ бы́ли ра́ды, когда́ (получа́ли/получи́ли) мо́й пода́рок. 11. Мы́ наконе́ц (конча́ли/ко́нчили) э́ту ску́чную рабо́ту и уже́ за́втра (бу́дем начина́ть/начнём) но́вую. 12. Мы́ тепе́рь ка́ждый де́нь (бу́дем конча́ть/ко́нчим) рабо́тать ра́но. 13. Я́ тебе́ бы́стро (бу́ду объясня́ть/объясню́) э́то пра́вило. 14. О́н (продава́л/про́дал) все́ свои́ ста́рые и гря́зные костю́мы. 15. —Ле́на, ты́ (запи́сывала/записа́ла) мо́й но́вый а́дрес? —Не́т ещё, я́ его́ сейча́с (бу́ду запи́сывать/запишу́).

C. *Give the correct Russian verb form of the words in parentheses, and translate the whole sentence into English.*

1. Во́т продавщи́ца, кото́рая (sold) мне́ э́ту кни́жную по́лку. 2. Ни́на (will work) в универса́льном магази́не; она́ (will sell)

[3] Оди́н его́ дру́г, a friend of his.

ме́бель. 3. Я́ (will sell) тебе́ моё вече́рнее пла́тье. 4. Я́ (will tell) Вади́му, что о́н пло́хо (did) э́тот перево́д. 5. Что́ ма́ма (answered) тебе́, когда́ ты́ (asked) её, о чём она́ (talked) со мно́й? 6. Когда́ ты́ (will answer) твоему́ дру́гу? 7. Я́ (will copy) моё упражне́ние. 8. —Вы́ уже́ (answered) ва́шему ученику́, от кото́рого вы́ (received) вчера́ письмо́? —Да́, я́ ему́ (answered) и (wrote) ему́ обо всём. 9. Мы́ (will write down) а́дрес ва́шего до́ктора. 10. Кто́ так хорошо́ (explained) ва́м э́то тру́дное пра́вило? 11. Весно́й они́ (will start) рабо́тать о́чень по́здно. 12. Они́ (will finish) сего́дня в три́ часа́. 13. Я́ (will tell) ва́м интере́сную исто́рию, кото́рую мне́ вчера́ (told) одна́ ми́лая де́вушка. 14. Э́тот молодо́й челове́к о́чень лю́бит (to ask) вопро́сы. 15. —Кто́ (copied) э́то упражне́ние? —Я́ (copied) его́. Я́ всегда́ (copy) то́, что я́ (write). 16. Вы́ часто (will receive) пи́сьма от меня́.

D. *Translate into Russian.*

1. When did he tell you that, before or after class? 2. When they (will) get my letter, I shall already be in Siberia. 3. Yesterday at the meeting he talked a lot, but said only one intelligent thing. 4. —From whom did you get this telegram? —I got it from Anna. 5. I shall explain this to you; I like explaining. 6. They will explain to you how to do this. 7. Here is a greeting from the Soviet Union. 8. Where is the answer from Professor Robinson? 9. Did he write to you from Odessa? 10. He wrote to me only from Leningrad. He wrote in his letter that the city was very beautiful and clean. 11. He wrote down their address. 12. Next year I shall start working in this small school. 13. I shall tell you all about my life. 14. Last year we received two letters from her from Italy, and one from France. 15. After dinner, when she finished talking about her son, her daughter, and her dog, she began telling us stories about her husband's mother. 16. We heard that he had received a letter from our old director, and that next year he will work in our factory. 17. All they know is that she will live alone, as she lived before the war. 18. They asked the young engineer whose those factories were. 19. Bob always got poor grades, but yesterday he got a good one. 20. If you don't write to her at once, she will not answer you. 21. When I (shall) write this article, I'll give it at once to my daughter; she will give it to her husband, and then they will give it to you. 22. As soon as you get it from them, you will give it to Vladimir. 23. Every month they will get the latest (last) books from London and from Moscow. 24. —What did you get from them? —From whom? From Vadim and Nina, of course! —Before I used to get good things, but now I got a hat from her, and nothing from him. Well, I don't care! 25. —When will you start working in the new office? —I shall start next year. 26. Everybody

will start working early tomorrow. 27. We got your wonderful present. Many thanks! 28. They told us the streets of this city were very dirty. 29. He said he would call us today. 30. They said they would answer us soon.

VOCABULARY

вече́рний evening (*adj.*)
второ́й second (*adj.*)
гря́зный dirty
да́ма lady
де́ньги (*pl.*) money
до́ллар dollar
отку́да from where
папиро́са cigarette
по́зже later
чи́стый clean

в бу́дущем году́ next year

UNIT 16

Genitive plural, 232. Uses of the genitive plural, 235. Numerals, 5-20, 238. Masculine nouns with zero ending in the genitive plural, 238. Time of day in hours, 240. Accusative plural, 241. Genitive as direct object of negated verbs, 243.

GRAMMAR

1. Genitive plural of nouns

There are three types of noun endings in the genitive plural; unlike most noun endings encountered so far, their selection is not generally determined by gender.

A. 1st type: bare stem ("zero ending"). The genitive plural form of nearly all hard neuter nouns, and of Fem. I nouns, hard and soft, is the bare stem of these nouns; this stem is obtained by dropping the final vowel sound of the nominative singular:

	Nominative Singular	*Genitive Plural*
Neut., hard	сло́во [slóv.ə]	слов [slóf.]
Fem. I, hard	рука́ [ruk.á]	рук [rúk.]
Fem. I, soft (Example 1)	неде́ля [ņiḑéļ.ə]	неде́ль [ņiḑéļ.]

In spelling, the final **-я** of the nominative singular is a sign both of the final vowel sound ([ə] in this example) and of the softness of the preceding consonant [ļ]; in the genitive plural, the final vowel sound is dropped, and the softness of the end consonant is then indicated by the sign **-ь** (*i.e.*, [ļə] is written **ля**; [ļ] final is written **ль**).

Example 2: [faṃíļij.ə]—[faṃíļij.] фами́лия—фами́лий

In spelling, the final letter **-я** of the nominative singular stands for [jə]. Dropping the final vowel sound to form the genitive plural leaves the sound [j] in final position; it is rendered by the letter **-й** (*i.e.*, [ijə] is written **-ия**; [ij] is written **-ий**.)

Similarly: [iḑéj.ə]—[iḑéj.] идéя—идéй

Neuter nouns in **-ие** follow the same pattern: [zdáņij.ə]—[zdáņij.] здáние—здáний.

Fleeting **о** *and* **е** *inserted in the genitive.* Those nouns which have "zero endings" in the genitive plural, *i.e.*, hard neuters and Fem. I, hard and soft, often have an inserted vowel **о** or **е** between two consonants in final position. Some of these are:

Nominative Singular	*Genitive Plural*
окнó [akn.ó]	óкон [ókən.]
крéсло [kŗésl.ə]	крéсел [kŗéşəl.]
письмó [pişm.ó]	пи́сем [píşəm.]
пóлка [pólk.ə]	пóлок [pólək.]
чáшка [ç̌ášk.ə]	чáшек [ç̌ášək.]
дéвушка [ḑévušk.ə]	дéвушек [ḑévušək.]
сестрá [şistr.á]	сестёр [şişţór.]

B. 2nd type (hard masculines): ending **-ов** added to the stem (pronounced [óf], or if unstressed, [əf]):

стол [stól]	стол**óв** [stal.óf]
студéнт [stuḑént]	студéнт**ов** [stuḑéntəf]

A variant of the ending **-ов** is **-ев**; masculine nouns ending in the nominative singular, in a vowel plus [j], spelled **-й**, take this ending: [ģirój]—[ģirój.əf] герóй—герó**ев**.

C. 3rd type: ending **-ей** added to the stem (pronounced [éj] if stressed; if unstressed, [əj]). This type includes soft masculines ending in **-ь**; masculines ending in **-ж, -ч, -ш,** and **-щ**; and Fem. II nouns (in **-ь**):

Examples:

учи́тель [uç̌íţiļ.]	учител**éй** [uç̌iţiļ.éj]
нож [nóš.]	нож**éй** [naž.éj]
врач [vraç̌.]	врач**éй** [vraç̌.éj]
товáрищ [taváŗišç̌.]	товáрищ**ей** [taváŗišç̌.əj]
пóле [póļ.ə]	пол**éй** [paļ.éj]
дверь [ḑy̧éŗ.]	двер**éй** [ḑy̧iŗ.éj]

The main classes of nouns may be grouped as follows according to the type of ending they take in the genitive plural (certain special cases of genitive plural formation will be given later):

GENITIVE PLURAL

		Type I	*Type II*	*Type III*
	Nominative Singular	Bare stem; "zero" ending	-ОВ/-ЕВ	-ЕЙ
Masc.	стол учи́тель геро́й нож		столо́в геро́ев	 учителе́й ноже́й
Neut.	сло́во по́ле зда́ние	слов зда́ний		 поле́й
Fem. I	ко́мната неде́ля фами́лия	ко́мнат неде́ль фами́лий		
Fem. II	дверь			двере́й

Drills

A. *The following are examples of the various types of genitive plurals. Identify the nominative singular of each, and mark its stress.*

Zero Ending	*Zero Ending— Fleeting Vowel Inserted*	-ОВ/-ЕВ	-ЕЙ
рек	студе́нток	студе́нтов	прия́телей
гор	таре́лок	домо́в	госте́й
мест	де́вочек	лесо́в	писа́телей
дач	ло́жек (spoons)	расска́зов	словаре́й
стен	ви́лок (forks)	ученико́в	дней
карти́н	гражда́нок	отцо́в	автомоби́лей
кварти́р	сосе́док	концо́в	това́рищей
жён	сестёр	ковро́в	враче́й
ламп	о́кон	геро́ев	ноже́й
карт	пи́сем	музе́ев	поле́й
учени́ц	кре́сел	ге́ниев	море́й
озёр	де́нег		двере́й
	ча́шек		ноче́й

B. *Place the following nouns in the genitive plural. Mark the stress. You may refer to the list in* A *above if necessary.*

дом	геро́й	мо́ре	же́нщина	музе́й	учени́ца
гость	ле́кция	слова́рь	ви́лка	газе́та	гражда́нка
де́вушка	сестра́	стена́	оте́ц	ге́ний	фами́лия
шко́ла	кни́га	лес	писа́тель	таре́лка	ви́лка
дверь	ло́жка	жена́	писа́тельница	нож	назва́ние
кре́сло	коне́ц	собра́ние	ковёр	учени́к	врач

2. Genitive plurals of adjectives and other modifiers

Adjectives and other modifiers end in **-ых/-их** for all genders (compare the genitive plural form of the third person pronoun, **их**).

Nominative Singular Masculine	*Genitive Plural (All Genders)*
но́вый	но́вых
кра́сный	кра́сных
си́ний	си́них
хоро́ший	хоро́ших
ру́сский	ру́сских
мой	мои́х
наш	на́ших
э́тот	э́тих
оди́н	одни́х

But весь (nominative plural все) has **всех**, and тот (nominative plural те) has **тех** in the genitive plural.

Drill

Change the following phrases from nominative plural to genitive plural.

но́вые учителя́	ва́ши ножи́	на́ши высо́кие зда́ния
после́дние гла́вы	э́ти ученики́	э́ти интере́сные ле́кции
хоро́шие учени́цы	э́ти широ́кие поля́	э́ти широ́кие озёра
англи́йские журна́лы	все́ но́вые автомоби́ли	на́ши краси́вые жёны
мои́ ста́рые роди́тели	все́ си́ние ковры́	

3. Uses of the genitive plural

Like the genitive singular, the genitive plural is used:

Possessively:

ко́мната сестры́—ко́мната сестёр.

After certain prepositions:

без окна́—без о́кон

от ва́шего до́ктора—**от** ва́ших докторо́в

кро́ме э́того студе́нта—**кро́ме** э́тих студе́нтов

до/по́сле уро́ка—**до/по́сле** уро́ков

для (for) мое́й сестры́—**для** мои́х сестёр

о́коло (near) э́того до́ма—**о́коло** э́тих домо́в

у сестры́—**у** сестёр.

With нет (**не́** бы́ло, не бу́дет):

У на́с **не́т** э́той кни́ги.—У на́с **не́т** э́тих кни́г.

With expressions of quantity: As has been seen in Unit 7, the genitive is used with indefinite expressions of quantity. The genitive *singular* is used with nouns denoting divisible matter, that is, substances which cannot be counted, but can be measured:

ско́лько воды́, вина́, хле́ба?

мно́го воды́, вина́, хле́ба

ма́ло воды́, вина́, хле́ба

The genitive *plural* is used with ско́лько, мно́го, ма́ло, and also with не́сколько (several) and сто́лько (so much, so many), when the noun denotes something that *can be counted:*

ско́лько стака́нов, ча́шек, ноже́й?

мно́го пи́сем, студе́нтов, ко́мнат

ма́ло кни́г, докторо́в, теа́тров

не́сколько журна́лов, де́вушек, автомоби́лей

сто́лько кни́г, веще́й, студе́нтов

Pattern Sentences

1. У Ива́на мно́го кни́г.
2. В Голла́ндии не́т го́р.
3. У меня́ ма́ло де́нег.
4. В на́шем до́ме не́т кварти́р.
5. Ма́ть не спала́ мно́го ноче́й.

6. В э́той ко́мнате не́сколько двере́й.
7. В ва́шей ку́хне ма́ло о́стрых ноже́й. Я ви́дел та́м то́лько два́ ножа́.
8. В э́том магази́не не́ было кра́сных карандаше́й.
9. Зде́сь ма́ло хоро́ших враче́й.
10. В Аме́рике мно́го больши́х озёр. Одно́ о́зеро о́коло на́шего го́рода.

1. Ivan has many books.
2. In Holland there are no mountains.
3. I have little money.
4. There are no apartments in our house.
5. The mother didn't sleep for many nights.
6. In this room there are several doors.
7. In your kitchen there are few sharp knives. I saw only two knives there.
8. In that store there were no red pencils.
9. There are few good physicians here.
10. In America there are many large lakes. One lake is near our town.

11. Я́ ча́сто за́втракаю у мо**и́х** ми́л**ых** учени́**ц**. — 11. I often have lunch at my charming pupils'.
12. Во́т оте́ц вс**е́х** э́т**их** ма́леньк**их** ма́льчик**ов**. — 12. Here is the father of all those little boys.
13. На собра́нии не́ было ни ва́ш**их**, ни мо**и́х** учени**ко́в**. — 13. Neither your pupils nor mine were at the meeting.
14. Никого́ та́м не́ было, кро́ме на́ш**их** профессор**о́в**. — 14. No one was there except our professors.
15. Ни́на не мо́жет жи́ть без сво**и́х** подр**у́г**. — 15. Nina can't live without her friends.
16. —Для кого́ вы́ купи́ли э́ти блу́зки? —Я́ купи́ла э́ти блу́зки для мо**и́х** сест**ёр**. — 16. —For whom did you buy those blouses? —I bought these blouses for my sisters.
17. Что́ вы́ бу́дете де́лать по́сле экза́мен**ов**? — 17. What will you be doing after the examinations?
18. О́н зна́ет сто́лько анекдо́т**ов**! — 18. He knows so many anecdotes!

Drills

A. *Place the words in parentheses in the proper case form.*

1. У на́с вчера́ бы́ло мно́го (интере́сный го́сть).
2. В э́том ме́сяце бы́ло ма́ло (хоро́ший де́нь).
3. В Ита́лии мно́го (ста́рый го́род).
4. Ле́том Ни́на прочита́ла не́сколько (интере́сный рома́н).
5. В э́том рома́не не́т (настоя́щий геро́й).
6. У на́с не́т (все́ э́ти журна́лы).
7. У на́с мно́го (нену́жная ве́щь).
8. В и́х кварти́ре не́сколько (больши́е ко́мнаты).

B. *Complete the following questions and answers in the plural, according to the model.*

	Вопро́с	**Отве́т**
Model:	У ва́с е́сть **кни́ги?**	Не́т, у на́с не́т **кни́г.**

Same for: словари́, тетра́ди, де́ньги, но́вости, сёстры, врачи́, у́мные студе́нты, вече́рние газе́ты, кра́сные кре́сла, о́стрые ножи́, хоро́шие учителя́.

C. *Translate into Russian.*

1. There are several large windows in your living room.
2. How many sisters does he have?
3. —How many pencils do you see on the table? —I see only three pencils.
4. —For whom did you buy these textbooks? —For my students.
5. There were no new letters on my desk.
6. How many blue plates and cups do you have?
7. We have neither blue cups nor plates.
8. There are no big forests near big cities.

9. —How many weeks did you stay (live) in the Crimea? —We stayed there three weeks.
10. New York has (in New York there are) several good libraries.
11. He knows many Russian words, but he speaks slowly.
12. I bought these books for my comrades.
13. Near those new summer cottages there are many woods.
14. Our students have few good textbooks.

4. Numerals 5 to 20

Numerals above 5, like other expressions of quantity, govern the genitive *plural*. Numerals from 11 to 19 are formed with the suffix **-надцать**; the first numeral loses final **-ь**, if any:

5	пять	13	трина́дцать
6	шесть	14	четы́рнадцать
7	семь	15	пятна́дцать
8	во́семь	16	шестна́дцать
9	де́вять	17	семна́дцать
10	де́сять	18	восемна́дцать
11	оди́ннадцать	19	девятна́дцать
12	двена́дцать	20	два́дцать

E.g.: пя́ть но́в**ых** дом**о́в**
де́сять ста́р**ых** город**о́в**
два́дцать сове́тск**их** журнали́ст**ов**

It will be remembered that the numerals 2, 3, and 4 take the genitive *singular*. But adjectives used with them are genitive *plural*:

три́ хоро́ш**их** ученик**а́**
четы́ре но́в**ых** заво́д**а**

With feminine inanimates the *nominative plural* may be used optionally:
три́ хоро́ш**их**/хоро́ш**ие** газе́ты

5. Masculine nouns with a zero ending in the genitive plural

A small number of hard masculine nouns have a zero ending in the genitive plural, that is, their genitive plural is identical with the nominative singular. These include the nouns **раз** (time, occasion), **солда́т** (soldier), **боти́нок** (shoe), and **глаз** (eye).

	ско́лько **ра́з**?	how many times?
	пя́ть **ра́з**	five times
But:	два́ **ра́за** (*gen. sing.*)	twice

As stated in Unit 13, the nominative plural of человéк (person) is лю́ди (people). The genitive plural is людéй. But with numerals (5 and above), as well as with скóлько and нéсколько, the genitive plural form человéк, identical with the nominative singular, is used:

—Скóлько тáм бы́ло **человéк?** —Тáм бы́ло сéмь **человéк.**
But: Тáм бы́ло мнóго **людéй.**
Óн жи́л у э́тих **людéй.**

The genitive plural of лéто (summer), лет, is used with numerals (5 and above) and *all* other expressions of quantity as a suppletive[1] genitive plural of год (year):

	скóлько **лéт**?	how many years?
	мнóго **лéт**	many years
	вóсемь **лéт**	eight years
But:	двá **гóда** (*gen. sing.*)	two years

Drills

A. *Read and translate.*

1. В э́том дóме шéсть удóбн**ых** кварт**и́р**.
2. У нáс сéмь мáленьк**их** кóмна**т**.
3. У отцá в кабинéте дéсять высóк**их** и больш**и́х** кни́жн**ых** пóл**ок**, а у меня́ в кóмнате тóлько двé мáленьк**их** пóлк**и**.
4. Я́ куплю́ пятнáдцать бéл**ых** чáш**ек**.
5. В нáшей библиотéке тóлько двáдцать францу́зск**их** кни́**г**.
6. —Скóлько вы́ заплати́ли за э́ту пласти́нку? —Я́ заплати́ла за неё пя́ть дóллар**ов**. Я́ никогдá не плачу́ бóльше. —Для когó вы́ купи́ли её? —Я́ купи́ла её для мои́х дочерéй.
7. —Скóлько стóит кóмната с вáнной в вáшей гости́нице? —Мы́ плáтим за кóмнату семнáдцать дóллар**ов** в недéлю.
8. —А скóлько вы́ плáтите? —Я́ плачу́ мéньше: тóлько оди́ннадцать дóлларов.
9. —Скóлько стóят вáши боти́нки? —Я́ заплати́ла за ни́х тринáдцать дóллар**ов**; я́ никогдá не плачу́ мéньше за боти́нки.
10. В недéле сéмь дн**éй**.
11. —Скóлько **человéк** бы́ло на собрáнии? —Тáм бы́ло пятнáдцать **человéк.**
12. —Скóлько **лéт** вы́ жи́ли в Еврóпе? —Мы́ тáм жи́ли двенáдцать **лéт.**
13. —Скóлько **рáз** вы́ бы́ли в Совéтском Сою́зе? —Я́ тáм бы́л пя́ть **рáз,** а моя́ женá тóлько двá **рáза.**
14. Здéсь нéт францу́зских **солдáт.**

[1] Suppletives are words unrelated in form but linked together in one declensional or conjugational pattern, *e.g.*, "be," "am," "was," etc., in English.

B. *Complete the following questions and answers in the plural, according to the model, varying the numeral of the answer.*

	Вопрóс	**Отвéт**
Model:	Скóлько у вáс **кóмнат?**	У нáс шéсть кóмнат.

Same for: крéсла, книжные пóлки, мáленькие лóжки, нóвые вúлки, сúние тарéлки, большúе ковры́, длúнные столы́, дорогúе лáмпы, ширóкие óкна.

C. *Translate into Russian.*

1. I saw several blue cars in the garage.
2. My sisters bought five red armchairs, and my brothers bought three green armchairs.
3. At the meeting yesterday I saw six Soviet reporters.
4. —How many knives do you see? —I see eight sharp knives.
5. I lived in England twenty years.
6. I don't know all these people.
7. I saw six people who were playing cards.
8. In my apartment there are five bright rooms.
9. My neighbor has three bright rooms.
10. —How many years have you worked here? —Three years. —And I have worked here nine years.
11. I have already read that book several times.
12. I've read it three times.
13. There were two soldiers at the concert.
14. There were no soldiers there.
15. I have no new shoes.

6. Time of day in hours

Котóрый чáс?	*What time is it?*
Чáс. (nom. sing.)	One o'clock.
Двá час**á**. (gen. sing.)	Two o'clock.
Трú час**á**.	Three o'clock.
Четы́ре час**á**.	Four o'clock.
Пя́ть час**óв**. (gen. pl.)	Five o'clock.
etc.	etc.
Двенáдцать час**óв**.	Twelve o'clock.

Бы́ло is used for the past (except one); бýдет for the future:

	Бы́ло двá часá.	It was two o'clock.
	Бы́ло дéсять часóв.	It was ten o'clock.
	Скóро **бýдет** дéсять часóв.	It will soon be ten o'clock.
But:	**Бы́л** чáс.	It was one o'clock.

В кото́ром часу́?	*At what time?*
В ча́с.	At one o'clock.
В два́ часа́.	At two o'clock.
etc.	etc.
В пя́ть часо́в.	At five o'clock.
etc.	etc.

Instead of the English system of using A.M. and P.M., the day is divided into four parts, designated by the genitives утра́, дня, ве́чера, and но́чи:

В ча́с дня́.	At 1:00 P.M.
В ше́сть часо́в ве́чера.	At 6:00 P.M.
В ча́с но́чи/утра́.	At 1:00 A.M.
В ше́сть часо́в утра́.	At 6:00 A.M.
etc.	

Drill

Translate into Russian.

1. In summer I like to get up at six o'clock.
2. In winter I usually get up later, sometimes at eight or even at nine.
3. Tomorrow is a holiday and I shall get up at ten.
4. —What time is it? —It is four o'clock.
5. And I thought it (was) already five.
6. —At what time did you have supper after the theater? —We had supper at eleven o'clock.
7. We usually have dinner exactly at seven o'clock.
8. Yesterday at one o'clock I had lunch with Boris and his wife.
9. —At what time did you see her? —At nine o'clock in the morning.
10. At ten P.M. he was not home yet.
11. It was two o'clock when I saw them.
12. It will soon be eight.

7. Accusative plural

We have seen (Unit 8, page 104) that in the masculine singular (but not in the other genders) the accusative coincides in form with the nominative for *inanimate* nouns and with the genitive for nouns *animate* in meaning.

In the plural, the animate-inanimate distinction and the rule that the accusative is like the nominative for inanimate nouns, and like the genitive for animate, applies to nouns of *all* genders.

ACCUSATIVE SINGULAR

Masc.	*Inan.:* Я́ ви́дел сто́л. *Anim.:* Я́ ви́дел **студе́нта.**	like *Nom. Sing.* like *Gen. Sing.*
Neut.	*Inan.:* Я́ ви́дел письмо́. *Anim.:* (Я́ ви́дел **дитя́.**)[2]	like *Nom. Sing.*
Fem. I	*Inan.:* Я́ ви́дел ко́мнату. *Anim.:* Я́ ви́дел **де́вушку.**	[u]-ending
Fem. II	*Inan.:* Я́ ви́дел две́рь. *Anim.:* Я́ ви́дел **до́чь.**	like *Nom. Sing.*

ACCUSATIVE PLURAL

Masc.	*Inan.:* Я́ ви́дел столы́. *Anim.:* Я́ ви́дел **студе́нтов.**	like *Nom. Pl.* like *Gen. Pl.*
Neut.	*Inan.:* Я́ ви́дел пи́сьма. *Anim.:* Я́ ви́дел **дете́й.**	like *Nom. Pl.* like *Gen. Pl.*
Fem. I	*Inan.:* Я́ ви́дел ко́мнаты. *Anim.:* Я́ ви́дел **де́вушек.**	like *Nom. Pl.* like *Gen. Pl.*
Fem. II	*Inan.:* Я́ ви́дел две́ри. *Anim.:* Я́ ви́дел **дочере́й.**	like *Nom. Pl.* like *Gen. Pl.*

Pattern Sentences

1. Ле́на купи́ла кра́сн**ую** ю́бк**у**, хотя́ у неё уже́ мно́го кра́сн**ых** ю́б**ок**.
2. Мы́ о́чень лю́бим э́т**у** ми́л**ую** де́вочк**у**.
3. Я́ люблю́ э́т**их** ми́л**ых** де́воч**ек**. Э́то до́чери люд**е́й**, кото́р**ых** я́ зна́ю мно́го **ле́т**.
4. —Вы́ зна́ете э́тот огро́мный заво́д? —Да́, я́ хорошо́ зна́ю э́тот заво́д, и я́ зна́ю его́ дире́ктор**а**.
5. Я́ зна́ю э́ти огро́мные заво́ды, и я́ хорошо́ зна́ю и́х директор**о́в**.

1. Lena bought a red skirt, although she already has many red skirts.
2. We like that sweet little girl very much.
3. I like those nice girls. They are the daughters of people whom I have known for many years.
4. —Do you know that huge plant? —Yes, I know that plant well and I know its director.
5. I know those huge plants and I know their directors well.

[2] The word дитя́ (child), which may be regarded as the only example of an animate neuter noun, is very rarely used in the singular.

6. Вчера́ я́ в пе́рвый ра́з ви́дела её **краси́вую сестру́**. — 6. Yesterday I saw her pretty sister for the first time.
7. Я́ уже́ не́сколько ра́з ви́дел её **краси́вых сестёр**. — 7. I've seen her pretty sisters several times already.
8. —Вы́ зна́ете **на́шу но́вую** машини́стку? —Я́ зна́ю **все́х ва́ших** машини́сток. — 8. —Do you know our new typist? —I know all your typists.

Drill

Put the words in parentheses into the correct form.

Зи́на ви́дела
- (ва́ша краси́вая блу́зка).
- (ва́ша краси́вая подру́га).
- (ва́ши краси́вые подру́ги).
- (э́тот ма́ленький го́род).
- (э́тот ма́ленький ма́льчик).
- (э́ти ма́ленькие ма́льчики).
- (э́ти ма́ленькие учени́цы).

Мы́ зна́ем
- (э́ти сове́тские журнали́сты).
- (э́та сове́тская газе́та).
- (э́та сове́тская журнали́стка).
- (э́ти сове́тские студе́нтки).

8. Genitive as direct object of negated verbs

The genitive case is generally used for the direct object of a negated verb, especially when referring to an entire class of things or to abstractions.

E.g.:	Я́ **не** е́м мя́са.	I eat no meat.
	О́н **не** зна́ет ру́сского языка́.	He doesn't know any Russian.
	Они́ никогда́ **не** чита́ют газе́т.	They never read the papers.
	Мы́ **не** получа́ем по́мощи.	We receive no help.
	Я́ **не** зна́ю зде́сь **ни** одно́й краси́вой де́вушки.	I don't know a single pretty girl here.
	Я́ **не** получи́л отве́та.	I got no answer.

However, in referring to a particular, individualized object or person, the accusative *may* be used, especially in colloquial speech.

E.g.:	О́н ещё **не** чита́л мою́ статью́.	He hasn't read my article yet.
	Я́ **не** зна́ю его́ жену́.	I don't know his wife.
	Я́ **не** куплю́ э́то кре́сло.	I won't buy this armchair.
	А́нна **не** лю́бит э́тот десе́рт.	Anna doesn't like this dessert.

Drill

Translate into Russian.

1. I never saw such big stores.
2. He drinks no milk.
3. Nobody likes Smirnov's daughter.
4. I didn't see his wife at the party.
5. Sonya doesn't like cheap restaurants.
6. We didn't see any good hotels there.
7. She never buys expensive blouses.
8. He doesn't like my mother.

CONVERSATION

В кото́ром часу́?

Андре́й. —Бо́б, вы́ должны́ бо́льше говори́ть по-ру́сски. Ва́м нужна́ пра́ктика. Два́ ра́за в неде́лю мы́ бу́дем разгова́ривать по-ру́сски. Сего́дня бу́дет пе́рвый уро́к. Я́ бу́ду игра́ть ро́ль детекти́ва и бу́ду задава́ть ва́м вопро́сы.

Боб. —Хорошо́. Но́ мне́ бу́дет тру́дно отвеча́ть на ва́ши вопро́сы: я́ зна́ю ма́ло сло́в и де́лаю мно́го оши́бок.

А. —Э́то ничего́. Слу́шайте. В до́ме на углу́ э́той у́лицы вчера́ огра́били (robbed) кварти́ру одно́й бога́той же́нщины. Бо́б, я́ хочу́ зна́ть, что́ вы́ вчера́ де́лали?

Б. —Я́ весь де́нь бы́л до́ма.

А. —**В кото́ром часу́** вы́ вста́ли?

Б. —Я́ вста́л **в се́мь часо́в.**

А. —Вчера́ бы́л пра́здник, вы́ могли́ вста́ть по́зже.

Б. —Я́ не люблю́ по́здно встава́ть.

А. —**В кото́ром часу́** вы́ за́втракали?

Б. —Я́ пи́л ко́фе с мое́й ма́терью **в во́семь часо́в,** как всегда́.

А. —Что́ вы́ де́лали **в оди́ннадцать часо́в?**

Б. —**В оди́ннадцать часо́в утра́** и́ли **ве́чера?**

А. —**Утра́.**

Б. —Я́ игра́л на роя́ле. Я́ сыгра́л не́сколько веще́й Бетхо́вена, но́ после́дней ве́щи я́ не ко́нчил.

А. —Почему́ вы́ не ко́нчили?

Б. —Потому́ что вдру́г позвони́л телефо́н.

А. —Аха́! **В кото́ром часу́** э́то бы́ло?

Б. —**Ро́вно в двена́дцать.**

А. —Кто́ ва́м звони́л?

Б. —Э́то бы́л мо́й ру́сский прия́тель, пиани́ст Во́льский. Мы́ ча́сто игра́ем у него́ дуэ́ты и кварте́ты.

А. —Ско́лько вре́мени вы́ с ни́м говори́ли?

Б. —Э́то ва́жно?

А. —Всё ва́жно. Но́ по́мните,[3] что вы́ должны́ говори́ть пра́вду. Всю пра́вду и то́лько пра́вду.

Б. —Коне́чно. Мы́ говори́ли ча́с.

А. —**В кото́ром часу́** вы́ ко́нчили говори́ть?

Б. —Мы́ ко́нчили говори́ть **в ча́с.**

А. —О чём вы́ с ни́м так до́лго говори́ли?

Б. —Снача́ла о́н рассказа́л мне́ не́сколько но́вых анекдо́тов, пото́м о́н сказа́л, что Сми́т и Бра́ун бу́дут у него́ **в де́вять часо́в,** и мы́ говори́ли о то́м, что́[4] мы́ бу́дем игра́ть ве́чером.

А. —И **в де́вять часо́в** вы́ бы́ли у Во́льского?

Б. —Да́, ро́вно **в де́вять.** Мы́ игра́ли три́ часа́, пото́м **в двена́дцать** мы́ у́жинали (бы́л о́чень хоро́ший у́жин) и **в два́ часа́** я́ бы́л до́ма, в крова́ти.

А. —Но́ вы́ мне́ сказа́ли, что вы́ весь де́нь бы́ли до́ма.

Б. —Да́, пра́вда! Я́ забы́л.

А. —Вы́ забы́ли? Но́ э́то о́чень, о́чень серьёзное де́ло! Кварти́ру огра́били **в ча́с утра́.** Но́, **кото́рый** тепе́рь **ча́с?**

Б. —Тепе́рь **пя́ть часо́в.**

А. —**Пя́ть часо́в!** Э́то коне́ц уро́ка. Мы́ бу́дем продолжа́ть на́ш прия́тный разгово́р в друго́й ра́з.

Б. —С удово́льствием! Большо́е спаси́бо за по́мощь! И я́ до́лжен сказа́ть, что вы́ не то́лько хоро́ший това́рищ и учи́тель, но́ и прекра́сный детекти́в.

Pronunciation Drill

bób, vɨ dalžní bóļšə gəvaŗíţ parúsķi. Vam nužná prákţikə. já búdu igráţ róļ detekţívə i búdu zədaváţ vám vaprósɨ.

xərašó. no mņé búḑit trúdnə atγiçáţ naváší vaprósɨ: já znáju málə slóf i ḑéləju mnógə ašíbək.

étə ņiçivó. slúšəjţi. vdóm̧i nəuglú étəj úļicɨ fçirá agráb̧iļi kvarţíru adnój bagátəj žénşçinɨ.

READING

На да́че у Ла́пиных

У меня́ е́сть подру́га Ни́на Ла́пина. Мы́ зна́ем друг дру́га уже́ мно́го ле́т: мы́ бы́ли вме́сте в шко́ле, а тепе́рь мы́ с не́й вме́сте в университе́те.

[3] Remember (imperative).
[4] О то́м, что́ . . . . about what . . . .

О́коло Москвы́, в о́чень краси́вом ме́сте, где́ мно́го поле́й и лесо́в, у роди́телей Ни́ны е́сть да́ча. Э́то огро́мный старомо́дный деревя́нный до́м. Вокру́г до́ма—большо́й са́д, в кото́ром расту́т огро́мные, ста́рые дере́вья.

В э́том большо́м, но́ ую́тном, до́ме мно́го больши́х и ма́леньких ко́мнат, мно́го дли́нных и у́зких коридо́ров, мно́го двере́й, балко́нов и вера́нд. Ме́бель в до́ме старомо́дная и никто́ да́же не зна́ет и не по́мнит, кто́ и когда́ её купи́л. В до́ме мно́го хоро́ших и плохи́х карти́н и кни́г, и везде́ мно́го ра́зных ну́жных и нену́жных веще́й.

Для меня́ всегда́ настоя́щий пра́здник жи́ть у Ла́пиных, у э́тих ми́лых, интере́сных люде́й.

Хозя́ин до́ма, Алекса́ндр Па́влович Ла́пин, изве́стный писа́тель. О́н написа́л не́сколько хоро́ших рома́нов и пье́с. Вы́, вероя́тно, чита́ли его́ рома́ны и мно́го ра́з ви́дели его́ и́мя в газе́те и чита́ли о нём мно́го хоро́ших веще́й (а иногда́ и плохи́х). Ла́пин весёлый и тёплый челове́к, что́[5] дово́льно необыкнове́нно для изве́стного писа́теля. О́н лю́бит люде́й, соба́к, лошаде́й, дете́й.[6] Во дворе́ его́ да́чи (дво́р о́чень большо́й) четы́ре соба́ки, две́ ло́шади и не́сколько ко́шек. Две́ ко́шки живу́т в до́ме.

Алекса́ндр Па́влович лю́бит приро́ду. Ле́том, когда́ пого́да хоро́шая, о́н лю́бит встава́ть ра́но, когда́ вся́ семья́ и го́сти ещё спя́т. Иногда́ о́н встаёт в ше́сть часо́в, а иногда́ да́же ра́ньше. Всё ти́хо вокру́г; то́лько пти́цы пою́т свои́ весёлые пе́сни. Ла́пин сиди́т на вера́нде на своём люби́мом ме́сте. О́н ви́дит ро́зовое не́бо, ви́дит, как встаёт со́лнце[7] и слу́шает пе́сни пти́ц. Как хорошо́ ра́ннее ле́тнее у́тро!

Го́сти и де́ти встаю́т по́зже. Но́ во́т о́н уже́ слы́шит и́х голоса́. У Ла́пиных всегда́ живёт[8] мно́го госте́й. Еле́на Бори́совна Ла́пина, как и её му́ж, лю́бит люде́й. У ни́х всегда́ мо́жно (one can) встре́тить писа́телей, поэ́тов, музыка́нтов, певцо́в и певи́ц. Та́м всегда́ мно́го молоды́х де́вушек, подру́г Ни́ны, и молоды́х люде́й, това́рищей Воло́ди, сы́на Ла́пиных. В до́ме мно́го шу́ма, весёлого сме́ха, интере́сных спо́ров и разгово́ров. Го́сти игра́ют в ка́рты на вера́нде, гуля́ют в саду́ и в лесу́, расска́зывают дру́г дру́гу мно́го анекдо́тов но́вых и ста́рых. Молоды́е лю́ди игра́ют в те́ннис, пою́т пе́сни, чита́ют стихи́ свои́х люби́мых поэ́тов, говоря́т об университе́те и о рабо́те.

[5] Which. Что́ (stressed) may be used as a relative pronoun without a definite antecedent.

[6] Genitive and accusative plural of де́ти.

[7] Sees the sun rising.

[8] As subject of the sentence, expressions of quantity, including numerals, often govern a verb which is neuter singular, particularly when they follow the verb.

Ве́чером все́ лю́бят сиде́ть в большо́м и ую́тном кабине́те Алекса́ндра Па́вловича, где́ у него́ мно́го фотогра́фий ра́зных знамени́тых люде́й и мно́го ре́дких и хоро́ших кни́г. Та́м го́сти чита́ют дру́г дру́гу свои́ ве́щи. Как мно́го хоро́ших расска́зов, стихо́в и пье́с я́ та́м слы́шала!

Я́ всю жи́знь бу́ду по́мнить э́тот весёлый, шу́мный до́м, э́ту семью́, и все́х замеча́тельных люде́й, кото́рых я́ та́м встре́тила.

Чита́йте э́ти вопро́сы и отвеча́йте на ни́х по-ру́сски.

1. Где́ э́та да́ча и чья́ она́? 2. Ско́лько вре́мени я́ зна́ю Ни́ну? 3. Опиши́те (describe) э́тот до́м. 4. Расскажи́те всё, что вы́ зна́ете о Ла́пине. 5. Когда́ о́н лю́бит встава́ть и что́ о́н де́лает у́тром? 6. Кого́ мо́жно (can one) встре́тить у Ла́пиных? 7. Что́ де́лают го́сти Ла́пиных це́лый де́нь? 8. Опиши́те кабине́т Ла́пина. 9. Что́ я́ слы́шала в э́том кабине́те? 10. Что́ я́ бу́ду по́мнить всю жи́знь?

EXERCISES

Translate into Russian.

1. —How much did you pay for that shirt? —I paid $5 for it; I never pay more for shirts. 2. I met him several times on a noisy, lively street in Paris. 3. —At what time did you meet him? —I met him yesterday at 7:00 P.M., and I shall meet him tomorrow at 10:00 A.M. 4. —How many Russian books do you have? —I have no Russian books. 5. Vadim has many sisters. 6. —Are there (any) tall houses in your street? —Yes, on my street there are several tall houses. 7. There were no mountains and no forests where we lived. 8. But there were many lakes, fields, and rivers. 9. —How many legs does a dog have? —A dog has four legs. 10. Near our house there are several good stores. 11. —For whom are you writing down that address? —I am writing it down for my sisters. 12. —For whom did you buy these coats? —I bought them for my secretaries. 13. Chekhov didn't write novels; he wrote (short) stories. 14. Bob has never read those stories. 15. I have never seen Chekhov's plays. 16. I never said such things. 17. He never said that. 18. My daughters were in the Caucasus eleven months ago. 19. I've told you twenty times not to do that. 20. Near the house (there) grow big trees. 21. (All) around the house there are many fields and woods.

VOCABULARY

анекдо́т anecdote
вера́нда porch, veranda
весёлый cheerful, lively, merry, gay
ви́лка fork
вокру́г (*adv. or prep.* + *gen.*) around, all around
двор yard, court
деревя́нный wooden
для (+ *gen.*) for, for the sake of
за (+ *acc.*) for (in exchange for)
изве́стный well-known
коридо́р hall, corridor
ко́шка cat
ло́жка spoon
ло́шадь (*fem.*) horse
не́бо (*pl.* **небеса́**) sky, heaven
не́сколько (+ *gen.*) several, some, a few
нож knife
о́коло (+ *gen.*) near, in the vicinity of
пев.е́ц (*gen.* **-ца́**; *fem.* **-и́ца**) singer
поэ́т poet
приро́да nature
пти́ца bird
раз time, occasion
ра́нний (*adj.*) early
ре́дкий rare
ро́вно exactly, precisely
роди́тели (*pl.*) parents
ро́зовый pink, rosy
смех laughter
солда́т soldier
со́лнце[9] sun
старомо́дный old-fashioned
стих (line of) verse
стихи́ verses
сто́лько (+ *gen.*) so much, so many
у́жин supper
ую́тный cosy
фотогра́фия photograph
шум noise
шу́мный noisy

Verbs

встава́ть (imperf., I: **вста.ю́, -ёшь**), **встать** (perf. I: **вста́н.у, -ешь**) to get up, stand up, arise
встреча́ть (imperf., I), **встре́тить** (perf., II: **встре́.чу, -тишь**) to meet, encounter
гуля́ть (imperf., I), **погуля́ть** (perf., I) to stroll, take a walk, go for walks
забыва́ть (imperf., I), **забы́ть** (perf., I: **забу́д.у, -ешь**) to forget
купи́ть (perf., II: **куплю́, ку́пишь**) to buy[10]
петь (imperf., I: **по.ю́, -ёшь**), **спеть** (perf., I) to sing
продолжа́ть (imperf., I) to continue, go on (+ *inf.*)
плати́ть (imperf., II: **плачу́, пла́тишь**), **заплати́ть** (perf., II) to pay (+ *dat. of person*): **п. за** + *acc.* to pay for
расти́ (imperf., I: **расту́, растёшь**), past: **рос, -ло́, -ла́, -ли́** to grow
у́жинать (imperf., I), **поу́жинать** (perf., I) to have supper

[9] The л of со́лнце is not pronounced. Also note that со́лнце is a *hard* neuter noun (gen. со́лнца, dat. со́лнцу, etc.). The **-е** of the nominative is in accord with Spelling Rule C.
[10] Купи́ть (perf.) is unusual in that it does not retain the prefix **по-** of the imperfective покупа́ть.

UNIT 17

GRAMMAR

1. Determinate and indeterminate imperfectives

Most Russian verbs have only one form of the imperfective aspect to express two kinds of meaning; this form is used:

For actions in actual progress at some particular time:

When I saw him, he *was reading.*
Когда́ я его́ ви́дел, о́н **чита́л.**

—What *is he doing* now? —He *is reading.*
Что́ о́н тепе́рь де́лает? О́н **чита́ет.**

For actions spoken of without reference to actual performance at any particular time; the action may be habitual, recurring at different times:

He *reads* a lot.	О́н мно́го **чита́ет.**
He *read* (used to read) a lot.	О́н мно́го **чита́л.**

Or it may be regarded as a potentiality, the statement being that someone is, or was, able to perform it:

He *reads* Russian (*i.e.,* he *can* read Russian).	О́н **чита́ет** по-ру́сски.
My father *read* Russian.	Мо́й оте́ц **чита́л** по-ру́сски.

It will be observed that in the above Russian sentences, the imperfective forms **чита́ет** present, and **чита́л** past, are used both in the first meaning (English: *is reading*, *was reading*), and in the second meaning (English: *reads*, *read*).

Unlike most other Russian verbs, one specific group of verbs has *two* kinds of imperfective forms for these two types of function. The verbs of this group are related in meaning: they describe different kinds of *going* and of *carrying*. In the case of these verbs, one of the imperfective forms (we will call it *determinate*) refers to the action of *going* or *carrying* in actual progress at some particular time and in a definite direction. The other form (we will call it *indeterminate*) is used when actual progress or definite direction are not implied. These forms denote actions of *going* or *carrying* that are habitual, recurring, potential, etc.

2. Verbs of going "by one's own means"

Russian uses one set of verbs for going by one's own means, without the help of any conveyance, and another set of verbs for riding in, or on, a car, train, horse, etc. (compare German *gehen* vs. *fahren*). Each of these two kinds of going may be referred to by an *indeterminate* or a *determinate imperfective* verb, as well as by a *perfective* verb (which will be given later in the lesson).

For going *by one's own means*, the two imperfective forms are as follows:

	Indeterminate	*Determinate*
Inf.:	**ходи́ть** (II)	**идти́** (I)
Pres.:	хожу́	иду́
	хо́дишь	идёшь
	хо́дит	идёт
	хо́дим	идём
	хо́дите	идёте
	хо́дят	иду́т
Past:	ходи́л, ходи́ло,	шёл, шло,
	ходи́ла, ходи́ли	шла, шли

One of the *indeterminate* forms is used to render *go* (on foot), *walk*, in such sentences as:

He *goes* to the library every day—хо́дит
He *went* (used to go) there every day—ходи́л
He *walks* a lot—хо́дит
Their little boy *walks* (can walk)—хо́дит

One of the determinate forms is used to render *am going*, *was going*, etc. (if the going is on foot), in such sentences as:

I *am going* home—иду́
When I saw him, he *was going* home—шёл

3. Adverbs and prepositional phrases of direction

There are two kinds of *where* in Russian. Where—**где**—refers only to *place in which* someone or something is or was, or some action is or was performed. *Where* in the sense of *whereto* (place *to which* something or someone is moving) is expressed by the word **куда́.**

A "**где** question" may be answered by a phrase with **в** or **на** and the name of the "place where" in the *locative* case:

	—*Where is* Ivan?	—**Где́** Ива́н?
	—He is *in the library.*	—О́н **в** библиоте́ке.
Or:	—He is *at a concert.*	—О́н **на** конце́рте.

A "**куда́** question" may be answered by a phrase with the same prepositions **в** or **на**; the name of the place (place *to* which someone or something moves) is in the *accusative* case:

—*Where* is Ivan going?	—**Куда́** идёт Ива́н?
—He is going *to the library.*	—О́н идёт **в** библиоте́ку.
—He is going *to* a concert.	—О́н идёт **на** конце́рт.

Phrases with **в** or **на** + locative express *location;* phrases with **в** or **на** + accusative express *direction.*

Questions with **где** and **куда́** may also be answered by adverbs.

In answer to **где**? *where*? (location), *here* is expressed by **здесь** or **тут**; *there*—by **там.**

In answer to **куда́**? *where*? (direction), *here* (coming this way) is expressed by **сюда́**; *there* (going away from here, going that way) is expressed by **туда́.**

Two commonly used adverbial forms express "home," one, **до́ма**, as location; the other, **домо́й**, as direction:

Location:

—*Where* is he? —He is *at home.* —**Где́** о́н? —О́н **до́ма.**

Direction:

—*Where* are you going?	—**Куда́** вы́ идёте?
—I am going *home.*	—Я́ иду́ **домо́й.**

Pattern Sentences

Ходи́ть

1. И́х ребёнок ещё не говори́т и не **хо́дит.** — Their child doesn't talk yet and it doesn't walk.
2. О́н о́чень ско́ро начнёт говори́ть и **ходи́ть.** — Very soon it will begin to talk and to walk.
3. Я́ всегда́ мно́го **хожу́**; я́ люблю́ **ходи́ть.** — I always walk a great deal; I like to walk.
4. Моя́ жена́ не лю́бит гото́вить, и мы́ ка́ждый де́нь **хо́дим** в рестора́н. — My wife doesn't like to cook, and every day we go to a restaurant.
5. Я́ люблю́ **ходи́ть** по гла́вной у́лице,[1] где́ мно́го магази́нов. — I like to walk on (along) the main street, where there are many stores.
6. Мы́ ра́ньше **ходи́ли** в теа́тр ра́з и́ли да́же два́ ра́за в[2] неде́лю, но́ тепе́рь мы́ **хо́дим** то́лько ра́з в ме́сяц. — We used to go to the theater once or even twice a week, but now we go only once a month.
7. Мо́й мла́дший сы́н **хо́дит** в э́ту шко́лу, а ста́рший **хо́дит** в университе́т. — My younger son goes to this school, and the elder one goes to the university.

Pattern Sentences

Идти́

1. —Зо́я, **куда́** ты́ **идёшь?** —Я́ **иду́** в кабине́т. Моя́ кни́га в кабине́те. — —Zoya, where are you going? —I'm going to the study. My book is in the study.
2. —**Куда́** вы́ **идёте?** —Мы́ **идём** в ту́ апте́ку. —Я́ то́же **туда́** иду́. — —Where are you going? —We're going to that drugstore. —I'm going there too.
3. Пора́ **идти́** обе́дать! Кто́ **идёт** со мно́й в рестора́н? — It's time to go for dinner! Who's coming (going) with me to the restaurant?
4. —**Куда́ идёт** Ко́ля? —О́н **идёт домо́й.** —Где́ его́ до́м? —О́коло шко́лы, на углу́. — —Where is Kolya going? —He's going home. —Where is his home? —Near the school, on the corner.
5. —Заче́м ко́шка **идёт** в ку́хню? —Она́ **идёт туда́** пи́ть молоко́. — —Why is the cat going to the kitchen? —It's going there to drink milk.
6. —Вы́ ви́дите, кто́ **сюда́ идёт?** —Да́, ви́жу. Э́то това́рищ Петро́в. — —Do you see who's coming here? —Yes, I see. It's Comrade Petrov.

[1] Ходи́ть in the sense of "to walk about" (without goal) takes the preposition **по** + dative, *e.g.*, Ходи́ть по у́лице, to walk on, along, up and down a street; ходи́ть по ко́мнате, to walk up and down a room; ходи́ть по го́роду, to walk about a town, etc.

[2] В + accusative, "per." Мы́ туда́ хо́дим ра́з в неде́лю. We go there once a (per) week.

7. —**Куда́** вы́ **идёте** по́сле уро́ка? —Я́ **иду́** в рестора́н. Я́ всегда́ за́втракаю в рестора́не.
8. Когда́ я́ **шёл** на ста́нцию, я́ встре́тил на́шего дире́ктора. О́н то́же **шёл туда́.**
9. Я́ ви́дел, как вы́ **туда́ шли́.**[3]
10. —Я́ ви́дел ва́с, когда́ вы́ **туда́ шли́.** Кто́ с ва́ми шёл? —Со мно́й **шла́** Ве́ра.
11. —**Куда́** вы́ спеши́те? —Я́ до́лжен бы́ть до́ма в пя́ть.
12. На́м пора́ **идти́ домо́й.**

7. —Where are you going after class? —I'm going to a restaurant. I always have lunch at a restaurant.
8. When I was on my way to the station, I met our director. He was going there too.
9. I saw you going there.
10. —I saw you when you were going there. Who was going with you? —Vera was going with me.
11. —Where are you hurrying? —I must be at home at five o'clock.
12. It's time for us to go home.

Drills

A. *Choose the correct form of the verbs in parentheses, and translate.*

1. С ке́м вы́ обыкнове́нно (хо́дите/идёте) в теа́тр?
2. Я́ обыкнове́нно (хожу́/иду́) оди́н.
3. Сего́дня ве́чером мы́ (хо́дим/идём) в кино́.
4. —Ва́ня, куда́ ты́ тепе́рь (хо́дишь/идёшь)? —Я́ (хожу́/иду́) на вера́нду.
5. Ка́к вы́ (хо́дите/идёте): ме́дленно и́ли бы́стро?
6. Я́ всегда́ (хожу́/иду́) бы́стро.
7. Я́ не люблю́ (ходи́ть/идти́) ме́дленно.
8. С ке́м вы́ (ходи́ли/шли́) вчера́, когда́ я́ ва́с встре́тил?
9. Я́ (ходи́л/шёл) с отцо́м.
10. Я́ вчера́ встре́тил Андре́я, когда́ о́н (ходи́л/шёл) в библиоте́ку.
11. Весно́й ба́бушка ка́ждый де́нь (ходи́ла/шла́) в па́рк.
12. Мы́ ча́сто (хо́дим/идём) в кино́.

B. *Form two series of sentences, one with* **Я́ иду́ . . .**, *the other with* **Я́ бы́л . . .**, *the correct preposition* (**в** *or* **на**), *and each of the nouns below in the proper case form:*

Model: Я́ иду́ в университе́т. Я́ бы́л в университе́те.

Same for: ко́мната, конце́рт, зда́ние, ле́кция, сад, уро́к, по́чта, заво́д, собра́ние, музе́й, парк.

C. *Choose the correct word in parentheses, and translate.*

1. Ива́н, (куда́/где́) ты́ идёшь?
2. Ни́на, (куда́/где́) ты́ рабо́таешь?
3. Ива́н Ива́нович, (куда́/где́) вы́ живёте?

[3] Ви́деть, как + verb—to see someone doing something. Note also: Я́ слы́шал, как о́н пе́л: I heard him singing.

4. (Куда́/где́) вы́ идёте?
5. Мы́ идём (туда́/та́м).
6. Вы́ то́же идёте (туда́/та́м)?
7. Мы́ за́втракали (туда́/та́м).
8. (Куда́/где́) рабо́тает Ива́н?
9. (Куда́/где́) о́н идёт?
10. О́н идёт (зде́сь/сюда́).
11. О́н живёт (зде́сь/сюда́).

D. *Translate the words in parentheses.*

1. —Куда́ (are going) де́ти? —Они́ (are going) в шко́лу.
2. —Куда́ ты́ (are going)? —Я́ (am going) на рабо́ту.
3. Ко́ля хо́чет (go) домо́й.
4. —С ке́м (was walking) Ве́ра? —Она́ (was walking) одна́.
5. Мы́ (were going) в кино́ и встре́тили Ива́на.
6. О́н то́же (was going) туда́.
7. Куда́ вы́ (are going) по́сле обе́да?
8. Мы́ (are going) в теа́тр.
9. Ко́ля идёт (home).
10. О́н бу́дет за́втракать (at home).
11. Мы́ идём (to the drugstore). На́м ну́жно купи́ть аспири́н (at the drugstore).
12. Мы́ идём (to the restaurant). Мы́ обе́даем (at the restaurant).
13. —Я́ иду́ (to the library). Вы́ то́же идёте (there)? —Да́, я́ тепе́рь рабо́таю (there).
14. Я́ ви́жу Ива́на; о́н идёт (here).
15. Я́ не зна́л, что о́н живёт (here).
16. Ко́шка всегда́ спи́т (here). Во́т она́ идёт (here).

4. Verbs of riding

As we have seen at the beginning of Section 2, Russian distinguishes two kinds of going: going by one's own means or walking, and riding in a car, train, on horseback, etc. Like the verb for going by one's own means, the basic verb which denotes riding also has two imperfective forms: *indeterminate* and *determinate:* it also has perfective forms, which will be given later. The two imperfective forms are as follows:

	Indeterminate	*Determinate*
Inf.:	**е́здить** (II)	**е́хать** (I)
Pres.:	е́зжу (pronounce [jéžžu])	е́ду
	е́здишь	е́дешь
	е́здит	е́дет
	е́здим	е́дем
	е́здите	е́дете
	е́здят	е́дут

The past tense of both verbs is regular: е́здил, etc; е́хал, etc.

5. Riding in a vehicle

The vehicle used in travel is expressed by **на** + *locative:*

е́хать на по́езде	to go by train
е́хать {на автомоби́ле / на маши́не}	to go by car
е́хать на авто́бусе	to go by bus

Мы́ е́хали в Москву́ на по́езде.
We were going by train to Moscow.

Я́ всегда́ е́зжу на рабо́ту на маши́не.
I always go to work by car.

But **в** + locative is normally used when it is a question of location, and not of use of a vehicle as a means for travel (compare English "by car" vs. "in a car"):

Мы́ сиде́ли **в** автомоби́ле.
We were sitting in a car.

Я́ встре́тил моего́ учи́теля **в** по́езде.
I met my teacher on the train.

Pattern Sentences

Е́здить

1. Я́ **е́зжу** в Оде́ссу два́ ра́за в го́д. В Оде́ссе живёт мо́й сы́н.
   I go to Odessa twice a year. My son lives in Odessa.
2. Мо́й му́ж ча́сто **е́здит** в Калифо́рнию. Его́ роди́тели живу́т в Калифо́рнии. О́н за́втра **е́дет** туда́.
   My husband often goes to California. His parents live in California. He is going there tomorrow.
3. Смирно́вы ка́ждое ле́то **е́здят** в Кры́м. И́х до́чь живёт в Крыму́. Они́ ско́ро туда́ **е́дут.**
   Every summer the Smirnovs go to the Crimea. Their daughter lives in the Crimea. They are going there soon.
4. Они́ лю́бят **е́здить** по го́роду в своём но́вом автомоби́ле.
   They like to ride around town in their new car.
5. Я́ живу́ далеко́ и ка́ждый де́нь **е́зжу** на рабо́ту на по́езде. Но́ сего́дня я́ **е́ду** на маши́не.
   I live far away, and every day I go to work by train. But today I am going by car.
6. Мы́ никогда́ не **е́здим** сли́шком бы́стро; э́то опа́сно.
   We never drive too fast; it's dangerous!
7. О́льга никогда́ не **е́здит** на метро́. Она́ **е́здит** то́лько на такси́.
   Olga never takes the subway. She takes only taxis.

Pattern Sentences

Е́хать

1. Я́ вчера́ **е́хал на** по́езде из Ленингра́да в Москву́. — Yesterday I was going by train from Leningrad to Moscow.
2. В по́езде я́ встре́тил Ми́ллера. О́н то́же **е́хал** туда́. — On the train I met Miller. He was going there too.
3. Послеза́втра я́ **е́ду** в дере́вню **на** автомоби́ле. Кто́ **е́дет** со мно́й? — Day after tomorrow I am going to the country by car. Who is coming with me?
4. —Как мно́го автомоби́лей! Куда́ **е́дут** все́ э́ти лю́ди? —Они́ **е́дут** на футбо́л. — —How many cars there are! Where are all those people going? —They are going to a football game.
5. Я́ ви́дел, как Ро́бертс **е́хал в** **своём но́вом** автомоби́ле. — I saw Roberts riding in his new car.
6. Его́ жена́ **е́хала** с ни́м. — His wife was riding with him.
7. Они́ **е́хали** о́чень бы́стро и не ви́дели меня́. — They were driving very fast, and didn't see me.
8. Из Оде́ссы мы́ **е́дем** в Ки́ев, и из Ки́ева мы́ **е́дем** в Москву́. — From Odessa we're going to Kiev, and from Kiev to Moscow.
9. —Мы́ **е́дем** за́втра во Флори́ду. —Ка́к вы́ туда́ **е́дете?** —Мы́ **е́дем на** маши́не. — —Tomorrow we are going to Florida. —How are you going there? —We are going by car.

Drills

A. *Choose the correct form of the verb in parentheses, and translate.*

1. Мы́ сего́дня (е́здим/е́дем) в Босто́н.
2. Мы́ ча́сто (е́здим/е́дем) туда́.
3. Я́ никогда́ не (е́зжу/е́ду) во Флори́ду.
4. Э́тот журнали́ст (е́здит/е́дет) в Берли́н не́сколько ра́з в го́д.
5. Здра́вствуйте! Куда́ вы́ сейча́с (е́здите/е́дете)? Я́ сейча́с (е́зжу/е́ду) на вокза́л.
6. Андре́й никогда́ не (е́здит/е́дет) бы́стро.
7. Мы́ лю́бим (е́здить/е́хать).

B. *Choose the correct form of the verb in parentheses, and translate.*

1. Вади́м (идёт/е́дет) в дере́вню.
2. Я́ за́втра (иду́/е́ду) в Филаде́льфию.
3. Я́ (иду́/е́ду) в столо́вую.
4. Соба́ка (идёт/е́дет) на вера́нду.
5. Мы́ (идём/е́дем) в Ло́ндон.
6. Я́ ви́дел, как Вади́м (шёл/е́хал) на автомоби́ле.
7. Когда́ вы́ (идёте/е́дете) в СССР?
8. А́нна (идёт/е́дет) в апте́ку.
9. Ма́ма (идёт/е́дет) в ку́хню.

C. *Translate into Russian.*

1. We are going to Europe.
2. We are going to the study.
3. Who is going to the country?
4. We are all going there by car.

5. Olga was riding very fast.
6. —Where are you going? —I am going to Boston.
7. —Is your wife going there too? —No, she is going to California.
8. We are going to the living room.
9. My grandmother is going to the garden. She likes to be in the garden.
10. The Kalinins are going to Odessa. Their daughter lives in Odessa.
11. They often go to London.
12. They're going there tomorrow.
13. They usually drive fast.
14. They were driving slowly when I saw them.
15. —Where do you go every summer? —We go to the country.
16. We are going there soon.
17. My husband goes to work by train, and I go by car.
18. Today I too am going by train.
19. Do you often go to Kiev?
20. I go there five or six times a year.

6. Adverbs and prepositional phrases of motion (continued)

A. Persons as goal of motion. In Section 3 it has been seen that Russian distinguishes location (**в** or **на** + locative) from direction (**в** or **на** + accusative).

If the goal is a person ("going to see someone," "to someone's place"), then direction is expressed by the preposition **к**; the name of the person visited is in the *dative:*

О́н идёт **к** до́ктору.	He is going to the doctor. He is going to the doctor's (house, office, etc.). He is going to see the doctor.

This usage corresponds to the locational **у** + *genitive:*

О́н тепе́рь **у** до́ктора. Now he is at the doctor's.

B. Motion from a place. Direction "from a place" is expressed by three prepositions, all governing the *genitive* case. These prepositions correspond in the following way to those used to express motion to a place:

	Going to			*Going from*		
Place	**в**	+ acc.	в дере́вню	**из**	+ gen.	**из** дере́вни
	на	+ acc.	на по́чту	**с**[4]	+ gen.	**с** по́чты
Person	**к**[4]	+ dat.	к до́ктору	**от**	+ gen.	**от** до́ктора

[4] **К** and **с** have the forms **ко** and **со** before certain words beginning with a double consonant, *e.g.*, **ко мне́** (to me), **ко все́м** (to everyone). **Со** is used before many words beginning with a double consonant, especially when the first consonant is **с** or **з**, *e.g.*, **со стола́**, "from the table."

The different prepositions and case forms expressing "being at, in," "going to," and "going from" present the following regular correspondences:

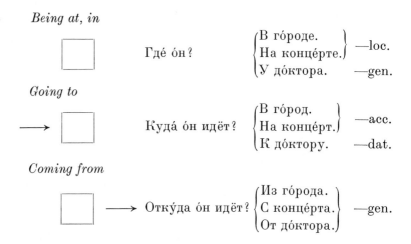

Being at, in

Где́ о́н? { В го́роде. / На конце́рте. } —loc.; У до́ктора. —gen.

Going to

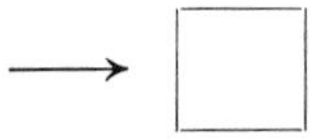

Куда́ о́н идёт? { В го́род. / На конце́рт. } —acc.; К до́ктору. —dat.

Coming from

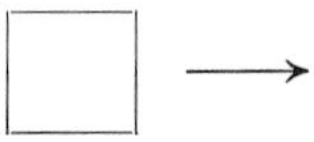

Отку́да о́н идёт? { Из го́рода. / С конце́рта. / От до́ктора. } —gen.

Adverbs of motion. Adverbs of place are distinguished from those which show motion to or from a place:

Place where		*Place to which*		*Place from which*	
где?	where?	куда́?	(to) where? whither?	отку́да?	from where? whence?
тут / здесь	here	сюда́	(to) here, hither	отсю́да	from here, hence
там	there	туда́	(to) there, thither	отту́да	from there, thence
до́ма	at home	домо́й	(to) home, homeward	и́з дому	from home

E.g.:
—Мы́ получи́ли письмо́ **от** Вади́м**а**.
—**Отку́да?**
—**Из** Ло́ндон**а**; о́н тепе́рь в Ло́ндоне и ча́сто на́м **отту́да** пи́шет.

"To go for something," "to go to get something" is expressed by a verb of motion + **за** and the instrumental:

Я́ иду́ в библиоте́ку **за** кни́г**ой**.
I'm going to the library *for a book.*

Я́ иду́ в кабине́т **за** карандаш**о́м**.
I'm going to the study *for a pencil.*

Pattern Sentences

1. —**К кому́** вы́ идёте сего́дня ве́чером? —Мы́ идём **к** Ни́не.	1. —To whose place are you going tonight? —We are going to Nina's.
2. Мы́ идём **к не́й** в се́мь часо́в.	2. We are going to her place at 7:00.
3. —**Отку́да** вы́ идёте? —Мы́ идём **от** Ни́ны. Мы́ **у неё** обе́дали.	3. Where are you coming from? —We're coming from Nina's. We had dinner at her place.
4. —Кому́ ты́ заплати́л э́ти пятна́дцать рубле́й? —Я́ заплати́л и́х до́ктору за визи́т.	4. —To whom did you pay those fifteen rubles? —I paid them to the doctor for a visit.
5. —Куда́ ты́ идёшь? —Я́ иду́ **к** до́ктору Смирно́ву.	5. —Where are you going? —I'm going to Dr. Smirnov's.
6. Я́ вчера́ бы́л **у** до́ктора. Я́ ча́сто хожу́ **к нему́.**	6. Yesterday I was at the doctor's. I often go to see him.
7. Ива́н идёт **от** до́ктора.	7. Ivan is coming from the doctor's.
8. —**Отку́да** вы́ идёте? —Мы́ идём **из** теа́тра. —Мы́ то́же идём **отту́да!** Стра́нно, что мы́ не ви́дели ва́с в теа́тре.	8. —Where are you coming from? —We're coming from the theater. —We're coming from there too! It's strange that we didn't see you at the theater.
9. Мы́ **шли́ в** ба́нк, а Кали́нины **шли́ из** ба́нка.	9. We were going to the bank, and the Kalinins were coming from the bank.
10. А́нна была́ **на** собра́нии. Когда́ она́ **шла́ с** собра́ния, она́ встре́тила Бори́са.	10. Anna was at the meeting. When she was coming away from the meeting, she met Boris.
11. Послеза́втра мы́ все́ идём **на** собра́ние.	11. Day after tomorrow we're all going to a meeting.
12. Газе́та лежа́ла **на** столе́, и я́ взяла́ её **со** стола́.	12. The newspaper was lying on the table, and I took it from the table.
13. —Куда́ вы́ идёте? —Я́ иду́ **на** по́чту **за** ма́ркой. —А я́ иду́ **с** по́чты. Я́ купи́л ма́рки **на** по́чте, а тепе́рь иду́ домо́й.	13. Where are you going? —I'm going to the post office for a stamp. —And I'm coming from the post office. I bought stamps at the post office, and now I'm on my way home.
14. —Бори́с, **заче́м** ты́ идёшь в магази́н? —Я́ иду́ **за** кра́сным вино́м.	14. —Boris, what are you going to the store for? —I'm going for red wine.

Drills

A. *Translate the words in parentheses.*

1. Мы́ идём (from the store).
2. Мы́ идём (to the store for a magazine).
3. Ни́на идёт (to the post office for a stamp).

4. Ни́на идёт (from the post office).
5. Я́ тепе́рь служу́ (at the post office).
6. Ма́ма е́дет (to Sonia's).
7. Она́ бу́дет жи́ть (at Sonia's).
8. Ма́ма е́дет сюда́ (from Sonia's).
9. Мы́ идём (to see Vadim).
10. Мы́ бу́дем обе́дать (at Vadim's).
11. Я́ иду́ (to see Ivan).
12. Я́ люблю́ рабо́тать (at Ivan's).
13. Кто́ идёт (to Dr. Smirnov's)?
14. Я́ бы́л вчера́ (at Dr. Smirnov's).
15. Зо́я идёт (to Lena's for a book).
16. Она́ тепе́рь живёт (at Lena's).

B. *Translate into Russian.*

1. Where are you coming from now?
2. We are coming from there.
3. I am coming from Dr. Smirnov's.
4. They are coming from Sonia's.
5. Andrew is coming from Anna's.
6. We are going to Moscow.
7. We live in Moscow.
8. We are coming from Moscow.
9. Anna is going to Leningrad.
10. She lives in Leningrad.
11. Where is she coming from now?
12. She is coming from Leningrad now.
13. —Where are they going? —They are going to the Ukraine.
14. They were in the Ukraine.
15. They are now coming from the Ukraine.
16. We are going to the concert.
17. We were at the concert.
18. We are now coming (away) from the concert.
19. Whom is this letter from? Where is it from?
20. The letter is from Olga, from the Caucasus.

7. Perfectives of going verbs, with prefix по-

Perfectives of the verbs "to go" (walk) and "to ride" are formed with the prefix **по-**:

	To go (*walk*)	*To go* (*ride*)
Inf.:	**пойти́**	**пое́хать**
Future:	пойду́ пойдёшь, etc.	пое́ду пое́дешь, etc.
Past:	пошёл, пошло́, etc.	пое́хал, etc.

These forms are used as perfectives of the verbs идти́ and е́хать, that is, they are used to denote a single trip. As with other perfectives, the "present" form of their conjugation has future meaning. Observe the difference in the use of these perfectives from that of the determinate imperfective:

Perfective

—Где́ Ива́н? —О́н **пошёл** в шко́лу.
—Where is Ivan? —He's *gone* to school.

Мо́й сы́н **пое́хал** в Ленингра́д.
My son *has gone* to Leningrad.

Determinate Imperfective

О́н **шёл** в шко́лу, когда́ я́ его́ встре́тил.
He *was on his way* to school when I met him.

Когда́ о́н **е́хал** в Ленингра́д, о́н встре́тил в по́езде Андре́я.
When he *was going* to Leningrad, he met Andrey on the train.

The determinate imperfective (бу́ду идти́, etc.) is seldom used in the future.

The present tense of идти́ (е́хать) *or* the future tense of пойти́ (пое́хать) may often be used interchangeably. This is similar to English:

За́втра я́ **пойду́** в музе́й.
Tomorrow I *shall go* to the museum.

Or:

За́втра я́ **иду́** в музе́й.
Tomorrow *I'm going* to the museum.

Here are several situations where the perfective future *must* be used:

If "going" in the future follows the completion of another action:

Я́ **напишу́** э́то письмо́ и **пойду́** на по́чту.
I shall write this letter and go to the post office.

Мы́ **пое́дем** с ва́ми, но́ ра́ньше мы́ **ко́нчим** на́шу рабо́ту.
We shall come with you, but first we shall finish our job.

With **когда́** or **е́сли** in a clause with future meaning:

Когда́ вы́ **пое́дете** в дере́вню, мы́ **пое́дем** с ва́ми.
When you *go* to the country, we *shall go* with you.

Я́ ещё не зна́ю, когда́ мы́ **пойдём** к Ве́ре.
I don't know yet when we *are going* to Vera's.

Е́сли бу́дет хоро́шая пого́да, мы́ **пойдём** ве́чером к Кали́нину.
If the weather is nice, we shall go to Kalinin's tonight.

Pattern Sentences

1. —Андре́й до́ма? —Не́т, его́ не́т, о́н **пошёл** к Бори́су за словарём.
   —Is Andrey at home? —No, he's not; he's gone to Boris's to get a dictionary.

2. —Бори́с живёт так далеко́! Вы́ ду́маете, что Андре́й **пошёл** пешко́м? —Да́, о́н лю́бит **ходи́ть.**
   —Boris lives so far away! Do you think that Andrey has gone on foot? —Yes, he likes to walk.

3. Я́ ви́дел его́, когда́ о́н **шёл** туда́. О́н **шёл** по пра́вой стороне́ у́лицы.
3. I saw him on his way (going) there. He was walking on the right side of the street.

4. —Где́ А́нна? —Она́ **пошла́** в магази́н за прови́зией. Вы́ не ви́дели её, когда́ она́ туда́ **шла́?**
4. —Where is Anna? —She's gone to the store for groceries. Didn't you see her on her way there?

5. Мы́ пообе́дали и **пошли́** в теа́тр.
5. We ate dinner and went to the theater.

6. Мы́ пообе́даем и **пойдём** в го́сти к А́нне.
6. We shall have dinner, and shall go and visit Anna.

7. —Куда́ вы́ **пошли́** по́сле теа́тра? —Мы́ **пошли́** пря́мо домо́й.
7. —Where did you go after the theater? —We went straight home.

8. —Мы́ поза́втракаем и **пойдём** в музе́й. Вы́ хоти́те **пойти́** с на́ми? —Спаси́бо, по́сле за́втрака я́ до́лжен **пойти́** к до́ктору.
8. —We shall have lunch and shall go to the museum. Do you want to come with us? —Thanks, after lunch I have to go to the doctor's.

9. Ива́н ко́нчит перево́д и **пойдёт** в кино́.
9. Ivan will finish his translation and go to the movies.

10. Я́ до́лжен за́втра **пое́хать** в дере́вню к ма́тери. Вы́ хоти́те **пое́хать** со мно́й?
10. Tomorrow I must go to the country to see Mother. Do you want to come with me?

11. За́втра я́ не могу́. Я́ **пое́ду** в дере́вню послеза́втра.
11. I can't tomorrow. I shall go to the country the day after tomorrow.

12. —Где́ Ива́н Ива́нович? —О́н **пое́хал** в Ки́ев. —Жена́ его́ **пое́хала** с ни́м? —Не́т, о́н **пое́хал** оди́н.
12. —Where is Ivan Ivanovich? —He's gone to Kiev. —Did his wife go with him? —No, he went alone.

13. Его́ жена́ прода́ст до́м и **пое́дет** к нему́ через неде́лю. Де́ти **пое́дут** с не́й.
13. His wife will sell the house and will join him in a week. The children will go with her.

14. Я́ ко́нчу статью́ через два́ дня́ и **пое́ду** отдыха́ть.
14. I shall finish the article in two days, and then go for a rest.

Drills

A. *Choose the correct form of the verb in parentheses and translate.*

1. Мне́ бы́ло ску́чно и я́ (шёл/пошёл) к Бори́су.
2. Я́ (шёл/пошёл) к нему́ по э́той у́лице.
3. Мы́ вчера́ (шли́/пошли́) в теа́тр.
4. Когда́ мы́ туда́ (шли́/пошли́), бы́ло хо́лодно.
5. О́льги не́т до́ма. Она́ (шла́/пошла́) в апте́ку за аспири́ном.
6. Я́ встре́тил её на у́лице, когда́ она́ туда́ (шла́/пошла́).
7. Почему́ ва́ш му́ж вдру́г (е́хал/пое́хал) в Ло́ндон?
8. Ско́лько дне́й о́н туда́ (е́хал/пое́хал)?

9. Когда́ вы́ (е́дете/пое́дете) в Ло́ндон, мы́ (е́дем/пое́дем) с ва́ми.
10. Я́ ко́нчу писа́ть э́тот рома́н через ме́сяц, и (е́ду/пое́ду) в Ме́ксику.
11. Они́ ку́пят до́м в Крыму́ и (е́дут/пое́дут) туда́ весно́й.

B. *Choose the proper form of the verbs* **пойти́** *or* **пое́хать,** *past or future.*

1. —Где́ Ко́ля? О́н ...... к това́рищу в Ки́ев.
2. Когда́ я́ ко́нчу кни́гу, я́ ...... в библиоте́ку, а пото́м я́ ...... домо́й.
3. Снача́ла мы́ ...... в столо́вую, а пото́м в кабине́т.
4. —Где́ Зи́на? —Она́ ...... в дере́вню.
5. —Кто́ ...... с не́й? —Она́ ...... одна́. —Тогда́ я́ то́же туда́ .... Вы́ ...... со мно́й? —Хорошо́, мы́ то́же ....
6. —Куда́ ...... ма́ма? —В ку́хню.

8. Idiomatic uses of the verb идти́

This verb is used in the following expressions and many others of a similar nature:

	Вре́мя идёт.	Time goes by (passes).
	Часы́ иду́т.	The watch (clock) is going.
	До́ждь идёт.	It is raining.
	Сне́г идёт.	It is snowing.
	Фи́льм (карти́на) идёт.	A movie is running.
	Пье́са идёт.	A play is running.
	По́езд идёт.	The train is going.
But:	Автомоби́ль **е́дет.**	The car is going.

Pattern Sentences

1. Как бы́стро **идёт** вре́мя! — 1. How rapidly time goes by!
2. Мне́ бы́ло ску́чно, и вре́мя **шло́** ме́дленно. — 2. I was bored and time passed slowly.
3. Вчера́ **шёл** до́ждь и сего́дня опя́ть **идёт** до́ждь! За́втра вероя́тно опя́ть бу́дет **идти́** до́ждь! — 3. Yesterday it was raining, and today it's raining again! Tomorrow it will probably rain again!
4. Зима́ была́ о́чень холо́дная и ка́ждый де́нь **шёл** сне́г. — 4. Winter was very cold, and it snowed every day.
5. Э́ти часы́ не **иду́т.** — 5. This watch is not running.
6. Мои́ часы́ **иду́т** пра́вильно, а ва́ши часы́ спеша́т. — 6. My watch is correct, and yours is fast.
7. Ка́к **иду́т** дела́? — 7. How are things going?
8. Пи́сьма иногда́ **иду́т** ме́дленно. — 8. Letters sometimes travel slowly.
9. Э́то письмо́, наприме́р, **шло́** пя́ть дне́й из Филаде́льфии. — 9. This letter, for example, took five days coming from Philadelphia.

10. Э́тот по́езд **идёт** бы́стро.
11. Отсю́да в Пари́ж телегра́мма **идёт** три́ часа́.
12. Фи́льм «До́н Жуа́н» **шёл** в це́нтре го́рода го́д тому́ наза́д. Тепе́рь о́н **бу́дет идти́** в э́том кино́.

10. This train is going fast.
11. From here to Paris a telegram takes three hours.
12. The film "Don Juan" was playing downtown a year ago. Now it will be running in this theater.

Drill

Translate into Russian.

1. Last year it rained almost every day.
2. My watch isn't running.
3. It snowed early in the morning.
4. Without you time will go slowly.
5. The trains are not running today.
6. It took the telegram five hours to get here.
7. This play was running two years ago.
8. I don't know what is playing in this theater.
9. In summer time goes fast.
10. Where does this train go?

READING

Кали́нины е́дут за́ город

Пикни́к.

Сего́дня пра́здник, и все́ Кали́нины, то́ есть ма́ть, оте́ц и сы́н, до́ма. Сего́дня отцу́ не ну́жно идти́ на слу́жбу, Ко́ле не ну́жно идти́ в шко́лу, а ма́тери—в магази́н за прови́зией.

Пого́да замеча́тельная: со́лнце све́тит (shines), не́бо си́нее. Но́ в го́роде шу́мно и ду́шно. Что́ Кали́нины бу́дут де́лать весь де́нь?

Анто́н Никола́евич пойдёт у́тром за газе́той и прочита́ет её с нача́ла до конца́. Пото́м о́н бу́дет смотре́ть телеви́зор, пото́м о́н возьмёт журна́л «Огонёк»[5] и пойдёт в сво́й кабине́т, где́ о́н, вероя́тно, бу́дет спа́ть до обе́да на своём зелёном дива́не. Ску́чно!

Ири́на Петро́вна бу́дет до́лго говори́ть по телефо́ну, снача́ла со свое́й ма́терью, пото́м с подру́гой, пото́м она́ пойдёт в ку́хню и начнёт гото́вить обе́д. По́сле обе́да она́ пойдёт к сосе́дке и бу́дет говори́ть с не́й о друго́й сосе́дке. Ску́чно!

Ко́ле, и́х сы́ну, то́же бу́дет о́чень ску́чно: оди́н его́ това́рищ пое́хал в дере́вню к свое́й ба́бушке; у друго́го това́рища гри́пп.

[5] A popular Soviet illustrated magazine.

Ко́ля бу́дет ходи́ть из ко́мнаты в ко́мнату и бу́дет с утра́ до ве́чера задава́ть отцу́ и ма́тери ма́ссу глу́пых вопро́сов.

Кали́нины мо́гут пойти́ в кино́, кото́рое о́коло и́х до́ма. Но́ та́м идёт ста́рая карти́на, кото́рую они́ уже́ ви́дели, а други́е кино́ сли́шком далеко́ от ни́х. Они́, коне́чно, мо́гут пойти́ в го́сти, но́ и э́то ску́чно.

И во́т что они́ реши́ли сде́лать: они́ пое́дут за́ город! Они́ все́ лю́бят приро́ду, а недалеко́ от Москвы́ е́сть замеча́тельные места́. Они́ пое́дут в Томи́лино.

До́м, где живу́т Кали́нины, не о́чень далеко́ от вокза́ла, и они́ пошли́ на вокза́л пешко́м. По доро́ге на вокза́л они́ встре́тили Ива́нова, кото́рый шёл со свои́м сы́ном Воло́дей за газе́той. Когда́ Кали́нины рассказа́ли Ива́нову о своём пла́не, Ива́нов вдру́г реши́л, что о́н с Воло́дей то́же пое́дет с ни́ми за́ город. Все́, а осо́бенно ма́льчики, бы́ли о́чень дово́льны.

Тепе́рь и́м ну́жно бы́ло спеши́ть, та́к как бы́ло уже́ дово́льно по́здно, и они́ могли́ опозда́ть на по́езд. Они́ пое́хали на вокза́л на авто́бусе.

На вокза́ле они́ купи́ли биле́ты. Кали́нин хоте́л заплати́ть за все́ биле́ты. Но́, по́сле до́лгих спо́ров, Ива́нов заплати́л за сво́й биле́т и за биле́т своего́ сы́на. Пото́м они́ спроси́ли, где́ по́езд, кото́рый идёт в Томи́лино. И́м сказа́ли но́мер платфо́рмы, и через три́ мину́ты они́ уже́ сиде́ли в удо́бном ваго́не, а через де́сять мину́т уже́ е́хали в Томи́лино.

Электри́ческий по́езд, на кото́ром они́ е́хали, шёл о́чень бы́стро. Роди́тели сиде́ли и разгова́ривали, а ма́льчики стоя́ли всё вре́мя у окна́ и смотре́ли на заво́ды, колхо́зы,[6] поля́ и леса́. Они́ с интере́сом смотре́ли на доро́гу, кото́рая шла́ паралле́льно с по́ездом. По э́той доро́ге е́хало мно́го автомоби́лей. Ма́льчики бы́ли о́чень дово́льны, что и́х по́езд идёт так бы́стро, а автомоби́ли е́дут ме́дленно.

Ро́вно через ча́с они́ уже́ бы́ли в Томи́лине. На вокза́ле они́ купи́ли хле́б, соси́ски, не́сколько са́ндвичей[7] с ма́слом, с ветчино́й и с колбасо́й. Они́ купи́ли та́кже пи́во, вино́, минера́льную во́ду и фру́кты.

С вокза́ла вся́ компа́ния пошла́ пря́мо в ле́с.

Как чу́дно в дере́вне! Во́здух чи́стый и све́жий. В лесу́ прохла́дно и ти́хо, то́лько пти́цы пою́т. Во́т серьёзный и гру́стный го́лос куку́шки (cuckoo): ку-ку́, ку-ку́. Е́сли вы́ хоти́те зна́ть, ско́лько ле́т вы́ ещё бу́дете жи́ть, вы́ должны́ сосчита́ть сколько ра́з куку́шка ска́жет ку-ку́. Но́ заче́м счита́ть? Заче́м зна́ть?

Они́ до́лго гуля́ли по ле́су, пото́м по по́лю. Бы́ло уже́ два́ часа́, когда́ они́ на́чали е́сть. Са́ндвичи и фру́кты бы́ли о́чень вку́сные, и

[6] Колхо́з, collective farm (abbreviation from коллекти́вное хозя́йство).
[7] Another popular word for "sandwich" is бутербро́д (from German).

всé éли с большúм аппетúтом, осóбенно мáльчики. Потóм онú лежáли и отдыхáли в высóкой травé. Пóсле óтдыха онú пошлú гулять по бéрегу рекú.

Нó как бы́стро идёт врéмя! Ужé почтú вéчер! Порá éхать обрáтно в гóрод. Кáк грýстно! И нáши друзья́ пошлú на вокзáл, óчень довóльные своúм днём.

Читáйте эти вопрóсы и отвечáйте на нúх по-рýсски.

1. Какáя былá погóда? 2. Почемý в гóроде бы́ло не осóбенно приятно? 3. Чтó Калúнин бýдет дéлать, éсли óн бýдет весь дéнь дóма? 4. Чтó бýдет дéлать егó женá? 5. Чтó бýдет дéлать Кóля? 6. Почемý Калúнины не пошлú в кинó, а решúли поéхать зá город? 7. Когдá онú встрéтили Ивáнова и Волóдю? 8. Кудá шёл Ивáнов? 9. Почемý вначáле Калúнины шлú, а не éхали? 10. Почемý онú потóм решúли поéхать на автóбусе? 11. Чтó онú сдéлали на вокзáле? 12. Что дéлали мáльчики в пóезде? На чтó онú смотрéли из окнá? 13. Чтó Калúнины купúли в Томúлине? 14. Опишúте (describe), кáк бы́ло в дерéвне, и чтó онú тáм дéлали? 15. Какóй гóлос у кукýшки? 16. Чтó нýжно дéлать, когдá слы́шишь,[8] как кукýшка кукýет? 17. Кáк шлó врéмя в дерéвне? 18. Почемý úм бы́ло грýстно и чéм онú бы́ли довóльны?

EXERCISE

Translate into Russian.

1. Every spring they go to Odessa. 2. Every day I go to school. 3. He likes to drive fast. 4. President Truman always walked fast. 5. When I saw her she was walking with Vadim. 6. I saw him going to the drugstore. 7. We shall have dinner, and then shall go to the movie, which is next door. 8. From the movie we shall go to a restaurant. 9. Are you going home? I shall come with you. 10. —Where are you going? —I am going to Odessa. —I shall come with you. 11. From Italy we'll go to the Soviet Union. 12. Where are you going? 13. We are going to the store. 14. We go to the store several times a day. 15. I have just been at the store. 16. I am coming from the store. 17. Where is Anna going? 18. She is going to the post office. 19. She is working at the post office. 20. She is coming from the post office. 21. Where are these young men going? 22. They are going to the factory. 23. They go there every day. 24. They work at the factory. 25. Now they are coming from the factory. 26. Day

[8] The second person singular of the verb is frequently used in the indefinite sense of "one," "you," "anyone," etc. In this use the pronoun subject is usually omitted.

after tomorrow we are going to see Professor Pavlov and his wife. 27. We shall have dinner at Professor Pavlov's. 28. We are coming from Professor Pavlov's. 29. Ivan is coming here from Leningrad. 30. Here is a letter from him. 31. And where is Olga coming from? 32. She is coming from Odessa. 33. Here is a letter from her. 34. She often goes to Odessa. 35. She goes there several times a year. 36. She was walking along the street with her husband. 37. They like to drive around the country. 38. How late it is! It's time to sleep.

VOCABULARY

автóбус bus
бáбуш.ка (*gen. pl.* **-ек**) grandmother
билéт ticket
ветчинá ham
винó wine
вокзáл terminal, station
грýстный mournful, sad
дéло affair, matter, business
делá (*pl.*) business, affairs
дождь (*masc.*) rain
дорóга road, way, route
дýшно stuffy
колбасá sausage
колхóз collective farm
мáр.ка (*gen. pl.* **-ок**) stamp
мáсло butter, oil
мáсса mass, great quantity of (*colloq.*)
обрáтно back, in return
опáсный dangerous
пешкóм on foot
пи́во beer
порá (+ *dat. and inf.*) it's time to
послезáвтра day after tomorrow
пря́мо straight, directly
соси́с.ка (*gen. pl.* **-ок**) frankfurter
сторонá side, direction
тáкже in addition, as well, likewise
травá grass
фрукт (a) fruit
фрýкты fruits, fruit (collective)
час.ы́ (*masc. pl.; gen.* **-óв**) watch, clock[9]
через (+ *acc.*) in, after, at the end of (a period of time); across
чýдно marvelous, wonderful

Verbs

опáздывать (imperf., I), **опоздáть** (perf., I) to be late; **опоздáть в клáсс** to be late for class; **опоздáть на пóезд** to be late for a train
позáвтракать (perf. of **зáвтракать,** I) to have breakfast, lunch
пообéдать (perf. of **обéдать,** I) to have dinner
решáть (imperf., I), **реши́ть** (perf., II: **реш.ý, -и́шь**) to decide
смотрéть (imperf., II: **смотрю́, смóтришь**), **посмотрéть** (perf., II) to watch, look; **смотрéть на** (+ *acc.*) to look at
спеши́ть (imperf., II: **спеш.ý, -и́шь**), **поспеши́ть** (perf., II) to hurry
считáть (imperf., I), **сосчитáть** (perf., I) to count; consider[10]

[9] The plural is used to denote a timepiece.
[10] Imperfective only in the sense of "consider," when it takes a predicate instrumental, *e.g.*, Я́ считáю Бори́са хорóшим студéнтом. Считáть is pronounced [ṣ̌č̣itáṭ].

Expressions

за́ город (to go) out of town, to the country
по доро́ге on the way
всё вре́мя all the time
то́ есть that is
с нача́ла до конца́ from beginning to end
с утра́ до ве́чера from morning to evening
идти́/ходи́ть/пойти́ в го́сти to go visiting, visit
Часы́ спеша́т. The watch (clock) is fast.

Vocabulary Note

The English preposition "for" corresponds in Russian to several prepositions governing different cases. Observe the following usage:

(1) For = for the sake of, purpose, goal, beneficiary—**для** + *gen.*

—**Для кого́** вы́ э́то купи́ли? —Я́ э́то купи́л **для ва́с.**
Э́то ко́мната **для госте́й.**
Э́то но́ж **для хле́ба.**

(2) For = in exchange for—**за** + *acc.*

Спаси́бо **за** **ва́шу** **по́мощь.**
Я́ заплати́ла до́ллар **за** **э́ту** **кни́гу.**

(3) For = go for, after, to get—**за** + *instr.*

Ива́н пошёл **за** **газе́той.**
Я́ иду́ в апте́ку **за** **аспири́ном.**

Vocabulary Review

Еда́—Food

суп
борщ
хлеб
ма́сло
мя́со
ветчина́
колбаса́
соси́ски
сыр
карто́фель (*masc. sing. only*)
фру́кты
са́хар
варе́нье

Напи́тки—Drink(s)

вода́
минера́льная вода́
молоко́
ко́фе
ви́ски
чай
пи́во
вино́
во́дка

UNIT 18

Imperative mood, 269. Ordinal numerals, 1 to 20, 274. Days of the week, 276. Accusative of time with* на *and* через*, 278. Going verbs with the prefixes* при- *and* у-*, 280.

GRAMMAR

1. The imperative mood

The imperative is the form of the verb used to express commands or requests: "Go!" "Write!" "Help me," etc.

The words emphasized in the examples below are imperatives:

Да́й мне́ каранда́ш.	*Give* me a pencil.
Закро́й две́рь.	*Close* the door.
Откро́й окно́.	*Open* the window.
Возьми́ тетра́дь.	*Take* your notebook.
Купи́ хле́ба.	*Buy* (some) bread.
Не забу́дь купи́ть хле́б.	*Don't forget* to buy bread.

The imperatives in the above examples are in the *singular;* they are used when speaking to one person addressed as **ты**.

Plural forms, corresponding to **вы**, both as the polite form and as the actual plural, are obtained by adding **-те** to the singular forms:

Singular, corresponding to ты	*Plural, corresponding to* вы
дай	да́й**те**
закро́й	закро́й**те**
откро́й	откро́й**те**
возьми́	возьми́**те**
купи́	купи́**те**
забу́дь	забу́дь**те**

A. Formation of the imperative. The imperative of very many verbs is the bare stem of the present (or perfective future) conjugation; other verbs add an [-i] to this stem to form their imperative.

(1) Verbs with stems ending in [-j]. The imperative is the bare stem:

	1st conjugation		*2nd conjugation*	
	чита́ю	[ç̦itáj.u]	стою́	[staj.ú]
	чита́ешь	[ç̦itáj.iš]	стои́шь	[sta(j).íš][1]
	чита́ет	[ç̦itáj.it]	стои́т	[sta(j).ít]
Imperative:	чита́**й**	[ç̦itáj.]	сто**й**	[stój.]
Pl.:	чита́**йте**		сто́**йте**	

(2) Verbs with stems ending in a consonant have imperatives which, depending on the type of accentuation, consist either:

of the bare stem (with the final consonant soft);
or of the stem with a stressed [-í] added.

Accent on the stem throughout:

	забу́ду	[zabúd.u]	
	забу́дешь	[zabúḑ.iš]	
	забу́дет	[zabúḑ.it]	
Imperative:	забу́**дь**	[zabúţ.]	Bare stem with final consonant soft.
Pl.:	забу́**дьте**		

Accent on ending throughout:

	говорю́	[gəvaŗ.ú]	
	говори́шь	[gəvaŗ.íš]	
	говори́т	[gəvaŗ.ít]	
Imperative:	говор**и́**	[gəvaŗ.í]	Stem + stressed [-í]
Pl.:	говор**и́те**		

Accent on ending in first person singular only:

	пишу́	[p̧iš.ú]	
	пи́шешь	[p̧íš.iš]	
	пи́шет	[p̧íš.it]	
Imperative:	пиш**и́**	[p̧iš.í]	Stem + stressed [-í]
Pl.:	пиш**и́те**		

(3) Changes in the stem ending of the first person singular form, which are frequent in verbs of the second conjugation, do not affect the imperative:

[1] The [-j] is weak before [i], or even not pronounced at all.

	сижу́	[şiž.ú]	куплю́	[kupļ.ú]
	сиди́шь	[şiḑ.íš]	ку́пишь	[kúp̧.iš]
	сидя́т	[şiḑ.át]	ку́пят	[kúp̧.at]
Imperative:	сиди́	[şiḑ.í]	купи́	[kup̧.í]

With second conjugation verbs the plural imperative is often the same as the second person plural present (or perfective future); *e.g.*: вы́ говори́те, you say; говори́те! speak! say! With such verbs the use or omission of the pronoun вы, as well as the intonation, often determines which form is indicated. With other second conjugation verbs the place of stress distinguishes the imperative: вы́ де́ржите, you hold; but держи́те! hold!

The following imperative forms require special attention:

Infinitive		*Imperative*	
быть	(future бу́ду)	будь, -те	be!
дава́ть	(imperf.)	дава́й, -те	give!
дать	(perf.)	дай, -те	give!
петь	(imperf.)	пой, -те	sing!
пить	(imperf.)	пей, -те	drink!
по́мнить	(imperf.)	по́мни, -те	remember![2]

The verbs е́хать and пое́хать are defective, and lack imperatives. The imperative forms поезжа́й, -те are used in the perfective.

B. Aspect with imperatives. Verbs of both aspects form imperatives. The perfective aspect is generally used for single, definite actions:

Напиши́те свою́ фами́лию!
Write your name!

Скажи́те мне́, куда́ вы́ идёте?
Tell me, where are you going?

Закро́й все́ о́кна!
Close all the windows!

The imperfective imperative is used for general rules, commands, or requests:

Пиши́ мне́ ча́сто.
Write me often.

Говори́те всегда́ пра́вду.
Always tell the truth.

[2] По́мни ends in [-i] to avoid a final double consonant.

The imperfective imperative is regularly used for *negative* commands:[3]

Не говори́те мне́, что́ я́ до́лжен де́лать!
Don't tell me what I have to do!

Не ду́майте, что о́н ва́м помо́жет.
Don't expect him to help you.

Pattern Sentences

1. **Повтори́те** э́то сло́во.
2. **Спроси́те** его́, когда́ о́н бу́дет до́ма.
3. **Откро́йте** тетра́ди; мы́ бу́дем писа́ть дикта́нт.
4. **Не де́лай** так мно́го оши́бок!
5. Вади́м, **закро́й,** пожа́луйста, две́рь! В коридо́ре о́чень шу́мно.
6. Вади́м, ты́ меня́ слы́шишь? **Слу́шай,** когда́ я́ с тобо́й разгова́риваю!
7. А́нна, **прочита́й** после́дний абза́ц. **Чита́й** гро́мко.
8. **Откро́йте** окно́; зде́сь так жа́рко!
9. **Не говори́те** таки́х ужа́сных веще́й!
10. **Не дава́йте** мне́ сове́тов. Я́ э́того не люблю́.
11. —**Да́йте** мне́ сове́т: что́ мне́[4] купи́ть Зи́не? —**Купи́те** е́й хоро́шую пласти́нку, но́ **не покупа́йте** е́й дороги́х пода́рков.
12. **Не забу́дьте** спроси́ть ва́шего бра́та, ка́к а́дрес Ива́на.
13. **Отвеча́йте** на все́ вопро́сы ко́ротко и я́сно.

1. Repeat this word.
2. Ask him when he'll be at home.
3. Open your notebooks; we are going to have dictation.
4. Don't make so many mistakes!
5. Vadim, please close the door. It's very noisy in the hall.
6. Vadim, do you hear me? Listen when I am talking to you!
7. Anna, read the last paragraph. Read loud.
8. Open the window; it's so hot here!
9. Don't say such terrible things!
10. Don't give me advice. I don't like it.
11. —Please give me advice: what can I buy Zina? —Buy her a nice record, but don't buy her any expensive presents.
12. Don't forget to ask your brother what Ivan's address is.
13. Answer all the questions briefly and clearly.

[3] The perfective imperative is used negatively in warnings, in the sense of "be careful not to":

Не потеря́й де́ньги, кото́рые я́ тебе́ да́л.
Don't lose the money I gave you.

The imperfective imperative is sometimes used to soften commands. This use is particularly common with a few verbs employed in polite suggestions and invitations:

Приходи́те к на́м. Come to see us.
Сади́тесь. Sit down.

[4] The infinitive with dative construction is used to express various shades of modality: necessity, obligation, possibility, etc.

E.g.: Что́ мне́ де́лать? What can I do? What should I do?
Куда́ мне́ идти́? Where should (can) I go?

The dative can be omitted when the reference is obvious, as in sentence 15 (page 273).

14. **Отве́тьте** неме́дленно на моё письмо́.	14. Answer my letter at once.
15. **Объясни́те,** пожа́луйста, э́тим молоды́м хозя́йкам, где́ покупа́ть све́жую ры́бу.	15. Please explain to these young housewives where they can buy fresh fish.
16. **Скажи́те** А́нне, что я́ уезжа́ю, но́ не **говори́те** когда́.	16. Tell Anna that I'm going away, but don't tell her when.
17. **Бу́дьте добры́, переда́йте** мне́ со́ль.	17. Be so kind as to pass me the salt.
18. **Бу́дьте** дово́льны те́м, что[5] у ва́с е́сть.	18. Be content with what you have.
19. **Расскажи́те** на́м о пье́се, кото́рую вы́ ви́дели в Городско́м теа́тре.	19. Tell us about the play which you saw at the City Theater.
20. **Извини́те,** но́ я́ не мо́г прийти́ вчера́.	20. Excuse me, but I couldn't come yesterday.
21. **В чём де́ло?** Почему́ вы́ смо́трите на сте́ну? **Смотри́те** в кни́гу!	21. What's the matter? Why are you looking at the wall? Look in your book!
22. **Посмотри́те,** что́ о́н де́лает!	22. Look what he's doing!
23. **Попроси́те** у ва́шего отца́ де́сять рубле́й.	23. Ask your father for ten rubles.
24. **Попроси́те** Бори́са прийти́ за́втра.	24. Ask Boris to come tomorrow.
25. **Спроси́те** его́, в кото́ром часу́ о́н мо́жет прийти́.	25. Ask him at what time he can come.

Drills

A. *Form imperatives, imperfective and perfective, of the following verbs.*

to do, read, write, explain, begin, finish, repeat, look, buy, open, shut, say, tell (narrate), show, go (walk), go (ride) (perfective only), take, give, be (imperfective only), forget, answer, sing (imperfective only), drink (imperfective only).

B. *Supply imperatives according to the model.*

Model: Попроси́ Бори́са закры́ть окно́.
—Бори́с, пожа́луйста, **закро́й** окно́.

1. Граждани́н, бу́дьте любе́зны, попроси́те ва́шего сосе́да закры́ть окно́.
   —Пожа́луйста, ... окно́.
2. Зи́на, скажи́ Вади́му, что́ о́н до́лжен прочита́ть.
   —Вади́м, ... после́днюю фра́зу.
3. А́нна, попроси́ Вади́ма объясни́ть тебе́ э́то пра́вило.
   —Вади́м, пожа́луйста, ...

[5] То́, что, that which, what, *e.g.*,—О́н говори́л **о то́м,** что о́н ви́дел. He talked about that which (what) he had seen.

4. Ива́н Ива́нович, попроси́те Алёшу откры́ть кни́гу и нача́ть чита́ть.
—Алёша, ...
5. Попроси́ роди́телей писа́ть на́м ча́сто.
—Пожа́луйста, ...
6. Попроси́те Ро́бертса рассказа́ть ва́м э́ту исто́рию.
—Господи́н Ро́бертс, пожа́луйста, ...
7. —Я́ хочу́ показа́ть ва́м на́ш но́вый до́м.
—Да́, пожа́луйста, ...
8. Попроси́ А́нну да́ть тебе́ де́ньги.
—А́нна, пожа́луйста ......
9. О́ля, е́сли ты́ хо́чешь взя́ть мою́ кни́гу, ... её.
10. Е́сли вы́ хоти́те повтори́ть уро́к, ... его́.
11. Е́сли вы́ хоти́те бы́ть та́м в два́ часа́, ... та́м в два́!
12. Е́сли вы́ хоти́те купи́ть э́то пла́тье, ... его́.
13. Е́сли вы́ хоти́те покупа́ть пла́тья в Пари́же, ... и́х та́м.
14. Е́сли ты́ до́лжен написа́ть реда́ктору, ... ему́.
15. Е́сли ты́ хо́чешь писа́ть расска́зы, ... расска́зы.
16. Е́сли ты́ хо́чешь говори́ть, ...!
17. Е́сли ты́ хо́чешь сказа́ть е́й, что ты́ её лю́бишь, ... е́й!

2. Ordinal numerals, 1 to 20

Cardinals	*Ordinals*	
оди́н, одно́, одна́	пе́рвый	first
два, две	второ́й	second
три	тре́тий	third
четы́ре	четвёртый	fourth
пять	пя́тый	fifth
шесть	шесто́й	sixth
семь	седьмо́й	seventh
во́семь	восьмо́й	eighth
де́вять	девя́тый	ninth
де́сять	деся́тый	tenth
оди́ннадцать	оди́ннадцатый	eleventh
двена́дцать	двена́дцатый	twelfth
трина́дцать	трина́дцатый	thirteenth
четы́рнадцать	четы́рнадцатый	fourteenth
пятна́дцать	пятна́дцатый	fifteenth
шестна́дцать	шестна́дцатый	sixteenth
семна́дцать	семна́дцатый	seventeenth
восемна́дцать	восемна́дцатый	eighteenth
девятна́дцать	девятна́дцатый	nineteenth
два́дцать	двадца́тый	twentieth

Ordinals are *adjectives*, and agree in gender, number, and case with the noun to which they refer:

> Э́то **деся́тая** глава́.
> This is the tenth chapter.
>
> Я́ то́лько что начала́ **деся́тую** главу́.
> I have just begun the tenth chapter.
>
> Во́т **седьмо́й** эта́ж.
> Here is the seventh floor.
>
> Мы́ живём на **седьмо́м** этаже́.
> We live on the seventh floor.

The ordinal **тре́тий** (third) has a special type of soft declension with stem [tŗ̧ę̧ţj-] in all forms except the nominative singular masculine. This declension is the same as that of the pronoun-adjective **чей, чьё, чья** (stem [ç̌j-]):

	SINGULAR			PLURAL
	Masculine	*Neuter*	*Feminine*	
Nom.	тре́тий	тре́тье	тре́тья	тре́тьи
Gen.	тре́тьего	like masc.	тре́тьей	тре́тьих
Dat.	тре́тьему	like masc.	тре́тьей	(тре́тьим)
Acc.	like Nom. or Gen.	тре́тье	тре́тью	like Nom. or Gen.
Instr.	тре́тьим	like masc.	тре́тьей	(тре́тьими)
Loc.	тре́тьем	like masc.	тре́тьей	(тре́тьих)

Pattern Sentences

1. Пётр **Пе́рвый,** и́ли, как его́ называ́ют, Пётр Вели́кий, основа́л го́род Петербу́рг.[6]
2. Ца́рь Никола́й **Второ́й** бы́л после́дним ру́сским царём.
3. Ца́рь Алекса́ндр **Тре́тий** бы́л отцо́м царя́ Никола́я **Второ́го.**
4. Англи́йский коро́ль Гео́рг **Шесто́й** бы́л отцо́м англи́йской короле́вы Елизаве́ты **Второ́й.**
5. У Ива́на **Четвёртого** (и́ли Ива́на Гро́зного, как его́ называ́ют), бы́ло се́мь жён.

1. Peter I, or, as he is called, Peter the Great, founded the city of St. Petersburg.
2. Tsar Nicholas II was the last Russian tsar.
3. Tsar Alexander III was the father of Tsar Nicholas II.
4. The English King George VI was the father of the English Queen Elizabeth II.
5. Ivan IV, or Ivan the Terrible (Dread), as he is called, had seven wives.

[6] Петербу́рг; in formal parlance Са́нкт Петербу́рг—St. Petersburg, later successively renamed Петрогра́д and Ленингра́д.

6. У англи́йского короля́ Ге́нриха **Восьмо́го** бы́ло то́лько ше́сть жён.	6. The English King Henry the Eighth had only six wives.
7. На пра́вой стороне́ у́лицы четы́ре до́ма. Мы́ живём в **четвёртом** до́ме.	7. On the right side of the street there are four houses. We live in the fourth house.
8. Мы́ живём на **седьмо́м** этаже́, а мои́ роди́тели живу́т на **девя́том.**	8. We live on the seventh floor, and my parents live on the ninth.

Drills

A. *Answer the following questions in Russian.*

1. Кто́ основа́л Петербу́рг?
2. Что́ вы́ зна́ете о царе́ Никола́е Второ́м?
3. Кто́ бы́л оте́ц Никола́я Второ́го?
4. Кто́ бы́л оте́ц Елизаве́ты Второ́й?
5. Ско́лько жён бы́ло у царя́ Ива́на Четвёртого?
6. А ско́лько бы́ло у англи́йского короля́ Ге́нриха Восьмо́го?
7. Кто́ тепе́рь короле́ва А́нглии?
8. На како́м этаже́ вы́ живёте?
9. На како́м этаже́ у на́с тепе́рь уро́к?

B. *Translate the words in parentheses.*

1. Я́ говорю́ о моём (second) сы́не.
2. Я́ пишу́ моему́ (second) сы́ну.
3. Мы́ чита́ем (the second) главу́.
4. О́н бы́л в Ло́ндоне со свое́й (second) жено́й.
5. Я́ повторя́ю э́то в (third) ра́з.
6. Я́ уже́ чита́ю (the third) ру́сскую кни́гу.
7. Мы́ купи́ли э́тот до́м на́шему (fourth) сы́ну.
8. Я́ ви́дел э́то сло́во на (the fifth) страни́це.
9. Мы́ живём на (the fourteenth) этаже́, а А́нна живёт на (the fifteenth).
10. Мы́ то́лько что ко́нчили (the seventeenth) уро́к в на́шем учёбнике и начина́ем (the eighteenth).
11. Мы́ живём в (the twentieth) ве́ке.

3. Days of the week

These are nouns, and follow the rules for gender and declension which apply to other nouns. They are not capitalized in Russian:

понеде́льник	Monday	пя́тница	Friday
вто́рник	Tuesday	суббо́та	Saturday
среда́	Wednesday	воскресе́нье	Sunday
четве́рг	Thursday		

Time when with days of the week is expressed by the preposition **в** + *accusative* (**во** with вто́ринк):

В пя́тницу я́ бы́л в теа́тре.
Во вто́рник я́ пое́ду в Ленингра́д.

про́шлый	last (literally "past")
э́тот	this
бу́дущий	next (literally "future")

В **про́шлую**[7] суббо́ту его́ не́ было до́ма.
В э́тот понеде́льник я́ бу́ду в Босто́не.
В **бу́дущую** сре́ду (note stress) я́ иду́ в теа́тр.

Dialogue

«Повторе́ние—ма́ть уче́нья» (*"Repetition is the mother of learning"*)
Дни́ неде́ли и ка́к и́х запо́мнить

А. —У меня́ плоха́я па́мять и мне́ тру́дно запо́мнить назва́ния дне́й неде́ли. Бу́дьте добры́, помоги́те мне́.

Б. —Э́то о́чень легко́ и про́сто. Е́сли хоти́те, я́ ва́м помогу́.

А. —Э́то бу́дет о́чень любе́зно с ва́шей стороны́. Но́ для э́того ну́жно мно́го вре́мени и терпе́ния.

Б. —Я́ э́то сде́лаю с больши́м удово́льствием. У меня́ е́сть своя́ систе́ма. Слу́шайте и повторя́йте. **Пе́рвый** де́нь неде́ли—э́то **понеде́льник. Понеде́льник**—э́то "Monday." "On Monday"—**в понеде́льньк.** Повтори́те два́ ра́за:

То́м **в понеде́льник** по́здно вста́л
И в шко́лу о́чень опозда́л.

А. (Повторя́ет).

Б. —О́чень хорошо́. Тепе́рь запо́мните, что второ́й де́нь неде́ли—**вто́рник.** Э́то про́сто и логи́чно, пра́вда?

А. —Да́, э́то легко́ запо́мнить: **второ́й** де́нь неде́ли—э́то **вто́рник.**

Б. "On Tuesday"—**во вто́рник.** Скажи́те два́ ра́за:

Мы́ **в понеде́льник** мно́го е́ли,
Во вто́рник я́ лежа́л в посте́ли.

А. (Повторя́ет).

Б. —По́сле **вто́рника** идёт тре́тий де́нь, **среда́.** Среда́—э́то середи́на (middle) неде́ли. "On Wednesday"—**в сре́ду.** Повтори́те два́ ра́за:

Мы́ идём к Бори́су **в сре́ду,**
Бу́дем е́сть бифште́кс к обе́ду.

[7] Note that these words appear with days in the *accusative* case. With months and years, however, they are in the *locative* case, *e.g.*, в про́шлом ме́сяце, в бу́дущем году́, etc.

А. (Повторя́ет).

Б. —Отли́чно. Тепе́рь **четвёртый** де́нь—**четве́рг.** Повтори́те три́ ра́за:

Мы́ **в четве́рг** в теа́тре бы́ли,
А что́ ви́дели—забы́ли.

А. (Повторя́ет).

Б. —Хорошо́. Како́й де́нь идёт по́сле четвёртого? Коне́чно **пя́тый!** Пя́тый де́нь—**пя́тница.** Повтори́те не́сколько ра́з:

В пя́тницу шёл до́ждь весь де́нь:
Мне́ рабо́тать бы́ло ле́нь.

А. (Повторя́ет).

Б. —Шесто́й де́нь—**суббо́та.** Сло́во «суббо́та» происхо́дит (comes) от сло́ва "Sabbath." Э́то легко́ запо́мнить. Пра́вда?

А. —Да́, э́то не тру́дно. Я́ уве́рен, что я́ запо́мню э́то сло́во без труда́. У ва́с е́сть сти́х для **суббо́ты**?

Б. —Е́сть:

Мы́ бу́дем отдыха́ть **в суббо́ту,**
Забу́дем шко́лу и рабо́ту.

А. —Я́ повторю́ э́то два́ ра́за. (Повторя́ет).

Б. —Отли́чно. Тепе́рь седьмо́й и после́дний де́нь, **воскресе́нье.**

А. —Э́то невозмо́жно запо́мнить!

Б. —Почему́ «невозмо́жно?» Всё возмо́жно. Я́ уве́рен, что вы́ легко́ э́то запо́мните. Е́сть така́я ру́сская погово́рка: «повторе́ние—ма́ть уче́нья.» Вы́ должны́ повтори́ть э́то сло́во не́сколько ра́з.

А. —Э́то коне́чно пра́вильно. А что́ зна́чит **«воскресе́нье»**?

Б. —Э́то зна́чит "resurrection." Тепе́рь повтори́те:

Воскресе́нье, воскресе́нье
Жду́ я́ с нетерпе́ньем.

А. Ура́! Я́ всё по́мню: понеде́льник, вто́рник, среда́, четве́рг, пя́тница, суббо́та, воскресе́нье! Ура́! Я́ ва́с о́чень благодарю́ за по́мощь. Э́то о́чень любе́зно с ва́шей стороны́.

Б. —Не сто́ит благода́рности. Я́ всегда́ ра́д ва́м помо́чь. Не забыва́йте погово́рку «повторе́ние—ма́ть уче́нья».

Назови́те всё дни́ неде́ли. Начни́те с понеде́льника.

4. Accusative of time with на and через

A. на with accusative. The preposition **на** is used with the *accusative* case to specify a period of time subsequent to an action such as going, giving, taking, lending, etc.:

Они́ **пое́хали** в Москву́ **на** неде́лю.
They went to Moscow for a week (to spend a week).

Я́ **взя́л** э́ту кни́гу **на** два́ дня́.
I took that book for two days (to keep it two days).

Questions of this type are formed with **на ско́лько** + *gen.*:

На ско́лько **вре́мени** о́н пое́хал в Москву́?
For how long has he gone to Moscow?

When the period of time is that of the duration of the action itself, the accusative *without* preposition is used. In such cases the English preposition "for" may usually be omitted.

—Ско́лько вре́мени вы́ чита́ли? —Я́ чита́л **три́ часа́.**
—(For) how long did you read? —I read (for) three hours.

B. Через with accusative. The preposition **через** is used with the accusative in the sense of "in" (but not "within"), "after," "at the end of."

Через неде́лю о́н пое́дет во Фра́нцию.
In (after—at the end of) a week he will go to France.

Drills

A. *Чита́йте э́ти вопро́сы и отвеча́йте на ни́х по-ру́сски.*

1. Како́й де́нь в середи́не неде́ли?
2. В како́й де́нь лю́ди отдыха́ют и хо́дят в це́рковь?
3. Како́й де́нь происхо́дит от сло́ва "Sabbath?"
4. Како́й пя́тый де́нь неде́ли?
5. В кото́ром часу́ у ва́с пе́рвый уро́к во вто́рник?
6. На ско́лько часо́в вы́ хо́дите в шко́лу?
7. В кото́ром часу́ вы́ обыкнове́нно встаёте в понеде́льник?
8. На ско́лько часо́в вы́ хо́дите в библиоте́ку?
9. Ско́лько часо́в в де́нь вы́ рабо́таете?
10. В кото́ром часу́ вы́ обы́чно обе́даете?
11. Воскресе́нье четвёртый де́нь неде́ли?
12. На ско́лько вре́мени вы́ е́дете в Сове́тский Сою́з?
13. На ско́лько дне́й вы́ взя́ли э́ту кни́гу?
14. Вы́ надо́лго е́дете в Аргенти́ну?
15. Через ско́лько вре́мени вы́ вернётесь?

B. *Переведи́те* (*translate*) *с англи́йского на ру́сский.*

1. I will take Anna's car for a few days.
2. I was in London for a few days last year.

3. I am going to Victor's for two hours.
4. I am going to work there for two hours.
5. I will return after two hours.
6. I am going to Europe in a week.
7. For how long are you going?
8. I am going for a month.
9. How long will you stay (live) at your sister's?
10. I am going to stay at her place for two weeks, not more.
11. We lived in the Ukraine for three years. We are going back there in four months.
12. —For how many months are you going there? —For two.

5. Going verbs with the prefixes при- and у-

In Unit 15 it was seen that the addition of a prefix to a basic verb may change both the aspect and the meaning of the verb.

The basic verbs of going take a variety of prefixes that express different shades of meaning: coming, going away, going out, leaving, arriving, etc. Thus, the prefix **при-** is added to going verbs to express the idea of "coming," "arriving," while the prefix **у-** is added to express "leaving," "going away." The distinction between going by one's own means and riding is retained with the compounds of these verbs. However, compound verbs of going possess *only one imperfective* form, which serves for both the *determinate* and *indeterminate* functions of the imperfective.

The two imperfective forms joined to a prefix produce compounds which have aspect as follows:

A. Verbs of coming, arriving.

Prefix + *indeterminate* imperfective → *compound imperfective*
при- + ходи́ть → **приходи́ть** (imperf.), to come, arrive (on foot)

Prefix + *determinate* imperfective → *compound perfective*
при- + идти́ → **прийти́** (also spelled **придти́**), to come, arrive (on foot)

The corresponding compounds for riding are formed with **-езжа́ть** (instead of the indeterminate imperfective е́здить) and **е́хать**:

при- + -езжа́ть → **приезжа́ть** (imperf.) to come, arrive (not on foot)
при- + е́хать → **прие́хать** (perf.)

The four verbs, all with the general meaning of "coming," "arriving," are conjugated as follows:

	Imperfective (*Present*)	*Perfective* (*Future*)
On foot	**приходи́ть** прихожу́ прихо́дишь прихо́дит прихо́дим прихо́дите прихо́дят	**прийти́** приду́ придёшь придёт придём придёте приду́т
By vehicle	**приезжа́ть** приезжа́ю приезжа́ешь приезжа́ет приезжа́ем приезжа́ете приезжа́ют	**прие́хать** прие́ду прие́дешь прие́дет прие́дем прие́дете прие́дут

Except for прийти́, the past tense is regularly formed from the infinitive. The past tense of прийти́ is like that of идти́:

пришёл, пришло́, пришла́, пришли́

The verb прие́хать lacks an imperative; the imperfective imperative приезжа́й, -те is used in its place.

Observe that the imperfective forms have both *indeterminate* and *determinate* functions:

Indeterm.: О́н ча́сто **прихо́дит** к на́м.
He often comes to see us.

Compare: О́н ча́сто **хо́дит** в теа́тр.
He often goes to the theater.

Determ.: Сего́дня о́н **прихо́дит** к на́м к обе́ду.
Today he's coming to our house for dinner.

Compare: Сего́дня о́н **идёт** в теа́тр.
Today he's going to the theater.

The "present" tense of the perfective has future meaning:

Perf.: Я́ ду́маю, что о́н **придёт.**
I think that he will come.

Compare: О́н говори́т, что **пойдёт** с на́ми в теа́тр.
He says that he will go to the theater with us.

B. Going away, leaving. Similarly, the prefix **у-** gives a set of verbs with the general meaning of "going away," "leaving:"

	Imperfective (Present)	*Perfective (Future)*
On foot	**уходи́ть** ухожу́ ухо́дишь etc.	**уйти́** уйду́ уйдёшь etc.
By vehicle	**уезжа́ть** уезжа́ю уезжа́ешь etc.	**уе́хать** уе́ду уе́дешь etc.

The past tense of уйти́ is ушёл, ушло́, ушла́, ушли́.

The perfective уе́хать lacks an imperative; the imperfective уезжа́й, -те is used in its place.

In summary:

		Imperfective	*Perfective*
Arriving (**при-**)	*on foot*	приходи́ть	прийти́
	by vehicle	приезжа́ть	прие́хать
Leaving (**у-**)	*on foot*	уходи́ть	уйти́
	by vehicle	уезжа́ть	уе́хать

Pattern Sentences

Приходи́ть, прийти́

1. Ка́ждый ра́з, когда́ я́ **прихожу́** в э́тот рестора́н, я́ встреча́ю э́того то́лстого господи́на.
2. Иногда́ о́н **прихо́дит** сюда́ со свое́й до́черью.
3. Смирно́вы ре́дко сюда́ **прихо́дят.**
4. Когда́ тётя жила́ бли́зко, она́ ча́сто ко мне́ **приходи́ла.**
5. Вчера́ Зо́я **пришла́** к обе́ду.
6. Профе́ссор Па́влов всегда́ **приходи́л** к на́м со свое́й жено́й.

1. Every time I come to this restaurant I meet that stout gentleman.
2. He comes here sometimes with his daughter.
3. The Smirnovs seldom come here.
4. When my aunt lived near, she used to come often to see me.
5. Yesterday Zoya came for dinner.
6. Professor Pavlov always came to see us with his wife.

7. Они́ всегда́ **приходи́ли** вме́сте.	7. They always came together.
8. В понеде́льник снача́ла **пришёл** о́н, а через ча́с **пришла́** она́.	8. On Monday he arrived first, and she arrived one hour later.
9. До́ктор до́лжен был **прийти́** в ча́с, но́ не **пришёл.**	9. The doctor was supposed to come at one, but didn't come.
10. Я́ **приду́** к ва́м в пя́тницу в четы́ре часа́.	10. I shall come to see you on Friday at four.
11. —Вы́ ду́маете, что Андре́й ско́ро **придёт?** —Через два́дцать мину́т.	11. —Do you think that Andrew will come soon? —In twenty minutes.
12. Они́ сказа́ли, что **приду́т** к на́м к обе́ду. **Приходи́те** то́же, е́сли ва́м удо́бно.	12. They said that they would come to our place for dinner. You come too, if it suits you.

Уходи́ть, уйти́

1. Я́ обыкнове́нно **ухожу́** с рабо́ты в пя́ть часо́в.	1. I usually leave work at five.
2. Почему́ Смирно́вы уже́ **ухо́дят?** Ещё рано́.	2. Why are the Smirnovs leaving already? It's still early.
3. Когда́ А́нна **уходи́ла,** она́ сказа́ла, что ско́ро опя́ть придёт.	3. When Anna was leaving, she said that she would soon come (back) again.
4. Она́ то́лько что **ушла́.** Её сы́н **ушёл** с не́й.	4. She has just left. Her son has left with her.
5. Я́ **уйду́** через два́ часа́.	5. I shall leave in two hours.
6. Все́ ско́ро **уйду́т,** и мы бу́дем одни́.	6. Everybody will leave soon and we shall be alone.
7. Е́сли вы́ бу́дете та́к говори́ть, мы́ **уйдём.**	7. If you are going to talk that way, we shall leave.

Drills

A. *Choose the correct verb and translate.*

Приходи́ть/прийти́

1. Зимо́й я́ (приходи́л/пришёл) домо́й в ше́сть.
2. Тепе́рь я́ всегда́ (прихожу́/приду́) ра́ньше.
3. А́нна вчера́ (приходи́ла/пришла́) к на́м в три́ часа́.
4. В кото́ром часу́ Андре́й сего́дня (приходи́л/пришёл) в библиоте́ку?
5. За́втра я́ (бу́ду приходи́ть/приду́) к ва́м ра́но у́тром.
6. Ле́том Ива́н (бу́дет приходи́ть/придёт) к на́м ча́сто.

Уходи́ть/уйти́

1. Секрета́рша сего́дня по́здно (уходи́ла/ушла́) из конто́ры.
2. Весно́й она́ (уходи́ла/ушла́) в четы́ре часа́.

3. Когда́ я́ рабо́тал на заво́де, я́ (уходи́л/ушёл) и́з дому[8] в пя́ть часо́в утра́.
4. Тепе́рь я́ (ухожу́/уйду́) и́з дому в во́семь.
5. Оте́ц (бу́дет уходи́ть/уйдёт) сего́дня рано из конто́ры.
6. Мы́ тепе́рь ка́ждый де́нь (бу́дем уходи́ть/уйдём) ро́вно в де́вять.

B. *Переведи́те с английского на русский.*

1. She used to come to the library at 12:00.
2. She used to leave the library at 2:00.
3. On Wednesday she always comes early and always leaves late.
4. I also come here often.
5. I leave every day at five.
6. I came earlier on Monday, and I left earlier.
7. I don't know yet when I shall come on Saturday and when I shall leave.
8. She went to the store.
9. I saw her going there.
10. She goes there every morning.
11. She left home ten minutes ago.
12. We shall leave soon.
13. When will you come?
14. I shall come on Tuesday.

Pattern Sentences

Приезжа́ть, прие́хать; уезжа́ть, уе́хать

1. Ра́ньше Смирно́вы **приезжа́ли** сюда́ ка́ждое ле́то.	1. Formerly the Smirnovs came here every summer.
2. Тепе́рь они́ бо́льше сюда́ не **приезжа́ют.**	2. Now they don't come here any more.
3. Когда́ мы́ жи́ли на берегу́ мо́ря, Ни́на ча́сто **приезжа́ла** к на́м на де́нь и́ли два́.	3. When we lived on the seashore, Nina often came to see us for a day or two.
4. Она́ обы́чно **приезжа́ла** в суббо́ту и **уезжа́ла** в понеде́льник ра́но у́тром.	4. She usually came on Saturday and went away early Monday morning.
5. Я́ сего́дня звони́л Ни́не, но́ мне́ сказа́ли, что она́ **уе́хала** не́сколько дне́й тому́ наза́д.	5. I telephoned Nina today, but they told me that she had gone away several days ago.
6. Из Оде́ссы мы́ е́дем в Я́лту парохо́дом.[9] Мы́ **приезжа́ем** туда́ в сре́ду у́тром.	6. From Odessa we go to Yalta by boat. We arrive there on Wednesday morning.

[8] Уходи́ть/уйти́ и́з дому, "to leave home." Contrast из до́ма, "out of the house."
[9] The instrumental case may also be used to express by what means one travels, *e.g.*: Мы́ е́дем в Вашингто́н по́ездом. We are going to Washington by train.

7. На́ш парохо́д **прихо́дит**[10] в де́вять часо́в утра́. — 7. Our boat arrives at 9:00 A.M.
8. Как то́лько мы́ **прие́дем,** мы́ сейча́с же позвони́м до́ктору Смирно́ву. — 8. As soon as we arrive, we shall call Dr. Smirnov at once.
9. На́м сказа́ли, что до́ктор Смирно́в **уе́хал** из Я́лты неде́лю тому́ наза́д. — 9. We were told that Dr. Smirnov had left Yalta a week ago.
10. Ива́н то́лько что **прие́хал** из А́фрики и **уезжа́ет** за́втра в Австра́лию. О́н **уезжа́ет** на два́ ме́сяца. — 10. Ivan has just arrived from Africa and is leaving tomorrow for Australia. He's going away for two months.
11. Мои́ роди́тели **уе́хали** в Евро́пу во вто́рник. Они́ **уе́хаи** на всё ле́то. — 11. My parents left for Europe on Tuesday. They've gone for the whole summer.
12. **Приезжа́йте** к на́м ча́сто. Мы́ всегда́ ра́ды ва́с ви́деть. — 12. Come and see us often. We are always glad to see you.

Drills

Replace the English verb in parentheses by the proper Russian verb form and translate.

при-

1. Мы́ вчера́ (came) в Нью-Йо́рк.
2. А́нна (came) с на́ми.
3. В э́тот ра́з мо́й оте́ц (didn't come) в го́род.
4. О́н (used to come) сюда́ ра́з в го́д.
5. А́нна всегда́ (came) с ни́м.
6. Мы́ иногда́ (came) одни́.
7. Я́ не зна́ю, когда́ мы́ опя́ть (will come) сюда́.
8. Когда́ вы́ (will come) к на́м в Кры́м?
9. Мы́ (will come) ле́том.
10. Мы́ (will come) ча́сто.

у-

1. Андре́й (left Moscow).
2. Зо́я (left) с ни́м.
3. Они́ (left) вме́сте.
4. Мы́ ско́ро (are leaving).
5. Когда́ вы́ (are leaving)?
6. Я́ (am leaving) через две́ неде́ли.
7. Они́ (are leaving) на две́ неде́ли.
8. Когда́ они́ (will leave), О́льга бу́дет жи́ть в и́х кварти́ре.
9. Е́сли зде́сь бу́дет о́чень жа́рко, мы́ (will leave).

[10] Observe the use of the "walking" form of the verb for the movement of boats and trains (but not cars or other vehicles).

READING

Челове́к, у кото́рого не́т па́мяти

Леони́д Па́влович Соро́кин ста́рый дру́г семьи́. О́н ча́сто приходи́л к моему́ отцу́, а тепе́рь о́н ча́сто прихо́дит ко мне́. Я́ говорю́, что о́н прихо́дит «ко мне́,» а не «к на́м,» потому́ что мо́й му́ж, Серге́й Фёдорович, не лю́бит Соро́кина. Ему́ ску́чно с ни́м разгова́ривать, и о́н обыкнове́нно ухо́дит, как то́лько слы́шит его́ го́лос. Я́ ду́маю, что Леони́д Па́влович э́то зна́ет и, поэ́тому, предпочита́ет приходи́ть, когда́ моего́ му́жа не́т до́ма. Меня́ о́н лю́бит как до́чь. Мне́ его́ жа́ль, о́н тако́й ста́рый и одино́кий. Никому́ о́н не ну́жен.

С Соро́киным не о́чень легко́ разгова́ривать. О́н о́чень лю́бит задава́ть вопро́сы, но́ о́н пло́хо слы́шит, что́ ему́ отвеча́ют и́ли забыва́ет, что́ вы́ ему́ то́лько что сказа́ли и через мину́ту опя́ть задаёт то́т же вопро́с.

Сего́дня я́ была́ одна́, когда́ вдру́г позвони́л звоно́к. Наве́рно э́то Леони́д Па́влович. Открыва́ю две́рь. Та́к и е́сть! Э́то о́н. Во́т на́ш разгово́р.

Я —Здра́вствуйте, ми́лый дру́г! Как хорошо́, что вы́ пришли́. О́чень ра́да ва́с ви́деть. Ну́, что́ у ва́с но́вого?

С. —Ничего́ у меня́ не́т но́вого, Со́нечка,[11] ста́рость и бо́льше ничего́. А что́ у ва́с но́вого, мо́й а́нгел? Я́ так давно́ ва́с не ви́дел.

Я —Ну ка́к давно́? Вы́ ведь[12] бы́ли зде́сь во вто́рник, а сего́дня четве́рг. Вы́ бы́ли зде́сь позавчера́.

С. —Позавчера́? Не по́мню, мо́й а́нгел, не по́мню. У меня́ тепе́рь совсе́м не́т па́мяти; я́ всё забыва́ю. А где́ же на́ш дорого́й Серге́й Фёдорович?

Я —Я́ ведь ва́м во вто́рник сказа́ла, что о́н в суббо́ту уе́хал в Ме́ксику.

С. —Я́ не слы́шу. Куда́ о́н уе́хал?

Я —В Ме́ксику, в Ме́ксику!

С. —А заче́м о́н туда́ пое́хал?

Я —Я́ ва́м всё позавчера́ рассказа́ла. Ему́ нужны́ ра́зные докуме́нты и материа́лы для статьи́. О́н пи́шет большу́ю статью́ об экономи́ческом положе́нии Ме́ксики во вре́мя войны́.

С. —Во вре́мя како́й войны́?

Я —Во вре́мя второ́й мирово́й войны́.

[11] Со́нечка, affectionate diminutive of Со́фья.

[12] Ведь is used to support a statement. Depending on the context, ведь may be translated by: *since, but, as you know, of course,* or it may sometimes be omitted in translation. The word ведь is never stressed.

С. —Как интере́сно! А ра́зве в Ме́ксике то́же е́сть экономи́ческое положе́ние?

Я —Ну что́ вы́ спра́шиваете, Леони́д Па́влович! Коне́чно е́сть. Везде́ е́сть экономи́ческое положе́ние! Сена́тор Фо́кс (вы́ о нём, коне́чно, слы́шали) неда́вно прие́хал из Ме́ксики и написа́л об э́том вопро́се о́чень интере́сную статью́. Сена́тор жи́л та́м це́лую неде́лю, и тепе́рь о́н настоя́щий экспе́рт. Я́ прочита́ла его́ статью́ с больши́м интере́сом. Вы́ её чита́ли?

С. —Не́т, Со́нечка, не чита́л. Мне́ тепе́рь тру́дно чита́ть; я́ пло́хо ви́жу и па́мять у меня́ тепе́рь то́же не о́чень хоро́шая. Расскажи́те мне́, что́ о́н та́м пи́шет, и́ли да́йте мне́ статью́, и я́ са́м её прочита́ю. А отку́да прие́хал э́тот Но́кс?

Я —О́н при́ехал из Ме́ксики, как я́ ва́м то́лько что сказа́ла, и фами́лия его́ не Но́кс, а Фо́кс.

С. —Всё равно́, Но́кс и́ли Фо́кс. Так о́н прие́хал из Москвы́? И Серге́й Фёдорович тепе́рь в Москве́! Статью́ Серге́я Фёдоровича о Москве́ я́, коне́чно, прочита́ю. Я́ уве́рен, что она́ бу́дет о́чень интере́сная. О́н наве́рно бу́дет в Кремле́ и бу́дет говори́ть с Ле́ниным. Позвони́те мне́, Со́нечка, как то́лько Серге́й Фёдорович прие́дет из Москвы́. Мне́ о́чень интере́сно послу́шать его́ расска́зы.

Я —Послу́шайте, Леони́д Па́влович, ра́зве вы́ не зна́ете, что Ле́нин уже́ не в Кремле́, а в мавзоле́е на Кра́сной пло́щади?

С. —В мавзоле́е? А я́ не зна́л? Но́ э́то не ва́жно; Серге́й Фёдорович мо́жет говори́ть с ни́м в мавзоле́е.

Я —Леони́д Па́влович! Ну что́ вы́ говори́те!

С. —Не слы́шу. Что? Ну́, тепе́рь я́ ухожу́. Я́ до́лжен идти́, Со́нечка. В два́ часа́ ко мне́ придёт оди́н студе́нт. О́н прихо́дит ко мне́ три́ ра́за в неде́лю и я́ помога́ю ему́ писа́ть рабо́ту[13] об экономи́ческом положе́нии во вре́мя войны́ в . . . не по́мню где́. Не понима́ю, ка́к я́ мо́г э́то забы́ть. Ну́, до свида́ния, мо́й а́нгел. Большо́е спаси́бо за интере́сные но́вости. За́втра я́ опя́ть приду́ к ва́м. Хорошо́?

Я —Коне́чно, приходи́те.

Сла́ва Бо́гу, бе́дный Соро́кин наконе́ц ушёл. Но́, Бо́же мо́й, что́ мне́ де́лать? Тепе́рь, когда́ о́н зна́ет, что му́жа не́т, о́н бу́дет приходи́ть ка́ждый де́нь.

Я́ сейча́с напишу́ му́жу о на́шем интере́сном разгово́ре, кото́рый вы́, мо́й чита́тель, то́лько что прочита́ли. И, хотя́ мне́ и[14] о́чень жа́ль Соро́кина, но́ ни за́втра ни послеза́втра меня́ весь де́нь не бу́дет до́ма.

[13] Рабо́та (here) paper.

[14] The conjunction **и** often follows хотя́ (хотя́ и), *although, though, even if, in spite of the fact that.*

Читайте эти вопросы и отвечайте на них по-русски.

1. Почему́ Леони́д Па́влович ча́сто прихо́дит к Со́не? 2. У него́ е́сть семья́? 3. Почему́ Со́ня не ухо́дит (как э́то де́лает её му́ж), когда́ прихо́дит Соро́кин? 4. Что́ о́н обыкнове́нно де́лает у Со́ни? 5. Почему́ она́ была́ одна́, когда́ Соро́кин к не́й пришёл? 6. Соро́кин давно́ её не ви́дел? 7. Почему́ о́н не зна́л, что Серге́й Фёдорович уе́хал? 8. Кто́ му́ж Со́ни, и почему́ о́н в Ме́ксике? 9. Кака́я война́ была́ до второ́й миро́вой войны́? 10. Ско́лько вре́мени жи́л сена́тор Фо́кс в Ме́ксике? 11. О чём о́н пи́шет в свое́й статье́? 12. Почему́ Соро́кин тепе́рь ма́ло чита́ет? 13. Вы́ зна́ете, где́ Кра́сная пло́щадь? 14. Ка́к вы́ ду́маете, Леони́д Па́влович хорошо́ помога́ет студе́нту? 15. Почему́ мы́ не зна́ем, о како́й стране́ пи́шет э́тот студе́нт? 16. Что́ бу́дет за́втра, когда́ Соро́кин придёт к Со́не?

EXERCISES

A. *Give a suitable Russian word or phrase for the English in parentheses.*

1. Мы́ придём (to see you) за́втра у́тром. 2. По́сле ле́кции о́н пришёл (to see me). 3. О́н бы́л (at my place) в три́ часа́. 4. О́н ско́ро (left my place). 5. Они́ бу́дут ра́ды, когда́ о́н (will leave them). 6. Когда́ вы́ придёте (to see us)? 7. Бы́ло по́здно, когда́ Ни́на (left her). 8. Е́сли ты́ за́втра бу́дешь (at home), я́ приду́ (to your place) и бу́ду обе́дать (at your place). 9. О́н вчера́ в пе́рвый ра́з пришёл (to Vadim's) и (left him) через ча́с. 10. Я́ бы́л (at Anna's), когда́ Зи́на пришла́ (to her place). 11. Я́ прие́ду (in two hours). 12. Я́ бу́ду рабо́тать (for two hours). 13. Я́ уйду́ (after two hours). 14. Я́ приду́ (at two o'clock). 15. Мы́ уезжа́ем (in a week). 16. Мы́ бу́дем жи́ть та́м (for a week). 17. Мы́ уезжа́ем (for a week). 18. Она́ пришла́ (for an hour). 19. Она́ сиди́т у на́с уже́ (for three hours). 20. О́льга пришла́ к на́м (for a book). 21. О́н бу́дет зде́сь (until Tuesday or Wednesday). 22. (After the theater) мы́ пойдём пря́мо домо́й.

B. *Переведи́те на ру́сский язы́к.*

1. Last month when he arrived from Madrid, he came at once to see us. 2. She just came from the director. 3. From his study she came to my room. 4. They left school early today. 5. From where

did he come, from Odessa or from Leningrad? 6. When I came to his room, he wasn't there. 7. Next month he will get (arrive) here from Africa. 8. I am leaving in two days. 9. When they leave Boston next year, who is going to live in their house? 10. She left the concert before the end. 11. She had just left for Moscow for a week. 12. We came here from France. 13. —When did he leave there? —Last Wednesday. 14. Come and see us on Monday. 15. Memorize the names of the days of the week. 16. Be so kind (as to) help me. 17. Excuse me, I have no time. 18. As soon as you arrive in London, write to all your friends. 19. Take this money and give it to your sons. 20. Don't give money to small children.

VOCABULARY

***абза́ц** paragraph
а́нгел angel
бифште́кс beefsteak
Бог[15] God
вели́кий great
возмо́жно possible
коро́ль (*masc.*) king
короле́ва queen
любе́зный gracious, pleasant, polite
***мавзоле́й** mausoleum
***Ме́ксика** Mexico
мину́та minute
мирово́й world (*adj.*)
наве́рно probably, surely
надо́лго for a long time
невозмо́жно impossible
нетерпе́ние impatience
одино́кий lonely
отли́чный excellent
парохо́д ship, steamboat
повторе́ние repetition
***погово́рка** (*gen. pl.* **-ок**) saying, proverb
позавчера́ day before yesterday
положе́ние position, situation
посте́ль (*fem.*) bed, bedding
пра́вильный correct
ра́зве? can it be that . . . ? (expresses surprise or disbelief)
ра́зве . . . не? surely?
рубль (*masc.*) ruble
середи́на middle
соль (*fem.*) salt
ста́рость (*fem.*) old age
терпе́ние patience
уве́рен, -а, -ы sure, certain
уче́нье study, studying
це́рк.овь (*fem., gen.* **-ви**) church
чита́тель (*fem.* **-ница**) reader
эта́ж floor, story
я́сный clear

Verbs

благодари́ть (imperf., II: **благодар.ю́, -и́шь**), **поблагодари́ть** (perf., II) to thank (+ *acc. of person thanked;* **за** + *acc. of object of thanks*)

[15] The word Бог has the vocative (special form for direct address) Бо́же!

ждать (imperf., I: **жд.у, -ёшь**), **подожда́ть** (perf., I) to wait for[16]
запомина́ть (imperf., I), **запо́мнить** (perf., II: **запо́мн.ю, -ишь**) to memorize, learn (by heart)
извиня́ть (imperf., I), **извини́ть** (perf., II: **извин.ю́, -и́шь**) to excuse
называ́ть (imperf., I), **назва́ть** (perf., I: **назов.у́, -ёшь**) to name, call
осно́вывать (imperf., I), **основа́ть** (perf., I, **осну.ю́, -ёшь**) to found, establish
передава́ть (imperf., I: **переда.ю́, -ёшь**), **переда́ть** (perf., like **дать**) to transfer, pass, hand on, transmit, convey
повторя́ть (imperf., I), **повтори́ть** (perf., II: **повтор.ю́, -и́шь**) to repeat
помо́чь (perf. of **помога́ть,** I: like **мочь**) to help (+ *dat. of person helped*)
послу́шать (perf. of **слу́шать,** I) to listen, obey (+ *acc.*)
предпочита́ть (imperf., I) to prefer
проси́ть (imperf., II: **прошу́, про́сишь**), **попроси́ть** (perf., II) to ask (for), request, beg (for)[17]

Expressions

с ва́шей стороны́ on your part
Бу́дьте добры́ . . . } Be so good as to (+ *imper. or infin.*)
Бу́дьте любе́зны . . . }
к обе́ду to dinner, for dinner
Мне́ бы́ло ле́нь (+ *infin.*) I didn't feel like . . .; I felt too lazy to . . .
Что́ зна́чит . . . ? What does . . . mean?
Не сто́ит (благода́рности). Don't mention it.
Мне́ его́ (*acc.*) **бы́ло жа́ль.** I felt sorry for him.
то́т же, та́ же, то́ же the same[18]
Та́к и е́сть. So it is.
Сла́ва Бо́гу! Thank God!
Бо́же мо́й! My God! My goodness!

[16] With the verb ждать, masculine and neuter nouns are normally in the genitive. Feminine nouns, in particular animates, show a strong tendency to take the accusative rather than the genitive, *e.g.*:

Я́ жду́ по́езда. I'm waiting for a train.
But: Я́ жду́ жену́. I'm waiting for my wife.

[17] Проси́ть/попроси́ть takes the *accusative* of the person asked + the *infinitive* of the favor asked, *e.g.*, Я́ попроси́л А́нну мне́ помо́чь. But when an object is requested, it is put in the *accusative* case, while the person from whom it is requested is then expressed by **у** + *genitive*, *e.g.*, Я́ попроси́л у А́нны кни́гу.
Note that спра́шивать/спроси́ть means "to ask a question." It governs the *accusative* of the person asked, or **у** + *genitive*.

[18] *E.g.*, Они́ обе́дали в **том же** рестора́не, что мы́. They ate in the same restaurant that we did.

UNIT 19

GRAMMAR

1. Verbs in -ся

Many Russian verbs add the suffix **-ся** (or **-сь**) to all their forms. The addition of this suffix often serves to indicate that the action of the verb is not directed toward an object; in other words, that the verb is *intransitive*. Thus the suffix **-ся** is often added to verbs which are normally transitive, to denote their intransitive uses.

A. Verbs used with or without -ся. One example of such a verb is начина́ть—нача́ть (to begin, start); with **-ся**: начина́ться—нача́ться. The forms without **-ся** are used only when the action is directed toward an object:

Я́ **на́чал** э́ту рабо́ту в де́вять часо́в утра́.
I *started* that work at 9:00 A.M.

Учи́тель **начина́ет** уро́к с объясне́ния грамма́тики.
The teacher *begins* the lesson with a grammar explanation.

If there is no object, then the forms with **-ся** must be used:

Моя́ рабо́та **начина́ется** в де́вять часо́в.
My work *starts* at 9:00.

Уро́к **начина́ется** с объясне́ния грамма́тики.
The lesson *begins* with a grammar explanation.

Similarly with конча́ться—ко́нчиться; открыва́ться—откры́ться; закрыва́ться—закры́ться:

Хозя́ин **открыва́ет** магази́н в де́вять часо́в.
The owner *opens* his store at 9:00.

Его́ магази́н **открыва́ется** в де́вять часо́в.
His store *opens* at 9:00.

Я́ ме́дленно **закрыва́ю** две́рь.
I *close* the door slowly.

Две́рь ме́дленно **закрыва́ется.**
The door *is closing* slowly.

Some verbs acquire a *reflexive* meaning with the **-ся** suffix (the action of the verb is directed toward the subject itself):

	Ма́ть **одева́ет** ребёнка.	The mother dresses the child.
But:	Ма́ть **одева́ется.**	The mother is dressing (herself).
	Я́ **мо́ю** посу́ду.	I am washing the dishes.
But:	Я́ **мо́юсь.**	I am washing (myself).

Sometimes this reflexive meaning becomes a *reciprocal* meaning, when several subjects perform an action and are also objects of this action:

Мы́ о́чень ре́дко **ви́димся.**
We see each other very seldom.

Они́ ча́сто **встреча́лись** зимо́й.
They often met in the winter.

A number of verbs occur *only* with the **-ся** suffix; many of these describe *emotions* or behavior expressing emotion:

боя́ться	to fear, be afraid of
наде́яться	to hope
смея́ться	to laugh

In English such verbs may sometimes have an object, *e.g.*, "to fear," but not in Russian. Боя́ться takes the *genitive* case (compare English "be afraid *of*"):

Э́тот учени́к **бои́тся** экза́мен**а**.
That student is afraid of the exam.

The predicate complement of the verb каза́ться, "to seem," is in the instrumental:

О́н мне́ **каза́лся** очень **молоды́м.**
He seemed (looked) very young to me.

Они́ на́м **ка́жутся стра́нными.**
They seem strange to us.

But more often this verb is used in the third person singular as an impersonal:

Мне́ **ка́жется,** что мы́ сде́лали оши́бку.
I think (it seems to me) that we've made a mistake.

Also parenthetically between commas:

Вы́, **ка́жется,** зна́ете мою́ сестру́?
I believe you know my sister?

In the third person the suffix **-ся** sometimes denotes that an action is *normally* or *correctly* done in a certain way:

Ка́к **пи́шется** э́то сло́во?
How is this word written (spelled)?

Э́то сло́во **пи́шется** та́к.
This word is written (spelled) so.

Э́то сло́во **произно́сится** та́к.
This word is pronounced so.

B. Conjugation of verbs in -ся. To verb forms ending in a consonant (hard or soft), **-ся** is added (**-сь** is added to forms ending in vowels). Observe that verbs which take **-ся** (**-сь**) may belong to either conjugation.

Conjugation of **мы́ться** (I), "*to wash (oneself)*"

мо́юсь	мо́емся
мо́ешься	мо́етесь
мо́ется	мо́ются

Past: мы́лся, мы́лось, мы́лась, мы́лись
Imperative: мо́йся, мо́йтесь

Note on pronunciation: the combinations **-ться** (in the infinitive) and **-тся** (third person singular and plural) are pronounced [c:ə], *i.e.*, a long ц + ə.

Conjugation of **боя́ться** (II), "*to fear*," "*be afraid of*"

бою́сь	бои́мся
бои́шься	бои́тесь
бои́тся	боя́тся

Past: боя́лся, боя́лось, боя́лась, боя́лись
Imperative: бо́йся, бо́йтесь

The verbs смея́ться, "to laugh," and наде́яться, "to hope," drop the vowel **я** in the present tense and all forms derived from the present, such as the imperative:

смея́ться, *"to laugh"*		**наде́яться,** *"to hope"*	
смею́сь	смеёмся	наде́юсь	наде́емся
смеёшься	смеётесь	наде́ешься	наде́етесь
смеётся	смею́тся	наде́ется	наде́ются
Past: смея́лся, смея́лась, etc.		*Past:* наде́ялся, наде́ялась, etc.	
Imperative: сме́йся, сме́йтесь		*Imperative:* наде́йся, наде́йтесь	

Pattern Sentences

1. На на́шей у́лице **откры́лся** но́вый рестора́н.
2. Я́ зна́ю челове́ка, кото́рый его́ **откры́л.**
3. Э́тот рестора́н **открыва́ется** в по́лдень и **закрыва́ется** в по́лночь.
4. Я́ хоте́л[1] **откры́ть** две́рь, но́ она́ почему́-то не **открыва́лась.**
5. Его́ рабо́чий де́нь **начина́ется** в во́семь утра́ и **конча́ется** в во́семь ве́чера.
6. Я́ то́чно не зна́ю, ка́к **пи́шутся** и ка́к **произно́сятся** не́которые слова́.
7. Мне́ **ка́жется,** что я́ **пишу́** и **произношу́** и́х непра́вильно.
8. Ра́ньше о́н **каза́лся** мне́ о́чень счастли́**вым** челове́**ком**, а тепе́рь о́н мне́ **ка́жется** о́чень несча́стн**ым.**
9. На́м с жено́й **показа́лось,** что вы́ недово́льны на́ми.
10. Мы́ случа́йно **встре́тились** с Вади́мом на ле́кции.
11. У́тром ма́ть **мо́ет** и **одева́ет** дете́й, а пото́м сама́ **мо́ется** и **одева́ется.**
12. Ве́чером, по́сле у́жина, ма́ть **раздева́ет** и **мо́ет** дете́й, а пото́м сама́ **раздева́ется** и **мо́ется.**

1. On our street a new restaurant has opened.
2. I know the man who opened it.
3. That restaurant opens at noon, and closes at midnight.
4. I tried to open the door, but for some reason it wouldn't open.
5. His work day starts at 8:00 A.M. and finishes at 8:00 P.M.
6. I don't know exactly how some words are spelled and how they are pronounced.
7. It seems to me that I spell and pronounce them wrong.
8. He used to seem a very happy person to me, but now he seems very unhappy.
9. It seemed to my wife and me that you were displeased with us.
10. We met Vadim by chance at a lecture.
11. In the morning the mother washes and dresses the children, and then washes and dresses herself.
12. In the evening, after supper, the mother undresses and washes the children, and then undresses and washes herself.

[1] Here хоте́ть should be translated as "to try."

13. За́втра я́, как обы́чно, вста́ну ра́но, **помо́юсь, оде́нусь** и поза́втракаю.
13. Tomorrow, as usual, I will get up early, wash, dress, and have breakfast.

14. Э́ти сёстры **одева́ются** одина́ково.
14. Those sisters dress alike.

15. Она́ **бои́тся** всего́ и всех, а её му́ж ничего́ и никого́ не **бои́тся.**
15. She is afraid of everything and everybody, but her husband is not afraid of anything or anyone.

16. Ива́н **бои́тся провали́ться** на экза́мене, и поэ́тому мно́го **занима́ется.**
16. Ivan is afraid of failing the exam, so he studies hard.

17. О́н **наде́ется** получи́ть хоро́шие отме́тки.
17. He is hoping to get good marks.

18. —Ско́лько вре́мени о́н **занима́лся** матема́тикой? —Я́ то́чно не зна́ю, но́ **ка́жется** о́чень до́лго.
18. —How long did he study mathematics? —I don't know exactly, but it seems a very long time.

19. Мы́ **наде́ялись,** что о́н придёт, но́ о́н не пришёл.
19. We hoped that he would come, but he didn't.

20. —Все́ лю́бят, когда́ Ни́ночка **смеётся:** у неё тако́й весёлый сме́х и тако́е смешно́е выраже́ние лица́!
20. —Everyone likes (it) when Ninochka laughs; she has such a merry laugh, and such a funny expression!

Drills

A. *Отве́тьте на э́ти вопро́сы по-ру́сски.*

1. Ско́лько вре́мени вы́ занима́етесь[2] ру́сским языко́м?
2. С ке́м вы́ занима́етесь?
3. Над ке́м смеётся ва́ш това́рищ?
4. Кого́ и́ли чего́ вы́ бои́тесь?
5. Что́ вы́ должны́ де́лать, когда́ вы́ встаёте?
6. Е́сли вы́ хоти́те получа́ть хоро́шие отме́тки, что́ вы́ должны́ де́лать?
7. Что́ должна́ де́лать ма́ть у́тром и ве́чером, е́сли у неё е́сть ма́ленький ребёнок?
8. Ва́с одева́ет ма́ть и́ли вы́ са́ми одева́етесь?

B. *Change the verbs in parentheses to the correct form of the present, past, or future as appropriate, and translate.*

1. Я́ (боя́ться) ва́с.
2. Вы́ меня́ (боя́ться)?
3. На́ши де́ти на́с совсе́м не (боя́ться).
4. Мы́ (наде́яться), что вы́ к на́м прие́дете. Почему́ вы́ не прие́хали?
5. Ни́на (наде́яться), что она́ вы́держит экза́мен.

[2] Ско́лько вре́мени, like давно́, takes the present tense in Russian when the reference is to a period of time beginning in the past and coming up to the present, *e.g.*, Ско́лько вре́мени вы́ уже́ зде́сь **живёте**? How long have you been living here? etc.

6. Концéрты ра́ньше (начина́ться) в дéвять.
7. Концéрт (нача́ться) через пя́ть мину́т.
8. Магази́ны тепéрь (закрыва́ться) в шéсть часóв.
9. Я́ вчера́ (просну́ться) в вóсемь часóв. Я́ бы́стро (помы́ться), (одéться) и пошёл в шкóлу.
10. Тепéрь я́ всегда́ (просыпа́ться) в сéмь часóв. Я́ бы́стро (встава́ть), (мы́ться) и (одева́ться).
11. Всé урóки обыкновéнно (конча́ться) в 4 ч., нó вчера́ они́ (кóнчиться) в 3.
12. За́втра урóки (кóнчиться) как всегда́.

C. *Choose one of the following verbs in* **-ся** *and employ it in the proper form:* **боя́ться, закрыва́ться, занима́ться, каза́ться, надéяться, одева́ться, открыва́ться, смея́ться.**

1. Пётр ещё не пришёл, нó я́ ......, что óн придёт.
2. Бори́с óчень мнóго ......; óн хотéл получи́ть хорóшие отмéтки.
3. Егó отéц ужа́сный человéк, и я́ ра́ньше ...... егó. Нó тепéрь я́ егó бóльше не ....
4. Ра́ньше мнé ......, что Бóб хорóший студéнт, а тепéрь мнé ......, что óн лени́вый.
5. Всé егó костю́мы óчень дороги́е; óн óчень хорошó ....
6. Они́ ......, что вы́ скóро приéдете к ни́м.
7. Óльга ......, что вы́ придёте, нó вы́ не пришли́.
8. Мы́ бу́дем ...... всю нóчь: за́втра у на́с экза́мены.
9. —Почему́ вы́ не закры́ли двéрь? —Э́та двéрь не ....
10. —Почему́ вы́ не открыва́ете э́то окнó? —Потому́ что онó не .... —Я́ егó открóю. Вóт ви́дите, онó ....
11. Я́ ......, что óн не придёт! Óн мнé óчень ну́жен.
12. Бу́дем ......, что всё бу́дет хорошó.
13. Всé ......, что ва́м бу́дет ску́чно на э́той лéкции.
14. Дéти ужé вста́ли, нó они́ ещё не .... Они́ ...... через дéсять мину́т.

2. Люби́ть и нра́виться, "to like" and "to love."

In addition to the verb **люби́ть,** introduced in earlier lessons, Russian has another verb with the general meaning "to like," "to love"; this is the verb **нра́виться.**

As we have seen, the verb люби́ть is transitive and takes a direct object, *e.g.*, —Я́ люблю́ ма́му. With нра́виться, on the other hand, the "person liking something" is denoted by a noun or pronoun in the *dative* case, while the person or object liked is the subject of the sentence in the *nominative* case. (In other words, a construction with нра́виться says that something or someone "appeals *to me, to him*," etc.; "is pleasing *to me, to him*," etc.)

Люби́ть, "*to love.*"

Я́ люблю́ свою́ ма́ть.	I love my mother.
Ива́н лю́бит О́льгу.	Ivan loves Olga.
Мы́ лю́бим свою́ страну́.	We love our country.

Люби́ть, "*to like,*" "*be fond of.*"

In expressing personal taste, habit, preference rather than judgment:

Я́ люблю́ сы́р.	I like cheese.
А́нна лю́бит жёлтый цве́т.	Anna likes the color yellow.
Я́ люблю́ Шекспи́ра.	I like Shakespeare.
Мо́й сы́н лю́бит му́зыку.	My son likes music.

This use is also common with infinitives:

Я́ люблю́ рабо́тать.
I like to work.

Ни́на лю́бит говори́ть, но́ не лю́бит чита́ть.
Nina likes to talk, but does not like to read.

Нра́виться *expresses judgment, impression, evaluation.*

Remember that with нра́виться the person "who likes" is in the *dative* case; the person or thing "liked" is in the *nominative:*

Мне́ нра́вится ва́ша после́дняя статья́.
I like your latest article.

А́нн**е** нра́вится моё но́вое пла́тье.
Anna likes my new dress.

Ива́н**у** нра́вятся э́ти но́вые дома́.
Ivan likes those new houses.

Мне́ не нра́вится ва́ш отве́т.
I don't like your answer.

—**Кому́** нра́вится э́та шля́па? —**Никому́.**
—Who likes this hat? —No one.

На́м не о́чень нра́вится на́ш но́вый нача́льник.
We don't like our new superior very much.

Ни́на нра́вится Вади́м**у**.
Vadim likes Nina (she appeals to him).

Вади́м нра́вится Ни́н**е**.
Nina likes Vadim (he appeals to her).

Aspects and tenses. Both **люби́ть** and **нра́виться** form perfectives with **по-**. With **люби́ть** the perfective has an inchoative meaning (to begin, get to, come to like something or someone):

Я́ ра́ньше не **люби́л** Ита́лии, а тепе́рь я́ **полюби́л** её.
Formerly I didn't like Italy, but now I've gotten to like it.

The past tense of the perfective **понра́виться** speaks of a favorable reaction upon first contact (continuing, unless otherwise specified, into the present):

—Ка́к ва́м понра́вилась пе́рвая ле́кция? —Мне́ о́чень понра́вилась.
—How did you like the first lecture? —I liked it very much.

Ма́тери не понра́вилось, ка́к е́й отве́тил сы́н.
The mother didn't like the way her son answered her.

Мне́ понра́вилась и́х до́чь.
I liked their daughter (she made a good impression on me).

Тури́стам о́чень понра́вился Пари́ж.
The tourists liked Paris very much.

Perfective future:

Е́сли мне́ не понра́вится в Финля́ндии—я́ уе́ду.
If I don't like it in Finland, I shall leave.

The past tense of the imperfective нра́виться rather suggests liking in the past, no longer experienced in the present ("I used to like"):

Мне́ о́чень нра́вился э́тот рома́н, когда́ я́ была́ молодо́й.
I used to like that novel very much when I was young.

Бори́су в то́ вре́мя нра́вилась Ни́на.
Boris liked Nina at that time.

With both люби́ть and нра́виться (and some other verbs like наде́яться, хоте́ть, etc.), the word о́чень is used for increased intensity (*never* о́чень мно́го).

Я́ **о́чень** люблю́ свою́ ма́ть.
Студе́нтке **о́чень** нра́вится э́тот молодо́й профе́ссор.
На́м **о́чень** понра́вился фи́льм, кото́рый мы́ вчера́ ви́дели.

Drills

A. *Give the suitable form of the following verbs, and supply a pronoun whenever needed:* **нра́виться, понра́виться; люби́ть, полюби́ть**

1. Влади́мир ...... занима́ться но́чью.
2. Мы́ ...... гуля́ть в лесу́.

3. Мне́ не ...... тво́й но́вый костю́м.
4. Когда́ я́ уви́дел Ло́ндон в пе́рвый ра́з, о́н мне́ о́чень не ....
5. Мне́ тепе́рь ...... на́ш профе́ссор.
6. На́м ......, ка́к ва́ш бра́т вчера́ сыгра́л ва́льсь Чайко́вского.
7. На́ш де́душка не о́чень ...... Чайко́вского.
8. Мо́й бра́т ви́дел вчера́ пье́су Лео́нова, и она́ ...... не ......, хотя́ о́н ...... э́того писа́теля.
9. Вчера́ на вечери́нке О́льга говори́ла то́лько с Бори́сом. Ка́жется, о́н о́чень ....
10. Купи́ пла́тье то́лько, е́сли оно́ ....
11. О́льга ...... шокола́д.
12. —Ива́н Ива́нович, ка́к .... вчера́шний конце́рт? —Та́к себе.

B. *Translate into Russian.*

1. I like your young friend; he is intelligent.
2. Formerly I used to like that newspaper, but now I no longer like it.
3. —How do you like this cheese? —So-so; I am not very fond of cheese.
4. If we don't like (it) in the mountains, we shall go to the seashore. My parents like both the mountains and seashore.
5. I like to study at night; at night it is so quiet!
6. —Do you like this novel? —Yes, I read it not long ago and liked it very much. I like that author.
7. Our teacher is very fond of Turgenev's novel, "Fathers and Children," but his students don't like Turgenev.
8. I liked that novel very much when I read it for the first time.
9. Last year we travelled around Europe; I liked France and Italy very much.
10. —How do you like our new teacher? —Not very much. He likes to ask the students difficult questions.

3. Dative, locative, and instrumental plural of nouns, adjectives, and pronoun-adjectives

These cases have only one plural form for all three genders. The following table presents the endings of these case forms:

	Nouns	*3rd Person Pronouns*	*Adjectives*	*Pronoun-Adjectives*	
Dat.	**-ам/-ям**	им	**-ым/-им**	**-им**	**-ем**
Loc.	**-ах/-ях**	их	**-ых/-их**	**-их**	**-ех**
Instr.	**-ами/-ями**	и́ми	**-ыми/-ими**	**-ими**	**-еми**

A. Nouns.

	Nominative Singular	*Nominative Plural*	*Dative Plural*	*Locative Plural*	*Instrumental Plural*
Masc.	до́ктор учи́тель геро́й	доктора́ учителя́ геро́и	доктора́м учителя́м геро́ям	доктора́х учителя́х геро́ях	доктора́ми учителя́ми геро́ями
Neut.	окно́ по́ле	о́кна поля́	о́кнам поля́м	о́кнах поля́х	о́кнами поля́ми
Fem. I	де́вушка ку́хня	де́вушки ку́хни	де́вушкам ку́хням	де́вушках ку́хнях	де́вушками ку́хнями
Fem. II	крова́ть	крова́ти	крова́тям	крова́тях	крова́тями

The following nouns have dative, locative, and instrumental plural forms which follow the nominative *plural:*

Nominative Singular	*Nominative Plural*	*Dative Plural*	*Locative Plural*	*Instrumental Plural*
брат	бра́тья	бра́тьям	бра́тьях	бра́тьями
стул	сту́лья	сту́льям	сту́льях	сту́льями
перо́	пе́рья	пе́рьям	пе́рьях	пе́рьями
де́рево	дере́вья	дере́вьям	дере́вьях	дере́вьями
лист (leaf)	ли́стья	ли́стьям	ли́стьях	ли́стьями
сын	сыновья́	сыновья́м	сыновья́х	сыновья́ми
друг	друзья́	друзья́м	друзья́х	друзья́ми
сосе́д	сосе́ди	сосе́дям	сосе́дях	сосе́дями
вре́мя	времена́	времена́м	времена́х	времена́ми
и́мя	имена́	имена́м	имена́х	имена́ми
мать	ма́тери	матеря́м	матеря́х	матеря́ми
дочь	до́чери	дочеря́м	дочеря́х	дочерьми́
(ребёнок)	де́ти	де́тям	де́тях	детьми́
(челове́к)	лю́ди	лю́дям	лю́дях	людьми́

The distinct instrumental ending **-ьми́** serves for four nouns: дочерьми́, детьми́, людьми́, and лошадьми́ (horses).

B. Adjectives and pronoun-adjectives.

Nominative Plural	*Dative Plural*	*Locative Plural*	*Instrumental Plural*
но́вые	но́вым	но́вых	но́выми
си́ние	си́ним	си́них	си́ними
хоро́шие	хоро́шим	хоро́ших	хоро́шими
ру́сские	ру́сским	ру́сских	ру́сскими
мои́	мои́м	мои́х	мои́ми
на́ши	на́шим	на́ших	на́шими
одни́	одни́м	одни́х	одни́ми
э́ти	э́тим	э́тих	э́тими
те	тем	тех	те́ми
все	всем	всех	все́ми

C. Time expressions with по and dative plural.

Мы́ всегда́ до́ма **по** вечер**а́м.**
Evenings we're always at home.

По четверг**а́м** я́ хожу́ в кино́.
On Thursdays I go to the movies.

О́н тепе́рь рабо́тает **по** ноч**а́м.**
He works nights now.

Pattern Sentences

Dative Plural

1. Я́ посла́л де́ньги мо**и́м** дорог**и́м** роди́тел**ям.** — I sent money to my dear parents.
2. Ни́на купи́ла пода́рки вс**е́м** сво**и́м** тёт**ям.** — Nina bought presents for all her aunts.
3. Учи́тельница объясня́ла пра́вила но́в**ым** учени**ка́м.** — The teacher was explaining the rules to the new pupils.
4. Глу́п**ым** лю́д**ям** ча́сто ка́жется, что они́ у́мные. — Silly people often think that they are intelligent.
5. Мы́ ча́сто хо́дим в го́сти к на́ш**им** сосе́д**ям.** — We often go visiting our neighbors.

Drill

Supply correct forms of the dative plural.

1. В э́том кла́ссе у́мные студе́нты и студе́нтки. Кому́ учи́тель объясня́ет пра́вила? .... и ....
2. У на́с е́сть но́вые друзья́. Кому́ мы́ пи́шем? Мы́ пи́шем ....

3. Ту́т живу́т мои́ дороги́е роди́тели. Я́ ча́сто хожу́ к ....
4. У Ни́ны е́сть хоро́шие подру́ги. Ни́на покупа́ет пода́рки ....
5. Мои́ бра́тья и сёстры живу́т далеко́. Я́ ча́сто пишу́ .... и ....
6. Все́ мои́ профессора́ задаю́т мне́ вопро́сы. Я́ отвеча́ю ....

Pattern Sentences

Locative Plural

1. В э́**тих** но́в**ых** дом**а́х** живу́т бога́тые лю́ди. — There are rich people living in those new houses.
2. Колхо́зники и колхо́зницы живу́т в колхо́з**ах**. Они́ рабо́тают в колхо́зн**ых** пол**я́х**, сад**а́х** и лес**а́х**. — Men and women collective farmers live in kolkhozes. They work in the kolkhoz fields, gardens, and woods.
3. В бога́т**ых** колхо́з**ах** е́сть мя́со, ры́ба, моло́чные проду́кты и о́вощи. — In well-to-do kolkhozes they have meat, fish, milk products, and vegetables.
4. Расскажи́те на́м о но́в**ых** францу́зск**их** пье́с**ах** и фи́льм**ах**, кото́рые вы́ ви́дели во Фра́нции. — Tell us about the new French plays and films which you saw in France.
5. Я́ ду́маю, что мы́ говори́м о т**е́х** же лю́д**ях**. — I believe that we're talking about the same people.
6. Я́ о́чень люблю́ Соединённые Шта́ты. Я́ мно́го ле́т живу́ в Соединённ**ых** Шта́т**ах**. — I am very fond of the United States. For many years I have been living in the United States.

Drill

Read the statement and answer the question which follows in terms of the statement.

1. Я́ люблю́ мои́х у́мных, приле́жных студе́нтов. О ко́м я́ ду́маю?
2. Андре́й никогда́ не жи́л в больши́х города́х. В каки́х города́х о́н жи́л?
3. У меня́ е́сть хоро́шие друзья́. О ко́м я́ ча́сто говорю́?
4. Она́ лю́бит дороги́е, удо́бные гости́ницы. Где́ она́ лю́бит жи́ть?
5. В э́том го́роде огро́мные заво́ды. Где́ рабо́тают э́ти рабо́чие?
6. У А́нны е́сть свои́ де́ньги. О чём она́ мно́го ду́мает?
7. Моя́ ма́ть лю́бит мои́х дете́й. О ко́м она́ всем расска́зывает?
8. Профе́ссор зна́ет все́ э́ти фа́кты. О чём о́н пи́шет?

Pattern Sentences

Instrumental Plural

1. Мы́ слу́шаем и слы́шим уш**а́ми**. — We listen and hear with our ears.
2. Мы́ ви́дим и смо́трим глаз**а́ми**. — We see and look with our eyes.
3. —Чём мы́ берём ве́щи? —Мы́ берём и́х па́льц**ами**. — —What do we take things with? —We take them with our fingers.

4. Ра́ньше лю́ди всё де́лали рук**а́ми**, а тепе́рь всё де́лают маши́н**ами**.

4. Formerly people used to do everything with their hands, but now they do everything with machines.

5. —Как**и́ми** нож**а́ми** мясни́к ре́жет мя́со? —О́н ре́жет ра́зн**ыми** нож**а́ми**—больш**и́ми** и ма́леньк**ими**.

5. —What kind of knives does the butcher cut meat with? —He cuts with different kinds of knives—big and little ones.

Instrumental with the preposition **с**

1. —**С ке́м** Серёжа и Алёша бы́ли на вечери́нке? —Они́ бы́ли та́м **с те́ми** же ми́л**ыми** де́вушк**ами**, **с** кото́р**ыми** они́ бы́ли на ле́кции.
2. Вчера́ мы́ бы́ли в теа́тре и случа́йно встре́тились **с** на́ш**ими** ста́р**ыми** друзь**я́ми** Лунёв**ыми**.
3. Я́ вчера́ обе́дала в рестора́не **со** вс**е́ми** мо**и́ми** бра́ть**ями** и сёстр**ами** и **с** и́х деть**ми́**.

1. —With whom were Seryozha and Alyosha at the party? —They were there with the same nice girls with whom they were at the lecture.
2. Yesterday we went to the theater and by chance met our old friends, the Lunyovs.
3. Yesterday I had dinner at a restaurant with all my brothers and sisters and their children.

Drill

Place the words in the right-hand column in the instrumental.

О́н э́то сде́лал	ма́ленькие ножи́ свои́ ру́ки си́ние и кра́сные карандаши́ свои́ то́лстые па́льцы
Мы́ рабо́тали та́м с (со)	молоды́е доктора́ сове́тские писа́тели хоро́шие инжене́ры у́мные де́вушки все́ учителя́ но́вые друзья́ ва́ши сыновья́

4. Prepositions за, перед, над, под, ме́жду with the instrumental[3]

A. За, behind, beyond, on the other side of.

За на́ш**им** до́м**ом** е́сть са́д.
Behind our house there is a garden.

За рек**о́й** е́сть ма́ленькая дере́вня.
There is a small village on the other side of the river.

[3] Two of these prepositions, **за** and **под**, also take the accusative case when they express direction; this will be treated in Unit 24.

О́н сиде́л **за мно́й.**
He sat behind me.

Ива́н шёл **за мно́й.**
Ivan walked behind me (he followed me).

It will be remembered that **за** with the instrumental is also used to express "going for," "going to buy," "going to get," etc.:

Ива́н пошёл в магази́н **за** хле́б**ом.**
Ivan went to the store for bread.

Ива́н пришёл **за** мн**о́й.**
Ivan came for me (to get me).

Idioms with **за***:*

за́ городом
(be) out of town, in the country

сиде́ть за столо́м
to be at the table

за грани́цей
(be) abroad

B. Перед, in front of; before (for place and time).

Place:

Перед до́**мом** стоя́л автомоби́ль.
In front of the house stood a car.

Time:

Перед уро́**ком** мы́ кури́ли в коридо́ре.
Before class we smoked in the hall.

Перед is close in its time sense to **до** (+ genitive); **до** means "before" (any time before), while **перед** is used mostly for "just before" or "immediately before."

Я́ мно́го рабо́тал **до** обе́д**а.**
I worked a lot before dinner (all the time before; unspecified).

Я́ вы́мыл ру́ки **перед** обе́д**ом.**
I washed my hands before dinner (when dinner was ready).

C. Над, above, over.

Над гор**а́ми** ту́чи.
There are clouds above the mountains.

На́ша кварти́ра **над** магази́н**ом.**
Our apartment is over the store.

Idioms with **над:**

рабо́тать над, *to work at.*

О́н на́чал **рабо́тать над** но́**вым** рома́н**ом.**
He started working at a new novel.

смея́ться над, *to laugh at, make fun of.*

На́ш учи́тель никогда́ не **смеётся над** на́**шими** оши́бк**ами.**
Our teacher never makes fun of our mistakes.

D. Под, below, under, underneath.

Кни́га лежа́ла **под** стол**о́м.**
The book was lying under the table.

The forms **передо, надо,** and **подо** (instead of перед, над, and под), are required before the pronoun **мной.**

Передо мно́й стена́. Надо мно́й потоло́к. Подо мно́й по́л.

E. Ме́жду, between, among.

На́ш университе́т стои́т **ме́жду** рек**о́й** и городск**и́м** па́рк**ом.**
Our university stands between the river and the city park.

Э́то **ме́жду на́ми,** коне́чно.
This, of course, is between us.

Pattern Sentences

1. У ка́ждого челове́ка должна́ бы́ть кры́ша **над** голов**о́й.**
2. **Над на́ми** ту́чи, а та́м, **над** зелё**ными** лес**а́ми** и пол**я́ми**, си́нее не́бо.
3. Его́ това́рищи всегда́ смея́лись **над ни́м.**
4. О́н никогда́ не расска́зывает, **над че́м** о́н рабо́тает.
5. Как прия́тно, когда́ **под** ног**а́ми** мя́гкий ковёр!
6. Чья́ э́то ма́ленькая соба́чка[4] та́м **под** де́рев**ом**?
7. Как хорошо́ в жа́ркий де́нь **под** э́**тими** ста́р**ыми** дере́вь**ями**!
8. **За** на́**шим** до́м**ом** ма́ленький дво́р, а **перед** до́м**ом** са́д.

1. Every man must have a roof over his head.
2. There are (storm) clouds above us, but over there, above the green woods and fields, there is blue sky.
3. His comrades were always laughing at him.
4. He never tells what he's working at.
5. How pleasant to have a soft carpet under one's feet!
6. Whose is that little dog over there under the tree?
7. How nice it is on a hot day under these old trees!
8. In back of our house there's a small yard, and in front of the house a garden.

[4] Соба́чка, diminutive of соба́ка, "dog." For diminutives, see Appendix B.

9. Хоро́шие де́ти всегда́ мо́ют ру́ки **перед** обе́д**ом**.
10. На́ш до́м стои́т **ме́жду** шко́л**ой** и ба́нк**ом**.
11. По-мо́ему, его́ но́вая пьє́са о́чень ску́чная; но́ э́то, коне́чно, **ме́жду на́ми!**
12. **Ме́жду** по́лк**ой** и окн**о́м** стои́т ма́ленький сто́лик,[5] и на нём ва́за **с** цвет**а́ми**.
13. Моя́ соба́чка Дэ́зи лю́бит спа́ть **под** э́**тим** ма́леньк**им** сто́лик**ом**.[5]
14. Же́ня пришла́ к Ри́те **за** сове́т**ом**.
15. Мы́ уже́ сиде́ли **за** стол**о́м**, когда́ вдру́г пришёл Ко́ля. О́н пришёл ко мне́ **за** папиро́с**ами**.

9. Good children always wash their hands before dinner.
10. Our house stands between a school and a bank.
11. In my opinion, his new play is very dull, but that, of course, is between us!
12. Between the bookshelf and the window stands a small table, and on it a vase with flowers.
13. My little dog Daisy likes to sleep under that little table.
14. Zhenya came to Rita for advice.
15. We were already seated at table, when suddenly Kolya arrived. He had come to me for cigarettes.

Drills

A. *Fill in suitable prepositions.*

1. Моя́ крова́ть стои́т ...... окно́м и по́лкой.
2. ...... на́шим до́мом гара́ж.
3. ...... на́ми кры́ша.
4. О́н рабо́тает ...... но́вым рома́ном.
5. О́н говори́л с профе́ссором ...... ле́кцией.
6. Смирно́вы живу́т ...... угло́м.
7. Зо́я пришла́ ...... обе́дом и ушла́ ...... обе́да.
8. Ма́ть посла́ла меня́ ...... молоко́м.
9. Я́ пришёл к ва́м ...... сове́том.
10. Журна́л лежа́л ...... кре́слом.

B. *Complete the sentences by putting the words on the right in the proper case.*

Больши́е ту́чи бы́ли над ......

на́ша река́.
ма́ленькие дома́.
си́нее мо́ре.
на́ши го́ловы.
высо́кие дере́вья.
я.
ты/вы.
он.
мы.
они́.

[5] Сто́лик, diminutive of стол.

CONVERSATION

Кла́ссная ко́мната, 9 часо́в утра́.

Учи́тельница. —До́брое у́тро!

Класс. —До́брое у́тро!

Уч. —Ка́к вы́ пожива́ете сего́дня? Ка́к дела́?

Класс. —О́чень хорошо́. —Та́к себе. —Не осо́бенно хорошо́. —Ничего́.

Уч. —Како́й чуде́сный де́нь сего́дня, пра́вда? Почти́ весна́!

Класс. —Мм . . . да́—

Уч. —Я́ ви́жу, вы́ ещё не совсе́м просну́лись и ещё не все́ собра́лись: не́т ни Ви́ктора, ни Алекса́ндра, ни . . . А! во́т они́!

Ви́ктор и Алекса́ндр. —Пожа́луйста извини́те, что мы́ опозда́ли!

Уч. —Ну́, ничего́, вы́ опозда́ли то́лько на три́ мину́ты. Та́к, тепе́рь все́ ту́т. Уро́к начина́ется. Откро́йте кни́ги. Я́ наде́юсь, что вы́ все́ хорошо́ зна́ете всё, что вы́ должны́ бы́ли пригото́вить на сего́дня. Наде́юсь, что расска́з ва́м понра́вился. Вы́ всё по́няли? Фили́пп, над че́м вы́ смеётесь? Начни́те чита́ть.

Фили́пп. —«Бы́ло ра́ннее весе́ннее у́тро. Москва́ ещё спала́.»

Уч. —Та́к. Не пло́хо, но́ произноше́ние ещё не совсе́м хоро́шее. В сло́ве «Москва́» «о» произно́сится всегда́ как «а». Повтори́те э́то сло́во ещё ра́з. Да́, тепе́рь почти́ хорошо́. Вы́ ведь все́ зна́ете э́то пра́вило фоне́тики? Не забыва́йте его́. Э́то о́чень ва́жно. Ну́, како́е е́сть пра́вило?

Класс. —Когда́ не́т ударе́ния на «о», «о» произно́сится как «а.» Мы́ зна́ем пра́вило, но́ на́м нужна́ пра́ктика.

Уч. —Коне́чно, нужна́. Но́ не забыва́йте пра́вила. Не́лли, тепе́рь вы́ чита́йте.

Не́лли. —«Москва́ ещё спала́. На у́лицах и в дома́х бы́ло ти́хо. То́лько в одно́м до́ме, за Москво́й-реко́й . . . »

Уч. —Совсе́м не пло́хо, но́ мя́гкое «л» (э́л) в сло́ве «то́лько» вы́ произно́сите твёрдо, как «л» (э́л) в сло́ве «по́лка.» Произнеси́те не́сколько ра́з «ско́лько,» «то́лько,» «ско́лько,» «то́лько.» А когда́ вы́ пи́шете э́ти слова́, не забыва́йте писа́ть мя́гкий зна́к по́сле «л».

Не́лли. —Ско́лько, то́лько, ско́лько, то́лько. Дово́льно?

Уч. —Дово́льно. Тепе́рь закро́йте кни́ги. Кто́ из ва́с по́мнит, каки́ми слова́ми начина́ется расска́з, и что́ идёт да́льше? А́нна, начни́те расска́зывать.

А́нна. —Бы́ло ра́ннее весе́ннее у́тро. Москва́ ещё спала́.

Уч. —Что́ да́льше? Я́ ва́м помогу́. Я́ бу́ду задава́ть ва́м вопро́сы: На како́м заво́де рабо́тал молодо́й и тала́нтливый меха́ник Алексе́й Ко́лосов?

А́нна. —Я́ не по́мню всёх сло́в и всёх выраже́ний.

Уч. —Почему́ вы́ не по́мните? Расска́з коро́ткий и о́чень просто́й. Я́ ду́маю, что вы́ недоста́точно занима́етесь. Вы́ должны́ бо́льше рабо́тать над зада́ниями.

А́нна. —Но́ в э́том расска́зе о́чень мно́го но́вых сло́в, и не́которые слова́ о́чень дли́нные и и́х тру́дно запо́мнить и произнести́.

Уч. —О́льга, мо́жет быть вы́ по́мните?

О́льга. —Прости́те, я́ не могла́ приготовить уро́ка, потому́ что у моего́ бра́та была́ вечери́нка, а вчера́ днём моя́ соба́чка Де́зи . . .

Уч. —О́льга! Дово́льно! Я́ ва́с не спра́шиваю о соба́чке. Ли́за, отве́тьте вы́ на мо́й вопро́с.

Ли́за. —Извини́те, я́ не по́мню вопро́са. Пожа́луйста повтори́те его́ ещё ра́з.

Уч. —На како́м заво́де рабо́тал молодо́й и тала́нтливый меха́ник Алексе́й Ко́лосов?

Ли́за. —Мне́ ка́жется, что о́н рабо́тал на большо́м автомоби́льном заво́де.

Уч. —Пра́вильно. Я́ ви́жу, что вы́ вчера́ занима́лись. Тепе́рь Бо́б, расскажи́те вы́ на́м: кто́ помога́л Алексе́ю Ко́лосову в его́ рабо́те?

Класс. —Бо́ба не́т в кла́ссе.

Уч. —Его́ не́т? А что́ с ни́м? Кто́ из ва́с зна́ет?

Класс. —Мы́ не зна́ем. Мо́жет быть о́н ещё спи́т.

Оди́н учени́к. —Мне́ ка́жется, что я́ ви́дел его́ в после́дний ра́з позавчера́ в теа́тре на пье́се Че́хова «Три́ сестры́.»

Друго́й учени́к. —А я́ ви́дел его́ вчера́. Мы́ бы́ли вме́сте в кино́ и ви́дели замеча́тельный япо́нский фи́льм. В э́том фи́льме япо́нский при́нц лю́бит европе́йскую де́вушку, но́ оте́ц при́нца и ма́ть э́той де́вушки . . .

Уч. —Вы́ мне́ э́то расска́жете по́сле уро́ка, а сейча́с я́ хочу́ зна́ть, кто́ помога́л Андре́ю Ко́лосову, когда́ Андре́ю нужна́ была́ по́мощь? Ни́на, бу́дьте добры́, отве́тьте мне́.

Ни́на. —Когда́ Андре́ю Ко́лосову нужна́ была́ по́мощь, ему́ всегда́ помога́л его́ ста́рый прия́тель, с кото́рым во вре́мя войны́ о́н бы́л вме́сте на фро́нте.

Уч. —Ни́на, не смотри́те в кни́гу. Закро́йте её и да́йте её мне́. Та́к, тепе́рь отвеча́йте.

Ни́на. —Пожа́луйста, объясни́те мне́, что́ зна́чит «предпочита́ть». Я́ не могу́ расска́зывать без э́того сло́ва.

Уч. —Я́ уже́ два́дцать ра́з ва́м э́то объясня́ла . . . Кто́ по́мнит моё объясне́ние?

Класс. —Я́! Я́! Я́!

Уч. —О́чень хорошо́. Тепе́рь возьми́те тетра́ди и пиши́те дикта́нт. Слу́шайте внима́тельно. У Андре́я Ко́лосова была́ хоро́шая . . . (Звоно́к.)

Уч. —Ка́к, уже́?! Ну́, хорошо́. Мы́ ко́нчим дикта́нт в друго́й ра́з. Пригото́вьте на за́втра второ́й расска́з, прочита́йте две́ главы́ и переведи́те два́дцать предложе́ний. По́мните, что вы́ должны́ мно́го занима́ться ка́ждый де́нь, а не то́лько перед экза́менами. До свида́ния. До за́втра.

Класс. —До за́втра.

Чита́йте э́ти вопро́сы и отвеча́йте на ни́х по-ру́сски.

1. Почему́ ученики́ хотя́т спа́ть? 2. Почему́ Ви́ктор и Алекса́ндр говоря́т «извини́те»? 3. Они́ о́чень опозда́ли? 4. Ка́к ну́жно произноси́ть слова́ Москва́, Оде́сса, Сове́тский Сою́з? 5. У Ни́ны хоро́шее произноше́ние? 6. Ученики́ должны́ были то́лько чита́ть в кла́ссе? 7. О ко́м бы́л расска́з, кото́рый учи́тельница и́м задала́? 8. Почему́ пе́рвая учени́ца не могла́ отве́тить на вопро́с? 9. Почему́ учи́тельница взяла́ кни́гу у Ни́ны? 10. Почему́ учи́тельница не хоте́ла отве́тить на вопро́с Ни́ны? 11. О чём бы́л фи́льм, кото́рый ви́дел оди́н из ученико́в? 12. Что́ все́ должны́ сде́лать на за́втра?

READING

В шко́лу—Going to School

Почему́ сего́дня Пе́тя
Просыпа́лся де́сять ра́з?
Потому́ что о́н сего́дня
Поступа́ет в пе́рвый кла́сс.[6]

О́н просну́лся но́чью тёмной.
Бы́ло то́лько три́ часа́.
О́н ужа́сно испуга́лся (got frightened),
Что уро́к у́ж начался́.

О́н оде́лся в две́ мину́ты,
Бы́стро к две́ри побежа́л (ran).
Па́па побежа́л за Пе́тей,
У двере́й его́ догна́л (caught up).

За стено́й сосе́ди вста́ли,
Э́лектри́чество зажгли́ (turned on),
За стено́й сосе́ди вста́ли,
А пото́м опя́ть легли́ (went to bed).

Разбуди́л о́н всю́ кварти́ру,
До утра́ засну́ть не мо́г.
Да́же ба́бушка просну́лась,
Начала́ чита́ть уро́к.

Его́ де́душке присни́лось (dreamt),
Что у ка́рты о́н стоя́л,
И не мо́г поня́ть, где́ Во́лга,
И не зна́л о́н, где́ Ура́л.

Почему́ сего́дня Пе́тя
Просыпа́лся де́сять ра́з?
Потому́ что о́н сего́дня
Поступа́ет в пе́рвый кла́сс.

(Adapted from A. Barto)

[6] Enrolls in the first grade.

Pronunciation Drill

pəç̌imú şivóḑņə p̧ẹ́ţə
prəsɨpálşə ḑẹ́şiţ rás?
pətamú štə ón şivóḑņə
pəstupáit fp̧érvəj klás.
ón prasnúlşə nóç̌ju ţómnəj.
bɨ́lə tóļkə tŗi ç̌isá.
ón užásnə ispugálşə,
štə urók úš nəç̌alşá.

EXERCISES

A. *Read the following sentences and translate.*

1. Оди́н ста́рый профе́ссор начина́л все́ свои́ ле́кции всегда́ те́ми же слова́ми. 2. Все́ его́ ле́кции начина́лись одина́ково. 3. —Други́ми слова́ми, они́ все́ бы́ли ску́чные? —Не́т, не всегда́. 4. По вечера́м о́н лю́бит занима́ться в свое́й ти́хой ко́мнате. 5. —С ке́м вы́ занима́лись зимо́й? —Снача́ла оди́н, а пото́м с хоро́шим учи́телем. 6. —Че́м она́ тепе́рь занима́ется? —Матема́тикой и ру́сским языко́м. 7. А́нна Семёновна люби́ла одева́ться и всегда́ чуде́сно одева́лась. 8. О́н смеётся надо все́м, и э́то совсе́м не смешно́. 9. —Я́ наде́юсь, что вы́ прие́дете к на́м в дере́вню? —Бою́сь, что не прие́ду: я́ поступи́л на но́вую слу́жбу, и тепе́рь у меня́ о́чень мно́го рабо́ты. 10. Мне́ ка́жется о́чень стра́нным, что о́н та́к бои́тся люде́й, и что лю́ди боя́тся его́. 11. Не наде́йтесь на него́: о́н ничего́ для ва́с не сде́лает. 12. Ма́ть всегда́ говори́ла сы́ну: «Не бо́йся никого́, и никто́ тебе́ ничего́ плохо́го не сде́лает.» 13. Я́ ви́жу, что О́ля купи́ла цветы́, но́ бою́сь, что она́ забы́ла купи́ть папиро́сы. 14. Снача́ла помо́йтесь и оде́ньтесь, а пото́м начни́те рабо́тать. 15. Я́ не зна́ю, что́ мне́ де́лать: моя́ две́рь не закрыва́ется! 16. Я́ ра́ньше ча́сто встреча́л Зи́ну в ра́зных места́х, а тепе́рь мы́ с не́й никогда́ не встреча́емся. 17. Мо́жет быть вы́ случа́йно зна́ете а́дрес граждани́на Петро́ва? 18. —В кото́ром часу́ вы́ вста́нете за́втра? —За́втра я́ вста́ну в во́семь часо́в. 19. —Когда́ вы́ пошлёте пода́рок ва́шим роди́телям? —Не зна́ю, когда́ я́ его́ пошлю́; ведь я́ его́ ещё не купи́л. 20. Переда́йте пожа́луйста приве́т от меня́ все́м на́шим хоро́шим друзья́м.

B. *Translate into Russian.*

1. The armchair is in front of us. 2. The sofa is behind us. 3. —Where are you standing? —I am standing between the window

and the table. 4. In front of me is a yellow armchair; behind me is the green sofa. 5. I am standing in front of the green sofa, behind the yellow armchair. 6. —Where is the ceiling? —The ceiling is over us. 7. There is a soft, expensive rug; the rug is beneath the table and the sofa. 8. Our Aunt Vera needs money; she has come to us for money. 9. The mother washes and dresses her younger children, but the elder children already wash and dress without her help. 10. You have written these words incorrectly! These words are spelled this way! 11. Do not fear, but hope. 12. Today I met my old friends by chance on the subway. 13. —When will you get up tomorrow? —I will get up early. 14. I have a great deal of work and I must start studying early. 15. —How long did you work on this book? —I worked for a long time, almost five years. 16. If you want to come to see me, tell me and I will be at home. 17. Those two girls dress alike. 18. I like this writer, but I didn't like his last novel. 19. We like to read in Russian, although we read slowly. 20. He always thinks about his friends, and sends money to all his friends. 21. —What do you do evenings? —I work with my sisters.

VOCABULARY

весённий spring (*adj.*)
внима́тельный attentive
всё-таки all the same, still, nevertheless
гро́мкий loud
дово́льно, доста́точно enough, rather
звон.о́к (*gen.* **-ка́**) bell
знак sign
мя́гкий (*pronounce* [m̡áxkəj]) soft
мясни́к butcher
недоста́точно insufficient(ly), not sufficient
не́которые certain (ones), some
непра́вильно incorrect(ly), wrong
о́вощи (*masc. pl.*, *gen. pl.* **овоще́й**) vegetables
одина́ково alike, identically, in the same way
папиро́са cigarette
по́лдень (*masc.*) noon
по́лночь (*fem.*) midnight
предложе́ние sentence, proposition, offer
принц prince
проду́кты (*masc. pl.*) produce, products
произноше́ние pronunciation
рабо́чий work (*adj.*), working; workman (*adj. used as noun*)
случа́йно by chance
Соединённые Шта́ты (Аме́рики)[7] United States (of America)
смешно́й funny
твёрдый hard, firm
тётя aunt
то́чно exactly[8]
ту́ча (storm) cloud
ударе́ние accent, stress
уж (уже́) already

[7] Abbreviated as США (U.S.A.), *indeclinable.*
[8] Ро́вно is used with numerals in the sense of "exactly," *e.g.*, ро́вно в се́мь часо́в, *but* Я́ то́чно не зна́ю, I don't know exactly.

у́ши (*nom. pl. of* **у́хо**) ears
цвет.о́к (*gen.* **-ка́**; *pl.* **цвет.ы́, -о́в,** etc.)[9] flower
чуде́сный marvellous, wonderful
япо́нский Japanese (*adj.*)

Verbs

(For other reflexive verbs see Section 1.)

буди́ть (imperf., II: **бужу́, бу́дишь**), **разбуди́ть** (perf., II) to awaken (*trans.*)
занима́ться (imperf., I) to study, be occupied with (+ *instr.*)
засыпа́ть (imperf., I), **засну́ть** (perf., I: **засн.у́, -ёшь**) to fall asleep
каза́ться (imperf., I: **кажу́сь, ка́жешься**), **показа́ться** (perf., I) to seem, appear (+ *instr.*)
мыть (imperf., I: **мо́.ю, -ешь**), **помы́ть** or **вы́мыть** (perf., I) to wash (*trans.*)
одева́ть (imperf., I), **оде́ть** (perf., I: **оде́н.у, -ешь**) to dress (*trans.*)
переводи́ть (imperf., II: **перевожу́, перево́дишь**), **перевести́** (perf., I: **перевед.у́, -ёшь**; past: **перевёл, перевело́,** etc.) to translate
поня́ть (perf. of **понима́ть,** I: **пойм.у́, -ёшь**; past: **по́нял, поняла́, по́няли**) to understand, comprehend, grasp
посла́ть (perf. of **посыла́ть,** I: **пошл.ю́, -ёшь**) to send
поступа́ть (imperf., I), **поступи́ть** (perf., II: **поступлю́, посту́пишь**) to enroll, enter (**в** *or* **на** + *acc.*)
произноси́ть (imperf., II: **произн.ошу́, -о́сишь**), **произнести́** (perf., I: **произнес.у́, -ёшь**; past: **произнёс, произнесло́,** etc.) to pronounce
просыпа́ться (imperf., I), **просну́ться** (perf., I: **просн.у́сь, -ёшься**) to wake up (*intrans.*)
ре́зать (imperf., II: **ре́ж.у, -ешь**) to cut, cut up
раздева́ть (imperf., I), **разде́ть** (perf., I: **разде́н.у, -ешь**) to undress (*trans.*)
собира́ть (imperf., I), **собра́ть** (perf., I: **собер.у́, -ёшь**) to collect, gather (*trans.*)
собира́ться, собра́ться to assemble (*intrans.*), come together; get ready to (+ *infin.*)

Expressions

та́к себе so-so
***провали́ться** (perf., II) **на экза́мене** to fail an exam
***вы́держать** (perf., I) **экза́мен** to pass an exam
наде́яться на (+ *acc.*) to hope for, rely on
сиде́ть за столо́м to be at the table
ничего́! not bad, all right, so-so; it doesn't matter
опа́здывать/опозда́ть на ча́с to be an hour late
Что́ идёт да́льше? What comes next?
Что́ с ни́м? What is the matter with him?
кто́ из ва́с? who of you?
До за́втра. Good-bye till tomorrow

[9] Note that the word for "color" is цвет; *plural* цвет.а́, -о́в, etc.

UNIT 20

GRAMMAR

1. Masculine nouns in -а and -я

A number of nouns denoting male persons end in **-а** or **-я** and are declined like feminine nouns with the same endings. Among these nouns are:

мужчи́на man (a male)
де́душка grandfather
дя́дя uncle
па́па papa

as well as most nicknames of men: Ко́ля (Никола́й), Са́ша (Алекса́ндр), Ва́ся (Васи́лий), Ва́ня (Ива́н), Бо́ря (Бори́с), etc.

Modifiers, verbs in the past tense, and pronouns in connection with these nouns take *masculine* endings:

Мо́й молодо́**й** дя́дя неда́вно приéха**л**; **о́н** бы́л в Нью-Йо́рке.
Я́ люблю́ сво**его́** молодо́**го** дя́дю.
На́ш де́душка жи́**л** в Москве́; я́ **его́** хорошо́ по́мню.

Pattern Sentences

1. Во́т семе́йная фотогра́фия. Э́тот высо́кий, худо́й **мужчи́на** с бородо́й —мо́й **де́душка,** а э́та ма́ленькая же́нщина с весёлым лицо́м—моя́ ба́бушка.	1. Here is a family photo. This tall thin man with a beard is my grandfather, and this little woman with a cheerful face is my grandmother.
2. Я́ о́чень люблю́ и сво**его́ де́душку** и свою́ ба́бушку.	2. I love both my grandfather and my grandmother very much.
3. В коридо́ре напра́во ко́мната мо**его́ де́душки,** а нале́во ко́мната мое́й ба́бушки.	3. In the hall to the right is my grandfather's room, and to the left is my grandmother's room.
4. В теа́тре тепе́рь идёт «**Дя́дя Ва́ня**» Че́хова.	4. Chekhov's "Uncle Vanya" is now playing at the theater.
5. —Вы́ ви́дели «**Дя́дю Ва́ню**»? —Да́, мы́ бы́ли вчера́ на «**Дя́де Ва́не**».[1]	5. —Have you seen "Uncle Vanya"? —Yes, we saw "Uncle Vanya" yesterday.
6. —Для кого́ О́ля купи́ла э́ти конфе́ты? —Она́ купи́ла и́х для **дя́ди Ко́ли** и для тёти Ка́ти.	6. —For whom did Olya buy this candy? —She bought it for Uncle Kolya and for Aunt Katya.
7. —Ко́ля, ты́ не зна́ешь,[2] где́ сейча́с **па́па** и ма́ма? —Не́т, я́ не ви́дел **па́пу** и ма́му весь де́нь.	7. —Kolya, do you know where Daddy and Mama are now? —No, I haven't seen Daddy and Mama all day.
8. Я́ бы́л вчера́ в кино́ с ма́мой, с **па́пой** и с **дя́дей Са́шей.**	8. Yesterday I went to the movies with Mama, Daddy, and Uncle Sasha.
9. —На кого́ ты́ смо́тришь? —Я́ смотрю́ на **па́пу.**	9. —Whom are you looking at? —I'm looking at Daddy.
10. В теа́тре почему́-то бы́ло мно́го **мужчи́н** и ма́ло же́нщин.	10. At the theater, for some reason, there were many men and few women.

Drills

A. *Чита́йте вопро́сы и отвеча́йте на ни́х:*

1. Вы́ хорошо́ зна́ете своего́ де́душку?
2. Како́й о́н челове́к?
3. Вы́ живёте вме́сте с ва́шим де́душкой и с ва́шей ба́бушкой?
4. У ва́с е́сть дя́дя?
5. У ва́шего дя́ди е́сть де́ти?
6. Ка́к сказа́ть по-ру́сски: "I like my daddy and my mama?"

[1] Мы́ бы́ли на «Дя́де Ва́не.» We saw "Uncle Vanya".

[2] Negative questions are very commonly used in Russian to ascertain or check bits of specific information such as place or time: Вы́ не ви́дели мою́ кни́гу? Did you see my book?

B. *Переведите с английского на русский.*[3]

1. Seventeen men and nine women work in this small plant.
2. Four men and three women work in our office.
3. Kolya has two uncles and two aunts.
4. Do you like your uncle and your aunt?
5. This is our uncle's house.
6. I remember well our grandfather and our grandmother.
7. Kolya writes often to his grandfather and to his grandmother.
8. They like Kolya and Katya very much.
9. —For whom did you buy these candies? —I bought them for Mama and Daddy.
10. She was talking with a small fat man and with a tall thin woman.
11. Whom are you looking at?
12. I am looking at my Uncle Vanya and at my Aunt Zina.

2. Genitive plural of nouns—miscellaneous categories

A. Nouns with nominative plural in -ья (see Unit 13, page 197). Most of these have genitive plural in **-ьев**. The three nouns which end in stressed **-ья́** in the nominative plural have stressed **-е́й** in the genitive plural:

Nominative Singular	*Nominative Plural*	*Genitive Plural*
стул	сту́лья	сту́льев
брат	бра́тья	бра́тьев
лист	ли́стья	ли́стьев
перо́	пе́рья	пе́рьев
де́рево	дере́вья	дере́вьев
пла́тье	пла́тья	пла́тьев
друг	друзья́	друзе́й
сын	сыновья́	сынове́й
муж	мужья́	муже́й

B. Feminines in consonant + -ня. These usually end in **-ен** (hard!) in the genitive plural:

	Nominative Singular	*Genitive Plural*
	пе́сня	пе́сен
	спа́льня	спа́лен
But:	дере́вня	дереве́нь
	ку́хня	ку́хонь

[3] To translate from a language, Russian uses **с** + genitive; to translate into a language, **на** + accusative.

C. Masculines in -ц. These end in **-ов** when the ending is stressed:

Nominative Singular	*Genitive Plural*
оте́ц	отцо́в
коне́ц	концо́в

Otherwise they end in **-ев**, according to Spelling Rule B:

ме́сяц	ме́сяцев
па́лец	па́льцев

D. Miscellaneous genitive plurals.

Nominative Singular	*Nominative Plural*	*Genitive Plural*
(ребёнок)	де́ти	дете́й
(челове́к)	лю́ди	люде́й[4]
сосе́д	сосе́ди	сосе́дей
мать	ма́тери	матере́й
дочь	до́чери	дочере́й
статья́	статьи́	стате́й
семья́	се́мьи	семе́й
и́мя	имена́	имён
вре́мя	времена́	времён

Pattern Sentences

1. В столо́вой вокру́г стола́ сто́ят ше́сть сту́л**ьев**.
2. Что́ э́то за дере́вья? Я́ никогда́ не ви́дел таки́х дере́в**ьев**!
3. У на́с в саду́ е́сть два́ таки́х де́рева. На э́тих дере́вьях уже́ мно́го кра́сных ли́ст**ьев**.
4. —Ско́лько у ва́с бра́т**ьев**? —У меня́ три́ бра́та. Все́ мои́ бра́тья живу́т о́коло Москвы́.
5. —Для чего́[5] ва́м сто́лько пе́р**ьев**? —Я́ люблю́ писа́ть ра́зными пе́рьями.

1. In the dining-room there are six chairs around the table.
2. What sort of trees are these? I've never seen such trees!
3. We have two trees of that kind in our garden. Those trees already have many red leaves.
4. —How many brothers do you have? —I have three brothers. All my brothers live near Moscow.
5. —What use do you have for so many pens? —I like to write with different (kinds of) pens.

[4] But челове́к (zero ending) after numerals, ско́лько and не́сколько.

[5] Both для чего́ and заче́м ("why?," "for what purpose") are more specific and more emphatic in stressing purpose than почему́, which means only "why?" Для чего́ and заче́м may often be used interchangeably. They are often used rhetorically to express surprise or disapproval, *e.g.*: Для чего́ (заче́м) ты́ купи́ла так мно́го хле́ба?

6. —Кто́ э́ти лю́ди? —Э́то на́ши друзья́. —Я́ не зна́л, что у ва́с сто́лько друз**е́й**.

6. —Who are those people? —They're our friends. —I didn't know that you had so many friends.

7. —Для кого́ вы́ купи́ли ша́хматы? —Я́ купи́л и́х для мои́х сын**ове́й**. —Все́ ва́ши сыновья́ игра́ют в ша́хматы? —Не́т, то́лько два́ сы́на.

7. —Whom did you buy the chess (set) for? —I bought it for my sons. —Do all your sons play chess? —No, only two.

8. —У ва́с е́сть де́ти? —Да́, е́сть. —Ско́лько у ва́с **дете́й?** —У на́с то́лько оди́н ребёнок.

8. —Do you have children? —Yes, I do. —How many children do you have? —We have only one child.

9. Когда́ **дете́й** не́т до́ма, для мат**е́рей** о́тдых. Ма́тери то́же должны́ иногда́ отдыха́ть.

9. When the children are not at home it's a rest (relief) for mothers. Mothers have to rest sometimes too.

10. —Для кого́ вы́ купи́ли э́тот до́м? —Я́ купи́ла его́ для мои́х доч**ере́й**. У меня́ две́ до́чери.

10. —For whom did you buy this house? —I bought it for my daughters. I have two daughters.

11. —**Ско́лько ра́з** вы́ бы́ли в теа́тре зимо́й? —Мы́ бы́ли четы́ре ра́за. А вы́? —Я́ бы́л то́лько оди́н ра́з!

11. —How many times have you been to the theater this winter? —We went four times. And you? —I went only once!

12. Вчера́ в и́х до́ме везде́ бы́ли лю́ди: в гости́ной бы́ло де́сять **челове́к,** в столо́вой бы́ло три́ челове́ка, **не́сколько челове́к** бы́ло в кабине́те и на вера́нде. То́лько в спа́льне не́ было ни одного́ челове́ка.

12. Yesterday there were people in their house everywhere: in the living room were ten people, in the dining room were three people, several people were in the study and on the porch. Only in the bedroom was there no one.

13. Де́ти пе́ли мно́го весёлых **пе́сен.**

13. The children sang many lively songs.

14. В на́шем но́вом до́ме бу́дет пя́ть **спа́лен.**

14. Our new house will have five bedrooms.

Drill

Translate the words in parentheses.

1. На́м ну́жно купи́ть (new chairs).
2. У на́с о́чень ма́ло (chairs).
3. В моей ко́мнате то́лько два́ (chairs).
4. Ско́лько (chairs) у ва́с?
5. У Ни́ны не́сколько (brothers).
6. Я́ не зна́ю её (brothers).
7. У меня́ три́ (brothers).
8. Почему́ все́ (leaves) жёлтые?
9. На э́том де́реве мно́го жёлтых (leaves).
10. Чьи́ э́ти (pens)?
11. Я́ ви́жу то́лько два́ (pens).
12. У меня́ не́т (pens).
13. В и́х саду́ ма́ло (trees).
14. О́коло на́шего до́ма четы́ре (trees).
15. Я́ люблю́ (trees).
16. У на́с зде́сь не́т (friends).
17. Где́ все́ ва́ши (friends)?
18. У на́с зде́сь то́лько два́ (friends).

19. Я́ не зна́ю её (sons).
20. Я́ не зна́л, что у неё е́сть (sons).
21. У неё два́ (sons) и две́ (daughters).
22. Вы́ зна́ете мно́го ру́сских (songs)?
23. Я́ бы́л в Пари́же то́лько два́ (times), а Зи́на была́ та́м мно́го (times). Ско́лько (times) вы́ та́м бы́ли?
24. Мы́ ви́дели в Берли́не ру́сских (soldiers).

3. Nouns of nationality

Russian, as we know, has adjectives of nationality (америка́нский, англи́йский, etc.), e.g.: америка́нский го́род, англи́йская газе́та, etc. These adjectives, however, are used only as modifiers. Referring to persons of a given nationality, *nouns* of nationality *must* be used, *e.g.*:

	He is an American.	О́н америка́нец.
Or:	He is American.	
	She is an American.	Она́ америка́нка.
Or:	She is American.	
	He is an Englishman.	О́н англича́нин.
Or:	He is English.	
	She is an Englishwoman.	Она́ англича́нка.
Or:	She is English.	

The only exception to the above is the Russian nationality; the forms ру́сск.ий, -ая, -ие are used both as modifiers and as nouns denoting Russian nationals, *e.g.*:

He is Russian.	Он ру́сский.	Они́ ру́сские.
She is Russian.	Она́ ру́сская.	

as well as:

ру́сский журна́л, ру́сская кни́га

Most nouns of nationality are formed either like америка́нец, америка́нка or like англича́нин, англича́нка, that is, with one of two types of suffixes:

A. Masculine singular **-ец**, plural **-цы**; feminine singular **-ка**, plural **-ки**.

Note that the **е** of the suffix **-ец** is dropped in case forms other than the nominative singular, thus in the genitive singular америка́н.**ца**; genitive plural **-цев**. In the feminine genitive singular америка́н.**ки**; genitive plural **-ок**.

B. Masculine singular **-анин/-янин**; (for declension of this type see Section 4 below), feminine **-анка/-янка**.

Observe that neither nouns nor adjectives of nationality are capitalized in Russian.

4. Declension of masculine nouns in -анин -янин

Masculine nouns ending in **-анин/-янин** are declined regularly in the singular. In the plural, however, they have a special declension based on a shortened stem ending in **-ан./-ян.** The nominative plural ends in **-ане/-яне**; genitive plural in **-ан/-ян** (zero ending); dative plural in **-анам/-янам,** etc.

To this group belong:

англича́нин, Englishman	nom. pl. англича́не
славяни́н, Slav	nom. pl. славя́не
граждани́н, citizen	nom. pl. гра́ждане
христиани́н, Christian	nom. pl. христиа́не
крестья́нин, peasant	nom. pl. крестья́не

The noun господи́н, "Mr.," "sir," etc., has the nominative plural господа́, genitive plural госпо́д, "sirs," "gentlemen," "ladies and gentlemen," etc.

The noun хозя́ин, "host," "master," etc., has the nominative plural хозя́ева, "host and hostess," "master and mistress," "hosts," "masters," etc.; genitive plural хозя́ев.

Pattern Sentences

1. —То́м Сми́т **америка́нец** и́ли **англича́нин?** —О́н, ка́жется, **ангича́нин.**
2. —Ка́к вы́ ду́маете, Не́лли Сми́т **англича́нка** и́ли **америка́нка?** —Она́ **америка́нка.** —Отку́да вы́ зна́ете? —Она́ мне́ сама́ э́то сказа́ла.
3. Я́ зна́ю не́сколько о́чень краси́вых **америка́нок.**
4. Не́которые **америка́нцы** и не́которые **англича́не** хорошо́ говоря́т на иностра́нных языка́х.[6]

1. —Is Tom Smith American or English? —I think he's English.
2. —Do you think Nelly Smith is English or American? —She's American. —How do you know? —She told me so herself.
3. I know several very beautiful American women.
4. Some Americans and some Englishmen speak foreign languages well.

[6] Говори́ть **на** (+ locative) to speak (in) a language. This construction, in contrast to the form with **по-**, must be used when the word язы́к occurs in the sentence:

—**На како́м** языке́ вы́ говори́те до́ма?—Мы́ говори́м **по-ру́сски.**

О́н говори́т **на мно́гих** языка́х.

—**На како́м** языке́ вы́ написа́ли э́ту статью́?—**По-англи́йски.**

5. На приёме у Орло́вых бы́ли ра́зные иностра́нцы. Та́м бы́ло не́сколько **англича́н,** не́сколько **францу́зов** и не́сколько **америка́нцев.**

5. At the reception at the Orlovs' there were different kinds of foreigners. There were several Englishmen, several Frenchmen, and several Americans.

6. —С ке́м вы́ хоти́те меня́ познако́мить? —Я́ хочу́ познако́мить ва́с с одни́м о́чень интере́сным **англича́нином.** Мне́ ка́жется, что вы́ с ни́м ещё не знако́мы.

6. —Whom do you want me to meet (Whom do you want to introduce me to)? —I want you to meet a very interesting Englishman. I don't think that you know him yet.

7. Ю́рий Гага́рин **ру́сский.** О́н сове́тский **граждани́н.** О́н **славяни́н.**

7. Yuri Gagarin is a Russian. He is a Soviet citizen. He is a Slav.

8. Еле́на Гага́рина **ру́сская.** Она́ сове́тская **гражда́нка.** Она́ **славя́нка.**

8. Yelena Gagarin is a Russian. She is a Soviet citizen. She is a Slav.

9. Гага́рины **ру́сские.** Они́ сове́тские **гра́ждане.** Они́ **славя́не.**

9. The Gagarins are Russian. They are Soviet citizens. They are Slavs.

10. **Не́мцы** лю́бят пи́ть пи́во. Пи́во в Герма́нии о́чень хоро́шее.

10. Germans like to drink beer. The beer in Germany is very good.

11. Мо́й сосе́д **ру́сский,** а его́ жена́ **не́мка.** Они́ говоря́т дру́г с дру́гом иногда́ по-ру́сски, а иногда́ по-неме́цки.

11. My neighbor is Russian and his wife is German. They sometimes talk Russian together and sometimes German.

12. Оди́н мо́й знако́мый **францу́з** о́чень лю́бит шути́ть. Его́ шу́тки ча́сто о́чень смешны́е.

12. A Frenchman whom I know is very fond of joking. His jokes are often very amusing.

Drills

A. *Переведи́те с ру́сского на англи́йский.*

1. На приёме у президе́нта бы́ло мно́го иностра́нцев, и мы́ весь ве́чер говори́ли на ра́зных иностра́нных языка́х.
2. Мы́ вчера́ познако́мились с одни́м францу́зом, кото́рый рабо́тает в Объединённых На́циях (the United Nations).
3. Оди́н из госте́й бы́л мо́й ста́рый знако́мый, кото́рого я́ не ви́дела мно́го ле́т.
4. Я́ была́ о́чень ра́да опя́ть встре́тить э́того знако́мого.
5. На́ш учи́тель матема́тики не́мец, а жена́ его́ францу́женка.
6. Францу́женки хорошо́ одева́ются и хорошо́ гото́вят.
7. В про́шлом году́ мы́ сде́лали о́чень прия́тное путеше́ствие: мы́ два́ ме́сяца е́здили по Испа́нии. На́м о́чень понра́вился испа́нский наро́д.
8. На́м осо́бенно понра́вились испа́нские крестья́не. В Мадри́де, в теа́тре, мы́ ви́дели не́сколько краси́вых испа́нок и испа́нцев.
9. Я́ хочу́ рассказа́ть ва́м об одно́м интере́сном слу́чае.
10. Э́то случи́лось во вре́мя одного́ из мои́х путеше́ствий по А́фрике.

11. —Вы́ поёте знако́мую мело́дию. Что́ э́то? —Я́ са́м не зна́ю, что́ я́ пою́.
12. В Сове́тском Сою́зе живёт мно́го славя́н, но́ не все́ славя́не живу́т в Сове́тском Сою́зе.

B. *Переведи́те с англи́йского на ру́сский.*

1. Anna is English, and her husband is French.
2. —Is Vadim's wife French or American? —His wife is American and he himself is Russian.
3. The English like to play tennis.
4. Americans like steak.
5. Did you speak with these Englishmen?
6. No, I spoke only with these Frenchmen and Frenchwomen.
7. There are many Slavs here.
8. —Who are these peasants? —They are Italians.
9. There are many peasants in Italy.
10. I like Italians.

5. Review of declension in the plural

A. Nouns. The following are the basic types of noun declension in the plural:

		Masculine		*Neuter*		*Feminine* I		*Feminine* II
		Hard	Soft	Hard	Soft	Hard	Soft	
Nom.	**-ы/-и, -а/-я**	столы́[7]	го́сти[9]	дела́	поля́	жёны[11]	ку́хни	две́ри
Gen.	**-ов/-ев,** zero, **-ей**	столо́в[8]	госте́й	дел	поле́й[10]	жён[12]	ку́хонь[13]	двере́й
Dat.	**-ам/-ям**	стола́м	гостя́м	дела́м	поля́м	жёнам	ку́хням	дверя́м
Acc.	Inanimate like Nominative; animate like Genitive.							
Instr.	**-ами/-ями**	стола́ми	гостя́ми	дела́ми	поля́ми	жёнами	ку́хнями	дверя́ми[14]
Loc.	**-ах/-ях**	стола́х	гостя́х	дела́х	поля́х	жёнах	ку́хнях	дверя́х

[7] дома́, леса́, профессора́ (see Unit 13, page 195); англича́не, господа́, хозя́ева (see Section 4 above).

[8] карандаше́й, враче́й, това́рищей, etc. (see Unit 16, page 233); ме́сяцев, па́льцев (see Section 2 above); раз, солда́т, глаз, etc. (see Unit 16, page 238); англича́н, господ́, хозя́ев (see Section 4 above).

[9] учителя́ (see Unit 13, page 195)

[10] пла́тьев.

[11] кни́ги, да́чи, etc. (Spelling Rule A).

[12] таре́лок, де́вушек, etc. (see Unit 16, page 233).

[13] неде́ль, дереве́нь, etc. (see Unit 16, page 232); фами́лий, фотогра́фий (see Unit 16, page 232); стате́й, семе́й, etc. (see Section 2 above); спа́лен, пе́сен (see Section 2 above).

[14] людьми́, детьми́, лошадьми́.

SPECIAL GROUPS

	Masculine	*Masculine and Neuter*	*Neuter*	*Feminine*
Nom.	друзья́[15]	бра́тья[16] (пе́рья)	имена́[17] (like дела́)	ма́тери[18] (like две́ри)
Gen.	друзе́й	бра́тьев	имён	матере́й
Dat.	друзья́м	бра́тьям	имена́м	матеря́м
Acc.	Inanimate like Nominative; animate like Genitive.			
Instr.	друзья́ми	бра́тьями	имена́ми	матеря́ми
Loc.	друзья́х	бра́тьях	имена́х	матеря́х

B. Pronouns, adjectives, and pronoun-adjectives.

	3rd Person Pronouns	*Hard Adjectives*	*Soft Adjectives*	*Possessives*	*Demonstratives*	
Nom.	они́	но́вые	си́ние	мои́	э́ти	те
Gen.	их	но́вых	си́них	мои́х	э́тих	тех
Dat.	им	но́вым	си́ним	мои́м	э́тим	тем
Acc.	их	Inanimate like Nominative; animate like Genitive.				
Instr.	и́ми	но́выми	си́ними	мои́ми	э́тими	те́ми
Loc.	(н)их	но́вых	си́них	мои́х	э́тих	тех

"Mixed" adjectives with stems ending in **г**, **к**, **х**, **ж**, **ч**, **ш**, and **щ** are declined in the plural with the written endings of soft adjectives (си́ний): ру́сск**ие**, etc., хоро́ш**ие**, etc.

Like мои́ are declined твои́, свои́, на́ши, and ва́ши.

Like э́ти are declined одни́ and чьи.

Like те is declined все.

6. Adjectival words expressing quantity

The adverbs мно́го, немно́го, ско́лько, сто́лько, and не́сколько have corresponding adjectival forms; the last three are used only in case forms other than the nominative:

[15] Мужья́ and сыновья́ are declined like друзья́.
[16] Сту́лья, ли́стья ("leaves") пе́рья, and дере́вья are declined like бра́тья.
[17] Времена́ and others are declined like имена́. For singular see Unit 12, page 178.
[18] До́чери is declined like ма́тери (but instrumental plural дочерьми́). For singular see Unit 12, page 178.

мно́гие, мно́гих, мно́гим, etc.
(no nom.), ско́льких, ско́льким, etc.
(no nom.), не́скольких, не́скольким, etc.

The use of these forms may be seen from the following examples:

Ско́лько музе́ев вы́ ви́дели в Евро́пе?
But: В **ско́льких** музе́ях вы́ бы́ли?

Я́ ви́дел **мно́го** стра́н (**не́сколько** стра́н).
But: Та́м бы́ли лю́ди из **мно́гих** стра́н (**не́скольких** стра́н).

Мно́го differs from мно́гие (*e.g.*, мно́го студе́нтов—мно́гие студе́нты) in that мно́го means simply "many," "a large number," whereas мно́гие implies part of a total (many, but not all). In this sense мно́гие is less than все, but more than не́которые (some, a number, a few), thus:

Все́ америка́нские студе́нты зна́ют англи́йский язы́к, **мно́гие** зна́ют оди́н иностра́нный язы́к, а **не́которые** зна́ют два́ и́ли да́же три́ иностра́нных языка́.

The words все, мно́гие, не́которые, and немно́гие are often used without a noun, the word "people" (лю́ди) being then understood:

Мно́гие бы́ли недово́льны э́той пье́сой.
Не́которые её совсе́м не по́няли.

The adverb ма́ло has no corresponding declined form. Немно́гие (cf. немно́го, "a few") is used instead: в немно́гих слу́чаях—in (a) few cases.

The singular form мно́гое, declined, is used in the sense of "many things":

В э́той стране́ мно́гое мне́ нра́вится.

Pattern Sentences

1. Ру́сские о́чень лю́бят игра́ть в ша́хматы, и мно́г**ие** игра́ют хорошо́.	1. The Russians are very fond of playing chess, and many (of them) play it well.
2. У мно́г**их** италья́нцев хоро́шие голоса́, но́ не у все́х.	2. Many Italians have good voices, but not all.
3. Васи́лий Ша́пкин крестья́нин. У него́, как у мно́г**их** крестья́н, тяжёлая жи́знь.	3. Vasili Shapkin is a peasant. Like many peasants, he has a hard life.
4. Оди́н из мои́х друзе́й хорошо́ говори́т на не́скольк**их** языка́х.	4. One of my friends speaks several languages well.
5. Во вре́мя на́шего путеше́ствия по Фра́нции мы́ познако́мились с не́скольк**ими** англича́нами и с не́скольк**ими** америка́нцами.	5. During our trip through France we met several English people and several Americans.

6. Не́которые из ни́х бы́ли о́чень симпати́чные лю́ди, и я́ иногда́ пишу́ не́которым из ни́х.	6. Some of them were very likable people, and I sometimes write to some of them.
7. В Пари́же мы́ бы́ли в не́скольких хоро́ших рестора́нах. В одно́м из ни́х я́ познако́милась с не́сколькими о́чень симпати́чными францу́зами.	7. In Paris we went to several good restaurants. In one of them I met some very nice Frenchmen.
8. В не́которых слу́чаях о́н быва́ет пра́в, но́ не во все́х.	8. In some cases he is right, but not in all.

7. Verbs of lying, sitting, and standing: ложи́ться/лечь, сади́ться/сесть, станови́ться/стать

These three verbs are unique in that their *imperfectives* are **-ся** verbs, but the *perfectives* lack **-ся**. All three are verbs which denote the assuming of a physical position: lying, sitting, and standing.[19] The conjugation of ложи́ться/лечь and сади́ться/сесть is parallel:

ложи́ться/лечь "*to lie down*"

Imperfective **ложи́ться**		*Perfective* **лечь**	
Present		*Future*	
ложу́сь	ложи́мся	ля́гу	ля́жем
ложи́шься	ложи́тесь	ля́жешь	ля́жете
ложи́тся	ложа́тся	ля́жет	ля́гут
Past		*Past*	
ложи́лся, ложи́лось, etc.		лёг, легло́, легла́, легли́	
Imperative		*Imperative*	
ложи́сь!	ложи́тесь!	ляг!	ля́гте!

сади́ться/сесть "*to sit down*"

Imperfective **сади́ться**		*Perfective* **сесть**	
Present		*Future*	
сажу́сь	сади́мся	ся́ду	ся́дем
сади́шься	сади́тесь	ся́дешь	ся́дете
сади́тся	садя́тся	ся́дет	ся́дут

[19] As such they must be kept distinct from verbs which denote remaining in a physical condition: лежа́ть, "to be lying," сиде́ть, "to be sitting," стоя́ть, "to be standing." For a tabular representation of the relation of these two groups of verbs, see Unit 25, page 448.

Past		*Past*	
сади́лся, сади́лось, etc.		сел, се́ло, се́ла, се́ли	
Imperative		*Imperative*	
сади́сь!	сади́тесь!	сядь!	ся́дьте!

станови́ться/стать, *"to take a standing position"*, *"to become"*

Imperfective **станови́ться**		*Perfective* **стать**	
Present		*Future*	
становлю́сь	стано́вимся	ста́ну	ста́нем
стано́вишься	стано́витесь	ста́нешь	ста́нете
стано́вится	стано́вятся	ста́нет	ста́нут
Past		*Past*	
станови́лся, станови́лось, etc.		стал, -о, -а, -и	
Imperative		*Imperative*	
станови́ сь!	станови́тесь!	стань!	станьте!

The verb станови́ться/стать means "to take up a standing position," "to place oneself (standing)." As such it should be distinguished from встава́ть/встать, which means "to stand up," "to get up," "to arise":

Снача́ла о́н стоя́л ря́дом со мно́й, а пото́м о́н **ста́л** о́коло О́льги.
At first he was standing near me, and then he stood (took a standing position) near Olga.

О́н **вста́л** с дива́на и се́л на сту́л.
He got up from the sofa and sat on a chair.

The verb станови́ться/стать is most common in the sense of "become." In this use it may take an adverb, or a predicate noun or adjective in the *instrumental:*

Стано́вится хо́лодн**о**.
It's getting cold.

О́н ста́л изве́стн**ым** исто́рик**ом**.
He became a well-known historian.

О́льга ста́ла хоро́ш**ей** хозя́йк**ой**.
Olga has become a good housekeeper.

Pattern Sentences

1. Дéти! Порá **ложи́ться!**	1. Children, it's time to go to bed!
2. Зимóй дéти **ложи́лись** (спáть) в вóсемь часóв, а мáть **ложи́лась** в оди́ннадцать.	2. In winter the children went to bed at 8:00, and the mother at 11:00.
3. Нáши дéти всегдá **ложáтся** в дéвять.	3. Our children always go to bed at 9:00.
4. Илья́ Ильи́ч **ложи́тся** рáно, просыпáется пóздно и дóлго **лежи́т** в кровáти.	4. Ilya Ilyich goes to bed early, wakes up late, and stays in bed a long time.
5. Пóсле обéда Илья́ Ильи́ч **ложи́тся** на дивáн и читáет газéту.	5. After dinner Ilya Ilyich lies down on the sofa and reads the paper.
6. Мы́ всé обыкновéнно **ложи́мся** рáно. Нó вчерá мы́ **легли́** довóльно пóздно: Андрéй **лёг** в двенáдцать, а Зи́на **леглá** в чáс.	6. Usually we all go to bed early. But yesterday we went to bed rather late. Andrey went to bed at 12:00, and Zina at 1:00.
7. Спокóйной нóчи! Я́ иду́ спáть.[20] Я́ люблю́ рáно **ложи́ться.**	7. Good night! I am going to bed. I like to go to bed early.
8. Зáвтра ну́жно бу́дет **лéчь** рáньше. Я́ **ля́гу** в дéсять и надéюсь, что вы́ всé рáно **ля́жете.** Дéти **ля́гут** в сéмь.	8. Tomorrow we must go to bed earlier. I will go at 10:00 and I hope that you will all go early. The children will go at 7:00.
9. Собáка Мáшка лю́бит **лежáть** на э́том крéсле, поэ́тому никтó на негó не **сади́тся.**	9. The dog Mashka likes to lie on this armchair, and therefore no one sits on it.
10. Я́ никогдá не **сажу́сь** на э́тот сту́л: на нём неудóбно **сидéть.** На негó никтó не **сади́тся.**	10. I never sit on this chair; it is not comfortable (to sit on). No one sits on it.
11. —**Сади́тесь,**[21] пожáлуйста, почему́ вы́ **стои́те?** Вы́ не хоти́те **сéсть?** —Спаси́бо, я́ **ся́ду,** когдá всé **ся́дут.** Нó я́ вообщé предпочитáю **стоя́ть.**	11. —Sit down, please; why are you standing? Don't you want to sit down? —Thank you; I'll sit down when everyone does. But in general I prefer to stand.
12. —Почему́ Ивáн Ивáнович **сéл** óколо Зи́ны? —Мнé кáжется, что э́то Зи́на **сéла** óколо Ивáна Ивáновича. Онá лю́бит **сидéть** óколо негó.	12. —Why has Ivan Ivanovich taken a seat near Zina? —It seems to me it's Zina (who) has taken a seat near Ivan Ivanovich. She likes to sit near him.
13. —**Ся́дьте** у окнá,[22] здéсь так жáрко!	13. Sit by the window, it's so hot here!

[20] Идти́/пойти́ спать is used only for a single time (ходи́ть спать is never used), *e.g.*, Иди́ спáть! or О́н сейчáс идёт спáть, Go to bed! or He's going to bed now. Лéчь спáть (perfective) is also said of going to bed once, *e.g.*, Я́ хочу́ лéчь спáть, I want to go to bed. Ложи́ться (спáть) (imperfective) is used in general, *e.g.*, Я́ бу́ду тепéрь рáно ложи́ться спáть, From now on I'll be going to bed early.

[21] The imperfective imperative of this verb is preferable as a polite invitation.

[22] **У** + genitive is used of objects (normally impenetrable) to mean "by," "at," "very close to": **у** доски́, at the blackboard; **у** стены́, by the wall, etc.

14. —Где́ вы́ **се́ли** на по́езд? —Я́ **се́л** на ма́ленькой ста́нции о́коло Москвы́.	14. —Where did you take the train? —I took it at a small station near Moscow.
15. —Ко́ля, почему́ ты́ ту́т **стои́шь?** Ты́ всегда́ **стано́вишься** ме́жду мно́й и окно́м!	15. —Kolya, why are you standing here? You always get (stand) between me and the window!
16. **Стано́вится** хо́лодно. Закро́йте, пожа́луйста, окно́.	16. It's getting cold. Please shut the window.
17. Е́сли ва́м **ста́нет** хо́лодно, закро́йте окно́.	17. If you get cold, shut the window.
18. Я́ бою́сь, что ско́ро **ста́нет** темно́.	18. I am afraid that it will soon get dark.
19. Бо́б **ста́л** хоро́ш**им** студе́нт**ом**; о́н тепе́рь хорошо́ занима́ется.	19. Bob has become a good student; he is studying well now.
20. Не́лли **ста́ла** плох**о́й** студе́нтк**ой**: она́ не хо́чет занима́ться.	20. Nelly has become a poor student: she won't study.

Drill

Переведи́те с англи́йского на ру́сский.

1. It is getting cold.
2. It got cold.
3. Soon it will get cold.
4. If you get cold, I'll shut the window.
5. —Where do you prefer to sit? —I prefer to sit near you.
6. —Kolya, when did you (*familiar*) go to bed yesterday? —We all went to bed early.
7. Today I shall go to bed at 10:00, and the others will go to bed at 12:00.
8. My son wants to become a doctor.
9. He became a famous actor.

8. The verb есть (to eat)

Есть is conjugated like the verb **дать**, with the exception of the third person plural. But note that есть is *imperfective present;* дать is *perfective future:*

	Perfective Future of **дать** (*to give*)	*Imperfective Present of* **есть** (*to eat*)
	дам	ем
	дашь	ешь
	даст	ест
	дади́м	еди́м
	дади́те	еди́те
	даду́т	ед**я́**т
Past:	дал, да́ло, дала́, да́ли	ел, е́ло, е́ла, е́ли
Imperative:	дай, да́йте	ешь, е́шьте

Есть has two perfectives: one, **поéсть** (to have a meal, have some-thing to eat); the other always transitive—used with an object—**съéсть** (to eat up, consume a specific quantity). **Съéсть** has its own secondary imperfective, **съедáть** (to eat a certain quantity of food—often, as a rule).[23]

—Вы́ ужé éли? —Дá, éл.

Мы́ **поéли** и пошли́ в кинó.

Я́ **съéл** двá кускá хлéба. Обыкновéнно я́ **съедáю** тóлько оди́н.

The same usage applies to пить (imperfective)—вы́пить (perfective, to drink up a certain quantity)—выпивáть (imperfective, to drink a certain quantity, often, as a rule).[24]

Я́ тóлько что **пи́л** кóфе.

Я́ **вы́пил** двé чáшки кóфе. Обыкновéнно я́ **выпивáю** тóлько однý.

Pattern Sentences

1. —Чтó ты́ **éшь** и чтó ты́ **пьёшь?** —Рáзве ты́ не ви́дишь? Я́ **éм** хлéб с мáслом и с колбасóй и **пью́** пи́во.

1. —What are you eating and drinking? —Can't you see? I'm eating bread, butter, and sausage and I'm drinking beer.

2. —Скóлько рáз в дéнь вы́ **еди́те?** —Мы́ **еди́м** три́ рáза в дéнь, и за едóй мы́ **пьём** винó и́ли пи́во.

2. —How many times a day do you eat? —We eat three times a day and with our food (meals) we drink wine or beer.

3. У нáшего сы́на Ми́ши óчень хорó-ший аппети́т—óн **éст** и пьёт цéлый дéнь.

3. Our son Misha has a very good appetite—he eats and drinks all day long.

4. Сегóдня к зáвтраку óн **съéл** четы́ре сáндвича и **вы́пил** три́ стакáна молокá.

4. For breakfast today he ate four sand-wiches and drank three glasses of milk.

5. —Гдé ты́ сегóдня **éл?** —Я́ **éл** дóма. Я́ **поéл** и пришёл пря́мо сюдá.

5. —Where did you eat today? —I ate at home. I ate and came straight here.

6. —Ни́на, хóчешь **éсть?** —Нéт, спа-си́бо, я́ ужé **éла.** —Чтó ты́ **éла?** —Я́ **éла** сáндвичи. —Скóлько сáндвичей ты́ **съéла?** —Я́ **съéла** двá и **вы́пила** чáшку кóфе.

6. —Nina, are you hungry? —No thanks, I've eaten already. —What did you eat? —I ate sandwiches. —How many sandwiches did you eat? —I ate two and drank a cup of coffee.

[23] There is another verb, кýшать (I), perf. покýшать, which also means "to eat." It is used chiefly in invitations to eat, *i.e.*, in the second person singular and plural and in the first person plural. This verb should *never* be used of the speaker alone in the first person singular.

[24] Note that *all* perfective verbs with the prefix вы- have the stress on вы-, but the corresponding imperfective verbs *never* have the stress on вы-.

7. Я́ обыкнове́нно **съеда́ю** два́ са́ндвича за за́втраком и **выпива́ю** ча́шку и́ли две́ ко́фе.
8. Как то́лько я́ **пое́м,** я́ приду́ к ва́м. Подожди́те меня́, и мы́ вме́сте пойдём в кино́.
9. Снача́ла **пое́шь,** а пото́м пойди́ игра́ть.
10. Когда́ моя́ жена́ уе́дет, я́ **бу́ду е́сть** в рестора́не.

7. Usually I eat two sandwiches for breakfast and drink a cup or two of coffee.
8. As soon as I have eaten, I'll come to your place. Wait for me and we'll go to the movies together.
9. Eat first, and then go and play.
10. When my wife goes away, I'm going to eat in a restaurant.

Drill

Переведи́те на ру́сский язы́к.

1. He never eats bread.
2. —Vadim, what are you (*familiar*) eating? I am eating meat and (= with) potatoes.
3. —Ivan Ivanovich, where do you usually eat? —We always eat at home.
4. I ate and went to work.
5. I ate two steaks!
6. He often eats two steaks at dinner.
7. The French drink a lot of wine.
8. Some Frenchmen drink two bottles of wine a day.
9. Kolya, drink up your milk!
10. I ate all the meat you gave me.

CONVERSATION

Познако́мьтесь пожа́луйста

Я —Ма́рья Васи́льевна, вы́ зна́ете Серге́я Ива́новича Ка́рпова?

М.В. —Не́т, я́ с ни́м не знако́ма, но́ я́ мно́го слы́шала о нём.

Я —Вы́ хоти́те с ни́м познако́миться?

М.В. —С больши́м удово́льствием!

Я —Серге́й Ива́нович! Ма́рья Васи́льевна Ша́пкина зде́сь. Вы́ говори́ли, что хоти́те с не́й познако́миться.

С.И. —Да́, бу́ду о́чень ра́д. Я́ слы́шал о не́й мно́го хоро́шего.

Я —Во́т, познако́мьтесь пожа́луйста: Серге́й Ива́нович, Ма́рья Васи́льевна.

I —Maria Vasilyevna, do you know Sergey Ivanovich Karpov?

M.V. —No, I don't know him, but I have heard a great deal about him.

I —Would you like to meet him?

M.V. —I would be very glad to!

I —Sergey Ivanovich! Maria Vasilyevna Shapkina is here. You said that you would like to meet her.

S.I. —I would be very happy to. I've heard many fine things about her.

I —Let me introduce you, then. Sergey Ivanovich, Maria Vasilyevna.

С.И. —О́чень прия́тно! Я́ так мно́го о ва́с слы́шал.

S.I. —How do you do? (I'm pleased to meet you). I've heard so much about you.

М.В. —О́чень ра́да с ва́ми познако́миться.

M.V. —How do you do? (I'm very glad to meet you).

На приёме у Орло́вых

А. —Я́ звони́л ва́м в пя́тницу ве́чером, Ма́рья Васи́льевна, но́ мне́ никто́ не отве́тил. Ва́с не́ было до́ма?

Б. —В пя́тницу? А́х, да́! Я́ была́ на приёме у Орло́вых.

А. —Я́ та́к и ду́мал! У ни́х бы́ло мно́го госте́й?

Б. —Да́, у ни́х бы́л большо́й приём. Орло́вы о́чень гостеприи́мные лю́ди. Они́ лю́бят принима́ть и принима́ют о́чень хорошо́.

А. —Да́, я́ э́то слы́шал от о́бщих друзе́й. Я́ с ни́ми са́м не знако́м. Кто́ у ни́х бы́л?

Б. —Как всегда́, мно́го иностра́нцев. Орло́в ведь рабо́тает в Объединённых На́циях (United Nations).

А. —Вы́ со все́ми уже́ бы́ли знако́мы?

Б. —Мно́гих я́ уже́ зна́ла, а с не́которыми я́ познако́милась в то́т ве́чер.

А. —Ва́м та́м бы́ло ве́село?

Б. —Ка́к ва́м сказа́ть? Я́ сама́ не зна́ю . . . Да́, дово́льно ве́село.

А. —Но́ мне́ ка́жется, что в ва́шем го́лосе не́т большо́го энтузиа́зма.

Б. —Вы́ пра́вы. Энтузиа́зма не́т. Во-пе́рвых, я́ вообще́ не люблю́ больши́х приёмов . . .

А. —А во-вторы́х?

Б. —Во-вторы́х, мне́ ну́жно бы́ло весь ве́чер говори́ть на иностра́нных языка́х, а мне́ э́то немно́жко тру́дно.

А. —Я́ э́то отли́чно понима́ю. А са́ми хозя́ева зна́ют иностра́нные языки́?

Б. —Да́, они́ до́лго жи́ли в Евро́пе и говоря́т на не́скольких языка́х. Когда́ рабо́таешь в ООН,[25] э́то о́чень ва́жно.

А. —Коне́чно. Так с ке́м же вы́ та́м познако́мились?

Б. —Та́м бы́л францу́зский мини́стр иностра́нных де́л, с кото́рым меня́ познако́мил хозя́ин. Мы́ пошли́ в кабине́т хозя́ина, се́ли та́м на дива́н и до́лго говори́ли, по-францу́зски, коне́чно. Мы́ говори́ли немно́жко о поли́тике и та́кже о совреме́нной литерату́ре. Э́тот францу́з о́чень культу́рный челове́к. О́н всё чита́л и всё зна́ет. О́н мне́ о́чень понра́вился.

А. —Но́ э́то ведь бы́ло интере́сно?

[25] ООН (U.N.), abbreviation of Организа́ция Объединённых На́ций (United Nations Organization). Рабо́таешь, "you work." The second person singular is often used in the indefinite sense of "one," "you," "a person," etc. The pronoun subject (ты) is then usually omitted.

Б. —О́чень, но́ э́то ещё не всё. Пото́м хозя́йка познако́мила меня́ с то́лстым испа́нцем. О́н, ка́жется, бы́л профе́ссором исто́рии, а тепе́рь ста́л диплома́том. О́н мне́ до́лго расска́зывал о полити́ческом положе́нии в Испа́нии. По-испа́нски, коне́чно!

А. —По-мо́ему э́то всё о́чень интере́сно.

Б. —Коне́чно. Но́ э́то ещё не всё. Пото́м я́ познако́милась с о́чень прия́тной и элега́нтной да́мой. Э́та да́ма—италья́нка. Она́ рабо́тает в италья́нской делега́ции. Она́ о́чень мно́го путеше́ствовала по всему́ све́ту и расска́зывала мне́ ра́зные интере́сные исто́рии, кото́рые с не́й случа́лись во вре́мя э́тих путеше́ствий. Всё э́то по-италья́нски, коне́чно. Пото́м шёл о́бщий разгово́р о поли́тике на все́х языка́х. По́сле э́того приёма я́ два́ дня́ лежа́ла в посте́ли и не сказа́ла ни одного́ сло́ва.

А. —Всё, что вы́ расска́зали, мне́ о́чень нра́вится; я́ люблю́ тако́е о́бщество. Мне́ о́чень жа́ль, что я́ не знако́м с Орло́выми.

Б. —Я́ ва́с с удово́льствием с ни́ми познако́млю.

Чита́йте э́ти вопро́сы и отвеча́йте на ни́х.

1. Кому́ звони́л А.? 2. В како́й де́нь о́н е́й звони́л? 3. Кто́ ему́ отве́тил? Почему́? Где́ она́ была́ в то́т ве́чер? 4. Где́ рабо́тает Орло́в? 5. Что́ М. В. говори́т об Орло́вых? 6. От кого́ А. уже́ слы́шал о ни́х? 7. Кто́ бы́л на их приёме? 8. Та́к как Ма́рья Васи́льевна не была́ знако́ма со все́ми гостя́ми, что́ е́й ну́жно было сде́лать? 9. На како́м языке́ она́ говори́ла ве́сь ве́чер? 10. С ке́м её познако́мил хозя́ин? 11. О чём она́ говори́ла с э́тим францу́зом? 12. Что́ она́ о нём ду́мает? 13. Что́ она́ рассказа́ла о да́ме, с кото́рой она́ познако́милась? 14. Что́ М. В. де́лала по́сле приёма? 15. Что́ сказа́л А., когда́ о́н всё это услы́шал?

SUPPLEMENTARY READING

Анекдо́т о Берна́рде Шо́у и о Че́стертоне

Берна́рд Шо́у, знамени́тый англи́йский писа́тель и драмату́рг, не е́л ни мя́са ни ры́бы. О́н бы́л вегетариа́нцем и е́л то́лько о́вощи, фру́кты и моло́чные проду́кты. Вообще́ о́н е́л ма́ло и бы́л о́чень худо́й.

Его́ дру́г, писа́тель и журнали́ст Ги́льберт Че́стертон, о́чень люби́л е́сть. О́н е́л мно́го и бы́л о́чень то́лстый.

Одна́жды, в Ло́ндоне, бы́л съе́зд писа́телей и журнали́стов. На э́тот съе́зд прие́хало мно́го иностра́нцев из ра́зных стра́н ми́ра.

Приéхали францу́зы, нéмцы, италья́нцы, америкáнцы и други́е иностра́нцы.

Съéзд бы́л óчень интерéсный. Бы́ло мнóго интерéсных доклáдов на рáзные литерату́рные тéмы; пóсле доклáдов, обы́чно, начинá-лись спóры. Спóрили о рáзных литерату́рных теóриях и о литерату́рной кри́тике.

Цéнтром óбщего внимáния бы́л почти́ всегдá Бернáрд Шóу. Всé слу́шали егó с больши́м внимáнием, а мнóгие дáже запи́сывали афори́змы, парадóксы и шу́тки знамени́того писáтеля. Вокру́г негó всегдá бы́ло вéсело, и всé мнóго смея́лись.

Англичáне, как э́то всé знáют, óчень гостеприи́мный нарóд. Они́ óчень хорошó принимáли свои́х инострáнных гостéй. В Лóндоне бы́ло мнóго приёмов, банкéтов, обéдов.

На однóм такóм обéде Шóу сидéл за столóм ря́дом с Чéстер-тоном. Шóу, как обы́чно, мáло éл и мнóго смея́лся и шути́л со свои́ми совéдями. Чéстертон же[26] говори́л мáло и, как всегдá, мнóго éл. Мóжет быть Чéстертону бы́ло немнóжко неприя́тно, что Шóу бы́л цéнтром óбщего внимáния, а мóжет быть óн прóсто хотéл пошути́ть, нó óн вдру́г сказáл ти́хо, нó тáк, что мнóгие могли́ егó слы́шать: «Éшьте бóльше, Шóу, и говори́те мéньше; вы́ такóй худóй, что э́ти инострáнцы бу́дут потóм писáть в свои́х статья́х, что в Áнглии гóлод.» Шóу немéдленно отвéтил ему́ со смéхом: «Вы́ прáвы, Чéстертон. Я́ знáю, что писáтели и журнали́сты ужáсные лю́ди! Нó вы́ знáете, чегó я́ ещё бою́сь? Я́ бою́сь, что они́ тáкже напи́шут, что в Áнглии гóлод, потому́ что Чéстертон так мнóго éст!»

Читáйте э́ти вопрóсы, отвечáйте на ни́х.

1. Чтó такóе вегетариáнец? 2. На лóндонский съéзд приéхали делегáты тóлько из Еврóпы? 3. Бы́ло мнóго полити́ческих спóров на съéзде? 4. О чём мнóго спóрили? 5. Когдá начинáлись спóры? 6. Почему́ Бернáрд Шóу бы́л цéнтром óбщего внимáния? 7. Чéс-тертон серьёзно боя́лся, что журнали́сты напи́шут, что в Áнглии гóлод? 8. Почему́ óн э́то сказáл? 9. Вы́ бы́ли в Áнглии? 10. Вы́ хорошó знáете англичáн? 11. Чтó вы́ о ни́х ду́маете? 12. Вы́ читáли Бернáрда Шóу, и́ли каки́е егó пьéсы вы́ ви́дели?

EXERCISES

A. *Combine each phrase of column A with each phrase of column B, putting the words of column B into the correct case form:*

[26] Chesterton, on the other hand. . .

A	B
Я́ зна́ю	у́мный англича́нин.
Она́ познако́милась с	у́мные англича́не.
Мы́ говори́ли о (об)	э́ти америка́нцы.
Она́ пи́шет	краси́вая америка́нка.
Мы́ бы́ли у	молодо́й францу́з.
	молода́я францу́женка.
	сове́тские гра́ждане.
	ста́рый америка́нец.
	тво́й дя́дя.
	люби́мая ба́бушка.
	ми́лый де́душка.
	Серёжа.
	ста́рый крестья́нин.
	ста́рые крестья́не.
	ру́сские солда́ты.

B. *Переведи́те на ру́сский язы́к.*

There was a big reception at Dr. Smirnov's, our acquaintance's. At that reception we met (got acquainted with) many interesting people. There were many men and women whom I had never yet seen. I spoke for a long while with a very funny, fat Italian, who was sitting on the sofa. I sat down in an armchair next to him. I speak a little Italian. He told funny stories about Italy. We laughed a great deal and had a very good time. I also spoke with my host's uncle, who had just arrived from Germany. He is German and his wife is Italian, but they lived all their life in England, and at home they speak many languages. He told me that not only his wife, but he himself likes to cook, and he told me how to cook fish. I listened to him with great interest. There were also Englishmen and Russians there. It was a very pleasant reception, and it seemed to me that everybody was very pleased. I've been there many times and it has always been pleasant. I hope that there will be many such receptions.

C. *Переведи́те на ру́сский язы́к.*

1. One of my friends has just returned from England. 2. How do you say that in Russian? 3. At dinner we spoke about you. 4. What kind of a magazine is that? 5. I am acquainted with that Englishman. 6. —How do you know that he didn't want to see you? —He told me that himself. 7. —We had a very good time last night. —I thought so. 8. My son wants to become a teacher. 9. In December it gets dark early, and we go to bed early. 10. Ivan works a great deal now and goes to bed late. Yesterday, for example, he went to bed at two o'clock.

VOCABULARY

америка́н.ец (*fem.* **-ка**) American
англича́н.ин (*pl.* **-е**; *fem.* **-ка**) Englishman (-woman)
борода́ beard
вообще́ in general
Герма́ния Germany
го́лод hunger, famine
гостеприи́мный hospitable
граждани́н (*pl.* **гра́ждане**); *fem.* **гражда́нка** citizen (citizeness)
де́душка (*masc.*) grandfather
дя́дя (*masc.*) uncle
еда́ food
знако́мый familiar; (*as a noun*) acquaintance
иностра́нный foreign
иностра́н.ец (*fem.* **-ка**) foreigner
испа́н.ец (*fem.* **-ка**) Spaniard
испа́нский Spanish
италья́н.ец (*fem.* **-ка**) Italian
италья́нский Italian (*adj.*)
конфе́та a piece of candy
конфе́ты (*pl.*) candy
крестья́н.ин (*pl.* **-е**; *fem.* **-ка**) peasant
культу́ра culture
культу́рный cultural, cultured
литерату́ра literature
литерату́рный literary
мужчи́на (*masc.*) man, male[27]
наро́д nation, people
неме́дленно immediately
не́м.ец (*fem.* **-ка**) German
неме́цкий German (*adj.*)
немно́го, немно́жко a little (+ *gen.*)[28]
о́бщий general, common, mutual
о́бщество society; company
одна́жды once, at one time
па́па (*masc.*) papa, daddy
приём reception
путеше́ствие travel
свет world
семе́йный family (*adj.*)
симпати́чный likable, appealing
славяни́н (*pl.* **славя́не**; *fem.* **славя́нка**), Slav
слу́чай (pronounce [slúčij]) case, incident, event; chance
совреме́нный contemporary, modern
съезд convention, assembly
тяжёлый (**тяжело́**) heavy, hard (of life)
францу́.з (*fem.* **-женка**) Frenchman (woman)
худо́й thin, lean, emaciated
ша́хматы (*fem. pl.*) chess
шу́т.ка (*gen. pl.* **-ок**) joke

Verbs

быва́ть (imperf., I) to be, occur, happen, visit,[29] to frequent
знако́мить (imperf., II: **знако́м.лю, -ишь**), **познако́мить** (perf., II) to introduce, acquaint (+ *acc. of person introduced;* **с** + *instr. of person to whom introduced*); **знако́миться, познако́миться,** to meet, be introduced to (**с** + *instr.*)
принима́ть (imperf., I), **приня́ть** (perf., I: **приму́, при́мешь**; past: **при́нял, при́няло, приняла́, при́няли**) to accept, receive, take (advice, medicine, etc.)
путеше́ствовать (imperf., I: **путеше́ству.ю, -ешь**) to travel

[27] The word мужчи́на is used mostly in contrast to же́нщина. When there is no contrast челове́к is much used, not only in the sense of "person," "human being," but also "man," "male person," *e.g.*, «Кто́ э́тот челове́к?» "Who is that man?" Note also «молодо́й челове́к,» "a young man."
[28] Contrast to ма́ло (little, few). Ма́ло has a limiting meaning; немно́го is more positive.
[29] All these meanings are frequentative, that is, they have the implication "occasionally," "sometimes," "often," etc.

случа́ться (imperf., I), **случи́ться,** (perf., II: **случи́тся**) to happen, occur
шути́ть (imperf., II: **шучу́, шу́тишь**), **пошути́ть** (perf., II) to joke

Expressions

Ка́к сказа́ть по-ру́сски . . . ? How do you say . . . in Russian?
знако́м, -а, -ы с (+ *instr.*) acquainted with
Отку́да вы́ зна́ете? How do you know?
оди́н из мои́х друзе́й one of my friends[30]
не́которые из мои́х друзе́й some of my friends[30]
Что́ э́то за (+ *nom.*)? What (kind of) . . . is that?
за за́втраком at breakfast
Я́ та́к и ду́мал. That's just what I thought.
Мне́ бы́ло ве́село. I had a good time.
во-пе́рвых first, in the first place
во-вторы́х second, in the second place
ни оди́н (одно́, одна́) not a single (one)

Vocabulary Review and Supplement

Expressions of Politeness

Приве́тствия—Greetings

Здра́вствуй, -те! Hello!
До́брое у́тро! Good morning!
До́брый де́нь (ве́чер)! Good afternoon (evening)!
Ка́к {**ты́ помива́ешь?** / **вы́ помива́ете?**} How are you? How have you been?
Хорошо́. Ничего́. Та́к себе. Нехорошо́. Пло́хо. Well. Fair. So-so. Not so well. Poor.
Что́ у тебя́ (ва́с) но́вого? What's new?
Ка́к дела́? How are things?
О́чень ра́д(а) тебя́ (ва́с) ви́деть! I'm very glad to see you!

Проща́ние—Farewell

До свида́ния! Good-bye (till I see you again)!
До ско́рого (свида́ния)! See you soon!
Проща́й, -те! Good-bye!
Всего́ хоро́шего! All the best!
Споко́йной но́чи! Good night!
Пожа́луйста, переда́йте приве́т ва́шей жене́! Please give my regards to your wife!

Пожела́ния—Good wishes

Жела́ю успе́ха! Good luck!
Счастли́вого пути́! Bon voyage!

[30] Note also: оди́н мо́й дру́г, a friend of mine; не́которые мои́ друзья́, some friends of mine.

Фо́рмы ве́жливости; про́сьбы—Forms of politeness; requests

Пожа́луйста (+ *imper.*) Please . . .

Бу́дьте добры́ (любе́зны) (+ *imper. or inf.*) Be so kind as to . . .

Мо́жно ва́с попроси́ть (+ *inf.*)? May I ask you to . . .

Мо́жно ва́с попроси́ть переда́ть мне́ са́хар? May I ask you to pass me the sugar?

Сади́тесь пожа́луйста. Please sit down.

Бу́дьте как до́ма. Make yourself at home.

Приходи́те к на́м в сре́ду. Come and see us on Wednesday.

(Большо́е) спаси́бо (за + *acc.*). (Many) thanks for . . .

Благодарю́ ва́с (за + *acc.*). Thank you for . . .

(Я́ ва́м) о́чень благода́рен (за + *acc.*). I am very grateful for . . .

Не́т, спаси́бо. No, thank you.

Вы́ о́чень любе́зны. You are very kind.

Пожа́луйста. You're welcome.

Не́ за что. ⎫
Не сто́ит благода́рности. ⎭ Don't mention it.

Вопро́сы

Ка́к ва́ша фами́лия? What is your (last) name?

Ка́к ва́ше и́мя-о́тчество? What is your first name and patronymic?

Ка́к ва́ш а́дрес? What is your address?

Ка́к ва́ш но́мер телефо́на? What is your telephone number?

Когда́ ва́с мо́жно ви́деть? When may I see you?

Когда́ к ва́м мо́жно прийти́? When may I come and see you?

Ка́к лю́ди знако́мятся—Introductions

Позво́льте/разреши́те ва́с познако́мить с мои́м дру́гом Ива́ном Ива́новичем Ива́новым. Let me introduce my friend Ivan Ivanovich Ivanov.

Позво́льте/разреши́те ва́м предста́вить моего́ дру́га Ива́на Ива́новича Ива́нова. May I present my friend Ivan Ivanovich Ivanov (to an older or more important person).

О́чень ра́д(а) с ва́ми познако́миться. ⎫ How do you do?
О́чень прия́тно. ⎭ (I'm very pleased to meet you.)

Извине́ния—Apologies

Извини́те, пожа́луйста. Excuse me, please.

Прости́те. Excuse me.

Прости́те за беспоко́йство. Excuse me for bothering you.

Извини́те (прости́те) меня́. Forgive me.

Пожа́луйста. ⎫
Что́ вы́! ⎬ Certainly.
Ради Бо́га! ⎭

UNIT 21

Conjugation of verbs, review and supplement, 337. Мо́жно *and* нельзя́, 350. *Perfective verbs* захоте́ть, уви́деть, услы́шать, *and* смочь, 352. *Numerals, 20-199,* 354. *Age,* 355.

GRAMMAR

1. Conjugation of verbs

It has been seen earlier that the conjugation pattern of a Russian verb is not determined by its infinitive. The ending of the infinitive does not generally indicate what type of endings (first or second conjugation) the verb takes in the present (or the perfective future) tense. On the other hand, the stem found in the conjugation may differ to a greater or lesser extent from the stem of the infinitive.

In practical terms, it is advisable to memorize for each verb, in addition to its infinitive, also the first and second singular forms from which, except for a very small number of irregular verbs, the other forms can be derived. It will, however, be helpful for the student to have an over-all view of the more important patterns of conjugation and of their variations in both the stem and personal endings.

A. The stem. In the different forms of a verb its stem appears in two variants; one of them is found in the infinitive and the past tense, the other in the present (or perfective future) and in the imperative (they will be hereafter referred to as the *infinitive-past stem* and the *present stem*).

In verbs of the first conjugation, the present stem may end either in a vowel followed by the sound [j] or in a consonant; the vowel + [j] type of stem is more common. In the second conjugation, the consonantal stem-ending is typical and only a few verbs have present stems ending in a vowel + [j].

(1) *First conjugation, present stems in vowel + [j].* The verb **чита́ть** may serve as an example of a first conjugation verb with the present stem ending in a vowel + [j]. One will also see from the presentation below that the infinitive and the past tense have one stem—in this case [č̦itá-]—and that the present stem, which is [č̦itáj-], is also found in the imperative:

Inf.	чита́ть	[č̦itá.ţ]	*Inf.-past stem:* [č̦itá-]
Past	чита́л	[č̦itá.l]	
Pres.	чита́ю	[č̦itáj.u]	*Present stem:* [čitáj-]
	чита́ешь	[č̦itáj.iš]	
	чита́ет	[č̦itáj.it]	
	чита́ем	[č̦itáj.im]	
	чита́ете	[č̦itáj.iţi]	
	чита́ют	[č̦itáj.ut]	
Imperative	чита́й	[č̦itáj]	

Most (but not all) first conjugation verbs with infinitives in **-ать/-ять** are conjugated like **чита́ть** and have present stems in [aj]. This pattern is, in particular, that of the numerous prefixed imperfective verbs with **-ыв-** or **-ив-** inserted before the infinitive ending; these verbs fall into the **чита́ть** type of conjugation regardless of the conjugation pattern of the corresponding perfective verb, *e.g.*:

Imperfective	*Perfective*
пока́з**ыв**ать: пока́зываю, пока́зываешь . . .	показа́ть: покажу́, пока́жешь . . .
запи́с**ыв**ать: запи́сываю, запи́сываешь . . .	записа́ть: запишу́, запи́шешь . . .
откр**ыв**а́ть: открыва́ю, открыва́ешь . . .	откры́ть: откро́ю, откро́ешь . . .
спра́ш**ив**ать: спра́шиваю, спра́шиваешь . . .	спроси́ть: спрошу́, спро́сишь . . .

With only a few exceptions, first conjugation verbs with infinitives in **-еть** (*e.g.* име́ть, "to have") and **-ять** (*e.g.* гуля́ть, "to take a walk," "stroll"), have present stems in [j], differing from the **чита́ть** type only in the vowel preceding the [j], *e.g.*:

Inf.	име́ть	[im̦ẹ́.ţ]	*Stem:* [im̦ẹ́-]	гуля́ть	[gul̦á.ţ]	*Stem:* [gul̦á-]
Past	име́л	[im̦ẹ́.l]		гуля́л	[gul̦á.l]	
Pres.	име́ю	[im̦ẹ́j.u]	*Stem:* [im̦ẹ́j-]	гуля́ю	[gul̦áj.u]	*Stem:* [gul̦áj-]
	име́ешь	[im̦ẹ́j.iš]		гуля́ешь	[gul̦áj.iš]	
	. . . . . .	. . . . . .		. . . . . .	. . . . . .	
Imperative	име́й	[im̦ẹ́j]		гуля́й	[gul̦áj]	

Among first conjugation verbs with present stems in vowel + [j] there are several groups presenting special patterns of variation between the two stems: the present and the infinitive-past.

(a) Verbs in **-овать.** These verbs, like совéтовать, "to advise," replace the [-ova-] element of the infinitive-past stem by the element [-uj-] in the present:

Inf.	совéтовать	[saɣétəvə.ţ]	*Stem:* [saɣétəvə-]
Past	совéтовал	[saɣétəvə.l]	
Pres.	совéтую	[saɣétuj.u]	*Stem:* [saɣétuj-]
	совéтуешь	[saɣétuj.iš]	
	совéтует	[saɣétuj.it]	
	совéтуем	[saɣétuj.im]	
	совéтуете	[saɣétuj.iţi]	
	совéтуют	[saɣétuj.ut]	
Imperative	совéтуй	[saɣétuj]	

The same pattern is found in numerous verbs of foreign origin ending in **-и́ровать,** like телефони́ровать, "to telephone":

Inf.	телефони́ровать	[ţiļifaņírəvə.ţ]	*Stem:* [ţiļifaņírəvə.-]
Past	телефони́ровал	[ţiļifaņírəvə.l]	
Pres.	телефони́рую	[ţiļifaņíruj.u]	*Stem:* [ţiļifaņíruj.-]
	телефони́руешь	[ţiļifaņíruj.iš]	
Imperative	телефони́руй	[ţiļifaņíruj]	

It must be remembered that only verbs in **-овать** (and some in **-евать**) present the feature described above, *not* those in **-ывать/-ивать** or **-ава́ть.**

(b) Verbs in **-ава́ть.** Verbs in **-ава́ть,** with the stress on the last syllable (all imperfective), drop the element [va] in the present stem:

	Inf.	дава́ть	[davá.ţ]	*Stem:* [davá-]
	Past	дава́л	[davá.l]	
	Pres.	даю́	[daj.ú]	*Stem:* [daj-]
		даёшь	[daj.óš]	
		даёт	[daj.ót]	
		даём	[daj.óm]	
		даёте	[daj.óţi]	
		даю́т	[daj.út]	
But:	*Imperative*	дава́й	[daváj]	

(One will recall that the corresponding perfective is the irregularly conjugated verb да́ть: дам, дашь, даст, дади́м, дади́те, даду́т; *imperative* да́й.)

(c) Verbs in **-ыть.** These verbs, *e.g.*, мыть, "to wash," which are all monosyllabic (prefixed perfectives, like вы́мыть, however, may have two syllables), change the [í] vowel of the infinitive and the past to [oj] in the present:

Inf.	мыть	[mɨ́.ţ]	*Stem:* [mɨ́.-]
Past	мыл	[mɨ́.l]	
Pres.	мо́ю	[móju.]	*Stem:* [mój.-]
	мо́ешь	[mój.iš]	
	мо́ет	[mój.it]	
	мо́ем	[mój.im]	
	мо́ете	[mój.iţi]	
	мо́ют	[mój.ut]	
Imperative	мой	[mój]	

A verb rarely used in its non-prefixed form, крыть, "to cover," is conjugated like мыть; so are its prefixed perfectives, откры́ть, to open, закры́ть, to close, and some others; откры́ть has the perfective future forms откро́ю, откро́ешь.

(d) Verbs in **-ить** (monosyllabic: one consonant + **-ить**). A group of verbs with infinitives consisting of a consonant + **-ить,** like пить, "to drink," have present stems formed with this consonant and [j]:

Inf.	пить	[p̧í.ţ]	*Stem:* [p̧i-]
Past	пил	[p̧í.l]	
Pres.	пью	[p̧j.ú]	*Stem:* [p̧j-]
	пьёшь	[p̧j.óš]	
	пьёт	[p̧j.ót]	
	пьём	[p̧j.óm]	
	пьёте	[p̧j.óţi]	
	пьют	[p̧j.út]	
But: Imperative	пей	[p̧ẹ́j]	

This pattern is preserved in prefixed perfective forms which may have two syllables, *e.g.* вы́пить (вы́пью).

Note that the verb **жить,** "to live," does *not* belong to this group.

(2) *First conjugation verbs with consonantal present stems.* A number of verbs of the first conjugation have present stems which end, not in a vowel + [j], but in a consonant; some of these verbs have infinitives in **-ать,** like the verb ждать, "to wait":

Inf.	ждать	[ždá.ţ]	*Stem:* [ždá-]
Past	ждал	[ždá.l]	
Pres.	жду	[žd.ú]	*Stem:* [žd-]
	ждёшь	[žḑ.óš]	
	ждёт	[žḑ.ót]	
	ждём	[žḑ.óm]	
	ждёте	[žḑ.óţi]	
	ждут	[žd.út]	
Imperative	жди	[žḑ.í]	

Consonantal present stems in the first conjugation often present irregularities in their formation; the following are examples of such irregularities in verbs with infinitives in **-ать/-ять**:

брать, to take, *imperfective*
Inf. брать; *Past* брал — *Stem:* [brá-]
Pres. беру́, берёшь etc.; *Imperative* бери́ — *Stem:* [b̡er-]

взять, to take, *perfective*
Inf. взять; *Past* взял — *Stem:* [vz̡á-]
Fut. возьму́, возьмёшь etc.; *Imperative* возьми́ — *Stem:* [vaz̡m-]

нача́ть, to begin, *perfective*
Inf. нача́ть; *Past* на́чал — *Stem:* [nac̡a-]
Fut. начну́, начнёшь etc.; *Imperative* начни́ — *Stem:* [nač̡n-]

поня́ть, to understand, *perfective*
Inf. поня́ть; *Past* по́нял — *Stem:* [pon̡a-]
Fut. пойму́, поймёшь etc.; *Imperative* пойми́ — *Stem:* [pojm-]

уста́ть, to become tired, *perfective*
Inf. уста́ть; *Past* уста́л — *Stem:* [ustá-]
Fut. уста́ну, уста́нешь etc.; *Imperative* уста́нь — *Stem:* [ustán-]

Consonantal present stems are found in all verbs with infinitives in **-уть**; these verbs are of the first conjugation and are mostly perfective; they present no irregularities in their conjugation. The verb верну́ть, "to return" (transitive, perfective), may serve as example:

Inf.	верну́ть	*Stem:* [v̡irnú.-]
Past	верну́л	
Fut.	верну́	*Stem:* [v̡irn.-]
	вернёшь, etc.	
Imperative	верни́	

One may also note that verbs with the following infinitive endings (all first conjugation) have consonantal present stems: **-ереть, -ти́, -сть,** and **-чь.**

(3) *Second conjugation.* The most frequent infinitive endings in the second conjugation are **-еть** and **-ить.** Both these endings occur in the first conjugation as well; however, first conjugation verbs in **-ить** are mostly those of the monosyllabic пить group. Some verbs in **-ать** belong to the second conjugation; nearly all have stems ending in **ж, ч, ш,** or **щ.**

With only a few exceptions, second conjugation verbs have present stems ending in a consonant. Generally, irregularities are much less frequent in the second conjugation than in the first.

(4) *Consonant alternations.* Many verbs of both conjugations appear, in their different forms, with different end consonants of the stem; thus [s] is found in писа́ть, писа́л, but [š] in пишу́; [d] in сиде́ть, сиде́л, but [ž] in сижу́. These consonants are said to "alternate." Alternations of consonants occur not only in verbs, but in other series of words as well. A parallel may be found in English, with the difference that English spelling does not usually reflect the alternations of sounds observed in pronunciation; thus:

in pre*ss* and pre*ss*ure, [s] alternates with [š]
in plea*s*e and plea*s*ure, [z] alternates with [ž]
in na*t*ive and na*t*ural, [t] alternates with [č] etc.

In Russian the following consonantal sounds may alternate:

с [s], х [x]	with ш [š]	писа́ть—пишу́; маха́ть—машу́ (to wave)
з [z], д [d], г [g]	with ж [ž]	ре́зать—ре́жу; сиде́ть—сижу́; могу́—мо́жешь
т [t], к [k]	with ч [č̦]	лете́ть—лечу́ (to fly); пла́кать—пла́чу (to weep)
ст [st], ск [sk]	with щ [ș̌č̦]	прости́ть—прощу́ (to forgive); полоска́ть—полощу́ (to rinse)

In addition, the group of consonantal sounds known as the "labials," [p], [b], [v], [f], and [m], may appear followed by an [l̦], that is, as [pl̦], [bl̦], [vl̦], etc. One finds alternations of this type in:

купи́ть—куплю́ п [p̦]—пл [pl̦]
люби́ть—люблю́ б [b̦]—бл [bl̦]
ста́вить—ста́влю в [v̦]—вл [vl̦] etc.

Consonant Alternations in the First and in the Second Conjugations. It is important to remember that when there is consonant alternation in verbs of the first conjugation, *e.g.*, [s]—[š] in писа́ть—пишу́, the consonant found in the first person singular form ([š] in пишу́) also appears in the other personal forms: пи́шешь, пи́шет, etc.

In the second conjugation, on the other hand, the alternate consonant is found in the first person singular only, the other personal forms having the same consonant as the infinitive. This may be seen in the following examples:

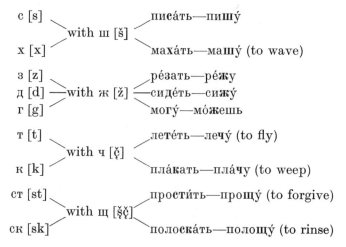

	1st conjugation				*2nd conjugation*			
Inf.	писа́ть	[s]	дрема́ть (to doze)	[m]	проси́ть	[ş]	люби́ть	[b̦]
Past	писа́л		дрема́л		проси́л		люби́л	
Pres.	пишу́	[š]	дремлю́	[mļ]	прошу́	[š]	люблю́	[bļ]
	пи́шешь		дре́млешь		про́сишь	[ş]	лю́бишь	[b̦]
	пи́шет		дре́млет		про́сит		лю́бит	
	пи́шем		дре́млем		про́сим		лю́бим	
	пи́шете		дре́млете		про́сите		лю́бите	
	пи́шут		дре́млют		про́сят		лю́бят	

(5) *Verbs with infinitives in* **-чь.** Verbs belonging to this group, all of the first conjugation, have a distinct pattern of consonant alternation. The roots of these verbs all end in either [g] or [k] (historically, the ending [č̦] derives from [g + ţ] or [k + ţ]). In the conjugation, [g] alternates with [ž] and [k] with [č̦] according to the following pattern:

Inf.	мочь [č̦] (from [gţ])		печь [č̦] (from [kţ], to bake)	
Past	мог, могла́	[g]	пёк, пекла́	[k]
Pres.	могу́	[g]	пеку́	[k]
	мо́жешь	[ž]	печёшь	[č̦]
	мо́жет		печёт	
	мо́жем		печём	
	мо́жете		печёте	
	мо́гут	[g]	пеку́т	[k]

Note the past tense, masculine, forms **мог** and **пёк**; this feature, the absence of **-л** in masculine (but, neuter, **-ло**; feminine, **-ла** and, plural, **-ли**) is common to all verbs with infinitives in **-чь.**

(6) *The three "key forms" of a verb.* It has been stated earlier that three forms of every verb, the infinitive and the first and second persons singular, should be memorized as the "key forms" from which one can predict all the others. The following examples will serve to show this:

1	2	3	4	5	6	7
зна́ть	идти́	писа́ть	мо́чь	говори́ть	лежа́ть	ходи́ть
зна́ю	иду́	пишу́	могу́	говорю́	лежу́	хожу́
зна́ешь	идёшь	пи́шешь	мо́жешь	говори́шь	лежи́шь	хо́дишь

Determining the Ending. Whether a verb is of the first or the second conjugation may be seen from the vowel in the ending of the second person singular; the vowel **е** (examples 1, 2, 3, and 4) means first conjugation, while **и** (examples 5, 6, and 7) means second. In two instances, the infinitive ending indicates that the verb is of the first conjugation: **-ти** (example 2) and **-чь** (example 4).

In the first conjugation, the ending of the third person plural is **-ют** if the first person singular ends in **-ю**: зна́ю—зна́ют (example 1); it is **-ут** if the first person singular ends in **-у**: иду́—иду́т (examples 2, 3, and 4). In the second conjugation, **-ю** in the first person singular corresponds to **-ят** in the third person plural: говорю́—говоря́т (example 5); and **-у** to **-ат**: лежу́—лежа́т (example 6). However, verbs with consonant alternations (example 7) have **-у** in the first person singular but **-ят** in the third person plural: хожу́—хо́дят.

Finding the Stem. In the first conjugation the stem is the same in the six personal forms except for verbs ending in **-чь** (example 4). The special pattern of alternation in these verbs was described before; it will be remembered that the final consonant of the stem of the first person singular appears again in the third person plural: могу́—мо́гут. In the second conjugation, on the other hand, consonant alternations appear in the first person singular only; the final consonant of the second person singular is maintained in the remaining forms (example 7, д in the second person singular, хо́дишь, and in the rest of the conjugation: хо́дит, хо́дим, хо́дите, хо́дят).

Determining the Position of the Stress. The stress in the conjugation of a verb may be fixed on the stem (example 1), or fixed on the ending (examples 2, 5, and 6), or it may shift from the ending in first singular to the stem in the other forms (examples 3, 4, and 7). It is, consequently, the position of the stress in the second person singular that determines its position in the remaining forms.

Irregular Verbs. There are only four verbs in Russian whose endings deviate from the two types known as the first and second conjugation (they also present certain irregularities in consonant alternations). The conjugation patterns of these verbs cannot be derived from the three "key forms"; the complete conjugation of each of these verbs must be committed to memory. These four verbs are:

дать	**есть**	**хоте́ть**[1]	**бежа́ть** (to run)[1]
дам	ем	хочу́ (1st)	бегу́ (1st)
дашь	ешь	хо́чешь (1st)	бежи́шь (2nd)
даст	ест	хо́чет (1st)	бежи́т (2nd)
дади́м	еди́м	хоти́м (2nd)	бежи́м (2nd)
дади́те	еди́те	хоти́те (2nd)	бежи́те (2nd)
даду́т	едя́т	хотя́т (2nd)	бегу́т (1st)

[1] These two verbs mix forms of the first and second conjugations as indicated.

B. New verbs, according to conjugation patterns.

(1) *First conjugation verb with infinitive in* **-еть**:

имéть (имé.ю, -ешь, imperf.), "to have" (no perfective)[2]

Drills

Переведи́те на англи́йский.

1. Когдá мы́ бýдем **имéть** удовóльствие вáс ви́деть?
2. Зимóй нýжно **имéть** тёплое пальтó.
3. Они́ **имéют** возмóжность поéхать в Еврóпу на три́ мéсяца.
4. Я́ **имéю** прáво дéлать, чтó хочý.
5. Я́ **имéл** слýчай нéсколько рáз говори́ть с дирéктором вáшего институ́та.
6. Перевóдчик дóлжен **имéть** хорóшие словари́.

Переведи́те на рýсский.

1. You have no right to talk like that!
2. I had the pleasure of meeting your daughter.
3. We never had the opportunity to talk about this matter.
4. You ought to have an evening dress.
5. One must have friends.

(2) *First conjugation verbs with infinitives in* **-овать/-евать.**

путешéствовать (imperf., I: **путешéству.ю, -ешь**), to travel
совéтовать (imperf., I: **совéту.ю, -ешь**), **посовéтовать** (perf., I) (+ *dative of person*) to advise, give advice to
совéтоваться (imperf., I: **совéту.юсь, -ешься**), **посовéтоваться** (perf., I) (**с** + *instrumental*), to consult (with)
танцевáть[3] (imperf., I: **танцý.ю, -ешь**), to dance
интересовáть (imperf., I: **интересý.ю, -ешь**) (+ *accusative of person*), to interest
интересовáться (imperf., I: **интересý.юсь, -ешься**), **поинтересовáться** (perf., I) (+ *instrumental*), to be interested in
телефони́ровать (imperf., I: **телефони́ру.ю, -ешь**) **потелефони́ровать** (perf., I) (+ *dative*), to telephone

Pattern Sentences

1. —Ивáн Ивáнович, вы́ мнóго **путешéствуете?** —Мы́ с женóй **путешéствуем** кáждый гóд.	1. —Ivan Ivanovich, do you travel much? —My wife and I travel every year.

[2] This verb is commonly used with abstract nouns (see "Expressions" in the Vocabulary of this unit). It is also used instead of the **у** + genitive construction where an infinitive is required (*e.g.*, sentences nos. 2 and 6 in the first drill above).

[3] The infinitive ending of this verb is spelled -евать since unstressed **о** may not be written after **ц** (Spelling Rule B).

2. В прóшлом годý мы́ **путешéствовали** по всéй Еврóпе.
3. Катю́ша мóжет **танцевáть** с утрá до вéчера. Онá чáсто **танцýет** с Бори́сом.
4. Нáши друзья́ **интересýются** нарóдными тáнцами и хорошó и́х **танцýют.**
5. —Вы́ хорошó **танцýете?** —Я́ **танцýю** как слóн.
6. Я́ **совéтую** моéй дóчери Катю́ше мéньше **танцевáть** и бóльше занимáться.
7. Мнóгие врачи́ **совéтуют** свои́м пациéнтам мéньше éсть и пи́ть и бóльше занимáться спóртом. Э́то хорошó для здорóвья.
8. Я́ хочý **посовéтоваться** с вáми об однóм óчень вáжном дéле.
9. Вчерá мóй отéц бы́л у своегó врачá. Врáч **посовéтовал** емý принимáть горя́чую вáнну кáждый вéчер и двá рáза в дéнь принимáть аспири́н.
10. Я́ не **совéтую** вáм покупáть в тóм магази́не—тáм всё óчень дóрого.
11. —Чтó вáс **интересýет?** —Меня́ **интересýют** нóвые пьéсы, а мою́ сестрý **интересýет** нóвая мýзыка.
12. —**Чéм интересýются** э́ти мáльчики? —Нéкоторые **интересýются** тóлько спóртом и мáло занимáются, а другие **интересýются** всéм.
13. —Я́ дóлжен **потелефони́ровать** А́нне. —Почемý ты́ так чáсто éй **телефони́руешь?** —Я́ **телефони́рую** éй рáз в недéлю!

2. Last year we travelled all over Europe.
3. Katyusha can dance from morning to evening. She often dances with Boris.
4. Our friends are interested in folk dances, and dance them well.
5. —Do you dance well? —I dance like an elephant.
6. I advise my daughter Katyusha to dance less and study more.
7. Many doctors advise their patients to eat and drink less and to go in more for sports. It is good for the health.
8. I want to consult you about a very important matter.
9. Yesterday my father went to see his doctor. The doctor advised him to take a hot bath every evening and to take aspirin twice a day.
10. I advise you against shopping in that store; everything there is very expensive.
11. —What are you interested in? —I am interested in new plays, and my sister is interested in new music.
12. —What are those boys interested in? —Some are interested only in sports and study little; others are interested in everything.
13. —I must telephone Anna. —Why do you telephone her so often? —I telephone her once a week!

Drill

Переведи́те с англи́йского на рýсский.

1. My teacher advises me to talk less and read more.
2. —Do you advise Ivan and Olga to go to England? —No, I don't advise (it).
3. He likes to consult with me about everything.

4. What can they advise us?
5. I know what they will advise you.
6. I like to dance with Tania, but we dance so seldom.
7. They dance only folk dances.
8. I like to travel and I travel a great deal.
9. I am very (much) interested in folk literature.
10. He is not interested in his students.
11. —What are you interested in? —The theater.
12. —Why don't you ever phone us? Don't we interest you? —I shall call you twice a week. All right?

(3) *First conjugation verbs with infinitives in* **-ава́ть.**[5]

узнава́ть (imperf., I: **узна.ю́, -ёшь**), **узна́ть** (perf., I: **узна́.ю, -ешь**),[6] to recognize; to find out, learn (about)
уства́ть (imperf., I: **уста.ю́, -ёшь**), **уста́ть** (perf., I: **уста́н.у, -ешь**), to grow tired, weary

Pattern Sentences

1. Я́ встре́тил Ива́на на у́лице и не **узна́л** его́, та́к о́н **измени́лся** с тех по́р, как я́ его́ ви́дел.
2. Стра́нно, что она́ меня́ никогда́ не **узнаёт!**
3. Я́ напишу́ Та́не, как то́лько **узна́ю** её а́дрес.
4. Я́ то́лько что **узна́л,** что Ви́ктор уе́хал за грани́цу.
5. **Узна́йте,** пожа́луйста, когда́ прихо́дит по́чта.
6. Я́ о́чень **уста́л.**[7] Я́ ля́гу на полчаса́, немно́жко отдохну́, а пото́м мы́ поу́жинаем.
7. Катю́ша, ты́ о́чень **уста́ла**: ты́ сли́шком мно́го танцева́ла! Ты́ должна́ немно́го отдохну́ть!
8. —Скажи́те мне́, когда́ вы́ **уста́нете** —мы́ мо́жем продолжа́ть на́шу рабо́ту по́сле обе́да. —Я́ скажу́ ва́м, е́сли **уста́ну.**

1. I met Ivan on the street and didn't recognize him, he had changed so since I saw him.
2. It's strange that she never recognizes me!
3. I will write Tanya as soon as I find out her address.
4. I have just learned that Victor has gone abroad.
5. Please find out when the mail arrives.
6. I am very tired. I shall lie down for half an hour and rest a bit, and then we shall have supper.
7. Katyusha, you are very tired: you've been dancing too much! You must rest a little!
8. —Tell me when you get tired—we can continue our work after dinner. —I'll tell you if I get tired.

[5] This group also includes the imperfective verbs дава́ть (to give) and встава́ть (to get up), given in preceding lessons.
[6] Note that the distinction between the imperfective present and the perfective future of this verb is one of place of stress: узнаю́, I recognize, find out, *but* узна́ю, I shall recognize, shall find out.
[7] Note that the perfective past of this verb is used with present meaning: Я́ уста́л, I am tired.

Drill

Переведи́те на ру́сский.

1. Zoya had changed so much that I didn't recognize her.
2. I don't think that you will recognize us; we have changed a great deal.
3. I know that she went abroad, but I must find out exactly where she went.
4. Please find out where he lives.
5. She gets tired very quickly.
6. I am tired this evening; I'll go to bed early.

(4) *First conjugation verbs with infinitives in* **-нуть.**

отдохну́ть (perf. of **отдыха́ть,** I: **отдохн.у́, -ёшь;** past **отдохну́л,** etc.), to rest, rest up, get rested

привыка́ть (imperf., I), **привы́кнуть** (perf., I: **привы́кн.у, -ешь;** past: **привы́к, -ло, -ла, -ли,** (**к** + *dat., or imperf. infinitive*), to get used to, grow accustomed to

отвыка́ть (imperf., I), **отвы́кнуть** (perf., I: **отвы́кн.у, -ешь;** past: **отвы́к, -ло, -ла, ли,** (**от** + *gen., or imperf. infinitive*), to grow unaccustomed to, lose the habit of

возвраща́ть (imperf., I), **верну́ть** (perf., I: **верн.у́, -ёшь;** past: **верну́л,** etc.),[8] to return (*trans.*), give back

возвраща́ться, верну́ться,[8] to return (*intrans.*), go back, come back

Note the absence of the **л** ending in the past tense, masculine, in привы́к and отвы́к.

Pattern Sentences

1. Я́ всегда́ **возвраща́ю** кни́ги, кото́рые беру́ у знако́мых.
2. —**Верну́ла** ва́м А́нна пятна́дцать рубле́й, кото́рые взяла́ у ва́с тре́тьего дня́? —Не́т ещё. Она́ сказа́ла, что **вернёт** и́х в суббо́ту.
3. Я́ ча́сто **возвраща́юсь** домо́й вме́сте с мои́м сосе́дом.
4. —А́нна уже́ **верну́лась** из Босто́на? —Не́т, она́ **вернётся** послеза́втра.
5. Лунёву бы́ло тру́дно **привы́кнуть к** сиби́рск**ому** кли́мату, но́ в конце́ концо́в о́н к нему́ **привы́к.** О́н **привы́к** и **к** жаре́ и **к** хо́лоду.

1. I always return books which I borrow from friends.
2. —Has Anna returned the fifteen rubles which she borrowed from you day before yesterday? —Not yet. She said that she would return them on Saturday.
3. I often return home with my neighbor.
4. —Has Anna come back from Boston? —No, she will come back day after tomorrow.
5. It was hard for Lunyov to get used to the Siberian climate, but in the end he got used to it. He got used both to the heat and the cold.

[8] The perfectives have the alternate forms возврати́ть (II: возвра.щу́, -ти́шь) and возврати́ться.

6. Мы́ уже́ **привы́кли**[9] **к** на́шей но́вой учи́тельнице, и она́, ка́жется, **привы́кла**[9] к на́м.
7. Мне́ тру́дно **привыка́ть к** но́вым места́м и **к** но́вым лю́дям.
8. Тёте Ве́ре бы́ло тру́дно **привы́кнуть к** но́вой жи́зни.
9. Тётя так до́лго жила́ в дере́вне, что она́ совсе́м **отвы́кла от** городско́й жи́зни и **от** о́бщества.
10. Мо́жно ко всему́ привы́кнуть.

6. We're already used to our new teacher, and she, it seems, is used to us.
7. I have difficulty getting used to new places and new people.
8. It was hard for Aunt Vera to get used to her new life.
9. Aunty lived so long in the country that she became unaccustomed to city life and society.
10. One can get used to everything.

Drill

Переведи́те на ру́сский.

1. —Have you got used to me? —Yes, we've got used to you.
2. Kolya has got used to heat and to cold.
3. I can't get used to this city!
4. I will return your book when I finish it. I always return books.
5. In the winter we always returned home early and went to bed early.
6. I will return at 10:00 sharp. When will you come back?
7. She returned from abroad two weeks ago.
8. We always come back together.
9. I must return your newspaper; I've finished it.
10. We came back from school early today.

(5) *First conjugation verb* **умере́ть.**

умира́ть (imperf., I), **умере́ть** (perf., I: **умр.у́, -ёшь,** past: **у́мер, у́мерло, умерла́, у́мерли**), to die

Note the absence of the **л** ending in the past tense, masculine.

Pattern Sentences

1. Мо́й де́душка **у́мер** в про́шлом году́, а ба́бушка **умерла́** два́ го́да тому́ наза́д.
2. Роди́тели Ни́ны **у́мерли** во вре́мя войны́.
3. Ты́ бу́дешь пла́кать, когда́ я́ **умру́.**
4. Мы́ все́ **умрём.** Но́ заче́м ду́мать о сме́рти?
5. Э́ти ста́рые дере́вья ме́дленно **умира́ют.**

1. My grandfather died last year, and grandmother died two years ago.
2. Nina's parents died during the war.
3. You will weep when I die.
4. We shall all die. But why think about death?
5. These old trees are slowly dying.

[9] Notice that the perfective past of this verb may correspond to English present: "to be used to."

Drill

Переведите на русский.

1. When he dies, his sons will get all his money.
2. When I die, my children will get nothing.
3. My aunt, my mother's sister, died seven years ago.
4. His grandfather died not long ago.
5. We are dying from the heat!
6. My uncle is not afraid of death, but he doesn't want to die.

2. Мо́жно and нельзя́

Мо́жно (**мо́жно было/будет**) means "one can," "one may," "it is possible to," etc. It takes an infinitive:

Где́ **мо́жно** купи́ть папиро́сы?
Where can one buy cigarettes?

Вы́ ду́маете, что **мо́жно** будет его́ ви́деть за́втра?
Do you think that one can see him tomorrow?

О́н сказа́л всё, что **мо́жно** было об э́том сказа́ть.
He said everything that could be said about that.

Мо́жно is used also to request permission:

Мо́жно зде́сь кури́ть?
May one (I) smoke here? (Is smoking permitted here?)

The person for whom permission is requested is often omitted as obvious. When specified, the person is named in the *dative:*

Мо́жно **мне́** взя́ть э́ту кни́гу?
May I take that book?

Мо́жно **на́м** с Ива́ном прийти́ к ва́м сего́дня ве́чером?
May Ivan and I come to see you this evening?

Нельзя́ (**нельзя́ было/будет**)) is the negative of **мо́жно:**

В э́том ваго́не **мо́жно** кури́ть, а в то́м **нельзя́.**
In this (railroad) car one may smoke, and in that one one may not.

Нельзя́ often corresponds to English "must not," "not supposed to."

Вра́ч сказа́л, что мне́ **нельзя́** пи́ть вино́.
The doctor said that I must not drink wine.

The words **возмо́жно** and **невозмо́жно** also denote possibility or impossibility. But only **мо́жно** and **нельзя́** may be used in requesting or granting permission, and only **возмо́жно** may be used in sentences of the type "Возмо́жно, что. . . " It is possible that. . .," *e.g.*, Возмо́жно, что о́н сего́дня не придёт на уро́к.

Pattern Sentences

One can—one cannot (possible—impossible)

1. Где́ **мо́жно** купи́ть хоро́ший шокола́д?
2. Зде́сь **нельзя́** купи́ть хоро́шего шокола́да.
3. Что́ **мо́жно** купи́ть за де́сять це́нтов?
4. За э́ти де́ньги тепе́рь ничего́ **нельзя́** купи́ть.
5. **Нельзя́** сказа́ть, что э́то о́чень хоро́шая статья́.

1. Where can one buy good chocolate?
2. One cannot buy good chocolate here.
3. What can one buy for ten cents?
4. You cannot buy anything now for that sum.
5. One can't say that this is a very good article.

May—may not (permitted—not permitted)

1. **Мо́жно** попроси́ть ва́с переда́ть мне́ со́ль и пе́рец?
2. —**Мо́жно** зада́ть ва́м оди́н вопро́с? —Пожа́луйста.
3. Во вре́мя ле́кции **нельзя́** задава́ть вопро́сов, а по́сле ле́кции **мо́жно.**
4. —**Мо́жно мне́** взя́ть бана́н? —Коне́чно!
5. —**Мо́жно** Ива́ну взя́ть э́ту кни́гу? —**Мо́жно.**
6. —**Мо́жно** се́сть ря́дом с ва́ми? — Коне́чно, **мо́жно!**

1. May I ask you to pass me the salt and pepper?
2. —May I ask you a question? — Please do.
3. You may not ask questions during the lecture, but after the lecture you may.
4. —May I take a banana? —Certainly!
5. —May Ivan take this book? —He may.
6. —May I sit down beside you? —Of course you may!

Drills

A. *Переведи́те с ру́сского на англи́йский.*

1. —Что́ **мо́жно** купи́ть в э́том магази́не? —Всё что хоти́те.
2. Вы́ ду́маете, что **мо́жно** будет ско́ро уйти́?
3. Вра́ч сказа́л, что де́душке **нельзя́** мно́го е́сть.
4. Ему́ тепе́рь **мо́жно** е́сть мя́со то́лько ра́з в неде́лю.
5. Ра́ньше ему́ **мо́жно** было е́сть ско́лько о́н хоте́л.
6. **Нельзя́** сказа́ть, что Петро́в о́чень у́мный челове́к!
7. **Нельзя́** привы́кнуть к э́тому шу́му!
8. Ко всему́ **мо́жно** привы́кнуть.

9. **Нельзя́** поня́ть, чего́ о́н хо́чет.
10. —Па́па, **мо́жно** на́м взя́ть тво́й автомоби́ль? —Тебе́ **мо́жно,** а Ни́не **нельзя́.**

B. *Переведи́те с англи́йского на ру́сский.*

1. —May I say one word? —Certainly.
2. It can be said that he's a very good poet, but it can't be said that he is a good teacher.
3. It's not possible to buy even a newspaper here!
4. It will soon be possible to go to the country.
5. You (one) can't believe him!
6. Can you live here?
7. It can't be said yet what kind of student he is.

3. Perfective verbs захоте́ть, уви́деть, услы́шать, смочь

The perfective verbs **захоте́ть** (imperf. хоте́ть, to want, wish), **уви́деть** (imperf. ви́деть, to see), **услы́шать** (imperf. слы́шать, to hear), and **смочь** (imperf. мочь, to be able) are used as follows:

In most cases calling for the use of the future, in particular after **когда́** and **е́сли,** the perfective is used. The imperfective future of **мочь** is never used, that of the other three verbs very rarely:

Мы́ **уви́дим,** кака́я бу́дет пого́да за́втра.
We shall see tomorrow what the weather is like.

Скажи́ мне́, когда́ ты́ **захо́чешь** е́сть.
Tell me when you feel like eating.

Е́сли я́ **смогу́,** я́ да́м ва́м де́ньги в понеде́льник.
If I can I shall give you the money on Monday.

The perfectives **захоте́ть, уви́деть,** and **услы́шать** refer to the moment when a desire is conceived or a sight or sound caught:

Я́ посмотре́л из окна́ и **уви́дел,** что идёт до́ждь.
I looked out of the window, and saw that it was raining.

Я́ вдру́г **захоте́л** пла́кать и пошёл в свою́ ко́мнату.
I suddenly felt like crying and went to my room.

Я́ **уви́дел** его́ то́лько, когда́ о́н бы́л уже́ передо мно́й.
I saw him only when he was already in front of me.

Pattern Sentences

Смочь, захоте́ть

1. Я́ бою́сь, что не **смогу́** хорошо́ объясни́ть э́то пра́вило.	1. I am afraid I shall not be able to explain this rule well.

2. Я́ ничего́ ему́ не обеща́л, но́ я́ сказа́л, что я́ да́м ему́ де́нег, е́сли **смогу́.**	2. I didn't promise him anything, but I told him that I would give him some money if I could.
3. Андре́й обеща́л прийти́, е́сли **смо́жет.**	3. Andrey promised to come if he can make it.
4. О́н наде́ется, что **смо́жет** да́ть мне́ отве́т во вто́рник.	4. He hopes that he will be able to give me an answer on Tuesday.
5. Я́ приду́, когда́ **захочу́!**	5. I shall come when I feel like it!
6. Е́сли вы́ **захоти́те** меня́ ви́деть за́втра, позвони́те мне́, и я́ приду́.	6. If you feel like seeing me tomorrow, phone me, and I shall come.
7. —Ко́ля, е́сли ты́ **захо́чешь** е́сть, возьми́ хле́б, ма́сло и кусо́к сы́ра.	7. Kolya, if you get hungry (feel like eating), take some bread, butter, and a piece of cheese.
8. Я́ уверен́, что Зо́я не **смо́жет** прийти́ за́втра.	8. I am sure that Zoya will not be able to come tomorrow.

Уви́деть, услы́шать

1. Она́ **услы́шала** голоса́ и пошла́ к две́ри.	1. She heard voices and went to the door.
2. Я́ вдру́г **услы́шал** гро́мкий кри́к.	2. I suddenly heard a loud cry.
3. Я́ на́чал переводи́ть статью́, но́ **уви́дел,** что без словаря́ не смогу́ э́того сде́лать.	3. I started to translate the article, but saw that without a dictionary I wouldn't be able to do it.
4. Я́ **уви́дел** Бори́са, когда́ о́н бы́л ещё далеко́.	4. I caught sight of Boris while he was still far away.
5. Я́ **услы́шал** об э́том вчера́ в пе́рвый ра́з.	5. I heard about that yesterday for the first time.
6. Я́ ви́дел Ни́ну вчера́ в три́ часа́ и **уви́жу** её за́втра в четы́ре.	6. I saw Nina yesterday at three, and shall see her tomorrow at four.
7. Я́ **уви́жу** его́ за́втра в два́ часа́, **услы́шу,** что́ о́н мне́ ска́жет и тогда́ **уви́жу,** что́ я́ смогу́ для него́ сде́лать.	7. I shall see him tomorrow at two o'clock, I shall hear what he has to tell me, and then I shall see what I can do for him.

Drills

A. *Translate the words in parentheses, and then the whole sentence into English.*

1. Как то́лько я́ (shall hear) о то́м, что́ случи́лось на собра́нии, я́ ва́м сейча́с же всё расскажу́.
2. Зи́на (heard) вчера́ хоро́ший анекдо́т и рассказа́ла его́ мне́.
3. Е́сли вы́ (should hear) интере́сный анекдо́т, расска́жите его́ мне́.
4. Мы́ шли́ вчера́ по на́шей у́лице и вдру́г (heard) ужа́сный кри́к.
5. Мы́ не в пе́рвый ра́з (heard) тако́й кри́к.
6. Я́ (saw) вчера́ Ро́бертса и (shall see) его́ опя́ть во вто́рник.

7. Е́сли через ча́с вы́ (will feel like) погуля́ть—скажи́те мне́.
8. Я́ ещё не зна́ю, когда́ я́ (shall be able) прийти́ к ва́м.
9. Я́ наде́юсь, что вы́ (will be able) прийти́ в суббо́ту.

B. *Чита́йте и переводи́те.*

1. С тех по́р, как О́ля поступи́ла на но́вую слу́жбу, она́ та́к устаёт, что ложи́тся спа́ть сра́зу по́сле у́жина.
2. —До каки́х по́р вы́ бу́дете сего́дня рабо́тать? —Я́ бу́ду рабо́тать до обе́да, и́ли до тех по́р, пока́ не уста́ну.
3. Я́ до сих по́р не могу́ поня́ть, ка́к о́н мо́жет так мно́го рабо́тать!
4. Одна́ моя́ знако́мая испа́нка о́чень хорошо́ танцу́ет испа́нские наро́дные та́нцы и поёт испа́нские пе́сни. Никто́ не зна́ет сто́лько пе́сен, как она́.
5. —Ты́ по́мнишь, что́ посове́товал дя́де Ми́ше знамени́тый вра́ч, у кото́рого о́н бы́л в Берли́не? —О́н посове́товал ему́ ходи́ть два́ часа́ в де́нь.
6. Я́ сего́дня мно́го рабо́тал и о́чень уста́л. Я́ пришёл домо́й, вы́пил два́ стака́на горя́чего ча́я с лимо́ном и с ро́мом, при́нял аспири́н и лёг в посте́ль.
7. Е́сли я́ захочу́ ещё стака́н ча́я—я́ попрошу́ жену́.
8. Зинаи́да Миха́йловна то́лько что приняла́ горя́чую ва́нну. Она́ о́чень уста́ла и легла́ на дива́н отдохну́ть.
9. Я́ не приму́ у ва́с э́тих де́нег! Возьми́те и́х обра́тно!
10. Внача́ле Ива́ну и А́нне бы́ло тру́дно привы́кнуть к городско́й жи́зни, но́ тепе́рь они́ не то́лко привы́кли к не́й, но́ да́же лю́бят её!
11. Сади́тесь на э́то кре́сло; на э́том кре́сле о́чень удо́бно сиде́ть.
12. Тепе́рь о́чень ра́но стано́вится темно́.
13. Вы́ ви́дите как уже́ ста́ло темно́!
14. По-мо́ему Ви́ктор ста́л хоро́шим ученико́м.
15. Е́сли ва́м ста́нет хо́лодно, я́ да́м ва́м сво́й пиджа́к.

4. Numerals, 20-199

	Cardinal	*Ordinal*
20	два́дцать	двадца́тый
21	два́дцать оди́н (одно́, одна́)	два́дцать пе́рвый
22	два́дцать два́ (две́)	два́дцать второ́й
23	два́дцать три́	два́дцать тре́тий
24	два́дцать четы́ре	два́дцать четвёртый
25	два́дцать пя́ть	два́дцать пя́тый
	etc.	etc.
30	три́дцать	тридца́тый
31	три́дцать оди́н (одно́, одна́)	три́дцать пе́рвый
	etc.	etc.
40	со́рок	сороково́й
50	пятьдеся́т	пятидеся́тый
60	шестьдеся́т	шестидеся́тый

70	се́мьдесят	семидеся́тый
80	во́семьдесят	восьмидеся́тый
90	девяно́сто	девяно́стый
100	сто	со́тый
101	сто́ оди́н (одно́, одна́)	сто́ пе́рвый
110	сто́ де́сять	сто́ деся́тый
125	сто́ два́дцать пя́ть	сто́ два́дцать пя́тый
	etc.	etc.

The nominative singular (or other cases as appropriate) is used with **оди́н** and all compound numerals the last part of which is **оди́н** (21, 31, 101, etc.): два́дцать оди́н студе́нт, 21 students; три́дцать одна́ де́вушка, 31 girls, etc. The *genitive singular* is used with compound numbers the last part of which is **два (две), три, четы́ре** (22, 43, 104, etc.): со́рок два́ до́ма, 42 houses; шестьдеся́т три го́рода, 63 cities. Other cardinal numbers take the *genitive plural:* сто́ де́сять дете́й, 110 children, etc.

Compound ordinals (21st, 135th, etc.) are formed with the *cardinal* of the first part (or parts) and the *ordinal* of the final part. Only the last part is declined:

Мы́ живём на два́дцать пе́рвом этаже́.
О́н живёт на сто́ три́дцать пя́той у́лице.

Пятьдеся́т (50), шестьдеся́т (60), се́мьдесят (70) and во́семьдесят (80) are compounds of пять, шесть, etc., but the second element -де́сят lacks **-ь.** Ordinals of these numerals replace the **ь** of the first numeral element with **и**: пятидеся́тый, etc.

5. Age

—Ско́лько **ва́м** ле́т? —How old are you?

—**Мне́** три́дцать оди́н го́д. —I am thirty-one.
—**Мне́** со́рок четы́ре го́да. —I am forty-four.
—**Мне́** пятьдеся́т ше́сть ле́т. —I am fifty-six.

Note that the dative case is used of the person (or object) whose age is given. The last element of the numeral governs the choice of noun: оди́н го́д; два́, три́, четы́ре го́да; пя́ть, ше́сть ле́т, etc.

The past and future use the neuter singular **бы́ло** and **бу́дет** (unless the final part of the numeral is **оди́н**).

Тогда́ Ива́ну **бы́ло** два́дца́ть пя́ть ле́т.
Ivan was twenty-five then.

Сестре́ ско́ро **бу́дет** два́дцать пя́ть ле́т.
My sister will soon be twenty-five.

Pattern Sentences

1. —**Ско́лько ле́т** ва́шим де́тям? —**Моему́** мла́дшему сы́ну Бори́су **два́дцать ле́т,** Андре́ю **два́дцать оди́н го́д,** а **мое́й** до́чери О́льге **два́дцать два́ го́да.**
2. —Мо́жно ва́с спроси́ть, **ско́лько ле́т ва́м** и **ско́лько ле́т** ва́шей жене́? —**Мне́ со́рок пя́ть ле́т,** а жене́ **со́рок оди́н го́д. Е́й** ско́ро **бу́дет со́рок два́ го́да.**
3. —**Э́тому** де́реву **сто́ ле́т!**
4. —Де́душке на́шего сосе́да **сто́ два́ го́да,** а ба́бушке **девяно́сто де́вять ле́т!**
5. Вади́му **бы́ло два́ го́да,** когда́ мы́ сюда́ прие́хали. Тепе́рь **ему́** ско́ро бу́дет **двена́дцать ле́т!**
6. Тепе́рь **двадца́тый** ве́к. Мы́ живём в **двадца́том** ве́ке.
7. Мы́ живём на **три́дцать шесто́й** у́лице.

1. —How old are your children? —My youngest son Boris is twenty, Andrey is twenty-one, and my daughter Olga is twenty-two.
2. —May I ask you how old you are and how old your wife is? —I am forty-five, and my wife is forty-one. She will soon be forty-two.
3. That tree is a hundred years old!
4. —Our neighbor's grandfather is a hundred and two years old, and the grandmother is ninety-nine!
5. Vadim was two years old when we came here. Now he will soon be twelve!
6. It's the twentieth century now. We are living in the twentieth century.
7. We live on Thirty-sixth Street.

Drill

Переведи́те на ру́сский язы́к.

1. Turgenev's parents had a house in which there were forty rooms.
2. Our teacher is twenty-seven, and her mother is fifty-nine.
3. Tolstoy was eighty-three when he died.
4. Some students are interested in Russian literature of the nineteenth century.
5. —What are you interested in? —I'm interested in Russian writers of the twentieth century.
6. Turgenev and Dostoevski lived and wrote in the nineteenth century.
7. In this skyscraper (высо́тное зда́ние) there are forty-two floors.
8. I have just found out that his office is on the fortieth floor, opposite the elevator.
9. I shall see him there tomorrow at eleven o'clock, when he returns from Boston.
10. I don't remember on which street in New York my friend lives: on 120th Street or 121st Street.
11. The Roberts live on 76th Street and their parents on 98th.
12. I'm telling you that for (**в** + accusative) the twentieth time!
13. We live in a skyscraper on the thirty-fifth floor.
14. My mother lives on the eighth floor.
15. Peter I lived in the eighteenth century.

READING

Моя́ сосе́дка

Нельзя́ сказа́ть, что моя́ сосе́дка Ве́ра Васи́льевна плоха́я же́нщина, но́ и нельзя́ сказа́ть, что она́ о́чень до́брый и прия́тный челове́к.

Во-пе́рвых, Ве́ра Васи́льевна лю́бит спле́тни (gossip). Спле́тничать (to gossip)—э́то её люби́мое заня́тие, и язы́к у неё дово́льно зло́й. Во-вторы́х, она́ о́чень лю́бит дава́ть сове́ты. Це́лый де́нь то́лько и слы́шишь: "Я́ ва́м сове́тую, сде́лайте э́то; я́ ва́м сове́тую, не де́лайте э́того." В-тре́тьих, она́ лю́бит расска́зывать о ра́зных у́жасах, о неприя́тных слу́чаях, смертя́х, сканда́лах и так да́лее и так да́лее.

Ве́ра Васи́льевна знако́ма не то́лько со все́ми жильца́ми на́шего до́ма, но́ почти́ все́ жильцы́ сосе́дних домо́в её хоро́шие знако́мые, и она́ зна́ет всё, что у ни́х происхо́дит.

В пя́тницу она́ пришла́ ко мне́, се́ла на своё люби́мое ме́сто у окна́, та́к чтобы ви́деть всё, что происхо́дит на у́лице (мы́ живём на второ́м этаже́) и сра́зу начала́ расска́зывать:

—Зна́ете, вчера́ я́ возвраща́лась домо́й от Лунёвых. (Кста́ти, Лизаве́та, сестра́ Лунёва, о́чень измени́лась. Она́ ста́ла тако́й стра́нной. Но́ я́ ва́м об э́том расскажу́ пото́м.) О чём я́ говорила́? А́х, да́! Я́ возвраща́лась ве́чером домо́й, бы́ло уже́ дово́льно по́здно, и вдру́г ви́жу, идёт Катю́ша Ле́бедева! И идёт она́ не одна́, а с Бори́сом Ка́рповым. Вы́ зна́ете Ка́рповых? Э́то жильцы́, кото́рые живу́т на седьмо́м этаже́. И́х кварти́ра пря́мо про́тив ли́фта. Вы́ и́х зна́ете! У Наста́сьи Ива́новны Ка́рповой о́чень гро́мкий и неприя́тный го́лос, и она́ лю́бит на все́х крича́ть. У ни́х две́ ко́шки.

—Не́т, не зна́ю ни Катю́шу Ле́бедеву, ни Ка́рповых, ни и́х ко́шек. И како́е мне́ де́ло, что́ все́ э́ти лю́ди де́лают?

—Ка́к, како́е де́ло?! Стра́нный вы́ челове́к! Ничего́ и никого́ вы́ не зна́ете и зна́ть не хоти́те. Никто́ ва́с не интересу́ет! Прости́те меня́, но́ та́к нельзя́ жи́ть. Ну́жно принима́ть уча́стие в жи́зни други́х.

Я́ е́й ничего́ не отве́тила: она́ всё равно́ не поймёт и начнёт спо́рить. И она́ продолжа́ла.

—Вы́ слы́шали, что инжене́р Ма́слов у́мер?

—Како́й инжене́р Ма́слов? Я́ не зна́ю никако́го инжене́ра Ма́слова.

—Ну что́ вы́ говори́те! Вы́ не зна́ете Ма́слова, кото́рый живёт, то́ есть жи́л, на на́шей у́лице, в тре́тьем до́ме от угла́? О́н жи́л на пе́рвом этаже́ и ве́чером, по́сле слу́жбы, люби́л сиде́ть у окна́. Мы́ с ни́м ча́сто разгова́ривали, когда́ его́ ста́рой тётки не быва́ло до́ма. Жена́ Ма́слова умерла́ не́сколько ле́т тому́ наза́д (о́н о́чень люби́л свою́ жену́), и к нему́ из дере́вни прие́хала на неде́лю его́ ста́рая тётка. Она́ прие́хала на неде́лю и, поду́майте, до сих по́р живёт у него́! Она́ меня́ почему́-то ненави́дит. За что́? Оди́н Бо́г зна́ет! А како́й у неё язы́к! Я́ никогда́ не зна́ла же́нщины с таки́м злы́м языко́м! Я́ е́й сове́тую верну́ться в дере́вню, а она́ мне́ говори́т, что э́то не моё де́ло! И оди́н ра́з она́ да́же попроси́ла меня́ к ни́м бо́льше не приходи́ть и не телефони́ровать и́м! Ужа́сная же́нщина! Я́ её про́сто ненави́жу.

—Прости́те меня́, но́ я́ не понима́ю, ка́к вы́ могли́ посове́товать е́й верну́ться в дере́вню? Како́е ва́м де́ло? Како́е пра́во вы́ име́ете та́к говори́ть! Я́ отли́чно понима́ю, что она́ ва́с не лю́бит.

—Вы́ её не зна́ете, вы́ не зна́ете, како́й у неё хара́ктер. Я́ ча́сто говори́ла Ма́слову: —«Андре́й Петро́вич, ну́, почему́ э́та ста́рая ве́дьма (hag, witch) у ва́с живёт? У ва́с така́я ску́чная жи́знь! Я́ ва́м о́чень сове́тую сказа́ть е́й, что у ва́с для неё не́т ме́ста. Бу́дьте си́льным челове́ком. Ну́, ра́зве э́то жи́знь?» А о́н, бе́дный, бы́л тако́й до́брый и сла́бый челове́к. О́н говори́л: —«Но́ э́то совсе́м не та́к! Во-пе́рвых, Варва́ра хоро́шая же́нщина, а во-вторы́х, у неё кро́ме меня́ никого́ на све́те не́т. Кро́ме того́, я́ привы́к к не́й, и она́ привы́кла ко мне́, и куда́ она́, бе́дная, тепе́рь пое́дет?» А я́ ему́ говори́ла: —«Вы́ никого́ не ви́дите, вы́ не принима́ете уча́стия в жи́зни други́х. Та́к нельзя́ жи́ть. Во́т увиди́те, что э́то пло́хо для ва́с ко́нчится!» И во́т, сего́дня я́ узна́ла, что Ма́слов у́мер!

—Да́, жи́знь не лёгкая ве́щь. Но́ кака́я свя́зь ме́жду сме́ртью Ма́слова и его́ тёткой?

—Ну́, что́ вы́, Зинаи́да Миха́йловна! Ну что́ э́то была́ за жи́знь для него́, несча́стного!

Пото́м Ве́ра Васи́льевна начала́ говори́ть на одну́ из свои́х люби́мых те́м; о то́м как бы́ло когда́-то и ка́к тепе́рь. Она́ начала́ издалека́.

—Да́, в моё вре́мя всё бы́ло по-друго́му. Когда́, наприме́р, мне́ бы́ло шестна́дцать ле́т, а мое́й сестре́ О́ле бы́ло семна́дцать, мы́ должны́ были ложи́ться спа́ть в де́вять часо́в. На́м нельзя́ бы́ло возвраща́ться по́здно домо́й, и на́м нельзя́ бы́ло танцева́ть с ке́м мы́ хоте́ли. А тепе́рь де́вушки де́лают, что́ хотя́т. Они́ танцу́ют с молоды́ми людьми́, кото́рых и́х роди́тели да́же не зна́ют, и возвраща́ются домо́й в любо́е вре́мя. А бе́дные роди́тели ничего́ свои́м де́тям да́же не говоря́т: они́ тепе́рь и́х боя́тся. Во́т, наприме́р, ва́ша Ни́ночка. Ни́ночке четы́рнадцать ле́т, пра́вда? Я́ зна́ю, что она́ хоро́шая де́вочка, я́ зна́ю, что она́ помога́ет ва́м по хозя́йству, но́, дорога́я Зинаи́да Миха́йловна! Я́ ведь ва́ш дру́г, пра́вда? Я́ ва́м о́чень сове́тую . . .

—Дорога́я Ве́ра Васи́льевна, е́сли вы́ хоти́те бы́ть мои́м дру́гом, я́ ва́м о́чень сове́тую не дава́ть мне́ сове́тов и не расска́зывать мне́ о дела́х други́х люде́й. Ла́дно?

Она́ посмотре́ла на меня́ и уви́дела, что я́ не шучу́. Пото́м посмотре́ла на часы́ и сказа́ла: —«Бо́же мо́й! Как по́здно! Споко́йной но́чи, дорога́я! Переда́йте приве́т Ни́ночке». Но́ когда́ она́ была́ уже́ у две́ри, она́ сказа́ла: «Ах, да́! Я́ забы́ла ва́м рассказа́ть про Лизаве́ту Луне́ву! Ну́, э́то бу́дет в друго́й ра́з. Я́ не забу́ду. Ва́м э́то бу́дет интере́сно.» И она́ ушла́.

Что́ она́ расска́зывает други́м обо мне́? Хотя́, должна́ пра́вду сказа́ть, меня́ э́то не осо́бенно интересу́ет.

Чита́йте э́ти вопро́сы и отвеча́йте на ни́х.

1. Что́ мо́жно сказа́ть о Ве́ре Васи́льевне? Что́ она́ лю́бит? О чём она́ лю́бит расска́зывать? 2. Кого́ она́ зна́ет? 3. Где́ её люби́мое ме́сто в мое́й кварти́ре и почему́? 4. Что́ она́ рассказа́ла про Катю́шу Ле́бедеву и про Ка́рповых? 5. Где́ кварти́ра Ка́рповых? 6. Что́ сказа́ла Ве́ра Васи́льевна, когда́ она́ услы́шала, что я́ не зна́ю всё́х э́тих люде́й? 7. Что́ она́ рассказа́ла мне́ про инжене́ра Ма́слова? 8. Почему́ его́ ста́рая тётя Варва́ра живёт у него́? 9. Что́ Ве́ра Васи́льевна о не́й говори́т? 10. Что́ она́ рассказа́ла о свои́х разгово́рах с Ма́словым? 11. Что́ она́ посове́товала тётке? Лю́бят э́ти две́ же́нщины дру́г дру́га? 12. На каку́ю те́му моя́ сосе́дка пото́м начала́ говори́ть? 13. Что́ я́ е́й посове́товала? 14. О чём я́ поду́мала, когда́ она́ наконе́ц ушла́?

EXERCISES

Переведи́те на ру́сский.

1. When will you give me back my book? 2. I shall return it in two days. All right? 3. I returned to Moscow after a long trip. 4. When is your husband coming back from France? 5. We live opposite the park. 6. My room is opposite Olga's room. 7. I am tired. Good night! 8. —Where is Mama? —She's gone to bed. 9. —May I take part in your conversation? —No, you may not. 10. If I can, I shall find out where he lives. 11. Smirnov is abroad; he will return here next year. 12. He will let us know as soon as he returns. 13. It was very hard for me to get used to this city, but I got used to it. 14. She is not used to such noise. 15. By the way, you can take any book you want. 16. I took a bath, and now good night! 17. This book doesn't interest me. 18. I shall phone you tomorrow.

VOCABULARY

ва́нна bath
век (*nom. pl.* **-а́**) century, age
городско́й city, urban, municipal
горя́чий (*adv.* **горячо́**) hot[10]
до́брый kind, good-hearted
жара́ hot weather, heat
жил.е́ц (*gen.* **-ьца́,** *fem.* **-и́ца**) lodger, tenant
заня́тие occupation
заня́тия (*pl.*) occupations, studies, classes
здоро́вье health
злой evil, vicious
издалека́ from afar
крик cry, shout
кста́ти by the way, à propos
ла́дно (*colloq.*) all right, O.K.
лифт elevator
луна́ moon
любо́й any (at all)
наро́дный national; folk
никако́й no, none (at all)
***пе́р.ец** (*gen.* **-ца**) pepper
про (+ *acc.*) about, concerning
про́тив (+ *gen.*) opposite, against
связь (*fem.*) link, tie, connection
си́льный strong
сла́бый weak
***слон** elephant
сра́зу at once, immediately
та́н.ец (*gen.* **-ца**) dance
тётка aunt, auntie
у́жас horror, terror
уча́стие participation, part
хо́лод cold
чтобы as to, in order to
шокола́д chocolate

Verbs

(For other verbs see Paragraphs 2 and 3 above, pages 350 and 352.)

изменя́ться (imperf., I), **измени́ться** (perf., II: **изменю́сь, изме́нишься**) to change (*intrans.*), be altered
крича́ть (imperf., II: **крич.у́, -и́шь**), **кри́кнуть** (perf., I: **кри́кн.у, -ешь**) to cry out, shout
обеща́ть (imperf., I) to promise (+ *dat. of person*)
отдохну́ть (perf. of **отдыха́ть**, I: **отдохн.у́, -ёшь**) to rest (up), get rested
пла́кать (imperf., I: **пла́ч.у, -ешь**) to weep, cry
пробы́ть (perf., I: **пробу́д.у, -ешь**; past: **про́был, -о, пробыла́, про́были**) to stay, spend (some time)
происходи́ть (imperf., II: **происхо́дит**), **произойти́** (perf., I: **произойдёт**; past: **произошло́**) to occur, happen; be derived from, proceed

Expressions

сади́ться/се́сть на по́езд to take a (the) train
с тех по́р since then

[10] Жа́ркий applies to weather only: жа́ркая пого́да; жа́ркий де́нь, клима́т, etc. Горя́чий applies to objects: горя́чий ко́фе, ча́й, су́п, etc.
* Students are not required to memorize words preceded by an asterisk.

с тех пóр, как . . . since the time when
до какúх пóр? how long, how far, till when?
до тех пóр till then
до сих пóр so far, this far, till now, still
трéтьего днé day before yesterday
по-другóму otherwise, differently
éхать за граню́цу (*acc.*) to go abroad
бы́ть за грани́цей (*instr.*) to be abroad
дáть (+ *dat.*) **знáть** to let someone know
покá . . . не (+ *perf. past or future*) until[11]
тóлько и слы́шишь . . . you hear nothing but . . .
в-трéтьих third, in the third place
и так дáлее (и т. д.) and so forth (etc.)
принимáть учáстие to take part
принимáть/приня́ть вáнну to take a bath
принимáть/приня́ть аспири́н to take aspirin
никогдá в жи́зни never in (my) life
когдá-то once, at one time
помогáть по хозя́йству to help around the house
Спокóйной нóчи. Good night
имéть удовóльствие (+ *inf.*) to have the pleasure
имéть возмóжность (+ *inf.*) to have the possibility
имéть слу́чай (+ *inf.*) to have a chance

[11] *E.g.* Я́ бу́ду рабóтать, **покá** ты́ **не** придёшь.

UNIT 22

GRAMMAR

1. The interrogative particle ли

The interrogative particle **ли** is used in indirect questions which may be answered by "yes" or "no," *i.e.*, in subordinate clauses comparable to those introduced in English by "whether" or "if." Note that the word **éсли** *must not be used in such clauses.* (A good test of the difference when translating from English is the possibility of replacing "if" by "whether"; when "whether" may be used in English, then **ли** must be used in Russian; otherwise "if" = **éсли. Ли** is always unstressed, and falls second in its clause, after the key word of the question:

Я́ не знáю,
О́н меня́ спрáшивает,
Мнé нýжно знáть,
Вы́ мóжете мнé сказáть, } приéхал **ли** ужé Ивáн.

Ли follows the key word of the indirect question, often but not necessarily a verb:

Спроси́те егó, мнóго **ли** óн читáет.
Я́ хочý знáть, хорошó **ли** игрáл Рахмáнинов.
Ктó знáет, дóма **ли** óн?

Note that clauses with **ли,** like other subordinate clauses, are set off by commas.

Ли is sometimes used in direct questions which may be answered by "yes" or "no," especially in negative questions analogous to polite English requests beginning with "Wouldn't you?" "Couldn't you?" etc.

Не зна́ете **ли** вы́, где́ живёт до́ктор Петро́в?
Wouldn't you know where Dr. Petrov lives?

Не мо́жете **ли** вы́ мне́ помо́чь?
Couldn't you help me?

In direct questions generally, **ли** expresses speculation, wonder, or doubt.

По́мнил **ли** о́н, что́ я́ ему́ сказа́л?
Зна́ет **ли** о́н об э́том?

Pattern Sentences

1. Вы́ не зна́ете, мо́жет **ли** Андре́й одолжи́ть мне́ сво́й фотоаппара́т? **Е́сли** о́н мне́ его́ за́втра одо́лжит, я́ верну́ его́ через де́нь.
2. Кто́ мо́жет мне́ сказа́ть, е́сть **ли** зде́сь хоро́шая гости́ница?
3. Кто́ зна́ет, хоро́шая **ли** э́то гости́ница?
4. Я́ не зна́ю, поняла́ **ли** Та́ня, что́ я́ е́й говори́л по телефо́ну. **Е́сли** она́ ва́с спро́сит, в чём де́ло, объясни́те е́й.
5. Я́ не по́мню, лю́бит **ли** Ва́ня я́блоки. **Е́сли** о́н лю́бит, я́ ему́ куплю́ два́ фу́нта я́блок.
6. —Я́ не зна́ю, смогу́ **ли** я́ ва́м помо́чь. —Я́ бу́ду ва́м о́чень благода́рен, **е́сли** вы́ смо́жете.
7. Спроси́ дя́дю Ми́шу, хо́чет **ли** о́н пойти́ в кино́ с на́ми. **Е́сли** о́н хо́чет, то́[1] мы́ его́ подождём.
8. **Е́сли** у па́пы бу́дут де́ньги во вто́рник, о́н коне́чно мне́ и́х да́ст, но́ я́ не зна́ю, **бу́дут ли** у него́ де́ньги.
9. Не хоти́те **ли** вы́ ещё ча́шку ча́ю?

1. Do you know whether Andrey can lend me his camera? If he lends it to me tomorrow, I shall return it a day later.
2. Who can tell me if there is a good hotel here?
3. Who knows whether this is a good hotel?
4. I don't know if Tanya understood what I told her on the telephone. If she asks you what it is, explain it to her.
5. I don't remember if Vanya likes apples. If he does, I shall buy him two pounds.
6. —I don't know whether I shall be able to help you. —I'll be very grateful to you if you can.
7. Ask Uncle Misha if he wants to come to the movies with us. If he wants to, then we'll wait for him.
8. If Papa has any money on Tuesday, of course he'll give it to me, but I don't know if he'll have any.
9. Wouldn't you like another cup of tea?

[1] Concluding clauses in "if" sentences often start with **то́** (stressed) when the concluding clause follows the "if" clause. Compare English: If . . . *then* . . .

Drills

A. *Change the statements into indirect questions using the particle* **ли.**

Model: Здéсь éсть пóчта. Óльга спроси́ла, éсть ли здéсь пóчта.

Ивáн бы́л на завóде. ____________
Э́то прáвда. ____________
Я́ живу́ здéсь. ____________

Model: Ты́ получи́л письмó. Ивáн хóчет знáть, получи́л ли ты́ письмó.

У А́нны éсть дéньги. ____________
Дéньги у А́нны. ____________
Вы́ хоти́те чáю. ____________
Э́то нáш учи́тель. ____________
Здéсь бы́л дóждь. ____________

B. *Переведи́те на ру́сский.*

1. Do you know if Petrov has returned from Moscow? If he has returned, I hope he will call me.
2. Ask Olga if she needs a black dress. If she needs one, I can give her mine.
3. I don't remember whether Boris was in class.
4. The professor asked Tanya if she had read *Anna Karenina.*
5. Who knows if she has money?
6. We don't know if they want to go to the country. If they wish, they can come with us.
7. Do you know if Ivan is at home?
8. I asked him if he worked much.

2. The particles -то and -нибудь

Interrogative pronouns and adverbs are combined with the particles **-то** and **-нибудь,** producing two series of compounds:

чтó-то	something
чтó-нибудь	something, anything
ктó-то	somebody, someone
ктó-нибудь	someone, anyone
гдé-то	somewhere
гдé-нибудь	somewhere, anywhere
кудá-то	(to) somewhere
кудá-нибудь	(to) somewhere, anywhere
какóй-то	some kind of
какóй-нибудь	some (any) kind of

почему́-то for some reason
почему́-нибудь for some (any) reason

The series with **-то** is used in referring to objects, persons, places, directions, etc., that are definite and identifiable, but that the speaker is unable (or unwilling) to identify:

О́н **что́-то** чита́л.
He was reading *something* (he knew what it was, but I couldn't see).

Кто́-то позвони́л.
Someone has rung the bell (I don't know yet who it is).

Я́ его́ **где́-то** уже́ встреча́л.
I have met him *somewhere* before (I don't recall where it was).

О́н **куда́-то** е́дет за́втра.
He is going *somewhere* tomorrow (he knows, but didn't tell me where).

Мне́ ну́жно ва́м **что́-то** сказа́ть.
I must tell you *something* (I know what it is, but I shall tell you a little later).

The compounds with **-нибудь** express indefiniteness; the object, person, place, direction, etc., does not have a definable identity:

Я́ го́лоден; е́сть у тебя́ **что́-нибудь** в ку́хне?
I'm hungry; do you have *anything* in the kitchen (any kind of food, whatever it is)?

Кто́-нибудь звони́л?
Did *anyone* call?

Мы́ мо́жем пообе́дать **где́-нибудь** в го́роде.
We can have dinner *somewhere* in town (we shall choose the place later; for the time being it is "any place").

Ле́том они́ всегда́ уезжа́ют **куда́-нибудь** в Евро́пу.
In summer they always go to *some place* in Europe (each time to a different place, so that no single name can indicate where they go).

The compound forms with **что, кто, како́й,** and **чей** are declined:

О́н **с ке́м-то** разгова́ривает.
He is talking to someone.

О́н **от кого́-то** получи́л письмо́.
He has received a letter from someone.

Они́ **о чём-то** говори́ли.
They were talking about something.

Ты́ **кому́-нибудь** говори́л об э́том?
Did you tell anyone about it?

Я́ не зна́ю, где́ о́н живёт; я́ **кого́-нибудь** спрошу́.
I don't know where he lives; I will ask someone.

Да́йте мне́ **каку́ю-нибудь** кни́гу.
Give me a book (some book or other).

Я́ нашёл **чью-то** кни́гу на моём столе́.
I found someone's book on my desk.

The forms **когда́-то** and **когда́-нибудь** show a distinction in meaning similar to that of the pairs listed above, but the proper English translation of **когда́-то** with a verb in the past tense will be "once," "one day," "at one time," etc.:

Я́ **когда́-то** хорошо́ игра́л в те́ннис.
At one time I played tennis well.

Когда́-то лю́ди всё де́лали рука́ми.
Once people used to do everything with their hands.

Я́ наде́юсь, что **когда́-нибудь** бу́дет ми́р на земле́.
I hope that some day there will be peace on earth.

Я́ **когда́-нибудь** всё ва́м расскажу́.
Some time I shall tell you everything.

Pattern Sentences

1. —**Кто́-нибудь** е́дет в го́род? —Не́т, никто́.
2. —**Кто́-нибудь** мне́ звони́л? —Да́, **кто́-то** звони́л, но́ не сказа́л своего́ и́мени.
3. —Вы́ **кого́-нибудь** встре́тили, когда́ шли́ сюда́? —Да́, я́ встре́тил **како́го-то** старика́.
4. Скажи́те мне́ **что́-нибудь** прия́тное!
5. Я́ **кому́-то** да́л сво́й ру́сско-англи́йский[2] слова́рь, и тепе́рь не по́мню кому́.
6. —Я́ наде́юсь, что у **кого́-нибудь** е́сть сего́дняшняя газе́та. —Да́, я́ её ви́дел у **кого́-то.**

1. —Is anyone going to town? —No, no one.
2. —Did anybody call me? —Yes, somebody called, but he didn't give his name.
3. —Did you meet anyone on your way here? —Yes, I met an old man.
4. Tell me something nice!
5. I gave someone my Russian-English dictionary, and now I don't remember whom.
6. —I hope that someone's got today's paper. —Yes, I saw someone with it.

[2] The first part of a compound adjective ends in **-o**, and is not declined.

7. Я́ хочу́ **куда́-нибудь** пойти́ сего́дня ве́чером.
8. За́втра ве́чером мои́х роди́телей не бу́дет до́ма; они́ **куда́-то** иду́т.
9. Вади́м **что́-то** нашёл, но́ не говори́т что́.
10. Я́ потеря́л часы́. Е́сли **кто́-нибудь** и́х найдёт, скажи́те мне́.
11. Не покупа́й чемода́на, а возьми́ **чёй-нибудь.**
12. Я́ нашёл **че́й-то** портфе́ль в свое́й ко́мнате.

7. I want to go somewhere this evening.
8. Tomorrow evening my parents won't be at home; they're going somewhere.
9. Vadim has found something, but he doesn't say what.
10. I lost my watch. If anyone finds it, tell me.
11. Don't buy a suitcase, but take someone else's.
12. I found someone's briefcase in my room.

Drills

A. *Add the suffix* **-то** *or* **-нибудь** *according to the sense.*

1. Бы́л вчера́ кто́-...... на ле́кции Петро́ва?
2. Кто́-...... мне́ сказа́л, что вы́ та́м бы́ли.
3. Вы́ мо́жете рассказа́ть мне́ что́-...... интере́сное?
4. У кого́-...... е́сть папиро́сы?
5. Я́ где́-...... об э́том уже́ слы́шал.
6. О́н ещё не зна́ет, пое́дет ли о́н куда́-...... ле́том.
7. Вы́ бы́ли где́-...... вчера́ ве́чером?
8. Хо́чет кто́-...... пойти́ со мно́й?
9. Сего́дня у́тром кто́-...... ва́м звони́л.
10. Я́ где́-...... его́ уже́ ви́дел.
11. Я́ наде́юсь, что я́ где́-...... найду́ э́то письмо́.

B. *Переведи́те с англи́йского на ру́сский.*

1. When you go to the store, buy me something.
2. Somebody wrote to my mother about that matter.
3. Do you know anyone who has recently been in the Soviet Union?
4. I heard that someone had just returned from there.
5. —Where is Grandmother? —She went somewhere.
6. He wrote to someone about that question.
7. Somebody's money is lying on the floor.
8. If you find anything interesting in the newspaper, read it to me.
9. Olga found somebody's hat.
10. Buy me some magazine (or other).
11. I've lost my briefcase somewhere.
12. For some reason he doesn't like me.

3. Prepositions of place or direction (supplement)

As has already been explained, the preposition **у** (+ genitive) expresses possession as well as location ("at someone's place"—see Unit 10, page 143). In the same way, **к** (+ dative) expresses "going to someone," "going to someone's place" (see Unit 17, page 257).

When used with words denoting physical objects, these two prepositions have the same basic meaning, although the usage may seem slightly different. **У** (+ genitive) denotes close proximity to an object; **к** (+ dative) denotes motion to the vicinity of an object or toward an object:

У with genitive

Сту́л стои́т **у** стен**ы́**.
The chair is standing by the wall.

Я́ люблю́ сиде́ть **у** окн**а́**.
I like to sit by the window.

Учи́тель стои́т **у** доск**и́**.
The teacher is standing at the blackboard.

К with dative

Позвони́л звоно́к. Хозя́ин пошёл **к** две́р**и**.
The bell rang, and the host went to the door.

Учени́к пошёл **к** доск**е́**.
The student went to (toward) the blackboard.

The preposition **ми́мо** (+ genitive) means "by," "past:"

Лю́ди шли́ **ми́мо** це́ркв**и**.
People were walking past the church.

The preposition **через** (+ accusative) means "across," "through:"

Мы́ шли́ **через** па́рк.
We were going through the park.

4. Verbs of motion with prefixes of direction

Verbs of motion prefixed with **при-** (coming to, arriving in), and **у-** (going away, leaving) were given in Unit 18. These verbs appear in regular imperfective-perfective pairs (*e.g.*, уходи́ть-уйти́), without the imperfective indeterminate-imperfective determinate distinction. They are derived as follows:

From imperfective indeterminate:
  ходи́ть-**у**ходи́ть—*imperfective*
From imperfective determinate:
  идти́ (contracted to -йти́)-**у**йти́—*perfective*

Besides **при-** and **у-**, a number of other prefixes may be added to the basic forms. It must be noted, however, that in prefixed verbs, not éздить, but the variant form **-езжáть** is used (cf. приезжáть and уезжáть); this form *never* occurs without a prefix.

Among the more important prefixes other than **при-** and **у-** are:

в- (во-, въ-)
Going (coming) in, entering

	not by vehicle	*by vehicle*
Imperf.:	входи́ть	въезжáть
Perf.:	войти́	въéхать
(*Perf. Past:*	вошёл, вошлá, etc.)	
	(with **в** + *acc.*)	

Мы́ **вошли́** в до́м.[4]
We entered the house.

Они́ **въезжáют** во дво́р.
They are driving into the yard.

вы-
Going (coming) out, exiting

	not by vehicle	*by vehicle*
Imperf.:	выходи́ть	выезжáть
Perf.:	вы́йти[3]	вы́ехать[3]
(*Perf. Past:*	вы́шел, вы́шла, etc.)	
	(with **из** + *gen.*)	

Мы́ **вы́шли** из до́ма.[4]
We left the house.

Мы́ **вы́ехали** из го́рода.
We drove out of the city.

под- (подо-, подъ-)
Approaching, coming up to

	not by vehicle	*by vehicle*
Imperf.:	подходи́ть	подъезжáть
Perf.:	подойти́	подъéхать
(*Perf. Past:*	подошёл, подошлá, etc.)	
	(with **к** + *dat.*)	

О́н **подошёл** к окну́.
He went up to the window.

от- (ото-, отъ-)
Moving away

	not by vehicle	*by vehicle*
Imperf.:	отходи́ть	отъезжáть
Perf.:	отойти́	отъéхать
(*Perf. Past:*	отошёл, отошлá, etc.)	
	(with **от** + *gen.*)	

О́н **отошёл** от окнá.
He moved away from the window.

Another important prefix is **за-**:

заходи́ть/зайти́
заезжáть/заéхать
} to call on, to drop in to see (for a brief informal visit) (**к** + dative); to call for, come for (**за** + instrumental)

По́сле обéда мы́ **зайдём** к вáм.
After dinner we'll drop in to see you.

Они́ **зайду́т** за нáми, и мы́ вмéсте пойдём поу́жинать.
They'll come for us and together we'll go to supper.

[3] The prefix **вы-** is never stressed in the imperfective, but always stressed in the perfective, in all forms. Note especially: **о́н вы́шел**, *he went out.*

[4] Observe that these verbs are intransitive and require the use of a preposition. (The corresponding English verb ("enter," "leave," etc.) may be transitive.)

The prefix **про-** has the meaning of "by," "past":

проходи́ть/пройти́ проезжа́ть/прое́хать	to go (come) by, past, through, pass (+ **ми́мо** + genitive—by, past) (+ **через** + accusative—through)

Они́ **прошли́** ми́мо на́с.
They passed us.

Де́нь **прошёл** бы́стро.
The day passed rapidly.

Мы́ **прошли́** через па́рк.
We walked through the park.

The prefix **пере-** has the meaning of "across":

переходи́ть/перейти́ переезжа́ть/перее́хать	to cross (+ accusative)

Мы́ **перешли́** у́лицу.
We crossed the street.

Pattern Sentences

1. Ра́ньше мы́ **выходи́ли** ка́ждый ве́чер, а тепе́рь мы́ о́чень ре́дко **выхо́дим.**
2. У Ива́на была́ инфлуэ́нца; о́н вчера́ **вы́шел** в пе́рвый ра́з.
3. Ка́ждый де́нь я́ **выхожу́** и́з дому в во́семь.
4. —Где́ Ко́ля? —О́н то́лько что **вы́шел** из ко́мнаты.
5. —Мо́жно **войти́?** —Пожа́луйста, **войди́те!**
6. Когда́ о́н **вошёл** в ко́мнату, она́ **вы́шла** (из ко́мнаты).
7. Я́ никогда́ не **вхожу́** в его́ кабине́т.
8. По доро́ге домо́й я́ **зашёл** в большу́ю апте́ку на гла́вной у́лице.
9. О́н ча́сто **захо́дит** ко мне́ «на мину́ту», а пото́м сиди́т о́чень до́лго. Я́ никогда́ не **захожу́** к нему́.
10. —**Зайди́те** ко мне́ по доро́ге в университе́т. —Хорошо́, я́ **зайду́** к ва́м, но́ не надо́лго.

1. We used to go out every evening, but now we go out very seldom.
2. Ivan had influenza; yesterday he went out for the first time.
3. Every day I leave home at eight.
4. —Where is Kolya? —He just stepped out of the room.
5. —May I come in? —Please come in!
6. When he entered the room, she left it.
7. I never go into his study.
8. On the way home I stopped in at a large drugstore on the main street.
9. He often drops in to see me "for a minute," and then stays a long time. I never drop in at his place.
10. —Stop in to see me on your way to the university. —All right, I'll stop in, but not for long.

11. Кто́ был э́тот стари́к, кото́рый к тебе́ **подошёл** в рестора́не?
12. Я́ наде́юсь, что он не **подойдёт** к на́м.
13. Мы́ должны́ будем **пройти́** через его́ ко́мнату.
14. Как бы́стро **прошёл** э́тот го́д!

11. Who was that old man who came up to you in the restaurant?
12. I hope he will not come up to us.
13. We shall have to pass through his room.
14. How quickly this year has gone by!

Drill

A. *Choose the proper form of the verbs* **выходи́ть/вы́йти, выезжа́ть/вы́ехать, входи́ть/войти́,** *and translate into English.*

1. Ни́на то́лько что ...... из ко́мнаты.
2. До́ктор сказа́л А́нне, что е́й ещё нельзя́ ....
3. Ка́ждое у́тро я́ ...... в се́мь часо́в.
4. Мы́ должны́ ...... о́чень ра́но, е́сли мы́ хоти́м прие́хать в Босто́н пока́ ещё светло́.
5. Она́ ...... в свою́ ко́мнату и через мину́ту ...... отту́да.
6. Откро́йте две́рь и ...... в мо́й кабине́т.
7. Да́ма и соба́чка ...... в магази́н.
8. Они́ ско́ро ...... из магази́на.
9. Я́ ...... и́з дому через полчаса́.
10. Когда́ вы́ ...... из ко́мнаты, закро́йте две́рь.
11. Когда́ мы́ ...... из го́рода, мы́ остано́вимся и поза́втракаем.
12. Они́ ...... из Москвы́ в понеде́льник.

B. *Choose the proper form of the verb* **заходи́ть/зайти́,** *and translate into English.*

1. Мо́жно ...... к ва́м на пя́ть мину́т?
2. Я́ тепе́рь ча́сто ...... к нему́ по доро́ге домо́й.
3. Вчера́ о́н ...... ко мне́ за кни́гой.
4. У́тром Ни́на ...... к подру́ге, но́ её не́ было до́ма.
5. Она́ тепе́рь ре́дко ...... к на́м.
6. Я́ тепе́рь живу́ бли́зко и бу́ду ча́сто ...... к ва́м.
7. ...... ко мне́ сего́дня ве́чером.
8. Я́ ...... за ва́ми, и мы вме́сте пойдём в кино́.

C. *Choose the proper form of the verbs* **подходи́ть/подойти́, отходи́ть/отойти́,** *and translate into English.*

1. ...... к столу́ и возьми́те кни́гу.
2. По́сле уро́ка о́н ...... ко мне́, за́дал вопро́с и сейча́с же ...... от меня́.
3. Я́ никогда́ не ...... к его́ пи́сьменному столу́.
4. Она́ ...... к доске́ и начала́ писа́ть, пото́м она́ ...... от доски́ и се́ла.
5. Мы́ ча́сто и́х встреча́ем, но́ никогда́ не ...... к ни́м.
6. Я́ ...... к не́й, е́сли она́ бу́дет одна́.

5. Verbs of carrying

As with verbs of going, Russian has two series of verbs of carrying, one for carrying on foot (corresponding to **ходи́ть/идти́**), the other in a vehicle (hauling, transporting, corresponding to **е́здить/е́хать**).

Also like the going verbs, the basic verbs denoting carrying have two kinds of imperfectives: a determinate, denoting carrying on one trip in one direction; and an indeterminate, denoting carrying in general, on more than one trip, or in more than one direction. Compare:

to go (*not by vehicle*):

Indeterminate Imperfective	*Determinate Imperfective*	*Perfective*
ходи́ть	**идти́**	**пойти́**
хожу́	иду́	пойду́
хо́дишь, etc.	идёшь, etc.	пойдёшь, etc.

to carry (*not by vehicle*):

носи́ть	**нести́**	**понести́**
ношу́	несу́	понесу́ (fut.)
но́сишь	несёшь	понесёшь, etc.
но́сит	несёт	
но́сим	несём	
но́сите	несёте	
но́сят	несу́т	
Past: носи́л, etc.	Past: нёс, несло́, несла́, несли́	Past: понёс, понесло́, etc.

Indeterminate imperfective **носи́ть** (*more than one direction*):

Ма́ть **ходи́ла** по ко́мнате и **носи́ла** больно́го ребёнка.

The mother was walking about the room, carrying the sick child.

Determinate imperfective **нести́** (*one direction*):

Она́ **шла́** по у́лице и **несла́** в руке́ паке́т.

She was walking along the street carrying a package in her hand.

Perfective **понести́**:

О́н взя́л у неё паке́т и **понёс** его.[5]

He took the package from her and carried it.

[5] The perfectives with **по-** sometimes have an inchoative meaning, emphasizing the beginning of the action, *e.g.*: По́езд останови́лся и через мину́ту опя́ть **пошёл**. The train stopped, and after a minute started again. But: Ива́н **пошёл** на почту; Ivan *went* to the post office.

to go (*by vehicle*):

Indeterminate Imperfective	*Determinate Imperfective*	*Perfective*
е́здить	**е́хать**	**пое́хать**
е́зжу	е́ду	пое́ду
е́здишь, etc.	е́дешь, etc.	пое́дешь, etc.

to carry (*by vehicle*):

вози́ть	**везти́**	**повезти́**
вожу́	везу́	повезу́ (fut.)
во́зишь	везёшь	повезёшь, etc.
во́зит	везёт	
во́зим	везём	
во́зите	везёте	
во́зят	везу́т	
Past: вози́л, etc.	Past: вёз, везло́, везла́, везли́	Past: повёз, повезло́, etc.

Indeterminate imperfective **вози́ть**:

Такси́ **е́здят** по го́роду и **во́зят** пассажи́ров.
Taxis drive about the city and transport passengers.

Determinate imperfective **везти́**:

Во́т **е́дет** пусто́е такси́; оно́ никого́ не **везёт.**
There goes an empty taxi; it's not carrying anybody.

Perfective **повезти́**:

Когда́ он **пое́дет** на ю́г, о́н **повезёт** с собо́й ста́рого отца́.
When he goes south, he will take his old father along.

Prefixed compounds of verbs of carrying. Like prefixed compounds of verbs of motion, the compounds of the verbs of carrying have *only two* forms: *imperfective* and *perfective*. Imperfectives are formed by adding a prefix to the imperfective *indeterminate;* perfectives by adding a prefix to the imperfective *determinate:*

	to bring	*to take/carry away*	*to take to*
(when walking)			
Imperf.	приноси́ть	уноси́ть	относи́ть
Perf.	принести́	унести́	отнести́
(when riding)			
Imperf.	привози́ть	увози́ть	отвози́ть
Perf.	привезти́	увезти́	отвезти́

The conjugation is the same as for the simple (non-prefixed) verbs:

Bringing

(*when walking*)

Imperfective *Inf.* приноси́ть		*Perfective* *Inf.* принести́	
Present		*Future*	
приношу́	прино́сим	принесу́	принесём
прино́сишь	прино́сите	принесёшь	принесёте
прино́сит	прино́сят	принесёт	принесу́т
Past		*Past*	
приноси́л, etc.		принёс, принесл.о́, -а́, -и́	

Bringing

(*when riding*)

Imperfective *Inf.* привози́ть		*Perfective* *Inf.* привезти́	
Present		*Future*	
привожу́	приво́зим	привезу́	привезём
приво́зишь	приво́зите	привезёшь	привезёте
приво́зит	приво́зят	привезёт	привезу́т
Past		*Past*	
привози́л, etc.		привёз, привезл.о́, -а́, -и́	

Ка́ждый ра́з, когда́ о́н **прихо́дит** к на́м, о́н на́м что́-нибудь **прино́сит.**
Every time he comes to see us he brings us something.

За́втра о́н **придёт** к на́м и **принесёт** на́м расска́зы Че́хова.
Tomorrow he will come to see us and will bring us Chekhov's stories.

Ка́ждый ра́з, когда́ о́н **приезжа́ет** из Пари́жа, о́н **приво́зит** игру́шки де́тям.
Every time he comes from Paris he brings toys for the children.

О́н **прие́дет** за́втра из Пари́жа и **привезёт** ва́м пода́рок.
Tomorrow he will arrive from Paris, and will bring you a present.

Compounds with **от-** have the meaning of to take (carry, drive, etc.) someone or something to a given place, invariably specified:

Отнеси́те э́ти таре́лки в ку́хню.
Take these plates to the kitchen.

Вы́ мо́жете **отвезти́** меня́ на вокза́л?
Can you drive (take) me to the station?

Compounds with **у-** simply mean "take away," with the place often unspecified:

Унеси́ э́ти гря́зные таре́лки отсю́да.
Take these dirty dishes away from here.

Носи́ть meaning "to wear." The indeterminate imperfective **носи́ть** has the secondary meaning "to wear" (habitually), "to wear around:"

Зимо́й я́ всегда́ **ношу́** тёплое пальто́.
I always wear a warm overcoat in winter.

Почему́ вы́ не **но́сите** шля́пы?
Why don't you wear a hat?

But: Почему́ вы́ не в но́вом пальто́?
Why aren't you wearing your new coat (now)?

Pattern Sentences

Носи́ть, нести́.

1. Студе́нты **хо́дят** из кла́сса в кла́сс и **но́сят** свои́ кни́ги.	1. The students go from class to class and carry their books.
2. Я́ уже́ два́ дня́ **ношу́** с собо́й э́то письмо́ и забыва́ю его́ посла́ть.	2. For two days I've been carrying this letter around and forgetting to mail it.
3. Во́т **идёт** стари́к и **несёт** тяжёлый паке́т. Бе́дный стари́к!	3. Here comes an old man carrying a heavy package. Poor old man!
4. —Куда́ ты́ **идёшь** и кому́ ты́ **несёшь** э́ти чу́дные цветы́? —Я́ **иду́** к Со́не и **несу́** ей э́тот буке́т.	4. —Where are you going and to whom are you taking those marvellous flowers? —I'm going to Sonya's and taking her this bouquet.
5. В понеде́льник, когда́ я́ **шёл** на по́чту, я́ встре́тил Лунёвых. Они́ то́же **шли́** туда́ и **несли́** посы́лки. О́н **нёс** две́ тяжёлых посы́лки, а она́ **несла́** одну́ лёгкую.	5. On Monday, when I was on my way to the post office, I met the Lunyovs. They were going there too and were carrying packages. He was carrying two heavy packages and she was carrying one light one.
6. Ле́том де́вушки **но́сят** све́тлые пла́тья.	6. In summer girls wear light-colored dresses.

Drill

Replace the blank by the correct form of the verb.

1. Я́ ви́дел О́льгу на у́лице. Она́ ...... цветы́.
2. Она́ ра́ньше всегда́ ...... с собо́й мно́го де́нег.
3. О́н тепе́рь ча́сто ...... тяжёлые паке́ты.
4. Я́ не зна́ю, куда́ он шёл и что́ о́н ....
5. Я́ не люблю́ ...... с собо́й мно́го кни́г, но́ иногда́ я́ и́х ....
6. Мы́ ...... э́ти кни́ги в библиоте́ку.

Pattern Sentences

A. **Приноси́ть, принести́, etc.**

1. Ка́ждый ра́з, когда́ они́ **прихо́дят** к на́м, они́ на́м что́-нибудь **прино́сят.**	1. Every time they come to see us they bring us something.
2. Когда́ я́ **прихожу́** к ни́м, я́ всегда́ что́-нибудь и́м **приношу́.**	2. When I go to see them, I always take them something.
3. Я́ бу́ду **приходи́ть** к ва́м ка́ждое у́тро и бу́ду **приноси́ть** ва́м газе́ту.	3. I shall come to see you every morning and shall bring you a paper.
4. Я́ не зна́ю, **придёт** ли о́н во вто́рник и **принесёт** ли о́н пласти́нку, кото́рую о́н обеща́л. Наде́юсь, что о́н не забу́дет её **принести́.**	4. I don't know if he'll come on Tuesday and bring the record which he promised. I hope he won't forget to bring it.
5. —Что́ вы́ **принесли́?** —Я́ **принёс** две́ буты́лки вина́, а Со́ня **принесла́** всё, что ну́жно к обе́ду.	5. —What have you brought? —I've brought two bottles of wine, and Sonya has brought everything we need for dinner.
6. **Уйди́** отсю́да и **унеси́** отсю́да все́ твои́ игру́шки!	6. Get out of here and take all your toys!
7. **Отнеси́** и́х в де́тскую и́ли в ку́хню, куда́ хо́чешь, и игра́й та́м!	7. Take them to the nursery or the kitchen, wherever you like, and play there!

B. **Вози́ть/везти́; привози́ть/привезти́, etc.**

1. Поезда́ **во́зят** пассажи́ров. Они́ **во́зят** и́х на се́вер, на ю́г, на восто́к и на за́пад.	1. Trains carry passengers. They carry them north, south, east, and west.
2. Андре́й **е́дет** на Сре́дний Восто́к и **везёт** с собо́й свою́ семью́. О́н ещё никогда́ не́ был на восто́ке.	2. Andrey is going to the Middle East and is taking his family with him. He has never yet been in the East.
3. Я́ ча́сто **е́зжу** на ю́г и **вожу́** туда́ свою́ до́чь. Моя́ ма́ть живёт на ю́ге. Она́ лю́бит ю́жный кли́мат.	3. I often go south and take my daughter there. My mother lives in the South. She likes the southern climate.

4. Пя́ть дне́й в неде́лю я́ у́тром **отвожу́** дете́й в шко́лу, а ве́чером **привожу́** и́х из шко́лы домо́й. — 4. In the morning, five days a week, I take the children to school, and in the evening I bring them home from school.

5. Когда́ я́ **вёз** и́х вчера́, начался́ до́ждь, и я́ бы́стро **привёз** и́х домо́й. — 5. When I took them yesterday, it started to rain, and I brought them home at once.

6. Моя́ сестра́ **прие́хала** из За́падной Герма́нии и **привезла́** на́м все́м пода́рки. — 6. My sister came from Western Germany and brought us all presents.

7. Ка́ждый ра́з, когда́ она́ **приезжа́ет** отту́да, она́ на́м что́-нибудь **приво́зит.** — 7. Every time she comes from there she brings us something.

8. Когда́ вы́ **прие́дете** из Кры́ма, пожа́луйста, **привези́те** на́м фотогра́фию ва́шей семьи́. — 8. When you come from the Crimea, please bring us a photograph of your family.

9. Когда́ вы́ **пое́дете** на вокза́л, пожа́луйста, **отвези́те** туда́ э́тот чемода́н. — 9. When you drive to the station, please take this suitcase there.

10. Они́ уе́хали на Кавка́з и увезли́ туда́ все́ свои́ ве́щи. — 10. They went off to the Caucasus and and took all their things there.

Drills

A. *Choose the correct word in parentheses and give the correct form.*

1. Куда́ вы́ е́хали сего́дня и куда́ вы́ (вози́ть/везти́) дете́й в во́семь часо́в утра́?
2. —Вы́ ча́сто (вози́ть/везти́) дете́й к мо́рю в про́шлом году́? —Да́, мо́й му́ж ча́сто и́х (вози́ть/везти́).
3. Бори́с е́хал на автомоби́ле и (вози́ть/везти́) куда́-то свою́ ма́ть.
4. —Почему́ ты́ всегда́ (носи́ть/нести́) с собо́й э́тот тяжёлый портфе́ль? —Я́ ре́дко его́ (носи́ть/нести́).
5. Зо́я, что́ ты́ (носи́ть/нести́), и что́ (носи́ть/нести́) Бори́с, когда́ я́ ва́с встре́тил?
6. Я́ не ви́жу, что́ о́н (носи́ть/нести́).
7. Через полчаса́ я́ (относи́ть/отнести́) кни́ги в библиоте́ку.
8. Пожа́луйста, (относи́ть/отнести́) молоко́ на ку́хню.
9. Е́сли вы́ е́дете на вокза́л, (отвози́ть/отвезти́) меня́ туда́.
10. Я́ тепе́рь ка́ждый де́нь (отвози́ть/отвезти́) дете́й в шко́лу.
11. Ра́ньше о́н всегда́ (привози́ть/привезти́) на́м что́-нибудь из загран́ицы.
12. О́н обеща́л, что когда́ о́н вернётся, о́н что́-нибудь на́м (привози́ть/привезти́).
13. Вчера́ о́н прие́хал и ничего́ на́м не (привози́ть/привезти́).
14. Когда́ я́ верну́сь из Пари́жа, я́ ва́м что́-нибудь (привози́ть/привезти́).
15. За́втра о́н придёт к обе́ду и (приноси́ть/принести́) вино́.
16. Когда́ о́н прихо́дит к обе́ду, о́н всегда́ что́-нибудь (приноси́ть/принести́).
17. Ива́н уе́хал в Кры́м и (увози́ть/увезти́) с собо́й все́ свои́ кни́ги.

B. *Give the correct form of the verb compound:* (**при-, у-, от-**) **-носи́ть, -нести́**; **-вози́ть, -везти́.**

1. О́н обеща́л, что придёт за́втра и ...... свою́ статью́.
2. О́н пришёл, но́ ничего́ не ......
3. Приходи́ к на́м за́втра и ...... на́м твою́ статью́.
4. Е́сли ты́ е́дешь на автомоби́ле, ты́ мо́жешь ...... э́тот паке́т на по́чту.
5. Е́сли я́ пое́ду на автомоби́ле, я́ ...... паке́т на по́чту.
6. О́н обеща́л ...... мне́ из Пари́жа мо́дное пла́тье.
7. Приезжа́й к на́м в дере́вню и ...... твою́ сестру́.
8. Я́ прие́ду к ва́м в понеде́льник и ...... сестру́.
9. Я́ наде́юсь, что она́ ско́ро уе́дет отсю́да и ...... своего́ сы́на.
10. Она́ уе́хала и ...... сы́на.
11. Мы́ ...... ва́м из Евро́пы что́-нибудь интере́сное.
12. Что́ я́ могу́ ва́м ...... из Ме́ксики? ...... мне́ пожа́луйста мексика́нскую ва́зу.

6. Verbs of leading

Like other unprefixed verbs of motion, the basic verb denoting leading has two imperfectives: *indeterminate* and *determinate.*

to lead, take, bring (*a person or an animal*)

	Indeterminate Imperfective	*Determinate Imperfective*	*Perfective*
	Present		*Future*
	води́ть	**вести́**	**повести́**
	вожу́[6]	веду́	поведу́
	во́дишь, etc.	ведёшь, etc.	поведёшь, etc.
Past:	води́л, etc.	Past: вёл, вел.о́, -а́, -и́	Past: повёл, повел.о́, -а́, -и́

Indeterminate imperfective **води́ть:**

Она́ ка́ждый де́нь **во́дит** своего́ ма́ленького сы́на в па́рк.
Every day she takes her little son to the park.

Determinate imperfective **вести́:**

Она́ **шла́** по у́лице и **вела́** за́ руку своего́ ма́ленького сы́на.
She was walking along the street leading her young son by the hand.

Compounds with **при-, у-, от-,** etc. have only a single imperfective (formed from the *indeterminate* imperfective) and a perfective (formed from the *determinate* imperfective). The meaning is analogous to the compounds of **носи́ть/нести́** and **вози́ть/везти́:**

Imperfective:

Она́ лю́бит **приводи́ть** домо́й все́х свои́х подру́г.
She likes to bring all her friends home.

[6] This form coincides with the first person singular of **вози́ть,** "to transport."

Perfective:

Óн **пришёл** к нáм и **привёл** своегó млáдшего брáта.
He came to see us and brought his younger brother.

These verbs have many abstract idiomatic meanings, *e.g.*, **вести́ войну́,** to carry on war; **вести́ разговóр,** to carry on a conversation; **проводи́ть/провести́ врéмя, лéто,** to spend time, the summer, etc.

Pattern Sentences

1. Внýчка **вóдит** тепéрь кáждый дéнь свою́ бáбушку в пáрк погуля́ть.	1. The granddaughter takes her grandmother to the park every day now for a walk.
2. Зимóй, когдá внýчка рабóтала, онá **води́ла** бáбушку в пáрк тóлько двá рáза в недéлю.	2. In winter, when the granddaughter was working, she took her grandmother to the park only twice a week.
3. Я́ ви́дел, как онá **велá** её тудá сегóдня рáно ýтром.	3. I saw her taking her there early this morning.
4. Ни́на, **уведи́** детéй отсю́да; они́ ужáсно шумя́т! **Отведи́** и́х в дéтскую.	4. Nina, take the children away (from here); they're making a terrible noise! Take them to the children's room.
5. Вчерá вéчером Лунёв **пришёл** к чáю и **привёл** свою́ сестрý.	5. Last evening Lunyov came to tea and brought his sister.

Some additional comments on verbs of motion. Observe that all the above verbs belonging to the *indeterminate imperfective* series of unprefixed verbs of motion are second conjugation: **ходи́ть, éздить, носи́ть, вози́ть, води́ть.** They all have consonant mutations in the first person singular: хожý, éзжу, ношý, вожý, вожý. All except **éздить** have shifting stress in the present.

The corresponding members of the *determinate imperfective* series are first conjugation (consonant stems): **идти́, éхать, нести́, везти́, вести́.** All of their infinitives end in **-ти́** (except **éхать**). The past tenses must be learned specially: **шёл (шло), нёс (неслó), вёз (везлó), вёл (велó);** only **éхал** is formed regularly.

Simple *perfectives* which do not specify direction are formed with **по-** and the *determinate* imperfective, *e.g.*, they are conjugated like the determinate imperfective except that their "present" tense form has future meaning. All of them may have an inchoative meaning, *i.e.*, the *beginning* of the going, carrying, or leading is emphasized. This inchoative meaning is especially marked with **понести́, повезти́,** and **повести́. Пойти́** and **поéхать** may or may not emphasize beginning action, e.g.:

Пóезд вдрýг **пошёл.**	The train suddenly started.
Óн взя́л чемодáн и **понёс** егó.	He took the suitcase and started to carry it.

7. Translation of "to take" and "to bring"

As has been seen, "to take" is very often rendered in Russian by an appropriate verb of carrying or leading. This is the case when something or someone is to be moved from one place to another:

Унеси́те э́ти кни́ги.
Take these books away.

Отнеси́те и́х куда́ хоти́те.
Take them wherever you wish.

Отведи́те э́того господи́на в его́ ко́мнату.
Take this gentleman to his room.

With **брать/взять** the emphasis is rather on taking something to use it:

Я́ **взя́л** э́ту кни́гу у Бори́са.
I took that book from Boris.

Я́ **взя́л** э́ту кни́гу в библиоте́ке.
I took the book at (from) the library.

In these two sentences Boris or the library functions as a source of supply; the emphasis is not on moving the book from place to place, but on having it available to read.

Learn the idiom **бра́ть/взя́ть с собо́й,** "to take along:"

Вы́ **взя́ли с собо́й** портфе́ль?
Did you take your briefcase along (with you)?

Принима́ть/приня́ть is used in some expressions equivalent to English phrases with "take:"

п. уча́стие (в + locative)	to take part in
п. ва́нну	to take a bath
п. лека́рство	to take medicine

"To bring" corresponds to a verb of carrying, or leading, with the prefix **при-**:

Принеси́те вино́; у на́с не́т вина́. Bring . . . .
Привези́ мне́ что́-нибудь из Пари́жа. Bring. . . .
Приведи́те к на́м ва́шу до́чь; мы́ хоти́м с не́й познако́миться. Bring . . . .

Drill

Translate the words in parentheses.

1. Вади́м (brought) стака́н молока́ из ку́хни.
2. Вади́м (brought) ва́м что́-то из Ита́лии.

3. Я́ (shall bring) тебе́ газе́ту на вера́нду.
4. Я́ (shall bring) тебе́ за́втра цветы́ из дере́вни.
5. О́льга (brought) подру́гу к обе́ду.
6. Она́ всегда́ (brings) кого́-нибудь к обе́ду.
7. (Take) э́ту кни́гу в библиоте́ку.
8. (Take) э́тот чемода́н на вокза́л.
9. Ма́ма (took) посу́ду в столо́вую.
10. Кто́ (took) моё пальто́?
11. Я́ (shall take) за́втра автомоби́ль Ива́на.

8. Prepositions of position and motion

A. Position.

(1) *Prepositions with the locative case.*

в

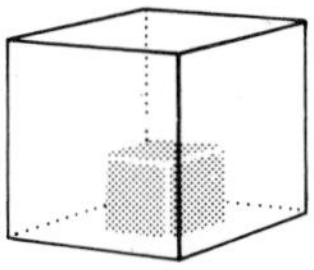

Position 1

на

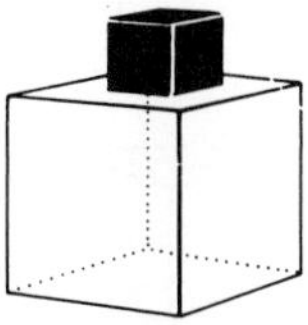

Position 2

(2) *Prepositions with the instrumental case.*

над

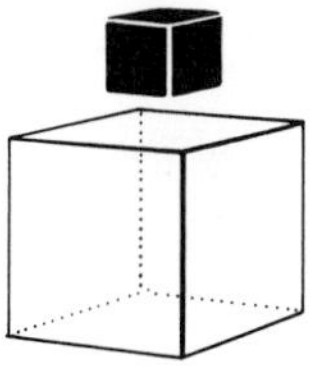

Position 3

под

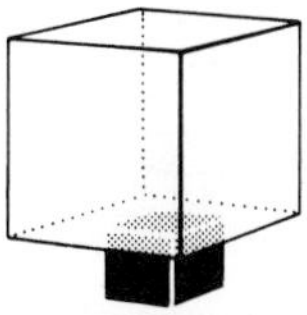

Position 4

перед

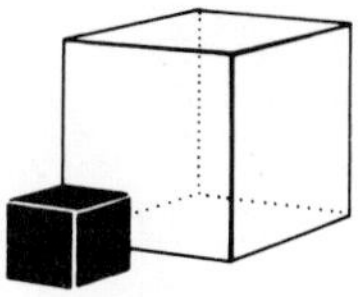

Position 5

за

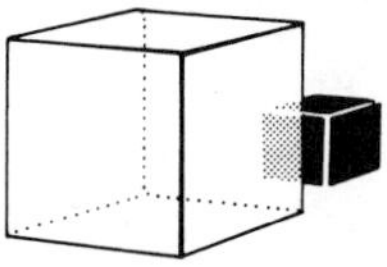

Position 6

ме́жду

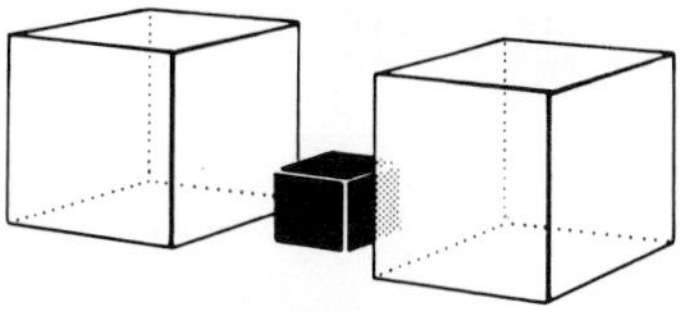

Position 7

(3) *Prepositions with the genitive case.* Prepositions of location governing the genitive describe proximity or closeness, but do not specify exact position.

Immediate proximity is indicated by **у**. **О́коло** is used to denote any position "nearby," "in the neighborhood." **Вокру́г** is used in reference to a circle going around some object.

у

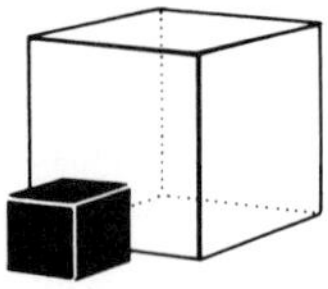

Position 8a

о́коло

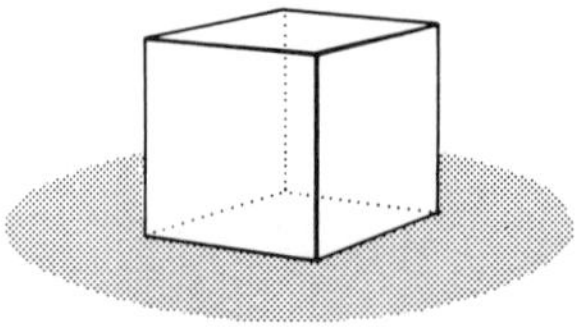

Position 8b

вокру́г

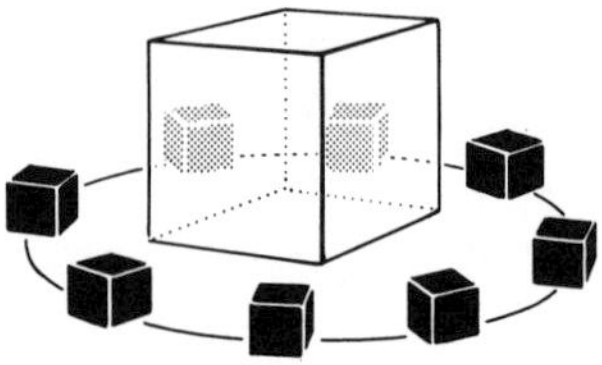

Position 8c

B. Motion.

(1) *Moving into position.* The positions described above will now be considered as goals of motion: moving into position in, on, at, etc. The number of each diagram refers to the number of the corresponding diagrams in Section A above.

	Motion	*Position Reached*
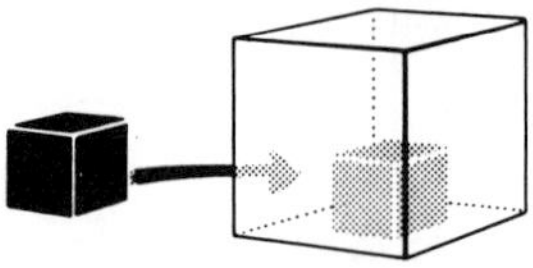	Position 1 **в** + acc.	**в** + loc.
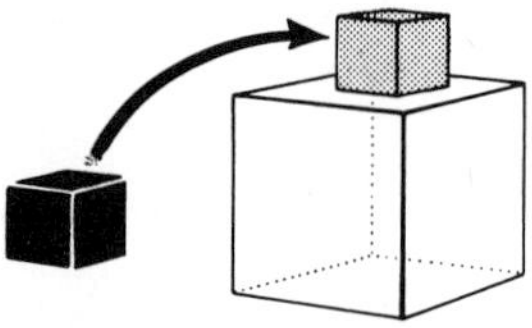	Position 2 **на** + acc.	**на** + loc.
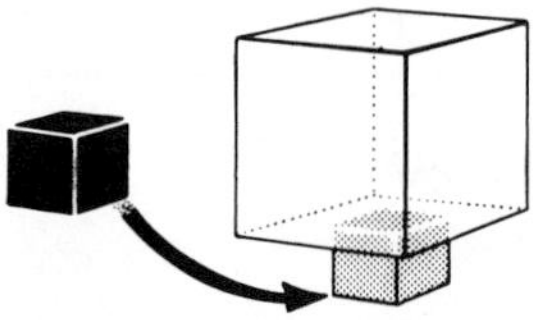	Position 4 **под** + acc.	**под** + instr.
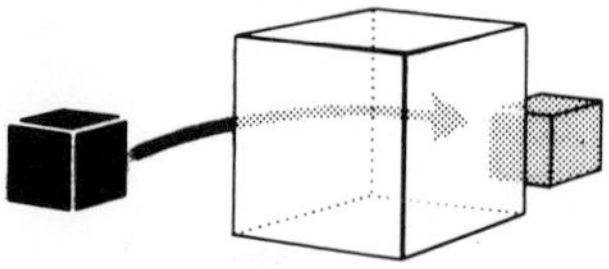	Position 6 **за** + acc.	**за** + instr.

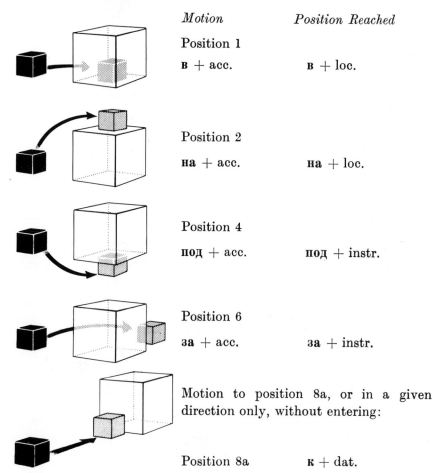

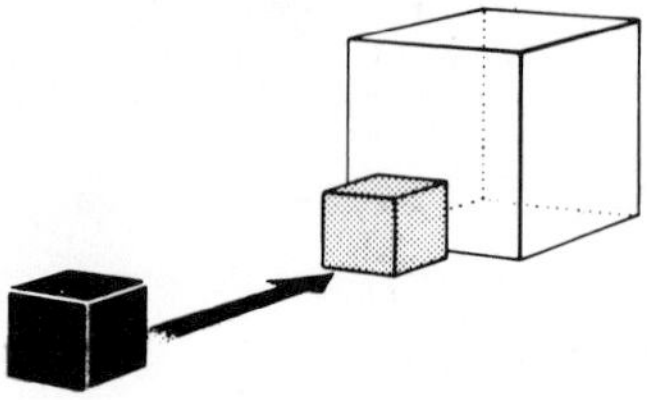

Motion to position 8a, or in a given direction only, without entering:

Position 8a **к** + dat.

Prepositions of Position

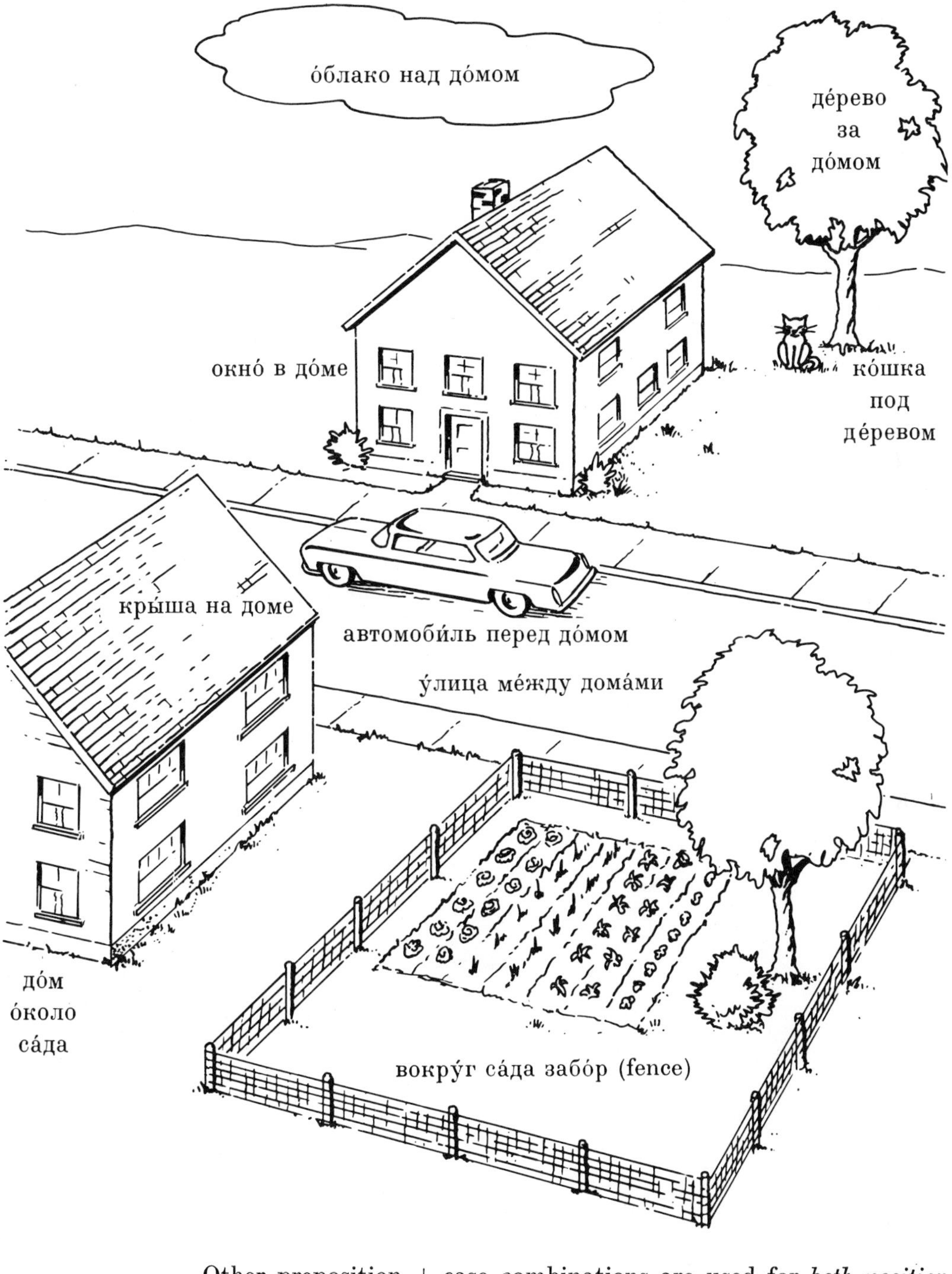

Other preposition + case combinations are used for *both position and motion* into position: **над, перед,** and **ме́жду** + instrumental; and **о́коло** and **вокру́г** + genitive.

(2) *Moving away from or out of position.* For motion away from or out of something, the following prepositions are used, all governing the genitive:

Position	*Moving out of Position*	
в + loc. (Pos. 1)	**из**	+ gen.
на + loc. (Pos. 2)	**с**	
под + instr. (Pos. 4)	**из-под**	
за + instr. (Pos. 6)	**из-за**	
у + gen. (Pos. 8)	**от**	

Most important are the three series:

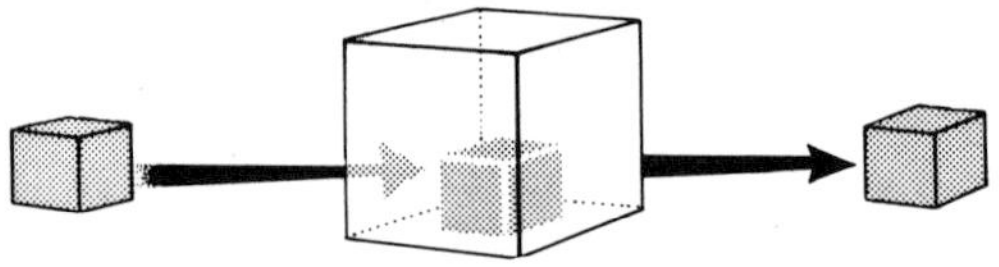

(a)	**в** + acc. Moving to Position 1	**в** + loc. Position 1	**из** + gen. Moving from Position 1

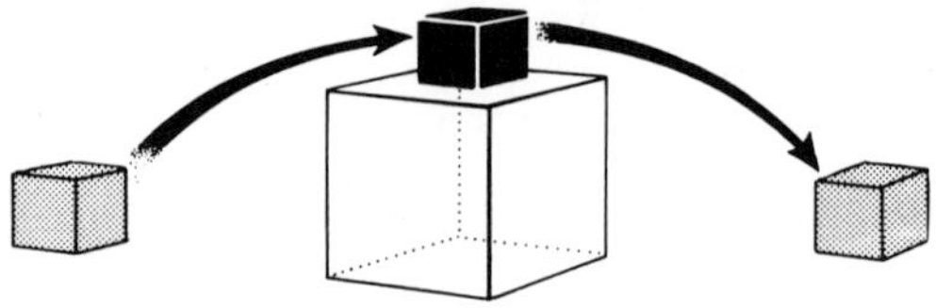

(b)	**на** + acc. Moving to Position 2	**на** + loc. Position 2	**с** + gen. Moving from Position 2

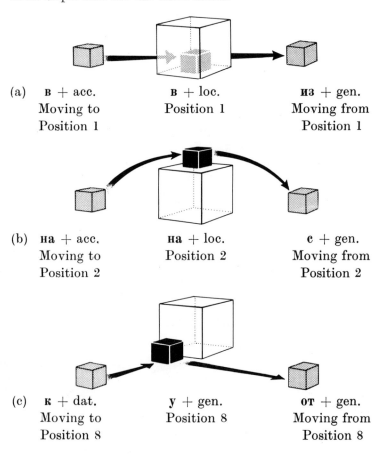

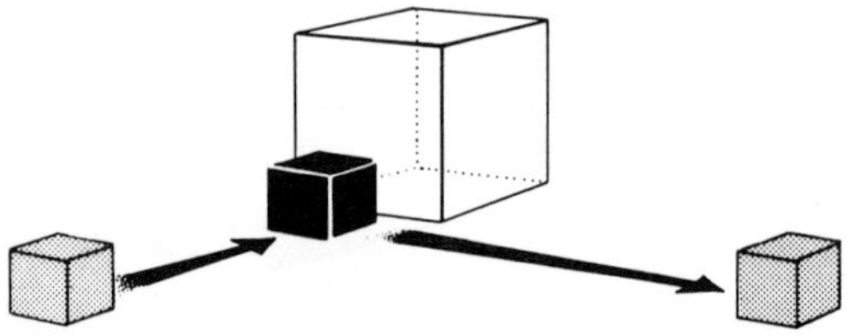

(c)	**к** + dat. Moving to Position 8	**у** + gen. Position 8	**от** + gen. Moving from Position 8

(3) *Movement other than into or out of position.*

(a) **Через** + accusative: across, through, via

(b) **По** + dative: motion within a space not directed to any goal (walking back and forth in a room, strolling in a city, a park, etc.). This is also used to denote motion (which may or may not have a direction) *along* a road, street, by a stream, etc.

(4) *Expression of limits* (*in space or time*).

от ... до	from ... to (space or time)
с ... до	from ... to (time; see Unit 26)

All these prepositions take the genitive.

Prepositions of Motion

3. Óн идёт че-рез плóщадь.

4. Óн прохóдит ми́мо цéркви.

5. Óн подхóдит к рестора́ну и вхóдит в рестора́н.

2. Óн пьёт ча́й у дру́га и разгова́ривает с дру́гом. Потóм óн ухóдит от дру́га. Óн идёт по у́лице, и выхóдит на плóщадь.

6. Óн сади́тся на сту́л (за стóл) и éст. Потóм óн пла́тит, встаёт со сту́ла, идёт к двéри и выхóдит из рестора́на.

1. Ива́нов идёт к дру́гу.

7. Потóм óн гуля́ет по па́рку.

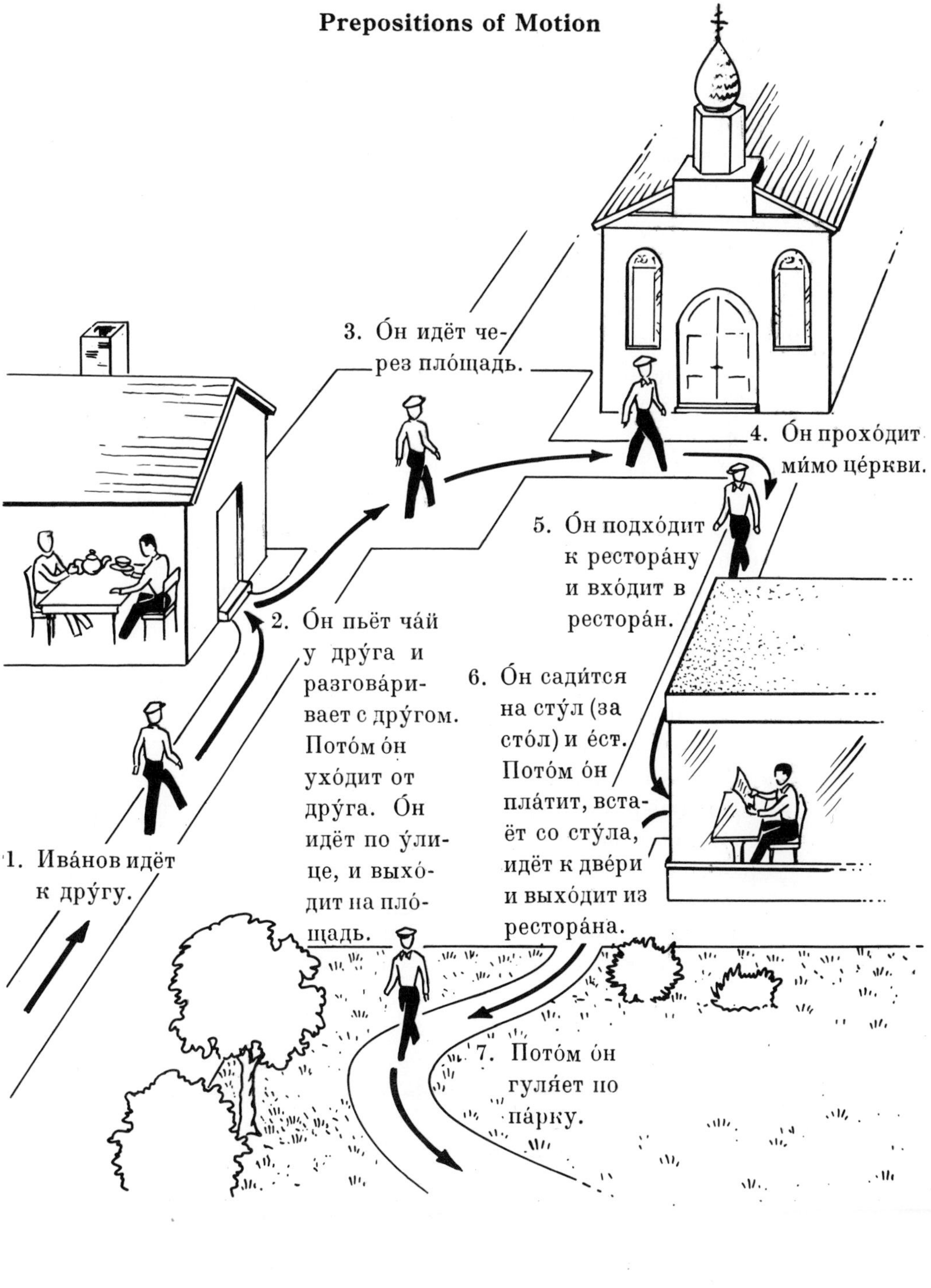

READING

На остано́вке авто́буса

Я́ стоя́л на углу́ гла́вной у́лицы и жда́л авто́буса «А». По гла́вной у́лице всегда́ хо́дят то́лпы люде́й. Одни́ несу́т в рука́х портфе́ли и́ли су́мки, други́е несу́т паке́ты, не́которые веду́т за́ руку дете́й.

Я́ стоя́л и жда́л, а лю́ди проходи́ли ми́мо. Они́ ходи́ли из магази́на в магази́н, заходи́ли в апте́ки и рестора́ны. К гости́нице подъезжа́ли такси́, и из такси́ выходи́ли лю́ди со свои́ми чемода́нами. Одни́ входи́ли в гости́ницу, а други́е выходи́ли из гости́ницы, сади́лись в такси́ и уезжа́ли. Не́которые покупа́ли газе́ты и спо́рили о после́дних полити́ческих новостя́х, и́ли о футбо́льном ма́тче ме́жду туре́цкой кома́ндой и сове́тской кома́ндой «Локомоти́в.» Одни́ серди́лись, други́е смея́лись, не́которые покупа́ли цветы́, кото́рые на друго́м углу́ продава́ла то́лстая стару́ха в платке́.

На э́той у́лице всегда́ мо́жно встре́тить знако́мых. Во́т по друго́й стороне́ идёт Лунёв со свое́й сестро́й Лизаве́той. О́н несёт како́й-то тяжёлый паке́т. Вероя́тно, о́н несёт на по́чту посы́лку для племя́нницы, кото́рая живёт в ма́леньком селе́ в Восто́чной Сиби́ри.

А во́т идёт Ве́ра Васи́льевна с како́й-то стару́шкой,[7] кото́рая несёт небольшо́й чемода́н. Е́сли не ошиба́юсь, э́то тётка инжене́ра Ма́слова, кото́рый неда́вно у́мер. Ве́ра Васи́льевна что́-то о́чень энерги́чно е́й объясня́ет. Куда́ она́ ведёт э́ту стару́шку с печа́льным лицо́м? Вероя́тно на вокза́л. Они́ прохо́дят ми́мо меня́, но́ сла́ва Бо́гу, меня́ не замеча́ют.

Како́й-то молодо́й челове́к с бородо́й, кото́рый нёс портфе́ль, подошёл ко мне́ и спроси́л, не зна́ю ли я́ кото́рый ча́с? Я́ сказа́л ему́, и о́н пошёл да́льше. Кто́ э́тот молодо́й ге́ний? Поэ́т? Писа́тель? Чита́ет ли кто́-нибудь его́ про́зу и́ли его́ поэ́зию? Е́сть ли у него́ де́ньги на обе́д? Что́ о́н нёс в своём портфе́ле? Мо́жет быть како́й-нибудь замеча́тельный рома́н, кото́рый сде́лает его́ знамени́тым. А мо́жет быть о́н тала́нтливый учёный и сде́лал како́е-нибудь ва́жное откры́тие, и я́ ско́ро уви́жу его́ портре́т на пе́рвых страни́цах газе́т?

Ми́мо меня́ прошла́ молода́я де́вушка. Она́ несла́ в руке́ ма́ленький буке́т. Она́ о́чень спеши́ла. Её кто́-то жда́л. А что́ е́сли э́тот «кто́-то» до́лго жда́л и ушёл, и тепе́рь они́ бо́льше никогда́ не уви́дятся? Како́ печа́льный коне́ц!

[7] Стару́шка, diminutive of стару́ха.

К останóвке, гдé я́ стоя́л, оди́н за други́м подъезжáли автó-бусы: «Б,» «К,» «П,» всé крóме «А,» тогó, котóрого я́ ждáл! Автó-бусы остана́вливались. Они́ привози́ли и увози́ли пассажи́ров. Одни́ пассажи́ры выходи́ли из автóбусов, други́е входи́ли в ни́х, и автóбусы éхали дáльше. Одни́ везли́ пассажи́ров на ю́г, други́е везли́ и́х на сéвер, на зáпад, на востóк.

Пошёл дóждь. Я́ всё стоя́л[8] и ждáл своегó автóбуса. Я́ стоя́л под дождём и дýмал о рáзных вещáх: откýда, напримéр, мóй автóбус знáет, что я́ егó ждý и поэ́тому не спеши́т за мнóй при-éхать? Ктó всé э́ти лю́ди, котóрые хóдят по э́той ýлице, подхóдят к витри́нам, вхóдят в магази́ны, нóсят покýпки, сýмки, портфéли? Откýда они́ пришли́ и кудá пойдýт отсю́да? Ждёт ли и́х ктó-нибудь дóма?

Нó гдé же мóй автóбус? Чтó с ни́м случи́лось?

Вóн тáм, перед витри́ной какóго-то магази́на, стои́т высóкая молодáя жéнщина с собáчкой. Онá мнé нрáвится. Онá смóтрит на каки́е-то вéщи в витри́не. Хóчет ли онá чтó-нибудь купи́ть, и́ли прóсто смóтрит? Вóт онá вхóдит в магази́н и через нéкоторое врéмя выхóдит оттýда с покýпками. Онá перехóдит ýлицу и подхóдит к другóй витри́не. Онá останови́лась на минýту у витри́ны и вошлá в магази́н. Éсть ли у неё мýж? Чéм óн занимá-ется? Óн вероя́тно занимáет вáжное положéние и, вероя́тно, óн óчень занятóй человéк, а онá, мóжет быть, цéлый дéнь бывáет однá? Лю́бит ли óн её? Éсть ли у ни́х дéти? Какóй у неё гóлос? Какóго цвéта её кóмната? Éсли онá поéдет на автóбусе, подойдёт ли онá к останóвке, гдé я́ стою́, и ся́дет ли онá в тóт же автóбус что я́?

Жéнщина вы́шла из магази́на, останови́ла такси́ и уéхала. Я́ бóльше никогдá её не уви́жу!

Óколо меня́ стоя́л какóй-то стари́к. Я́ егó рáньше не замéтил. Я́ сказáл емý, что я́ ужé полчасá ждý автóбуса «А.» Стари́к посмотрéл на меня́ с удивлéнием и сказáл, что проéхало нéсколько автóбусов «А», и óн не понимáет, кáк я́ мóг и́х не ви́деть.

Читáйте э́ти вопрóсы и отвечáйте на ни́х.

1. Чтó я́ дéлал на глáвной ýлице? 2. Расскажи́те, чтó дéлают лю́ди на большóй центрáльной ýлице? 3. Расскажи́те о тóм, каки́х знакóмых я́ тáм ви́дел и чтó они́ дéлали? 4. Опиши́те (describe) молодóго человéка, котóрый ко мнé подошёл, чтó óн нёс, чтó я́ о нём дýмал. 5. Расскажи́те о дéвушке, котóрая прошлá ми́мо меня́. 6. Чтó я́ дýмал о моём автóбусе? 7. Ктó мнé понрá-вился? 8. Чтó я́ хотéл знáть про э́ту жéнщину? 9. Почемý я́ не замéтил своегó автóбуса?

[8] Я́ всё стоя́л, I kept standing.

EXERCISE

Переведите на русский.

1. I am going to the North and am taking my family there. 2. We shall live in the North for a year. 3. Our doctor told our granddaughter that she may not go out yet. 4. When you go out, please shut the window. 5. The old woman entered the room and came up to me. 6. —Who was that tall young man who approached you on the street? —It was my grandson. 7. I shall go into the house; it is raining. 8. When I come to see you on Tuesday, I'll bring you the latest magazines. 9. He came from the West and brought a nice toy for our little son. 10. Hello, Vanya! Where are you going and what are you carrying? 11. I am going to my grandmother's and am taking her apples and candies. 12. Our grandson came for us, and we went together to the opera. 13. She used to drop in on us quite often. 14. Yesterday she dropped in for a few minutes and brought her niece and her nephew. 15. My husband was walking along our street and found a watch. 16. I never find anything. 17. When I go to school I usually go through the park. 18. I will cross the street at the corner. 19. I don't know if my nephew is bringing me anything from Northern Italy. 20. —Why does this scientist always carry his briefcase with him? —I didn't notice it. 21. My niece, who lives in the South, never wears hats. 22. It began to rain; I stopped a taxi, the taxi stopped, I got (went) in and went home.

VOCABULARY

буке́т bouquet
***витри́на** shop window
внук grandson
вну́ч.ка (*gen. pl.* **-ек**) granddaughter
вон over there (at a rather great distance)
восто́к east
восто́чный eastern, oriental
***де́тская** (*adj. used as noun*) children's room, nursery
занято́й busy, occupied
за́пад west
за́падный western
игру́ш.ка (*gen. pl.* **-ек**) toy, plaything
***кома́нда** team
матч match, game
остано́в.ка (*gen. pl.* **-ок**) stop (bus)
паке́т package
пассажи́р, *fem.* **-ка** passenger
печа́льный sad
плат.о́к (*gen. sing.* **-ка́**) kerchief, shawl, handkerchief
племя́нник nephew
племя́нница niece
поку́п.ка (*gen. pl.* **-ок**) purchase
полчаса́ half an hour
портре́т portrait, picture
портфе́ль (*masc.*) briefcase
посы́л.ка (*gen. pl.* **-ок**) parcel, package

се́вер north
се́верный northern
село́ (*nom. pl.* **сёла,** *gen. pl.* **сёл**) village, town
сре́дний middle, center, average
стари́к old man
стару́ха old woman
су́м.ка (*gen. pl.* **-ок**) bag, purse
толпа́ crowd
***туре́цкий** Turkish
удивле́ние surprise, amazement
учёный scholarly, scientific; (*adj. used as noun*) scholar, scientist
фотоаппара́т camera
чемода́н suitcase
юг south
ю́жный southern
энерги́чный energetic
я́блок.о (*nom. pl.* **-и,** *gen. pl.* **я́блок**) apple

Verbs

замеча́ть (imperf., I), **заме́тить** (perf., II: **заме́.чу, -тишь**) to notice, observe
занима́ть (imperf., I), **заня́ть** (perf., I: **займ.у́, -ёшь;** past: **за́нял, -о, заняла́, за́няли**) to occupy
находи́ть (imperf., II: **нахожу́, нахо́дишь**), **найти́** (perf., I: **найд.у́, -ёшь;** past: **нашёл, нашло́,** etc.) to find
находи́ться to be located
ода́лживать (imperf., I), **одолжи́ть** (perf., II: **одолжу́, одо́лжишь**) to lend
ока́нчивать (imperf., I), **око́нчить** (perf., II: **око́нчу, око́нчишь**) to finish, graduate
оставля́ть (imperf., I), **оста́вить** (perf., II: **оста́в.лю, -ишь**) to leave (*trans.*)
остана́вливать (imperf., I), **останови́ть** (perf., II: **остан.овлю́, -о́вишь**) to stop (*trans.*)
остана́вливаться, останови́ться to stop (*intrans.*)
ошиба́ться (imperf., I), **ошиби́ться** (perf., I: **ошиб.у́сь, -ёшься;** past: **оши́бся, оши́блась,** etc.) to make a mistake, be mistaken
серди́ться (imperf., II: **сержу́сь, се́рдишься**), **рассерди́ться** (perf., II) to get angry (**на** + *acc.*) at
теря́ть (imperf., I), **потеря́ть** (perf., I) to lose

Expressions

с собо́й with oneself, along
на се́вер, на ю́г, на восто́к, на за́пад (to the) north, south, east, west
на се́вере, на ю́ге, на восто́ке, на за́паде in the north, south, east, west
из-за грани́цы from abroad
за́ руку by the hand
Начался́ до́ждь. / **Пошёл до́ждь.** It began to rain.

Vocabulary Review

Семья́-Family

па́па	сын (pl. сыновья́)	двою́родный бра́т	cousin	внук, вну́чка
ма́ма	дочь (pl. до́чери)	двою́родная сестра́	cousin	дя́дя
оте́ц (pl. отцы́)	брат (pl. бра́тья)	де́душка		тётя
мать (pl. ма́тери)	сестра́ (pl. сёстры)	ба́бушка		племя́нник
				племя́нница

UNIT 23

GRAMMAR

1. Short forms of adjectives

Adjectives in Russian, as in English, have two uses, the attributive and the predicative. The adjective is used attributively in:

> В на́шем го́роде е́сть **краси́вые** зда́ния.
> In our town there are *beautiful* buildings.

It is used predicatively in:

> Э́ти зда́ния о́чень **краси́вые.**
> These buildings *are* very *beautiful.*

Most Russian adjectives have special forms known as *short* or *predicative*, which are used when an adjective plays the part of a predicate. The short (predicative) form is mandatory for certain adjectives when they are used predicatively; it is merely optional for many others.

A. Forms of short adjectives. Short adjectives have the following endings:

Masc.:	*zero* instead of **-ый/-ий/-о́й:**	краси́в, хоро́ш, мо́лод.
Neut.:	**-о** instead of **-ое/-ее:**	краси́во, хорошо́, мо́лодо.
Fem.:	**-а** instead of **-ая:**	краси́ва, хороша́, молода́.
Pl.:	**-ы/-и** instead of **-ые/-ие:**	краси́вы, хороши́, мо́лоды.

Note that shifts of stress are frequent with short forms. Common are stress shifts to the ending, particularly in the feminine singular.

Only one predicate adjective has a soft stem: син**ь**, си́н**е**, син**я́**, си́н**и**.

The masculine short form is a base stem form. The stem of a number of adjectives ends in a consonantal cluster, and many of these adjectives insert a vowel **е** or **о** in the masculine short form:

интере́сн.ый	интере́с**ен**	у́мн.ый	ум**ё**н
холо́дн.ый	хо́лод**ен**	лёгк.ий	лёг**о**к etc.
больн.о́й	бо́л**ен**		

Since short adjectives are used only as predicatives, they agree with the subject of the sentence and therefore occur in the *nominative* case *only*.

B. Optional use of the short forms. The following illustrates the optional use of the short form:

> Э́тот па́рк о́чень **краси́вый** or (short form) **краси́в.**
> Э́то зда́ние о́чень **краси́вое** or (short form) **краси́во.**
> Э́та це́рковь о́чень **краси́вая** or (short form) **краси́ва.**
> Э́ти цветы́ о́чень **краси́вые** or (short form) **краси́вы.**

It is not possible to give any hard and fast rules for the choice between the long and the short (predicative) form for an adjective used predicatively. One may observe, however, that:

(1) The short forms generally suggest a more formal style, while the long ones are more colloquial, and are used more frequently.

(2) The short forms are often preferred when the adjective does not denote a permanent, intrinsic quality, but one that appears only as temporary, or limited to certain circumstances, or present if some special point of view is taken, a special purpose considered, etc.

> И́х са́д бы́л о́чень **краси́в** весно́й. (Time)
> О́н тогда́ бы́л **мо́лод.** (Time)
> Э́ти цветы́ бу́дут **краси́вы** на столе́ в на́шей гости́ной. (Circumstance)
> О́н **мо́лод** для э́той ро́ли. (Purpose)
> О́н **ста́р** для э́той рабо́ты. (Purpose)

The adjectives ма́ленький (small) and большо́й (large) lack short forms. The short forms of ма́лый (small) and вели́кий (great) are often used instead in the sense of "too small" or "too big" for a particular purpose:

> Хотя́ э́та кварти́ра не **ма́ленькая,** но́ она́ **мала́** для на́с.
> Э́тот костю́м мне́ **вели́к.**

The neuter short form of the adjective also serves as the adverb:

Adverb:

О́н **свобо́дно** говори́т по-ру́сски.
He speaks Russian *freely* (*fluently*).

Predicate adjective:

Э́то ме́сто **свобо́дно.**
This seat is *free* (*not taken*).

Many adjectives lack short forms entirely. Among these are almost all soft adjectives (после́дний, весе́нний, etc.), all adjectives ending in **-ский** (ру́сский, америка́нский, etc.), ordinal numerals (пе́рвый, второ́й, etc.), and many others. Such adjectives use only long forms in the predicate.

On the other hand, the adjective **рад** (glad) has only short forms: рад, ра́до, ра́да, ра́ды.

Note that the forms **как** (how) and **так** (so) are used with the *short forms* of adjectives; the forms **како́й** and **тако́й** with the *long forms:*

Она́ **така́я** краси́вая же́нщина!
Она́ была́ **так** краси́ва в но́вом бе́лом пла́тье.

C. Mandatory use of the short forms. A few adjectives must always be used in the short form in the predicate, or are used with a distinct shade of meaning. Some of these are:

(1) Занято́й (long form) means "busy" in general:

О́н о́чень **занято́й** челове́к.	He is a very busy man.

За́нят (short form) means "busy," "occupied" at a given moment:

О́н тепе́рь **за́нят.**	He is busy now.

The same distinction applies to свобо́дный "free" (long form)—свобо́ден (short form).

Я́ сейча́с **за́нят,** но́ ве́чером я́ бу́ду **свобо́ден.**

(2) Здоро́вый (long form) means "healthy," "enjoying good health."
Здоро́в (short form) means "being well" at a given time.
Similarly, больно́й (long form) means "ailing," "having poor health" (used also as a noun, больно́й means "a patient").
Бо́лен (short form) means "being sick" at, or during, a specified time.

—Я́ слы́шал, что ва́ша жена́ была́ **больна́** (ill).
—Да́, и она́ и де́ти бы́ли **больны́;** у ни́х была́ инфлуэ́нца, но́ тепе́рь они́ уже́ все́ **здоро́вы** (well) (short form).
Вообще́ на́ши де́ти о́чень **здоро́вые** (healthy) (long form).

(3) Любе́зный (long form) means "gracious," "courteous" (in general).

Ива́н Ива́нович о́чень **любе́зный** челове́к.
Ivan Ivanovich is a very gracious person.

Любе́зен (short form) means "kind," "courteous" (in a given situation).

О́н бы́л о́чень **любе́зен** со мно́й.
He was very nice (considerate, courteous) to me.

Благода́рный (long form) means "grateful," "thankful" (in general).

Как ма́ло **благода́рных** люде́й на све́те!
How few grateful people there are in the world!

Благода́рен (short form) means "thankful" (in a particular situation).

Они́ бы́ли на́м о́чень **благода́рны** за по́мощь.
They were very grateful for our help.

Бу́дьте **любе́зны,** переда́йте мне́ са́хар. Спаси́бо, я́ ва́м о́чень **благода́рен.**
Be so kind as to pass me the sugar. Thank you, I am very grateful to you.

(4) Пра́вый (long form) means "right" (as opposed to "left").
Прав (short form) means "right" (as opposed to "wrong").

Вы́ бы́ли **пра́вы,** когда́ сказа́ли, что бу́дет до́ждь.
You were right when you said that it was going to rain.

The following adjectives are normally used in the short form when the adjective is predicative:

знако́м, знако́мо, знако́ма, знако́мы	acquainted
дово́лен, дово́льно, дово́льна, дово́льны	satisfied, content
свобо́ден, свобо́дно, свобо́дна, свобо́дны	free
здоро́в, здоро́во, здоро́ва, здоро́вы	well, healthy
бо́лен, больно́, больна́, больны́	sick, ill
любе́зен, любе́зно, любе́зна, любе́зны	kind, gracious
добр, добро́, добра́, добры́	kind
благода́рен, благода́рно, благода́рна, благода́рны	grateful
за́нят, за́нято, занята́, за́няты	busy, occupied[1]
уве́рен, уве́рено, уве́рена, уве́рены	sure[1]
удивлён, удивлено́, удивлена́, удивлены́	surprised[1]
согла́сен, согла́сно, согла́сна, согла́сны	agreed

[1] За́нят, уве́рен, удивлён are actually past passive participles (explained in Unit 27), but their predicative use does not differ from any other adjectives presented in this lesson.

гото́в, гото́во, гото́ва, гото́вы	ready
прав, пра́во, права́, пра́вы	right, correct
похо́ж, похо́же, похо́жа, похо́жи	similar, resembling
го́лоден, го́лодно, голодна́, го́лодны	hungry
сча́стлив, сча́стливо, сча́стлива, сча́стливы	happy, lucky

Pattern Sentences

1. **Свобо́да** хоро́шая ве́щь. Все́ лю́бят **свобо́ду.**
2. Мо́й прия́тель Пти́цын **свобо́дный** челове́к: у него́ не́т ни жены́ ни дете́й.
3. —Е́сли вы́ бу́дете **свобо́дны** в бу́дущую сре́ду, приходи́те к на́м. —Большо́е спаси́бо, но́ мне́ тру́дно сказа́ть зара́нее, бу́ду ли я́ **свобо́ден.**
4. Ни́ночка обеща́ла мне́, что бу́дет **свобо́дна** во вто́рник ве́чером.
5. Я́ нашёл **свобо́дное** ме́сто и се́л.
6. Э́то ме́сто **свобо́дно.**
7. Сми́т тепе́рь дово́льно **свобо́дно** говори́т по-ру́сски.
8. До́ктор Смирно́в о́чень **занято́й** челове́к.
9. К сожале́нию Ви́ктор бу́дет **за́нят** в воскресе́нье и не смо́жет прийти́.
10. Как жа́ль, что Зо́я была́ **занята́** в сре́ду ве́чером.
11. Ве́ра Васи́льевна была́ о́чень **удивлена́,** когда́ услы́шала э́ту но́вость.
12. Мно́гие бы́ли **удивлены́.** На мно́гих ли́цах мо́жно бы́ло ви́деть **удивле́ние.**
13. Профе́ссор Па́влов бы́л **бо́лен** в про́шлом ме́сяце, но́ тепе́рь о́н **здоро́в.**
14. —Вы́ **уве́рены,** что ва́ша жена́ **согла́сна** с ва́ми? —Да́, я́ соверше́нно **уве́рен** в э́том.
15. Мы́ с О́льгой соверше́нно **согла́сны** с отцо́м, но́ ма́ть с ни́м не **согла́сна.**

1. Freedom is a fine thing. Everyone likes freedom.
2. My friend Ptitsyn is a free man: he has neither wife nor children.
3. —If you are free next Wednesday, come to see us. —Thank you very much, but it's hard for me to tell in advance if I'll be free.
4. Ninochka promised me that she'd be free Tuesday evening.
5. I found a vacant seat and sat down.
6. This seat is vacant.
7. Smith speaks Russian quite fluently now.
8. Dr. Smirnov is a very busy man.
9. Unfortunately Victor will be busy on Sunday and won't be able to come.
10. It's too bad that Zoya was busy Wednesday night.
11. Vera Vasilievna was very surprised when she heard that piece of news.
12. Many people were surprised. One could see surprise on many faces.
13. Professor Pavlov was sick last month, but now he's well.
14. —Are you sure that your wife agrees with you? —Yes, I am absolutely sure of it.
15. Olga and I are in complete agreement with Father, but Mother does not agree with him.

16. Вы́ бы́ли **пра́вы,** когда́ сказа́ли, что Зо́я опозда́ет на ле́кцию.	16. You were right when you said that Zoya would be late to the lecture.
17. Коне́чно, я́ всегда́ **пра́в!**	17. Of course, I am always right!
18. По-мо́ему вы́ о́чень **похо́жи на ва́шего отца́.**	18. To me you look very like your father.
19. Ра́зве? А все́ говоря́т, что я́ **похо́ж на** ма́ть, а сестра́ **похо́жа на** отца́.	19. Really? But everyone says that I look like my mother, and my sister looks like Father.
20. Я́ о́чень **го́лоден.** Е́сли обе́д не **гото́в,** пойдём в рестора́н. Зо́я, ты́ **гото́ва** идти́?	20. I am very hungry. If dinner isn't ready, let's go to a restaurant. Zoya, are you ready to go?
21. Обе́д бу́дет **гото́в** через де́сять мину́т, и мы́ смо́жем пое́сть, хотя́ я́ совсе́м не **голодна́.**	21. Dinner will be ready in ten minutes, and we can eat, although I'm not the least bit hungry.

Drills

A. *Переведи́те на ру́сский.*

1. We are glad that you could come.
2. I don't agree with you that Ivan is a poor student.
3. Are you satisfied with my work?
4. —Olga, are you sure of that? —Yes, I am absolutely sure.
5. I am busy this evening, and I don't know when I will be free. I never know in advance; I am a very busy person.
6. —I think that this seat is taken. —Yes, you are right.
7. I am very grateful to you for your help. You are very kind.
8. This young man is a little young for that role.
9. This suit is too small for you.
10. All these dresses are either too large or too small for me.
11. I was sure that they would come. But they didn't come.
12. Is supper ready? We are very hungry.

B. *Choose from the following predicate adjectives one which makes correct sense, and supply the proper form:* **го́лоден, удивлён, похо́ж, согла́сен, уве́рен, любе́зен, гото́в, за́нят, свобо́ден**

1. Я́ не ...... с ва́ми, что о́н тако́й глу́пый. —А О́льга ...... со мно́й.
2. Мы́ бы́ли о́чень ......, когда́ о́н сказа́л, что о́н не зна́ет, кто́ бы́л Толсто́й.
3. Ни́на была́ ......, что пришёл то́лько Вади́м: она́ была́ ......, что Бори́с то́же придёт.
4. Я́ совсе́м не ......, что о́н по́нял, что́ я́ сказа́л. А вы́ ......, что о́н меня́ по́нял?
5. Ва́ша статья́ уже́ ......?
6. Мо́й сы́н о́чень ...... на меня́.
7. —Америка́нские города́ не ...... на европе́йские, пра́вда? —Да́, я́ ...... с ва́ми.

8. Бу́дьте ......, принеси́те мне́ воды́.
9. —Ни́на ничего́ ещё не е́ла, и она́ о́чень .... Обе́д ......? —Да́, всё ....
10. Е́сли вы́ бу́дете ...... за́втра ве́чером, приходи́те к на́м.
11. Ве́ра не мо́жет прийти́; она́ ....
12. Все́ бы́ли о́чень ......, что ва́с не́ было у Орло́вых.
13. Я́ сказа́л и́м зара́нее, что мы́ бу́дем ...... в сре́ду.
14. —Зо́я, ты́ ......, что Серге́й придёт к обе́ду? —Да́, я́ ......, и я́ бу́ду о́чень ......, е́сли о́н не придёт.

2. Months of the year

The names of the months are all masculine in gender. **В** + *locative* is used to express "in such and such a month":

	Name of Month	*In*
January	янва́рь	в январе́
February	февра́ль	в феврале́
March	март	в ма́рте
April	апре́ль	в апре́ле
May	май	в ма́е
June	ию́нь	в ию́не
July	ию́ль	в ию́ле
August	а́вгуст	в а́вгусте
September	сентя́брь	в сентябре́
October	октя́брь	в октябре́
November	ноя́брь	в ноябре́
December	дека́брь	в декабре́

Note also:

в про́шлом / в э́том / в бу́дущем } декабре́, ма́е, и т. д. — last / this / next } December, May, etc.

Drill

Напиши́те отве́ты на э́ти вопро́сы.

1. Како́й тепе́рь ме́сяц?
2. Како́й пе́рвый ме́сяц го́да? Како́й после́дний?
3. Каки́е ле́тние ме́сяцы вы́ зна́ете?
4. В како́м ме́сяце начина́ется уче́бный (school) го́д?
5. В како́м ме́сяце о́н конча́ется?
6. В како́м ме́сяце вы́ роди́лись?
7. В како́м ме́сяце де́нь рожде́ния Вашингто́на?
8. Како́й ва́ш люби́мый ме́сяц?
9. В како́м ме́сяце начина́ется весна́?

10. В каком месяце начинается лето?
11. Какой первый зимний месяц?
12. В каких месяцах тридцать дней, а в каких тридцать один день?

3. Reflexive pronoun себя́

The reflexive pronoun **себя́** (oneself) refers back to the subject of the sentence. It has no nominative case. It corresponds to all three persons and both numbers in English ("myself," "himself," "ourselves," "themselves," etc.).

Gen.	себя́
Dat.	себе́
Acc.	себя́
Instr.	собо́й (-о́ю)
Loc.	себе́

E.g.: Я́ купи́л всё э́то для **себя́** (for myself).
Когда́ мне́ ску́чно, я́ расска́зываю **себе́** (to myself) анекдо́ты.
О́н о́чень дово́лен **собо́й** (with himself).
Она́ никогда́ не ду́мает о **себе́** (about herself).

Себя́ is used as the object of transitive verbs which otherwise are normally not reflexive, that is, which only in exceptional cases direct action back to the subject:

Никто́ **себя́** не зна́ет.
No one knows himself.

Она́ о́чень лю́бит **себя́.**
She is very fond of herself.[2]

Note especially: **чу́вствовать себя́,** to feel (oneself):

—Ка́к вы́ **себя́ чу́вствуете?**
How are you feeling?

—Я́ **чу́вствую себя́** о́чень хорошо́.
I am feeling very well.

Note also the idiom **с собо́й,** "along," "with oneself":

Возьми́ **с собо́й** тёплое пальто́.
Take a warm coat along (with you).

О́н возьмёт **с собо́й** портфе́ль.
He will take a briefcase along.

[2] The suffix **-ся**, rather than **себя́,** appears with many verbs which are normally or always reflexive, *e.g.*, о́н мо́ет**ся**, he is washing (himself). Note that English frequently omits the reflexive pronoun with such verbs.

4. Intensive pronoun сам

This pronoun corresponds to the various English *intensive* pronouns in -self: "myself," "yourself," "himself," "ourselves," "themselves," etc., used to identify or emphasize a particular noun or pronoun. **Сам** is declined like **оди́н:**

	SINGULAR			PLURAL
	Masculine	*Neuter*	*Feminine*	*All Genders*
Nom.	сам	само́	сама́	са́ми
Gen.	самого́	like masc.	само́й	сами́х
Dat.	самому́	like masc.	само́й	сами́м
Acc.	like Nom. or Gen.	само́	саму́ (самоё)	like Nom. or Gen.
Instr.	сами́м	like masc.	само́й	сами́ми
Loc.	само́м	like masc.	само́й	сами́х

The intensive pronoun must not be confused with the reflexive pronoun **себя́,** although both have the same form in English; the intensive pronoun identifies, isolates, or emphasizes:

Я́ **са́м** не зна́ю.
I don't know myself (I myself don't know).

But: Я́ **себя́** не зна́ю.
I don't know myself (I have no knowledge of myself).

Pattern Sentences

1. Во́т идёт **са́м** дире́ктор!
2. Я́ получи́л письмо́ от **самого́** президе́нта.
3. Вы́ должны́ э́то сказа́ть **самому́** профе́ссору.
4. Зи́не никто́ не помога́ет; она́ всё де́лает **сама́.**
5. Я́ никогда́ не чита́л **само́й** кни́ги, но́ я́ слы́шал о не́й.
6. Я́ говори́л об э́том не с **само́й** Зи́ной, а с её сестро́й.
7. Я́ иногда́ ненави́жу **себя́.**
8. По́сле экза́мена Зи́на была́ о́чень недово́льна **собо́й.**
9. Когда́ я́ уезжа́л из Москвы́, я́ сказа́л **себе́,** что я́ до́лжен ско́ро верну́ться.

1. Here comes the director himself!
2. I got a letter from the president himself.
3. You must tell that to the professor himself.
4. No one helps Zina; she does everything herself.
5. I have never read the book itself, but I've heard about it.
6. I discussed it not with Zina herself, but with her sister.
7. Sometimes I hate myself.
8. After the exam Zina was very dissatisfied with herself.
9. When I was leaving Moscow, I told myself that I must return soon.

Drill

Переведите на ру́сский.

1. I did that myself.
2. He bought that picture for himself.
3. Tell that to the director himself!
4. They are always very satisfied with themselves!
5. My teacher told me that herself.
6. I myself don't know what I want.
7. Don't think so much about yourself! It's bad for the health.
8. Did you bring your briefcase with you?
9. Take a coat with you; it will be cold.
10. Who understands himself?
11. I shall take you along.
12. Buy yourself a new hat!

5. Expressions of health

Learn the following words and expressions:

здоро́вый челове́к	a healthy person
больно́й челове́к	a sick person
бо́лен, больна́, больны́	(be) sick, ill
здоро́в, -а, -ы.	(be) well
чу́вствовать себя́ хорошо́/пло́хо/лу́чше/ху́же и т. д.	to feel well/ill/better/worse, etc.
Мне́ хорошо́/пло́хо/лу́чше/ху́же и т. д.	I am (feel) well/ill/better/worse, etc.
Мне́ ста́ло хорошо́/пло́хо, лу́чше/ху́же и т. д.	I got well/ill/better/worse, etc.
боле́ть (imperf., I: боле́.ю, -ешь)	to be sickly, ailing, get sick (often or for a period of time)
Ива́н ча́сто боле́ет.	Ivan is often ill.
боле́ть (imperf., II: бол.и́т, -я́т)	to hurt, pain
У меня́ боли́т голова́/живо́т/нога́ и т. д.	I have a headache/a stomach-ache; my foot hurts, etc.
Что́ с ва́ми?	What's the matter with you?
Что́ у него́?	What (illness) does he have?
У него́ ревмати́зм/гри́пп/боле́знь се́рдца и т. д.	He has rheumatism/grippe/heart disease, etc.
О́н простуди́лся.	He caught a cold.
Я́ просту́жен(а).	I have a cold.
Всё прошло́.	It's all (illness, pain) gone away.
Э́та боле́знь прошла́.	That illness went away.

Pattern Sentences

1. Смирно́в бы́л о́чень **бо́лен** в феврале́. О́н вообще́ о́чень **больно́й** челове́к.
   Smirnov was very sick in February. He is generally a very sick man.
2. Ко́ля сего́дня немно́го **нездоро́в**: о́н **просту́жен** и **у него́** ма́ленькая **температу́ра.** Но́ вообще́ о́н о́чень **здоро́вый** ребёнок, и я́ уве́рен, что за́втра **всё пройдёт.**
   Kolya is a trifle unwell today: he has a cold and has a little temperature. But in general he's a very healthy child, and I am sure it will all be gone tomorrow.
3. Моя́ тётя уве́рена, что она́ **серьёзно больна́,** но́ по мне́нию до́ктора она́ соверше́нно **здоро́вая** же́нщина.
   My aunt is sure that she's seriously ill, but in the doctor's opinion she's a completely healthy woman.
4. Ве́рочка **простуди́лась** и **у неё бы́л гри́пп.** Она́ была́ **больна́** четы́ре дня́. Она́ ча́сто **боле́ет.** А я́ никогда́ не **боле́ю.**
   Verochka caught cold and got the grippe. She was sick for four days. She gets sick often. But I never get sick.
5. —**Ка́к ва́ше здоро́вье?** —Спаси́бо, **не пло́хо.** Вчера́ **мне́ бы́ло дово́льно пло́хо,** но́ сего́дня **я́ чу́вствую себя́ лу́чше.**
   —How is your health? —Thanks, not bad. Yesterday I felt rather sick, but today I feel better.
6. —**Ка́к себя́ чу́вствует** ва́ша ма́ть? —Спаси́бо, она́ тепе́рь **хорошо́ себя́ чу́вствует.**
   —How is your mother feeling? —Thanks, she's feeling well now.
7. Мо́й сосе́д бы́л **бо́лен** це́лую неде́лю. В про́шлую сре́ду ему́ **ста́ло ху́же,** и мы́ отвезли́ его́ в **больни́цу.**
   My neighbor was sick for a whole week. Last Wednesday he got worse, and we took him to the hospital.
8. —**Что́ у него́?** —**У него́ боле́знь се́рдца.**
   —What does he have? —He has heart disease.
9. —**Что́ с ва́ми?** —**У меня́ боли́т голова́.**
   —What's the matter with you? —I have a headache.
10. —Вчера́ **у меня́ боле́ла нога́,** а сего́дня **боли́т живо́т.**
    —Yesterday my foot hurt, and today I have a stomach-ache.

Drills

A. *Choose the word which makes correct sense and give the proper form:* **боле́ть, больно́й, бо́лен, здоро́в.**

1. Вчера́ у меня́ ...... голова́.
2. Во вто́рник у Ни́ны ...... глаза́.
3. Тепе́рь у Ива́на ...... у́ши.
4. Е́сли у неё опя́ть бу́дет что́-нибудь ......, она́ не придёт.
5. В суббо́ту у меня́ о́чень ...... пра́вая рука́.
6. Е́сли у ва́с бу́дут ...... глаза́, пойди́те к врачу́.
7. Бе́дная А́нна! Она́ была́ ...... и не могла́ выходи́ть це́лую неде́лю.

8. В э́то вре́мя го́да все́ ....
9. Андре́й, е́сли ты́ за́втра ещё бу́дешь ......, позвони́ мне́.
10. Мне́ сказа́ли, что они́ ста́рые и ...... лю́ди.
11. Я́ была́ ......, но́ тепе́рь я́ совсе́м ...... и могу́ выходи́ть.
12. До́ктор говори́т, что па́па о́чень ...... челове́к.
13. У на́с весёлые, ... де́ти.
14. Они́, сла́ва Бо́гу, никогда́ не ....
15. Ива́н бы́л просту́жен, но́ тепе́рь о́н уже́ ....

B. *Choose the proper form of the following words:* **себя́ чу́вствовать**; **мне́/ему́, и т. д. пло́хо/хорошо́/ху́же/лу́чше.**

1. —Ка́к вы́ ....? —Спаси́бо, я́ .... хорошо́.
2. —Ка́к .... сего́дня ва́ш бра́т? —О́н .... пло́хо.
3. Е́сли вы́ бу́дете пло́хо ...., позвони́те врачу́.
4. Вчера́ О́льга пло́хо ...., а сего́дня е́й ......, и она́ мо́жет вы́йти.
5. Во вто́рник Бори́су бы́ло о́чень ......, и мы́ отвезли́ его́ в больни́цу.
6. К сожале́нию ему́ сего́дня ......, и мы́ не зна́ем, когда́ о́н смо́жет вы́йти из больни́цы.
7. Я́ наде́юсь, что за́втра о́н бу́дет .... немно́го ....

6. Образова́ние—Education: verbs of learning, studying, and teaching

A. **Учи́ть** (II: учу́, у́чишь), "to teach," "learn."

1. "*To teach*": person taught in accusative; subject matter taught in dative (or infinitive):

Учи́тель у́чит на́с ру́сск**ому** язык**у́**.
The teacher teaches us Russian.

Ма́ть у́чит ребёнка **ходи́ть.**
The mother teaches the child to walk.

Учи́тель у́чит на́с **говори́ть** и **писа́ть** по-ру́сски.
The teacher teaches us to speak and write Russian.

2. "*To learn (memorize)*"; thing learned in accusative:

Учени́к у́чит уро́к.
The student learns the lesson.

Актёр у́чит ро́ль.
The actor learns his part.

B. **Учи́ться** (II: учу́сь, у́чишься), "to learn," "study," "go to school": subject matter in dative (or infinitive):

Где́ у́чится ва́ш сы́н?
Where does your son study (go to school)?

Мóй сы́н ýчится в Москóвском университéте.
My son studies at Moscow University.

Óн лю́бит учи́ться.
He likes to study.

—Кáк óн ýчится? —Óн ýчится óчень хорошó.
—How is he doing in school? —Very well.

—**Чемý** вы́ тепéрь ýчитесь? —Я́ учýсь рýсск**ому** язык**ý** и математи́к**е**.
—What are you studying now? —I am studying Russian and mathematics.

Мои́ сёстры **ýчатся танцевáть.**
My sisters are learning to dance.

Óн **учи́лся** мýзык**е** у хорóшего учи́теля.
He studied music with a good teacher.

C. **Научи́ть** (perf., II: научý, наýчишь) (accusative of person; dative or infinitive of subject) "to teach," "impart" knowledge or skill.

Ивáн **научи́л** меня́ говори́ть по-рýсски.
Ivan taught me to speak Russian.

Мáть **научи́ла** нáс вс**емý**.
Mother taught us everything.

D. **Научи́ться** (perf., II: научýсь, наýчишься) (+ dative or infinitive) "to learn," "to acquire" knowledge or skill.

Я́ **научи́лся** рýсск**ому** язык**ý** у Ивáна.
I learned Russian from Ivan.

Мы́ **научи́лись** вс**емý** у мáтери.
We learned everything from our mother.

Я́ поéду в Итáлию, когдá **научýсь** говори́ть по-италья́нски.
I shall go to Italy when I have learned to speak Italian.

E. **Изучáть** (imperf., I), **изучи́ть** (perf., II: изучý, изýчишь) (+ accusative) "to study" a subject, a question, etc. (perfective past implies that mastery has been acquired).

—Чтó вы́ изучáете? —Я́ изучáю кáрт**у** (э́т**у** проблéм**у**, рýсск**ий** язы́к, и т. д.).
—What are you studying? —I am studying the map (this problem, Russian, etc.).

Бори́с изучи́л плáн гóрода.
Boris mastered the map of the city.

F. **Занима́ться** (imperf., I), "to study" a given subject (instrumental case); also used of doing homework, preparing for class, etc.

—**Чём** вы́ занима́етесь? —**Ру́сским языко́м.**
—What are you studying? —Russian.

—Где́ вы́ занима́етесь? —У себя́ в ко́мнате.
—Where do you study (do your homework)? —In my room.

More broadly, **занима́ться** (+ instrumental) is used to describe the practice of a profession:

—**Чём** занима́ется ва́ш оте́ц? —О́н архите́ктор.
—What does your father do? —He's an architect.

G. **Преподава́ть** (imperf., I: conjugated like **дава́ть**), "to teach," "give instruction in;" subject matter in the accusative; person(s) taught in the dative:

Где́ вы́ преподаёте?
Where do you teach?

Кто́ ва́м преподаёт матема́тику?
Who teaches you mathematics?

Что́ преподаёт э́тот преподава́тель?
What does that teacher teach?

Observe that with **учи́ть** (= "to teach;" see paragraph A1 above) the person(s) taught must always be specified in the accusative, while with **преподава́ть** the person(s) taught may be specified (in the dative) or only implied.

Dialogue

—Где́ **преподаёт** Петро́в?	—Where does Petrov teach?
—В на́шей шко́ле. О́н прекра́сный **преподава́тель.**	—In our school. He is an excellent teacher.
—Что́ о́н **преподаёт?**	—What does he teach?
—Му́зыку. Я́ **учу́сь** у него́.	—Music. I study under him.
—Я́ не зна́л, что вы́ **у́читесь** в э́той шко́ле, и я́ не зна́л, что вы́ **у́читесь** му́зыке.	—I didn't know you were studying at that school, and I didn't know that you were learning music.
—О́ да́, и я́ о́чень мно́го **занима́юсь,** но́ мне́ ещё до́лго ну́жно бу́дет **учи́ться.**	—Oh, yes, and I study very hard, but I still have a long way to go (a lot to learn).
—Вы́ **изуча́ете** компози́цию и гармо́нию?	—Are you studying composition and harmony?
—Коне́чно. Когда́ я́ око́нчу э́ту шко́лу, я́ поступлю́ в консервато́рию и бу́ду та́м **учи́ться** три́ го́да.	—Of course. When I finish this school I shall enter the conservatory and shall study there for three years.

—А потóм бýдете давáть концéрты?
—Надéюсь. А мóжет быть бýду **преподавáть** мýзыку.

—And then you will give concerts?
—I hope so. Or perhaps I'll teach music.

Drill

Translate into Russian.

1. My sister teaches in this school.
2. She likes to teach.
3. I am teaching him to play the piano.
4. He studied a great deal.
5. We are studying this new map.
6. I like to study in my room.
7. Dr. Smirnov studied at this university.
8. I am learning to speak Russian.
9. Where did you learn to play tennis so well? Who taught you?
10. I have been studying this problem for a whole month.

CONVERSATION

Об учéнии

А. —Здрáвствуйте, Зинаи́да Михáйловна! Рáд вáс ви́деть! Кáк вы́ поживáете? Кáк дéти?

Б. —Спаси́бо, всё хорошó. Нó дéти ужé не дéти, а совсéм взрóслые.

А. —Дá, врéмя идёт бы́стро. А чтó они́ дéлают? Гдé ýчатся?

Б. —Мóй стáрший, Ми́ша, в ию́не окóнчил десятилéтку[3] и в сентябрé поступи́л в университéт.

А. —На какóм факультéте[4] óн ýчится?

Б. —На медици́нском.

А. —На медици́нском нелегкó и нýжно учи́ться мнóго лéт.

Б. —Дá, нó óн лю́бит учи́ться и ýчится хорошó. Óн получи́л стипéндию, тáк что егó учéние нáм ничегó не стóит. Я́ не знáю, кáк бýдет потóм, нó на пéрвом кýрсе[5] óн óчень мнóго рабóтает. Óн тепéрь изучáет анатóмию и иногдá занимáется до пóздней нóчи. Нó óн óчень довóлен. Егó всегдá интересовáла медици́на и, крóме тогó, óн знáет, что врачи́ óчень нужны́.

А. —Конéчно! Странá растёт. Всё нýжно. А гдé ýчится вáш млáдший сы́н?

Б. —Вади́м ещё не кóнчил семилéтки.[3] Сейчáс, на кани́кулы, óн поéхал в колхóз и рабóтает тáм. Óн проведёт тáм ию́ль и áвгуст.

[3] There are two types of secondary schools in the Soviet Union. **Десятилéтка** (ten-year school) prepares the student for the university (medicine, law, philosophy, etc.), while **семилéтка** (seven-year school) gives the student a minimum required education and prepares him for vocational schools.

[4] **Факультéт,** a school within a university.

[5] **Пéрвый кýрс,** first year in a school of higher education.

Пока́ о́н провёл та́м то́лько две́ неде́ли и о́чень все́м дово́лен. О́н принима́ет акти́вное уча́стие в колхо́зной жи́зни и мно́гому та́м у́чится.

А. —Чему́ же о́н та́м у́чится?

Б. —О́н изуча́ет практи́ческую жи́знь, у́чится жи́ть в коллекти́ве, у́чится по́льзоваться маши́нами (тра́ктором и комба́йном). В колхо́зе е́сть инструктора́, кото́рые у́чат шко́льников, всё и́м объясня́ют и пока́зывают.

А. —О́н в большо́м колхо́зе?

Б. —Да́, колхо́з дово́льно большо́й. У ни́х мно́го земли́ и скота́. Вади́м о́чень лю́бит приро́ду и живо́тных. О́н в ка́ждом письме́ пи́шет мне́ про одну́ коро́ву, кото́рую зову́т[6] «Черну́шка» (Blackie). О́н её про́сто обожа́ет. О́н пи́шет, что о́н изучи́л все́ её привы́чки, что она́ о́чень у́мная и понима́ет ка́ждое его́ сло́во. Я́ не зна́ла, что коро́ва тако́е у́мное живо́тное.

А. —О́н вероя́тно бу́дет хоро́шим агроно́мом и́ли ветерина́ром.

Б. —О́н ещё са́м не зна́ет, ке́м[7] о́н хо́чет бы́ть. О́н та́кже о́чень лю́бит поэ́зию и пи́шет стихи́. Мо́жет бы́ть о́н бу́дет поэ́том? Э́то то́же неплохо́е заня́тие. Поэ́ты ведь то́же нужны́. Пра́вда?

А. —Коне́чно, нужны́. А где́ Ни́ночка? Что́ она́ де́лает?

Б. —Ни́ночка око́нчила педагоги́ческий институ́т и в октябре́ уе́хала в Казахста́н.[8] Она́ живёт в небольшо́м селе́ и преподаёт в се́лькой шко́ле. Она́ у́чит ребя́т ру́сскому языку́, арифме́тике и вообще́ всему́. Она́ та́м то́лько четы́ре ме́сяца и уже́ научи́ла и́х дово́льно свобо́дно и пра́вильно говори́ть по-ру́сски.

А. —Во́т, молоде́ц! А я́ по́мню её, когда́ она́ сама́ была́ ещё совсе́м ма́ленькой, и я́ учи́л её говори́ть! Ско́лько е́й тепе́рь ле́т?

Б. —Ей уже́ два́дцать два́ го́да.

А. —Бо́же мо́й, ка́к вре́мя идёт! Ра́д слы́шать, что у ва́с всё хорошо́.

Б. —Да́, сла́ва Бо́гу, жа́ловаться не могу́.

Чита́йте э́ти вопро́сы и отвеча́йте на ни́х.

1. В како́м ме́сяце Ми́ша око́нчил десятиле́тку? 2. Что́ о́н сде́лал в сентябре́? 3. Бу́дет ли его́ уче́ние до́рого сто́ить его́ роди́телям? 4. Почему́ о́н поступи́л на медици́нский факульте́т? 5. В како́й шко́ле у́чится Вади́м? 6. Ско́лько ему́ ле́т? 7. Каки́е ме́сяцы о́н проведёт в колхо́зе? 8. Чему́ о́н та́м у́чится? 9. Что́

[6] Кото́рую зову́т (past: зва́ли), whose name is . . . Ка́к тебя́ зову́т, де́вочка? What is your name, little girl? This is a very frequent and very informal expression used only for animates. For more formal address, Ка́к и́мя (ка́к и́мя-о́тчество)? Ка́к фами́лия? are used. For inanimates the question is: Ка́к называ́ется? *e.g.*, Ка́к называ́ется э́та пло́щадь? or Ка́к назва́ние э́того уче́бника?

[7] Russian idiom has **ке́м** о́н бу́дет; **ке́м** о́н хо́чет бы́ть; note the use of the instrumental.

[8] **Педагоги́ческий институ́т,** teachers' college. Kazakhstan, a Soviet republic in Central Asia.

о́н пи́шет в свои́х пи́сьмах? 10. Ке́м о́н бу́дет? 11. Что́ де́лает до́чь Зинаи́ды Миха́йловны? 12. Како́й результа́т её преподава́ния? 13. Чему́ вы́ са́ми у́читесь? 14. Ке́м вы́ хоти́те бы́ть?

READING

Она́ обожа́ет говори́ть о себе́

Вы́ ещё не всё зна́ете про Ве́ру Васи́льевну.

Одна́ из её люби́мых те́м, э́то те́ма о здоро́вье. Она́ о́чень интересу́ется боле́знями все́х, но́ бо́льше всего́ она́ лю́бит говори́ть о свои́х боле́знях.

По-мо́ему, она́ о́чень здоро́вая же́нщина, но́ она́ всегда́ жа́луется на своё здоро́вье все́м, кто то́лько хо́чет её слу́шать.

Е́сли, не да́й Бо́г, вы́ задади́те Ве́ре Васи́льевне бана́льный вопро́с: «Ка́к пожива́ете?», вы́ сейча́с же от неё услы́шите, что, хотя́ она́ вообще́ не лю́бит жа́ловаться и никогда́ не жа́луется, она́ должна́ сказа́ть, что она́ пло́хо себя́ чу́вствует; в понеде́льник она́ была́ совсе́м больна́: у неё весь де́нь боле́ла голова́ и боле́ло го́рло. Ве́чером е́й ста́ло немно́го лу́чше, но́ но́чью е́й ста́ло опя́ть ху́же. Она́ всю но́чь принима́ла аспири́н, пила́ горя́чий ча́й с лимо́ном, но́ ничего́ не помога́ло. Во вто́рник она́ весь де́нь лежа́ла в посте́ли. В сре́ду у неё боле́ли у́ши. Снача́ла боле́ло пра́вое у́хо, а пото́м и ле́вое, и она́, коне́чно, соверше́нно не могла́ спа́ть. Пото́м, сла́ва Бо́гу, э́то прошло́. Но́ в четве́рг у неё та́к боле́ли но́ги и спина́, что она́ совсе́м не могла́ ходи́ть и её хоте́ли отвезти́ в больни́цу. К сча́стью е́й ста́ло немно́жко лу́чше, и ве́чером она́ пошла́ к сосе́дям. У сосе́дей бы́ли го́сти, Лунёвы. У Лунёва ужа́сный ревмати́зм, но́ не тако́й, как у неё. И так да́лее, и так да́лее . . .

Я́ бо́льше никогда́ не спра́шиваю её «ка́к пожива́ете» и ва́м сове́тую э́того не де́лать.

Чита́йте э́ти вопро́сы и отвеча́йте на ни́х.

1. О чём В. В. бо́льше всего́ лю́бит говори́ть? 2. Что́ она́ говори́т о своём хара́ктере? Чего́ она́ никогда́ не де́лает? 3. Что́ у неё боле́ло в понеде́льник? 4. Ка́к е́й бы́ло но́чью, и что́ она́ де́лала? 5. Что́ у неё боле́ло в сре́ду? 6. Почему́ в четве́рг её хоте́ли отвезти́ в больни́цу? 7. Почему́ её туда́ не отвезли́? 8. Что́ она́ рассказа́ла о ве́чере того́ дня́? 9. Како́е у ва́с здоро́вье? 10. Ско́лько ра́з в э́том году́ вы́ бы́ли больны́? 11. Что́ ну́жно де́лать, когда́ у челове́ка грипп?

EXERCISES

Переведите на русский.

1. —How is your father feeling now? —Thank you, fortunately he is better today. 2. Unfortunately, our grandmother is feeling worse today. In the doctor's opinion, she is very sick. 3. My aunt was sick and my uncle took her to the hospital, and now I've learned that my uncle himself is sick. 4. Their cow is sick. They are afraid that she will die—poor animal! 5. I don't feel well this evening; I have a headache. 6. —Where did you study? —I studied at Moscow University, and besides I studied for a year in England. I studied history. 7. —Does your son like to study? —Yes, very much. 8. —We are studying French this year. —What textbook do you use? —We are using a new textbook; I've forgotten its name. 9. Every year we spend our vacation at the seashore. We adore the sea! 10. My father spent this summer in the mountains. He adores mountains! 11. My aunt often complains of her health; she is a very sick woman. 12. It's impossible to tell in advance who will receive a scholarship for next year. 13. My father's birthday is in August, and my mother's in September. 14. —Tell me something about yourself. —I myself don't know what to tell you. 15. It is a bad habit to speak about oneself. 16. The dog is a very intelligent animal. 17. Your daughter, according to my wife, looks very like you. 18. This city resembles Paris. 19. This kolkhoz has much land and much cattle. 20. If, God forbid, you tell her that she is wrong, she will hate you. 21. Thank Heaven, Grandfather is better today. 22. It is fortunate that we took him to the hospital.

VOCABULARY

боле́знь (*fem.*) disease, illness
больни́ца hospital
взро́слый (*adj. used as noun*) adult
го́рло throat
живо́т stomach, belly
живо́тное (*adj. used as noun*) animal
зара́нее in advance
земля́ (*gen. pl.* **земе́ль**) earth, land
инстру́ктор (*nom. pl.* **-а́**), *fem.* **-ша** (practical) instructor
кани́кулы (*fem. pl. only*) school holidays, vacation
коро́ва cow
лу́чше better
мно́гое (*declined as a neut. adj.*) much, many things
образова́ние education
поэ́зия poetry
практи́ческий practical
преподава́ние teaching

привы́ч.ка (*gen. pl.* **-ек**) habit
ребя́та (*nom. pl.; gen. pl.* **ребя́т**) kids, fellows (*colloq.*)
рожде́ние birth, birthday
свобо́да freedom, liberty
свобо́дный free
свобо́дно freely, fluently
се́льский village (*adj.*)
се́рдце heart
скот livestock, cattle
соверше́нно completely, practically, absolutely
спина́ back (of an animate being)
***стипе́ндия** scholarship
температу́ра temperature
уче́ние study, learning, schooling, education
у́ши (*nom. pl. of* **у́хо**) ears
ху́же worse
шко́льн.ик, *fem.* **-ица** schoolboy (girl)

Verbs

жа́ловаться (imperf., I: **жа́лу.юсь, -ешься**), **пожа́ловаться** (perf., I) to complain (+ *dat.*) to; (**на** + *acc.*) of, about
обожа́ть (imperf., I) to adore, worship
по́льзоваться (imperf., I: **по́льзу.юсь, -ешься**), **воспо́льзоваться** (perf., I) to use, take advantage of (+ *instr.*)
проводи́ть (imperf., II: **провожу́, прово́дишь**), **провести́** (perf., I: **провед.у́, -ёшь;** past: **провёл, провело́,** etc.) to pass, spend (time)
рожда́ться (imperf., I), **роди́ться** (perf., II: **рожу́сь, роди́шься;** past: **роди́лся, родил.о́сь, -а́сь, -и́сь**) to be born
чу́вствовать (imperf., I: **чу́вству.ю, -ешь**), **почу́вствовать** (perf., I) to feel (*trans.*)
чу́вствовать себя́ to feel (*intrans.:* well, ill, etc.)

Expressions

к сча́стью fortunately
к сожале́нию unfortunately
уве́рен в (+ *loc.*) sure of
похо́ж на (+ *acc.*) look like, resemble
Пойдём! Let's go!
де́нь рожде́ния birthday
Молоде́ц! (used for men and women) Good boy/girl! Good for you (him, her)!
бо́льше всего́ most of all
всём, кто то́лько хо́чет to everyone who is the least bit willing
Не да́й Бо́г! God forbid!
по мнению (+ *gen.*) in the opinion of . . . , according to . . .
кро́ме того́ besides (*adv.*), in addition

UNIT 24

GRAMMAR

1. The hypothetical mood

The particle **бы** is used with verbs in the forms of the past tense (or the infinitive) to express the *hypothetical mood* (also called the conditional or subjunctive).

The sentence «Я́ пошёл бы в теа́тр» is in the hypothetical mood; the form «**пошёл бы**» means that the speaker considers going to the theater as a possibility, as something he might do (or might have done), would like (or would have liked) to do, would do (or would have done), circumstances permitting.

These meanings may be contrasted with those expressed by the *indicative mood*, which is used to state that an action was, is, or will actually be performed: Я́ пошёл (went) в теа́тр, Я́ иду́ (am going) в теа́тр, Я́ пойду́ (will go) в теа́тр; or in questions, *e.g.*, Вы́ пойдёте в теа́тр? etc.

It must be clearly understood that in hypothetical constructions (past tense forms plus **бы**), the verb is *not* past in meaning; it is actually neither past, nor present, nor future, since this construction does not have the means to differentiate tenses.

The hypothetical mood in conditions. It has been seen earlier that the word **е́сли** in Russian (like *if* in English) means that one event is contingent on another one:

Е́сли оте́ц мне́ пришлёт де́ньги, я́ куплю́ автомоби́ль.
If Father sends me the money, I shall buy a car.

In this example, both verbs (**куплю́** and **пришлёт**) are in the future tense and the indicative mood. Substituting the hypothetical mood for the indicative, we have:

> **Е́сли бы** оте́ц присла́л мне́ де́ньги, я́ **бы** купи́л автомоби́ль.

This construction emphasizes the hypothetical nature of the condition; the speaker here has no particular reason to believe that the money will be forthcoming and is merely expressing a wish or speculating on what he would do if he did receive it. The indicative (Е́сли оте́ц пришлёт . . . я́ куплю́) would suggest, on the other hand, that there is some reason for expecting or hoping that the money will arrive.

The Russian hypothetical construction does not differentiate between conditions that, however improbable, might come true, and those that are known to have failed (or are regarded as impossible); only the context can indicate whether the condition is possible or contrary to fact. The sentence above, given a context, may correspond in English either to "If Father *sent* (or *would send*) me the money, I *would buy* a car" (possible, though perhaps unlikely), or to "If Father *had sent* me the money, I *would have bought* a car" (impossible).

A clearly "unreal" condition is stated in the phrase "If I were you . . .":

> **Е́сли бы** я́ бы́л на ва́шем ме́сте, я́ **бы** ему́ э́того не расска́зывал.
> If I were in your place, I shouldn't have told him that.

The words **е́сли бы** or the particle **бы** alone are often used colloquially as expressions of a wish, hope, uncertainty, tentative consideration, etc.

> Хорошо́ (было) **бы** пое́хать куда́-нибудь к мо́рю.
> It would be nice to go somewhere to the seaside.

> На́до (было) **бы** написа́ть отцу́; мы́ давно́ ему́ не писа́ли.
> I think (or: Don't you think) we ought to write to Father; it has been a long time since we wrote to him.

In questions:

> Где́ **бы** на́м пообе́дать сего́дня?
> Where could we (or: I wonder where we could) have dinner tonight?

> Куда́ **бы** на́м пойти́ ве́чером?
> Where could we (or: I wonder where we could) go tonight?

Very often the phrase я́ хоте́л бы is used rather than the more assertive я́ хочу́; the difference between the two is very much the same as that between "I would like to" and "I want to."

A variant of the hypothetical construction is used in Russian in sentences of the type: "John wants Peter to come." This is rendered as:

Ива́н хо́чет, **чтобы** Пётр **пришёл.**

In this construction the subordinate clause is introduced by **чтобы** (**что** combined with the **бы** particle), and the verb in this clause is in the past tense form (not past in *meaning*).

Observe that **хоте́ть** is used with the infinitive in sentences of the type: Я́ хочу́ прочита́ть э́ту кни́гу; or Бори́с хо́чет прочита́ть э́ту кни́гу; in such sentences the person who wants and the person who will read are the same. Contrast: **Я́** хочу́, чтобы **Бори́с** прочита́л э́ту кни́гу; here the persons are different and the hypothetical mood must be used.

The same pattern is followed with other verbs, such as telling, writing, requesting, commanding, etc.:

Я́ скажу́ ему́, **чтобы** о́н **принёс** кни́гу.
I shall tell him to bring the book.

О́н мне́ написа́л, **чтобы** я́ **привёз** кни́ги.
He wrote me to bring the books.

Purpose clauses. The word **чтобы** or the prepositional construction **для того́, чтобы** is generally used to express the purpose of an action ("in order that," "in order to"); the verb in the subordinate clause then has the past tense form when there are different subjects in the two clauses:

Я́ да́л ему́ де́нег (для того́), **чтобы** о́н **мо́г** пое́хать на Кавка́з.
I gave him money so that he could go to the Caucasus.

Я́ не зна́ю, что́ я́ до́лжен сде́лать, **чтобы** она́ наконе́ц **отве́тила** на письмо́ ма́тери.
I don't know what I must do so that she will finally answer her mother's letter.

If the subject in the two clauses is the same, the *infinitive* is used:

О́н мно́го занима́ется (для того́), **чтобы** хорошо́ **сда́ть** (pass) экза́мены.
He studies a great deal (in order) to get good grades on his exams.

Она́ идёт в магази́н (для того́), **чтобы** всё **купи́ть** на за́втра.
She is going to the store (in order) to buy everything for tomorrow.

2. The English conditional and its equivalent in Russian

As has already been pointed out (Unit 15, page 227), in Russian the tense used in reported discourse is the same as in the original statement, *e.g.*:

> Ivan speaking: «Я́ приду́ за́втра.»
> Reported: Ива́н сказа́л, что **придёт** за́втра.
> (Contrast English: He said that he *would* come.)

The English auxiliary verb *would* thus corresponds to the Russian future in past reported speeches,[1] and not, as in the examples in Section 1, to the hypothetical mood.

A third use of English "would" is to denote habitual action in the past; this corresponds to the Russian *imperfective past:*

> О́н ка́ждый де́нь **приходи́л** к на́м.
> Every day he *would* come to see us.

Care must be taken when translating "would" into Russian to determine whether the future, imperfective past, or the hypothetical mood is appropriate.

Pattern Sentences

Hypothetical conditions: **е́сли бы.**

1. **Е́сли бы** у меня́ **бы́ло** мно́го де́нег, мне́ не ну́жно **бы́ло бы** рабо́тать.	1. If I had a lot of money, I wouldn't have to work.
2. **Е́сли бы** вы́ вчера́ **сказа́ли,** что ва́м нужны́ де́ньги, я́ бы ва́м сего́дня и́х **принёс.**	2. If you had said yesterday that you needed money, I would have brought it to you today.
3. Они́ **купи́ли бы** э́того Рембра́ндта, **е́сли бы** у ни́х **бы́ло** бо́льше де́нег.	3. They would have bought that Rembrandt if they had had more money.
4. Как **бы́ло бы** хорошо́, **е́сли бы** вы́ **прие́хали** к на́м, когда́ мы́ жи́ли на да́че! Почему́ вы́ не прие́хали?	4. How nice it would have been if you had come to see us when we were living in the country! Why didn't you?
5. —Как жа́ль, что вы́ вчера́ не́ были у Смирно́вых! —**Е́сли бы** я́ **зна́л,** что вы́ та́м бу́дете, я́ **бы** то́же **пришёл.**	5. —Too bad you weren't at the Smirnovs' yesterday! —If I had known that you would be there, I would have come too.

[1] The same rule applies to constructions which are not, strictly speaking, reported speeches, and for which there is no actual "original statement"; the principles involved, however, are the same as if an actual statement had been made, *e.g.*, Я́ ду́мал, что о́н **придёт.** I thought that he *would* come.

6. Что́ **бы** вы́ **сде́лали, е́сли бы** о́н ва́м сказа́л, что вы́ ему́ бо́льше не нужны́?	6. What would you do if he should tell you that he doesn't need you any-more?
7. Что́ **бы** мы́ **де́лали** без ва́с?[2]	7. What would we do without you?

Wishes, commands, etc.: **чтобы.**

1. Я́ хочу́, **чтобы** Па́вел **написа́л** обо всём сво́им роди́телям.	1. I want Paul to write to his parents about everything.
2. **Я́ хочу́, чтобы** ты́ **отве́тил** на мо́й вопро́с.	2. I want you to answer my question.
3. Учи́тель **хо́чет, чтобы** мы́ **сде́лали** э́тот перево́д на за́втра.	3. The teacher wants us to do that translation for tomorrow.
4. Они́ **хотя́т, чтобы** я́ и́м **принёс** два́дцать пя́ть до́лларов во вто́рник.	4. They want me to bring them $25 on Tuesday.
5. Мы́ о́чень **хоти́м,** чтобы вы́ **пришли́** к на́м в э́то воскресе́нье к обе́ду.	5. We would very much like you to come to our house this Sunday for dinner.
6. Мы́ все́ **хоти́м, чтобы** вы́ на́м **сыгра́ли** балла́ду Шопе́на.	6. We all want you to play a ballade by Chopin for us.
7. Ири́на **про́сит, чтобы** я́ **привёз** е́й часы́ из Швейца́рии.	7. Irene is asking me to bring her a watch from Switzerland.
8. Ива́н **написа́л** мне́, **чтобы** я́ **привёз** ему́ но́вые пласти́нки.	8. Ivan wrote me to bring him some new records.
9. **Я́ сказа́л** Со́не, **чтобы** она́ **купи́ла** цвето́в.	9. I told Sonya to buy some flowers.

Purpose clauses: **чтобы.**

1. Принеси́те мне́ письмо́, **чтобы** я́ **мо́г** его́ подписа́ть.	1. Bring me the letter so that I can sign it.
2. **Для того́ чтобы купи́ть** биле́ты в теа́тр, ва́м ну́жно бу́дет пое́хать в го́род.	2. In order to buy tickets for the theater, you'll have to go downtown.
3. **Чтобы** о́н со мно́й не **спо́рил,** я́ сра́зу скажу́ ему́, что я́ с ни́м согла́сен.	3. To keep him from arguing with me, I'll tell him right away that I agree with him.
4. **Для того́, чтобы** свобо́дно **говори́ть** по-ру́сски, ва́м нужна́ пра́ктика.	4. In order to speak Russian fluently, you need practice.
5. **Чтобы** Пе́тя лу́чше **е́л,** ма́ть расска́зывает ему́ ска́зки за обе́дом.	5. So that Petya should eat better (more), his mother tells him fairy-tales at dinner.

[2] In this sentence the condition with е́сли бы is implied. Compare: Что́ бы мы́ де́лали, е́сли бы ва́с не́ было?

Wishes, advice, etc. with **бы.**

1. Я́ **бы́л бы** ра́д его́ ви́деть.
2. Как **бы́ло бы** хорошо́ пое́хать к мо́рю в таку́ю пого́ду!
3. На́до **бы** написа́ть дя́де Ва́не! Мы́ так давно́ ему́ не писа́ли.
4. О́н не до́лжен **бы́л бы** э́того говори́ть.
5. Вы́ **бы пошли́** погуля́ть.
6. Я́ **бы хоте́л** забы́ть своё про́шлое.
7. Как **бы́ло бы** хорошо́, е́сли **бы** вы́ **могли́** к на́м прийти́ в воскресе́нье! Вы́ придёте?
8. Бы́ло бы хорошо́, е́сли бы вы́ ему́ помогли́.

1. I would be glad to see him.
2. How nice it would be to go to the seashore in such weather!
3. We ought to write to Uncle Vanya! We haven't written to him for such a long time.
4. He shouldn't have said that.
5. You should go for a walk.
6. I would like to forget my past.
7. How nice it would be if you could come to see us on Sunday! Will you come?
8. It would be good if you would help him.

Drills

A. *Translate the words in parentheses into Russian.*

1. Мы́ о́чень хоти́м, (you to come) в суббо́ту.
2. Моя́ ма́ть хо́чет, (me to write) отцу́.
3. Я́ не зна́ю, что́ сде́лать, (that he should speak) бо́льше по-ру́сски!
4. Они́ (would have been) о́чень ра́ды ва́с ви́деть.
5. Бы́ло бы хорошо́, (if he would come).
6. Вы́ должны́ попроси́ть его́, (that he should bring) пятьдеся́т рубле́й.
7. (In order to write) перево́д, мне́ ну́жен слова́рь.
8. О́н хоте́л, (me to read) ему́ э́то письмо́. Но́, (in order to read) э́то иисьмо́, мне́ ну́жно взя́ть его́ у сестры́.
9. Они́ та́к (would like) пое́хать на Кавка́з!

B. *Translate into Russian.*

1. He said that he would buy me a present.
2. If he had the money, he would have bought me a present. But unfortunately he has no money!
3. If he has (will have) the money tomorrow, he'll buy me something.
4. How nice it would have been if you had written to Olga! Why didn't you write to her?
5. I would like to see him.
6. In order to see him, you must go to Moscow.
7. Mother doesn't want me to go to Moscow.
8. She wants to go there herself.
9. I wrote to her in (to) Kiev to bring us Ukrainian books.
10. You should have written to her husband.

3. Verbs of placing

Russian makes a sharp distinction between placing something in a standing position and placing it in a lying position. The student translating English verbs such as "to put" or "to place" must make this distinction.

Transitive verbs of placing are related to corresponding intransitive verbs of standing or lying:

	Intransitive Verbs (*Being in a Position*)	*Transitive Verb* (*Putting into Position*)	
		Imperfective	*Perfective*
Standing:	стоя́ть (II: сто.ю́, -и́шь)	ста́вить (II: ста́в.лю, -ишь)	поста́вить (II: поста́в.лю, -ишь)
Lying:	лежа́ть (II: леж.у́, -и́шь)	класть[3] (I: клад.у́, -ёшь; *Past:* кла́л, -о, -а, -и)	положи́ть[3] (II:положу́, поло́жишь)

Transitive verbs of placing take the prepositions **в** or **на** with the accusative, or **к** with the dative, or adverbs of direction:

> Я́ **положи́л** э́то письмо́ **на** пи́сьменный сто́л, и оно́ ещё та́м **лежи́т.**
> I put (laid) that letter on the desk, and it's still lying there.
>
> **Поста́вьте** э́тот сту́л **сюда́.** Пу́сть о́н зде́сь **стои́т.**
> Put (stand) this chair here. Let it stand here.

4. Prepositions за and под with accusative

The prepositions **за** and **под** take the *instrumental* case to indicate location (see Unit 19, page 303). When they indicate direction of motion, however, they take the *accusative:*

> Я́ поста́вил портфе́ль **за** кре́сл**о**. Во́т о́н стои́т **за** кре́сл**ом.**
> Я́ положи́л газе́ту **под** кни́г**у**. Она́ лежи́т **под** кни́г**ой.**

Note the following expressions:

е́хать за́ город[4]	to go out of town, go to the country
жи́ть за́ городом	to live in the country
е́хать за грани́цу	to go abroad (literally, beyond the border)
жи́ть за грани́цей	(instr.) to live abroad

[3] The imperfective-perfective pair класть/положи́ть is a third irregular pair (like говори́ть/сказа́ть and бра́ть/взя́ть). Note the relationship between the perfective по**лож**и́ть, "to put in a lying position," "put down," and **леж**а́ть, "to lie."

[4] Prepositions sometimes take the stress from the noun, especially in certain common adverbial expressions; note also: Кни́га упа́ла **на́ пол**. The book fell on the floor.

Pattern Sentences

1. Ты́ забы́ла **положи́ть** на сто́л ло́жки и забы́ла **поста́вить** стака́ны для воды́.	1. You forgot to put spoons on the table and to put out water glasses.
2. —Кто́ **поста́вил** на сто́л э́ту пусту́ю буты́лку? —Э́то я́ **поста́вила** её. Мне́ показа́лось, что она́ по́лная.	2. —Who put this empty bottle on the table? —I did. I thought it was full.
3. Я́ **поста́влю** э́то кре́сло в кабине́т; оно́ мо́жет **стоя́ть** в кабине́те.	3. I'll put that easy chair in the study; it can stand in the study.
4. Не **клади́** все́ э́ти ве́щи на дива́н, а **положи́** и́х в шка́ф. Они́ должны́ **лежа́ть** в шкафу́.	4. Don't put all those things on the sofa, but put them in the cupboard. They must stay in the cupboard.
5. Я́ **положи́л** письмо́ на тво́й пи́сьменный сто́л, туда́, куда́ я́ всегда́ **кладу́** пи́сьма. Во́т оно́ **лежи́т.**	5. I put the letter on your desk, in the place where I always put letters. There it is.
6. Я́ **поста́вил** твою́ кни́гу на по́лку. Во́н она́ **стои́т.**	6. I put your book on the shelf. There it is.
7. —Куда́ О́льга **кладёт** де́ньги? —Она́ всегда́ **кладёт** де́ньги **за** э́ту ва́зу. Ви́дишь, они́ **лежа́т за ва́зой.**	7. —Where does Olga put money? —She always puts it behind this vase. You see, it's lying behind the vase.
8. Ма́ма **поло́жит** твои́ платки́ в шка́ф **за** руба́шки. По́мни, что они́ **бу́дут лежа́ть за** руба́шк**ами** на второ́й по́лке.	8. Mamma will put your handkerchiefs in the cupboard behind the shirts. Remember that they'll be lying behind the shirts on the second shelf.
9. Я́ **поста́влю** боти́нки **под** крова́ть. Ты́ и́х найдёшь **под** крова́т**ью.**	9. I shall put my shoes under the bed. You'll find them under the bed.
10. Мо́крый зо́нтик **стои́т за** кре́сл**ом.** Кто́ **поста́вил** зо́нтик **за** кре́сло? Не **ста́вьте** его́ **туда́!**	10. A wet umbrella is standing back of the armchair. Who put an umbrella back of the armchair? Don't put it there!
11. Не **ста́вь** пусты́е буты́лки **под** сто́л!	11. Don't put empty bottles under the table!

Drills

A. *Replace the blank with a suitable verb* (**класть/положи́ть, ста́вить/поста́вить, лежа́ть, стоя́ть**).

1. —Кто́ ...... э́ти пи́сьма на мо́й сто́л? —Ве́ра ...... и́х сюда́.
2. —Почему́ ты́ всегда́ ...... все́ пи́сьма на мо́й сто́л? —Я́ обыкнове́нно ...... и́х сюда́, потому́ что я́ не зна́ю куда́ и́х ....
3. Чьи́ пи́сьма ...... на моём столе́?
4. —Вади́м, куда́ ты́ ...... ви́ски? —Я́ ...... его́ туда́, куда́ я́ всегда́ его́ ....
5. Е́сли хоти́те, я́ сейча́с ...... ви́ски в буфе́т, туда́, где́ ...... во́дка.
6. Возьми́те э́ти докуме́нты и ...... и́х в шка́ф, а слова́рь ...... на по́лку туда́, где́ ...... францу́зские кни́ги.

B. *Translate into Russian.*

1. Children, don't put empty glasses under the table!
2. And don't put them under the armchair!
3. Put them on the table.
4. Glasses should not stand under a table.
5. Boris, why did you put this old newspaper behind the sofa?
6. I don't know where to put old newspapers.
7. I've put the salt behind the bread.
8. Who has put my pencil under the dictionary?
9. Vanya ran behind the garage.
10. Why were his toys behind the garage?
11. I've put the chair behind the tree.
12. You see? It's standing behind the tree.

5. Going verbs, continued

Three more commonly used verbs of motion have paired imperfective forms: *determinate* and *indeterminate* (see Unit 17, page 249):

	Indeterminate Imperfective	*Determinate Imperfective*	*Perfective*
to run			
Inf.	**бе́гать** (I)	**бежа́ть**[5]	**побежа́ть** (I)
Pres.	бе́гаю	бегу́	*Fut.* побегу́
	бе́гаешь	бежи́шь	побежи́шь
	etc.	......	......
		бегу́т	побегу́т
to fly			
Inf.	**лета́ть** (I)	**лете́ть** (II)	**полете́ть** (II)
Pres.	лета́ю	лечу́	*Fut.* полечу́
	лета́ешь	лети́шь	полети́шь
	etc.	......	......
		летя́т	полетя́т
to sail, float, swim			
Inf.	**пла́вать** (I)	**плыть** (I)	**поплы́ть** (I)
Pres.	пла́ваю	плыву́	*Fut.* поплыву́
	пла́ваешь	плывёшь	поплывёшь
	etc.	etc.	etc.

[5] The verb **бежа́ть** is irregular: most of its forms are second conjugation, but the first person singular and third person plural are first conjugation.

Prefixed compounds of these verbs are formed analogous to those of other verbs, *e.g.*, прилета́ть/прилете́ть, to come (arrive) by flying; улета́ть/улете́ть, to fly away, etc. Note the stress shift in imperfective compounds of бе́гать: прибега́ть/прибежа́ть, to come running. Imperfective compounds of пла́вать are found with -плыва́ть: подплыва́ть/подплы́ть, to sail (swim) toward.

Pattern Sentences

Лета́ть/лете́ть (у-, при-, вы-).

1. Над на́шим го́родом це́лый де́нь **лета́ют** самолёты.	1. All day airplanes fly over our town.
2. Посмотри́те, как ни́зко **летя́т** э́ти два́ самолёта!	2. Look how low those two planes are flying!
3. Я́ **лета́ю** в Оде́ссу по де́лу два́ ра́за в ме́сяц.	3. I fly to Odessa twice a month on business.
4. За́втра я́ **лечу́** туда́. Моя́ секрета́рша **лети́т** со мно́й.	4. Tomorrow I'm flying there. My secretary is coming with me.
5. Е́сли я́ **вы́лечу** в се́мь утра́, я́ **прилечу́** в Оде́ссу в де́сять.	5. If I set out at seven, I shall land in Odessa at ten.
6. Я́ обы́чно **вылета́ю** и **прилета́ю** в э́то вре́мя.	6. I usually leave and arrive by plane at that time.
7. Со́ня не лю́бит **лета́ть**; она́ предпочита́ет е́здить по́ездом и́ли парохо́дом.	7. Sonya doesn't like to fly; she prefers to travel by train or by boat.
8. Мо́й племя́нник **прилете́л** вчера́ у́тром из Се́верной А́фрики и ве́чером **улете́л** в Ю́жную Аме́рику.	8. My nephew flew in yesterday morning from Northern Africa and left by plane in the evening for South America.
9. Вре́мя **лети́т** бы́стро.	9. Time flies quickly.

Бе́гать/бежа́ть (при-, у-, в-, вы-).

1. Как мно́го эне́ргии у дете́й! Они́ **бе́гают** це́лый де́нь и никогда́ не устаю́т.	1. How much energy children have! They run about all day long and never get tired.
2. Куда́ **бегу́т** э́ти ма́льчики?	2. Where are those boys running?
3. Я́ ви́дел, как Ива́н Ива́нович **бежа́л** по у́лице. Я́ останови́л его́ и спроси́л: «Куда́ вы́ **бежи́те**?» О́н останови́лся и отве́тил: «Я́ **бегу́** на вокза́л; я́ бою́сь опозда́ть на по́езд.»	3. I saw Ivan Ivanovich running down the street. I stopped him and asked, "Where are you running?" He stopped and answered, "I am running to the station; I'm afraid I'll be late for the train."
4. Вероя́тно, когда́ о́н **прибежа́л** на вокза́л, по́езд уже́ ушёл.	4. When he arrived at the station, the train had probably left already.

5. Мы́ с Ни́ной стоя́ли и споко́йно разгова́ривали. Вдру́г **вбежа́л** в ко́мнату Ко́ля с телегра́ммой в руке́.
6. Ни́на прочла́[6] телегра́мму и **вы́бежала** из ко́мнаты.
7. Еле́на Ива́новна так мно́го вчера́ говори́ла, что я́ **убежа́л.**

5. Nina and I were standing talking peacefully. Suddenly Kolya ran into the room with a telegram in his hand.
6. Nina read the telegram and ran out of the room.
7. Yelena Ivanovna talked so much yesterday that I rushed (ran) away.

Пла́вать/плыть (**до-**,[7] **у-**, **под-**).

1. —Вы́ любите **пла́вать?** —О́чень, но́ я́ пло́хо **пла́ваю.**
2. Бори́с вчера́ сли́шком мно́го **пла́вал** и о́чень уста́л.
3. Я́ **плы́л** полчаса́ до того́ ма́ленького о́строва. Я́ ду́мал, что я́ никогда́ не **доплыву́ до** него́.
4. Огро́мная ры́ба **подплыла́** к бе́регу и бы́стро **уплыла́.**

1. —Do you like to swim? —Very much, but I swim badly.
2. Boris swam too much yesterday and got very tired.
3. I swam for half an hour to that small island. I thought I'd never reach it.
4. A huge fish swam up to the shore and quickly swam away.

Drills

Choose the correct form.

A. **Лета́ть/лете́ть**

1. Я́ люблю́ (лета́ть/лете́ть), но́ я́ ре́дко (лета́ю/лечу́).
2. Я́ слы́шал, что вы́ куда́-то (лета́ете/лети́те) сего́дня ве́чером.
3. Да́, я́ (лета́ю/лечу́) в Я́лту.
4. Посмотри́те! Куда́ (лета́ют/летя́т) э́ти самолёты?
5. В кото́ром часу́ вы́ вчера́ (прилета́ли/прилете́ли)?
6. Дя́дя Ми́ша ча́сто (прилета́л/прилете́л) к на́м на Кавка́з.

B. **Бе́гать/бежа́ть**

1. Соба́чка лю́бит (бе́гать/бежа́ть).
2. Э́та соба́ка (бе́гает/бежи́т) домо́й.
3. Я́ ви́дел у́тром Серёжу. О́н куда́-то (бе́гал/бежа́л).
4. О́н (прибега́л/прибежа́л) ко мне́ сего́дня у́тром.
5. И́х соба́ка ча́сто (убега́ет/убежи́т) от ни́х.
6. Я́ ду́маю, что она́ ско́ро опя́ть (убега́ет/убежи́т).
7. Она́ всегда́ (прибега́ет/прибежи́т) обра́тно.

[6] The perfective verb прoче́сть is interchangeable with the perfective verb прочита́ть: past: прочёл, прочло́, прочла́, прочли́; future.: проч.ту́, -тёшь.

[7] Доплыва́ть/доплы́ть + до + genitive, *cf.* доходи́ть/дойти́ + до + genitive, to reach; get as far as.

C. **Пла́вать/плыть**

1. Я́ люблю́ (пла́вать/плы́ть).
2. Ле́том я́ ка́ждый де́нь (пла́вал/плы́л) в о́зере.
3. Оди́н ра́з, когда́ я́ (пла́вал/плы́л) к бе́регу, я́ уви́дел ры́бу, кото́рая (пла́вала/плыла́) ко мне́. Она́ посмотре́ла на меня́, и бы́стро (уплыва́ла/уплыла́) от меня́.

READING

А́х, е́сли бы у него́ был поря́док!

Ива́н Ива́нович Пти́цын живёт за́ городом и ка́ждый де́нь е́здит на слу́жбу, снача́ла по́ездом, а пото́м на метро́.

Чтобы не опа́здывать на слу́жбу, о́н до́лжен встава́ть о́чень ра́но и ка́ждый де́нь, кро́ме выходно́го дня́, о́н ста́вит буди́льник на ше́сть часо́в. А о́сенью и зимо́й в э́то вре́мя на дворе́ быва́ет хо́лодно и темно́ как но́чью.

У Пти́цына была́ бы дово́льно споко́йная и да́же лёгкая жи́знь, е́сли бы о́н встава́л сра́зу, когда́ звони́т буди́льник, и е́сли бы у него́ бы́л поря́док в веща́х. Тогда́ о́н всегда́ приходи́л бы во́время на рабо́ту, ему́ не ну́жно было бы ка́ждый ра́з спеши́ть, и у него́ не́ было бы неприя́тных разгово́ров ни со свои́м нача́льником на слу́жбе, ни до́ма со свое́й хозя́йкой. У́тром о́н мо́г бы споко́йно приня́ть ду́ш, мо́г бы споко́йно побри́ться и споко́йно поза́втракать. Но́ э́того почти́ никогда́ не быва́ет.

Возьмём для приме́ра одно́ у́тро, и во́т что мы́ уви́дим и услы́шим.

Буди́льник звони́т ро́вно в ше́сть и бу́дит Пти́цына. Пти́цын просыпа́ется, открыва́ет оди́н гла́з, берёт буди́льник, кладёт его́ под поду́шку и неме́дленно опя́ть засыпа́ет. Бе́дный буди́льник беспоко́ится и гро́мко ти́кает под поду́шкой, но́ разбуди́ть Пти́цына не мо́жет.

Через не́которое вре́мя Пти́цын просыпа́ется от сту́ка в две́рь. Э́то стучи́т Ве́ра Васи́льевна, его́ хозя́йка, вдова́, у кото́рой о́н снима́ет ко́мнату. Пти́цын слы́шит за две́рью её неприя́тный, гро́мкий го́лос.

Хозя́йка. (кричи́т) —Ива́н Ива́нович! Пора́ встава́ть! Вы́ опя́ть опозда́ете на слу́жбу. Ва́м не сты́дно?

Пти́цын. (гро́мко, чтобы она́ слы́шала) —Я́ встаю́! Я́ уже́ почти́ гото́в.

Хозя́йка. —Почти́ гото́в! Ха́, ха́! Ка́к ва́м не сты́дно! А я́, как то́лько услы́шала ва́ш буди́льник, сра́зу поста́вила кофе́йник на плиту́. Кофе́йник уже́ полчаса́ стои́т на плите́. А вы́ зна́ете, ско́лько я́ должна́ плати́ть за га́з?

Пти́цын. (гро́мко) —Зна́ю, зна́ю, всё тепе́рь до́рого сто́ит. (Не о́чень гро́мко, та́к, чтобы она́ не слы́шала) —Наприме́р моя́ ко́мната. (Гро́мко) —Ве́ра Васи́льевна, сними́те пожа́луйста кофе́йник с плиты́ и поста́вьте его́ на сто́л. Я́ бу́ду гото́в через пя́ть мину́т. Я́ уве́рен, что ко́фе бу́дет ещё горя́чий.

Хозя́йка. —Зна́ю я́ ва́ши пя́ть мину́т. (Ухо́дит).

Пти́цын встаёт с крова́ти и начина́ет спеши́ть. О́н бежи́т в ва́нную, бы́стро мо́ется (у него́ не́т вре́мени чтобы приня́ть ду́ш), чи́стит зу́бы, бре́ется и бежи́т обра́тно в свою́ ко́мнату, чтобы оде́ться. О́н надева́ет руба́шку, хо́чет наде́ть брю́ки, но́ не мо́жет и́х найти́. О́н по́мнит, что ве́чером положи́л и́х на кре́сло. Где́ же они́? Ока́зывается, они́ упа́ли за кре́сло. О́н нахо́дит и́х за кре́слом в дово́льно печа́льном ви́де, надева́ет и́х и начина́ет иска́ть га́лстук. О́н и́щет га́лстук мину́т пя́ть.[8] Ока́зывается, га́лстук упа́л за дива́н. О́н нахо́дит его́ за дива́ном. Куда́ же о́н поста́вил ве́чером свои́ боти́нки? О́н по́мнит, что о́н сиде́л на то́м сту́ле, когда́ и́х снима́л. О́н и́щет и́х и, наконе́ц, нахо́дит оди́н боти́нок в одно́м углу́, а друго́й в друго́м. Пиджа́к его́ в ужа́сном ви́де, та́к как на нём всю но́чь спала́ ко́шка хозя́йки. Наконе́ц о́н гото́в и бежи́т на[9] ку́хню.

Та́м его́ ждёт хозя́йка. Она́ давно́ сняла́ кофе́йник с плиты́ и, пока́ Пти́цын пьёт холо́дный ко́фе, она́ произно́сит це́лую ре́чь.

Хозя́йка. —Я́ не могу́ убира́ть ко́мнату, в кото́рой всегда́ тако́й беспоря́док. Вы́ ничего́ не кладёте в шка́ф, и всё броса́ете на́ пол: бельё, чи́стое и гря́зное, носки́, чи́стые и гря́зные, кни́ги, газе́ты. Всё лежи́т на полу́! Спи́чки и оку́рки (cigarette butts) вы́ броса́ете под сто́л, под дива́н, за дива́н. А вчера́, когда́ я́ убира́ла ко́мнату, я́ нашла́ за дива́ном ка́рты и две́ руба́шки. И вы́ зна́ете, что́ вы́ ещё сде́лали? Вы́ вчера́ поста́вили мо́крый зо́нтик в у́гол ко́мнаты, на парке́т (parquet floor)! Вы́ не в пе́рвый ра́з его́ туда́ ста́вите! Я́ всегда́ ста́влю сво́й зо́нтик в у́гол в пере́дней. Я́ не хочу́, чтобы мо́крые и́ли да́же сухи́е зонты́ стоя́ли в ко́мнатах. Они́ должны́ стоя́ть в пере́дней. Вы́ меня́ слы́шите? А мо́крую шля́пу вы́ положи́ли на но́вое кре́сло! Пожа́луйста, клади́те ва́ши ве́щи на ме́сто.

—О́ Го́споди! —говори́т Пти́цын. О́н выпива́ет ча́шку холо́дного ко́фе, съеда́ет кусо́к сухо́го хле́ба, надева́ет пальто́ и выбега́ет и́з дому. Когда́ о́н прибега́ет на вокза́л, после́дний ваго́н его́ по́езда бы́стро прохо́дит ми́мо него́.

[8] About five minutes. Inverting the noun and the numeral is one method (a colloquial one) of indicating approximation.

[9] The preposition **на** is common with ку́хня.

Читáйте э́ти вопрóсы и отвечáйте на ни́х.

1. Почему́ Пти́цын дóлжен так рáно вставáть? 2. Всегдá ли óн стáвит буди́льник на шéсть часóв? 3. Чтó бы́ло бы, éсли бы óн срáзу вставáл, когдá буди́льник егó бу́дит? 4. Чтó óн дéлает, когдá звони́т буди́льник? 5. Чтó óн слы́шит за двéрью? 6. Чтó онá ему́ говори́т? 7. Чтó óн хóчет, чтобы онá сдéлала с кофéйником? 8. Чтó óн дéлает, когдá встаёт? 9. Чтó óн дéлает в вáнной? 10. Почему́ óн не мóжет бы́стро одéться? 11. Чтó случи́лось с брю́ками и с гáлстуком? Гдé óн и́х нашёл? 12. Почему́ хозя́йка не хóчет убирáть егó кóмнату? 13. Чтó óн сдéлал с мóкрым зонтóм? 14. Чтó óн сдéлал с мóкрой шля́пой? 15. Ктó вáс бу́дит у́тром? 16. Продолжáете ли вы́ лежáть в кровáти, и́ли срáзу встаёте? 17. Бросáете ли вы́ вáши вéщи нá пол, и́ли кладёте и́х на мéсто? 18. Чтó вы́ дéлаете с вáшим зонтóм? 19. Ктó убирáет вáшу кóмнату?

EXERCISES

Переведи́те на ру́сский язы́к.

1. If you want me to come on Tuesday, I shall come and read you the second part of the letter. 2. I asked Boris to write to the director of your school. He hasn't answered his letter yet. 3. I want Olga to buy an evening dress. 4. If there were a park opposite our house, we would go there to walk. 5. Her brothers see each other very seldom. 6. If Nina had had a choice, she would have chosen another apartment, but she had no choice! 7. He doesn't want me to go with him to the Middle East. 8. Take off your coat, put your wet hat on the table, and put your wet umbrella in the corner. 9. I shall take off my coat, put my hat on the table, and put my umbrella in the corner. 10. Don't put all these bottles on the floor! Put them in the cupboard, there where I usually put them. 11. I am sure that if he had wanted to get a good grade, he would have studied all day Sunday. 12. If they had always helped each other, their life would have been easier. 13. We would have helped them if we could have. 14. I would very much have loved to live in some eastern country. 15. The saleslady asked me whether I wanted the black shoes or the blue ones. 16. We shall go to the country on Wednesday if the weather is nice. 17. We would have gone to the country if the weather had been nice. 18. I shall take off my hat. 19. I put the newspaper on the table underneath the book. 20. Your pen fell behind the piano.

VOCABULARY

бельё underwear, linen, laundry
беспоря́д.ок (*gen.* **-ка**) disorder
буди́льник alarm clock
ваго́н railroad car
вдова́ widow
вид appearance, condition, air, view, aspect
во́время on time
газ gas
га́лстук necktie
душ shower
зонт, зо́нтик umbrella
зуб tooth
***кофе́йник** coffeepot
мо́крый wet
нос.о́к (*gen.* **-ка́**) sock
оде́жда clothing
о́стров (*nom. pl.* **-а́**) island
пере́дняя (*adj. used as noun*) vestibule, anteroom
пиджа́к jacket, suitcoat
плита́ stove
поду́ш.ка (*gen. pl.* **-ек**) pillow
по́лный full (+ *gen.*)
поря́д.ок (*gen.* **-ка**) order
про́шлое (*adj. used as noun*) the past
пусто́й empty
речь (*f.*) speech
самолёт airplane
ска́з.ка (*gen. pl.* **-ок**) fairy-tale
спи́ч.ка (*gen. pl.* **-ек**) match
споко́йный peaceful, calm
стук knock, rap
сухо́й dry
шкаф (*loc.* **в шкафу́**) cupboard, closet

Verbs

беспоко́иться (imperf., II: **беспоко́.юсь, -ишься**) to worry, be concerned
бри́ться (imperf., I: **бре́.юсь, -ешься**), **побри́ться** (perf., I) to shave (oneself)
броса́ть (imperf., I), **бро́сить** (perf., II: **бро́шу, бро́сишь**) to throw, fling; to throw away, give up, abandon
иска́ть (imperf., I: **ищу́, и́щешь**) to look for, seek
надева́ть (imperf., I) **наде́ть** (perf., I: **наде́н.у, -ешь**) to put on
ока́зываться (imperf., I), **оказа́ться** (**ока́жется**) to turn out (to be)
па́дать (imperf., I), **упа́сть** (perf., I: **упад.у́, -ёшь**) to fall
снима́ть (imperf., I), **снять** (perf., I: **сниму́, сни́мешь**) to take off; rent
стуча́ть (imperf., II: **стуч.у́, -и́шь**), **постуча́ть** (perf., II) to knock, rap
***ти́кать** (imperf., I) to tick
убира́ть (imperf., I), **убра́ть** (perf., I: **убер.у́, -ёшь**) to clean up, off; tidy
чи́стить (imperf., II: **чи́щу, чи́стишь**), **почи́стить** (perf., II) to clean

Expressions

по де́лу on business
(по)е́хать за́ город to drive out of town
бы́ть за́ городом to be out of town
выходно́й де́нь day off, holiday

(по)ста́вить буди́льник на (+ *acc.*) to set an alarm clock for
на дворé out of doors
возьмём let's take
за двéрью on the other side of the door
вáм не сты́дно? Aren't you ashamed?
на мéсто to its proper place
на мéсте in its place; on the spot

Vocabulary Review

Одéжда—Clothing

пальтó шля́па шáпка (cap) платóк

Мужскáя одéжда

мужскóй костю́м
пиджáк
брю́ки (*gen. pl.* брюк)
рубáшка
жакéт (sport jacket)
носóк (*nom. pl.* носки́)
боти́нок (*nom. pl.* боти́нки; *gen. pl.* боти́нок)

Жéнская одéжда

дáмский костю́м
жакéт
ю́бка
плáтье
блу́зка
чулóк (*nom. pl.* чу́лки; *gen. pl.* чулóк) stocking
ту́фля (*nom. pl.* ту́фли; *gen. pl.* ту́фель) shoe, slipper

UNIT 25

***Comparative adjectives and adverbs,* 425. *Superlative adjectives,* 434. *The verbal prefixes* по-, про-, *and* за-, 439. *Translation of "let,"* 441. *Vocabulary Review: Verbs of Position,* 448.**

GRAMMAR

1. Comparative adjectives and adverbs

The adjectives and adverbs given in earlier lessons were in the *positive* degree. Besides the positive degree, Russian, like English, also has a *comparative* degree (formed in English with the ending *-er: bigger, taller, sooner;* or with the word *more: more interesting*). Russian and English also have a *superlative* degree (formed in English with the ending *-est: biggest, tallest, soonest;* or with the word *most: most interesting*). The following are some examples of Russian comparatives (they are given beside the corresponding positive forms):

Positive Degree		*Comparative Degree*	
но́вый	new	нове́е	newer
дли́нный	long	длинне́е	longer
большо́й	large, big	бо́льше	larger, bigger
бы́стрый	fast	быстре́е	faster

Comparatives are indeclinable: their endings do not change to express gender, number, or case. The same form serves as comparative both of the adjective and of its corresponding adverb; *e.g.*, **быстре́е** means both "more rapid" and "more rapidly." Most comparatives are formed with the ending **-ее** (sometimes shortened to **-ей**), like **нове́е** from **но́вый**, and **длинне́е** from **дли́нный**.[1] Others are

[1] The stress shifts to the ending **-ее** if the adjective has a monosyllabic stem, *e.g.*, нове́е; it does not shift when the stem has more than one syllable, *e.g.*, краси́вее.

formed with **-е**,[2] *e.g.*, бо́льше from большо́й, or бога́че from бога́тый. In the latter type (one **-е**) consonant mutations occur, as in **бога́тый—бога́че** or **молодо́й—моло́же,** etc.; these consonant changes and irregular formations will be given below.

In a statement of comparison, such as *He is younger than I*, or *The Volga is longer than the Don,* English "than I" or "than the Don" may be rendered in Russian in two different ways:

(1) With the second term of a comparison in the same case as the first term to which it is compared; the second term is placed in a subordinate clause introduced by **чем:**

> **Во́лга** длинне́е, чем **До́н.** (two nominatives).
> The Volga is longer than the Don.
>
> О́н помога́ет **мне́** бо́льше, чем **ва́м.** (two datives).
> He helps me more than (he does) you.

(2) With the second term of comparison, which is part of the main clause, in the *genitive:*

> Во́лга длинне́е До́н**а.**
> The Volga is longer than the Don.
>
> Ва́ш костю́м нове́е мо**его́.**
> Your suit is newer than mine.

The latter construction (with the genitive) obviously serves only for declinable words; it may be used in comparing someone or something to the subject of the sentence (or sometimes to the direct object, particularly when the direct object is inaminate):

> О́н умне́е **меня́.** (comparison with subject).
> He is more intelligent than I.
>
> Я́ люблю́ **мя́со** бо́льше **ры́бы.** (comparison with object).
> I like meat better than fish.

Otherwise the construction with **чем** is mandatory; thus:

(1) Comparison between adverbs:

> О́н говори́т **по-ру́сски** лу́чше, чем **по-англи́йски.**
> He speaks Russian better than English.

(2) Comparison between infinitives:

> **Говори́ть** по-ру́сски трудне́е, чем **чита́ть.**
> It's harder to speak Russian than to read it.

[2] The comparative ending **-е** is never stressed.

(3) Comparison between adverbial clauses:

В Крыму́ теплée, чем **в Москвé.**
It's warmer in the Crimea than in Moscow.

A. Use of comparatives. Comparatives have two uses: predicative and adverbial.

Predicative use.

Э́та шля́па **дешéвле** тóй (or чем тá).
This hat is *cheaper* than that one.

Тó здáние **вы́ше** э́того (or чем э́то).
That building is *taller* than this one.

Нáша стáрая кварти́ра былá **дешéвле,** нó **мéньше** э́той.
Our old apartment was *cheaper* but *smaller* than this one.

Adverbial use. The comparative forms are also used adverbially; thus **интерéснее** is the comparative of the adjective **интерéсный** and also of the adverb **интерéсно.**

Adjectival use:

Егó доклáд бы́л **интерéсный,** нó доклáд Петрóва бы́л ещё **интерéснее.**
His report was interesting, but Petrov's was still *more interesting.*

Adverbial use:

О́н говори́т **интерéсно,** нó пи́шет ещё **интерéснее.**
He speaks *interestingly*, but he writes still *more interestingly.*

B. Comparatives with бóлее and мéнее. An alternative means for expressing comparison in Russian is provided by the words **бóлее** (more) and **мéнее** (less), placed before an adjective in the positive degree which is declined; they require the use of the construction with **чем:**

Э́та гости́ница **бóлее дорогáя,** чем тá, в котóрой мы́ живём.
This hotel is more expensive than the one in which we live.

Мы́ жи́ли в **мéнее дорогóй** гости́нице, чем тá, в котóрой жи́ли Кали́нины.
We lived in a less expensive hotel than the one in which the Kalinins lived.

Generally comparisons with **бóлее** are less idiomatic than those using the comparative forms; in some instances, however, the use of

бо́лее may be preferable, or even necessary, as in the case when a comparative appears in the attributive function (*i.e.*, not predicatively or adverbially):

Мне́ ну́жен **бо́лее о́стрый** но́ж.
I need a sharper knife.

Я́ никогда́ не чита́л **бо́лее интере́сной** кни́ги.
I have never read a more interesting book.

Comparatives with the prefix **по-** are often used in requests, commands, suggestions, etc., indicating, *without any specific comparison*, the wish for better, more, quicker, cheaper, etc.:

Купи́ **побо́льше** моро́женого: они́ приду́т со свои́ми детьми́.
Buy more (be sure to buy enough) ice-cream; they are bringing their children.

Приходи́те к на́м **поча́ще.**
Come to see us more often.

Не́т ли у ва́с чего́-нибудь **подеше́вле?**
Don't you have anything (a bit) cheaper?

Да́й мне́ но́ж **поостре́е.**
Give me a sharper knife.

C. Consonant mutations and irregularities in the comparatives in -е. Comparatives ending in **-е** (not **-ее**) often undergo changes of the final consonant of the stem. These follow the usual pattern of consonant mutations and are the same mutations as those which occur in the present conjugation of verbs (see Unit 21, page 342).

г > **ж**	доро**г**о́й—доро́**ж**е	dearer, more expensive
х > **ш**	ти́**х**ий—ти́**ш**е	quieter
х > **ш**	су**х**о́й—су́**ш**е	drier
т > **ч**	бога́**т**ый—бога́**ч**е	richer, wealthier
д > **ж**	моло**д**о́й—моло́**ж**е	younger
ст > **щ**	про**ст**о́й—про́**щ**е	simpler
	ча́**ст**ый—ча́**щ**е	oftener
	чи́**ст**ый—чи́**щ**е	cleaner
	то́л**ст**ый—то́л**щ**е	thicker, fatter
в > **вл**	дешёвый—деше́**вл**е	cheaper

A number of adjectives have a **-к-**, or **-ок-**, element between the stem and the ending; in the comparative form some adjectives preserve the **-к-** element (which undergoes a mutation and appears as **ч**), while in others it disappears; the **-ок-** element always disappears:

-к- changes to **ч**:

гро́мкий—гро́мче	louder
жа́ркий—жа́рче	hotter
лёгкий—ле́гче	lighter, easier
мя́гкий—мя́гче	softer

-к- disappears; final stem consonant changed:

т > ч	коро́ткий—коро́че	shorter
з > ж	бли́зкий—бли́же	nearer
	ни́зкий—ни́же	lower
	у́зкий—у́же	narrower
д > ж	ре́дкий—ре́же	more rarely, less often

-ок- disappears:

высо́кий—вы́ше	higher, taller
широ́кий—ши́ре	wider, broader

Observe also the following comparatives formed with **-ше** or **-же**:

глубо́кий—глу́бже	deeper
далёкий—да́льше	farther, further
по́здний (по́здно)—по́зже	later
ра́нний (ра́но)—ра́ньше	earlier
то́нкий—то́ньше	thinner
до́лгий (до́лго)—до́льше	longer (in time)
ста́рый—ста́рше	older

A small number of adjectives have special attributive forms made without **бо́лее.** In most of these the comparative stem is distinct from that of the positive:

Positive	*Comparative Attributive*	*Predicative and Adverbial*	
хоро́ший	лу́чший	лу́чше	better
плохо́й	ху́дший	ху́же	worse
ста́рый	ста́рший	ста́рше	older, elder, senior
молодо́й	мла́дший	мла́дше, моло́же	younger, junior
большо́й	бо́льший[3]	бо́льше[4]	bigger, larger; more
ма́ленький	ме́ньший	ме́ньше[4]	smaller; less, fewer

[3] Note the distinction in place of stress between the positive **большо́й** and the comparative **бо́льший.**

[4] **Бо́льше** serves as the comparative form of both **большо́й** (big) and **мно́го** (much, many). Similarly, **ме́ньше** is the comparative of both **ма́ленький** and **ма́ло.**

Attributive:

Сего́дня мы́ нашли́ **лу́чший** рестора́н.
Today we found a better restaurant (better than our usual one).

Predicative:

Э́тот слова́рь **лу́чше** ва́шего.

Adverbial:

О́н пи́шет **лу́чше** меня́, но́ ме́дленнее.

Pattern Sentences

Predicate and Adverbial Comparatives

1. Ленингра́д **краси́вее** Москвы́.
2. Ва́ш до́м **нове́е** на́шего.
3. Ле́на **умне́е** О́льги.
4. О́льга **глупе́е** Ле́ны.
5. Вади́м, хотя́ **моло́же, сильне́е** Бори́са.
6. Бори́с **ста́рше** и **вы́ше,** но́ **слабе́е его́.**
7. Ю́жное не́бо **сине́е** се́верного.
8. Сего́дня немно́жко **тепле́е, чем** бы́ло вчера́. Но́ говоря́т, что за́втра бу́дет опя́ть **холодне́е.**
9. **Ти́ше!** Не шуми́те!
10. Говори́те немно́жко **гро́мче**—я́ ва́с пло́хо слы́шу.

1. Leningrad is more beautiful than Moscow.
2. Your house is newer than ours.
3. Lena is more intelligent than Olga.
4. Olga is stupider than Lena.
5. Vadim, though younger, is stronger than Boris.
6. Boris is older and taller, but weaker than he is.
7. The southern sky is bluer than the northern one.
8. Today it's a bit warmer than yesterday. But they say that tomorrow will be colder again.
9. Quiet(er)! Don't make noise!
10. Speak a little louder. I can't hear you well.

Attributive with **бо́лее** *or* **ме́нее.**

1. Поговори́м на **бо́лее интере́сную** те́му!
2. Пообе́даем в **бо́лее дешёвом** рестора́не. Рестора́н про́тив моего́ до́ма **деше́вле** э́того.
3. Я́ счита́ю, что э́то **ме́нее ва́жный** вопро́с, чем то́т, о кото́ром мы́ говори́ли вчера́.
4. В э́тот ра́з мы́ останови́лись в **бо́лее дорого́й** гости́нице.

1. Let's talk about a more interesting subject!
2. Let's dine in a cheaper restaurant. The restaurant across from my house is cheaper than this one.
3. I consider this question less important than the one we talked about yesterday.
4. This time we stopped (stayed) at a more expensive hotel.

Drills

A. *Complete the sentences.*

Семёновы богаче { я. / ты. / он. / она́. / мы. / вы. / они́. / до́ктор Смирно́в. / на́ша но́вая учи́тельница. / Ива́н Петро́вич Андре́ев. / ва́ши друзья́. / ва́ши подру́ги. }

Москва́ бо́льше { Оде́сса. / Ки́ев. / ва́ша столи́ца. / э́тот го́род. }

B. *Supply the comparatives of the adjectives in boldface and then give their opposites in the comparative, according to the model.*

	Opposite comparatives	
Model: Ива́н **си́льный,** но́ Па́вел **сильне́е** Ива́на.	**Ива́н**	**слабе́е.**
1. Дне́пр **дли́нный,** но́ Во́лга	......	......
2. Мы́ **бога́тые,** но́ Рокфе́ллер	......	......
3. Воло́дя **высо́кий,** но́ Серёжа	......	......
4. Моя́ кварти́ра **хоро́шая,** но́ ва́ша	......	......
5. Ка́тя **у́мная,** но́ Зи́на	......	......
6. Мне́ **удо́бно** прийти́ в два́, но́ в три́ мне́	......	......
7. Мо́й костю́м **дорого́й,** но́ тво́й	......	......
8. Я́ пишу́ **пло́хо,** но́ ты́ пи́шешь	......	......
9. Мы́ живём **далеко́,** но́ вы́ живёте	......	......
10. Ла́вка **бли́зко,** но́ апте́ка	......	......
11. Моё пла́тье **коро́ткое,** но́ твоё	......	......
12. Моя́ ко́мната **тёмная,** но́ твоя́	......	......
13. Сего́дня **тепло́,** но́ вчера́ бы́ло	......	......
14. Си́няя ю́бка **широ́кая,** но́ чёрная	......	......
15. Зи́на поёт **хорошо́,** но́ ты́ поёшь	......	......

C. *Supply correct forms of the comparative.*

1. До́ктор Смирно́в (хоро́ший), чем до́ктор Кры́мов.
2. Я́ (пло́хо) гото́влю, чем Ли́за.
3. Толсто́й писа́л Войну́ и ми́р (до́лго), чем А́нну Каре́нину.
4. Си́няя ю́бка (коро́ткая) чёрной.
5. Я́ живу́ (далеко́) от университе́та, чем вы́.
6. Мне́ (легко́) чита́ть по-францу́зски, чем говори́ть.

7. Э́то вечéрнее плáтье (нóвое) тогó.
8. Алёша (ýмный) Ви́ктора.
9. Вóлга (широ́кая) Днепрá.
10. Нáша ýлица (ýзкая) вáшей.
11. Рекá Амазóнка (дли́нная) Вóлги.
12. Вáш дóм (высóкий) нáшего.
13. Э́та горá (ни́зкая) тóй.
14. Нáша гости́ная (большáя) столóвой.
15. Э́ти боти́нки (дешёвые) чёрных.
16. Твоя́ кварти́ра (дорогáя) моéй.
17. Ктó (си́льный), Бори́с и́ли Вади́м?
18. Вади́м (слáбый) Бори́са.
19. Нáши сосéди (богáтые) нáс.
20. Мы́ (бéдные) нáших сосéдей.

D. Adverbs and conjunctions with the comparative. **Горáздо** is used with comparatives for emphasis much as the word **óчень** is used with adjectives or adverbs in the positive degree; óчень трýдный—**горáздо труднéе** (much harder); óчень высóкий—**горáздо вы́ше** (much higher); óчень мнóго—**горáздо бóльше** (much—or many—more).

Ещё means "still (more)":

О́н óчень ýмный, нó егó брáт **ещё умнéе.**
He is very intelligent, but his brother is still more so.

Всё before a comparative adjective means "more and more," "all the time":

Дни́ станóвятся **всё корóче.**
The days keep getting shorter.

На скóлько? means "by how much?" The answer is also made with **на:**

—**На скóлько** вы́ **стáрше** меня́? —**На двá гóда.**
—How much older are you than I? —Two years.

—**На скóлько** страни́ц вы́ прочитáли **бóльше,** чем я́?
—Я́ прочитáл на оди́ннадцать страни́ц **бóльше.**
—How many pages more than I did you read?
—I read eleven pages more.

Чем . . . тем is equivalent to English "the . . . the" with comparatives:

Чем бóльше, **тем** лýчше.
The more the better.

Чем скорéй, **тем** лýчше.
The sooner the better.

Pattern Sentences

Горáздо *with comparatives.*

1. Лéтом в Срéдней А́зии **горáздо жáрче,** чем в Крымý.

1. In summer it's much hotter in Central Asia than in the Crimea.

2. Сове́тский Сою́з **гора́здо бо́льше** и **бога́че** По́льши.	2. The Soviet Union is much larger and wealthier than Poland.
3. Кавка́зкие го́ры **гора́здо вы́ше** Ура́льских и Кры́мских го́р.	3. The Caucasus Mountains are much higher than the Urals or those of the Crimea.
4. Ура́льские го́ры **гора́здо ни́же** Кавка́зских.	4. The Ural Mountains are much lower than those of the Caucasus.
5. Э́ти рабо́чие рабо́тают тепе́рь **гора́здо быстре́й,** но́ всё же недоста́точно бы́стро.	5. These workers work much faster now, but still not fast enough.

Ещё *with comparatives.*

1. Хотя́ Дне́пр и о́чень дли́нная река́, но́ Во́лга **ещё длинне́е** (Днепра́).	1. Though the Dnieper is a very long river, the Volga is still longer (than the Dnieper).
2. Вчера́ бы́ло жа́рко, но́ сего́дня, ка́жется, бу́дет **ещё жа́рче.**	2. It was hot yesterday, but I think today will be still hotter.
3. Мы́ живём о́чень бли́зко от университе́та, но́ вы́ живёте **ещё бли́же.**	3. We live very close to the university, but you live still closer.

Всё *with comparatives.*

1. О́н **всё ре́же** и **ре́же** быва́ет в на́шем го́роде.	1. He visits our city more and more rarely.
2. Тепе́рь **всё ча́ще** и **ча́ще** идёт сне́г.	2. It snows more and more often now.
3. Алёша занима́ется **всё ме́ньше** и **ме́ньше.**	3. Alyosha is studying less and less.

На ско́лько *with comparatives.*

1. —**На ско́лько** э́та кварти́ра **доро́же** ста́рой? —Она́ **доро́же на** пятна́дцать до́лларов в ме́сяц.	1. —How much more expensive is this apartment than the old one? —It's $15 a month more.
2. Мы́ живём тепе́рь в **бо́лее дешёвой** кварти́ре. Она́ **на** три́дцать рубле́й **деше́вле** ва́шей.	2. We're now living in a cheaper apartment. It's thirty rubles cheaper than yours.
3. **На ско́лько** ле́т Ни́на **моло́же** О́льги? —Она́ **моло́же на** четы́ре го́да.	3. —How much younger is Nina than Olga? —She is four years younger.

Чем . . . тем *with comparatives.*

1. **Чем бо́льше** вы́ бу́дете говори́ть по-ру́сски, **тем лу́чше** вы́ бу́дете говори́ть.	1. The more you (will) speak Russian, the better you will speak it.
2. **Чем скоре́е** о́н вернётся, **тем лу́чше.**	2. The sooner he comes back, the better.

Drill

Переведи́те на ру́сский.

1. How much younger is your brother than you (are)?
2. He is two years younger than I (am).
3. —How much older is your son than mine? —He is much older.
4. —How much shorter is the second story than the first one? —Three pages.
5. —How much closer do you live to the border than we do? —Forty-two kilometers.
6. —How many kilometers farther from (**от** + genitive) the border is your town than theirs? —Only a few (several) kilometers.
7. —How many more books do you have now than you had before? —Fifty or sixty.
8. The sooner you (will) finish this book, the sooner you'll start another one.
9. The oftener I see him the less I like him.
10. He makes mistakes more and more often.
11. I like meat much more than fish.
12. He writes many more letters than I do.
13. The grandmother talks much more than the granddaughter.
14. She talks more and more.

2. Superlative adjectives

One type of superlative is formed by adding **-ейший** or **-айший** to the stem of the adjective.[5] This superlative usually does *not imply* any comparison, but merely asserts a very high degree of the quality in question:

в **ближа́йшем** вре́мени
in the very near future

Very often this form of the superlative has an emotional coloring:

Э́то **интере́снейшая** рабо́та!
That's extremely interesting work!

Я́ то́лько что ви́дел **замеча́тельнейший** фи́льм!
I've just seen the most wonderful film!

Another type of superlative is formed by using **са́мый** with the positive degree of the adjective. *Both* **са́мый** and the adjective itself are declined:

Э́то **са́мая дорога́я** гости́ница в го́роде.
This is *the most expensive* hotel in town.

Мы́ живём в **са́мой интере́сной** ча́сти на́шего го́рода.
We live in *the most interesting* part of our city.

[5] The ending is regularly **-ейший**, but **-айший** is used after **ж, ч, ш**, occurring as the result of mutation of the final stem consonant, *e.g.*, ближа́йший, велича́йший, глубоча́йший, тиша́йший, etc.

Вы́ купи́ли мне́ **са́мую интере́сную** кни́гу, кото́рую я́ когда́-либо чита́л.
You bought me *the most interesting* book I have ever read.

This type of superlative, unlike that in **-ейший** or **-айший,** is used chiefly to denote superiority to others (contrast English "the most" = **са́мый,** as opposed to "a most" = **-ейший/-айший**):

Э́то **са́мая интере́сная** кни́га на э́ту те́му.
This is *the most interesting* book on the subject.

Э́то **интере́снейшая** кни́га!
This is *a most interesting* book.

The forms **лу́чший, ху́дший, ста́рший,** and **мла́дший** are frequently used with superlative meaning:

мо́й лу́чший дру́г	my best friend
мо́й ста́рший бра́т	my elder (or eldest) brother

Са́мый is also used with these comparatives and makes the statement somewhat stronger:

О́н **са́мый лу́чший** учени́к в кла́ссе.
He is the (very) best student in the class.

О́н **са́мый ста́рший** из э́тих ма́льчиков.
He is the eldest of those boys.

Pattern Sentences

Superlatives in **-ейший/-айший.**

1. О́н за́дал мне́ **глупе́йший** вопро́с.	1. He asked me an extremely foolish question.
2. Лунёв рассказа́л на́м **интере́снейшую** исто́рию.	2. Lunyov told us a most interesting story.
3. Его́ де́душка **умне́йший** стари́к.	3. His grandfather is an extremely clever old man.
4. Дире́ктор произнёс на банке́те **длинне́йшую** ре́чь.	4. The director gave a terribly long speech at the banquet.
5. Пу́шкин **велича́йший** ру́сский поэ́т.	5. Pushkin is the greatest Russian poet.
6. В Сре́дней А́зии нахо́дятся **высоча́йшие** го́ры. Они́ вы́ше все́х го́р в ми́ре.	6. In Central Asia there are very high mountains. They are the highest (higher than any other) mountains in the world.

Superlatives with **са́мый.**

1. Во́лга **са́мая дли́нная** река́ в Евро́пе.	1. The Volga is the longest river in Europe.

2. **Са́мые высо́кие** го́ры в СССР нахо́дятся о́коло грани́цы Афганиста́на. Э́ти го́ры **гора́здо вы́ше** Кавка́зских го́р.

2. The highest mountains in the U.S.S.R. are located near the frontier of Afghanistan. These mountains are much higher than those of the Caucasus.

3. Байка́л **са́мое большо́е** о́зеро Сове́тского Сою́за, и в пе́снях его́ да́же называ́ют мо́рем. Э́то **са́мое глубо́кое** о́зеро в ми́ре. Не́т о́зера **глу́бже** Байка́ла.

3. Baikal is the largest lake in the Soviet Union, and in songs it is even called a sea. It is the deepest lake in the world. There is no deeper lake than Baikal.

4. —**Са́мое лу́чшее** что вы́ мо́жете сде́лать, э́то верну́ть ему́ э́то письмо́.

4. —The best thing that you can do is to return that letter to him.

5. Я́ разгова́ривал вчера́ с **са́мым у́мным** челове́ком, кото́рого я́ когда́-либо зна́л.

5. Yesterday I talked to the most intelligent man I have ever known.

Лу́чший, ху́дший

1. Андре́й **лу́чший** учени́к в кла́ссе, а Ива́н **ху́дший.**

1. Andrey is the best pupil in the class, and Ivan is the poorest.

2. Э́то **лу́чшая** кни́га, кото́рую я́ когда́-либо чита́л.

2. That's the best book that I have ever read.

Drills

A. *Переведи́те на англи́йский.*

Не́сколько сло́в о геогра́фии Сове́тского Сою́за.

Сове́тский Сою́з **гора́здо бо́льше** други́х европе́йских стра́н, и о́н та́кже **бо́льше** Соединённых Шта́тов и Кита́я.

Са́мые дли́нные ре́ки СССР в его́ Азиа́тской ча́сти—в Сиби́ри. **Са́мая дли́нная** река́ в Евро́пе—э́то Во́лга. Во́лга **длинне́е** и **ши́ре** Днепра́ и До́на и **длинне́е** и **ши́ре** Дуна́я (Danube) и Ре́йна (Rhine).

Ура́льские го́ры образу́ют (form) на се́вере грани́цу ме́жду европе́йской и азиа́тской ча́стью СССР. Они́ **ни́же** Кавка́зских го́р. Кавка́зские го́ры нахо́дятся ме́жду Чёрным и Каспи́йским моря́ми. Они́ **гора́здо вы́ше** Ура́льских. Мы́ уже́ зна́ем, что **са́мая высо́кая** гора́ на Кавка́зе—э́то Эльбру́с. Монбла́н (Mont Blanc), са́мая высо́кая гора́ в за́падной Евро́пе, ни́же Эльбру́са. Е́сть го́ры та́кже в Крыму́. Кры́м нахо́дится на се́вере Чёрного мо́ря. Кры́мские го́ры то́же **ни́же** Кавка́зских.

Населе́ние СССР **бо́льше** населе́ния Соединённых Шта́тов.

Са́мые больши́е города́ Сою́за нахо́дятся в его́ европе́йской ча́сти. Москва́, столи́ца Сою́за, **гора́здо бо́льше** Вашингто́на, но́ **гора́здо ме́ньше** Нью-Йо́рка. В Москве́ **бо́льше** жи́телей, чем в Вашингто́не.

B. *Читáйте вопрóсы и отвечáйте на ни́х.*

1. Прáвильно ли сказáть, что Вóлга сáмая дли́нная рекá Совéтского Союза?
2. Чтó мóжно сказáть об Урáльских горáх?
3. Éсть ли в зáпадной Еврóпе гóры вы́ше Монблáна?
4. Чтó вы́ знáете об Эльбрýсе?
5. Гдé нахóдится Кры́м?
6. Гдé нахóдится Кавкáз?
7. Чтó вы́ знáете о населéнии Совéтского Союза?
8. В какóй чáсти СССР нахóдятся сáмые больши́е городá?
9. В какóй из столи́ц бóльше жи́телей, в Вашингтóне и́ли в Москвé?

C. *Translate the words in parentheses.*

1. Какáя (longest) ýлица в э́том гóроде?
2. Какóй из э́тих домóв (oldest)?
3. Вади́м танцевáл вчерá с (most pretty) дéвушкой.
4. Андрéй лю́бит (the silliest) дéвушку из всéх.
5. Я́ пишý э́то письмó моемý (most intelligent) студéнту.
6. Я́ расскáзывал о моём (oldest) дрýге.
7. Зелёное плáтье (most expensive) из всéх.
8. Вади́м (much taller) Ивáна.
9. Алёша (much more intelligent) Лéны.

Set expressions with the superlative.

сáмое лýчшее
the best (thing)

сáмое хýдшее
the worst (thing)

сáмое глáвное
the most important (thing), the main thing

в лýчшем/хýдшем слýчае
at best (worst)

с величáйшим удовóльствием
with the greatest pleasure

в ближáйшем бýдущем
in the very near future

в ближáйшие дни́
in the next few days

в ближáйшем ресторáне, магази́не, и т. д.
in the nearest restaurant, store, etc.

бо́льше всего́[6]
most of all, more than anything else

бо́льше все́х[6]
most of all, more than anyone else

Pattern Sentences

1. **Са́мое лу́чшее,** что вы́ мо́жете сде́лать, э́то написа́ть письмо́ самому́ дире́ктору.
2. Да́, я́ то́же ду́маю, что э́то бу́дет **са́мое лу́чшее.** Я́ напишу́ ему́ в **ближа́йшие дни́.**
3. **В ху́дшем слу́чае** о́н ва́м не отве́тит.
4. **В ху́дшем слу́чае** я́ опозда́ю к нача́лу его́ ре́чи.
5. Мы́ зашли́ в **ближа́йший** рестора́н и пое́ли та́м.
6. **Бо́льше всего́** мо́й сы́н лю́бит му́зыку. О́н игра́ет на роя́ле **лу́чше всё́х** свои́х друзе́й.
7. Молодо́й италья́нский певе́ц пе́л **лу́чше всё́х. Лу́чше всего́** о́н пе́л неаполита́нские серена́ды.

1. The best thing you can do is to write to the director himself.
2. Yes, I think too that would be the best. I'll write to him in the next few days.
3. The worst that can happen is that he won't answer you.
4. At worst I'll miss (be late for) the beginning of his speech.
5. We stopped at the nearest restaurant and ate there.
6. Most of all my son likes music. He plays the piano better than any of his friends.
7. The young Italian singer sang the best of anyone. Best of all he sang Neapolitan serenades.

Drills

A. *Переведи́те с ру́сского на англи́йский.*

1. Профе́ссор счита́ет Вади́ма свои́м лу́чшим студе́нтом.
2. Ленингра́д бли́же к грани́це, чем Москва́.
3. Мно́гие счита́ют Петра́ Вели́кого велича́йшим ру́сским царём.
4. Как то́лько верну́сь, я́ сейча́с же расскажу́ обо всём э́том мои́м лу́чшим друзья́м.
5. Мы́ зашли́ в ближа́йшую ла́вку, купи́ли лу́чшее вино́, како́е у ни́х бы́ло, и верну́лись домо́й.
6. О́н отве́тил мне́ глупе́йшим письмо́м, кото́рое я́ ему́ верну́, как то́лько его́ уви́жу.
7. Я́ люблю́ все́х и́х дете́й, но́ бо́льше всё́х я́ люблю́ Ве́рочку.
8. Я́ бо́льше всего́ люблю́ говори́ть по-францу́зски.
9. Са́мое лу́чшее бу́дет никому́ об э́том не говори́ть.
10. Наде́юсь, что о́н поговори́л с ни́м о са́мом гла́вном.
11. Мы́ ля́жем сего́дня гора́здо ра́ньше, чем обы́чно, та́к как за́втра ну́жно бу́дет о́чень ра́но встать.

[6] These forms, though comparative, are frequently used in the function of an adverbial and predicative superlative. Note also: **лу́чше всего́,** better than anything else; **лу́чше всё́х,** better than anyone else.

12. —На ско́лько э́та доро́га коро́че то́й? —Э́та доро́га, ка́жется, на пя́ть киломе́тров коро́че.
13. Но́вый слова́рь доро́же ста́рого на ше́сть рубле́й; пра́вда, о́н то́лще, то́ есть полне́е. Ста́рый деше́вле, но́ то́ньше: о́н ме́нее по́лный.
14. Грани́ца ме́жду Сове́тским Сою́зом и Кита́ем длинне́е, чем грани́ца ме́жду Соединёнными Шта́тами и Кана́дой.
15. Я́ зайду́ к ва́м в ближа́йшие дни́.
16. Зинаи́да Миха́йловна миле́йший челове́к.
17. Я́ получи́л интере́снейшее письмо́ от одного́ неме́цкого учёного.
18. К чёрту всё! Ну́жно жи́ть веселе́й.
19. О́н тепе́рь рабо́тает гора́здо бо́льше, чем ра́ньше, но́ всё же недоста́точно.

B. *Переведи́те на ру́сский.*

1. Most of all Petrov likes to play chess. He plays the best (better than anyone) in our town.
2. I shall finish the article in the next few days.
3. The best that you can do is to write to him at once.
4. I shall help you with the greatest pleasure.
5. At the worst I shall be a few minutes late.
6. A young French journalist told me that the war in Africa would end in the near future.
7. I told him the main thing.
8. He is my best friend.
9. —How much more do you pay for your room than I do? —Ten rubles more.
10. He's a most wonderful person!

3. The verbal prefixes по-; про-; за-

По-. Many verbs may form a perfective using the prefix **по-**. With some verbs, this prefix, while it changes the aspect, does not affect the meaning of the basic verb; the following are among imperfective-perfective pairs in which the two forms differ in aspect only:

Imperfective	*Perfective*
обе́дать	пообе́дать
за́втракать	поза́втракать
сове́товать	посове́товать
ве́рить	пове́рить
etc.	

With very many verbs, on the other hand, **по-** produces perfectives meaning *limited duration:* an action has been performed, or a state or condition has lasted "for a while" and then has been terminated, but without any goal, result, or conclusion having been reached.

Some verbs may have a **по-** perfective besides a perfective signifying actual completion:

Прочита́ть (always with a direct object) means to complete the reading of a certain amount of written or printed matter; **почита́ть** (with or without a direct object) means to do some reading, to read for a while; similarly:

погуля́ть	to go for a walk, walk for a while
порабо́тать	to do some work
поговори́ть	to have a talk
поспа́ть	to take a nap

Perfectives with **по-** are especially frequent with verbs describing actions that do not ordinarily lead to any result or completion; such are verbs of state or condition, in particular, verbs of position (sitting, lying, standing):

сиде́ть—посиде́ть	to sit for a while
лежа́ть—полежа́ть	to lie (rest) for a while
стоя́ть—постоя́ть	to stand for a while

Unlike other prefixes, **по-** gives *perfective* verbs when added to indeterminate imperfectives of motion:

походи́ть	to walk for a while (perf.)
пое́здить	to drive for a while (perf.)

But contrast: **приходи́ть, уходи́ть,** etc. which are *imperfective.*

Про-. Verbs of state or condition (including sitting, lying, standing) may also be prefixed with **про-**; forms with **про-** are used when it is felt that the time spent in a state or condition (or position) has been long (sometimes excessively long); these verbs are transitive, and the time spent must always be indicated in the accusative (if not necessarily expressed in units of time):

О́н **просиде́л** у на́с весь ве́чер.
О́н **пролежа́л** два́ ме́сяца в больни́це.
О́н **простоя́л** всю́ доро́гу.
О́н **про́жил** всю́ жи́знь в Москве́.

Note also: **побы́ть—пробы́ть,** to stay, spend some time somewhere.

За-. A special class of perfectives denotes only the start of an action; such perfectives are known as inchoatives. They are formed with several prefixes, among which is the prefix **за-**:

игра́ть—заигра́ть	to start playing
говори́ть—заговори́ть	to speak up, begin to speak
боле́ть—заболе́ть	to fall ill

This prefix is not always inchoative, of course, *e.g.* **заходи́ть—зайти́,** "to drop in to see."

Pattern Sentences

Verbal prefixes **по-, про-** *and* **за-:**

1. По́сле обе́да мы́ **заговори́ли** о бо́лее интере́сных веща́х.	1. After dinner we began to talk about more interesting things.
2. Орке́стр **сыгра́л** танго́ и **заигра́л** каку́ю-то бо́лее весёлую мело́дию.	2. The orchestra played through a tango and struck up a more cheerful melody.
3. Ребёнок **засмея́лся,** а пото́м вдру́г **запла́кал.** О́н немно́го **попла́кал** и на́чал е́сть.	3. The child began to laugh and then suddenly began to cry. He cried for a while and began to eat.
4. Я́ **полежу́** и мо́жет быть **посплю́** немно́го, а пото́м мы́ **поговори́м.**	4. I shall lie down a bit and perhaps sleep a bit, and then we'll have a talk.
5. **Почита́йте** пока́ газе́ту—я́ ско́ро верну́сь.	5. Meanwhile read the paper a while; I'll soon be back.
6. Я́ **посижу́** и **покурю́,** а ты́ пока́ оде́нься.	6. I'll sit and smoke for a while; in the meantime you get dressed.
7. О́н **про́жил** всю́ жи́знь на Да́льнем Восто́ке.	7. He lived all his life in the Far East.
8. О́н **пролежа́л** в больни́це не́сколько ме́сяцев.	8. He spent several months in the hospital.

4. Inclusive imperative ("let us") and 3d person imperative ("let him," etc.)

"Let us," that is, an invitation or command to perform an action in which the speaker will participate, may be rendered by a verb in the future tense of the first person plural without a pronoun subject; when one person is addressed by the formal **вы,** or when several persons are addressed, **-те** is added.

Perfective future:

Пойдём! (пойдёмте!)
Let's go!

Возьмём (возьмёмте) маши́ну и **пое́дем.**
Let's take the car, and let's go.

Imperfective future:

Positive:

Бу́дем наде́яться.
Let's hope.

The imperfective is more frequent when the meaning is negative, "Let's not."

Negative:

Не бу́дем об э́том спо́рить.
Let's not argue about that.

With imperfective verbs it is, however, more common to use the *infinitive* preceded by **дава́й** or **дава́йте** (the imperative of **дава́ть**); **дава́й/дава́йте** may also be used together with *future tense* forms of both aspects:

Дава́й/те писа́ть.
Let's write.

Дава́й/те бу́дем ходи́ть гуля́ть вме́сте ка́ждое у́тро.
Let's go for a walk together every morning.

Дава́й/те поговори́м об э́том де́ле.
Let's have a talk about this matter.

Unprefixed verbs of motion are used in the first person plural of the *present* tense as the inclusive imperative:

Идём/те! / Е́дем/те!	Let's go!
Бежи́м/те	Let's run!

In the third person, singular and plural ("let him," "let her," "let them"), **пусть** (or, more colloquially, **пуска́й**) is used:

Пу́сть она́ придёт.
Let her come (Tell her to come; or I don't mind if she comes).

Е́сли о́н мне́ не ве́рит, **пуска́й** спро́сит у моего́ отца́.
If he doesn't believe me, let him ask my father.

Pattern Sentences

First person plural, perfective future.

1. Ко́нчим перево́д. На́м оста́лось то́лько три́ стро́чки.	1. Let's finish the translation. We have only three lines left.
2. Начнём рабо́тать. Пора́!	2. Let's start work! It's time!
3. Пойдём ве́чером в кино́. Ла́дно?	3. Let's go to the movies this evening. O.K.?
4. Уйдёмте отсю́да! Мне́ ску́чно.	4. Let's get out of here! I'm bored.
5. Зайдём к Ива́ну.	5. Let's go to see Ivan.
6. Пое́дем за́ город.	6. Let's go out of town.
7. Напи́шем А́нне.	7. Let's write Anna.

Дава́й(те).

1. Дава́йте говори́ть то́лько по-ру́сски!	1. Let's speak only Russian!

2. Дава́й(те) напи́шем пье́су!	2. Let's write a play!
3. Дава́йте чита́ть.	3. Let's read.
4. Дава́йте занима́ться.	4. Let's study.
5. Дава́й(те) сде́лаем э́тот перево́д вме́сте.	5. Let's do that translation together.

Пусть (пуска́й) + *third person.*

1. Пу́сть А́нна да́ст ва́м сво́й слова́рь.	1. Let Anna give you her dictionary (tell her to).
2. Пу́сть Андре́й са́м э́то сде́лает.	2. Let Andrey do that himself.
3. Е́сли они́ хотя́т, пуска́й приведу́т своего́ дру́га.	3. If they want to, let them bring their friend.
4. Пу́сть (она́) говори́т, что́ хо́чет.	4. Let her say what she wants.
5. Пу́сть все́ э́то зна́ют.	5. Everyone ought to know that.

Drill

Переведи́те с англи́йского на ру́сский.

1. Let him do what he wants!
2. Let her tell you what she saw.
3. Let them think what they want.
4. Let's play.
5. Let's go abroad!
6. Let's start studying. It's time!
7. Let's go to the restaurant.
8. Let's finish the article.
9. Let's tell them about our plans.
10. Let them come if they want.
11. Let's not think about war.
12. Let's write to him today.
13. Let Anna buy the newspaper this evening.
14. Let's not talk about it.

CONVERSATION

Чем бо́льше я́ тебя́ зна́ю, тем ме́ньше я тебя́ понима́ю

Ви́ктор. —А́, Алёша! Ра́д тебя́ ви́деть! Сади́сь в то́ кре́сло! Мы́ тепе́рь всё ре́же и ре́же ви́димся, а когда́ ви́димся, то то́лько и́здали, на ле́кциях. Зимо́й ты́ заходи́л ко мне́ гора́здо ча́ще. Ты́, по-мо́ему, да́же в клу́бе не́ был бо́льше ме́сяца. В чём де́ло?

Алёша. —У меня́ ма́сса рабо́ты. Я́ занима́юсь с ра́ннего утра́ и до по́зднего ве́чера. Я́ тепе́рь ложу́сь по́зже и встаю ра́ньше и всё-же у меня́ не́т доста́точно вре́мени не то́лько, чтобы ходи́ть в го́сти, но́ да́же чтобы газе́ту почита́ть! Возьмём для приме́ра сего́дняшний де́нь. Сего́дня воскресе́нье, пра́вда? Я́ вста́л в ше́сть, как то́лько позвони́л буди́льник. Я́ при́нял холо́дный ду́ш, побри́лся, оде́лся, вы́пил стака́н ча́ю, съе́л кусо́к хле́ба с колбасо́й, се́л за сто́л и просиде́л за столо́м весь де́нь. И то́лько тепе́рь вы́шел на полчаса́.

Ви́ктор. —Ты́ сумасше́дший! Ты́ всегда́ рабо́таешь бо́льше все́х и хо́чешь бы́ть лу́чше все́х. Чем бо́льше я́ тебя́ зна́ю, тем ме́ньше я́ тебя́ понима́ю. Мне́ ка́жется, что е́сли я́ проживу́ с тобо́й сто́ ле́т, я́ всё равно́ не пойму́, что́ ты́ за челове́к! Кста́ти, мо́жно узна́ть, над че́м ты́ рабо́таешь?

Алёша. —Я́ рабо́таю сейча́с над рефера́том и хочу́ поскоре́й ко́нчить его́, чтобы прочита́ть его́ на после́днем семина́ре. Я́ нашёл гора́здо бо́льше интере́сных материа́лов, чем я́ ду́мал и, поэ́тому, я́ рабо́таю над рефера́том до́льше, чем хоте́л. Рефера́т оказа́лся длинне́й, но́ зато́ гора́здо интере́сней. В ближа́йшие не́сколько дне́й я́ бу́ду о́чень за́нят. Во́т и всё.

Ви́ктор. —Ты́ молоде́ц! Настоя́щий учёный! Но́ что́ э́то за жи́знь? Коне́чно, э́то де́ло вку́са, но́, по-мо́ему, та́к нельзя́ жи́ть. Жи́знь сли́шком коротка́. Ну́жно же иногда́ поговори́ть с прия́телем, поигра́ть в ша́хматы, послу́шать му́зыку, вы́йти с де́вушкой потанцева́ть. Но́ ты́, ви́дно, бо́льше всего́ лю́бишь тру́д. Чу́вство до́лга в тебе́ сильне́е всего́. До́лг пре́жде всего́!

Алёша. —Ты́ о́чень похо́ж на мою́ сестру́ Ле́ну. Она́ говори́т то́ же са́мое. Я́ слы́шу от неё те́ же слова́. Она́ счита́ет меня́ сухи́м и ску́чным челове́ком. А я́ счита́ю, что она́ гора́здо скучне́й меня́. Но́, как ты́ говори́шь, э́то де́ло вку́са, а о вку́сах не спо́рят. Пу́сть она́ говори́т, что́ хо́чет. И ты́ мо́жешь ду́мать, что́ хо́чешь. Мне́ всё равно́.

Ви́ктор. —Ты́ говори́шь, что я́ похо́ж на Ле́ну, а Ле́ну ты́ счита́ешь ску́чной? Зна́чит, и я́ ску́чный? Спаси́бо за комплиме́нт! Но́ лу́чше не бу́дем спо́рить о то́м, кто́ скучне́й, кто́ интере́сней, кто́ глупе́й, кто́ умне́й. Заче́м? Дава́й лу́чше поговори́м о чём-нибудь бо́лее прия́тном и бо́лее интере́сном. Что́ ты́ бу́дешь де́лать на пра́здниках? У на́с ведь бу́дут три́ свобо́дных дня́. Ты́ куда́-нибудь пое́дешь на э́ти дни́?

Алёша. —Не ду́маю, хотя́ я́ и получи́л приглаше́ние от Смирно́вых. Они́ приглаша́ют меня́ прие́хать к ни́м на да́чу и пожи́ть у ни́х не́сколько дне́й. Они́ тепе́рь живу́т на берегу́ Балти́йского мо́ря. Они́ пи́шут, что у ни́х бу́дет о́чень интере́сное о́бщество:

ра́зные изве́стные лю́ди: Васи́лий Кузнецо́в—изве́стный спортсме́н, Гали́на Зо́рина—певи́ца, како́й-то арти́ст Большо́го теа́тра и ещё каки́е-то знамени́тости.

Ви́ктор. —И ты́ не при́нял э́того приглаше́ния? Стра́нный ты́ челове́к! Я́ бы пое́хал, е́сли бы меня́ пригласи́ли! Смирно́вы—миле́йшие лю́ди, и говоря́т, что у Зо́риной замеча́тельнейший го́лос. Не лу́чше ли бы́ло бы тебе́ пое́хать туда́, чем сиде́ть в ду́шном го́роде?

Алёша. —Не́т, не пое́ду. Я́ поблагодари́л за приглаше́ние и написа́л, что прие́хал бы с велича́йшим удово́льствием, е́сли бы кани́кулы бы́ли подлинне́е. Э́то бы́ло бы друго́е де́ло. Но́ та́к—не сто́ит. Смирно́вы живу́т тепе́рь гора́здо да́льше, чем жи́ли пре́жде, почти́ у фи́нской грани́цы. Э́то о́чень дли́нное путеше́ствие; я́ не смо́г бы верну́ться ра́ньше среды́ и потеря́л бы мно́го вре́мени. А что́ ты́ бу́дешь де́лать?

Ви́ктор. —Я́ ещё не реши́л. Я́ бы о́чень хоте́л пое́хать в прия́тном о́бществе куда́-нибудь за́ город. Хорошо́ бы погуля́ть на све́жем во́здухе, попла́вать в ре́чке, полежа́ть на зелёной траве́ под зелёными дере́вьями, послу́шать, ка́к пти́цы пою́т. Про́сто забыва́ешь, что е́сть цветы́, дере́вья, трава́, сло́вом—приро́да. Я́ уже́ счита́ю часы́, когда́ всё э́то уви́жу. Ну́жно бы поча́ще е́здить за́ город.

Алёша. —Да́, бы́ло бы хорошо́ провести́ де́нь в дере́вне. Э́то не плоха́я мы́сль.

Ви́ктор. —Так почему́ же на́м не пое́хать? Пое́дем! Пое́дем хо́ть в па́рк культу́ры и о́тдыха. Э́то гора́здо бли́же и про́ще, чем е́хать на фи́нскую грани́цу. Вы́едем ра́но у́тром и, е́сли хо́чешь, вернёмся ве́чером пора́ньше. Ла́дно?

Алёша. —А рефера́т? И я́ ведь, кро́ме того́, уже́ на́чал рабо́тать над диссерта́цией . . . Я́ потеря́ю це́лый де́нь, и мне́ пото́м бу́дет трудне́е . . .

Ви́ктор. —К чёрту всё! Оди́н де́нь на во́здухе да́ст тебе́ бо́льше эне́ргии, си́л и мы́слей, чем витами́ны, кото́рые врачи́ сове́туют на́м принима́ть. Е́дем?

Алёша. —Ре́чка, дере́вья, си́нее не́бо. Е́дем! То́лько не говори́ ничего́ Ле́не. Пу́сть она́ ду́мает, что я́ сижу́ в библиоте́ке.

Чита́йте вопро́сы и отвеча́йте на ни́х.

1. Всегда́ ли Ви́ктор и Алёша так ре́дко ви́делись? 2. Ско́лько вре́мени Алёша не́ был в клу́бе? 3. Когда́ Алёша тепе́рь занима́ется? 4. О́н тепе́рь ложи́тся и встаёт в то́ же вре́мя, как пре́жде? 5. Почему́ Алёша тепе́рь не чита́ет газе́т? 6. Ка́к о́н провёл воскресе́нье? 7. Что́ сказа́л Ви́ктор, когда́ услы́шал э́тот расска́з?

8. Ка́к А. объясня́ет своё поведе́ние (behavior)? 9. Почему́ его́ рефера́т бу́дет длинне́е, чем о́н ду́мал? 10. Кака́я филосо́фия жи́зни у В., и что́ о́н говори́т о вку́сах А.? 11. Что́ говори́т Ле́на? 12. От кого́ А. получи́л приглаше́ние, и что́ бы́ло в письме́? 13. Почему́ о́н не при́нял приглаше́ния? 14. Что́ В. хоте́л бы сде́лать на пра́здниках? 15. Что́ об э́том пла́не ду́мает А.? 16. Ка́к реаги́рует (reacts) В., когда́ о́н слы́шит, что А. никуда́ не хо́чет е́хать? 17. Че́м конча́ется э́тот разгово́р?

EXERCISE

Переведи́те на ру́сский.

1. —How old is this little boy? —He is only five years old. He is two years younger than my son. 2. The climate of that country is much worse and colder than the climate of our country. 3. We live a little closer to the border than you. 4. His elder sister is seven years older than he. 5. I have never heard him play, but they say that he plays much better than his father. 6. Our kolkhoz is wealthier than yours; and theirs is still wealthier. 7. He promised to return in an hour, but he returned much later. 8. When I return from the Ukraine, I shall tell you more interesting stories than those which you've just heard. 9. Nature is much richer in Southern Russia than in Northern Russia. 10. She always used to go to bed late, but yesterday she went to bed still later. 11. Sit down near me and let's have a talk. 12. We shall sit and smoke for a while until he returns. 13. He sat down at his table, worked for a while, and went to the restaurant. 14. The longer you (will) work at your novel, the better your novel will be. 15. I've read a most interesting story. 16. This is the most interesting story that we've read. 17. Let's go to the movies this evening. 18. Let them pay for the tickets. 19. He is seventy-five years old already; if he were younger, he would travel more. 20. I paid $67 for this suit; formerly I used to pay much less for suits. 21. In our village there are 173 inhabitants; in yours, 127. In your village there are 46 inhabitants fewer. 22. I saw Nina from afar. 23. —Everyone will think you are crazy if you don't accept their invitation! —Let them think what they wish! 24. Victor has not yet accepted the invitation which we sent him two and a half weeks ago. 25. But I hope he will accept it and will come for the holidays. 26. Let's go to the country tomorrow. 27. You're crazy! I have to work on my article.

VOCABULARY

арти́ст, *fem.* **-ка** performing artist (singer, dancer, etc.)
ви́дно apparent(ly), evident(ly)
вкус taste
всё-же still, all the same
долг debt; moral duty (*no pl. in this sense*)
жи́тель (*masc.*), *fem.* **-ница** inhabitant
доста́точно enough, sufficiently
зато́ on the other hand, however
***знамени́тость** (*fem.*) celebrity
и́здали from afar
киломе́тр kilometer
когда́-либо ever, at any time
ла́в.ка (*gen. pl.* **-ок**) shop, small store
мысль (*fem.*) thought, idea
населе́ние population
недоста́точно insufficient(ly), not enough
пре́жде formerly, before (*adv.*)
приглаше́ние invitation
ре́ч.ка (*gen. pl.* **-ек**) small river, stream
си́ла power, force (often used in plural)
спортсме́н athlete
строка́, стро́чка line (of writing or print)
сумасше́дший crazy, insane, mad (person), madman
хоть if only
чу́вство (*gen. pl.* **чувств**) feeling

Verbs

остава́ться (imperf., I: **оста.ю́сь, -ёшься**), **оста́ться** (perf., I: **оста́н.усь, -ешься**) to remain, stay, be left
приглаша́ть (imperf., I), **пригласи́ть** (perf., II: **пригла.шу́, -си́шь**) to invite
шуме́ть (imperf., II: **шум.лю́, -и́шь**) to make noise

Expressions

произноси́ть/произнести́ ре́чь (*f.*) to give (deliver) a speech
бли́зко от (+ *gen.*) near (to)
бли́же к (+ *dat.*) nearer to
с утра́ до ве́чера from morning till evening
три́ (пя́ть, и т. д.) с полови́ной three (five, etc.) and a half
Ти́ше! Quiet! Silence!
когда́ . . . то́ when . . . then
сего́дняшний де́нь today (used as noun)
Во́т и всё. That's all (there is to it).
ра́ньше всего́ / **пре́жде всего́** } first of all
то́ же са́мое the same (thing)
на пра́здники for the holidays
на пра́здниках during the holidays
принима́ть/приня́ть приглаше́ние to accept an invitation
сло́вом in a word
К чёрту! The devil with it!
К чёрту всё! To the devil with everything!
на во́здухе in the (open) air

Vocabulary Review: Verbs of Position

	I *Being in a Standing, Sitting, or Lying Position*		II *Taking a Standing, Sitting, or Lying Position*		III *Putting Something or Someone in a Standing, Sitting, or Lying Position*	
	Imperf.	*Perf.*	*Imperf.*	*Perf.*	*Imperf.*	*Perf.*
	стоя́ть	по—	встава́ть	встать	ста́вить	по—
	стою́	про—	встаю́	вста́ну	ста́влю	
	стои́шь		встаёшь	вста́нешь	ста́вишь	
A *Standing*	стоя́л		встава́л	встал	ста́вил	
			станови́ться	стать		
			становлю́сь	ста́нешь		
			стано́вишься	ста́нет		
			станови́лся	стал		
	сиде́ть	по—	сади́ться	сесть	сажа́ть[8]	посади́ть[8]
B *Sitting*	сижу́	про—	сажу́сь	ся́ду	сажа́ю	посажу́
	сиди́шь		сади́шься	ся́дешь	сажа́ешь	поса́дишь
	сиде́л		сади́лся	сел	сажа́л	посади́л
	лежа́ть	по—	ложи́ться	лечь	класть	положи́ть
C *Lying*	лежу́	про—	ложу́сь	ля́гу	кладу́	положу́
	лежи́шь		ложи́шься	ля́жешь	кладёшь	поло́жишь
	лежа́л		ложи́лся	лёг	клал	положи́л

[8] These verbs mean "to seat," also "to sow" (seeds).

UNIT 26

Declension of numerals, 449. *Cardinal and ordinal numerals, review and completion*, 452. **Óба, óбе, "both,"** 456. *Dates*, 457. *Fractions*, 458. *Time of day*, 459. *Time in schedules*, 462. *Expressions of time (review and supplement)*, 462.

GRAMMAR

1. Declension of numerals

Like nouns, pronouns, and adjectives, Russian numerals are declined.

A. Declension of 1.

	Masculine	*Neuter*	*Feminine*
Nom.	оди́н	одно́	одна́
Gen.	одного́	like Masc.	одно́й
Dat.	одному́	like Masc.	одно́й
Acc.	like Nom. or Gen.	одно́	одну́
Instr.	одни́м	like Masc.	одно́й
Loc.	одно́м	like Masc.	одно́й

B. Declension of 2, 3, and 4.

	2 *Masc.–Neut.*	*Fem.*	**3**	**4**
Nom.	два	две	три	четы́ре
Gen.	двух		трёх	четырёх
Dat.	двум		трём	четырём
Acc.	Like Nom. or Gen.			
Instr.	двумя́		тремя́	четырьмя́
Loc.	двух		трёх	четырёх

Note the stem in oblique cases of **два-две: дву-**; of **три: трё-тре-**.

C. Declension of numerals above 4 ending in -ь. These are declined like Fem. II nouns in the *singular:*

	5	8
Nom.	пять	во́семь
Gen.	пяти́	восьми́
Dat.	пяти́	восьми́
Acc.	пять	во́семь
Instr.	пятью́	восемью
Loc.	пяти́	восьми́

D. Phrases "Numeral + Noun." As we know, after 2, 3, and 4 nouns are in the genitive *singular;* after **5** and above in the genitive *plural, e.g.*, два́ стола́, три́ кни́ги, четы́ре окна́; *but:* пя́ть столо́в, ше́сть кни́г, се́мь о́кон, etc.

These rules apply only when the numeral is in the *nominative* case, that is, most commonly when the word group "numeral + noun" is the subject of a sentence:

Мои́ **два́** бра́та живу́т зде́сь.
На по́лке стоя́т **два́дцать пя́ть** кни́г.

Used in other case forms than the nominative (and the accusative, which is treated below), the numeral and the noun appear in the case form required, the noun in the *plural* of the case.

Gen.	Во́т до́м мо**и́х** дв**у́х** профессор**о́в.**
Dat.	Я́ написа́л дв**у́м** профессор**а́м.**
Instr.	Я́ говори́л с дв**умя́** профессор**а́ми.**
Loc.	Мы́ говори́ли о дв**у́х** профессор**а́х.**

In the accusative case of the group "numeral + noun," the animate–inanimate distinction applies to all genders for the numbers 2, 3, and 4: inanimate is like nominative; animate is like genitive.

Inanimate:	Я́ ви́дел **два́** до́ма (**две́** кни́ги).
Animate:	Я́ ви́дел **дву́х** студе́нтов.

The numbers 5 and above, however, have but one form of the accusative for *both* animate and inanimate:

Inanimate:	Я́ ви́дел **пя́ть** домо́в.
Animate:	Я́ ви́дел **пя́ть** студе́нтов.

Summary Table of Numeral Declensions

1. **Два (две), три, четы́ре** *with inanimate nouns.*

Nom.	Во́т (**два́, три́, четы́ре**) до́ллара, (**две́**) шля́пы.
Gen.	У меня́ нет (**дву́х, трёх, четырёх**) до́лларов, шля́п.
Dat.	Я́ ра́д[1] э́тим (**дву́м, трём, четырём**) до́лларам, шля́пам.

[1] **Ра́д** + dative, to be glad of (glad to get/to see)

Acc.	Я́ получи́л (**два́, три́, четы́ре**) до́ллара, (**две́**) шля́пы.
Instr.	Что́ я́ сде́лаю с (**двумя́, тремя́, четырьмя́**) до́лларами, шля́пами?
Loc.	Я́ ду́маю о (**двух, трёх, четырёх**) до́лларах, шля́пах.

2. **Два** (**две**), **три, четы́ре** *with animate nouns.*

Nom.	Во́т на́ши (**два́, три́, четы́ре**) ма́льчика, (**две́**) де́вочки.
Gen.	Э́то кни́ги для (**дву́х, трёх, четырёх**) ма́льчиков, де́вочек.
Dat.	Ко́ля пи́шет (**дву́м, трём, четырём**) ма́льчикам, де́вочкам.
Acc.	Я́ зна́ю (**дву́х, трёх, четырёх**) ма́льчиков, де́вочек.
Instr.	Мы́ бы́ли та́м с (**двумя́, тремя́, четырьмя́**) ма́льчиками, де́вочками.
Loc.	Мы́ говори́м о (**дву́х, трёх, четырёх**) ма́льчиках, де́вочках.

3. *Numerals above* **5** (*ending in soft sign*): *nominative and accusative are alike* (*no distinction for animate and inanimate*); *genitive, dative, and locative all end in* **-и́**.

Nom.	Во́т пя́ть **столо́в, по́лок, студе́нтов.**
Gen.	Зде́сь не́т пяти́ столо́в, по́лок, студе́нтов.
Dat.	Я́ подошёл к пяти́ стола́м, по́лкам, студе́нтам.
Acc.	Я́ ви́жу пя́ть **столо́в, по́лок, студе́нтов.**
Instr.	Что́ мне́ де́лать с пят**ью́** стола́ми, по́лками, студе́нтами?
Loc.	Мы́ говори́м о пяти́ стола́х, по́лках, студе́нтах.

E. Approximation is expressed by о́коло + genitive:

Я́ та́м жи́л о́коло **дву́х** ле́т.
I lived there about two years.

У меня́ бы́ло о́коло пят**и́** рубл**е́й**.
I had about five rubles.

F. Declension of compound cardinal numerals. All parts of a compound cardinal numeral are declined, *e.g.*:

ме́ньше двадцат**и́** тр**ёх** фу́нтов
less than 23 pounds

о́коло тридцат**и́** пят**и́** киломе́тров
about 35 kilometers

It will be recalled that in the nominative and accusative inanimate, the final part of a compound numeral determines the case and number of the following noun:

В э́том кла́ссе два́дцать **оди́н** студе́н**т** (nom. sing.).
Я́ ви́жу на ка́рте три́дцать **два́** го́род**а** (gen. sing.).
На собра́нии бы́ли со́рок **пя́ть** учител**е́й** (gen. pl.).

When possessives (**мои́, на́ши,** etc.) and demonstratives (**э́ти** and **те**), and some adjectives such as **пе́рвые, после́дние, други́е,** etc., *precede* numerals, they agree with the *numeral* in case:

Вы́ чита́ли **все́ мои́ три́** рома́на?
Я́ прочита́л **ва́ши пя́ть** кни́г.
Вы́ зна́ете **мои́х трёх** дочере́й?
Я́ познако́мился со **все́ми твои́ми пятью́** детьми́.
Я́ чита́л его́ **пе́рвые два́** рома́на.

2. Cardinal and ordinal numerals, review and completion

	Cardinal	*Ordinal*
0	ноль (masc.), нуль (masc.)	нулево́й, нулево́й
1	оди́н, одно́, одна́	пе́рвый
2	два, две	второ́й
3	три	тре́тий
4	четы́ре	четвёртый
5	пять	пя́тый
6	шесть	шесто́й
7	семь	седьмо́й
8	во́семь	восьмо́й
9	де́вять	девя́тый
10	де́сять	деся́тый
11	оди́ннадцать	оди́ннадцатый
12	двена́дцать	двена́дцатый
13	трина́дцать	трина́дцатый
14	четы́рнадцать	четы́рнадцатый
15	пятна́дцать	пятна́дцатый
16	шестна́дцать	шестна́дцатый
17	семна́дцать	семна́дцатый
18	восемна́дцать	восемна́дцатый
19	девятна́дцать	девятна́дцатый
20	два́дцать	двадца́тый
21	два́дцать оди́н (одно́, одна́)	два́дцать пе́рвый
22	два́дцать два́ (две́)	два́дцать второ́й
	etc.	etc.
25	два́дцать пя́ть	два́дцать пя́тый
	etc.	etc.
30	три́дцать	тридца́тый
40	со́рок	сороково́й
50	пятьдеся́т	пят**и**деся́тый
60	шестьдеся́т	шест**и**деся́тый
70	се́мьдесят	сем**и**деся́тый
80	во́семьдесят	восьм**и**деся́тый

	Cardinal		*Ordinal*
90	девяно́сто		девяно́стый
100	сто		со́тый
200	две́сти		двухсо́тый
300	три́ста	(gen. sing. ста)	трёхсо́тый
400	четы́реста	(gen. sing. ста)	четырёхсо́тый
500	пятьсо́т	(gen. pl. сот)	пят**и**со́тый
600	шестьсо́т	(gen. pl. сот)	шест**и**со́тый
700	семьсо́т	(gen. pl. сот)	сем**и**со́тый
800	восемьсо́т	(gen. pl. сот)	восьм**и**со́тый
900	девятьсо́т	(gen. pl. сот)	девят**и**со́тый
1,000	(одна́) ты́сяча (fem. noun)		ты́сячный
2,000	две́ ты́сячи (gen. sing.: ты́сячи)		двухты́сячный
	etc.		etc.
5,000	пя́ть ты́сяч (gen. pl.: ты́сяч)		пятиты́сячный
			etc.
1,000,000	миллио́н (masc. noun)		миллио́нный

Observe that the teens drop the soft sign (ь) after the first numeral element. The numerals 50, 60, 70, and 80 retain the soft sign in the middle (after the first numeral element), but have *no* soft sign at the end. There are never two soft signs in a Russian numeral in the nominative case.

Сто (100) has the form ста in all cases except the nominative and accusative. Like сто are declined со́рок (40) and девяно́сто (90).

Пятьдеся́т (50), шестьдеся́т (60), се́мьдесят (70), and во́семьдесят (80) are declined like пять, though they lack final **-ь** in the nominative and accusative. In the genitive, dative, and locative all of them replace the **-ь** of the first numeral element with **-и**, *e.g.*, пятьдеся́т: genitive–dative–locative, пят**и́**десят**и**; in the instrumental they have **-ью**: пят**ью́**десят**ью**.

Numerals for 100, 200, 300, 400, 500, etc., have both parts declined, *e.g.*, две́сти, двухсо́т, двумста́м, две́сти, двумяста́ми, двухста́х; or пятьсо́т, пятисо́т, пятиста́м, пятьюста́ми, пятиста́х.

Ты́сяча (1,000) is declined as a hard feminine noun; миллио́н (1,000,000) as a hard masculine. These two numerals always govern the genitive plural, regardless of the case of the numeral itself, *e.g.*: С ты́сячей солда́т. В миллио́не слу́ча**ев** (in a million cases).

The higher ordinals generally are formed by combining the *genitive* of the cardinal of the first numeral element with the ordinal of the second, *e.g.*, пятидеся́тый, шестидеся́тый, двухсо́тый, пятиты́сячный, etc. Note the forms with double accents: трёхсо́тый, четырёхты́сячный, etc.

It will be recalled that ordinals are adjectives, and are declined as adjectives. All of them are hard adjectives, except тре́тий (for the declension of which see Unit 18, page 275). Cardinals ending in **-ь** drop **-ь** before adding the adjective ending **-ый (-о́й)**.

With compound ordinals, only the final part is declined as an ordinal adjective. All other parts are *cardinals*, and remain in the *nominative* case:

> На́ша конто́ра нахо́дится на **два́дцать пя́том** этаже́.
> Я́ ва́м э́то уже́ говори́л сто́ ра́з; я́ повторя́ю э́то в **сто́ пе́рвый** и в после́дний!

Drills

A. *Translate the following cardinal or ordinal numerals.*

1. Два́дцать де́вять.
2. Со́рок во́семь.
3. Се́мьдесят се́мь.
4. Девяно́сто седьмо́й.
5. Сто́ двена́дцать.
6. Сто́ два́дцать де́вять.
7. Сто́ со́рок девя́тый.
8. Со́тый.
9. Сто́ се́мьдесят второ́й.
10. Сто́ семидеся́тый.
11. Две́сти сорокво́й.
12. Двухсо́тый.
13. Четы́реста шестьдеся́т четы́ре.
14. Четырёхсо́тый.
15. Четы́реста шестьдеся́т четвёртый.
16. Пятьсо́т два́.
17. Пятисо́тый.
18. Семьсо́т со́рок второ́й.
19. Восьмисо́тый.
20. Ты́сяча девятисо́тый.
21. Ты́сяча девятьсо́т шестьдеся́т четвёртый.
22. Ты́сячный.
23. Две́ ты́сячи восемьсо́т пятьдеся́т оди́н.
24. Ше́сть ты́сяч две́сти со́рок седьмо́й.
25. Две́сти три́дцать три́ ты́сячи семьсо́т девяно́сто во́семь.
26. Три́ миллио́на восемьсо́т се́мьдесят ше́сть ты́сяч три́ста со́рок два́.
27. Пя́ть биллио́нов шестьсо́т двена́дцать миллио́нов.

B. *Переведи́те на англи́йский.*

1. Я́ не по́нял э́**тих** пят**и́** стро́к.
2. Мы́ останови́лись на шестьдеся́т четвёрт**ой** и́ли шестьдеся́т пя́т**ой** строк**е́**.
3. В э́том то́лстом то́ме ты́сяча три́ста два́дцать се́мь страни́ц.
4. Я́ ду́мал, что зде́сь ме́ньше ты́сяч**и трёхсо́т** двадцат**и́** сем**и́** страни́ц.
5. Прочита́йте ты́сяча три́ста два́дцать седьм**у́ю** страни́цу.
6. Я́ прочита́л ты́сяч**у** страни́ц.
7. В Москве́ бо́льше пят**и́** миллио́н**ов** жи́тел**ей**, а в Ленингра́де о́коло **трёх** миллио́н**ов**.
8. Во́т статьи́ на́**ших** дв**у́х** корреспонде́нт**ов**.
9. Э́то тетра́ди мо**и́х трёх** ученик**о́в**.
10. Я́ даю́ уро́ки **трём** ученик**а́м**.
11. С э́тими **тремя́** ученик**а́ми** я́ прочита́л нача́ло **тре́тьего** уро́ка на́шего уче́бника.
12. Я́ говори́л ва́м о мо**и́х трёх** ученик**а́х**.

13. Вы́ ка́жется зна́ете мо**и́х трёх** ученик**о́в.**
14. Мы́ бу́дем по́льзоваться **тремя́** учёбник**ами.**
15. На э́той у́лице **четы́ре** ме́бельн**ых** магази́н**а**.
16. Мы́ бы́ли во вс**е́х четырёх** магази́н**ах**, но́ не нашли́ того́, что на́м ну́жно.
17. Мы́ наде́емся, что найдём всё в четвёрт**ом** магази́н**е**, та́к как о́н са́мый большо́й из **четырёх** магази́н**ов**.
18. У Ко́ли пя́ть това́рищ**ей**.
19. О́н получа́ет пи́сьма от сво**и́х** пят**и́** това́рищ**ей** и ча́сто пи́шет сво**и́м** пят**и́** това́рищ**ам**.
20. О́н вероя́тно расска́зывал ва́м об э́т**их** пят**и́** това́рищ**ах**.
21. О́н учи́лся в шко́ле с э́т**ими** пять**ю́** това́рищ**ами**.
22. У меня́ не́т двадцат**и́** пят**и́** копе́**ек**.
23. Что́ мо́жно сде́лать с двадцат**ью́** пят**ью́** копе́йк**ами**?
24. Почему́ вы́ говори́те о двадцат**и́** пят**и́** копе́йк**ах**?
25. Я́ прочита́л об э́том на два́дцать пя́т**ой** страни́це.
26. Э́тому селу́ сто́ ле́т.
27. Э́тому де́реву бо́льше **ста́** ле́т.
28. —Моско́вском**у** университе́ту ка́жется две́сти ле́т? —Не́т, ему́ бо́льше **двухсо́т** ле́т.
29. На э́той страни́це о́коло пят**и́**десят**и** стро́к.
30. Мы́ останови́лись **на** пят**и**деся́т**ой** строке́.
31. Мо́й оте́ц провёл о́коло десят**и́** ле́т в Сиби́ри.

C. *Read and write the following numerals as both cardinals (nominative) and ordinals (masculine singular nominative).*

Model. Cardinals: 1,781, ты́сяча семьсо́т во́семьдесят оди́н.
Ordinals: 1,781st, ты́сяча семьсо́т во́семьдесят пе́рвый.

11	33	69	141	666	2,000	1,000,000
16	37	70	200	777	7,300	2,000,000
14	40	77	225	800	22,112	8,600,000
20	44	88	300	999	59,550	10,397,654
21	50	90	330	1,000	100,000	
22	56	99	400	1,851	221,000	
30	60	100	515	1,962	532,000	

D. *Переведи́те с англи́йского на ру́сский.*

1. She cannot live without her three dogs.
2. She buys the best meat for her three dogs.
3. These are the wives of their four sons.
4. Zina is the wife of their fourth son.
5. Anna is their fourth daughter.
6. I didn't know the name of your fourth daughter.
7. I don't have \$7.
8. I don't have \$25.

9. Why do you speak about $25?
10. In a year there are 12 months, 52 weeks, 365 days.
11. Vladimir has 1,000 rubles, I have 1,500, and Zina has 2,292.
12. We have about $1,000.
13. Here is 102nd Street.
14. Who lives on 102nd Street?
15. Her husband is twenty-two years older than she is.
16. The new road is 139 kilometers longer than the old one.
17. In this city live 225,000 more inhabitants than in that one.
18. I read 1,010 pages less than Andrey.
19. In this town there are 1,335 homes.
20. In this small village there are only 162 homes, and in ours there are 112 homes.
21. This church is 400 years old.

3. О́ба/о́бе, "both"

This numeral is declined like **два/две,** but the feminine has the distinct stem **обе-** throughout. **О́ба/о́бе** governs the same cases as **два/две.**

	Masculine—Neuter	*Feminine*
Nom.	о́ба	о́бе
Gen.	обо́их	обе́их
Dat.	обо́им	обе́им
Acc.	Like Nom. or Gen.	
Instr.	обо́ими	обе́ими
Loc.	обо́их	обе́их

E.g.: Я́ прочёл **о́ба** журна́ла, кото́рые вы́ мне́ да́ли.
У **обе́их** на́ших дочере́й е́сть де́ти.
У на́с два́ до́ма; мы́ живём в **обо́их** дома́х.

Drills

A. *Переведи́те на англи́йский.*

1. Я́ прочёл о́бе газе́ты.
2. У Еле́ны Ива́новны два́ сы́на и две́ до́чери. О́ба её сы́на живу́т на ю́ге, а о́бе до́чери живу́т с ма́терью.
3. Я́ хорошо́ зна́ю обо́их сынове́й и обе́их дочере́й.
4. Я́ учи́лся в шко́ле с её обо́ими сыновья́ми, а моя́ сестра́ учи́лась с обе́ими дочерьми́.
5. Она́ ча́сто пи́шет свои́м обо́им сыновья́м.
6. Она́ ча́сто получа́ет пи́сьма от свои́х обо́их сынове́й.
7. Я́ написа́ла и ему́ и е́й.
8. Бори́с и исто́рик и матема́тик.

B. *Переведите на русский.*

1. I liked both pictures.
2. I want to buy both tables.
3. I wrote to both sisters.
4. He loves both his mother and his father.
5. I spoke with both professors.
6. I was there with both my sisters.
7. I bought these briefcases for both our boys.

4. Dates

Days of the month are expressed by the neuter ordinal (the noun **число́** "number," "date" is understood). The month is in the genitive (such and such date *of* the month):

—Как**о́е** сего́дня числ**о́**?
—What is the date today?

—Сего́дня два́дцать шест**о́е** июн**я**.
—Today is the twenty-sixth of June.

—Пе́рв**ое** октябр**я́**.
—October the first.

"Time when" (on such and such date) is expressed by the genitive:

Два́дцать шест**о́го** июн**я** мы́ поéдем на да́чу.
On June 26th we go to the country.

Заня́тия начина́ются пе́рв**ого** сентябр**я́**.
Classes begin on September 1.

Note that in Russian dates the numeral of the date always *precedes* the name of the month.

"From . . . to" is expressed by **от** + genitive . . . **до** + genitive.

От пятна́дцат**ого** ма́**я** **до** три́дцать пе́рв**ого** а́вгуст**а**.
From May 15 to August 31.

"From that date on" is expressed by **с** + genitive:

С пе́рв**ого** сентябр**я́** мы́ бу́дем в го́роде.

Years are expressed by ordinal numerals with the noun **год**:

Ты́сяча девятьсо́т со́рок пя́т**ый** **го́д**.
The year 1945.

Time when in years is expressed by the preposition **в** and the locative cases of the ordinal with **году́**.

В ты́сяча девятьсо́т со́рок пя́т**ом** году́. In 1945.

But when an exact date or more specific time of the year is given, the *genitive must* be used:

> Толсто́й роди́лся два́дцать восьм**о́го** а́вгуст**а** ты́сяча восемьсо́т два́дцать восьм**о́го** го́д**а** (1828 г.) и у́мер седьм**о́го** ноябр**я́** ты́сяча девятьсо́т дес**я́того** го́д**а** (1910 г.).
>
> Tolstoy was born on August 28, 1828, and died on November 7, 1910.

Drill

Переведи́те на ру́сский.

1. Today is December 25th.
2. We are going abroad on December 25th.
3. We shall be in Italy from May 15th to June 6th.
4. Who said that yesterday was the 15th?
5. What date will it be tomorrow, the 21st or the 22nd?
6. Our exam is on the 22nd.
7. Where were you in 1945?
8. In August, 1945, I was in the South.
9. —What date is it today? —It is September 28th.
10. This semester (семе́стр) began in September.
11. They say that it will rain from the 28th to the 30th.
12. It rained from the 15th to the 23rd.
13. In what month were you born?
14. I was born in February.
15. —In what year and on what date? —February 13, 1927.

5. Fractions

Following are several important Russian fractions; all of them take the genitive case.

пол; полови́на	one half, *e.g.*, по́л стака́на
(одна́) че́тверть (fem.)	one quarter, *e.g.*, че́тверть фу́нта
три́ че́тверти	three quarters, *e.g.*, три́ че́тверти го́да
(одна́) тре́ть (fem.)	one third, *e.g.*, тре́ть семе́стра
две́ тре́ти	two thirds, *e.g.*, две́ тре́ти доро́ги

Other fractions are formed with a *cardinal* numeral (feminine)[2] as the numerator, and an *ordinal* numeral (feminine)[2] as the denominator, *e.g.*, **одна́ пя́тая,** "one fifth," **две́ седьмы́х,** "two sevenths," **три́ деся́тых,** "three tenths."

Пол is used with measures. With precise measures, **пол** is spelled as one word together with the genitive of the noun-measure:

[2] The word **часть** (part), which is feminine in gender, is understood with fractions.

полчаса́, полдня́, полго́да, и т. д.
half an hour/a day/a year, etc.

When the measure is not precise, it is spelled separately:

по́л стака́на, по́л ча́шки, и т. д. half a glass/a cup, etc.

Полови́на (feminine noun) is generally used to denote half of something which is not itself a unit of measure:

полови́на де́нег, half of the money
полови́на веще́й, half of the things

Russian has a special term to denote $1\frac{1}{2}$. This is **полтора́** with masculine and neuter nouns; **полторы́** with feminine nouns. The noun following it is in the genitive singular:

Masc./Neut.	полтора́ го́да/рубля́/я́блока
Fem.	полторы́ неде́ли/мину́ты/ты́сячи

With other numerals:

for $2\frac{1}{2}$, $3\frac{1}{2}$, $4\frac{1}{2}$, два/три/четы́ре **с полови́ной,** followed by a noun in the genitive singular: два́ **с полови́ной** часа́; with five and above followed by a noun in the genitive plural: се́мь **с полови́ной** часо́в.

Полтора́ with numerals:

150	полтора́ста рубле́й
1,500	полторы́ ты́сячи жи́телей
150,000,000	полтора́ миллио́на челове́к

6. Time of day

Fractions of the hour:

че́тверть часа́	a quarter of an hour
полчаса́	half an hour
три́ че́тверти часа́	three quarters of an hour
полтора́ часа́	an hour and a half
два́ с полови́ной часа́	two and a half hours

The expression of hours in Russian has been presented in Unit 16 (page 240). The phrases "**два́ часа́,**" "**пя́ть часо́в,**" etc., denote an exact hour: 2:00, 5:00; also "**в два́ часа́,**" "**в пя́ть часо́в,**" at 2:00, at 5:00, etc. Periods of one hour, *i.e.*, the sixty minutes beginning at 12:00, 1:00, 2:00, etc., are denoted by *ordinal* numerals as follows:

пе́рвый ча́с	the hour beginning at 12 o'clock
второ́й ча́с	the hour beginning at 1 o'clock
тре́тий ча́с	the hour beginning at 2 o'clock
etc.	

Expressing time by means of ordinals is comparable to English "after three," "after four," etc.:

второй ча́с—во второ́м часу́ after one
тре́тий ча́с—в тре́тьем часу́ after two

More important, ordinal numerals for hours are used for "quarter past," "half past," as well as "so many minutes past" an hour:

—Кото́рый ча́с? —What time is it?

"*Past*" or "*after*": Nominative + genitive of *ordinal* of hour:

2:15 че́тверть тре́тьего (literally: "a quarter of the third hour")
2:30 полови́на[3] тре́тьего
3:05 пя́ть мину́т четвёртого
4:20 два́дцать мину́т пя́того

"*Of*" or "*to*": без + genitive of cardinals for minutes; hour (*cardinal*) in *nominative:*

2:45 без че́тверти три́ (quarter to three)
2:57 без трёх три́ (three minutes to three)
3:35 без двадцати́ пяти́ четы́ре (twenty-five minutes to four)

The illustration below represents a series of times between the hours of twelve and one (the hour hand is to the right of twelve). The various times given in Russian correspond to the different positions of the minute hand shown:

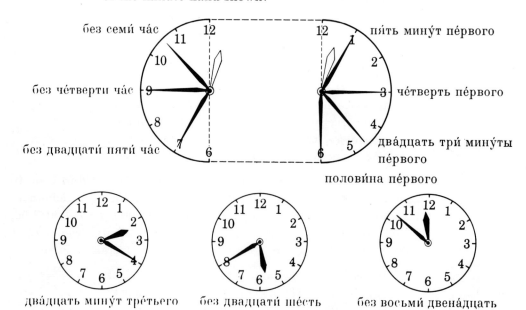

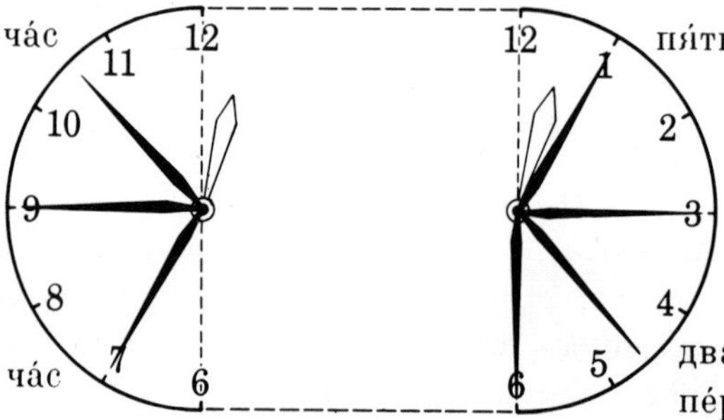

два́дцать мину́т тре́тьего

без двадцати́ ше́сть

без восьми́ двена́дцать

[3] **Полови́на** is used instead of **пол** for time of day.

два́дцать три́ мину́ты второ́го

без че́тверти три́

At what time?

—В кото́ром часу́? —At what time?

The answer employs the preposition **в**. **Полови́на** is preferably used in the locative case: **в полови́не:**

at 2:15 в че́тверть тре́тьего
at 2:30 в полови́не тре́тьего
at 3:05 в пя́ть мину́т четвёртого
at 4:20 в два́дцать мину́т пя́того

With **без** the preposition **в** is usually omitted; the *genitive* case is used:

at 2:45 без че́тверти три́
at 2:57 без трёх три́
at 3:35 без двадцати́ пяти́ четы́ре

Drills

A. *Переведи́те на англи́йский.*

1. Полови́на пе́рвого.
2. В полови́не пе́рвого.
3. Че́тверть пе́рвого.
4. Без че́тверти ча́с.
5. Без двадцати́ ча́с.
6. Де́сять мину́т второ́го.
7. Два́дцать пя́ть мину́т второ́го.
8. Без двадцати́ пяти́ два́.
9. Пя́ть мину́т тре́тьего.
10. В полови́не тре́тьего.
11. Без трёх (мину́т) три́.
12. Полови́на пя́того.
13. Полови́на седьмо́го.
14. В полови́не девя́того.
15. В полови́не оди́ннадцатого.
16. В че́тверть оди́ннадцатого.
17. Без че́тверти оди́ннадцать.
18. Без десяти́ (мину́т) оди́ннадцать.
19. Два́дцать три́ мину́ты деся́того.
20. В полови́не двена́дцатого.
21. Без двадцати́ трёх двена́дцать.
22. Два́дцать три́ мину́ты пе́рвого.

B. *Чита́йте по-ру́сски.*

7:30	2:15	5:30	7:15	9:50
at 7:30	3:15	5:15	7:45	9:58
1:30	3:30	5:45	at 8:30	at 11
at 1:30	3:40	6:30	at 9:30	at 10:50
1:15	3:45	7:30	at 9:10	at 10:30

7. Time in schedules

For *schedules* and *timetables* the time is often expressed by the hour followed by the number of minutes.

Ле́кция начина́ется в де́вять три́дцать.
The lecture starts at 9:30.

For transportation a twenty-four hour schedule is used:

По́езд ухо́дит в два́дцать три́ де́сять.
The train leaves at 23:10 (= 11:10 P.M.).

8. Expressions of time (review and supplement)

Different types of time expressions use different grammatical cases, some with prepositions, some without.

A. Accusative. The length of time an action endures is expressed by the *accusative* (*no* preposition).

О́н жи́л в Москве́ неде́л**ю**/вс**ю** зи́м**у**/це́лый ме́сяц.
He lived in Moscow (for) a week/a whole winter/ a whole month.

The preposition **на** + *accusative* expresses the duration of an implied state or condition which is to *follow* the action of the verb.

О́н прие́хал в Москву́ **на** неде́л**ю**/**на** вс**ю** зи́м**у**/**на** ме́сяц.
He came to Moscow for a week/for the whole winter/for a month (planning to stay a week, etc.).

A period of time at the end of which an action is performed is expressed by **через** + *accusative*.

Через неде́л**ю** мы́ поéдем за грани́цу.
In (after) a week we shall go abroad.

The time *when* a given action occurs is expressed differently, depending on several factors. One is the relative length of the unit of time.

With short units of time (minutes, hours, days) **в** + *accusative* is used:

в то́т моме́нт	at that moment
в ту́ мину́ту	at that minute
в то́т ча́с	at that hour
в три́ часа́	at 3:00
в то́т де́нь	that day
в пя́тницу	on Friday

Words meaning "time," "period," "epoch," "occasion," etc., also take **в** + *accusative:*

в то́ вре́мя	at that time
в ту́ эпо́ху	in that epoch
в то́т пери́од	at that period
в то́т ра́з	on that occasion

B. Instrumental. With parts of the day and seasons of the year, the *instrumental* is used.

вчера́ у́тр**ом**, за́втра ве́чер**ом**
про́шл**ым** ле́т**ом**, э́т**ой** весн**о́й**, бу́дущ**ей** о́сен**ью**

C. Locative. With longer periods of time (months, years, centuries) **в** + *locative* is used:

в про́шл**ом** ме́сяц**е**	last month
в э́т**ом** ме́сяц**е**	this month
в бу́дущ**ем** ме́сяц**е**	next month
в апре́л**е**	in April
в про́шл**ом** год**у́**	last year
в э́т**ом** год**у́**	this year
в бу́дущ**ем** год**у́**	next year
в ты́сяча девятьсо́т шестьдеся́т втор**о́м** год**у́**	in 1962
в двадца́т**ом** ве́к**е**	in the 20th century
в про́шл**ом** ве́к**е**	in the last century

на + *locative with weeks:*

на э́т**ой**/ на про́шл**ой**/ на бу́дущ**ей** неде́л**е**	this/last/ next week

D. Genitive. With dates, the *genitive* is used:

пятна́дцат**ого** апре́л**я**	on April 15
два́дцать тре́ть**его** январ**я́** ты́сяча девятьсо́т шестьдеся́т четвёрт**ого** го́д**а**	on January 23, 1964

When one unit of time falls within another, the second and larger unit is in the *genitive* (compare English "of"):

Сего́дня пе́рвое феврал**я́**.
Today is February 1 (the first of February).

в после́дний де́нь про́шл**ого** ме́сяц**а**
on the last day of last month

Drills

A. *Complete the sentence by translating the English phrases on the right.*

Я́ бы́л/бу́ду в Я́лте {
last year.
last month.
last January.
last week.
next week.
this week.
a month and a half.
a week and a half.
last summer.
last winter.
for the last time.
for a whole week.
the whole winter.
the whole month of May.
in May.
next year.
next spring.
this Wednesday.
this Sunday.
on Tuesday.

Я́ е́ду за грани́цу {
for the week.
for two weeks.
for two months.
for half a year.
for five months.
for a year and a half.
for three and a half years.

B. *Write out the numerals in the correct case; translate dates.*

Его́ конто́ра на 15; 19; 20; 21; 27; 30; 40; 50; 102 этаже́.
—На како́й э́то страни́це? —На 15; 19; 20; 21; 30; 33; 40; 50; 90; 102.
О́н роди́лся on May 1, 1923; in 1923; on Sept. 12, 1847; in 1947; on July 28, 1942; in 1692; in 1951.
Мы́ уезжа́ем на кани́кулы ме́жду (June 25 and 30); (July 1 and 5); (May 13 and 19); (August 20 and 22).
Мы́ пробу́дем за грани́цей от (August 15 to September 27); (October 1 to November 21); (January 3 to February 12).

C. *Translate the words in parentheses.*

1. О́н прие́хал (that day).
2. (At that hour) на у́лице никого́ не́ было.

3. Она́ пришла́ (at four).
4. (At that time) я́ ещё ходи́л в шко́лу.
5. (Next month) я́ пое́ду в Вашингто́н.
6. (Last month) я́ провёл два́ дня́ в Ки́еве.
7. Андре́й око́нчил семиле́тку (last year).
8. Мы́ ещё не зна́ем, куда́ мы́ пое́дем (next spring).
9. (Next week) моя́ тётя приезжа́ет сюда́.
10. —Мы́ идём в теа́тр (this week). —(On what day)? —(On Saturday.)
11. (Next week) у на́с бу́дут экза́мены. —(On what day)? —(On Tuesday.)
12. Толсто́й у́мер (in the twentieth century).
13. Она́ прие́хала (last week) и уезжа́ет (next week).
14. Каки́е знамени́тые писа́тели жи́ли (in the last century)?
15. Бы́ло о́чень хо́лодно (last January).

D. *Переведи́те на ру́сский.*

1. This year I am working much more than I worked last year.
2. I don't know yet what I will be doing next year.
3. Last month my sister arrived from China.
4. There will be many holidays this month.
5. I would like to go to the seashore next month.
6. It will be much warmer in a month.
7. We were at the seashore last week.
8. This week I must go to Kharkov for two weeks.
9. I will return next week.
10. They told us that they are going to the Crimea for a week, and that in a week they will come back here.
11. I will return from there in three days.
12. Last time I explained that rule to you.
13. Last summer we spent a month in the Caucasus, on the shore of the Black Sea.
14. Next summer we'll go to the mountains.
15. Next spring we want to go to the Ukraine.
16. I am going there for three days.

CONVERSATION

Прие́зд Еле́ны Ива́новны

(Ве́чер. Вокза́л. Больши́е часы́. На часа́х два́дцать пя́ть мину́т девя́того. Напра́во на стене́ расписа́ние поездо́в. Два́ молоды́х челове́ка, Смирно́в и Зло́бин.)

Смирно́в (Зло́бину). —А́, здра́вствуйте! Что́ вы́ ту́т де́лаете? Пришли́ встреча́ть кого́-нибудь и́ли куда́-нибудь е́дете?

Зло́бин. —Я́ пришёл встреча́ть одну́ знако́мую, кото́рая приезжа́ет из Ха́рькова. А что́ вы́ ту́т де́лаете?

С. —Я́ то́же встреча́ю одну́ знако́мую из Ха́рькова. Мо́жно спроси́ть, кто́ ва́ша знако́мая?

З. —Еле́на Ива́новна Во́лкова.

С. —Я́ то́же пришёл её встреча́ть!

З. —Я́ получи́л от неё письмо́, в кото́ром она́ пи́шет, что приезжа́ет во вто́рник, семна́дцатого декабря́, и про́сит меня́, её лу́чшего дру́га, встре́тить её. Но́ она́ забы́ла написа́ть в письме́, каки́м по́ездом она́ е́дет, и в кото́ром часу́ её по́езд прихо́дит! А мо́жет быть она́ вообще́ реши́ла оста́ться в Ха́рькове и забы́ла да́ть мне́ зна́ть.

С. —Я́ получи́л от неё то́чно тако́е же письмо́! Она́ пи́шет мне́ то́ же са́мое, что ва́м: она́ про́сит меня́, своего́ лу́чшего дру́га, встре́тить её и мне́ то́же не пи́шет, в кото́ром часу́ она́ приезжа́ет!

З. —Кака́я исто́рия! Вчера́ ве́чером я́ позвони́л на вокза́л и мне́ сказа́ли, что из Ха́рькова прихо́дит пя́ть поездо́в в де́нь! Е́сть два́ у́тренних по́езда: пе́рвый прихо́дит без десяти́ во́семь, второ́й в полови́не оди́ннадцатого; е́сть оди́н дневно́й в че́тверть пя́того, пото́м е́сть вече́рний по́езд, кото́рый прихо́дит без че́тверти де́вять (в два́дцать со́рок пя́ть) и после́дний, ночно́й, прихо́дит в оди́ннадцать (в два́дцать три́). (На стене́ расписа́ние поездо́в. Они́ остана́вливаются перед расписа́нием.) Во́т ви́дите, всё, как я́ ва́м говори́л.

С. —Да́, ви́жу. В кото́ром же часу́ вы́ сюда́ пришли́?

З. —Я́ боя́лся опозда́ть и пришёл в полови́не восьмо́го утра́. Я́ зде́сь с полови́ны восьмо́го!

С. —Несча́стный челове́к!

З. —Да́, глу́по. Но́ почему́ вы́ пришли́ то́лько тепе́рь? Отку́да вы́ зна́ли, что она́ приезжа́ет без че́тверти де́вять?

С. —Я́ зна́ю Еле́ну Ива́новну. Она́ не лю́бит ни ра́но встава́ть ни по́здно ложи́ться, и я́ реши́л поэ́тому, что она́ прие́дет вече́рним по́ездом.

З. —По́езд прихо́дит без че́тверти де́вять, а сейча́с уже́ без двадцати́ пяти́. Мы́ должны́ спеши́ть. У на́с оста́лось пя́ть мину́т, а мы́ да́же ещё не зна́ем но́мера платфо́рмы.

С. Я́ никогда́ не спешу́ и всегда́ прихожу́ во́время. У на́с е́сть ещё мно́го вре́мени. Я́ ду́маю, полчаса́, и́ли да́же три́ че́тверти.

З. —Я́ ва́с не понима́ю! Посмотри́те на часы́! Сейча́с уже́ без двадцати́ де́вять, а по́езд до́лжен прийти́ без че́тверти. У на́с е́сть то́лько пя́ть мину́т.

С. —Я́ хорошо́ зна́ю Еле́ну Ива́новну. Она́ всегда́ опа́здывает.

З. —Вы́ хоти́те сказа́ть, что по́езд опозда́ет, потому́ что на нём е́дет Еле́на Ива́новна?

(Го́лос громкоговори́теля.) Внима́ние! Внима́ние! По́езд из Ха́рькова опозда́ет на полчаса́ и придёт в два́дцать оди́н пятна́дцать.

С. —Ну́, во́т ви́дите, в че́тверть деся́того! Зна́чит, я́ бы́л пра́в! У на́с ещё мно́го вре́мени. Пойдёмте в буфе́т и вы́пьем за здоро́вье Еле́ны Ива́новны.

Чита́йте э́ти вопро́сы и отвеча́йте на ни́х.

1. Где́ встре́тились два́ молоды́х челове́ка? 2. Заче́м они́ о́ба пришли́ на вокза́л? 3. Пришли́ ли они́ о́ба в то́ же вре́мя? 4. Кото́рый ча́с на больши́х часа́х? 5. Что́ мы́ ви́дим на стене́ напра́во? 6. Что́ Еле́на Ива́новна написа́ла обо́им молоды́м лю́дям? 7. В како́й де́нь она́ должна́ была́ прие́хать и како́го числа́? 8. Что́ Смирно́в говори́т о Е. М.? 9. Что́ сказа́л громкоговори́тель?

READING

Я́лта, 2-о́е ию́ля 1961 г.[4]

Письмо́. Ча́сть пе́рвая.[5]

I. Я́лта

Дорого́й Па́вел!

Ты́ вероя́тно бу́дешь о́чень удивлён, когда́ полу́чишь э́то письмо́ от меня́, Матве́я Желя́бина. Сто́лько ле́т прошло́ с тех по́р, как мы́ с тобо́й ви́делись в после́дний ра́з.

Я́ то́лько что случа́йно узна́л тво́й а́дрес и реши́л сейча́с же тебе́ написа́ть. Мне́ так хо́чется мно́гое тебе́ рассказа́ть, мно́гое узна́ть о тебе́, и так хо́чется вме́сте с тобо́й вспо́мнить про́шлое! Я́ ду́маю, что э́то письмо́ бу́дет о́чень, о́чень дли́нное.

Я́ пишу́ тебе́, как ви́дишь, из Я́лты, где́ я́ провожу́ кани́кулы с мое́й семьёй. Мы́ провели́ зде́сь ле́то в про́шлом году́ и на́м та́к понра́вилась Я́лта, что мы́ реши́ли в э́том году́ опя́ть сюда́ прие́хать.

Мы́ прилете́ли сюда́ 21-ого ию́ня из Свердло́вска,[6] где́ мы́ живём. 23-го ию́ля конча́ется мо́й о́тпуск, и я́ до́лжен буду верну́ться в Свердло́вск и нача́ть опя́ть рабо́тать в больни́це; я́ та́м гла́вный вра́ч. Но́ семья́ моя́ пробу́дет зде́сь до 15-го а́вгуста.

[4] This date may also be abbreviated as 2/VII/61. In Russian dates the day comes first, then the month, then the year.

[5] Чтобы ле́гче бы́ло чита́ть э́то дли́нное письмо́, мы́ разделили/divided/ его́ на гла́вы.

[6] Sverdlovsk, a city in the Urals.

Я́ слы́шал, что ты́ жена́т и что у тебя́ сы́н и до́чь. Как хорошо́ бы́ло бы, е́сли бы ты́ прие́хал сюда́ с свое́й семьёй! Я́ не зна́ю, бы́л ли ты́ уже́ когда́-нибудь в Я́лте. Я́ уве́рен, что Я́лта тебе́ бы о́чень понра́вилась. Приро́да зде́сь чуде́сная: мо́ре, го́ры, везде́ ма́сса цвето́в. Така́я красота́ вокру́г, что тру́дно описа́ть.

Я́ пишу́ э́то письмо́ на балко́не, кото́рый выхо́дит[7] в са́д. Ви́д с балко́на замеча́тельный: за са́дом мо́ре, спра́ва и сле́ва го́ры. На одно́й горе́ ста́рая тата́рская дере́вня. Над голово́й глубо́кое, си́нее, ю́жное не́бо. Над мо́рем лета́ют и крича́т бе́лые ча́йки. Приезжа́й, Павлу́ша, и са́м посмотри́ на э́ту красоту́.

Семья́

Я́ забы́л тебе́ сказа́ть, что и я́ жена́т. Мою́ жену́ зову́т[8] Любо́вь. Лю́ба[9] чу́дный челове́к. Она́ краси́вая, у́мная и у неё золото́е се́рдце. У на́с две́ де́вочки и ма́льчик. О́бе де́вочки о́чень сла́вные и хорошо́ у́чатся. Ста́ршей, Ве́ре,[9] 11 ле́т, мла́дшей, Наде́жде[9] 9, а сы́ну 4 го́да. Мы́ пра́здновали его́ де́нь рожде́ния на про́шлой неде́ле. Сы́на зову́т Па́влом, в че́сть тебя́. Па́влик[10] то́лстый, о́чень смешно́й и задаёт ма́ссу заба́вных вопро́сов. Во́т тебе́ не́сколько приме́ров:

1. Ма́ма, кто́ роди́лся ра́ньше: ты́ и́ли я́?
2. Па́па, заче́м мне́ учи́ться чита́ть? Я́ всегда́ могу́ попроси́ть ма́му, и она́ прочита́ет мне́ всё, что мне́ захо́чется.
3. Почему́ со́лнце све́тит днём, а не но́чью, когда́ темно́? Е́сли бы оно́ свети́ло но́чью, бы́ло бы всегда́ светло́, и мне́ никогда́ не ну́жно было бы ложи́ться спа́ть.
4. Ма́ма, когда́ я́ роди́лся, я́ не уме́л говори́ть, ве́рно? Так ка́к же ты́ и па́па узна́ли, что меня́ зову́т Па́влик?
5. Ка́к лю́ди мо́гут ви́деть сны́? Ведь они́ спя́т с закры́тыми глаза́ми!
6. Па́па, а кто́ сильне́е: леопа́рд и́ли тра́ктор?

И та́к без конца́! О́н о́чень заба́вный па́рень, но́ пове́рь мне́, не всегда́ легко́ отвеча́ть на все́ его́ вопро́сы. Приезжа́й, Павлу́ша! Мы́ с тобо́й должны́ сно́ва познако́миться и познако́мить на́ши се́мьи. Бы́ло бы так хорошо́ на́м все́м ту́т собра́ться! Мо́жешь ли ты́ получи́ть о́тпуск?

Продолже́ние сле́дует (to be continued).

[7] Here this verb has the meaning of "look out on," "face."

[8] Ка́к его́ зову́т? What is his name? (literally, what do they call him?). The question (and reply) are less formal than Ка́к его́ и́мя/фами́лия? The reply uses the nominative or instrumental case: Его́ зову́т Па́вел/Па́влом.

[9] Любо́вь (diminutive, Лю́ба), Love; Ве́ра, Faith; Наде́жда, Hope.

[10] Diminutive of Па́вел.

Чита́йте э́ти вопро́сы и отвеча́йте на ни́х.

1. Почему́ Матве́й ду́мает, что Па́вел бу́дет удивлён, когда́ полу́чит от него́ письмо́? 2. Почему́ Матве́й то́лько тепе́рь пи́шет своему́ дру́гу? 3. Почему́ о́н пи́шет э́то письмо́? 4. Почему́ Желя́бины второ́й ра́з прово́дят кани́кулы в Я́лте? 5. Верну́тся ли все́ Желя́бины вме́сте в Свердло́вск? А е́сли не́т, то почему́? 6. Почему́ сы́на Матве́я зову́т Па́влом? 7. Куда́ выхо́дит балко́н, и како́й с него́ ви́д? 8. Запо́мнили ли вы́ како́й-нибудь вопро́с Па́влика, и како́й из ни́х ва́м бо́льше всего́ понра́вился? 9. Почему́ Матве́й так хо́чет, что́бы его́ дру́г прие́хал в Я́лту?

VOCABULARY

***буфе́т** buffet
ве́рно right, true; probably
***громкоговори́тель** (*masc.*) loudspeaker
дневно́й afternoon, daytime (*adj.*)
дура́к, *fem.* **ду́ра** fool
жена́т, -ы (**на** + *loc.*) married (to)[11]
за́мужем (**за** + *instr.*) married (to)[11]
заба́вный amusing, entertaining
закры́тый closed, shut[12]
золото́й gold (*adj.*), golden
копе́йка (*gen. pl.* **копе́ек**) copeck (1/100 of a ruble)
красота́ beauty
о́тпуск leave (from work), vacation
прие́зд arrival (by vehicle)
расписа́ние schedule
сон (*gen.* **сна**) sleep; dream
сла́вный (*colloq.*) fine, nice
сно́ва again, anew
сле́ва on (from) the left
спра́ва on (from) the right
страни́ца page
***тата́рский** Tartar (*adj.*)
том volume
у́тренний morning (*adj.*)
***ча́йка** (*gen. pl.* **ча́ек**) seagull
число́ number, date

Verbs

вспомина́ть (imperf., I), **вспо́мнить** (perf., II: **вспо́мн.ю, -ишь**) to recollect, recall
опи́сывать (imperf., I), **описа́ть** (perf., I: **опишу́, опи́шешь**) to describe
пра́здновать (imperf., I: **пра́зднy.ю, -ешь**) to celebrate
свети́ть (**свечу́, све́тишь**) to shine
хоте́ться (imperf.: **хо́чется**), **захоте́ться** (perf.: **захо́чется**) to want to, feel like (+ *dat. and inf.*). **Мне́ хо́чется е́сть,** I feel like eating, I am hungry

Expressions

расписа́ние поездо́в (train) timetable
тако́й же of the same sort
вы́пить за здоро́вье (+ *gen.*) to drink someone's health
зна́чит (*as adverb*) so then, then, hence
в честь (+ *gen.*) in someone's honor
ви́деть со́н to have a dream

[11] A man says Я́ жена́т, but a woman says Я́ за́мужем; a married couple says Мы́ жена́ты.
[12] The short form is obligatory in the predicate, *e.g.*, Две́рь закры́та.

UNIT 27

***Particiрles,* 470. *Hypothetical mood corresponding to English suffix "-ever,"* 484. *Conjunctions of time in subordinate clauses,* 485.**

GRAMMAR

1. Participles

Russian participles are words derived from verbs having the verbal characteristics of tense, past or present (but not future), and aspect, perfective or imperfective.

There are two kinds of participles:

Adjectival participles, which are similar to adjectives in form and function.

Adverbial participles, which are indeclinable and similar in function to adverbs.

A. Adjectival participles. Adjectival participles may be active or passive, past or present; they have the aspect of the verb from which they are derived.

(1) *Active adjectival participles, past.* The words in boldface in the sentences below are *past* active adjectival participles; they may replace a clause introduced by **кото́рый** and containing a verb in the *past* tense, imperfective or perfective, from which the participle is derived (in the following examples this clause is given in parentheses after each participle). It will be observed that participles agree, like adjectives, with the nouns they modify, in number, gender, and case.

Все́ мои́ хоро́шие студе́нты, **чита́вшие** (кото́рые чита́ли) э́ту кни́гу, говоря́т, что она́ о́чень интере́сная.

Я́ зна́ю писа́теля, **написа́вшего** (кото́рый написа́л) э́ту кни́гу.

Я́ познако́мился с одни́м америка́нским журнали́стом, до́лго **жи́вшим** (кото́рый до́лго жи́л) в Москве́.

Я́ написа́л письмо́ в Вашингто́н моему́ хоро́шему дру́гу, **бы́вшему** (кото́рый бы́л) неда́вно в Москве́ и **ви́девшему** (кото́рый ви́дел) та́м моего́ бра́та.

О́н спроси́л молодо́го челове́ка, **сиде́вшего** (кото́рый сиде́л) ря́дом с ни́м в авто́бусе, идёт ли э́тот авто́бус на Кра́сную пло́щадь.

Мы́ ви́дели де́вушку, **бежа́вшую** (кото́рая бежа́ла) по у́лице и гро́мко **пе́вшую** (кото́рая гро́мко пе́ла) каку́ю-то пе́сню.

Past active participles are formed from the past stem by dropping the **-л** ending and adding the suffix **-вш-** (in the case of some verbs **-ш-** only), then the adjective ending:

чита́(л)	чита́.**вш**.ий
написа́(л)	написа́.**вш**.ий
бы(л)	бы́.**вш**.ий
ви́де(л)	ви́де.**вш**.ий
сиде́(л)	сиде́.**вш**.ий
жи(л)	жи́.**вш**.ий
принёс	принёс.**ш**.ий

(2) *Active adjectival participles, present.* The words in boldface in the sentences below are *present* active participles; they may replace a clause introduced by **кото́рый** and containing a verb in the *present* tense from which the participle is derived; this clause is given in parentheses after the participle.

Я́ зна́ю инжене́ра, **рабо́тающего** (кото́рый рабо́тает) на э́том заво́де.

Она́ получи́ла письмо́ от свое́й сестры́, **живу́щей** (кото́рая живёт) в Москве́.

Мне́ нужна́ секрета́рша, **зна́ющая** (кото́рая зна́ет) ру́сский язы́к.

Молодо́й челове́к, **иду́щий** (кото́рый идёт) по то́й стороне́ у́лицы, похо́ж на ва́шего бра́та.

У на́с е́сть не́сколько студе́нтов, хорошо́ **говоря́щих** (кото́рые хорошо́ говоря́т) по-ру́сски.

Соба́ка подошла́ к челове́ку, **сидя́щему** (кото́рый сиди́т) у окна́.

Учё́бник для **начина́ющих** (для те́х, кто начина́ет) (for beginners).

Ваго́н для **куря́щих** (для те́х, кто ку́рит) (for smokers).

Present active participles are formed from the present tense conjugation stem as it appears in the third person plural; final **-т** is dropped, and to this stem is added the suffix **щ**, then an adjectival ending:

рабо́таю(т)	рабо́таю.щ.ий
живу́(т)	живу́.щ.ий
зна́ю(т)	зна́ю.щ.ий
иду́(т)	иду́.щ.ий
говоря́(т)	говоря́.щ.ий
сидя́(т)	сидя́.щ.ий

Drill

Replace adjectival participles by clauses with **кото́рый,** *and translate.*

Model: Актри́са, **игра́вшая** ро́ль Офе́лии, о́чень тала́нтлива.
Актри́са, **кото́рая игра́ла** ро́ль Офе́лии, о́чень тала́нтлива.

1. Я́ зна́ю да́му, **сидя́щую** про́тив на́с.
2. Вы́ по́мните де́вушку, **сиде́вшую** ря́дом с Серге́ем?
3. Ва́м ну́жно найти́ ги́да, **зна́ющего** португа́льский язы́к.
4. Я́ спроси́л одну́ же́нщину, **слы́шавшую** Ле́нина, хорошо́ ли о́н говори́л.
5. Мы́ познако́мились с писа́тельницей, мно́го **пи́шущей** о де́тях.
6. Учи́тельница, **даю́щая** мне́ уро́ки му́зыки—францу́женка.
7. Вы́ зна́ете люде́й, **сня́вших** кварти́ру на пя́том этаже́?
8. Да́ма, **снима́вшая** пальто́ когда́ вы́ вошли́, до́чь хозя́йки.
9. Господи́н, **покупа́вший** руба́шки и **кури́вший** большу́ю сига́ру, изве́стный певе́ц.
10. Я́ зна́ю ма́ленького ма́льчика, хорошо́ **игра́ющего** на роя́ле.
11. **Сидя́щий** в углу́ челове́к—бра́т мое́й сосе́дки.
12. Семья́, **жи́вшая** над на́ми, перее́хала в другу́ю кварти́ру.
13. Ты́ ви́дишь старика́, **иду́щего** с чемода́ном в руке́?
14. Мы́ ча́сто пи́шем сы́ну, **живу́щему** на Кавка́зе.
15. Андре́й зна́ет журнали́стку, **написа́вшую** э́ту статью́.
16. **Входя́щий** в ко́мнату челове́к—знамени́тый учёный.
17. **Воше́дшая** с ни́м же́нщина—его́ жена́.

(3) *Passive adjectival participles, past. Passive* adjectival participles, which can be derived from transitive verbs only, modify the *object* of an action; the agent by whom the action was performed may be described by a noun (or pronoun) in the instrumental case; thus:

Construction with *active* participle:

Журнали́ст, **написа́вший** статью́ . . .
The newspaperman who wrote the article . . .

Construction with *passive* participle:

Статья́, **напи́санная** журнали́стом . . .
The article written (which was written) by the newspaperman . . .

It will be observed that all the participles occurring in the examples below are derived from *perfective* verbs; past passive participles from *imperfective* verbs are rarely used.

In these sentences, the words in boldface are *past passive* adjectival participles:

Я́ прочита́л статью́, **напи́санную** мои́м знако́мым (кото́рую написа́л мо́й знако́мый).
Мы́ е́здили в Босто́н на автомоби́ле, неда́вно **ку́пленном** мои́м бра́том (кото́рый мо́й бра́т неда́вно купи́л).
Я́ ещё не получи́л **по́сланных** ва́ми кни́г (кни́г, кото́рые вы́ посла́ли).
Я́ возврати́л в библиоте́ку все́ **прочи́танные** мно́й кни́ги (все́ кни́ги, кото́рые я́ прочита́л).
Я́ чита́ю кни́гу, **взя́тую** мно́ю (кото́рую я́ взя́л) в библиоте́ке.
Портфе́ль, **привезённый** отцо́м (кото́рый привёз оте́ц) из А́нглии, мне́ о́чень нра́вится.
Я́ ви́дел письмо́, **подпи́санное** гла́вным реда́ктором (кото́рое подписа́л гла́вный реда́ктор).

Past passive participles are formed from the infinitive stem with, in the case of some verbs, the suffix **-нн-** (sometimes **-енн-**) and, in the case of others, **-т-**. Formation of these participles is complicated, and the student is advised to learn the forms below as vocabulary. Note that all the forms below are *perfective*.

The following are among the more frequently used forms:

Suffix **-нн-** (*mostly first conjugation*):

написа́ть	напи́санный	written (which was, has been written)
прода́ть	про́данный	sold
прочита́ть	прочи́танный	read (which has been read)
сказа́ть	ска́занный	said, spoken
показа́ть	пока́занный	showed
рассказа́ть	расска́занный	told, narrated
подписа́ть	подпи́санный	signed
сде́лать	сде́ланный	done, made
услы́шать	услы́шанный	heard
сыгра́ть	сы́гранный	played
потеря́ть	поте́рянный	lost

Suffix **-енн-** (*mostly second conjugation, often with consonant mutations similar to those in the first person singular*):

получи́ть	полу́ченный	received, obtained
купи́ть	ку́пленный	bought, purchased
поста́вить	поста́вленный	placed, stood
положи́ть	поло́женный	placed, set down
постро́ить	постро́енный	built
пригото́вить	пригото́вленный	prepared
око́нчить	око́нченный	finished
возврати́ть	возвращённый	returned, given back
окружи́ть	окружённый	surrounded
принести́	принесённый	brought (on foot)
привезти́	привезённый	brought (in a vehicle)
найти́	на́йденный	found

Suffix **-т-** (*occurs with a limited number of first conjugation verbs*):

заня́ть	за́нятый	occupied; busy
сня́ть	сня́тый	taken off; rented
забы́ть	забы́тый	forgotten
взя́ть	взя́тый	taken
за-/откры́ть	за-/откры́тый	closed/open, opened
оде́ть	оде́тый	dressed
уби́ть	уби́тый	killed
нача́ть	на́чатый	begun, started
вы́пить	вы́питый	consumed, drunk

(4) *Predicative forms of passive adjectival participles.* Passive adjectival participles, past and present, have predicative (short) forms which are mandatory when these participles are used predicatively. As with adjectives, the predicative forms are obtained by dropping the adjectival endings and adding zero for masculine, **-о** for neuter, **-а** for feminine, and **-ы** for plural. Past passive participles formed with the suffix **-нн-** preserve only the first **-н-** of this suffix:

Attributive		*Predicative*
напи́санный	*Masc.*	напи́сан
	Neut.	напи́сано
	Fem.	напи́сана
	Plural	напи́саны

Pattern Sentences

1. Э́то письмо́ бы́ло **напи́сано** мно́й в ма́е.	1. This letter was written by me in May.

2. Я́ ду́маю, что о́н бу́дет о́чень **удивлён** те́м, что услы́шит.	2. I think that he will be very amazed by what he is going to hear.
3. Аме́рика была́ **откры́та** Колу́мбом.	3. America was discovered by Columbus.
4. Э́тот писа́тель тепе́рь все́ми **забы́т.**	4. That writer is now forgotten by everyone.
5. Э́та телегра́мма была́ **полу́чена** в два́ часа́.	5. This telegram was received at two o'clock.
6. На́ш до́м **окружён** поля́ми и леса́ми.	6. Our house is surrounded by fields and woods.

Drill

Переведи́те на англи́йский.

1. Письмо́, **возвращённое** мне́ А́нной, лежи́т на полу́.
2. Почему́ э́то письмо́ бы́ло **возвращено́?**
3. Я́ не могу́ найти́ на ка́рте го́рода, **взя́того** враго́м.
4. Мо́жет быть вы́ по́мните, когда́ э́тот го́род бы́л **взя́т?**
5. Куда́ ты́ положи́ла проду́кты, **ку́пленные** на за́втра?
6. **Полу́ченные** вчера́ журна́лы лежа́т на сто́лике в кабине́те.
7. Ке́м была́ **ку́плена** карти́на, о кото́рой вы́ говори́ли?
8. Э́та карти́на была́ **ку́плена** одни́м музе́ем.
9. Э́тот до́м бы́л **постро́ен** в конце́ про́шлого ве́ка.
10. В нача́ле э́того ве́ка о́н бы́л **про́дан** бога́тому иностра́нцу.
11. На фотогра́фии де́душка и ба́бушка, **окружённые** детьми́ и вну́ками.
12. Сто́л, **поста́вленный** посреди́ ко́мнаты, занима́ет сли́шком мно́го ме́ста.
13. Куда́ вы́ положи́ли **прочи́танные** газе́ты?
14. Я́ уви́дел на дива́не кни́гу, **забы́тую** Ива́ном.
15. Всё э́то бы́ло **сде́лано** мои́м отцо́м.
16. Я́ никогда́ не забу́ду сло́в, **ска́занных** ва́ми.
17. Она́ бои́тся, что её сы́н бу́дет **уби́т** на фро́нте.
18. Кто́ ко́нчит **на́чатую** ва́ми рабо́ту?
19. Э́та кни́га была́ **напи́сана** и́м до войны́.

(5) *Passive adjectival participles, present.* Present tense passive participles are less common than the past tense forms discussed in the preceding paragraph; only a limited number of verbs, all transitive, produce this type of participle. While most *past* passive participles are formed from perfective verbs; all *present* passive participles are formed from *imperfective* verbs. Their use emphasizes that an action continues to be performed over a period of time. They are derived from present tense stems and have a vowel plus the suffix **-м-** (**-ем-** with most verbs of the first conjugation, **-им-** for those of the second conjugation).

Examples of passive, present tense, participial constructions:

> Я́ не чита́л кни́ги, **критику́емой** а́втором э́той статьи́ (кото́рую критику́ет а́втор . . .).
> I have not read the book criticized (under criticism) by the author of this article.

> Пра́вила, **изуча́емые** на́ми, ча́сто ка́жутся мне́ тру́дными (кото́рые мы́ изуча́ем . . .).
> The rules studied by us (which we are studying) often seem difficult to me.

More common than the pattern illustrated above, is the adjectival use of present passive participles with no agent in the instrumental case. Compare the passive construction with a passive participle and the agent in the instrumental:

> Во́т после́дний рома́н **люби́мого мно́й** писа́теля.
> (literally: "of the loved, or preferred, by me writer.")

with the more idiomatic construction in which the passive participle is used simply as a modifier:

> Во́т после́дний рома́н **моего́ люби́мого** писа́теля.
> (literally: "of my favorite, or preferred, writer.")

The following are among the more common present passive participles, used mostly as adjectives:

ви́деть, ви́димый	seen, visible, apparent
ви́деть, неви́димый	invisible
забыва́ть, незабыва́емый	unforgettable
называ́ть, называ́емый	called; так называ́емый, so-called, abbrev.: т.н.
уважа́ть, уважа́емый	respected, esteemed; уважа́емый, многоуважа́емый (much respected), or глубокоуважа́емый (deeply respected), followed by a name or title, is the standard official form of address in Russian —used in letters, in addressing a meeting, etc.
обходи́ть, необходи́мый	indispensable (from обходи́ть, "to by-pass," "get around")
обвиня́ть, обвиня́емый	(the) accused (the defendant in a criminal trial; used as a noun)

The present passive participle is also used in the predicative short form:

Его́ оте́ц был все́ми **люби́м** и **уважа́ем.**
His father was loved and respected by everyone.

B. Adverbial participles. In a sentence with one subject and two predicate verbs, one of these verbs may usually be replaced by an adverbial participle derived from it. Thus, in О́н сиде́л у окна́ и чита́л (He sat by the window and read), either verb may be replaced by an adverbial participle (сиде́л by си́дя, or чита́л by чита́я), producing the two variants:

О́н сиде́л у окна́ **чита́я** газе́ту.
He sat by the window *reading* the newspaper.

О́н чита́л газе́ту **си́дя** у окна́.
He read the newspaper *sitting* by the window.

In the first variant above, the action expressed by the verb, сиде́л, is given more prominence than the other action of the original sentence; the latter is now referred to by an adverbial participle, **чита́я,** which is a modifier describing the circumstances in which the action «сиде́л» is performed. The reverse is true of the second variant, where **си́дя** substituted for сиде́л is an adverbial modifier of the predicate, чита́л.

Adverbial participles are said to be *past* when they refer to actions performed prior to the action of the predicate verb, and *present* when their action is in progress at the time of the action of the predicate verb.

(1) *Past adverbial participles.* The words in boldface in the sentences below are "past" adverbial participles; each example is followed by the infinitive of the verb which appears here as an adverbial participle:

Прочита́в кни́гу, я́ верну́л её в библиоте́ку. (прочита́ть)
Having read the book, I returned it to the library.

Верну́в кни́гу, я́ пошёл в рестора́н. (верну́ть)
Having returned the book, I went to a restaurant.

Написа́в письмо́, я́ отнёс его́ на по́чту. (написа́ть)
Having written the letter, I took it to the post office.

Купи́в всё, что е́й бы́ло ну́жно, она́ пошла́ домо́й. (купи́ть)
Having bought all she needed, she went home.

Узна́в в како́й гости́нице о́н останови́лся, я́ посла́л ему́ телегра́мму. (узна́ть)
Having found out in what hotel he was staying, I sent him a wire.

Посла́в телегра́мму, я́ лёг спа́ть. (посла́ть)
Having sent the wire, I went to bed.

Приéхав в Москвý, я́ пошёл осмáтривать Крéмль. (приéхать)
Arriving (having arrived) in Moscow, I went to visit the Kremlin.

О́н ушёл, никомý не **сказáв** кудá óн идёт. (сказáть)
He left without telling (having told) anyone where he was going.

Не **получи́в** отвéта на моё письмó, я́ написáл емý опя́ть. (получи́ть)
Receiving no reply to my letter, I wrote to him again.

Past adverbial participles are derived from the past tense stem and take the suffix **-в**: написá(л)—написá**в**; прочитá(л)—прочитá**в**; купи́(л)—купи́**в**; узнá(л)—узнá**в**; получи́(л)—получи́**в**. (A less commonly used variant is formed with **-вши**: написáв—написá**вши**; прочитáв—прочитá**вши**; приéхав—приéха**вши**).

"Past" adverbial participles (referring to an action terminated before that of the predicate verb) are, as a general rule, derived from perfective verbs.

The use of a past adverbial participle instead of a verb for an action performed prior to the action of the predicate is a means of indicating that some connection is felt to exist between the two actions, the one referred to by the past adverbial participle being regarded as the circumstance that has caused, or made possible, necessary, desirable, etc., the action expressed by the predicate verb.

Drill

Replace the verbs in boldface by past adverbial participles and rework the sentence according to the example.

Model: О́н **написáл** свóй пéрвый ромáн и срáзу стáл знамени́тым.
Написáв свóй пéрвый ромáн, óн срáзу стáл знамени́тым.

1. О́н **прóжил** нéсколько лéт в Москвé и тепéрь хорошó говори́т по-рýсски.
2. О́н **получи́л** телегрáмму из Чикáго и сейчáс же тудá вы́ехал.
3. О́н **вы́пил** довóльно мнóго вóдки и нáчал грóмко и вéсело пéть.
4. Я́ **позáвтракал** и пошёл погуля́ть.
5. Мы́ **пообéдали** в ресторáне и пошли́ в кинó.
6. Мы́ **кóнчили** рабóтать и нáчали читáть газéту.
7. Я́ **написáл** письмó и пошёл погуля́ть.
8. Я́ **прочитáл** газéту и дáл её А́нне.
9. О́н **спроси́л** меня́, готóв ли обéд, и пошёл в столóвую.
10. Онá **началá** говори́ть и не моглá останови́ться.
11. Я́ **отвéтил** на её вопрóс и вы́шел из кóмнаты.
12. Зи́на **откры́ла** окнó и леглá на диван.

(2) *Present adverbial participles.* The words in boldface in the sentences below are present adverbial participles:

Ду́мая о де́тстве, я́ всегда́ вспомина́ю ба́бушку.
Thinking about my childhood, I always remember my grandmother.

Вспомина́я ба́бушку, я́ иногда́ пла́чу.
When I remember my grandmother, I sometimes cry.

О́н лю́бит чита́ть газе́ту, **лёжа** на дива́не.
He likes to read the paper lying on the sofa.

Чита́я газе́ту о́н лю́бит кури́ть.
When he reads the paper he likes to smoke.

Говоря́ со мно́й, о́н всё вре́мя смотре́л на часы́.
While talking with me, he constantly looked at his watch.

Не **получа́я** отве́та на на́ши пи́сьма, мы́ посла́ли телегра́мму.
Not receiving any answer to our letters, we sent a telegram.

Посыла́я телегра́мму, мы́ не спроси́ли когда́ она́ придёт.
When we sent the telegram, we didn't ask when it would arrive.

Не **зна́я** его́ а́дреса, я́ не мо́г посла́ть ему́ кни́гу.
I couldn't send him the book without knowing his address.

Отвеча́я на вопро́с учи́теля, учени́к сде́лал две́ оши́бки.
In answering the teacher's question, the pupil made two mistakes.

Де́лая оши́бки, о́н всегда́ красне́ет.
When he makes mistakes, he always blushes.

У на́с бы́ло мно́го вре́мени, и мы́ шли́ не **спеша́.**
We had a great deal of time and we walked along without hurrying.

Живя́ так далеко́, я́ ре́дко ви́жу мои́х роди́телей.
Living so far away, I seldom see my parents.

Negative adverbial participles in Russian often correspond to the English use of "without" and the verbal noun in "-ing," *e.g.*:

О́н отве́тил **не ду́мая.**
He answered without thinking.

Не говоря́ ни сло́ва, о́н вы́шел из ко́мнаты.
Without saying a word he left the room.

Не зна́я что́ сказа́ть, она́ спроси́ла, хо́чет ли о́н ещё ча́ю.
Not knowing what to say, she asked if he wanted some more tea.

Adverbial participles past and present may be used in constructions in which the main action is expressed by a verb in the infinitive; constructions of this type are impersonal:

Нельзя́ **переходи́ть** у́лицу, **чита́я** газе́ту. (Compare: О́н переходи́л у́лицу, **чита́я** газе́ту.)
One must not (ought not to) cross a street reading a newspaper.

Ле́том прия́тно **чита́ть, лёжа** на траве́.
In the summer it is pleasant to read lying on the grass.

Ко́нчив чита́ть кни́гу, на́до сейча́с же верну́ть её в библиоте́ку.
Having finished reading a book, one should at once return it to the library.

Present adverbial participles are formed from the present stem of the verb (third person plural, less **-ут/-ют** or **-ат/-ят**), to which is added the ending **-я** (**-а** after **ж, ч, ш, щ**):

начина́(ют)	начина́я	нес(у́т)	неся́
чита́(ют)	чита́я	ид(у́т)	идя́
говор(я́т)	говоря́	леж(а́т)	лёжа
ку́р(ят)	куря́	спеш(а́т)	спеша́

A number of perfective verbs (in particular the prefixed perfective forms of идти́, нести́, везти́) usually form their *past* adverbial participle on the pattern of the present adverbial participle, that is, not the past tense stem with the suffix **-в-**, but the present-future stem with **-я** (or **-а**):

Past adv. participle (*from perf.*)

уйти́: уйд(у́т)—**уйдя́** (having left)
принести́: принес(у́т)—**принеся́** (having brought)
отвезти́: отвез(у́т)—**отвезя́** (having driven to)

Pres. adv. participle (*from imperf.*)

уходи́ть: ухо́д(ят)—**уходя́** (leaving)
приноси́ть: проино́с(ят)—**принося́** (bringing)
отвози́ть: отво́з(ят)—**отвозя́** (driving to)

A. *Replace the clauses with* **когда́** *by present or past adverbial participles and rework the sentence according to the examples.*

Когда́ пацие́нт **говори́л** с врачо́м, о́н забы́л рассказа́ть ему́ о са́мом гла́вном.
Говоря́ с врачо́м, пацие́нт забы́л рассказа́ть ему́ о са́мом гла́вном.

1. **Когда́** о́н **жи́л** в Я́лте, о́н ча́сто е́здил в Севасто́поль.
2. **Когда́** она́ **говори́т** по телефо́ну, она́ всегда́ ку́рит.
3. **Когда́** я́ **приезжа́ю** в Нью-Йо́рк, я́ сейча́с же звоню́ ма́тери.

4. **Когда́** А́нна **расска́зывает** о свои́х де́тях, она́ всегда́ смеётся.
5. **Когда́** Алёша **слу́шает** му́зыку, о́н отдыха́ет.
6. **Когда́** о́н **отдыха́ет,** о́н слу́шает му́зыку.
7. **Когда́** она́ **ду́мает** о сы́не, она́ ча́сто пла́чет.
8. **Когда́** о́н **рабо́тает,** о́н никогда́ не шу́тит.
9. **Когда́** она́ **сняла́** пальто́, она́ вошла́ в гости́ную.
10. **Когда́** о́н **уходи́л,** о́н сказа́л, что ско́ро вернётся.

B. *Replace the first verb with a present or past adverbial participle, according to the model.*

Model: Ива́н **шёл** по у́лице и пе́л.
Идя́ по у́лице, Ива́н пе́л.

1. Она́ **сиде́ла** в кре́сле и говори́ла по телефо́ну.
2. О́льга **чита́ла** кни́гу и кури́ла.
3. О́н **прочита́л** кни́гу и да́л её мне́.
4. О́н **расска́зывал** о свое́й жи́зни в Сиби́ри и кури́л папиро́су за папиро́сой.
5. О́н **рассказа́л** всё и ушёл.
6. Она́ **снима́ла** пальто́ и разгова́ривала с Зо́ей.
7. Она́ **говори́ла** с Бори́сом и ве́село смея́лась.
8. О́н **сказа́л,** что ему́ ску́чно, и ушёл.
9. Она́ **поспала́** и начала́ рабо́тать.
10. Она **игра́ла** на роя́ле и пе́ла.

C. *Переведи́те на ру́сский.*

1. Speaking with me, she was looking at my husband.
2. Having said a few words, she left the room.
3. Having read the letter, he put it on the desk.
4. (While) reading the letter, he laughed.
5. Lying on the divan, he was looking at the wall.
6. While living with his family, he never worked.
7. He said it without thinking.
8. He was walking along the street, not seeing anyone.
9. Not knowing what to do, she stood near the door.
10. Having finished our work, we went home.

C. Participles from verbs in -ся. Active adjectival and adverbial participles, past and present, may be formed from verbs in **-ся.**

Adjectival participles from verbs in **-ся** preserve **-ся** in all forms (it is not contracted to **-сь** even after vowels). In the case of adverbial participles the ending always appears as **-сь.**

Past adverbial participles of **-ся** verbs are formed with the **-вши-** suffix (see page 471), to which **-сь** is added.

To take an example, the verb смея́ться (perfective, засмея́ться, "to burst out laughing," gives the following participial forms:

Act. adj., past imperf. masc.:	смея́вш.ийся	(*neut.:* -ееся; *fem.:* -аяся; *pl.:* -иеся)
Act. adj., past perf. masc.:	засмея́вш.ийся	
Act. adj., pres.:	смею́щ.ийся—(*neut.:* -ееся; *fem.:* -аяся; *pl.:* -иеся)	
Adverb, past perf.:	засмея́вшись	
Adverb, pres.:	смея́сь	

Active adjectival participles, present

На фотогра́фии бы́ло молодо́е, краси́вое, **смею́щееся** лицо́.
In the photograph was a young, handsome, laughing face.

Её ма́ленький сы́н подошёл на у́лице к незнако́мому **смею́щемуся** челове́ку и спроси́л его́, почему́ о́н смеётся.
Her little son went up on the street to a stranger who was laughing and asked him why he was laughing.

Adverbial participles, past

Засмея́вшись, ма́ть попроси́ла меня́ продолжа́ть расска́з.
Laughing (having broken out laughing), Mother asked me to continue the story.

Бы́стро **оде́вшись,** она́ пошла́ открыва́ть две́рь.
Having dressed quickly, she went to open the door.

Adverbial participles, present

Смея́сь, Ни́на рассказа́ла мне́ о то́м, что́ случи́лось вчера́.
Laughing, Nina told me about what happened yesterday.

Умыва́ясь и **одева́ясь,** Ко́ля ве́село пе́л.
Kolya was cheerfully singing while washing and dressing.

Verbs in **-ся** may correspond to English passives when the verb without **-ся** is transitive, *e.g.*:

Зде́сь **стро́ится** мно́го домо́в.
Many homes are being built here.

Э́то зда́ние **стро́илось** два́ го́да.
This building was under construction for two years.

Что́ **продаётся** в э́том магази́не?
What is sold in this store?

Ско́лько кни́г в го́д **пи́шется** в э́той стране́?
How many books a year are written in this country?

Such verbs may form active participles corresponding in meaning to English passives:

О́н подошёл к **стро́ющемуся** до́му.
He approached the building which was being constructed.

Мы́ ви́дели дово́льно большо́й до́м, **продаю́щийся** о́чень дёшево.
We saw a fairly large house for sale (which was being sold) at a very cheap price.

Drills

A. *Translate.*

Наде́жда Ви́кторовна за́мужем за архите́ктором Ковале́вским. Они́ живу́т в Сталингра́де.[1] Сталингра́д бы́л соверше́нно разру́шен во вре́мя войны́. Та́м тепе́рь стро́ится мно́го домо́в, шко́л, теа́тров и т. д. Мно́го зда́ний уже́ постро́ены, и стро́ится ещё мно́го но́вых.

Сыновья́ Ковале́вских, Андре́й и Бори́с, бы́ли в Сталингра́де, когда́ вра́г окружи́л го́род. Сталингра́д бы́л окружён со всё́х сторо́н. Тру́дно себе́ предста́вить, ка́к жи́ли лю́ди в го́роде, окружённом врага́ми!

Во вре́мя защи́ты Сталингра́да, ста́рший сы́н Ковале́вских, Андре́й, бы́л уби́т, а мла́дший, Бори́с, бы́л тяжело́ ра́нен. Портре́т уби́того сы́на виси́т над дива́ном в кабине́те отца́.

B. *Translate. Identify the participles in boldface as adjectival or adverbial, active or passive, present or past.*

1. Стару́ха, **снима́ющая** пальто́ в пере́дней—ба́бушка хозя́йки.
2. **Снима́я** пальто́, она́ ве́село разгова́ривала с вну́чкой.
3. **Сня́в** пальто́, она́ пошла́ в гости́ную.
4. **Входя́** в гости́ную, она́ заме́тила своего́ вну́ка, **стоя́щего** о́коло краси́вой молодо́й блонди́нки, **сидя́щей** на дива́не.
5. **Войдя́,** ба́бушка сра́зу подошла́ к ни́м и, не **говоря́** ни сло́ва, се́ла в кре́сло **стоя́вшее** ря́дом с дива́ном.
6. Мы́ осмотре́ли но́вый музе́й, **постро́енный** знамени́тым архите́ктором.
7. Э́тот музе́й бы́л **постро́ен** в про́шлом году́.
8. **Уби́тая** соба́ка лежа́ла на доро́ге. Никто́ не зна́ет, ке́м она́ была́ **уби́та.**
9. Во́т телегра́мма, то́лько что **полу́ченная** мно́й из Баку́.
10. Телегра́мма была́ **полу́чена** в два́ часа́.
11. Лю́ди, **получа́ющие** мно́го пи́сем, не всегда́ на ни́х отвеча́ют.
12. **Отвеча́я,** я́ всегда́ благодарю́ за **полу́ченное** мно́й письмо́.

C. *Translate and form participles with the words in italics:*

1. I know very well your cousin Anna *who lives* in Odessa.
2. *Living* there, I used to meet her and your cousin Paul quite often.
3. *Not speaking* Italian, I couldn't explain to him the mistakes *made* by him in his speech.

[1] Now Волгогра́д.

4. *Knowing* that he would come at half-past five, I placed the *signed* papers on the desk.
5. The director *who signed* them left the room *without saying* a word.
6. I saw a woman *who was smoking* a pipe.
7. *Smoking, crying, and talking,* she walked about the room.
8. Do you know that the man *who lives* downstairs is my cousin?
9. *Having taken* all our money, he went abroad.
10. *Having heard* the terrible news, her grandson and her granddaughter returned all the presents *received* from her.
11. I must finish the article *begun* last week.
12. He is a *forgotten* man.
13. Why does the woman *who is speaking* with your grandson shout so?
14. The house *which is being built* (use **-ся** form of verb) on the corner will obstruct (закро́ет) the view of (to) the river.
15. Tomorrow I will return the money *taken* by my cousin from (at) the bank.
16. The umbrella *found* by me is standing in the corner.

2. Hypothetical mood corresponding to English constructions with "no matter" or suffix "-ever."

The hypothetical mood (past tense with **бы**) with the particle **ни** is used where English adds the suffix "-ever" to pronouns and adjectives.

Кого́ **бы** о́н **ни** проси́л о по́мощи, никто́ не хоте́л ему́ помо́чь.
Whomever he asked (no matter whom he asked) for help, no one wanted to help him.

Где́ **бы** о́н **ни** жи́л, о́н всегда́ бы́л сча́стлив.
Wherever he lived (no matter where he lived), he was always happy.

Где́ **бы** я́ **ни́** был, я́ всегда́ по́мню мои́х друзе́й.
No matter where I am, I always remember my friends.

С ке́м **бы** о́н **ни** говори́л, о́н все́м расска́зывал о своём сы́не.
Whomever he talked to, he talked about his son.

Drill

Переведи́те на англи́йский.

1. Что́ бы она́ ни де́лала, она́ всё де́лает хорошо́.
2. Кому́ бы я́ об э́том ни расска́зывал, мне́ никто́ не ве́рит.
3. О ко́м бы о́н ни говори́л, о́н всех называ́ет дурака́ми.
4. Куда́ бы они́ ни приезжа́ли, они́ везде́ встреча́ли э́того челове́ка.
5. Кого́ бы я́ ни спра́шивал об Ива́не, никто́ ничего́ о нём не зна́ет.
6. Когда́ бы я́ её ни ви́дел, она́ всегда́ куда́-нибудь спеши́т.
7. Что́ бы я́ ни купи́ла сестре́, е́й никогда́ ничего́ не нра́вится.

3. Conjunctions of time in subordinate clauses

The Russian words **до, перед,** and **после** are prepositions. They may be used as conjunctions only by inserting the connective phrase **тó, как,** with **то** in the case governed by the preposition employed. These combinations are usually followed by an infinitive when one subject only is given. When there are two distinct subjects, they introduce a subordinate clause with a conjugated verb in the required tense.

До тогó, как принять решéние, я дóлжен посовéтоваться с отцóм.
Before making a decision, *I* must consult with Father (one subject).

Перед тéм, как уйти, мнé нýжно будет позвонить в контóру.
Before leaving *I* must call the office (one subject).

Я дóлжен с вáми поговорить **до тогó, как** óн придёт.
I must speak to you before *he* comes (will come) (two subjects).

Пóсле тогó, как óн вернýлся из-за границы, мы ни рáзу у негó нé были.
Since *he* has come back from abroad, *we* haven't been to see him once (two subjects).

Verbal nouns are sometimes used in place of such clauses:

Перед своим **отъéздом** óн зашёл к мáтери проститься.
Before his departure (before he left) he went to see his mother to say goodbye.

Пóсле вáшего **прихóда** Андрéй не сказáл ни слóва.
Since your arrival (since you came) Andrew hasn't said a word.

READING

Переведите на английский.

Перед тéм, как начáть говорить, доклáдчик посмотрéл на человéка, **стоявшего** спрáва от негó, потóм спросил о чём-то **стоявшую** слéва от негó и **курившую** дéвушку, и нáчал говорить. Я смотрéл на **говорившего** человéка, слýшал егó и мнé вдрýг стáло так скýчно, что я решил уйти. **Перед тéм, как** уйти, я сказáл **сидéвшему** у выхода господину, что я вернýсь тóлько **пóсле тогó, как говорящий** сейчáс дурáк перестáнет говорить. **Говоря** это, я вы́шел, **не заме́тив,** что о́коло **сиде́вшего** у вы́хода челове́ка сиде́ла жена́ **говори́вшего** и слы́шала, что я́ назва́л её му́жа дурако́м. Пото́м мне́ расска́зывали, что **услы́шав** мои́ слова́, она́ **смея́сь** сказа́ла **стоя́вшей** о́коло неё молодо́й же́нщине, что е́й всё равно́, ка́к я́ называ́ю её му́жа: та́к как, **бу́дучи** его́ ста́рым полити́ческим враго́м и **ви́дя,** како́й успе́х име́ла его́ ре́чь, я́ ничего́ друго́го не мо́г сде́лать, как уйти́, и что **называ́я** её му́жа дурако́м, я́ то́лько дока́зываю, что я́ са́м не осо́бенно умён. Я́ узна́л обо всём э́том из письма́, **полу́ченного** мно́й вчера́ и **напи́санного** одни́м мои́м дру́гом, то́же **бы́вшим** на собра́нии. Э́то письмо́ **бы́ло напи́сано** сра́зу **по́сле то́го, как** собра́ние ко́нчилось. **До того́, как** я́ получи́л э́то письмо́, я́ не зна́л, что́ произошло́ по́сле моего́ ухо́да. «Дру́г», **написа́вший** э́то письмо́, ду́мал, что **чита́я** письмо́, мне́ бу́дет неприя́тно узна́ть обо всём э́том, но́ **прочита́в** о **случи́вшемся,** я́ сейча́с же обо всём забы́л.

Письмо́. Ча́сть втора́я.

II. После́днее свида́ние. Мо́лодость.

Получи́в тво́й а́дрес, я́ неме́дленно се́л за письмо́ да́же не спроси́в себя́, о чём я́ бу́ду писа́ть. Написа́в пе́рвые не́сколько стро́к, я́ почу́вствовал, что мне́ та́к же легко́ тебе́ писа́ть, как когда́-то бы́ло легко́ говори́ть с тобо́й, и я́ реши́л писа́ть всё, что придёт в го́лову.

Стра́шно поду́мать, ско́лько ле́т мы́ с тобо́й не ви́делись! Мы́ ви́делись в после́дний ра́з в 1939 году́: ты́, я́, и ещё не́сколько бы́вших шко́льных това́рищей собрали́сь у Васи́лия Кузнецо́ва. По́мнишь? Э́то бы́ло в Москве́, 3-го ию́ня 1939 го́да. Ви́дишь, я́ да́же то́чно по́мню число́ и ме́сто! Я́ так я́сно всё по́мню, как бу́дто э́то бы́ло вчера́!

А ка́к лети́т вре́мя! С тех по́р прошло́ бо́льше двадцати́ ле́т!

Ви́дя, как бы́стро пролете́ли э́ти 20 ле́т, я́ представля́ю себе́, что сле́дующие 20 пролетя́т та́к же бы́стро, и мы́ с тобо́й ско́ро бу́дем старика́ми . . .

А ка́к мы́ ещё бы́ли мо́лоды в 1939 году́! Мы́ о́ба ещё учи́лись: я́ учи́лся на медици́нском факульте́те, а ты́ поступи́л в педагоги́ческий институ́т. Ты́ с ра́нних ле́т мечта́л ста́ть преподава́телем. Я́ по́мню, что тебя́ гла́вным о́бразом интересова́ло преподава́ние иностра́нных языко́в. Ты́ всегда́ говори́л о то́м, как зна́ние языко́в ва́жно и поле́зно в на́ше вре́мя. Бу́дучи хоро́шим ученико́м, ты́, ещё уча́сь в шко́ле, дава́л уро́ки неме́цкого. Мне́ по́мнится,[2] что в институ́те ты́ гла́вным о́бразом занима́лся англи́йским языко́м. Научи́лся ли ты́ свобо́дно говори́ть на э́том языке́? Тепе́рь э́то

[2] I seem to remember.

было бы так поле́зно! Я́ слы́шал, что е́сть большо́й спро́с на люде́й, зна́ющих англи́йский. Зна́я англи́йский, мо́жно бы́ть не то́лько поле́зным, но́ мо́жно та́кже и хорошо́ зараба́тывать.

Челове́к, да́вший мне́ тво́й а́дрес и живу́щий в то́й же гости́нице, что мы́, тебя́ ли́чно не зна́ет. О́н говори́т, что слы́шал от кого́-то, ка́жется, от како́го-то челове́ка, рабо́тающего где́-то с твои́м ро́дственником, что ты́ служи́л одно́ вре́мя перево́дчиком в Интури́сте.[3] Пра́вда ли э́то? Ещё кто́-то говори́л, что ты́ перевёл с англи́йского како́й-то совреме́нный рома́н, кото́рый бу́дто бы име́л зде́сь огро́мный успе́х.

Но́ э́то всё слу́хи, и я́ о́чень хочу́ поскоре́й услы́шать обо всём от тебя́ самого́.

III. Мечты́

Но́ вернёмся к на́шему после́днему свида́нию.

Собра́вшись в ма́ленькой ко́мнатке[4] у Кузнецо́ва, жи́вшего у каки́х-то свои́х ро́дственников на ве́рхнем этаже́ ста́рого четырёхэта́жного до́ма, си́дя на крова́ти и́ли на полу́, окружённые облака́ми таба́чного ды́ма, мы́ е́ли хле́б с колбасо́й, пи́ли пи́во и говори́ли и говори́ли . . . Смея́сь, спо́ря и куря́, мы́ мечта́ли о бу́дущем и стро́или грандио́зные пла́ны.

У ка́ждого бы́ли свои́ пла́ны, свои́ мечты́.

Мы́ с тобо́й мечта́ли о то́м, что, око́нчив уче́ние и до того́, как нача́ть серьёзно рабо́тать по специа́льности, мы́ вме́сте пое́дем попутеше́ствовать по на́шей огро́мной стране́. Чтобы лу́чше познако́миться с не́й и с жи́знью на́шего наро́да, мы́ собира́лись порабо́тать не́которое вре́мя в колхо́зах и на произво́дстве. Мы́ э́то счита́ли необходи́мым, та́к как, пожи́в и порабо́тав среди́ наро́да и познако́мившись с усло́виями жи́зни, мы́ смо́жем в бу́дущем принести́ стране́ бо́льше по́льзы.

Мы́ та́кже мечта́ли вме́сте посети́ть на́ш родно́й го́род, где́ мы́ о́ба родили́сь, игра́ли, учи́лись, где́ провели́ на́ше счастли́вое де́тство. По́мнишь, как детьми́[5] мы́ люби́ли бе́гать по поля́м и леса́м с сосе́дними ма́льчиками, как мы́ лови́ли пти́ц и игра́ли в войну́? По́мнишь, как мы́ возвраща́лись домо́й голо́дные, гря́зные, но́ счастли́вые? На́ши ма́тери не всегда́ встреча́ли на́с с улы́бкой; вме́сто улы́бки и поцелу́я на́с ча́сто жда́ло наказа́ние. Но́ на сле́дующий де́нь, несмотря́ на наказа́ние—всё опя́ть начина́лось снача́ла.

Да́, э́то бы́ло, мо́жет быть, лу́чшим вре́менем в мое́й жи́зни!

[3] Служи́ть, рабо́тать, etc., take the instrumental in the sense of "to serve as," "to work as." Интури́ст, Intourist, the Soviet travel agency (from иностра́нный тури́ст).

[4] Diminutive of ко́мната.

[5] Детьми́, as children.

IV. Войнá

В дéнь нáшей послéдней встрéчи никтó из нáс не мóг ни предвидеть ни предсказáть, что рóвно через трѝ мéсяца произойдёт мировáя катастрóфа—начнётся войнá со всéми её ýжасами, котóрых никтó тогдá не мóг себé дáже представить. Войнá положила конéц нáшим мечтáм. Онá по-свóему и инáче познакóмила нáс с нарóдом, с жизнью и смéртью; благодаря войнé мы научились переносить страдáния и научились не терять надéжды.

Ты неповéришь, Павлýша, нó гдé бы я ни был, чтó бы со мнóй ни случáлось, я всегдá вспоминáю тебя, нáше дéтство, и глáвным óбразом шкóлу, учителéй и шкóльных товáрищей.

Я вспоминáл об этом дáже на фрóнте, гдé я провёл бóльше трёх лéт, с 1941-го до 1944-го гóда; дáже в сáмые стрáшные дни, когдá нáша рóдина былá в серьёзной опáсности, когдá врáг иногдá окружáл нáс со всéх сторóн и когдá, иногдá, казáлось, что нéт надéжды на спасéние. Дá, стрáшное это было врéмя!

Во врéмя осáды и защиты Сталингрáда, я был серьёзно рáнен и пролежáл в гóспитале до середины 1945-го гóда. Когдá я ещё лежáл в гóспитале, я получил извéстие, что мóй отéц был убит на зáпадном фрóнте, а пóсле тогó, как я вышел из гóспиталя, я узнáл, что мáма умерлá в Ленингрáде во врéмя блокáды.

Во всé гóды войны я не знáл, гдé ты. Не мóг найти тебя и пóсле окончáния войны. Нó тепéрь, когдá я наконéц тебя нашёл, мнé так захотéлось поговорить с тобóй о прóшлом, обо всём, что мнé так дóрого, что я дóлжен был это сдéлать дáже до тогó, как я тебя увижу. Ты ведь единственный человéк, с котóрым я могý об этом поговорить.

Нó мнé давнó порá остановиться. Ответь поскорéе и приезжáй!

Твóй дрýг
Матвéй Желябин.

Читáйте эти вопрóсы и отвечáйте на них.

1. Был ли у Матвéя готóвый плáн в головé, когдá óн сéл за письмó? 2. Почемý óн пишет, что óни óба скóро бýдут старикáми? 3. Когдá Пáвел нáчал преподавáть? 4. Почемý совéтскому граждани́ну полéзно знáть англи́йский язык? 5. Почемý Матвéй почти ничегó не знáет о своём дрýге? 6. Почемý они собирáлись рабóтать в колхóзах и на произвóдстве? 7. Почемý óн так хотéл посмотрéть на свóй роднóй гóрод? 8. Окóнчив занятия, смогли ли они поéхать путешéствовать, как они об этом мечтáли? 9. Когдá началáсь вторáя мировáя войнá? 10. Собрáвшись у Кузнецóва, дýмали ли они, что скóро бýдет войнá? 11. О чём они дýмали?

VOCABULARY

благодаря́ (+ *dat.*) thanks to, because of
бу́дучи (*pres. adv. participle of* **быть**) being
бы́вший (*past adj. participle of* **быть**) former
ве́рхний top, upper
враг enemy
встре́ча meeting, encounter
вы́ход exit, way out
го́спиталь (*masc.*) (army) hospital
двою́родный бра́т cousin (male)
двою́родная сестра́ cousin (female)
де́тство childhood
докла́дч.ик, *fem.* **-ица** lecturer, speaker
дым smoke
еди́нственный the only (one)
***защи́та** defense
зна́ние knowledge
ина́че otherwise, different(ly)
изве́стие (piece of) news, information
ли́чный personal
мечта́ (day)dream, reverie
мо́лодость (*fem.*) youth
наде́жда hope; **наде́жда на** (+ *acc.*) hope for
наказа́ние punishment
необходи́мый essential, indispensable, necessary
о́блако (*gen. pl.* **облако́в**) cloud
оконча́ние termination, ending
опа́сность (*fem.*) danger
***оса́да** siege
по́льза use, profit
поле́зный useful, profitable
посреди́ (+ *gen.*) in the middle of
поцелу́й kiss
произво́дство production
ра́нний early
ро́дина homeland, fatherland
родно́й native, own
ро́дственн.ик, *fem.* **-ица** relative
свида́ние meeting, rendezvous
сле́дующий next, following
слух rumor; hearing
***спасе́ние** salvation
спрос demand; **спро́с на** (+ *acc.*) demand for
***среди́** (+ *gen.*) among, amidst
страда́ние suffering
стра́шный terrible, frightening
улы́б.ка (*gen. pl.* **-ок**) smile
***усло́вие** condition
успе́х success
ухо́д departure (on foot)
***четырёхэта́жный** four-storied
шко́льный school (*adj.*)

Verbs

***висе́ть** (imperf., II: **вишу́, виси́шь**) to hang (*intrans.*)
дока́зывать (imperf., I), **доказа́ть** (perf., I: **докажу́, дока́жешь**) to prove[6]
зараба́тывать (imperf., I), **зарабо́тать** (perf., I) to earn
лови́ть (imperf., II: **ловлю́, ло́вишь**) to catch
мечта́ть (imperf., I) to (day)dream, muse
окружа́ть (imperf., I), **окружи́ть** (perf., II: **окруж.у́, -и́шь**) to surround
переноси́ть (imperf., II: **переношу́, перено́сишь**), **перенести́** (perf., I: like **нести́**) to bear, endure

[6] The imperfective may mean only "try to prove." This weakening of force is common with many imperfectives.

переставáть (imperf., I: **переста.ю́, -ёшь**), **перестáть** (perf., I: **перестáн.у, -ешь**) to stop, cease (+ *inf.*)
подýмать (perf. of **дýмать,** I) to think
***попутешéствовать** (perf., I: **попутешéству.ю, -ешь**) to travel (a little, a while)
***посещáть** (imperf., I), **посети́ть** (perf., II: **посещý, посети́шь**) to visit
***почýвствовать** (perf. of **чýвствовать,** I: **почýвству.ю, -ешь**) to feel
предви́деть (imperf., II: **предви́жу, предви́дишь**) to foresee
предскáзывать (imperf., I), **предсказáть** (perf., I: **предскажý, предскáжешь**) to foretell, predict
представля́ть (imperf., I), **представить** (perf., II: **представ.лю, -ишь**) to present, represent; **п. себé** to imagine, suppose
пролетáть (imperf., I), **пролетéть** (perf., II: **проле.чý, -ти́шь**) to fly (past)
разрушáть (imperf., I), **разрýшить** (perf., II: **разрýш.у, -ишь**) to destroy
рáнить (imperf. and perf., II: **рáн.ю, -ишь**) to wound
собирáться (imperf., I), **собрáться** (perf., I: **собер.ýсь, -ёшься**) come together, assemble; to get ready to, prepare to, be going to (+ *inf.*)
стрóить (imperf., II: **стрó.ю, -ишь**), **пострóить** (perf., II) to build
убивáть (imperf., I), **уби́ть** (perf., I: **убью́, убьёшь**) to kill
уважáть (imperf., I) to respect
целовáть (imperf., I: **целý.ю, -ешь**), **поцеловáть** (perf., I) to kiss

Expressions

со всéх сторóн from all sides
сéсть за письмó to sit down to write a letter
тáк же . . . как (just) as . . . as
как бýдто (бы) as if
бýдто бы seemingly
глáвным óбразом for the most part, chiefly
по специáльности in one's field
несмотря́ на (+ *acc.*) in spite of
по-своéму in its (my, your, his) own way, in one's own way

APPENDIX A

DECLENSIONS

The tables below present the basic declension patterns for nouns, pronouns, pronoun-adjectives, and adjectives. Numerals have in general not been included, since they are summarized in Unit 26; some supplementary numeral forms are given in Appendix E.

1. Nouns

Masculines.

	Sing.		*Pl.*	
	Hard	Soft	Hard	Soft
Nom.	стол	дождь	столы́[4]	дожди́[4]
Gen.	стола́[1]	дождя́[1]	столо́в[5]	дожде́й[5]
Dat.	столу́	дождю́	стола́м	дождя́м
Acc.	стол (an. до́ктора)	дождь (an. го́стя)	столы́ (an. докторо́в)	дожди́ (an. госте́й)
Instr.	столо́м[2]	дождём	стола́ми	дождя́ми
Loc.	столе́[3]	дожде́[3]	стола́х	дождя́х

It will be recalled that many masculines ending in the nominative singular in **о** + consonant or **е** + consonant drop the **о** or **е** in other cases of the singular and plural (except accusative singular inanimate); this is particularly true of nouns ending in **-ок** and **-ец**, e.g., кусо́к, genitive куска́; оте́ц, genitive отца́, etc.

[1] Genitive singular са́хару, шокола́ду, ча́ю, and some others in partitive sense.

[2] Instrumental singular has **-ем** instead of unstressed **-ом** after **ж, ч, ц, ш, щ,** *e.g.*, ме́сяц**ем**, това́рищ**ем**, etc.

[3] Locative singular в саду́, на берегу́, на мосту́, на полу́, в лесу́, в/на углу́, в году́, на краю́, and some others.

[4] Masculine plural has **-и** instead of **-ы** after **г, к, х, ж, ч, ш, щ,** *e.g.*, куски́, ножи́, etc. Many nouns end in **-а́/-я́** (stressed); леса́, дома́, города́, вечера́, берега́, голоса́, цвета́, адреса́, глаза́, поезда́, доктора́, профессора́, учителя́, etc. See Unit 13:4 page 195. Сосе́д, "neighbor," is soft throughout the plural: сосе́ди, сосе́дей, etc. Note also the plural of чёрт, "devil": че́рти, черте́й, etc.

[5] Genitive plural—see Units 16, page 232, and 20, page 315.

Masculine and neuter plurals in -ья. These are formed from a few masculine and neuter hard nouns: друг, муж, сын, стул, лист, перó, брат, дéрево, etc.

	Pl.	*Pl.*
Nom.	друзья́	сту́лья
Gen.	друзе́й	сту́льев
Dat.	друзья́м	сту́льям
Acc.	друзе́й	сту́лья (an. бра́тьев)
Instr.	друзья́ми	сту́льями
Loc.	друзья́х	сту́льях

Like друзья́ are declined мужья́ and сыновья́ (stress on ending and genitive in **-ей́**).

Like сту́лья are declined ли́стья, бра́тья, and дере́вья (stress on stem and genitive in **-ьев**).

Masculines in -анин/-янин. This type of declension is used for a few masculine animates, most of which denote nationality or place of origin (see page 319).

	Sing.	*Pl.*
Nom.	граждани́н	гра́ждане
Gen.	граждани́на	гра́ждан
Dat.	граждани́ну	гра́жданам
Acc.	граждани́на	гра́ждан
Instr.	граждани́ном	гра́жданами
Loc.	граждани́не	гра́жданах

Masculines in -ёнок, plural -я́та. Nouns in this class designate the young of animals.

	Sing.	*Pl.*
Nom.	котёнок (kitten)	котя́та
Gen.	котёнка	котя́т
Dat.	котёнку	котя́там
Acc.	котёнка	котя́т
Instr.	котёнком	котя́тами
Loc.	котёнке	котя́тах

To this group belongs ребёнок, "child." The plural ребя́та serves in colloquial speech in the meaning of "fellows," "kids," "guys" (де́ти "children" is the proper plural of ребёнок).

Plurals of господи́н and хозя́ин. The plurals of господи́н, "master," "sir," "Mr.," and хозя́ин, "host," "landlord," "owner," proprieter," are declined like the above group: nominative plural, господа́, хозя́ева; genitive plural, госпо́д, хозя́ев; dative plural, господа́м, хозя́евам, etc.

Neuters.

	Sing.		*Pl.*	
	Hard	Soft	Hard	Soft
Nom.	ме́сто	по́ле	места́[7]	поля́
Gen.	ме́ста	по́ля	мест[8]	поле́й[9]
Dat.	ме́сту	по́лю	места́м	поля́м
Acc.	ме́сто	по́ле	места́	поля́
Instr.	ме́стом	по́лем	места́ми	поля́ми
Loc.	ме́сте	по́ле[6]	места́х	поля́х

Neuters in -мя. To this class belong вре́мя, "time," и́мя, "first name," and a few other words.

	Sing.	*Pl.*
Nom.	и́мя	имена́
Gen.	и́мени	имён
Dat.	и́мени	имена́м
Acc.	и́мя	имена́
Instr.	и́менем	имена́ми
Loc.	и́мени	имена́х

Feminines.

Feminine I.

	Sing.		*Pl.*	
	Hard	Soft	Hard	Soft
Nom.	ко́мната	неде́ля	ко́мнаты[13]	неде́ли
Gen.	ко́мнаты[10]	неде́ли	ко́мнат[14]	неде́ль[14]
Dat.	ко́мнате	неде́ле[11]	ко́мнатам	неде́лям
Acc.	ко́мнату	неде́лю	ко́мнаты[13] (animate like gen.)	неде́ли
Instr.	ко́мнатой (-ою)[12]	неде́лей (-ею)	ко́мнатам	неде́лям
Loc.	ко́мнате	неде́ле[11]	ко́мнатах	неде́лях

[6] Neuters ending in **-ие** have **-ии** in the locative singular, *e.g.*, зда́н**ии**, собра́н**ии**, etc.

[7] Я́блоко (apple), плечо́ (shoulder), and коле́но (knee) end in **-и** in the plural. У́хо (ear) has the plural у́ши, уше́й, etc. Не́бо (sky, heaven) has the plural небеса́, небе́с, etc.

[8] Genitive plural may add fleeting **о** or **е**, *e.g.*, о́кон, пи́сем. О́блако has облако́в.

[9] Neuters ending in **-ие** have **-ий** in the genitive plural: зда́н**ий**, собра́н**ий**, etc. The genitive plural of пла́тье is пла́тьев.

[10] Genitive singular has **-и** instead of **-ы** after **г**, **к**, **х**, **ж**, **ч**, **ш** and **щ**, *e.g.*, кни́г**и**, да́ч**и**, etc.

[11] Feminines ending in **-ия** have **-ии** in dative and locative singular: Росс**ии**, фотогра́ф**ии**, etc.

[12] Instrumental singular has **-ей** (**-ею**) instead of unstressed **-ой** (**-ою**) after **ж**, **ч**, **ц**, **ш**, **щ**, *e.g.*, да́ч**ей**, у́лиц**ей**, etc.

[13] Nominative plural has **-и** instead of **-ы** after **г**, **к**, **х**, **ж**, **ч**, **ш**, and **щ**, *e.g.*, кни́г**и**, да́ч**и**, etc.

[14] Genitive plural—see Units 16, page 232, and 20, page 315.

Feminine II. These include all feminines ending in **-ь** in the nominative singular.

	Sing.	*Pl.*
Nom.	дверь	двéри
Gen.	двéри	дверéй
Dat.	двéри	дверя́м
Acc.	дверь	двéри
Instr.	двéрью	дверя́ми[15]
Loc.	двéри	дверя́х

Two fem. II nouns ending in **-овь** drop **о** in all cases other than the nominative-accusative and instrumental singular, *e.g.*, любóвь (love), genitive любви́, but instrumental любóвью; цéрковь (church), genitive цéркви, but instrumental цéрковью.

Feminine nouns мать and дочь.

	Sing.	*Pl.*
Nom.	мать	мáтери
Gen.	мáтери	матерéй
Dat.	мáтери	матеря́м
Acc.	мать	матерéй
Instr.	мáтерью	матеря́ми[16]
Loc.	мáтери	матеря́х

2. Pronouns

Personal pronouns.

				3rd pers.		
		1st pers.	*2nd pers.*	*Masc.*	*Neut.*	*Fem.*
Sing.	*Nom.*	я	ты	он	онó	онá
	Gen.	меня́	тебя́	егó	егó	её
	Dat.	мне	тебé	ему́	ему́	ей
	Acc.	меня́	тебя́	егó	егó	её
	Instr.	мной (-óю)	тобóй (-óю)	им	им	ей (éю)
	Loc.	мне	тебé	нём	нём	ней
Pl.	*Nom.*	мы	вы		они́	
	Gen.	нас	вас		их	
	Dat.	нам	вам		им	
	Acc.	нас	вас		их	
	Instr.	нáми	вáми		и́ми	
	Loc.	нас	вас		них	

[15] Instrumental plural of this noun has the alternate form дверьми́. Лóшадь has only лошадьми́. Note also instrumental plural людьми́ from лю́ди (people) and детьми́ from дéти (children).

[16] But дочерьми́ in instrumental plural.

Interrogative pronouns.

	кто? who?	что? what?
Nom.	кто	что
Gen.	кого́	чего́
Dat.	кому́	чему́
Acc.	кого́	что
Instr.	кем	чем
Loc.	ком	чём

3. Pronoun-adjectives

Possessive мой.

	Sing.			*Pl.*
	Masc.	*Neut.*	*Fem.*	
Nom.	мой	моё	моя́	мои́
Gen.	моего́	Like masc.	мое́й	мои́х
Dat.	моему́	Like masc.	мое́й	мои́м
Acc.	мой (an. моего́)	моё	мою́	мои́ (an. мои́х)
Instr.	мои́м	Like masc.	мое́й (-е́ю)	мои́ми
Loc.	моём	Like masc.	мое́й	мои́х

Like **мой** are declined **твой** and **свой.**

Possessive наш.

	Sing.			*Pl.*
	Masc.	*Neut.*	*Fem.*	
Nom.	наш	на́ше	на́ша	на́ши
Gen.	на́шего	Like masc.	на́шей	на́ших
Dat.	на́шему	Like masc.	на́шей	на́шим
Acc.	наш (an. на́шего)	на́ше	на́шу	на́ши (an. на́ших)
Instr.	на́шим	Like masc.	на́шей (-ею)	на́шими
Loc.	на́шем	Like masc.	на́шей	на́ших

Like **наш** is declined **ваш.**

Demonstrative э́тот.

	Sing.			*Pl.*
	Masc.	*Neut.*	*Fem.*	
Nom.	э́тот	э́то	э́та	э́ти
Gen.	э́того	Like masc.	э́той	э́тих
Dat.	э́тому	Like masc.	э́той	э́тим
Acc.	э́тот (an. э́того)	э́то	э́ту	э́ти (an. э́тих)
Instr.	э́тим	Like masc.	э́той (-ою)	э́тими
Loc.	э́том	Like masc.	э́той	э́тих

Like **э́тот** are declined the numeral **оди́н, одно́, одна́,** (stem **одн-**), and the intensive pronoun **сам, само́, сама́.** Besides the feminine singular accusative **саму́** the latter has a partly archaic form **самоё.**

Demonstrative тот.

	Sing.			*Pl.*
	Masc.	*Neut.*	*Fem.*	
Nom.	тот	то	та	те
Gen.	того́	Like masc.	той	тех
Dat.	тому́	Like masc.	той	тем
Acc.	тот (an. того́)	то	ту	те (an. тех)
Instr.	тем	Like masc.	той (то́ю)	те́ми
Loc.	том	Like masc.	той	тех

Весь, "all."

	Sing.			*Pl.*
	Masc.	*Neut.*	*Fem.*	
Nom.	весь	всё	вся	все
Gen.	всего́	Like masc.	всей	всех
Dat.	всему́	Like masc.	всей	всем
Acc.	весь (an. всего́)	всё	всю	все (an. всех)
Instr.	всем	Like masc.	всей (-е́ю)	все́ми
Loc.	всём	Like masc.	всей	всех

Interrogative possessive pronoun чей? whose?

	Sing.			*Pl.*
	Masc.	*Neut.*	*Fem.*	
Nom.	чей	чьё	чья	чьи
Gen.	чьего́	Like masc.	чьей	чьих
Dat.	чьему́	Like masc.	чьей	чьим
Acc.	чей (an. чьего́)	чьё	чью	чьи (an. чьих)
Instr.	чьим	Like masc.	чьей (-е́ю)	чьи́ми
Loc.	чьём	Like masc.	чьей	чьих

Reflexive pronoun себя́, "oneself."

Gen.	себя́
Dat.	себе́
Acc.	себя́
Instr.	собо́й (-о́ю)
Loc.	себе́

Reciprocal pronoun дру́г дру́га, "each other."

Gen.	дру́г дру́га
Dat.	дру́г дру́гу
Acc.	дру́г дру́га
Instr.	дру́г дру́гом
Loc.	дру́г (о) дру́ге[17]

[17] Other prepositions also come between the two words, *e.g.*, дру́г у дру́га; дру́г с дру́гом; etc.

4. Adjectives

Hard adjectives.

	Sing.			*Pl.*
	Masc.	*Neut.*	*Fem.*	
Nom.	но́вый[18]	но́вое	но́вая	но́вые
Gen.	но́вого	Like masc.	но́вой	но́вых
Dat.	но́вому	Like masc.	но́вой	но́вым
Acc.	но́вый (an. но́вого)	но́вое	но́вую	но́вые (an. но́вых)
Instr.	но́вым	Like masc.	но́вой (-ою)	но́выми
Loc.	но́вом	Like masc.	но́вой	но́вых

"Mixed" adjectives with stems ending in г, к, х. Since only и, never ы, can be written after г, к, and х, the masculine singular nominative (and inanimate accusative), the masculine and neuter singular instrumental, and the entire plural deviate in spelling from the hard adjective declension:

	Sing.			*Pl.*
	Masc.	*Neut.*	*Fem.*	
Nom.	ру́сский	ру́сское	ру́сская	ру́сские
Gen.	ру́сского	Like masc.	ру́сской	ру́сских
Dat.	ру́сскому	Like masc.	ру́сской	ру́сским
Acc.	ру́сский (an. ру́сского)	ру́сское	ру́сскую	ру́сские (an. ру́сских)
Instr.	ру́сским	Like masc.	ру́сской (-ою)	ру́сскими
Loc.	ру́сском	Like masc.	ру́сской	ру́сских

"Mixed" adjectives with stems ending in ж, ц, ч, ш, щ. Since only и, never ы, can be written after ж, ч, ш, щ, the same changes apply as for adjectives with stems in г, к, х. In addition, unstressed е, not о, must be written after ж, ч, ш, щ, *and* ц:

	Sing.			*Pl.*
	Masc.	*Neut.*	*Fem.*	
Nom.	све́жий	све́жее	све́жая	све́жие
Gen.	све́жего	Like masc.	све́жей	све́жих
Dat.	све́жему	Like masc.	све́жей	све́жим
Acc.	све́жий (an. све́жего)	све́жее	све́жую	све́жие (an. све́жих)
Instr.	све́жим	Like masc.	све́жей (-ею)	све́жими
Loc.	све́жем	Like masc.	све́жей	све́жих

[18] The ending for masculine singular nominative and accusative inanimate is **-о́й** when the stress is on the ending, *e.g.*, больш**о́й**.

Soft adjectives in -ний.

	Sing.			Pl.
	Masc.	*Neut.*	*Fem.*	
Nom.	си́ний	си́нее	си́няя	си́ние
Gen.	си́него	Like masc.	си́ней	си́них
Dat.	си́нему	Like masc.	си́ней	си́ним
Acc.	си́ний (an. си́него)	си́нее	си́нюю	си́ние (an. си́них)
Instr.	си́ним	Like masc.	си́ней (-ею)	си́ними
Loc.	си́нем	Like masc.	си́ней	си́них

Soft adjectives in -ий, -ье, -ья, -ьи. The ordinal numeral **тре́тий,** "third," follows a special declension, limited to a few adjectives. The pronoun **чей?** "whose?" (see above), also follows this declension.

	Sing.			Pl.
	Masc.	*Neut.*	*Fem.*	
Nom.	тре́тий	тре́тье	тре́тья	тре́тьи
Gen.	тре́тьего	Like masc.	тре́тьей	тре́тьих
Dat.	тре́тьему	Like masc.	тре́тьей	тре́тьим
Acc.	тре́тий (an. тре́тьего)	тре́тье	тре́тью	тре́тьи (an. тре́тьих)
Instr.	тре́тьим	Like masc.	тре́тьей (-ею)	тре́тьими
Loc.	тре́тьем	Like masc.	тре́тьей	тре́тьих

Possessive adjectives in -ин. Some nouns denoting specific persons and ending in **-а/-я** form possessive adjectives in **-ин**, **-ино**, **-ина**. These include nouns designating members of the family such as ма́ма (mama), ба́бушка (grandmother), де́душка (grandfather), тётя (aunt), дя́дя (uncle), etc.; feminine names: Ле́на, О́льга, Зо́я, etc.; and masculine nicknames: Ко́ля, Алёша, etc., *e.g.*, Э́то ма́мин сту́л. Во́т ма́мина шля́па. Где́ Ле́нино перо́? Э́то Алёшины кни́ги.

Declension of ма́мин, "Mama's."

	Sing.			Pl.
	Masc.	*Neut.*	*Fem.*	
Nom.	ма́мин	ма́мино	ма́мина	ма́мины
Gen.	ма́миного	Like masc.	ма́миной	ма́миных
Dat.	ма́миному	Like masc.	ма́миной	ма́миным
Acc.	ма́мин (an. ма́миного)	ма́мино	ма́мину	ма́мины (an. ма́миных)
Instr.	ма́миным	Like masc.	ма́миной (-ою)	ма́миными
Loc.	ма́мином	Like masc.	ма́миной	ма́миных

Declension of surnames in -ин and -ов/-ев. These were originally possessive adjectives similar to those described above. Today they have a mixed declension: some case forms have noun endings; others adjective endings:

	Sing.		*Pl.*
	Masc.	*Fem.*	
Nom.	Петро́в	Петро́ва	Петро́вы
Gen.	Петро́ва	Петро́вой	Петро́вых
Dat.	Петро́ву	Петро́вой	Петро́вым
Acc.	Петро́ва	Петро́ву	Петро́вых
Instr.	Петро́вым	Петро́вой	Петро́выми
Loc.	Петро́ве	Петро́вой	Петро́вых

Declension of surnames. Surnames (as well as first names) which denote males are declined in Russian *unless* they end in **-е**, **-и**, **-о**,[19] **-у** or stressed **-а́**. Other Russian masculine names *are* declined, *e.g.:*

Я́ зна́ю { Па́бло́ Пикассо́. / президе́нта Ке́ннеди. / Алекса́ндра Дюма́. }

Surnames which denote females are declined in Russian *only* when they end in **-ова/-ева, -ина** (see above), or **-а́я** or **-ская** (*i.e.*, as adjectives). No other names denoting women are declined, *e.g.:*

Я́ зна́ю { Джо́на Сми́та, *but* А́нну Сми́т. / Жа́на Море́ля, *but* Жа́нну Море́ль. / Ма́кса Блюменфельда, *but* Ли́зу Блюменфельд. / Никола́я Станке́вича, *but* Мари́ю Станке́вич. }

APPENDIX B

DIMINUTIVES

1. Diminutives of nouns

Russians have a strong tendency to use so-called diminutives either to express the smallness of an object, or to convey a certain emotional attitude (affection, intimacy, sometimes condescension) toward an object or a person. Diminutives are much used in speaking to children and animals, for example. Diminutives are also frequently used for food, thus: вода́—води́чка, во́дка—во́дочка, яйцо́ (egg)—яи́чко, ры́ба—ры́бка, кусо́к—кусо́чек, etc.

[19] But first names and family names ending in **-о** are sometimes declined as feminines, *e.g.*, Я зна́ю Михаи́ла Зо́щенку or Я зна́ю Михаи́ла Зо́щенко.

Diminutives end in **-ок**, **-ёк**, **-ик** for masculine, **-ко** for neuter, **-ка** for feminine. Final **г**, **к**, **х** of the stem become **ж**, **ч**, **ш** respectively:

друг—друж**о́к**
круг—круж**о́к** (circle; club or society)
го́род—город**о́к**
дом—до́м**ик**
ко́мната—ко́мнат**ка**
кварти́ра—кварти́р**ка**
у́лица—у́лич**ка**
стол—сто́л**ик** (especially in restaurants)
кни́га—кни́ж**ка** (this diminutive is as much used as the regular form)
рука́—ру́ч**ка** (also denotes a handle)
нога́—но́ж**ка** (also denotes the leg of a piece of furniture)
спина́—спи́н**ка** (also denotes the back of a chair or sofa)
стару́ха—стару́ш**ка**
стари́к—старич**ёк**
соба́ка—соба́**чка**

So-called diminutives of second degree take a variety of endings of two syllables, including **-очек** or **-ушек** for masculine; **-очка** or **-ушка** for feminine. They convey greater tenderness than diminutives of first degree, and are much used among members of a family group:

ма́ма—ма́мочка
дед—де́душка (this diminutive has become more common than the root word)
дя́дя—дя́дюшка
 etc.

The words ба́бушка, де́вушка, and де́вочка are actually secondary diminutives which have replaced the words from which they are derived.

Some secondary diminutives have a pejorative shade of meaning, *e.g.*, ма́льчик—мальчи́шка, "urchin;" де́вочка—девчёнка, "girlie," etc.

Russian also has augmentatives in **-ище**, **-ища**, denoting large size (or contempt); these are much less used, *e.g.*, дом—доми́ще, "a huge house"; рука́—ручи́ща, "a big strong hand," etc.

2. Diminutives of adjectives

Not only nouns, but also adjectives have diminutive forms. These diminutives have the same functions as have the diminutives of nouns, *i.e.*, to show small size, affection, etc., *e.g.*, ти́хонький, "nice and quiet"; ху́денький, "little and thin," etc.

The suffixes are: **-енький (-онький)** masculine, **-енькое (-онькое)** neuter, **-енькая (-онькая)** feminine.

но́вый—но́венький ми́лый—ми́ленький
си́ний—си́ненький кра́сный—кра́сненький
бе́лый—бе́ленький дешёвый—дешёвенький
глу́пый—глу́пенький у́мный—у́мненький
ста́рый—ста́ренький молодо́й—молоде́нький

From хоро́ший is formed хоро́шенький, "pretty."

Russian adjectives in **-ова́тый/-ева́тый** correspond to English adjectives ending in "-ish."

желтова́тый	yellowish
синева́тый	bluish
краснова́тый	reddish
слабова́тый	rather weak ("weakish")
глупова́тый	rather silly
теплова́тый	lukewarm, tepid

APPENDIX C

INDEX OF PREPOSITIONS

1. Prepositions with genitive

без, безо	without	Мы́ бы́ли в теа́тре **без** А́нн**ы**. Я́ пью ча́й **без** са́хар**а**. О́н сде́лал э́то **без** на́**шей** по́мощ**и**.
близ	near	**Близ** на́**шей** шко́л**ы** большо́й па́рк.
вдоль	along	Мы́ до́лго шли́ **вдо́ль** бе́рег**а** рек**и́**.
вме́сто	instead, in place of	**Вме́сто** письм**а́** о́н присла́л телегра́мму. **Вме́сто** А́нн**ы** пришла́ её сестра́.
вне	outside of	О́н до́лго жи́л **вне** Росси́**и**.
внутри́	inside of	Мы́ не зна́ли, что́ происхо́дит **внутри́** стран**ы́**.
во́зле	near, alongside	Апте́ка **во́зле** на́ш**его** до́м**а**.
вокру́г	around	Кто́-то всю но́чь ходи́л **вокру́г** до́м**а**. **Вокру́г** стол**а́** стоя́ли сту́лья.

впереди́	ahead of	О́н е́хал **впереди́** все́х.
для	for, for the sake of	Я́ э́то сде́лал **для** отца́. Э́то пло́хо **для** страны́. Во́т но́ж **для** хле́ба.
до	before, until, up to, as far as	**До** войны́ они́ жи́ли на Кавка́зе. Я́ бу́ду рабо́тать **до** пяти́. Мы́ дошли́ **до** це́ркви. We got as far as the church.
из	from (place), out of	Во́т письмо́ **из** Москвы́. О́н пьёт **из** буты́лки. Э́тот сто́л сде́лан **из** дорого́го де́рева (wood).
из-за	because of, from behind	Я́ опозда́л **из-за** Ива́на. Соба́ка вы́бежала **из-за** угла́.
кро́ме	besides, except	**Кро́ме** расска́зов, Че́хов писа́л пье́сы. **Кро́ме** О́льги, все́ бы́ли до́ма.
ми́мо	past, by	**Ми́мо на́с** прошёл высо́кий челове́к. Мы́ прое́хали **ми́мо** це́ркви.
о́коло	near, about	Я́ живу́ тепе́рь **о́коло** университе́та. У меня́ бы́ло **о́коло** пяти́ до́лларов.
от	from (a person), from the house of, away from; from . . . to; from (due to)	Во́т письмо́ **от** А́нны. Я́ иду́ **от** до́ктора. Отойди́ **от** окна́! **От** девяти́ до десяти́. Ско́лько киломе́тров от Москвы́ до Ки́ева? О́н дрожа́л **от** стра́ха. (He was trembling from fear.)
по́сле	after	**По́сле** у́жина мы́ бу́дем игра́ть в бри́дж. О́н пришёл **по́сле** слу́жбы.
посреди́	in the middle of	**Посреди́** разгово́ра она́ вдру́г замолча́ла (fell silent). До́м стоя́л **посреди́** па́рка.
про́тив	opposite; against, opposed to	Рестора́н **про́тив** теа́тра. Я́ **про́тив** э́того кандида́та.
ра́ди	for the sake of	Я́ э́то сказа́л **ра́ди ва́с.** О́н всё де́лает **ра́ди** де́нег.

с, со	from, off, down from; since; beginning with	Мы́ идём **с** конце́рта. Сними́ всё **со** стола́. Они́ сошли́ (got down) **с** авто́буса. Мы́ зде́сь **с** пя́того ма́я. **С** понеде́льника я́ бу́ду приходи́ть регуля́рно.
среди́	among, in the midst of	**Среди́** мои́х друзе́й мно́го враче́й. Я́ не заме́тил его́ **среди́** толпы́.
у	"to have;" at the house of; by, near, at	**У** до́ктора но́вый автомоби́ль. Мы́ обе́даем сего́дня **у** ба́бушки. Учи́тель стои́т **у** доски́.

2. Prepositions with dative

благодаря́	thanks to, due to	Жи́знь ста́ла ле́гче **благодаря́** прогре́ссу. Я́ смо́г э́то сде́лать **благодаря́** ва́шей по́мощи. О́н нашёл рабо́ту **благодаря́** зна́нию языко́в.
к, ко	to, toward (motion); to (going to a person), to the house of; by (time)	Я́ иду́ **к** дире́ктору. Автомоби́ль подъе́хал **к** до́му. Я́ ко́нчу рабо́ту **к** концу́ ме́сяца.
навстре́чу	toward, to meet	**Навстре́чу мне́** шла́ стару́ха. О́н вы́шел **навстре́чу** ма́тери.
по	about, along; according to; in the/on (time); distribution ("to each"); by (phone, mail, radio)	Мы́ це́лый де́нь е́здили **по** го́роду. Ко́шки лю́бят ходи́ть **по** кры́ше. **По** гла́вной у́лице ходи́ли то́лпы люде́й. **По**-мо́ему вы́ не пра́вы. Мы́ **по** вечера́м всегда́ до́ма. Я́ посла́л посы́лку **по** по́чте. О́н да́л ка́ждому **по** рублю́.
согла́сно	according to, in accordance with	**Согла́сно** э́тому до́говору . . . Всё бы́ло сде́лано **согла́сно** его́ жела́нию.

3. Prepositions with accusative

в, во	into, to (direction); per, a	Она́ вошла́ **в** ко́мнату. Маши́на въе́хала **во** дво́р. О́н рабо́тает во́семь часо́в **в** де́нь.
за	behind (direction); for (exchange); for (opposite of against)	Соба́ка побежа́ла **за** до́м. Кни́га упа́ла **за** кре́сло. Я́ плачу́ сто́ рубле́й **за** кварти́ру. В спо́ре я́ бы́л **за** О́льгу, а Ива́н бы́л про́тив неё.

на	on; to (direction); for (time); with comparison of quantities	Мы́ идём **на** собра́ние. Кто́ положи́л письмо́ **на** мо́й сто́л? Я́ е́ду в Ло́ндон **на** неде́лю. Э́то перево́д **на** за́втра. Бра́т **на** два́ го́да ста́рше меня́.
по	until (date), up to	Я́ бу́ду та́м с пе́рвого **по** пятна́дцатое. Зде́сь вода́ **по** коле́но (knee).
под	under (direction)	Положи́ де́ньги **под** кни́гу. Каранда́ш упа́л **под** сто́л.
про	about, concerning	О́н мне́ всё рассказа́л **про** сестру́.
с	about (with quantities)	Мы́ жи́ли та́м **с** неде́лю.
сквозь	through	Свéт прохо́дит **сквóзь** занаве́ску (curtain). Вода́ протекла́ (flowed) **сквóзь** потоло́к.
через	across, through; after, in (time); via, by way of	Мы́ живём **через** у́лицу. Они́ прое́хали **через** на́ш го́род. Ива́н вернётся **через** неде́лю. Я́ переда́л ему́ приглаше́ние **через** Ива́на.

4. Prepositions with instrumental

за	behind (static); go for/after; at (during) (with meals)	На́ше село́ **за** рекóй. Гара́ж **за** до́мом. Я́ иду́ **за** молокóм и **за** папиро́сами. Соба́ка бежа́ла **за** на́ми. **За** обе́дом мы́ говори́ли о поли́тике.
ме́жду	between, among	Я́ бу́ду до́ма **ме́жду** тремя́ и пятью́. Я́ сиде́л **ме́жду** Ива́ном и О́льгой. Э́то, коне́чно, **ме́жду на́ми**.
над, надо	above, over; (work) on; (laugh) at	На́ша кварти́ра **над** магази́ном. О́н рабо́тает **над** диссерта́цией. Почему́ ты́ смеёшься **над на́ми**?
перед, передо	before; in front of	О́н пришёл **перед** обе́дом. **Перед** на́шей да́чей—доро́га. **Передо мнóй** тру́дная пробле́ма.
под, подо	under (static)	Кни́га лежи́т **под** столóм. Она́ **под** влия́нием ма́тери.

с, со	with	Я́ бы́л в теа́тре **с** сестро́й. На столе́ стои́т ва́за **с** цвета́ми. О́н е́л **с** больши́м аппети́том. Я́ э́то сде́лаю **с** удово́льствием.

5. Prepositions with locative

в, во	in	Она́ тепе́рь **в** Москве́. Вы́ **во** всём пра́вы.
на	on; at (event); by (vehicles)	Кни́га **на** по́лке. Я́ ви́дел его́ **на** конце́рте. Я́ прие́хал **на** по́езде.
о, об, обо	about, concerning	Мы́ говори́ли **о** но́вой пье́се. Она́ забы́ла **обо** всём.
по	after, upon, on	**По** прие́зде о́н сейча́с же на́м позвони́л. **По** оконча́нии университе́та о́н поступи́л на слу́жбу.
при	at the time of; under (a ruler or government); in the presence of; attached to	**При** царе́ Никола́е Второ́м. О́н э́то сказа́л **при мне́**. **При** на́шем университе́те е́сть библиоте́ка.

APPENDIX D

SUFFIXES

1. Certain types of nouns denoting persons

A. Agent

(1) **-тель,** feminine **-тельница.** This suffix is added to verbal stems to denote persons performing an action or engaged in an occupation.

писа́тель, -ница	writer
учи́тель, -ница	teacher
преподава́тель, -ница	teacher

чита́тель, -ница	reader
строи́тель, -ница	builder

(2) The suffix **-ик**, feminine **-ица** (or **-ник/-ница**, **-чик/-чица**) also serves for nouns of agent or occupation:

лётч.ик, -ица	flier, pilot
носи́льщ.ик, -ица	porter
колхо́зн.ик, -ица	collective farmer
перево́дч.ик, -ица	translator

(3) The suffix **-ик** is also used to designate the practitioners of sciences with words of non-Russian origin. There is no special form for feminine:

исто́рик	historian
хи́мик	chemist
матема́тик	mathematician
фи́зик	physicist

(4) Many foreign words in *-ist* preserve this *-ist* in Russian; feminine in **-ка:**

социали́ст, -ка	socialist
коммуни́ст, -ка	communist
импрессиони́ст	impressionist

(5) Words formed in English with *-logist* lack the element *-ist* in Russian. There is no distinct feminine.

археолог	archaeologist
физио́лог	physiologist
зоо́лог	zoologist
био́лог	biologist

The corresponding science denoted by *-ology* in English has **-оло́гия** in Russian:

зооло́гия	zoology
физиоло́гия	physiology
филоло́гия	philology
биоло́гия	biology

(6) Words formed in English with *-ographer* correspond to Russian words with **-ограф.** There is no distinct feminine.

гео́граф	geographer
фото́граф	photographer
био́граф	biographer

The corresponding subject denoted in English by *-ography* has **-огра́фия** in Russian:

геогра́фия	geography
фотогра́фия	photography; also photograph
биогра́фия	biography

B. Origin.

(1) Patronymics. These end in **-ич** (feminine **-ична**) for fathers' Christian names ending in **-а/-я**; in **-ович/-евич** (feminine **-овна/-евна**) for all other fathers' names:

Никитич	son of Nikita	Никитична	daughter of Nikita
Ива́нович	son of Ivan	Ива́новна	daughter of Ivan
Алексе́евич	son of Alexey	Алексе́евна	daughter of Alexey

The actual pronunciation of those in **-ович/-евич** is usually slurred to [-ɨč̦]/[-ič̦] when the vowel **-о-** or **-е-** is not stressed, *e.g.*, [ivánɨč̦], [a̦lik̦șéič̦] etc. Feminines in **-овна/-евна** are also more or less slurred.

(2) The suffix **-анин/-янин** (feminine **-анка/-янка**) is used principally to denote certain nationalities or inhabitants of certain countries or cities:

англича́нин, англича́нка	Englishman (-woman)
армяни́н, армя́нка	Armenian
датча́нин, датча́нка	Dane
парижа́нин, парижа́нка	Parisian

The masculine plural of these end in **-ане/-яне** (see Unit 20, page 319).

(3) The suffixes **-ец**, feminine **-ка**, and **-ич**, feminine **-ичка**, are also used to denote inhabitants or natives of countries, regions, cities:

америка́нец, америка́нка	American
голла́ндец, голла́ндка	Dutchman
испа́нец, испа́нка	Spaniard
кавка́зец, кавка́зка	Caucasian
москви́ч, -ка	Muscovite

(4) The suffix **-ёнок** (plural **-я́та/-а́та**) is used for the names of young animals (see Appendix A):

котёнок, pl. котя́та	kitten
гусёнок, pl. гуся́та	gosling

2. Abstract nouns

A. Verbal nouns. These end in **-ние** (or **-нье**) for those classes of verbs which have past passive participles in **-нный**; the connecting vowel **-е-** or **-а-/-я-** remains the same, except that the **-ё-** of the participle becomes **-é-**. Intransitive verbs, which lack past passive participles, may nevertheless possess verbal nouns, formed analogously.[1]

понима́ние	(process of) understanding
объясне́ние	explanation
чте́ние	reading
гуля́нье	walking, strolling

[1] The student is warned that not all verbs form verbal nouns, nor can the exact meaning be predicted for those which do form them.

Verbal nouns end in **-тие** (**-тье**) for those groups of verbs which have a past passive participle in **-тый**:

откры́тие	discovery	заня́тие	occupation

Very often these nouns have come to denote not only the generalized process of verbal action, but also a specific case of it, *e.g.*, чте́ние, a given piece of reading; объясне́ние, a given explanation; откры́тие, a given discovery; поня́тие, an idea. Sometimes their meaning becomes entirely concrete, e.g., име́ние, an estate; расписа́ние, a timetable.

B. Other abstract nouns.

(1) The suffix **-ость** (feminine) (occasionally **-есть**) is added to adjectives (sometimes participles) to denote qualities:

ра́дость	joy	но́вость	newness; news
ста́рость	old age	глу́пость	stupidity, foolishness
мо́лодость	youth	све́жесть	freshness
бе́дность	poverty		

(2) The suffix **-ство** is added to nouns to form abstract nouns of quality, state, condition, etc.:

де́тство	childhood
родство́	kinship
знако́мство	acquaintance
о́бщество	society; a company
госуда́рство	state (from госуда́рь, sovereign)

(3) The foreign suffix **-изм** is used in words of foreign origin corresponding to English "-ism;" it is sometimes also used for words of native origin:

социали́зм	socialism	большеви́зм	Bolshevism
коммуни́зм	communism		

(4) The suffix **-ция** corresponds in words of foreign origin to English "-tion:"

на́ция	nation	цивилиза́ция	civilization
револю́ция	revolution	конститу́ция	constitution

(5) Suffixes **-оло́гия**, **-огра́фия**: see Para. 1 above.

3. Diminutives and Augmentatives—see Appendix B.

4. Adjectives

A. The suffix -ный (-но́й) is used to derive adjectives from nouns (mostly inanimate). The final stem consonant may change (see page 342).

ум—у́мный	intelligent
вкус—вку́сный	delicious, tasty
шум—шу́мный	noisy
страх—стра́шный	frightful
труд—тру́дный	difficult
ло́гика—логи́чный	logical

ме́сто—ме́стный	local
век—ве́чный	eternal
сон—со́нный	sleepy

This suffix is also used for some adjectives of foreign origin:

серьёзный	serious
консервати́вный	conservative
норма́льный	normal

This suffix sometimes has the form **-енный**, or **-онный**:

жизнь—жи́зненный	vital
о́бщество—обще́ственный	social
революция—революцио́нный	revolutionary

B. The suffix -ний (soft) is used for adjectives of time and a few adjectives of place; the form -шний is frequent in derivations from adverbs:

зима́—зи́мний	вчера́—вчера́шний
весна́—весе́нний	сего́дня—сего́дняшний
ле́то—ле́тний	за́втра—за́втрашний
о́сень—осе́нний	здесь—зде́шний (local, of here)
у́тро—у́тренний	тепе́рь—тепе́решний (present, of this time)
ве́чер—вече́рний	сосе́д—сосе́дний (neighboring)
по́здний	ра́нний

C. The suffix -ский (-ско́й) is used to derive adjectives from some animate nouns, as well as from inanimates. It is most common with adjectives of place:

жена́—же́нский	women's, feminine
муж—мужско́й	men's, masculine
Аме́рика—америка́нский	American
Нью-Йо́рк—нью-йо́ркский	New York (adj.)
Москва́—моско́вский	of Moscow

D. The suffix -и́ческий is used in many adjectives of foreign origin corresponding to English "-ic" or "-ical."

юмористи́ческий	электри́ческий
драмати́ческий	коммунисти́ческий
траги́ческий	социалисти́ческий
истори́ческий	капиталисти́ческий

E. The suffix **-им-** or **-ем-** is added to verbal stems to form adjectives (identical with the present passive participle: see Unit 27, page 475) comparable to English adjectives ending in "-able," "-ible." They are most common in the negative:

незабыва́емый	unforgettable
необъясни́мый	inexplicable

F. Possessive suffix **-ин**—see Appendix A.

G. Diminutives—see Appendix B.

APPENDIX E

NUMERALS: SUPPLEMENT

1. Collective numerals

Russian has a special set of numerals from two to ten, the so-called collective numerals: двóе, трóе, чéтверо, пя́теро, шéстеро, сéмеро, вóсьмеро, дéвятеро, дéсятеро. The numerals above 5 are relatively little used. They all (including двóе, трóе, and чéтверо) take the genitive plural.

Collectives are used with masculine animates when a group is thought of as a unit:

Трóе солдáт вы́шли и́з лесу.
Двóе нáших сосéдей бы́ли у нáс.
Её чéтверо сыновéй живýт заграни́цей.

Collectives are mandatory or at least preferable in the following cases:
a. With certain masculine animate nouns, including дéти and мужчи́ны.

У ни́х пя́теро детéй.
В контóре слýжат трóе мужчи́н.

b. With nouns which are used only in the plural:

трóе часóв	(часы́—clock, watch)
чéтверо сýток	(сýтки—24 hours)
двóе ворóт	(ворóта—gate)

c. With personal pronouns:

Нáс бы́ло двóе.	There were two of us.
И́х бýдет чéтверо.	There will be four of them.
Мы́ всé трóе бы́ли тáм.	All three of us were there.

d. With adjectives used as nouns, for 2, 3, 4:

Трóе рабóчих рабóтали во дворé.
Three workmen were working in the yard.
Двóе больны́х ждáли врачá.
Two patients were waiting for the doctor.

In oblique cases (except for accusative inanimate) collective numerals are usually replaced by the oblique cases of the cardinal numerals (see Unit 26), *e.g.*, двóе детéй, "two children," but двýх детéй—more common for "of the two children." If the collectives are declined, they take endings of the soft adjectives (двóе, трóе) or hard adjectives (чéтверо . . . дéсятеро). The accent shifts to the ending in declension: двóе, двои́х, двои́м, etc. In oblique cases the noun agrees with the numeral in case, *e.g.*, Мы́ подошли́ к дво**и́м** дéт**ям**.

2. Collective units

A second type of collective numeral is used for collective units (compare English "dozen," "score," "gross"). These are declined as hard or soft nouns; they always govern the genitive plural:

деся́ток	ten (eggs, fruit, etc.)
дю́жина	dozen (handkerchiefs, sheets, etc.)
со́тня	hundred (military unit, money, etc.)

E.g.: деся́ток папиро́с, два́ деся́тка, пя́ть деся́тков яи́ц (eggs), etc.; дю́жина платко́в, две́ дю́жины платко́в, пя́ть дю́жин, etc.; со́тня папиро́с, две́ со́тни, пя́ть со́тен, etc.

3. Adverbial numerals

a. One type describes action performed by a number of people *as a group*:

Они́ пришли́ к на́м втроём.	They came to see us, the three of them together.
В бри́дж игра́ют вчетверо́м.	Bridge is played by four people.
Мы́ бу́дем вдвоём весь ве́чер.	We will be alone (just the two of us) all evening.
Мы́ оста́лись вдвоём.	We were left alone.

b. With comparatives вдво́е, втро́е, вче́тверо, впя́теро, are used, or в два́ ра́за, в пя́ть ра́з, etc.

вдво́е (в два́ ра́за) бо́льше	twice as much
в ше́сть ра́з ме́ньше	six times as small

4. Substantivized numerals

These designate numerals used as nouns; cf. English "a one," "a three," etc., as in cards, or in numeral grades:

едини́ца	a one	шестёрка	a six	семёрка	a seven
дво́йка	a two	четвёрка	a four	восмёрка	an eight
тро́йка[1]	a three	пятёрка	a five	девя́тка	a nine
				деся́тка	a ten

The grading system in Russian schools goes from едини́ца to пятёрка: едини́ца corresponds to an F; пятёрка to an A.

5. Numerals used distributively

The preposition **по** is used with cardinal numerals in a distributive sense (compare English "one each," "three apiece," etc.). With the number **оди́н** (expressed or implied), **по** takes the dative; with other numerals it takes the accusative:

Оте́ц да́л сыновья́м **по** рубл**ю́** (masc. dat.).
The father gave his sons a ruble each.

Ка́ждый из на́с купи́л **по две́** кни́г**и**.
Each of us bought two books (apiece).

[1] Also used for a team of three horses abreast.

RUSSIAN-ENGLISH VOCABULARY

The following vocabulary is complete, except for a few words used in the readings which are similar in form and meaning in both Russian and English, and for certain numerals which are listed in Unit 26. The latter include ordinals above "tenth," as well as compound numerals denoting hundreds.

The number of the unit in which a given word or expression is first used appears in parentheses. This number is italicized when the unit gives important information concerning a word's inflection, usage, or meaning.

Perfective verbs are given following the corresponding imperfective verb with the same meaning. Imperfectives and perfectives are both marked as such.

First conjugation verbs like читáть are indicated simply by the number I, *e.g.*, объясня́ть, I. For other verbs of the first or second conjugations, the first and second persons singular are given after the infinitive, *e.g.*, сказáть (perf., I: скажý, скáжешь), or говори́ть (imperf., II: говор.ю́, -и́шь). Where prefixed perfectives are conjugated like the corresponding imperfectives, the conjugation pattern is given only for the imperfective, *e.g.*, писáть (imperf., I: пишý, пи́шешь), **на-** (perf., I). Imperative and past tense forms are given only when they cannot be derived according to the usual rules.

Forms of adverbs in **-o** are given in parentheses after the corresponding adjectives when their stress is distinct from that of the adjective, *e.g.*, лёгкий (легкó).

а and; but (*4*); **а тó** otherwise, or else
абзáц paragraph (18)
áвгуст August (*23*)
автóбус autobus, bus (17); **на автóбусе** by (on the) bus
автомоби́ль (*m.*) automobile, car (6); **на автомоби́ле** by car (17)
áвтор author (9)
áдрес (*nom. pl.* **-á**) address (7). **Кáк áдрес** (+ *gen.*)? What is the address of . . . ? (7)
аллó! Hello! (on the telephone) (11)
Амéрика America
америкáн.ец (*gen.* **-ца**) (*f.* **-ка,** *gen. pl.* **-ок**) American (*noun*) (*20*)
америкáнский American (*adj.*) (6)
áнгел angel (18)
Áнглия England (12)
англи́йский English (*adj.*) (10)
англичáн.ин (*decl. 20*) (*fem.* **-ка,** *gen. pl.* **-ок**) Englishman (-woman) (*20*)
анекдóт anecdote (16)
аппети́т appetite (11)
апрéль (*m.*) April (*23*)
аптéка drugstore (12)
арти́ст (*f.* **-ка**) (performing) artist, actor (25)
аудитóрия auditorium, lecture room (13)
Áфрика Africa (11)
ах! ah! oh! (3)

бáбуш.ка (*gen. pl.* **-ек**) grandmother (17)
банк bank (11)
бéгать (indeterm. imperf., I), **бежáть**

(determ. imperf.: **бегу́, бежи́шь, . . . бегу́т**), **побежа́ть** (perf.), to run (*24*)
бе́дный poor, unfortunate (13)
без (+ *gen.*) without (*10*)
бе́лый white (6)
бельё linen, laundry (24)
бер-, see **брать**
бе́рег (*loc.* **на берегу́;** *nom. pl.* **-á**) shore, bank (12)
беспоко́иться (imperf., II: **беспоко́.юсь, -ишься**) to worry, be concerned (*24*)
беспоря́д.ок (*gen.* **-ка**) disorder (24)
библиоте́ка library (5)
биле́т ticket (17)
бифште́кс beefsteak (18)
благодари́ть (imperf., II: **благодар.ю́, -и́шь**), **по-** (perf., II) (+ *acc.*) to thank (18) **б. за** (+ *acc.*) to thank for
благода́рный grateful (*23*); **б. за** (+ *acc.*) grateful for (23)
благода́рность (*f.*) gratitude. **Не сто́ит благода́рности.** Don't mention it (18).
бли́же nearer (*25*); **б. к** (+ *dat.*) nearer to (25)
бли́зко near(by) (5); **б. от** (+ *gen.*) near (to) (*prep.*) (25)
блонди́н (*f.* **-ка**, *gen. pl.* **-ок**) blond(e) (8)
блу́з.ка (*gen. pl.* **-ок**) blouse (13)
Бог God (18) **Бо́же мо́й!** My God! Good heavens! (18) **Сла́ва Бо́гу!** Thank God! (18)
бога́тый rich, wealthy (10)
боле́знь (*f.*) sickness, illness (23)
боле́ть (imperf., II: **боли́т, боля́т**) to ache, pain. **У меня́ боли́т голова́.** I have a headache (23).
боле́ть (imperf., I: **боле́.ю, -ешь**) to be ailing, get sick (often) (23), **за-** (perf., I), to be taken ill (*25*)
больни́ца hospital
больно́й sick, ill; a patient (*adj. used as noun*) (*23*)
бо́льше (+ *gen.*) more, bigger (8); **б. не** no more, no longer (10); **б. всего́ (всех)** most of all (23, *25*)
бо́льший bigger, larger, greater (25)
большо́й big, large (6); **большо́е спаси́бо** many thanks (10)
борода́ beard (20)
борщ borsch (soup) (11)
боти́н.ок (*gen.* **-ка;** *gen. pl.* **боти́нок**) shoe (13)
боя́ться (imperf., II: **бо.ю́сь, -и́шься**) (+ *gen.*) to fear, be afraid of (19)
брат (*nom. pl.* **бра́тья;** *gen. pl.* **бра́тьев**) brother (4, *20*)
брать (imperf., I: **бер.у́, -ёшь**), **взять** (perf., I: **возьм.у́, -ёшь**) to take (15), **бра́ть/взя́ть у** (+ *gen.*), take from (*15*)
бри́ться (imperf., I: **бре́.юсь, -ешься**), **по-** (perf., I) to shave (24)
броса́ть (imperf., I), **бро́сить** (perf., II: **бро́.шу, -сишь**) to throw, throw away; to give up, abandon (24)
брю́ки (*pl. only, gen. pl.* **брюк**) trousers (13)
брюне́т (*f.* **-ка**, *gen. pl.* **-ок**) brunet(te) (8)
буди́льник alarm clock (24)
буди́ть (imperf., II: **бужу́, бу́дишь**) (19), **разбуди́ть** (perf., II) (19) to awake (*trans.*)
бу́дто: как бу́дто (бы) as if (27); **бу́дто бы** seemingly (27)
бу́ду I shall be (*see* **быть**)
бу́дучи being (*27*)
бу́дущий future, next (14); **бу́дущее** (*adj. used as noun*) the future (25)
буке́т bouquet (22)
бума́га paper (2)
буты́л.ка (*gen. pl.* **-ок**) bottle (11)
буфе́т buffet (26)
бы particle indicating the hypothetical mood (see 24)
быва́ть (imperf., I) to be, happen, visit (sometimes, often), frequent. **Э́то быва́ет.** That (sort of thing) happens. (20)
бы́вший former (*27*)
бы́стро fast, quickly (8)
быть (imperf.) to be (*5, 14*); **б. в** (+ *loc.*) to wear (6)

в, во (+ *loc.*) in, inside, at (*5*); (+ *acc.*) to, into (*17*); per, a (*17*); (+ *acc. or loc.*) at, in (time) (*26*)
ваго́н railway car (24)
ва́жный important (12)
ва́нна bath (21); **принима́ть/приня́ть ва́нну** to take a bath (21)
ва́нная (*declined as an adj.*) bathroom (10)
ваш your, yours (*4, 12, 20*)

вбега́ть (imperf., I), **вбежа́ть** (perf., I: **вбегу́, вбежи́шь . . . вбегу́т**) to run in (*24*)
вдова́ widow (24)
вдруг suddenly (13)
вед-, see **вести́**
ведь but, why, you know, since, you realize (implies that a fact is well known or obvious) (*18*)
везде́ everywhere (11)
везти́ (determ. imperf., I: **вез.у́, -ёшь**; past **вёз, везло́**, *etc.*), **по-** (perf., I) to carry, take, drive (*22*)
век (*nom. pl.* **-а́**) century (21)
вели́кий great (18)
вера́нда porch, veranda (16)
ве́рить (imperf., II: **ве́р.ю, -ишь), по-** (perf., II) (+ *dat.*) to believe (14)
ве́рно right, true; probably (26)
верну́ть (perf., I: **верн.у́, -ёшь**) to return (*trans.*), give back (*21*); **верну́ться** to return (*intrans.*), go back, come back (*21*)
вероя́тно probably (5)
ве́рхний upper, top (27)
весёлый (**ве́село**) merry, lively, gay, cheerful (16). **Мне́ ве́село.** I'm having a good time (20).
весе́нний spring (*adj.*)
весна́ spring (11); **весно́й** in spring (11)
вести́ (determ. imperf., I: **вед.у́, -ёшь**; past **вёл, вело́**, *etc.*), **по-** (perf., I) to lead, take, conduct, carry on (*22*)
весь all, the whole; (*pl.*) every (*12, 20*); **весь де́нь** all day (7)
ве́т.ер (*gen.* **-ра**) wind; it's windy (11)
ветчина́ ham (17)
ве́чер (*nom. pl.* **-а́**) evening; evening party (7); **в де́вять часо́в ве́чера** at 9:00 p.m.; **ве́чером** in the evening (11)
вечери́н.ка (*gen. pl.* **-ок**) (informal) evening party (8)
вече́рний evening (*adj.*) (15)
вещь (*f.*) thing (13); work (of art, etc.) (14)
взро́слый adult (23)
взять (perf.), *see* **брать**
вид appearance, condition, air, view, aspect; **в. на** (+ *acc.*) view of (24)
ви́деть (imperf., II: **ви́жу, ви́дишь**) (11), **у-** (perf., II) (21) to see
ви́дно apparent(ly), evident(ly) (25)
ви́л.ка (*gen. pl.* **-ок**) fork (16)
вино́ wine (17)
висе́ть (imperf., II: **вишу́, виси́шь**) to hang (*intrans.*) (27)
витри́на shop window (22)
вкус taste (25)
вку́сный delicious, tasty (11)
вме́сте together (5)
вме́сто (+ *gen.*) instead of, in place of (23)
внима́ние attention (13)
внима́тельный attentive (19)
внук grandson (22)
вну́ч.ка (*gen. pl.* **-ек**) granddaughter (22)
во, *see* **в**
во́время on time (24)
во-вторы́х second, in the second place (20)
вода́ water (7)
води́ть (indeterm. imperf., II: **вожу́, во́дишь**), **вести́** (determ. imperf., I: **вед.у́, -ёшь**; past **вёл, вело́,** etc.), **повести́** (perf., I) to lead, take, conduct (*22*)
во́дка vodka (11)
вождь (*m.*) leader (12)
возвраща́ть (imperf., I), **возврати́ть** (perf., II: **возвра.щу́, -ти́шь**) or **верну́ть** (perf., I: **верн.у́, -ёшь**) to return (*trans.*), give back (*21*); **возвраща́ться, возврати́ться** or **верну́ться,** to return (*trans.*), go back, come back (*21*)
во́здух air (12); **на во́здухе** in the (open) air (25)
вози́ть (indeterm. imperf., II: **вожу́, во́зишь**), **везти́** (determ. imperf., I: **вез.у́, -ёшь**; past **вёз, везло́**, *etc.*), **повезти́** (perf., I) to carry, take, drive, transport (*22*)
возмо́жно possible (18, *21*)
возьм-, *see* **взять**
война́ war (10)
войти́ (perf.), *see* **входи́ть**
вокза́л terminal, large station (17); **на вокза́ле** at the station
вокру́г (*adv. or prep.* + *gen.*) around, all around (16)
вон over there (22)
вообще́ in general (20)
во-пе́рвых first, in the first place (20)
вопро́с question (6); **задава́ть/зада́ть в.** to ask a question (*13*)
восемна́дцать eighteen (*16, 26*)

во́семь eight (*16*, *26*)
во́семьдесят eighty (*22*, *26*)
воскресе́нье Sunday (*18*)
воспо́льзоваться (perf.), *see* **по́льзоваться**
восто́к east (22); **на в.** to the east; **на восто́ке** in the east
восто́чный eastern, oriental (22)
восьмо́й eighth (*18*)
вот here is (are); there is (are) (2). **Во́т и всё.** That's all (25).
враг enemy (27)
врач physician (16)
вре́мя (*n.*) time (7, decl. *12*); **во вре́мя** (+ *gen.*) during (12); **ско́лько вре́мени?** how long? (12); **вре́мя го́да** season (13)
всё (*n. sing.*) everything, all (3); **всё, что** everything that (7); **ра́ньше всего́** first of all (25); **о́н всё ду́мает** he keeps thinking; **Мне́ всё равно́.** It's all the same to me (11); **Во́т и всё.** That's all (25).
все (*pl.*) everyone, everybody, all (8)
всегда́ always (5)
всё-же still, all the same (25)
всё-таки still, nevertheless, all the same (19)
вспомина́ть (imperf., I), **вспо́мнить** (perf., II: **вспо́мн.ю, -ишь**) to recollect, recall (26)
встава́ть (imperf., I: **вста.ю́, -ёшь;** imperative **встава́йте**), **встать** (perf., I: **вста́н.у, -ешь**) to get up, stand up, arise (16)
встреча́ть (imperf., I) (19), **встре́тить** (perf., II: **встре́.чу, -тишь**) (24) to meet (*trans.*), encounter; **встреча́ться, встре́титься с** (+ *instr.*) to meet (with) (19)
вто́рник Tuesday (18)
второ́й second (15); **во-вторы́х** second, in the second place (20)
в-тре́тьих third, in the third place (21)
входи́ть (imperf., II: **вхожу́, вхо́дишь**), **войти́** (perf., I: **войд.у́, -ёшь;** past **вошёл, вошло́,** *etc.*) to go in, come in, enter (on foot) (*22*)
вчера́ yesterday (5)
вчера́шний yesterday's (6)
въезжа́ть (imperf., I), **въе́хать** (perf., I: **въе́д.у, -ешь;** imperative **въезжа́й/те**) to go in, drive in (*22*)
вы you (*2*)
выбега́ть (imperf., I), **вы́бежать** (perf., **вы́бегу, вы́бежишь . . . вы́бегут**) to run out (*24*)
выезжа́ть (imperf., I), **вы́ехать** (perf., I: **вы́ед.у, -ешь;** imperative **выезжа́й/те**) to drive out, set out (*22*)
вы́йти (perf.), *see* **выходи́ть**
вылета́ть (imperf., I), **вы́лететь** (perf., II: **вы́ле.чу, -тишь**) to fly out, set out by plane (*24*)
вы́мыть (perf.), *see* **мыть**
выраже́ние expression (13)
высо́кий high, tall (10)
вы́ход exit, way out (27)
выходи́ть (imperf., II: **выхожу́, выхо́дишь**), **вы́йти** (perf., I: **вы́йд.у, -ешь;** past **вы́шел, вы́шло,** *etc.*) to go out, set out, exit, come out (on foot) (*22*)
выходно́й де́нь day off, holiday (24)
вы́ше higher, taller (*25*)

газ gas (24)
газе́та newspaper (4)
га́лстук necktie (24)
гара́ж garage (6)
где where (2)
где́-нибудь, где́-то anywhere, somewhere (*22*)
ге́ний genius (9)
Герма́ния Germany (20)
герои́ня heroine (5)
геро́й hero (5)
гид guide (12)
глава́ chapter; head, chief (14)
гла́вный main, chief (13); **гла́вным о́бразом** for the most part, chiefly (27)
глаго́л verb (13)
глаз (*nom. pl.* **-а́;** *gen. pl.* **глаз**) eye (3)
глу́бже deeper (*25*)
глубо́кий deep (13)
глу́пый foolish, stupid, silly (9)
говори́ть (imperf., II: **говор.ю́, -и́шь**) (8, 14), to speak, talk; tell, say; perfs., *see* **сказа́ть** and **поговори́ть**
год (*loc.* **в году́;** *gen. pl.*, *see 16*) year; **в э́том году́** this year (12)
голова́ head (3)
го́лод hunger, famine (20)
голо́дный hungry (*23*)
го́лос (*nom. pl.* **-а́**) voice (11)
гора́здо much (used with comparatives) (*25*)

гора́ mountain (13)
го́рло throat (23)
го́род (*nom. pl.* **-а́**) city, town (3); **за́ город** to the country (17); **за́ городом** out of town (24)
городско́й city (*adj.*), urban
горя́чий (горячо́) hot (*21*)
го́спиталь (*m.*) (army) hospital (27)
господи́н (*nom. pl.* **господа́;** *gen. pl.* **госпо́д**) Mr., gentleman, master (*11*); (*in plural*) ladies and gentlemen (*20*)
госпожа́ Mrs. (*11*)
гостеприи́мный hospitable (20)
гости́ная (*declined as an adj.*) living-room (10)
гости́ница hotel (7)
гость (*m.*) guest (4); **ходи́ть/идти́/пойти́ в го́сти** to go visiting (17)
гото́вить (imperf., II: **гото́в.лю, -ишь**) (13), **при-** (perf., II) (14) to prepare, cook
гото́в/ый ready (13, *23*)
граждани́н (decl. *20*) (*f.* **гражда́н.ка,** *gen. pl.* **-ок**) citizen (12)
грамма́тика grammar (2)
грани́ца boundary, frontier (13); **(по)е́хать за грани́цу** to go abroad (21); **бы́ть за грани́цей** to be abroad (21)
гро́мкий loud (19)
громкоговори́тель (*m.*) loudspeaker (26)
гру́стный mournful, sad (17)
гря́зный dirty (15)
гуля́ть (imperf., I) (16), **по-** (perf., I) to stroll, take a walk

да yes (2); and; but (emphatic)
дава́ть (imperf., I: **да.ю́, -ёшь;** imperative: **дава́й/те**) (9), **дать** (perf., *see 15*; imperative: **дай/те**), to give; **д. зна́ть** (+ *dat.*) to let know (21); **дава́й(те)** let's (*25*)
давно́ long ago, long since (*7, 9, 11*). **Вы́ давно́ зде́сь?** Have you been here long? (7) **Давно́ пора́** (+ *inf.*). It's high time to . . .
да́же even (5)
да́лее further; **и так да́лее** and so forth (21); **и т. д.** etc. (21)
далеко́ far (away) (5); **д. от** (+ *gen.*) far from
да́льше farther, further (25). **Что́ идёт д.?** What comes next? (19) **идти́/е́хать д.** to go on, continue (one's journey, etc.)
да́ма lady (15)
дать (perf.), *see* **дава́ть**
да́ча summer house, cottage (12); **(по)е́хать на да́чу** to go to the country (for the summer, on weekends, etc.)
два (*m. and n.*), **две** (*f.*) two (*10, 26*)
два́дцать twenty (*16, 26*)
двена́дцать twelve (*16, 26*)
дверь (*f.*) door (7)
двор court, yard (16); **на дворе́** out of doors (24)
двою́родный бра́т (*f.* **двою́родная сестра́**) cousin (27)
де́воч.ка (*gen. pl.* **-ек**) (little) girl (13)
де́вуш.ка (*gen. pl.* **-ек**) girl, young girl (8)
девяно́сто ninety (*21, 26*)
девятна́дцать nineteen (*16, 26*)
девя́тый ninth (*18*)
де́вять nine (*16, 26*)
дед, де́душ.ка (*gen. pl.* **-ек**) grandfather (20)
действи́тельно indeed, in fact, actually (14)
дека́брь (*m.*) December (23)
де́лать (imperf., I) (5, 8), **с-** (perf., I) (14), to do, make. **Что́ на́м д.?** What are we to do? (14)
де́ло matter, affair, business (14); **дела́** (*pl.*) business (14). **В чём д.?** What is it? **Д. в то́м, что . . .** The thing is . . . (14) **Ка́к дела́?** How are you? How are things? **по де́лу** on business (24)
день (*m., gen.* **дня**) day (6) **До́брый д.!** Good day! (greeting) (3); **днём** in the daytime, in the afternoon (11); **весь д.** all day (7); **в два́ часа́ дня́** at 2:00 p.m. (16)
де́ньги (*pl. only, gen.* **де́нег**) money (15)
дере́вня village; country (6)
де́рево (*nom. pl.* **дере́вья;** *gen. pl.* **дере́вьев**) tree, wood (13, *20*)
деревя́нный wooden (16)
держа́ть (imperf., II: **держу́, де́ржишь**) to hold (11); **д. экза́мен** to take an exam (13)
деся́тый tenth (18)
де́сять ten (*16, 26*)
де́ти (*gen. pl.* **дете́й**) children (13)
де́тская (*adj. used as noun*) nursery, children's room (22)

де́тство childhood (27)
дешёвый (дёшево) cheap, inexpensive (7)
джаз jazz (9)
дива́н sofa, couch (11)
дире́ктор (*nom. pl.* **-а́**) director (9)
дли́нный long (12)
для (+ *gen.*) for, for the sake of (*16*)
дн-, *see* **день**
дневно́й afternoon, daytime (*adj.*); daily (26)
днём in the daytime; in the afternoon (11)
до (+ *gen.*) before; until, up to; as far as (*10*); **до свида́ния** good-bye (3)
до́бр/ый kind, good-hearted (21). **Д. де́нь** Good day! (greeting) (3) **Бу́дьте добры́** (+ *imperative*). Be so good as to . . . (17)
дово́льный (+ *instr.*) pleased, satisfied (with) (10, *23*); **дово́льно** rather, fairly, enough (10)
дождь (*m.*) rain (17). **Идёт д.** It's raining. (17); **под дождём** in the rain
дока́зывать (imperf., I), **доказа́ть** (perf., I: **докажу́, дока́жешь**) to prove (27)
докла́д report, speech (12); **чита́ть д.** to give a talk (12)
докла́д.чик (*f.* **-чица**) speaker, lecturer (27)
до́ктор (*nom. pl.* **-а́**) doctor (4)
долг debt; (moral) duty (no pl. in this meaning (25)
до́лгий long
до́лго long, for a long time (11)
до́лжен must, have to, ought to (*8*, *9*); **д. был** had to, was supposed to (8); **д. был бы** should have (24)
до́ллар dollar (15)
дом (*nom. pl.* **-а́**) house, building, home (2); **до́ма** at home (2); **домо́й** (to) home, homewards (*17*); **и́з дому** from home (*17*)
доплыва́ть (imperf., I), **доплы́ть** (perf., I: **доплыв.у́, -ёшь**) (**до** + *gen.*) to sail, swim (to, as far as), reach by swimming (*24*)
доро́га way, road, route (17); **по доро́ге** on the way
дорого́й (до́рого) dear; expensive (7)
дос.ка́ (*gen. pl.* **-ок**) blackboard, board (2)
доста́точно enough, sufficiently (25)
дочь (*f.*) daughter (4, decl. *12*, *20*)
друг (*nom. pl.* **друзья́**; *gen. pl.* **друзе́й**) friend (8, *20*)
друго́й another, a different, other (13); **по-друго́му** otherwise, differently (21)
ду́мать (imperf., I) (5, 8), **по-** (perf., I) (14), to think
дура́к (*f.* **ду́ра**) fool (26)
душ shower (24)
ду́шно stuffy; it's stuffy (17)
дым smoke (27)
дя́дя (*m.*) uncle (*20*)

Евро́па Europe (7)
европе́йский European (7)
ед-, *see* **е́хать; есть**
еда́ food (20)
еди́нственный the only (one) (27)
е́здить (indeterm. imperf., II: **е́зжу, е́здишь**), **е́хать** (determ. imperf., I: **е́д.у, -ешь; imperative** **езжа́й/те**), **пое́хать** (perf., I) to go, ride, drive (*17*)
ел ate (past tense of **есть**) (7)
е́сли if (10, *14*); **е́сли бы** if (*24*)
есть there is (are) (*7*); **то́ есть** that is (17); **У меня́ е́сть . . .** (+ *nom.*) I have . . . (*10*)
есть (imperf., 7, 8, *conj. 20*), **по-** (perf., *20*), **съ-** (perf. trans., *20*) to eat
е́хать (indeterm. imperf., I: **е́д.у, -ешь**), **по-** (perf., I) to go, ride, drive (*17*)
ещё still, yet (6); in addition, more, another (*10*); **кто́ ещё** who else? **что́ ещё** what else? **ещё оди́н** one more (10)

жа́ловаться (imperf., I: **жа́лу.юсь, -ешься**), **по-** (perf., I) (+ *dat.*) to complain to; (**на** + *acc.*) to complain (of) (23)
жаль: Жа́ль, что . . . It's too bad that . . . (6) **Как жа́ль!** What a pity! **Мне́ его́** (acc.) **жа́ль.** I feel sorry for him (18).
жара́ heat (21)
жа́ркий hot (of weather) (7) **Жа́рко.** It's hot. (7)
ждать (imperf., I: **жду, ждёшь**), **подожда́ть** (perf., I) (+ *gen. or acc.*, see *18*) to wait for (*18*)
же particle expressing identity, contrast, emphasis, emotional intensity, etc. **что́ же?** what then, but what? **где́ же?** just where? **то́т же** the same (18); **та́к же . . . как** just as . . . as (27)

жёлтый yellow (15)
жена́ (*nom. pl.* **жёны**) wife (4)
жена́т married (said of men; in plural of a married couple) (*26*); **ж. на** (+ *loc.*) married to
же́нщина woman (4)
жест gesture (11)
живо́т stomach, belly (23)
живо́тное (*adj. used as noun*) animal (23)
жизнь (*f.*) life (11)
жил.е́ц (*gen.* **-ьца́**) (*f.* **-и́ца**) lodger, tenant (21)
жи́тель (*m.*) (*f.* **-ница**) inhabitant (25)
жить (imperf., I: **жив.у́, -ёшь**) to live (9)
журна́л magazine (3)
журнали́ст (*f.* **-ка**, *gen. pl.* **-ок**) reporter, newspaper man (woman) (4)

за (+ *instr.*) behind, beyond, on the other side of; for (after) (*19*); (+ *acc.*) beyond, to the other side of (*27*); (in exchange) for (*16*). **Не́ за что.** Don't mention it. (10) **Что́ э́то за** (+ *nom.*)? What (kind of) . . . ? (22)
заба́вный amusing, entertaining (26)
забыва́ть (imperf., I), **забы́ть** (perf., I: **забу́д.у, -ешь**) to forget (16)
заво́д plant, factory (12)
заводско́й factory (*adj.*) (14)
за́втра tomorrow (10); **До з.** Goodbye until tomorrow. (19)
за́втрак breakfast; lunch (11)
за́втракать (imperf., I) (11), **по-** (perf., I) (17) to have breakfast, lunch
грани́ца abroad (22); **из заграни́цы** from abroad (22)
задава́ть (imperf., I: **зада.ю́, -ёшь;** imperative **задава́й/те**) (13), **зада́ть** (perf.; *conj.* like **дать**) (24): to assign; **з. вопро́с** to ask a question (13); **з. уро́к/и** to assign homework (13)
зада́ние assignment, task (13)
заинтересова́ть(ся) (perf.), *see* **интересова́ть(ся)**
зайти́ (perf.), *see* **заходи́ть**
закрыва́ть (imperf., I) (8), **закры́ть** (perf., I: **закро́.ю, -ешь**) (15) to close, shut
закры́т/ый closed, shut (26)
замеча́тельный wonderful, remarkable (12)
замеча́ть (imperf., I), **заме́тить** (perf., II: **заме́.чу, -тишь**) to notice, observe (22)
за́мужем married (of women only) (26); **з. за** (+ *instr.*) married to (26)
занима́ть (imperf., I), **заня́ть** (perf., I: **займ.у́, -ёшь;** past **за́нял,** etc.) to occupy (22); **занима́ться, заня́ться** to be occupied with, study (imperf. only) (+ *instr.*) (19, 23)
заня́тие occupation (21); **заня́тия** (*pl.*) studies, classes, occupations (21)
занято́й busy, occupied (22, *23*)
за́пад west (22); **на з.** to the west; **на за́паде** in the west
за́падный western (22)
запи́с.ка (*gen. pl.* **-ок**) note, jotting
запи́сывать (imperf., I) (13), **записа́ть** (perf., I: **запишу́, запи́шешь**) (15) to write down, note down
заплати́ть (perf.), *see* **плати́ть**
запомина́ть (imperf., I), **запо́мнить** (perf., II: **запо́мн.ю, -ишь**) to memorize, learn (by heart) (18)
зараба́тывать (imperf., I), **зарабо́тать** (perf., I) to earn (27)
зара́нее in advance, ahead (23)
засыпа́ть (imperf., I), **засну́ть** (perf., I) **засн.у́, -ёшь**) to fall asleep (19)
зато́ on the other hand, however (25)
заходи́ть (imperf., II: **захожу́, захо́дишь**), **зайти́** (perf., I: **зайд.у́, -ёшь;** past **зашёл, зашло́,** etc.) to call on, stop in, drop in (to see) (**к** + *dat.*) (*22*); to stop for (**за** + *instr.*) (*22*)
захоте́ть (perf.), *see* **хоте́ть**
заче́м why, what for (10)
защи́та defense (27)
звать (imperf., I: **зов.у́, -ёшь**) **на-** (perf., I), to name, call (+ *nom. or instr.*); **Ка́к его́ зову́т?** What is his name? (26) **Его́ зову́т Па́вел (Па́влом).** His name is Pavel (26).
звони́ть (imperf., II: **звон.ю́, -и́шь**), **по-** (perf., II) (14) to ring, telephone (+ *dat.*) (9)
звон.о́к (*gen.* **-ка́**) bell, ring (3)
зда́ние building (12)
здесь here (4)
здоро́в/ый healthy, well (*23*)
здоро́вье health (21); **Ка́к ва́ше здоро́вье?**

How is your health? (21) **(вы́)пить за з.** (+ *gen.*) to drink someone's health (26)

здра́вствуй(те)! hello! (4)

зелёный green (12)

земля́ (*gen. pl.* **земе́ль**) land, earth (23)

зима́ winter (6); **зимо́й** in winter (11)

зи́мний winter (*adj.*) (6)

злой evil, wicked, vicious, ill-tempered (21)

знак sign (19)

знако́мить (imperf., II: **знако́м.лю, -ишь**), **по-** (perf., II) to acquaint, introduce (*acc. and* **с** + *instr.*) (20); **знако́миться, по-** to be introduced, meet, make the acquaintance of (**с** + *instr.*) (20)

знако́м/ый familiar; an acquaintance (*adj. used as noun*) (20, *23*); **знако́м, -а, -ы с** (+ *instr.*) acquainted with (20, *23*). **Мы́ знако́мы.** We are acquainted. (20)

знамени́тость (*f.*) celebrity (25)

знамени́тый famous (13)

зна́ние knowledge (27)

знать (imperf., I) to know (5)

зна́чит (*as adv.*) so, then, hence (26). **Что́ зна́чит ...?** What does ... mean? (18)

зов-, *see* **звать**

золото́й gold, golden (26)

зонт, зо́нтик umbrella (24)

зуб tooth (24)

и and (2); also, too, as well (7); even (7); **и ... и** both ... and (4)

игра́ть (imperf., I) (6, 8), **сыгра́ть** (perf. trans., I) (14) to play; **и. на роя́ле** to play the piano (6); **и. в ша́хматы** to play chess (20); **и. в ка́рты** to play cards (14)

игру́ш.ка (*gen. pl.* **-ек**) toy (22)

идти́ (determ. imperf., I: **ид.у́, -ёшь;** past **шёл, шло,** etc.), **пойти́** (perf., I: **пойд.у́, -ёшь;** past **пошёл, пошло́,** etc.) to go, walk (*17*). **Идём (пойдём)!** Let's go (*23*). **Идёт до́ждь.** It's raining (17). **Фи́льм/пье́са идёт.** The picture/the play is running (playing) (17).

из (+ *gen.*) out of, from (15, *17*)

изве́стие (piece of) news, information (27)

изве́стный well-known (16)

извиня́ть (imperf., I), **извини́ть** (perf., II: **извин.ю́, -и́шь**) to excuse (18)

издалека́, и́здали from afar (21, 25)

изменя́ться (imperf., I), **измени́ться** (perf., II: **изменю́сь, изме́нишься**) to change (*intrans.*), be altered (21)

изуча́ть (imperf., I-), **изучи́ть** (perf., II: **изучу́, изу́чишь**) (+ *acc.*) to study, learn (12, *23*)

и́ли or (2); **и́ли ... и́ли** either ... or (5)

и́мя (*n.*) (first, Christian) name (7, decl. *12*); **Ка́к ва́ше и́мя?** What is your (first) name? (7)

ина́че otherwise, differently (27)

инжене́р engineer (9)

иногда́ sometimes (8)

иностра́н.ец (*gen.* **-ца**) (*f.* **-ка,** *gen. pl.* **-ок**) foreigner (20)

иностра́нный foreign (20)

инстру́ктор (*nom. pl.* **-а́**) (*f.* **-ша**) (practical) instructor (23)

интере́с interest (11); **и. к** (+ *dat.*) interest in

интере́сный interesting (5, 6)

интересова́ть (imperf., I: **интересу́.ю, -ешь**), **за-** (perf., I) to interest (+ *acc. of person, instr. of object of interest*) (21); **интересова́ться, за-** to be interested in (+ *instr.*) (21)

иска́ть (imperf., I: **ищу́, и́щешь**) to look for, seek (24)

испа́н.ец (*gen.* **-ца**) (*f.* **-ка,** *gen. pl.* **-ок**) Spaniard (20)

испа́нский Spanish (*adj.*) (20)

исто́рик historian (11)

исто́рия history; story, event (9)

Ита́лия Italy (12)

италья́н.ец (*gen.* **-ца**) (*f.* **-ка,** *gen. pl.* **-ок**) Italian (20)

италья́нский Italian (*adj.*) (20)

ию́ль (*m.*) July (*23*)

ию́нь (*m.*) June (*23*)

к, ко (+ *dat.*) to, toward; to the house of (*17, 22*)

кабине́т study (5)

Кавка́з Caucasus (3); **на Кавка́зе** in the Caucasus (12)

ка́ждый each, every (8)

каза́ться (imperf., I: **кажу́сь, ка́жешься**), **по-** (perf., I) to seem (+ *instr.*) (19)

как how, like, as (3); what do you mean?

(surprise); **как то́лько** as soon as (14); **та́к как** since, because, as (14); **как и** as well as, along with

ка́к-нибудь, ка́к-то anyhow, somehow (*22*)

како́й what (a); which; what kind of; how (6); **к. большо́й** how large, what a large (6); **к.-нибудь, к.-то** any, some, sort of (*22*)

кани́кулы (*pl. only, gen.* **кани́кул**) (school) vacation (23)

каранда́ш pencil (3)

ка́рта map; card (3); **игра́ть в ка́рты** to play cards (14)

карти́на picture; motion picture (5)

карто́фель (*m., no pl.*) potato(es) (11)

кварти́ра apartment (5)

киломе́тр kilometer (25)

кино́ (*n. indecl.*) movie house, cinema (*12*)

Кита́й China (11)

кита́йский Chinese (*adj.*)

класс class, classroom (2)

класть (imperf., I: **клад.у́, -ёшь;** past **клал,** etc.), **положи́ть** (perf., II: **положу́, поло́жишь**) to put, place, lay down (*24*)

кли́мат climate (12)

клуб club (12)

кни́га book (2)

кни́жный book (*adj.*) (10); **к. магази́н** bookstore (10); **кни́жная по́лка** bookshelf, bookcase (10)

ко, *see* **к**

ков.ёр (*gen.* **-ра́**) rug, carpet (10)

когда́ when (4, *14*); **к.-либо** ever, at all (25); **к.-нибудь, к.-то** at one time, at some time, one day (*22*)

колбаса́ sausage (17)

колхо́з collective farm (17)

колхо́зн.ик (*f.* **-ица**) collective farmer

колхо́зный collective farm (*adj.*)

кома́нда team (22)

ко́мната room (4)

кон.е́ц (*gen.* **-ца́**) end, finish (7); **в конце́** at the end (7); **в конце́ концо́в** in the end, in the last analysis

коне́чно of course, certainly (5)

househ конто́ра office (9)

конфе́та a piece of candy (20); **конфе́ты** (*pl.*) candy (20)

конце́рт concert (5); **на конце́рте** at a concert (5)

конча́ть (imperf., I) (8), **ко́нчить** (perf., II: **ко́нч.у, -ишь**) (15) to finish, end

копе́йка (*gen. pl.* **копе́ек**) copeck (1/100 of a ruble) (26)

коридо́р corridor, hall (16)

коро́ва cow (23)

короле́ва queen (18)

коро́ль (*m.*) king (18)

коро́ткий (**ко́ротко**) short, brief (12)

костю́м suit (6)

кото́рый (*rel. pron.*) who, which, that (*6*); (*interrog. pron.*) which (one)? (*6*) **К. ча́с?** What time is it? (16) **В кото́ром часу́?** At what time? (16)

ко́фе (*m. indecl.*) coffee (11)

кофе́йник coffee-pot (24)

ко́ш.ка (*gen. pl.* **-ек**) cat (16)

краси́вый beautiful, handsome, pretty (6)

кра́сный red (9)

красота́ beauty (26)

кре́сло armchair (6)

крестья́н.ин (decl. *20*) (*f.* **-ка,** *gen. pl.* **-ок**) peasant (*20*)

крик cry, shout (21)

крича́ть (imperf., II: **крич.у́, -и́шь**), **кри́кнуть** (perf., I: **кри́кн.у, -ешь**) to cry out, shout (21)

крова́ть (*f.*) bed (10)

кро́ме (+ *gen.*) except, besides (*prep.*) (10); **к. того́** besides (*adv.*) (23)

Крым (*loc.* **в Крыму́**) Crimea (12)

кры́ша roof (7)

кста́ти by the way; apropos (21)

кто who (3)

кто́-нибудь, кто́-то anybody, somebody (*22*)

куда́ where, whither (*17*)

куда́-нибудь, куда́-то somewhere (*22*)

культу́ра culture (20)

культу́рный cultured, cultural (20)

купи́ть (perf.), *see* **покупа́ть**

кури́ть (imperf., II: **курю́, ку́ришь**) to smoke (11)

кус.о́к (*gen.* **-ка́**) piece, bit (7)

ку́хня kitchen (4)

ла́в.ка (*gen. pl.* **-ок**) shop, small store (25)

ла́дно all right, O.K. (*colloq.*) (21)
ла́мпа lamp, electric light (2)
ле́вый left (11)
лёгкий (**легко́**) easy, light (6)
лежа́ть (imperf., II: **леж.у́, -и́шь**) to lie, be lying (11)
ле́кция lecture (12); **чита́ть ле́кцию** to give a lecture (12)
лени́вый lazy (10)
лень: Мне́ бы́ло л. (+ *inf.*) I didn't feel like . . . ; I felt too lazy to . . . (18)
лес (*loc.* **в лесу́**; *nom. pl.* **леса́**) woods, forest (12)
лета́ть (indeterm. imperf., I), **лете́ть** (determ. imperf., II: **лечу́, лети́шь**), **полете́ть** (perf., II) to fly (*24*)
ле́тний summer (*adj.*) (6)
ле́то summer (6); **ле́том** in summer (11); **пя́ть ле́т** five years (*16*)
лечь (perf.), *see* **ложи́ться**
ли, interrogative particle used in "yes-or-no" questions (*22*)
лимо́н lemon (11)
лист (*nom. pl.* **листы́**; *gen. pl.* **листо́в**) sheet (13); (*nom. pl.* **ли́стья**; *gen. pl.* **ли́стьев**, etc.) leaf (13, *20*)
литерату́ра literature (20)
литерату́рный literary (20)
лифт elevator (21)
лицо́ face; person (3)
ли́чный personal (27)
лови́ть (imperf., II: **ловлю́, ло́вишь**), **пойма́ть** (perf., I) to catch (27)
ложи́ться (imperf., II: **лож.у́сь, -и́шься**; imperative **ложи́.сь/тесь**), **лечь** (perf., I: **ля́гу, ля́жешь . . . ля́гут**; imperative **ля́г/те**; past **лёг, легло́**, etc.) to lie down, go to bed (*21*); **л. спа́ть** to go to bed (21)
ло́ж.ка (*gen. pl.* **-ек**) spoon (16)
ло́шадь (*f.*, *instr. pl.* **лошадьми́**) horse (16)
луна́ moon (21)
лу́чше better (23, *25*). **Мне́ л.** I am (feel) better (23); **л. всего́** (**всех**) best of all (*25*)
лу́чший better, best (*25*); **Всего́ лу́чшего!** All the best!
любе́зный kind, gracious (17, *23*). **Бу́дьте любе́зны** (+ *imperative*). Be so kind as to . . . (17)
люби́мый favorite, beloved (12, *27*)
люби́ть (imperf., II: **люблю́, лю́бишь**) to love, like (11, *19*)
любо́вь (*f.*, *gen.* **любви́**; *instr.* **любо́вью**) love (12)
любо́й any (whatsoever), any you like (21)
лю́ди (*pl.*, *gen. pl.* **люде́й**) people (*13*)

мавзоле́й mausoleum (18)
магази́н store, shop (9)
май May (23)
ма́ленький little, small (6)
ма́ло (+ *gen.*) little, few (*5*)
ма́льчик boy (13)
ма́ма mama (5)
ма́р.ка (*gen. pl.*, **-ок**) stamp (17)
март March (23)
ма́сло butter; oil (17)
ма́сса mass; great quantity of (*colloq.*) (17)
матч match, game (22)
мать mother (4, decl. *12*, *20*)
маши́на machine; car, auto (12)
машини́ст (*f.* **-ка**, *gen. pl.* **-ок**) machinist; typist (14)
ме́бель (*f. collect.*) furniture (10)
ме́дленно slowly (8)
ме́жду (+ *instr.*) between, among (19)
Ме́ксика Mexico (18)
мел chalk (11)
ме́ньше (+ *gen.*) less, fewer (*8*)
ме́ньший smaller (*25*)
ме́сто place, seat (11); **на м.** to its proper place (24); **на ме́сте** in its place; on the spot (24)
ме́сяц month; moon (8); **в э́том ме́сяце** this month (23)
метро́ (*n. indecl.*) subway (12); **на метро́** by subway
мечта́ (day)dream, reverie, fancy (27)
мечта́ть (imperf., I) to daydream, dream, muse
миллио́н million (*26*)
ми́лый nice, likeable, dear (9)
ми́мо (+ *gen.*) past, by (*22*)
мину́та minute (18)
мир world; peace (10)
мирово́й world (*adj.*) (18)
мла́дший younger, youngest (9, *25*)

мне́ние opinion; **по мне́нию** (+ *gen.*) in the opinion of . . . (23)
мно́го (+ *gen.*) much, many (5, *7*, *20*)
мно́гое (*declined as a neut. adj.*) much, many things (*23*)
мог-, мож-, *see* **мочь**
мо́да fashion, style (13)
мо́жет быть maybe, perhaps (10)
мо́жно it is possible to; one can (may) (*21*). **Мо́жно (мне́)?** May I? (*21*)
мой my, mine (*4*, *12*, *20*)
мо́крый wet (24)
молоде́ц! (*used both for men and women*) Good for you (him, her)! (23)
молодо́й young (6)
мо́лодость (*f.*) youth (27)
молоко́ milk (7)
моло́чный milk (*adj.*)
мо́ре sea (12)
Москва́ Moscow (3)
моско́вский (of) Moscow (12)
мост (*loc.* **на мосту́**) bridge (12)
мочь (imperf., I; **могу́, мо́жешь . . . мо́гут;** past **мог, могло́,** etc.) (*10*) **с-** (perf., I) (*21*) to be able (+ *inf.*); **я́ могу** I can (*10*); **я́ смогу́** I shall be able, shall manage (*21*); **мо́жет быть** maybe, perhaps (10). **Я́ не могу́ не** (+ *inf.*) I can't help . . . (11)
мо́ю(сь), *see* **мы́ть(ся)**
муж (*nom. pl.* **мужья́,** *gen. pl.* **муже́й**) husband (4, *20*)
мужчи́на (*m.*) man (male) (*20*)
музе́й museum (2)
му́зыка music (9)
музыка́нт musician (7)
мы we (3)
мысль (*f.*) thought, idea (25)
мыть (imperf., I: **мо́.ю, -ешь**), **по-** or **вы́-** (perf., I) to wash (*trans.*) (19), **мы́ться, по-** or **вы́-** to wash (oneself) (19)
мя́гкий soft (19)
мясни́к butcher (19)
мя́со meat (6)

на (+ *loc.*) on, at (5); (+ *acc.*) onto, to (16); (+ *acc.*) for (time) (18); by (with vehicles) (*17*)
наве́рно(е) likely, probably, for sure (18)
над, надо (+ *instr.*) above, over (19)
надева́ть (imperf., I), **наде́ть** (perf., I: **наде́н.у, -ешь**) to put on (24)
наде́жда hope; **н. на** (+ *acc.*) hope for, reliance in (27)
наде́яться (imperf., I: **наде́.юсь, -ешься**) to hope (19); **н. на** (+ *acc.*) to hope for, rely on
на́до (+ *inf.*) it is necessary to . . . , one must (has to) . . . (*10*); **Мне́ на́до** (+ *inf.*). I must (have to, need to) . . . (*10*).
надо, *see* **над**
надо́лго for a long time (22)
наза́д back; **(тому́) н.** ago (16)
назва́ние name, title (7); **Ка́к назва́ние** (+ *gen.*)? What is the name of (an object)? (7)
называ́ть (imperf., I), **назва́ть** (perf., I: **назов.у́, -ёшь**) to name, call (18)
найти́ (perf.), *see* **находи́ть**
наказа́ние punishment (27)
наконе́ц finally, at last (14)
нале́во on (to) the left (12)
населе́ние population (25)
написа́ть (perf.), *see* **писа́ть**
напра́во on (to) the right (12)
наприме́р for example (8)
наро́д nation, people (20)
наро́дный national, folk (21)
настоя́щий real, present (9)
находи́ть (imperf., II: **нахожу́, нахо́дишь**), **найти́** (perf., I: **найд.у́, -ёшь;** past **нашёл, нашло́,** etc.) to find; **находи́ться** to be located (22)
нача́ло beginning (7); **в нача́ле** (+ *gen.*) at the beginning of . . . (7)
нача́льник superior, chief, boss (9)
начина́ть (imperf., I) (8), **нача́ть** (perf., I: **начн.у́, -ёшь**) (15) to begin, start (+ *inf.*)
наш our, ours (*4*, *12*, *20*)
не not (*2*); **Не́ за что.** Don't mention it. (10)
не́бо (*pl.* **небеса́**) sky, heaven (16)
невозмо́жно impossible (18, 20)
неда́вно recently, not long ago (7)
недалеко́ not far (away) (6); **н. от** (+ *gen.*) not far from
неде́ля week (8)
недово́лен dissatisfied (10); **н.** (+ *instr.*) dissatisfied with . . .
недоста́точно insufficiently (19)

не́которые (*pl. adj.*) some, certain (ones) (*19*)
нельзя́ (+ *inf.*) it is impossible (forbidden); one can (may) (must) not (*21*); **н. не** (+ *inf.*) one can't help but . . .
неме́дленно immediately (20)
не́м.ец (*gen.* **-ца**) (*f.* **-ка,** *gen. pl.* **-ок**) German (20)
неме́цкий German (*adj.*) (20)
немно́го, немно́жко (+ *gen.*) a little
ненави́деть (imperf., II: **ненави́.жу, -дишь**) to hate (14)
необходи́мый essential, indispensable, necessary (27)
непло́хо not bad(ly) (11)
непра́в wrong (in predicate only) (14)
непра́вда untruth; (it is) not true (5)
непра́вильно incorrect(ly) (19)
неприя́тный unpleasant (8)
не́сколько (+ *gen. pl.*) several, a few, some, a number of (16, 20)
несмотря́ на (+ *acc.*) in spite of (27)
несча́стный unhappy, unfortunate (13)
нет no (2); (+ *gen.*) there is (are) no; (at end of sentence) not (7); **не́ту** (+ *gen.*) (*colloq.*) there is (are) no (7)
нетерпе́ние impatience (18); **с нетерпе́нием** impatiently
-нибудь, *see 22*
нигде́ nowhere (*8*)
ни́зкий low (10)
никако́й no, none (at all) (21)
никогда́ never (*8*)
никто́ no one (*8, 10*)
ничего́ nothing (*8, 10*); never mind; it doesn't matter; it's not so bad; so-so (19)
но but (5)
но́вый new (6); **Что́ (у ва́с) но́вого?** What's new (with you)?
но́вость (*f.*) news, a piece of news (14); **но́вости** (*pl.*) the news (14)
нога́ foot, leg (10)
нож knife (16)
но́мер (*nom. pl.* **-а́**) number; hotel room (12)
норма́льный normal (6)
нос (*loc.* **на носу́**) nose (3)
нос.о́к (*gen.* **-ка́**) sock (24)
ночно́й night (*adj.*)
ночь (*f.*) night (6); **но́чью** at night (11); **в два́ часа́ но́чи** at 2:00 A.M. (16); **Споко́йной но́чи!** Good night! (21)
ноя́брь (*m.*) November (23)
нра́виться (imperf., II: **нра́в.люсь, -ишься**), **по-** (perf., II) to please, like (*see 19*); **Мне́ нра́вится** (+ *nom.*) I like . . . (*19*).
ну well (interjection expressing mild surprise, impatience or encouragement) (5)
ну́жен necessary, needed (*10*); **Мне́ нужна́ кни́га.** I need a book (*10*). **Ну́жно** (+ *inf.*). It is necessary to; one must (has to, needs to) . . . (9). **Мне́ ну́жно** (+ *inf.*). I must (have to . . .) (*9*).

о, об, обо (+ *loc.*) about, concerning (*5*, 12)
обе́д dinner (10); **к обе́ду** to (for) dinner (18)
обе́дать (imperf., I); **по-** (perf., I) to dine, have dinner (11)
обеща́ть (imperf., I) (21) to promise (+ *dat. of person*)
о́блако (*gen. pl.* **облако́в**) cloud (27)
обо, *see* **о**
обожа́ть (imperf., I) (23) to adore, worship
о́браз image, picture; way, form; **гла́вным о́бразом** for the most part, chiefly (27)
обра́тно back, in return (17)
о́бщество (*gen. pl.* **о́бществ**) society; company (20)
о́бщий common, mutual, general (20)
объясне́ние explanation (13)
объясня́ть (imperf., I) (8), **объясни́ть** (perf., II: **объясн.ю́, -и́шь**) (15) to explain
обыкнове́нный ordinary, usual (12, 13)
обы́чно usually (9)
о́вощи (*pl., gen. pl.* **овоще́й**) vegetables (19)
огро́мный huge, enormous, immense (12)
ода́лживать (imperf., I), **одолжи́ть** (perf., II: **одолж.у́, -и́шь**) to lend (22)
одева́ть (imperf., I), **оде́ть** (perf., I: **оде́н.у, -ешь**) to dress (*trans.*) (19); **одева́ться, оде́ться** to dress (*intrans.*) (19)
оде́жда clothing (24)
оди́н one (*6, 12*); only, alone (*8, 12*); a certain; **одни́** only, alone; some, certain (*8, 12*); **ни оди́н** not a single (20); **одни́ . . . други́е** some . . . others (13); **оди́н его́ дру́г** a friend of his (*15*); **оди́н из его́ друзе́й** one of his friends (*20*)
одина́ково equally (19)

оди́ннадцать eleven (*16, 26*)
одино́кий lonely (18)
одна́жды once, at one time (20)
одни́, *see* **оди́н**
одолжи́ть, perf., *see* **ода́лживать**
о́зеро (*nom. pl.*, **озёра**) lake (13)
ока́зываться (imperf., I), **оказа́ться** (perf., I: **окажу́сь, ока́жешься**) to turn out (to be) (24); **О́н оказа́лся** (+ *instr.*). He turned out to be .... **Оказа́лось, что ....** It turned out that ....
ока́нчивать (imperf., I), **око́нчить** (perf., II: **око́нч.у, -ишь**) to complete, graduate from (+ *acc.*) (23)
окно́ (*gen. pl.* **о́кон**) window (2)
о́коло (+ *gen.*) near, about, approximately (*16, 26*)
окружа́ть (imperf., I), **окружи́ть** (perf., II: **окруж.у́, -и́шь**) to surround (27)
октя́брь (*m.*) October (23)
он he; it (*3, 4*)
она́ she; it (*3, 4*)
они́ they (*3, 4*)
оно́ it (*3, 4*)
опа́здывать (imperf., I), **опозда́ть** (perf., I) to be late (17); **о. в кла́сс** to be late for class; **о. на по́езд** to be late for the train; **о. на ча́с** to be an hour late
опа́сность (*f.*) danger (27)
опа́сный dangerous (17)
опи́сывать (imperf., I), **описа́ть** (perf., I: **опишу́, опи́шешь**) to describe (26)
опя́ть again (14)
оригина́льный original (9)
оса́да siege (27)
осе́нний autumn, fall (*adj.*)
о́сень (*f.*) autumn, fall; **о́сенью** in fall (11)
осно́вывать (imperf., I), **основа́ть** (perf., I: **осну.ю́, -ёшь**) to found, establish (18)
осо́бенно especially (12)
остава́ться (imperf., I: **оста.ю́сь, -ёшься**), **оста́ться** (perf., I: **оста́н.усь, -ешься**) to remain, stay, be left (25)
оставля́ть (imperf., I), **оста́вить** (perf., II: **оста́в.лю, -ишь**) to leave (*trans.*) (22)
остана́вливать (imperf., I), **останови́ть** (perf., II: **остановлю́, остано́вишь**) to stop (*trans.*); **остана́вливаться, останови́ться** to stop (*intrans.*) (22)
остано́в.ка (*gen. pl.* **-ок**) stop (22)
о́стров (*nom. pl.* **-а́**) island (24)
от (+ *gen.*) from, away from, from the house of (15, *17*)
отве́т answer, reply (9)
отвеча́ть (imperf., I) (9), **отве́тить** (perf., II: **отве́.чу, -тишь**) (15) to answer, reply (+ *dat. of persons or* **на** + *acc., see 15*)
отвози́ть (imperf., II: **отвожу́, отво́зишь**), **отвезти́** (perf., I: **отвез.у́, -ёшь;** past **отвёз, отвезло́,** etc.) to take, drive, transport (to) (*22*)
отвыка́ть (imperf., I), **отвы́кнуть** (perf., I: **отвы́кн.у, -ешь;** past **отвы́к, отвы́кло,** etc.) to grow unaccustomed to (**от** + *gen. or inf.*) (21)
отде́л department, division (13)
о́тдых rest, relaxation (8)
отдыха́ть (imperf., I) (8), **отдохну́ть** (perf., I: **отдохн.у́, -ёшь**) (21) to rest, relax
от.е́ц (*gen.* **-ца́**) father (4)
открыва́ть (imperf., I) (8), **откры́ть** (perf., I: **откро́.ю, -ешь**) (24) to open
откры́тие discovery (17)
откры́тый open, opened (26)
отку́да from where (*17*)
отли́чный excellent (18)
отме́т.ка (*gen. pl.* **-ок**) mark, grade (13)
относи́ть (imperf., II: **отношу́, отно́сишь**), **отнести́** (perf., I: **отнес.у́, -ёшь;** past **отнёс, отнесло́,** etc.) to take, carry (to, on foot) (*22*)
о́тпуск leave (from work), vacation (26)
отсю́да from here (*17*)
отту́да from there (*17*)
отходи́ть (imperf., II: **отхожу́, отхо́дишь**), **отойти́** (perf., I: **отойд.у́, -ёшь;** past **отошёл, отошло́,** etc.) to move away, withdraw (on foot), stand back (**от** + *gen.*) (*22*)
о́тчество patronymic (*11*)
офице́р officer (11)
о́чень very (3, *10*)
ошиба́ться (imperf., I), **ошиби́ться** (perf., I: **ошиб.у́сь, -ёшься;** past **оши́бся, оши́блось,** etc.) (22) to be mistaken
оши́б.ка (*gen. pl.* **-ок**) mistake, error; **(с)де́лать оши́бку** to make a mistake (14)

па́дать (imperf., I), **упа́сть** (perf., I: **упад.у́, -ёшь**; past **упа́л, -о, -а, -и**) to fall (24)
паке́т package (22)
па́л.ец (*gen.* **-ьца**) finger; toe (11)
пальто́ (*n. indecl.*) coat, overcoat (12)
па́мятник monument, memorial (7)
па́мять (*f.*) memory (11)
па́па papa (*20*)
папиро́са cigarette (15)
па́ра pair, couple (13)
па́р.ень (*gen.* **-ня**) (*colloq.*) fellow
парк park (6)
парохо́д ship, steamboat (18)
па́ртия game; political party (14)
пассажи́р (*f.* **-ка,** *gen. pl.* **-ок**) passenger (22)
пев.е́ц (*gen.* **-ца́**) (*f.* **-и́ца**) singer (16)
пе́рвый first (6); **в п. ра́з** (for) the first time (16); **во-пе́рвых** first, in the first place (20)
перево́д translation (10)
переводи́ть (imperf., II: **перевожу́, перево́дишь**) (5, *19*), **перевести́** (perf., I: **перевед.у́, -ёшь**; past **перевёл, перевело́,** etc.) (19) to translate
перево́д.чик (*f.* **-чица**) translator, interpreter (12)
перед, передо (+ *instr.*) before, in front of (*19*)
передава́ть (imperf., I: **переда.ю́, -ёшь**), **переда́ть** (perf., *conj. like* **дать**) to convey, transmit, give (18); **п. приве́т** to give, send (someone) one's regards (18)
пере́дняя (*adj. used as noun*) vestibule, anteroom (24)
переноси́ть (imperf., II: **переношу́, перено́сишь**), **перенести́** (perf., I: **перенес.у́, -ёшь**; past **перенёс, перенесло́,** etc.) to bear, endure, carry (over) (27)
перепи́сывать (imperf., I), **переписа́ть** (perf., I: **перепишу́, перепи́шешь**) to rewrite (15)
перестава́ть (imperf., I: **переста.ю́, -ёшь**), **переста́ть** (perf., I: **переста́н.у, -ешь**) to stop, cease (+ *inf.*) (27)
переходи́ть (imperf., II: **перехожу́, перехо́дишь**), **перейти́** (perf., I: **перейд.у́, -ёшь**; past **перешёл, перешло́,** etc.) to cross (*22*)
пе́р.ец (*gen.* **-ца**) pepper (21)
перо́ (*nom. pl.* **пе́рья,** *gen. pl.* **пе́рьев**) pen; feather (2)
пе́сня (*gen. pl.* **пе́сен**) song (13)
петь (imperf., I: **по.ю́, -ёшь**), **с-** (perf., trans., I) to sing (16)
печа́льный sad (22)
пешко́м on foot (17)
пи́во beer (17)
пиджа́к coat, jacket (13)
писа́ние writing (14)
писа́тель (*f.* **-ница**) writer (5)
писа́ть (imperf., I: **пишу́, пи́шешь**) (9), **на-** (perf., I) (14) to write
пи́сьменный сто́л desk (10)
письмо́ (*gen. pl.* **пи́сем**) letter (4)
пить (imperf., I: **пью, пьёшь**; imperative **пей/те**) (11), **вы́-** (perf., trans. ,I) (20) to drink; **(вы́)пить за здоро́вье** (+ *gen.*) to drink to the health of . . . (26)
пла́вать (indeterm. imperf., I), **плыть** (determ. imperf., I: **плыв.у́, -ёшь**), **поплы́ть** (perf., I) to float, sail, swim (*24*)
пла́кать (imperf., I: **пла́ч.у, -ешь**) to weep, cry (21)
план plan (14)
пласти́н.ка (*gen. pl.* **-ок**) phonograph record
плати́ть (imperf., II: **плачу́, пла́тишь**), **за-** (perf., II) to pay (+ *dat. of person*) (16); **(за)п. за** (+ *acc.*) to pay for (16)
плат.о́к (*gen.* **-ка́**) kerchief, handkerchief (22)
пла́тье (*gen. pl.* **пла́тьев**) dress (6)
племя́нник nephew (22)
племя́нница niece (22)
плита́ stove (24)
плохо́й (**пло́хо**) bad, poor (6); **Мне́ пло́хо.** I feel sick (23).
пло́щадь (*f.*) square (12)
по (+ *dat.*) about, around, along (motion) (*17*); **по го́роду** around (back and forth through) the city; **по у́лице** along the street
по-англи́йски (in) English (*5*); **говори́ть по-англи́йски** to speak English, in English (*5*)
побежа́ть (perf.), *see* **бежа́ть**
поблагодари́ть (perf.), *see* **благодари́ть**
по-ва́шему in your opinion
повезти́ (perf.), *see* **везти́**
пове́рить (perf.), *see* **ве́рить**
повести́ (perf.), *see* **вести́**
повторе́ние repetition (18)

повторя́ть (imperf., I) (18), **повтори́ть** (perf., II: **повтор.ю́, -и́шь**) (24) to repeat

поговори́ть (perf., II: **поговор.ю́, -и́шь**) (*25*), perf. of **говори́ть** = to speak, talk

погово́р.ка (*gen. pl.* **-ок**) saying, proverb (18)

пого́да weather; **Кака́я сего́дня п.?** What is the weather today? (6)

по́д, подо (+ *instr.*) under, below (19)

пода́р.ок (*gen.* **-ка**) gift (9)

подожда́ть (perf.), *see* **ждать**

подплыва́ть (imperf., I), **подплы́ть** (perf., I: **подплыв.у́, -ёшь**) to approach by sailing, swimming; to swim/sail up to (*24*)

подру́га (girl) friend (8)

по-друго́му otherwise, differently (21)

поду́мать (perf.), *see* **ду́мать**

поду́ш.ка (*gen. pl.* **-ек**) pillow (24)

подходи́ть (imperf., II: **подхожу́, подхо́дишь**), **подойти́** (perf., I: **подойд.у́, -ёшь;** past **подошёл, подошло́,** etc.) to approach, go (come) up, come near (on foot) (**к** + *dat.*) (*22*)

подъезжа́ть (imperf., I), **подъе́хать** (perf., I: **подъе́д.у, -ешь;** imperative **подъезжа́й/те**) to approach, drive up to (**к** + *dat.*) (*22*)

по́езд (*nom. pl.* **-а́**) train (13)

пое́хать (perf.), *see* **е́хать**

пожа́луйста please, if you please; you're welcome (3)

пожива́ть (imperf., I) to live, get along; **Ка́к вы́ пожива́ете?** How are you? (3)

поза́втракать (perf.), *see* **за́втракать**

позавчера́ day before yesterday (18)

позвони́ть (perf.), *see* **звони́ть**

по́здно late (7)

по́зже later (15, 25)

пойти́ (perf.), *see* **идти́**

пока́ so far, till now (14); **п. . . . не** (+ *perf.*) until (*21*)

пока́зывать (imperf., I) (9), **показа́ть** (perf., I: **покажу́, пока́жешь**) (15) to show

показа́ться (perf.), *see* **каза́ться**

покупа́тель (*f.* **-ница**) customer, shopper (13)

покупа́ть (imperf., I) (8), **купи́ть** (perf., II: **куплю́, ку́пишь**) (16) to buy

поку́п.ка (*gen. pl.* **-ок**) purchase (22)

пол (*loc.* **на полу́**) floor (2)

по́лдень (*m.*) noon (19)

по́ле field (4)

поле́зный useful (27)

полете́ть (perf.), *see* **лете́ть**

по́л.ка (*gen. pl.* **-ок**) shelf, bookshelf (2)

по́лночь (*f.*) midnight (19)

по́лный full (+ *gen.*) (*24*)

полови́на half (14, *26*); **три́ с полови́ной** three and a half

положе́ние position, situation (18)

положи́ть (perf.), *see* **класть**

полтор.а́ (*m.*), **-ы́** (*f.*) one and a half (*26*)

получа́ть (imperf., I) (13), **получи́ть** (perf., II: **получу́, полу́чишь**) (15) to receive, get, obtain

полчаса́ half an hour (22)

по́льза use, profit (27)

по́льзоваться (imperf., I: **по́льзу.юсь, -ешься**), **вос-** (perf., I) to use, take advantage of (+ *instr.*) (23)

по́мнить (imperf., II: **по́мн.ю, -ишь;** imperative **по́мни/те**) to remember (11)

помога́ть (imperf., I) (9), **помо́чь** (perf., I: **помогу́, помо́жешь . . . помо́гут** (18); imperative **помоги́/те;** past **помо́г, помогло́,** etc.) to help (+ *dat.*)

по-мо́ему in my opinion (14)

по́мощь (*f.*) help (10)

помы́ть(ся) (perf.) *see* **мы́ть(ся)**

понеде́льник Monday (18)

понести́ (perf.), *see* **нести́**

понима́ть (imperf., I) (8), **поня́ть** (perf., I: **пойм.у́, -ёшь**) (19) to understand, grasp, comprehend

понра́виться (perf.), *see* **нра́виться**

пообе́дать (perf.), *see* **обе́дать**

поплы́ть (perf.), *see* **плыть**

попроси́ть (perf.), *see* **проси́ть**

попутеше́ствовать (perf., I: **попутеше́ству.ю, -ешь**) to travel (for a while) (27)

пора́ (+ *dat. and inf.*) it is time to . . . (17); **с тех по́р** since then; **с тех по́р, как . . .** since the time when . . . ; **до каки́х по́р?** how long, how far, till when? **до тех по́р** till then; **до сих по́р** so far, thus far, till now, still (21)

портре́т portrait (22)

портфе́ль (*m.*) briefcase (22)

по-ру́сски (in) Russian; **чита́ть по-ру́сски** to read (in) Russian (*5*)

поря́д.ок (*gen.* **-ка**) order (24)
по-сво́ему in one's (its) own way (27)
посеща́ть (imperf., I), **посети́ть** (perf., II: **посе.щу́, -ти́шь**) to visit (27)
посла́ть (perf.), *see* **посыла́ть**
после́дний last, latest (6)
по́сле (+ *gen.*) after (10); (*adv.*) later, afterwards
послеза́втра day after tomorrow (17)
послу́шать (perf.), *see* **слу́шать**
посмотре́ть (perf.), *see* **смотре́ть**
посове́товать(ся) (perf.), *see* **сове́товать(ся)**
поспеши́ть (perf.), *see* **спеши́ть**
посреди́ (+ *gen.*) in the middle of (27)
поста́вить (perf.), *see* **ста́вить**
посте́ль (*f.*) bed, bedding (18)
постро́ить (perf.), *see* **стро́ить**
поступа́ть (imperf., I), **поступи́ть** (perf., II: **поступлю́, посту́пишь**) to enroll, enter (19)
постуча́ть (perf.), *see* **стуча́ть**
посу́да (*collect.*) dishes, china (13)
посыла́ть (imperf., I) (9), **посла́ть** (perf., I: **пошл.ю́, -ёшь**) (19) to send
посы́л.ка (*gen. pl.* **-ок**) package, parcel (22)
потеря́ть (perf.), *see* **теря́ть**
потол.о́к (*gen.* **-ка́**) ceiling
пото́м then, next, later (11)
потому́ что because (4)
поу́жинать (perf.), *see* **у́жинать**
похо́ж/ий similar, like; **п. на** (+ *acc.*) similar to, like; **О́н похо́ж на своего́ отца́.** He looks like his father (23).
поцелова́ть, perf. of **целова́ть**
поцелу́й kiss (27)
почему́ why (4); **почему́-то** for some reason (12)
почи́стить (perf.), *see* **чи́стить**
по́чта post-office; post, mail (12); **на по́чте** at the post office
почти́ almost, nearly (8)
почу́вствовать (perf.), *see* **чу́вствовать**
пошути́ть (perf.), *see* **шути́ть**
поэ́зия poetry (23)
поэ́т poet (16)
поэ́тому therefore (9)
прав right, correct (said of persons, in predicate only) (14, *23*); **О́н пра́в.** He's right (13, *23*).
пра́вда truth; justice (5, 13); **П., что . . .** It's true that . . . **Э́то пра́вда.** That's right (5).
пра́вило rule (9)
пра́вильный correct (3, 18)
пра́вый right (11)
пра́здник holiday (9); **на пра́здники** for the holidays (25)
пра́здновать (imperf., **пра́здну.ю, -ешь**) to celebrate (26)
пра́ктика practice (14)
практи́ческий practical (23)
предви́деть (imperf., II: **предви́.жу, -дишь**) to foresee (27)
предложе́ние sentence, proposition (19)
предпочита́ть (imperf., I) to prefer (+ *acc. or inf.*) (18)
предска́зывать (imperf., I), **предсказа́ть** (perf., I: **предскажу́, предска́жешь**) to foretell, predict (27)
представля́ть (imperf., I), **предста́вить** (perf., II: **предста́в.лю, -ишь**) to present, represent; **п. себе́** to imagine (27)
пре́жде formerly, before (*adv.*) (25)
президе́нт president (11)
прекра́сный fine, wonderful, excellent (7)
преподава́ние teaching (23)
преподава́ть (imperf., I: **препода.ю́, -ёшь;** imperative **преподава́й/те**) to teach (*23*)
прибега́ть (imperf., I), **прибежа́ть** (perf.: **прибегу́, прибежи́шь . . . прибегу́т**) to come running, rush up (*24*)
приве́т greeting(s) (9)
привози́ть (imperf., II: **привожу́, приво́зишь**), **привезти́** (perf., I: **привез.у́, -ёшь;** past **привёз, привезло́,** etc.) to bring (by vehicle) (*22*)
привыка́ть (imperf., I), **привы́кнуть** (perf., I: **привы́кн.у, -ешь;** past **привы́к, привы́кло,** etc.) to get used to (**к** + *dat. or inf.*) (21)
привы́ч.ка (*gen. pl.* **-ек**) habit (23)
приглаша́ть (imperf., I), **пригласи́ть** (perf., II: **пригла.шу́, -си́шь**) to invite (25)
приглаше́ние invitation (25)
пригото́вить (perf.), *see* **гото́вить**
прие́зд arrival (by vehicle) (26)
приезжа́ть (imperf., I), **прие́хать** (perf., I: **прие́д.у, -ешь,** imperative **приезжа́й/те**) to come, arrive (by vehicle) (*18*)

приём reception (20)
прийти́ (perf.), *see* **приходи́ть**
приле́жный diligent, studious (10)
прилета́ть (imperf., I), **прилете́ть** (perf., II: **приле.чу́, -ти́шь**) to fly in, arrive (by flying) (*24*)
принима́ть (imperf., I), **приня́ть** (perf., I: **приму́, при́мешь**) to accept, receive, take (20)
приноси́ть (imperf., II: **приношу́, прино́сишь**), **принести́** (perf., I: **принес.у́, -ёшь;** past **принёс, принесло́,** etc.) to bring (on foot) (*22*)
принц prince (19)
принце́сса princess
приро́да nature (16)
приходи́ть (imperf., II: **прихожу́, прихо́дишь**), **прийти́** (perf., I: **прид.у́, -ёшь;** past **пришёл, пришло́,** etc.) to come, arrive (on foot) (*18*)
прия́тель (*f.* **-ница**) friend (7)
прия́тный pleasant (6)
про (+ *acc.*) about, concerning (21)
пробы́ть (perf., I: **пробу́д.у, -ешь**) to stay, spend (some time) (21, *25*)
прова́ливаться (imperf., I), **провали́ться** (perf., II: **провалю́сь, прова́лишься**) to fail; **п. на экза́мене** to fail an exam (19)
проводи́ть (imperf., II: **провожу́, прово́дишь**), **провести́** (perf., I: **провед.у́, -ёшь;** past **провёл, провело́,** etc.) to spend/pass time, lead (through) (23)
продава́ть (imperf., I: **прода.ю́, -ёшь;** imperative **продава́й/те**) (9), **прода́ть** (perf., *conj. like* **дать**) (15) to sell
продав.е́ц (*gen.* **-ца**) salesman, sales clerk (13)
продавщи́ца saleslady (13)
продолжа́ть (imperf., I) to continue, go on (+ *inf.*) (16)
проду́кты (*m. pl.*) produce, products (19)
произво́дство production (27)
произноси́ть (imperf., II: **произношу́, произно́сишь**), **произнести́** (perf., I: **произнес.у́, -ёшь:** past **произнёс, произнесло́,** etc.) to pronounce; **п. ре́чь** to give a speech (19)
произноше́ние pronunciation (19)
происходи́ть (imperf., II: **происхожу́, происхо́дишь**), to come from (originate); **произойти́** (perf., I: **произойдёт;** past **произошёл, произошло́**) to occur, take place (21)
пройти́ (perf.), *see* **проходи́ть**
пролета́ть (imperf., I), **пролете́ть** (perf., II: **проле.чу́, -ти́шь**) to fly past (27)
проси́ть (imperf., II: **прошу́, про́сишь**), **по-** (perf., II) to ask for, beg (*18*)
прости́те pardon; forgive me (4)
просто́й simple (12); **про́сто** simply; only (10)
просыпа́ться (imperf., I), **просну́ться** (perf., I: **просн.у́сь, -ёшься**) to wake up (*intrans.*) (19)
про́тив (+ *gen.*) opposite, opposed to (21)
прохла́дно cool; it's cool (12)
проходи́ть (imperf., II: **прохожу́, прохо́дишь**), **пройти́** (perf., I: **пройд.у́, -ёшь;** past **прошёл, прошло́,** etc.) to cross, go through, finish; **п. ми́мо** (+ *gen.*) to pass (*22*); **Э́то пройдёт.** That will pass (23).
прочита́ть, проче́сть (perf.), *see* **чита́ть**
про́шлый past, last (12); **в про́шлом году́** last year (12); **про́шлое** (*adj. used as noun*) the past (24)
про́ще simpler (25)
пря́мо straight, direct(ly) (17)
пти́ца bird (16)
пусто́й (**пу́сто**) empty (24)
пусть, пуска́й let (*25*)
путеше́ствие travel, journey, trip (20)
путеше́ствовать (imperf., I: **путеше́ству.ю, -ешь**) to travel (20)
пье́са play, drama (8)
пятна́дцать fifteen (*16, 26*)
пя́тница Friday (18)
пя́тый fifth (18)
пять five (*16, 26*)
пятьдеся́т fifty (*21, 26*)

рабо́та work (5); **на рабо́те** at work (5)
рабо́тать (imperf., I) to work (5); **р. над** (+ *instr.*) to work at (on) (19)
рабо́чий work, working (*adj.*); workman (*adj. used as noun*) (19)
равно́: Мне́ всё равно́. I don't care (10).
рад glad (*5*); **Я́ э́тому ра́д.** I'm glad of that.

ра́дио (*n. indecl.*) radio (9)
раз (*gen. pl.* **раз**) time, occasion (16); **в пе́рвый р.** for the first time; **(оди́н) р.** once; **два́ ра́за** twice
разбуди́ть (perf.), *see* **буди́ть**
ра́зве can it be that . . . ? (expresses surprise or disbelief); **р. . . . не** surely (18)
разгова́ривать (imperf., I) to converse (11)
разгово́р conversation
раздева́ть (imperf., I), **разде́ть** (perf., I: **разде́н.у, -ешь**) to undress (*trans.*); **раздева́ться, разде́ться** to undress (*intrans.*) (19)
разме́р size, measure (13)
ра́зный various (13)
разруша́ть (imperf., I), **разру́шить** (perf., II: **разру́ш.у, -ишь**) to destroy (27)
ра́нить (imperf. and perf., II: **ра́н.ю, -ишь**) to wound (27)
ра́нний early (*adj.*) (27)
ра́но early (*adv.*) (7)
ра́ньше earlier, before (*adv.*) (12)
расписа́ние schedule; **р. поездо́в** train timetable (26)
рассерди́ться(perf.), *see* **серди́ться**
расска́з story, tale (10)
расска́зывать (imperf., I) (11), **рассказа́ть** (perf., I: **расскажу́, расска́жешь**) (15) to tell, narrate
расти́ (imperf., I: **раст.у́, -ёшь;** past **рос, росло́,** etc.) to grow (16)
ребён.ок (*gen.* **-ка**; *pl., see* **де́ти**) child (13)
ребя́та (*m. pl.: gen. pl.* **ребя́т**) (*colloq.*) fellows, kids (23)
револю́ция revolution (12)
ре́дкий rare, uncommon (16); **ре́дко** seldom, rarely (9)
ре́же less often, rarer (*25*)
ре́зать (imperf., I: **ре́ж.у, -ешь**) to cut (19)
рестора́н restaurant (7)
ре́ч.ка (*gen. pl.* **-ек**) stream, small river (25)
речь (*f.*) speech (24)
реша́ть (imperf., I), **реши́ть** (perf., II: **реш.у́, -и́шь**) to decide (17)
ро́вно exactly (with numerals) (16); **р. в се́мь (часо́в)** at 7:00 sharp (16)
ро́дина fatherland (27)
роди́тел.и (*pl., gen.* **-ей**) parents (16)
родно́й native, own (27)
ро́дствен.ник (*f.* **-ница**) relative (27)
рожда́ться (imperf., I), **роди́ться** (perf., II: **рожу́сь, роди́шься**) to be born (23)
рожде́ние birth, birthday (23); **де́нь рожде́ния** birthday; **на р.** for (on) one's birthday
ро́зовый pink, rosy (16)
роль (*f.*) role (12); **игра́ть р.** to play a part
рома́н novel (6)
Росси́я Russia (11)
рот (*gen.* **рта,** *loc.* **во рту́**) mouth (3)
роя́ль (*m.*) piano (6)
руба́ш.ка (*gen. pl.* **-ек**) shirt (13)
рубль (*m.*) ruble (18)
рука́ hand; arm (3); **за́ руку** by the hand (22)
ру́сский Russian; a Russian (6, *20*)
ры́ба fish (9)
ря́дом next door, beside, side by side; **р. с** (+ *instr.*) beside, next to, next door to (11)

с, со (+ *instr.*) with, together with (*11*); (+ *gen.*) off, down from, from (*17*); (+ *acc.*) about, approximately
сади́ться (imperf., II: **сажу́сь, сади́шься**), **сесть** (perf., I: **ся́д.у, -ешь;** past **сел, -о, -а, -и**) to sit down (21); **с. за сто́л** to sit down at the table; **с. на по́езд** to take a train
сала́т salad (11)
сам oneself, myself, himself, etc. (*14, 23*)
самолёт airplane (24)
са́мый the very, the most (13, *25*); **то́ же са́мое** the same thing (25)
са́хар sugar (11, 12)
све́жий (свежо́) fresh; cool, chilly; it is cool (6)
свет world, light (20)
свети́ть (imperf., II: **свечу́, све́тишь**) to shine (26)
све́тлый (светло́) light, bright (7)
свида́ние meeting, rendez-vous (27); **до свида́ния** good-bye (*lit.* till we meet again) (3)
свобо́да freedom (23)
свобо́дный free; fluent (23)
свой my, his, our, etc. (refers back to subject of sentence; *see 9*) (*12, 20*)

связь (*f.*) link, tie, connection (21)
сде́лать (perf.), *see* **де́лать**
себя́ oneself (*23*)
се́вер north (22); **на с.** to the north; **на се́вере** in the north
се́верный northern (22)
сего́дня today (5)
сего́дняшний today's (6); **с. де́нь** today (used as noun) (25)
седьмо́й seventh (18)
сейча́с now, just now; right away, just a minute (14); **с. же** at once, immediately (14)
секре́т secret (14)
секрета́рша secretary (4)
село́ (*nom. pl.* **сёла,** *gen. pl.* **сёл**) village, town (22)
се́льский village (*adj.*) (23)
семе́йный family (*adj.*) (20)
семна́дцать seventeen (*16, 26*)
семь seven (*16, 26*)
се́мьдесят seventy (*21, 26*)
семья́ (*gen. pl.* **семе́й**) family (9, *20*)
сентя́брь (*m.*) September (23)
серди́ться (imperf., II: **сержу́сь, се́рдишься**), **рас-** (perf., II) to get angry at (**на** + *acc.*) (22)
се́рдце (*gen. pl.* **серде́ц**) heart (*23*)
середи́на middle (18)
серьёзный serious (6)
сестра́ (*nom. pl.* **сёстры,** *gen. pl.* **сестёр**) sister (4)
сесть (perf.), *see* **сади́ться**
Сиби́рь (*f.*) Siberia (3)
сиде́ть (imperf., II: **сижу́, сиди́шь**) (11) to sit, be seated; **с. до́ма** to stay at home
си́ла power, force (25)
си́льный strong (21)
симпати́чный likeable, pleasant (20)
си́ний blue (6)
сказа́ть (perf., I: **скажу́, ска́жешь**), perf. of **говори́ть** = to say, tell (*14*); **Я́ хочу́ сказа́ть . . .** I mean (to say) . . . (14).
ска́з.ка (*gen. pl.* **-ок**) fairy-tale (24)
ско́лько (+ *gen.*) how much, how many (7, *20*); **с. вре́мени** how long (12)
ско́ро soon (5). **Скоре́й!** Hurry!
скот cattle, livestock (23)
ску́чный dull, boring (8). **Мне́ ску́чно.** I'm bored. (8)
сла́вный nice, likeable (26)
славяни́н (decl. *20*) (*f.* **славя́н.ка,** *gen. pl.* **-ок**) Slav (*20*)
сле́ва on (from) the left (26)
сле́дующий next, following (27)
сли́шком too, excessively (8)
слова́рь (*m.*) dictionary (4)
сло́во word (6); **сло́вом** in a word (25)
слон elephant (21)
слу́жба job, work; service (14)
служи́ть (imperf., II: **служу́, слу́жишь**), to serve (+ *dat.*); be employed, work (12)
слух rumor; hearing (27)
слу́чай case, incident, event; chance (20)
случа́йно by chance (19)
случа́ться (imperf., I), **случи́ться** (perf., II: **случи́тся**) to happen, occur (20)
слу́шать (imperf., I) (5, 8), **по-** (perf., I) (18) to listen to, obey (+ *acc.*)
слы́шать (imperf., II: **слы́ш.у, -ишь**) (11), **у-** (perf., II) (21) to hear
смерть (*f.*) death (11)
смех laughter (16)
смешно́й funny (19)
смея́ться (imperf., I: **сме.ю́сь, -ёшься**) to laugh (**над** + *instr.*) to laugh at, make fun of (19)
смотре́ть (imperf., II: **смотрю́, смо́тришь**), **по-** (perf., II) to look; **(по)с. на** (+ *acc.*) to look at (17)
смочь (perf.), *see* **мочь** (*21*)
сна, *see* **сон**
снача́ла at first (11)
снег (*loc.* **в снегу́;** *nom. pl.* **-а́**) snow (13); **Идёт сне́г.** It's snowing (17).
снима́ть (imperf., I), **снять** (perf., I: **сниму́, сни́мешь**) to take off; rent (24)
сно́ва again, anew (26)
со, *see* **с**
соба́ка dog (10)
собира́ть (imperf., I), **собра́ть** (perf., **собер.у́, -ёшь**) to collect, gather (*trans.*) (19); **собира́ться, собра́ться** to collect, assemble, come together, prepare to (*intrans.*) (19)
собра́ние meeting, gathering (12)
соверше́нно completely, perfectly (23)

сове́т advice, counsel; council (9)
сове́товать (imperf., I: **сове́ту.ю, -ешь**), **по-** (perf., I) to advise (someone + *dat. and inf.*) (21); **сове́товаться, по-** to consult with (**с** + *instr.*) (21)
сове́тский Soviet (7); **С. Сою́з** Soviet Union (3)
совреме́нный contemporary, modern (20)
совсе́м quite, entirely, completely (11); **с. не (не́т)** not at all (11); **не с.** not quite (11)
согла́сный agreed, in agreement (*23*)
Соединённые Шта́ты Аме́рики United States of America (19)
сожале́ние regret; **к сожале́нию** unfortunately (23)
солда́т (*gen. pl.* **солда́т**) soldier (16)
со́лнце sun (16)
соль (*f.*) salt (18)
сон (*gen.* **сна**) sleep; dream; **ви́деть с.** to have a dream (26)
со́рок forty (*21, 26*)
сосе́д (*pl.* **сосе́ди**) neighbor; **сосе́д.ка** (*gen. pl.* **-ок**) neighbor woman (10)
соси́с.ка (*gen. pl.* **-ок**) frankfurter (17)
сочине́ние composition (5)
сою́з alliance, union
спа́льня (*gen. pl.* **спа́лен**) bedroom (10)
спасе́ние salvation (27)
спаси́бо thank you (3); **с. за** (+ *acc.*) thanks for (16)
спать (imperf., II: **сплю, спишь**) to sleep (7, 11)
специа́льность (*f.*) speciality; **по специа́льности** in one's field (27)
спеши́ть (imperf., II: **спеш.у́, -и́шь**), **по-** (perf., II) to hurry, hasten; **Часы́ спеша́т.** The watch (clock) is fast (17).
спина́ back (of a person) (23)
спич.ка (*gen. pl.* **-ек**) match
споко́йный peaceful, calm (24). **Споко́йной но́чи!** Good night! (21)
спор argument (13)
спо́рить (imperf., II: **спо́р.ю, -ишь**), **по-** (perf., II) to argue (13)
спортсме́н athlete (25)
спра́ва on (from) the right (26)
спра́шивать (imperf., I) (8), **спроси́ть** (perf., II: **спрошу́, спро́сишь**) (15) to ask, question (*acc. or* **у** + *gen.*)
спрос demand; **с. на** (+ *acc.*) demand for (27)
сра́зу at once, immediately (21)
среда́ Wednesday (18)
среди́ among, amidst (27)
сре́дний average, medium, middle (22)
СССР (indecl.) U.S.S.R. (13)
ста́вить (imperf., II: **ста́в.лю, -ишь**), **по-** (perf., II) to put, stand (*trans.*) (*24*); **(по)с. буди́льник на** (+ *acc.*) to set an alarm clock for . . . (24)
стака́н glass, tumbler (7)
станови́ться (imperf., II: **становлю́сь, стано́вишься**), **стать** (perf., I: **ста́н.у, -ешь**) to stand (take up a standing position); to become (+ *instr.*) (*21*); **Мне́ ста́ло лу́чше.** I got better (23).
ста́нция station (12)
стари́к old man (22)
старомо́дный old-fashioned (16)
ста́рость (*f.*) old age (18)
стару́ха old woman (22)
ста́рше older (*25*)
ста́рший older, elder; oldest, eldest (8, *25*)
ста́рый old (6)
стать, perf., *see* **станови́ться**
статья́ (*gen. pl.* **стате́й**) article (5)
стена́ wall (2)
степь (*f.*) steppe, prairie (13)
стипе́ндия scholarship (23)
стих (line of) verse; **стихи́** verse(s) (16)
сто hundred (*21, 26*)
сто́ить (imperf., II: **сто́.ю, -ишь**) to cost, be worth (16)
стол table (2); **за столо́м** at the table (19)
столи́ца capital (city) (7)
столо́вая (*adj. used as noun*) dining-room (10)
сто́лько (+ *gen.*) so much, so many (16, 20)
сторона́ side; direction (17); **с ва́шей стороны́** on your part (18); **со всех сторо́н** from all sides (27)
стоя́ть (imperf., II: **сто.ю́, -и́шь**) to stand (5, 11)
страда́ние suffering (27)
страна́ country (7)
страни́ца page (26)
стра́нный strange (6)

стра́шный terrible, frightful (27)
стро́ить (imperf., II: **стро́.ю, -ишь**), **по-** (perf., II) to build (27)
строка́, стро́ч.ка (*gen. pl.* **-ек**) line (of writing) (25)
студе́нт (*f.* **-ка**) student (2)
стук knock, rap (24)
стул (*nom. pl.*, **сту́лья,** *gen. pl.* **сту́льев**) chair (2)
стуча́ть (imperf., II: **стуч.у́, -и́шь**), **по-** (perf., II) to knock, rap (24)
сты́дно: Мне́ сты́дно. I am ashamed (24).
суббо́та Saturday (18)
сумасше́дший insane, mad (person), madman (25)
су́м.ка (*gen. pl.* **-ок**) bag, purse (22)
сухо́й dry (24)
су́ше drier (*25*)
счастли́вый happy, fortunate (13, *23*)
сча́стье happiness, luck; **к сча́стью** fortunately (23)
счита́ть (imperf., I) to count, consider as (+ *instr.*) (17)
съезд convention (20)
сыгра́ть (perf.), *see* **игра́ть**
сын (*nom. pl.* **сыновья́,** *gen. pl.* **сынове́й**) son (4)
сыр cheese (7, 12)
сюда́ (to) here, hither (*17*)

так so, thus (4); that's right; **т. себе́** so-so (19); **т. как** since, because, as (12); **т. же . . . как** (just) as . . . as (27)
та́кже also, too, in addition (*17*)
тако́й such (2), so (*6*); **т. большо́й** so large (6); **т. же** similar, of the same sort (26)
такси́ (*n. indecl.*) taxi; **на т.** by taxi, in a taxi (12)
тала́нтливый talented (9)
там there, over there (2)
та́н.ец (*gen.* **-ца**) dance (21)
танцева́ть (imperf., I: **танцу́.ю, -ешь**), **по-** (perf., I) to dance (21)
таре́л.ка (*gen. pl.* **-ок**) plate (13)
тата́рский Tartar (26)
твёрдый firm, hard (19)
твой your, yours (*4, 12, 20*)
теа́тр theater (5)
телеви́зор television set (9)
телегра́мма telegram (9)
телефо́н telephone; **по телефо́ну** by (on the) telephone (9)
те́ма theme, subject; **на э́ту те́му** on that subject (11)
тёмный (темно́) dark; it is dark (7)
температу́ра temperature (23)
тепе́рь now (2)
тёплый (тепло́) warm; it's warm (6)
терпе́ние patience (18)
теря́ть (imperf., I), **по-** (perf., I) to lose (22)
тетра́дь (*f.*) notebook, copybook (13)
тётя, тёт.ка (*gen. pl.* **-ок**) aunt (19, 21)
ти́кать (imperf., I) to tick (24)
ти́хий quiet, low (in voice) (8)
ти́ше quieter (*25*); **Ти́ше!** Silence! (25)
то that (*4*); **то́, что** that which, what (*13*); **е́сли . . . , то́** if . . . , then; **когда́ . . . , то́** when . . . , then (25); **то́ есть** that is (17)
-то, *see 22*
тогда́ then, at that time (10, *11*)
то́же also, too (3, *17*)
толпа́ crowd (22)
то́лстый fat, stout (8)
то́лько only (4); **как т.** as soon as (*14*); **т. что** (have) just (14)
том volume (26)
тому́ наза́д ago (16)
то́нкий thin, fine, delicate (13)
тот that (one) (*4, 12, 20*); **т. же** the same (18); **то́, что** that which, what (*13*)
то́чно exactly (19); just like, just as if
трава́ grass (17)
тре́тий third (*18*); **тре́тьего дня́** the day before yesterday (21); **в-тре́тьих** third, in the third place (21)
три three (*10, 26*)
три́дцать thirty (*21, 26*)
трина́дцать thirteen (*16, 26*)
тру́б.ка (*gen. pl.* **-ок**) pipe (11)
труд work, labor (11); **с трудо́м** with difficulty (11)
тру́дный difficult, hard (6)
туда́ (to) there, thither (*17*)
туре́цкий Turkish (22)
тут here (2)
ту́ча (storm) cloud (19)
ты you, "thou" (intimate) (*4*)
ты́сяча thousand (*26*)

тяжёлый (тяжело́) heavy; hard (said of life, fate, etc.) (20)

у at the house (apartment, etc.) of (*10*); at, near, by (*22*); **У меня́ (е́сть)** (+ *nom.*). I have . . . . (*10*)
убега́ть (imperf., I), **убежа́ть** (perf.: **убегу́, убежи́шь . . . убегу́т**) to run away (*27*)
убива́ть (imperf., I), **уби́ть** (perf., I: **убью́, убьёшь**) to kill (27)
убира́ть (imperf., I), **убра́ть** (perf., I: **убер.у́, -ёшь**) (24) to clean up (off), tidy
уважа́ть (imperf. only, I) to respect (27)
уве́рен/ный sure, certain (18, *23*); **уве́рен в** (+ *loc.*) sure of
уви́деть (perf. of **ви́деть**), *see 21*
увози́ть (imperf., II: **увожу́, уво́зишь**), **увезти́** (perf., I: **увез.у́, -ёшь**; past **увёз, увезло́**, etc.) to carry, transport away (*22*)
у́гол (*gen.* **угла́**, *loc.* **в/на углу́**) corner, angle (12)
ударе́ние accent, stress (19)
удивле́ние surprise (22)
удивлён/ный surprised (*23*)
удо́бный comfortable, convenient (7); **Мне́ удо́бно.** I am comfortable.
удово́льствие pleasure (11)
уезжа́ть (imperf., I), **уе́хать** (perf., I: **уе́д.у, -ешь**; imperative **уезжа́й/те**), to go away, leave (in a vehicle) (*18*)
у́жас horror, terror (21)
ужа́сный horrible, terrible (13)
уже́ already (3); **у. не** no longer
у́же narrower (25)
у́жин supper (16)
у́жинать (imperf., I), **по-** (perf., I) to have supper (16)
у́зкий narrow, tight (8)
узнава́ть (imperf., I: **узна.ю́, -ёшь**), **узна́ть** (perf., I) to find out, learn (*21*)
уйти́ (perf.), *see* **уходи́ть**
Украи́на Ukraine; (12); **на Украи́не** in the Ukraine
улета́ть (imperf., I), **улете́ть** (perf., II: **уле.чу́, -ти́шь**) to fly away (*24*)
у́лица street (5); **на у́лице** on the street, outdoors
улы́б.ка (*gen. pl.* **-ок**) smile (27)
умира́ть (imperf., I), **умере́ть** (perf., I: **умр.у́, -ёшь**; past **у́мер, -ло**, etc.) to die (21)
у́мный (умно́) clever, intelligent (9)
универса́льный магази́н (универма́г) department store (13)
университе́т university (12)
уноси́ть (imperf., II: **уношу́, уно́сишь**), **унести́** (perf., I: **унес.у́, -ёшь**; past **унёс, унесло́**, etc.) to take away, carry away (on foot) (*22*)
упа́сть (perf.), *see* **па́дать**
упражне́ние exercise (9)
Ура́л Urals (12); **на Ура́ле** in the Urals
уро́к lesson (5); **на уро́ке** at the lesson, in class
усло́вие condition (27)
услы́шать, perf. of **слы́шать**
успе́х success (27)
устава́ть (imperf., I: **уста.ю́, -ёшь**), **уста́ть** (perf., I: **уста́н.у, -ешь**) to get tired; (in perf. past) to be tired (21)
у́тренний morning (*adj.*) (26)
у́тро morning (7); **у́тром** in the morning (11); **в де́вять часо́в утра́** at 9:00 a.m. (16); **с утра́ до ве́чера** from morning to evening (25)
у́хо (*nom. pl.* **у́ши**; *gen. pl.* **уше́й**) ear (10, *19*)
ухо́д departure (on foot) (27)
уходи́ть (imperf., II: **ухожу́, ухо́дишь**), **уйти́** (perf., I: **уйд.у́, -ёшь**; past **ушёл, ушло́**, etc.) to leave, go away (on foot) (*18*)
уча́стие participation (21)
уче́бник textbook (10)
учен.и́к (*f.* **-и́ца**) pupil, schoolboy (-girl) (*10*)
уче́ние (уче́нье) studies, studying, learning, schooling (18, 23)
учёный scholarly, scientific; (*adj. used as noun*) scholar, scientist (22)
учи́тель (*f.* **-ница**, *nom. pl.* **учителя́**) teacher (3)
учи́ть (imperf., II: **учу́, у́чишь**), **на-** (perf., II) to teach (*acc. of person; dat. of subject matter*); **учи́ться, на-** to learn, study (+ *dat.*) (*23*)
у́ши, *see* **у́хо**
ую́тный cosy (16)

фами́лия family name (4); **Ка́к ва́ша фами́лия?** What is your (last) name?

февра́ль (*m.*) February (23)
фильм film, motion picture (12)
фоне́тика phonetics (3)
фотоаппара́т camera (22)
фотогра́фия photograph (16)
Фра́нция France (12)
францу́.з (*f.* **-женка,** *gen. pl.* **-женок**) Frenchman (-woman) (20)
францу́зский French (*adj.*); **по-францу́зски** in French (7)
фрукт a fruit; **фру́кты** (*pl.*) fruits, fruit (*collect.*) (17)
фунт pound (7)
футбо́л football; soccer; **на футбо́ле** at a football game (5)

хара́ктер disposition, character (10)
хи́мик chemist (14)
хлеб bread (7)
ходи́ть (indeterm. imperf., II: **хожу́, хо́дишь**), **идти́** (determ. imperf., I: **ид.у́, -ёшь;** past **шёл, шло,** etc.), **пойти́** (perf., I: **пойд.у́, -ёшь;** past **пошёл, пошло́,** etc.) to go (on foot, perf.) (17)
хозя́ин (*f.* **хозя́йка,** *gen. pl.* **хозя́ек**) master, host, landlord, owner (11); **хозя́ева** (*m. pl.*) masters, etc.; *also* master and mistress, host and hostess, landlord and landlady, etc. (*20*)
хозя́йство household; management; business; economy (9); **помога́ть по хозя́йству** to help around the house (21)
хо́лод cold (21)
холо́дный (хо́лодно) cold (*adj.*) (6); **Хо́лодно.** It is cold (6). **Мне́ хо́лодно.** I am cold (9).
хоро́ший (хорошо́) good, fine, nice, well (6)
хорошо́ good, well, fine, all right (3); **Э́то х.** That's good. **Х., что . . .** It's good that . . . (3). **Мне́ х.** I feel well, good, all right (23).
хоте́ть (imperf., *conj. 10*), **за-** (perf., *21*) to want, wish; intend (+ *inf.*); **х. сказа́ть** to mean (14); **хоте́ться, за-** (see *26*)
хоть if only (25)
хотя́ (и) although (10)
худо́й thin, lean (20)
ху́дший worse, worst (*25*)
ху́же worse (23, *25*); **Мне́ х.** I am (feel) worse (23).

царь (*m.*) tsar (14)
цвет (*nom. pl.* **-а́**) color (7); **Како́го цве́та** (+ *nom.*)? What is the color of . . .? (7)
цвет.о́к (*gen.* **-ка́;** *nom. pl.* **цветы́**) flower (19)
целова́ть (imperf., I: **целу́.ю, -ешь**), **по-** (perf., I) to kiss (27)
це́лый (a) whole (6)
цена́ price (7); **Кака́я цена́** (+ *gen.*)? What is the price of . . . ? (7)
центр center (7)
це́рк.овь (*f.*, *gen.* **-ви,** *instr.* **-овью**) church (18)

чай tea (11, *12*)
ча́йка (*gen. pl.* **ча́ек**) gull (26)
час hour (14); **в ч.** at one o'clock (16); **Кото́рый ч.?** What time is it? **В кото́ром часу́?** At what time? (16); **часы́** (*pl.*) hours; clock, watch (17)
ча́сто often (9)
часть (*f.*) part (12)
ча́ш.ка (*gen. pl.* **-ек**) cup (10)
ча́ще more often, more frequently (*25*)
чей whose (*4, 18*)
челове́к (*pl.*, *see* **лю́ди**) man, person, human being (8)
чем . . . тем the . . . the (*25*)
чемода́н suitcase (22)
через (+ *acc.*) in, after, at the end of; **ч. ча́с** in an hour (*18*); across, through (*22*); **ч. у́лицу** across the street
чёрный black (6)
чёрт (*nom. pl.* **че́рти**) devil; **К чёрту!** The devil with it! (25)
честь (*f.*) honor; **в ч.** (+ *gen.*) in honor of (26)
четве́рг Thursday (18)
четвёртый fourth (18)
че́тверть (*f.*) quarter, one-fourth (*26*)
четы́ре four (*10, 26*)
четырёхэта́жный four-storied (27)
четы́рнадцать fourteen (*16, 26*)
число́ number; date (*26*)
чи́стить (imperf., II: **чи́щу, чи́стишь**), **по-** (perf., II) to clean (24)
чи́стый clean, pure (15)
чита́тель (*f.* **-ница**) reader (18)
чита́ть (imperf., I) (5, 8), **про-** (perf., I) (14)

or **прочéсть** (perf., I: **прочт.ý, -ёшь;** past **прочёл, прочлó,** etc.) (*24*) to read; **читáйте!** read! (3); **(про)ч. лéкцию** to lecture, give a lecture (12); **(про)ч. доклáд** to give a talk, report (12)

чище cleaner (*25*)

чтéние reading (*noun*) (6)

что what; that (*3, 5, 15*); **Чтó э́то (такóе)?** What is this (that)? (3) **Чтó э́то за** (+ *nom.*)? What, what kind of . . . is that? (22) **Чтó дéлать?** What can one do? What should we do? (10) **Чтó нáм дéлать?** What can (should) we do? (14) **Чтó такóе . . . ?** What is . . . ? **Чтó с вáми?** What is the matter with you? (23)

чтобы (in order) to (that) (*24*)

чтó-нибудь, чтó-то anything, something (*22*)

чýвство (*gen. pl.* **чувств**) feeling (25)

чýвствовать (imperf., I: **чýвству.ю, -ешь**), (23) **по-** (perf., I) (27) to feel; **Кáк вы́ себя́ чýвствуете?** How do you feel? **Я́ себя́ чýвствую хорошó.** I feel well (23).

чýдный, чудéсный wonderful, marvellous (17, 19)

чулóк (*gen. pl.* **чулóк**) stocking (24)

шáхматы (*pl. only, gen.* **шáхмат**) chess; **игрáть в ш.** to play chess (20)

шестнáдцать sixteen (*16, 26*)

шестóй sixth (18)

шесть six (*16, 26*)

шестьдеся́т sixty (*21, 26*)

ши́ре wider, broader (*25*)

ширóкий wide, broad (8)

шкаф (*loc.* **в шкафý**) cupboard; closet (24)

шкóла school (5)

шкóльный school (*adj.*) (27)

шкóль.ник (*f.* **-ница**) schoolboy (-girl) (23)

шля́па hat (6)

шоколáд chocolate (21,*12*)

шум noise (16)

шумéть (imperf., II: **шум.лю́, -и́шь**) to make noise, be noisy (25)

шýмный noisy (16)

шути́ть (imperf., II: **шучý, шýтишь**), **по-** (perf., II) to joke (20)

шýт.ка (*gen. pl.* **-ок**) joke (20)

эгои́ст (*f.* **-ка,** *gen. pl.* **-ок**) egoist, selfish person (14)

экзáмен examination (5); **держáть э.** to take an exam (13); **вы́держать э.** to pass an exam.; **провали́ться на экзáмене** to fail an exam (19)

энерги́чный energetic (22)

этáж floor, story (18)

э́тот this, that (*4, 12, 20*); **Э́то . . . .** This (that) is . . . (*2*).

ю́б.ка (*gen. pl.* **-ок**) skirt (13)

юг south (22); **на ю.** to the south; **на ю́ге** in the south

ю́жный southern (22)

я́блоко (*nom. pl.* **я́блоки,** *gen. pl.* **я́блок**) apple (22)

язы́к language, tongue (12, *20*)

янвáрь (*m.*) January (23)

япóнский Japanese (19)

я́сный clear (18)

ENGLISH-RUSSIAN VOCABULARY

As in the Russian-English Vocabulary, the numbers in parentheses refer to the units in which words or expressions are first used or are explained. Where the number is italicized, additional information on inflection or on usage may be found by referring to the unit indicated.

Verbs are designated as imperfective (imperf.), or perfective (perf.), except when two verbs related in form are given together: in the latter case the first verb of the pair is always imperfective, the second always perfective. Verb conjugation patterns are not given in this vocabulary; they can be found by referring to the Russian-English Vocabulary, or to the units listed after the verbs.

All cardinal numerals are given except the compound forms denoting the hundreds. Ordinals are given up to "tenth" only. Other numerals can be found by referring to Unit 26.

a (*not translated—see 2*); **(a certain)** оди́н; како́й-то (*22*); **(any)** како́й-нибудь (*22*); **(not a single)** ни оди́н (*20*); **(per)** в (+ *acc.*) (*17*)
A.M. утра́ **(in the morning)** (*16*); но́чи **(at night)** (*16*)
able, to be мочь (*10*), с- (*21*)
about (concerning) о, об, обо (+ *loc.*) (*5*, *12*), про (+ *acc.*) (*21*); **(approximately)** о́коло (+ *gen.*) (*26*); **a. five students** студе́нтов пя́ть (*colloq.*), *or* о́коло пяти́ студе́нтов; **a. the town** по го́роду; **a. the room** по ко́мнате (*17*)
above над (+ *instr.*) (*19*)
abroad, to go (по)е́хать за грани́цу; **to be a.** бы́ть за грани́цей (*21*)
accent ударе́ние, акце́нт (19)
to accept принима́ть, приня́ть (*20*)
accident, by случа́йно (19)
acquaintance (friend) знако́м/ый (*20*)
acquainted with знако́м с (+ *instr.*) (*20*)
across через (+ *acc.*) (*22*)
addition, in ещё (*10*); кро́ме того́ (23)
address а́дрес (*nom. pl.* -а́) (7); **What is the a. of . . . ?** Ка́к а́дрес (+ *gen.*)? (7)
to adore обожа́ть (imperf. only) (23)
adult взро́слый (23)
advance, in зара́нее (23)
advertisement объявле́ние (8)
advice сове́т (9)
to advise сове́товать, по- (*21*)
affair де́ло (14)
afraid of, to be боя́ться (imperf. only) (+ *gen.*) (*19*)
Africa А́фрика (11)
after по́сле (+ *gen.*) (*10*); **(at the end of a period of time)** через (+ *acc.*) (*18*); **(afterwards)** пото́м, по́сле (11)
afternoon, in the днём (11); (*adj.*) дневно́й (26); **Good a.!** До́брый де́нь!
again опя́ть (14); ещё ра́з; **(anew)** сно́ва (26)
against (opposed to) про́тив (+ *gen.*) (21)
age, old ста́рость (*f.*) (18); **What is your a.?** Ско́лько ва́м ле́т?
ago (тому́) наза́д (16)
to agree: I a. with you. Я́ с ва́ми согла́сен (*23*).
air во́здух (12)
airplane самолёт (24)

alarm clock будильник (24); **to set an a. c. for . . .** (по)ставить будильник на (+ *acc.*) (24)
alike (in the same way) одинаково (19)
all весь (*12*); **(everyone)** все (*8, 20*); **(everything)** всё (*7, 14*); **a. (everything) that . . .** всё, что . . . (*7*); **a. the** весь, це́лый (6); **not at a.** совсе́м не (не́т) (11); **a. the same** всё-таки (19); **in a.** всего́; **a. day (long)** весь де́нь (7); **a. night (long)** всю но́чь (7); **a. right** хорошо́ (3), ла́дно (21); **first of a.** ра́ньше/пре́жде всего́ (25); **best of a.** лу́чше всего́ (все́х) (25). **That's a.** Во́т и всё! (25)
almost почти́ (8)
alone оди́н (*8, 20*)
along (the street, river, etc.) по (+ *dat.*) (*17*); **to take a.** взя́ть с собо́й (22)
already уже́ (3, 7)
also и (*7*); то́же (3, *17*); та́кже (*17*)
although хотя́ (и) (*10*)
always всегда́ (5)
am, *see* **be**
America Аме́рика (5)
American (*adj.*) америка́нский (6)
American, an америка́н.ец, *f.* -ка (*20*)
among ме́жду (+ *instr.*) (*19*)
amusing заба́вный (26)
and и (2, *3*); а (*3*)
anecdote анекдо́т (16)
angel а́нгел (18)
angry, to get серди́ться, рас- (*22*)
animal живо́тное (23)
announcement объявле́ние (8)
another друго́й (13); **(in addition)** ещё (*10*); **one a.** дру́г дру́га (*13*)
answer отве́т (9); **to a.** отвеча́ть (9), отве́тить (*15*)
any како́й-нибудь (*22*), любо́й (21)
anyone, anybody кто́-нибудь (*22*); **not . . . a.** никто́ не (*8, 10*)
anything что́-нибудь (*22*); **not . . . a.** ничего́ не (*8, 10*)
anywhere где́-нибудь (*22*); **(go)** куда́-нибудь (*22*); **not . . . a.** нигде́ не (*8*); **not (go) a.** никуда́ не
apartment кварти́ра (5)
apparent(ly) ви́дно (25)
to appear (seem) каза́ться, по- (*19*)
appetite аппети́т (11)
apple я́блоко (*22*)
to approach (on foot) подходи́ть, подойти́ к (+ *dat.*) (*22*); **(not on foot)** подъезжа́ть, подъе́хать к (+ *dat.*) (*22*)
approximately о́коло (+ *gen.*) (*26*)
April апре́ль (*m.*) (23)
apropos кста́ти (21)
are, *see* **be**
to argue спо́рить, по- (13)
argument спор (13)
arm рука́ (2)
armchair кре́сло (6)
around вокру́г (+ *gen.*) (*16*); **(with numerals)** о́коло (+ *gen.*) (*26*); **to walk a. town** ходи́ть по го́роду (*17*)
arrival (on foot) прихо́д; **(not on foot)** прие́зд (26)
to arrive (on foot) приходи́ть, прийти́ (18); **(not on foot)** приезжа́ть, прие́хать (*18*); **(flying)** прилета́ть, прилете́ть (*24*)
article статья́ (5)
artist (performer) арти́ст, *f.* -ка (25)
as как (4); **(because)** та́к как (12); **as soon as** как то́лько (14); **as . . . as** та́к же . . . как (27); **as if** как бу́дто (бы) (27)
ashamed: I am a. Мне́ сты́дно (24).
Asia А́зия (11)
to ask спра́шивать (8), спроси́ть (*15*); **to a. for** проси́ть, по- (*18*); **to a. a question** задава́ть/зада́ть вопро́с (*13*)
asleep, to fall засыпа́ть, засну́ть (19)
assemble (*trans.*) собира́ть, собра́ть (*19*); (*intrans.*) собира́ться, собра́ться (*19*)
to assign задава́ть (*13*), зада́ть (*24*)
assignment зада́ние (13)
at в (+ *loc.*) (*5*); на (+ *loc.*) (*5, 12*); у (+ *gen.*) (*10*); **(near)** у (+ *gen.*) (*22*); **a. the house of (a.—'s)** у (+ *gen.*) (*10*); **a. home** до́ма (2); **a. once** сейча́с же (14), сра́зу (21); **a. last** наконе́ц (14); **a. that time** в то́ вре́мя (17), тогда́ (10); **a. one o'clock** в ча́с (*17*); **(a. a given time of day—*see 26*)**
athlete спортсме́н (25)
attention внима́ние (13)
attentive внима́тельный (19)
auditorium аудито́рия (13)
August а́вгуст (23)

aunt тётя (19)
author áвтор (9)
automobile автомоби́ль (*m.*) (6), маши́на (12); **by a.** на автомоби́ле, на маши́не (17)
autumn óсень (11); (*adj.*) осе́нний; **in a.** óсенью (11)
to awake (*trans.*) буди́ть, раз- (*19*); (*intrans.*) просыпáться, проснýться (*19*)
awful(ly) ужáсно (13)

back (in return) обрáтно (17); **(of a person)** спинá (23)
bad плохóй (плóхо) (5, 6); **not b.** неплóхо; **It's too b. that ....** Жáль, что ... (6).
badly плóхо (5); **not b.** неплóхо
bag сýмка (22)
bank банк (12); **(of a river, etc.)** бéрег (12)
bath вáнна (21); **to take a b.** принимáть/приня́ть вáнну (21)
bathroom вáнная (10)
to be *usually not translated in present tense, see 2; past, see 7; future, see 17;* **there is, there are (pointing)** вот (*2*), **(not pointing)** есть (*10*); **there is (are) not** нет (+ *gen.*) (*10*); **to b. (often, sometimes)** бывáть (imperf.) (*20*)
to bear переноси́ть, перенести́ (*27*)
beard боротá (20)
beautiful краси́вый (6)
beauty красотá (26)
because потомý что (4)
to become станови́ться, стать (+ *instr.*) (*21*)
bed кровáть (*f.*) (10), постéль (*f.*) (18); **to go to b.** ложи́ться/лéчь спáть (*21*)
bedroom спáльня (10)
beefsteak бифштéкс (18)
beer пи́во (17)
before до (+ *gen.*) (*10, 19*); перед (+ *instr.*) (*19*); **(earlier)** рáньше (12), прéжде (25)
to beg for проси́ть, по- (*18*)
to begin (*trans.*) начинáть (8), начáть (*15*); (*intrans.*) начинáться, начáться (*19*); **It began to rain.** Начался́ дóждь (23).
beginning начáло (7); **in/at the b. (first)** сначáла (11); **in/at the b. of** в начáле (+ *gen.*) (7)
behind за (+ *instr.*) (*19*); (+ *acc.*) (*27*)
being бýдучи (*27*)
to believe вéрить, по- (+ *dat.*) (*14*)
bell звонóк (3, 19)
beneath под (+ *instr.*) (*19*); (+ *acc.*) (*24*)
besides (*prep.*) крóме (+ *gen.*) (10); (*adv.*) крóме тогó (23)
best (сáмый) лýчший (*25*); **the b. thing** сáмое лýчшее (25); **b. of all** лýчше всегó (всéх) (*25*)
better лýчший (*25*); лýчше (23, *25*); **I feel b.** Мнé лýчше (23).
between мéжду (+ *instr.*) (*19*)
beyond за (+ *instr.*) (*19*); (+ *acc.*) (*24*)
big большóй (6)
bigger бóльший (*25*); бóльше (*25*)
bird пти́ца (16)
birth рождéние (23)
birthday дéнь рождéния (23); **for (on) one's b.** на рождéние
black чёрный (6)
blackboard доскá (2)
blond(e) блонди́н, *f.* -ка (8)
blouse блýзка (13)
blue си́ний (6)
book кни́га (2)
bookcase пóлка (2), кни́жная пóлка (10)
bookstore кни́жный магази́н (10)
bored: I am b. Мнé скýчно (8).
boring скýчный (8)
born, to be рождáться, роди́ться (*23*)
borsch борщ (11)
Boston Бостóн (5)
both óба, óбе (*26*); **b. . . . and** и . . . и (4)
bottle буты́лка (11)
boundary грани́ца (13)
bouquet букéт (22)
boy мáльчик (13)
bread хлеб (7)
breakfast зáвтрак (11); **to have b.** зáвтракать (11), по- (17)
bridge мост; **on the b.** на мостý (12)
brief корóткий (кóротко) (12)
briefcase портфéль (*m.*) (22)
bright свéтлый (светлó) (7)
to bring, *see 22*
broad широ́кий (широкó) (8)
broader ши́ре (*25*)
brother брат (4, *20*)
brunet(te) брюнéт, *f.* -ка (8)

buffet буфе́т (26)
to build стро́ить, по- (*27*)
building зда́ние (12)
bus авто́бус (17); **by b.** на авто́бусе
business де́ло, дела́ (*pl.*) (14); **on b.** по де́лу (24), по дела́м
busy занято́й, за́нят (22, *23*)
but но (*5*); а (*4*); **(except)** кро́ме (+ *gen.*) (10)
butcher мясни́к (19)
butter ма́сло (17)
to buy покупа́ть (*8*), купи́ть (*16*)
by *instr. case* (*11*); **(near)** у (+ *gen.*) (*22*); **(past)** ми́мо (+ *gen.*) (*22*); **(by vehicle)** на (+ *loc.*) (*17*); **by (phone, radio, etc.)** по (+ *dat.*)

to call (by phone) звони́ть (*9*), по- (+ *dat.*) (*15*); **to c. on (for)** заходи́ть, зайти́ (*22*); **(to name)** звать, на- (*26*)
calm споко́йный (24)
camera фотоаппара́т (22)
can мочь (*10*), с- (*21*); **one c.** мо́жно (*21*); **one cannot** нельзя́ (*21*); **One can't help but . . . .** Нельзя́ не (+ *inf.*). **I can't help but . . . .** Я́ не могу́ не (+ *inf.*).
candy конфе́ты (*f. pl.*); **(a piece)** конфе́та (20)
capital столи́ца (7)
car автомоби́ль (*m.*) (6), маши́на (12); **(railway) c.** ваго́н (24); **by c.** на автомоби́ле, на маши́не (17)
card ка́рта (5); **to play cards** игра́ть в ка́рты (14)
care: I don't c. Мне́ всё равно́ (10).
carpet ковёр (10)
to carry, *see 22*
case слу́чай (20)
cat ко́шка (16)
to catch лови́ть (imperf.) (*27*), пойма́ть (perf.)
cattle скот (*collect.*) (23)
Caucasus Кавка́з (11); **in the C.** на Кавка́зе (12)
ceiling потоло́к (2)
to celebrate пра́здновать (imperf.) (26)
celebrated знамени́тый (13)
celebrity знамени́тость (*f.*) (25)
center центр (7)
century век (*nom. pl.* -а́) (21)
certain (sure) уве́рен/ный (18, *23*) **c. of** уве́рен в (+ *loc.*) (*23*); **a c.** оди́н (8), како́й-то (*22*); **c. (ones)** не́которые (*19*)
chair стул (2); **(armchair)** кре́сло (6)
chalk мел (11)
chance, by случа́йно (19)
to change (*intrans.*) изменя́ться, измени́ться (*21*)
chapter глава́ (14)
character хара́ктер (10)
charming ми́лый (9)
cheap дешёвый (дёшево) (7)
cheaper деше́вле (*25*)
cheerful весёлый (ве́село) (16)
cheese сыр (7, *12*)
chemist хи́мик (14)
chess ша́хматы (*pl. only*); **to play c.** игра́ть в ша́хматы (20)
chief (*adj.*) гла́вный (13); (*noun*) нача́льник (9)
child ребёнок (*pl.*, *see* **children**) (13)
childhood де́тство (27)
children де́ти (*13*)
China Кита́й (11)
chocolate шокола́д (21, *12*)
choice вы́бор (13)
Christian name и́мя (*n.*) (*7*, *12*, *20*)
church це́рковь (*f.*) (*18*)
cigarette папиро́са (15)
citizen граждани́н, *f.* гражда́нка (*11*, *12*, *20*)
city го́род (*nom. pl.* -а́) (3); (*adj.*) городско́й (21)
class класс (2); уро́к (3)
classroom класс (2)
clean чи́стый (15); **cleaner** чи́ще (*25*)
to clean чи́стить, по- (*24*); **to c. up (off)** убира́ть, убра́ть (*24*)
clear я́сный (18)
climate кли́мат (12)
clock часы́ (*pl.*) (17)
close бли́зко (5); **c. to** бли́зко от (+ *gen.*) (25); **closer** бли́же; **c. to** бли́же к (+ *dat.*) (*25*)
to close (*trans.*) закрыва́ть (8), закры́ть (*15*); (*intrans.*) закрыва́ться, закры́ться (*19*)
closed закры́т/ый (*26*)
closet шкаф (24); **in the c.** в шкафу́
clothing оде́жда (24)

cloud óблако (27); **storm c.** тýча (19)
club клуб (12)
coast бéрег (*nom. pl.* -á) (12); **on the c.** на берегý (12)
coat (overcoat) пальтó (*n. indecl.*) (*12*); **(jacket)** пиджáк (13)
coffee кóфе (*m. indecl.*) (*11*)
coffee-pot кофéйник (24)
cold холóдный (хóлодно); (*noun*) хóлод (21); **It is c.** Хóлодно (6). **I am c.** Мнé хóлодно (9).
to collect (*trans.*) собирáть, собрáть (*19*); (*intrans.*) собирáться, собрáться (*19*)
collective farm колхóз (17); (*adj.*) колхóзный
collective farmer колхóзн.ик, *f.* -ица
color цвет (*nom. pl.* -а) (7). **What c. is . . . ?** Какóго цвéта (+ *nom.*) (7)
to come (on foot) приходи́ть, прийти́ (*18*); **(not on foot)** приезжáть, приéхать (*18*); **to c. in, out, up to, etc.** (*see 22*); **to c. back,** *see* **return** (*intrans.*)
comfortable удóбный (7); **I am c.** Мнé удóбно (7).
common (mutual) óбщий (20)
company óбщество (20)
to complain жáловаться, по- (*23*)
completely совсéм (11); совершéнно (23)
compliment комплимéнт; **Thanks for the compliment!** Спаси́бо за комплимéнт! (8)
composition сочинéние (5)
comrade товáрищ (11)
concerning о, об, обо (+ *loc.*) (*5, 12*); про (+ *acc.*) (21)
concert концéрт (5); **at the c.** на концéрте (5)
condition услóвие (27)
connection связь (*f.*) (21)
to consider считáть (imperf.) (*17*)
to consult совéтоваться с (+ *instr.*) (*21*), по- (*21*)
contemporary совремéнный (20)
to continue продолжáть (imperf.) (16)
convenient удóбный (7)
convention съезд (20)
conversation разговóр (4)
to converse разговáривать (imperf.) (11)
to cook готóвить (*13*), с-
cool: It's cool. Прохлáдно (12). Свежó (6).
copeck копéйка (*26*)
corner ýгол (12); **in the c.** в углý; **on the c.** на углý
correct (of things) прáвильный (18)
correspondent корреспондéнт, *f.* -ка (8)
corridor коридóр (16)
to cost стóить (imperf.) (*16*)
cosy уютный (16)
cottage (summer) дáча (12); **at the c.** на дáче
couch дивáн (11)
could, *see* **can**
council, counsel совéт (9)
to count считáть (imperf.) (17)
country (nation) странá (7); **country(side)** дерéвня (6); **to go to the country** éздить/éхать/поéхать в дерéвню/на дáчу/зá город (17)
couple пáра (13)
course, of конéчно (5)
court двор (16)
cousin (male) двою́родный брáт; **(female)** двою́родная сестрá (27)
cow корóва (23)
Crimea Крым; **in the C.** в Крымý (12)
to cross переходи́ть, перейти́ (*22*)
crowd толпá (22)
cry крик (21)
to cry (out) кричáть, кри́кнуть (*21*); **(to weep)** плáкать (imperf.) (*21*)
culture культýра (20)
cultured, cultural культýрный (20)
cup чáшка (10)
cupboard шкаф, (24); буфéт; **in the c.** в шкафý
customer покупáтель, *f.* -ница (13)
to cut рéзать (imperf.) (*19*)

daddy пáпа
daily дневнóй (26)
dance тáнец (21)
to dance танцевáть, по- (*21*)
danger опáсность (*f.*) (27)
dangerous опáсный (17)
dark тёмный (темнó) (7); **It is d.** Темнó (7).
date числó; **What is the d. today?** Какóе сегóдня числó? (*26*)

daughter дочь (4, *12*, *20*)
day день (6); **all d. (long)** весь де́нь (7); **in the daytime** днём (11); **d. off** выходно́й де́нь (24); **d. after tomorrow** послеза́втра (17); **d. before yesterday** позавчера́ (18), тре́тьего дня́ (21). **Good d.! (greeting)** До́брый де́нь! **What d. is it today?** Како́й сего́дня де́нь?
daydream мечта́ (27)
daytime, in the днём (11)
daytime (*adj.*) дневно́й (26)
deal, a great мно́го (+ *gen.*) (*5*)
dear дорого́й (до́рого) (7); **dearer** доро́же (*25*)
death смерть (*f.*) (12)
debt долг (25)
December дека́брь (*m.*) (23)
to decide реша́ть, реши́ть (*17*)
deep глубо́кий (13); **deeper** глу́бже (*25*)
defense защи́та (27)
delicious вку́сный (11)
demand спрос, **d. for** спро́с на (+ *acc.*) (27)
department отде́л (13); **d. store** универса́льный магази́н (универма́г) (13)
departure (on foot) ухо́д (27)
to describe опи́сывать, описа́ть (*26*)
desk стол (2), пи́сьменный сто́л (10)
to destroy разруша́ть, разру́шить (*27*)
devil чёрт (25)
dictionary слова́рь (4)
to die умира́ть, умере́ть (*21*)
different друго́й (13); **(various)** ра́зный (13)
differently ина́че; по-друго́му (21)
difficult тру́дный (6)
difficulty, with с трудо́м (11)
diligent приле́жный (10)
to dine обе́дать (11), по- (17)
dining-room столо́вая (10)
dinner обе́д (10); **at d.** за обе́дом; **to (for) d.** к обе́ду (18); **to have d.,** *see* **to dine**
diplomat диплома́т (11)
direct(ly) пря́мо (17)
director дире́ктор (*nom. pl.* -а́) (9), нача́льник (9)
dirty гря́зный (15)
discovery откры́тие (14)
to discuss говори́ть о (+ *loc.*) (5, 8), по- (25)
dish таре́лка (13); **dishes** посу́да (*collect.*) (13)
disorder беспоря́док (24)
displeased, dissatisfied недово́лен (*10*)
disposition хара́ктер (10)
division отде́л (13)
to do де́лать (5, 8), с- (14)
doctor до́ктор (*nom. pl.* -а́) (4) врач (16)
dog соба́ка (10)
dollar до́ллар (15)
Don Дон (*12*); **on the D.** на Дону́
door дверь (*f.*) (7, *13*); **out of doors (static)** на у́лице (7), на дворе́ (24)
down from (off) с (+ *gen.*) (17)
dream сон (*26*); **(daydream)** мечта́ (27); **to have a d.** ви́деть со́н (26); **to daydream** мечта́ть (*imperf.*) (27)
dress пла́тье (6, *20*)
to dress (*trans.*) одева́ть, оде́ть (*19*); (*intrans.*) одева́ться, оде́ться (*19*)
drier су́ше (*25*)
to drink пить (7, *11*), вы́- (*20*)
to drive (= to ride), *see 17, 18*; **to d. (someone),** *see 22*
to drop in to see заходи́ть, зайти́ к (+ *dat.*) (*22*)
drugstore апте́ка (12)
dry сухо́й (су́хо) (24)
dull ску́чный (8)
during во вре́мя (+ *gen.*) (12)
duty долг (*no pl.*) (25)

each ка́ждый (8); **e. other** дру́г дру́га (*13*)
ear у́хо (10, *19*)
early (*adv.*) ра́но (7); (*adj.*) ра́нний (27); **It's e.** Ра́но (7); **earlier** ра́ньше (*12*, *25*)
to earn зараба́тывать, зарабо́тать (27)
easier ле́гче (*25*)
east восто́к; **to the e.** на восто́к; **in the e.** на восто́ке (22)
eastern восто́чный (22)
easy лёгкий (легко́) (6); **It's e. to ....** Легко́ (+ *inf.*) (*8*)
to eat есть (imperf.) (*7*, *8*, *20*), по- (perf.) (*25*), съ- (perf.) (*20*); **to e. breakfast, lunch, supper,** *see* **breakfast, lunch, supper**; **to e. dinner,** *see* **dine.**
education образова́ние (23)
eight во́семь (*17*, *26*)

eighteen восемна́дцать (*17, 26*)
eighth восьмо́й (18)
eighty во́семьдесят (*21, 26*)
either . . . or и́ли . . . и́ли (5)
elder ста́рший (*25*)
eldest (са́мый) ста́рший (8, *25*)
elephant слон (21)
elevator лифт (21)
eleven оди́ннадцать (*17, 26*)
else: who e.? кто́ ещё? **what e.?** что́ ещё? **or e.** а то́
empty пусто́й (пу́сто) (24)
end коне́ц (7); **at the e. of** в конце́ (+ *gen.*) (7); **in the e., in the final analysis,** в конце́ концо́в
to end (*trans.*) конча́ть (8), ко́нчить (*15*); (*intrans.*) конча́ться, ко́нчиться (19)
to endure переноси́ть, перенести́ (*27*)
enemy враг (27)
engineer инжене́р (9)
England А́нглия (12)
English (*adj.*) англи́йский (10); **(language)** англи́йский язы́к; **(in) E.** по-англи́йски (*5*); **the E.** англича́не (*20*)
Englishman англича́нин (*20*)
Englishwoman англича́нка (*20*)
enough дово́льно (19), доста́точно (25)
to enter (on foot) входи́ть, войти́ в (+ *acc.*); (*22*); **(not on foot)** въезжа́ть, въе́хать в (+ *acc.*) (*22*); **(enroll in)** поступа́ть, поступи́ть в/на (+ *acc.*) (19)
entertaining заба́вный (26)
entirely совсе́м (11), соверше́нно (23)
equally одина́ково (19)
error оши́бка (14)
especially осо́бенно (12)
essential необходи́мый (27)
etc. и т. д. (и так да́лее) (21)
Europe Евро́па (5)
European европе́йский (7)
even да́же (5), и (7)
evening ве́чер (*nom. pl.* -а́) (7); **in the e.** ве́чером (11); **e. party** вечери́нка (8); (*adj.*) вече́рний (15); ве́чер (7), **Good e.!** До́брый ве́чер!
ever (in questions) когда́-нибудь (*22*), когда́-либо (25); **not e.** никогда́ не (*8*)
every ка́ждый (8); все (*8, 20*)
everybody, everyone все (*8, 20*); **e. who** все́, кто . . .
everything всё; **e. that** всё, что . . . (7)
everywhere везде́ (11)
evident(ly) ви́дно (25)
evil (*adj.*) злой (21)
exactly то́чно (21); **(with numerals)** ро́вно (16, *21*)
examination экза́мен (5); **to take an e.** держа́ть экза́мен (13); **to pass an e.** вы́держать экза́мен; **to fail an e.** провали́ться на экза́мене (19)
example, for наприме́р (8)
excellent отли́чный (18); **(fine)** прекра́сный (7)
except кро́ме (+ *gen.*) (10)
to excuse извиня́ть, извини́ть (*18*); **E. me!** Извини́те! (18). Прости́те! (4)
exercise упражне́ние (9)
exit вы́ход (27)
expensive дорого́й (до́рого) (7); **more e.** доро́же (*25*)
to explain объясня́ть (8), объясни́ть (*15*)
explanation объясне́ние (13)
expression выраже́ние (13)
eye глаз (*nom. pl.* -а́; *gen. pl.* глаз) (3)

face лицо́ (20)
fact факт; **in f.** действи́тельно
factory заво́д; **at the f.** на заво́де (12); (*adj.*) заводско́й (14)
to fail прова́ливаться, провали́ться; **to f. an exam** провали́ться на экза́мене (19)
fairly (rather) дово́льно (10)
fairy-tale ска́зка (24)
fall (autumn) о́сень; **in f.** о́сенью (11); (*adj.*) осе́нний
to fall па́дать, упа́сть (*24*); **to f. asleep** засыпа́ть, засну́ть (*19*)
falsehood непра́вда (5)
familiar знако́м/ый (20)
family семья́ (9, *20*); (*adj.*) семе́йный (20); **f. name** фами́лия; **What is your f. name?** Ка́к ва́ша фами́лия? (4)
famous знамени́тый (13)
far (away) далеко́; **f. from** далеко́ от (+ *gen.*); **not f. (away)** недалеко́ (6);

so f. (to now, up to here) до сих пóр (21); **from f.** издалекá (21), и́здали (25)
farther дáльше (*25*)
fashion мóда (13)
fast бы́стрый (8); **The clock is f.** Часы́ спешáт (17).
fat тóлстый (8)
father отéц (4, *7*)
fatherland рóдина (27)
fatter тóлще (*25*)
favorite люби́мый (12)
to fear боя́ться (imperf.) (*19*)
February феврáль (*m.*) (23)
to feel—often expressed by an impersonal construction + *dat.*, (*see 9, 23*); (*trans.*) чу́вствовать, по- (*23*); (*intrans.*) чу́вствовать себя́ (imperf.); **How do you f.?** Кáк вы́ себя́ чу́вствуете? **I f. well.** Я́ хорошó себя́ чу́вствую (23); **to f. like (want)** хотéть (*10*), за- (*21*); хотéться, за- (*26*)
feeling чу́вство (25)
fellow пáрень (14)
few мáло (+ *gen. pl.*) (*16*); **a f.** нéсколько (+ *gen. pl.*) (*16, 20*); немнóгие (*nom. pl.*) (*20*)
fewer мéньше (+ *gen. pl.*) (*25*)
field пóле (4)
fifteen пятнáдцать (*17, 26*)
fifth пя́тый (18)
fifty пятьдеся́т (*21, 26*)
film фильм (12)
finally наконéц (14)
to find находи́ть, найти́ (*22*); **to f. out, learn** узнавáть, узнáть (*21*)
fine хорóший (хорошó) (6); прекрáсный (7); слáвный (26); **(delicate, thin)** тóнкий (13)
finger пáлец (11)
to finish (*trans.*) кончáть (8), кóнчить (*15*); (*intrans.*) кончáться, кóнчиться (*19*)
firm твёрдый (19)
first пéрвый (6); **at f.** сначáла (11); **f. name** и́мя (*n.*) (7, *12, 20*); **What is your f. name?** Кáк вáше и́мя? (7); **the f. time** пéрвый рáз (16); **for the f. time** в пéрвый рáз (16); **in the f. place** во-пéрвых (20)
fish ры́ба (9)
five пять (*16, 26*)
to float, *see 24*
floor пол (2, *12*); **(story)** этáж (18)
flower цвет.óк (*nom. pl.*, -ы́) (*19*)
fluently свобóдно (23)
to fly, f. in, out, away, past, etc., *see 24, 27*
folk (*adj.*) нарóдный (21)
following слéдующий (27)
fond of, to be люби́ть (imperf., *11, 19*)
food едá (20)
fool дурáк, *f.* ду́ра (26)
foolish глу́пый (9)
foot ногá (10); **on f.** пешкóм (17)
football футбóл; **at a f. game** на футбóле (5); **to play f.** игрáть в футбóл
for (f. the sake of) для (+ *gen.*) (*16*); **(in exchange f.)** за (+ *acc.*) (*16*); **(a period of time)** *simple acc.* (*18*), на (+ *acc.*) (*18*); **(= to get)** за (+ *instr.*) (*17*)
forbidden, it is нельзя́ (+ *inf.*) (*20*)
force си́ла (25)
foreign инострáнный (20)
foreigner инострáн.ец, *f.* -ка (20)
to foresee предви́деть (imperf.) (*27*)
forest лес (*nom. pl.* -á) (*12, 13*); **in the f.** в лесу́
to foretell предскáзывать, предсказáть (*27*)
to forget забывáть, забы́ть (*16*)
fork ви́лка (16)
former бы́вший (27)
formerly рáньше (12), прéжде (25)
fortunate счастли́вый (13)
fortunately к счáстью (23)
forty сóрок (*21, 26*)
to found оснóвывать, основáть (*18*)
four четы́ре (*10, 26*)
fourth четвёртый (18)
fourteen четы́рнадцать (*17, 26*)
France Фрáнция (12)
free свобóдный (*23*)
freedom свобóда (23)
French (*adj.*) францу́зский (7); **(language)** францу́зский язы́к; **(in) F.** пофранцу́зски; **the F.** францу́зы (20)
Frenchman францу́з (20)
Frenchwoman францу́женка (20)
frequently чáсто (9); **more f.** чáще (*25*)

fresh свéжий (свежó) (6)
Friday пя́тница (18)
friend прия́тель, *f.* -ница (7); друг (8, *20*), *f.* подрýга (8)
frightening стрáшный (27)
from (a person) от (+ *gen.*) (*15, 17*); **(out of)** из (+ *gen.*) (*15, 17*); **down f.** с (+ *gen.*) (*17*); **f. where** откýда (*15, 17*); **f. the house of** от (+ *gen.*) (*17*)
front of, in перед (+ *instr.*) (19)
frontier грани́ца (13)
fruit, a фрукт; **fruit** (*collect.*) фрýкты (*pl.*) (*17*); (*adj.*) фруктóвый
full пóлный (*24*)
fun весéлье; **to make f. of** смея́ться (imperf.) над (+ *instr.*) (*19*)
funny смешнóй (19)
furniture мéбель (*f. collect.*) (10)
further дáльше (*25*)
future (*adj.*) бýдущий (*14*); **the f.** бýдущее (*25*); **in the near f.** в ближáйшем бýдущем (25)

game (contest) матч (22); пáртия (14)
garage гарáж (6)
garden сад (*12*); **in the g.** в садý
gas газ (24)
gay весёлый (вéсело) (16)
general (*adj.*) óбщий (20); **in g.** вообщé (20)
genius, a гéний (9)
gentleman господи́н (*11, 20*)
German (*adj.*) немéцкий (20); **G. language** немéцкий язы́к; **in G.** по-немéцки (20); **a G.** нéмец, *f.* нéмка (20)
Germany Гермáния (20)
gesture жест (11)
to get (receive) получáть, получи́ть (*13*); **(arrive on foot)** приходи́ть, прийти́ (*21*); **(not on foot)** приезжáть, приéхать (*21*); **to g. up** вставáть, встать (*16*); **(to become)** станови́ться, стать (+ *instr.*) (*21*); **to g. dressed** одевáться, одéться (*19*); **to g. undressed** раздевáться (*19*); **to g. used** привыкáть, привы́кнуть (*21*)
gift подáрок (9)
girl дéвушка (8); **(little) g.** дéвочка (13)
to give давáть (*9*), дать (*15*); **to g. back,** *see* **return** (*trans.*); **to g. up (doing something)** переставáть, перестáть (+ *inf.*) (*27*)
glad рад (*51*); **I'm g. of that.** Я́ э́тому рáд.
glass (tumbler) стакáн (7)
to go, *see 17, 18, 22*; **let's g.** идём, пойдём (*23*); **to g. away,** *see 18*; **to g. in, out, up to, away, through, past, across,** *see 22*; **to g. back,** *see* **return** (*intrans.*); **to g. on, continue** продолжáть (+ *inf.*) (imperf.) (16); **to g. to bed** ложи́ться/лéчь спáть (*21*)
God Бог (18). **Thank God!** Слáва Бóгу! (18)
gold(en) золотóй (26)
good хорóший (хорошó) (4, 6); **It's g. that . . . .** Хорошó, что . . . . (4). **That's g.** Э́то хорошó (4). **G. morning!** Дóброе ýтро! (7). **G. night!** Спокóйной нóчи! (21). **G. for you (him, her, etc.)!** Молодéц! (23); **g.-hearted** дóбрый (21)
good-bye до свидáния (3), прощáй(те)! **g. till tomorrow** до зáвтра (19)
grade (mark) отмéтка (13)
grammar граммáтика (2)
granddaughter внýчка (22)
grandfather дед, дéдушка (*20*)
grandmother бáбушка (17)
grandson внук (22)
grass травá (17)
grateful благодáрный (*23*)
great большóй (6); вели́кий (18); **a g. deal** мнóго (+ *gen.*) (*5*); **greater** бóльший, бóльше (*25*)
green зелёный (12)
greeting(s) привéт (9); **to give (someone) g. from . . .** передáть п. от . . . (+ *gen.*)
ground земля́ (23)
to grow (*intrans.*) расти́ (imperf.) (*21*); **(to become)** станови́ться, стать (*21*)
guest гость (*m.*) (4)
guide гид (12)

habit привы́чка (23)
half полови́на (14, *26*); пол (*26*); **h. an hour** полчасá (22); **one and a h.** полторá (*26*); **five and a h.** пять с полови́ной (25)
hall коридóр (16); **(vestibule)** перéдняя (24)

ham ветчина́ (17)
hand рука́ (2); **by the h.** за́ руку (22)
handkerchief плато́к (22)
handsome краси́вый (6)
to hang (*intrans.*) висе́ть (imperf.) (*27*)
to happen случа́ться, случи́ться (*20*); **to h. sometimes/often** быва́ть (imperf.) (*20*)
happy счастли́вый (13, *23*)
hard тру́дный (6); **(firm)** твёрдый (19); **h. life** тяжёлая жи́знь (20); **It is h. to ....** Тру́дно (+ *inf.*) (*8*)
hardly: h. anyone почти́ никто́ (6); **h. anything** почти́ ничего́ (6)
hard-working приле́жный (10)
hat шля́па (6)
to hate ненави́деть (imperf.) (*14*)
to have у (+ *gen.*) (*10*); **I h. ...** У меня́ (е́сть) (+ *nom.*) (*10*). **I h. no ...** У меня́ не́т (+ *gen.*) (*10*). **I h. to ...** Я́ до́лжен (+ *inf.*) (*8*); Мне́ на́до (ну́жно) (+ *inf.*) (*10*); **to h. breakfast, lunch, supper,** *see* **breakfast, lunch, supper; to h. dinner,** *see* **dine; to h. a talk** поговори́ть (perf.) (*25*); **to h. a nap** поспа́ть (perf.) (*25*)
he он (*2, 12*)
head голова́ (3, 10); **(chief)** глава́
headache: I have a h. У меня́ боли́т голова́ (23).
health здоро́вье (21); **How is your h.?** Ка́к ва́ше здоро́вье? (21)
healthy здоро́в/ый (*23*)
to hear слы́шать (*11*), у- (*21*)
heart се́рдце (*23*)
heat жара́ (21)
heaven не́бо (16)
heavy тяжёлый (тяжело́) (20)
hello здра́вствуй(те) (*4*); **(on the telephone)** алло́ (11)
help по́мощь (*f.*) (10)
to help помога́ть (*9*), помо́чь (*18*) (+ *dat.*); **One can't h. but ...** Нельзя́ не (+ *inf.*). **I can't h. but ...** Я́ не могу́ не (+ *inf.*) (11).
her, hers её (*7*)
here тут (2), здесь (4); **h. is (are)** вот (*2*); **(to) h., hither** сюда́ (*17*); **from h.** отсю́да (*17*)
hero геро́й (5)
heroine герои́ня (5)
herself, *see* **self**
high высо́кий (10); **higher** вы́ше (*25*)
himself, *see* **self**
his его́ (*7*)
history исто́рия (9)
historian исто́рик (11)
to hold держа́ть (imperf.) (*11*)
holiday пра́здник (9); **(day off)** выходно́й де́нь (24); **for the holidays** на пра́здники (25); **school holidays** кани́кулы (pl.) (*23*)
home дом (*nom. pl.* -а́) (2); **at h.** до́ма (2); **(to) h., homewards** домо́й (*17*); **from h.** и́з дому (*17*)
honor честь (*f.*); **in h. of** в че́сть (+ *gen.*) (26)
hope наде́жда (27)
to hope наде́яться (imperf.) (*19*); **to h. for** наде́яться на (+ *acc.*) (19)
horror у́жас (21)
horrible ужа́сный (13)
horse ло́шадь (*f.*) (16, *20*)
hospitable гостеприи́мный (20)
hospital больни́ца (23); го́спиталь (*m.*) (27)
host хозя́ин (11, *20*)
hostess хозя́йка (9)
hot (of weather) жа́ркий (7); **It's h.** Жа́рко (7); **(of objects)** горя́чий (горячо́) (21); **hotter (of weather)** жа́рче (*25*)
hotel гости́ница (7)
hour час (14); **half an h.** полчаса́ (22)
house дом (*nom. pl.* -а́) (2); **at the h. of** у (+ *gen.*) (*10*); **to the h. of** к (+ *dat.*) (*17*); **from the h. of** от (+ *gen.*) (*15*); **to help around the h.** помога́ть по хозя́йству (21)
housewife хозя́йка (9)
how как (3); како́й (*with adjectives in long form*) (6); **h. much, h. many** ско́лько (+ *gen.*) (7, 15); **h. large!** како́й большо́й! (6); **h. long (time)?** ско́лько вре́мени? (12); **H. much is (are) ....** Ско́лько сто́ит (сто́ят)? (16). **H. are you?** Ка́к вы́ пожива́ете? (3)
however зато́ (25)
huge огро́мный (12)
hundred сто (*21, 26*)

hunger го́лод (20)
hungry голо́дный (*23*)
to hurry спеши́ть, по- (*17*); **H. up!** Скоре́й!
to hurt (*intrans.*) боле́ть (imperf.) (*23*)
husband муж (3, *20*)

I я (2)
idea мысль (*f.*) (25), иде́я
identically одина́ково (19)
if е́сли (10, *14*, *24*); **in indirect questions** ли (*22*); **in hypothetical conditions** е́сли бы (*24*)
ill бо́лен (*23*)
illness боле́знь (*f.*) (23)
to imagine (suppose) представля́ть/предста́вить себе́ (*27*)
immediately сра́зу (21), неме́дленно (20)
immense огро́мный (12)
impatience нетерпе́ние (18)
important ва́жный (12)
impossible невозмо́жно (18, *20*); **it is i.** нельзя́ (*20*); невозмо́жно (*20*)
in в (+ *loc.*) (*5*); **with expressions of time,** *see 26*; **in front of** перед (+ *instr.*) (19)
incident слу́чай (20)
incorrectly непра́вильно (19)
inexpensive дешёвый (дёшево) (7)
information изве́стие (27)
infrequently ре́дко (9)
inhabitant жи́тель, *f.* -ница (22)
insane (person) сумасше́дший (25)
instead of вме́сто (+ *gen.*) (23)
instructor инстру́ктор (*nom. pl.* -а́), *f.* -ша (23)
insufficiently недоста́точно (19)
intelligent у́мный (умно́) (9)
interest интере́с (11); **i. in** интере́с к (+ *dat.*)
to interest интересова́ть, за- (*21*); **to be interested in** интересова́ться, за- (+ *instr.*) (*21*)
interesting интере́сный (5, 6)
interpreter перево́дч.ик, *f.* -ица (12)
into в (+ *acc.*) (*17*)
to introduce знако́мить, по- (*20*); **to be introduced** знако́миться, по- (*20*)
invitation приглаше́ние (25)
to invite приглаша́ть, пригласи́ть (*25*)
is, *see* **be**
island о́стров (24)
it э́то (*2*); он, оно́, она́ (*4*); **with impersonals not translated** *see 7, 9*
Italian (*adj.*) италья́нский (12); **I. language** италья́нский язы́к; **in I.** по-италья́нски (12); **(an) I.** италья́н.ец, *f.* -ка (20)
Italy Ита́лия (12)
its его́ (*7*); её (*7*)
itself, *see* **self**

jacket пиджа́к (13)
January янва́рь (*m.*) (23)
Japanese (*adj.*) япо́нский (19)
jazz джаз (9)
joke шу́тка (20)
to joke шути́ть, по- (*20*)
journalist журнали́ст, *f.* -ка (4)
July ию́ль (*m.*) (23)
June ию́нь (*m.*) (23)
just (only) то́лько (4); **(exactly)** ро́вно (16); **have j.** то́лько что (+ *past tense*) (14)

to keep (hold) держа́ть (imperf.) (*11*)
kerchief плато́к (22)
Kiev Ки́ев
to kill убива́ть, уби́ть (*27*)
kilometer киломе́тр (25)
kind ми́лый (9); до́брый (21); любе́зный (*18*, *23*); **Be so k. as to ....** Бу́дьте добры́ (*18*, *23*). Бу́дьте любе́зны (*18*, *23*) (+ *imperative*). **What k. of . . . ?** Како́й . . . ? (6); Что́ э́то за (+ *nom.*)? (20)
king коро́ль (18)
kiss поцелу́й (27)
to kiss целова́ть, по- (*27*)
kitchen ку́хня (4, *20*)
knife нож (16)
knock стук (24)
to knock стуча́ть, по- (*24*)
to know знать (imperf.) (5, 8)
knowledge зна́ние (27)
kolkhoz колхо́з (17)

labor (work) труд (11)
lady да́ма (15); **ladies and gentlemen** господа́ (*20*)
lake о́зеро (*13*)

lamp ла́мпа (2)
land земля́ (23); **(country)** страна́ (7)
landlady хозя́йка (9)
landlord хозя́ин (11, *20*)
language язы́к (12, *20*)
large большо́й (6)
larger бо́льший, бо́льше (*25*)
last после́дний (6); **at l.** наконе́ц (14); **(past)** про́шлый (12); **(in) l. year** в про́шлом году́ (12); **l. name** фами́лия (4); **What is your l. name?** Ка́к ва́ша фами́лия? (4)
late (*adv.*) по́здно (7); (*adj.*) по́здний; **It's l.** По́здно (7). **to be l.** опа́здывать, опозда́ть (*17*, *19*); **later** по́зже (15, *25*), поздне́е; **(afterwards)** пото́м (11), по́сле; **latest** после́дний (6)
to laugh смея́ться (imperf.) (*19*); **to l. at** смея́ться над (+ *instr.*) (*19*)
laughter смех (16)
laundry бельё (24)
to lay down класть (imperf.), положи́ть (perf.) (*24*)
lazy лени́вый (10). **I felt too l. to ....** Мне́ бы́ло ле́нь (+ *inf.*) (18).
leader вождь (*m.*) (12)
leaf лист (13, *20*)
to learn учи́ться, на- (+ *dat.*) (*23*); **(to find out)** узнава́ть, узна́ть (*21*); **(to memorize)** запомина́ть, запо́мнить (*18*)
leave (vacation) о́тпуск (26)
to leave (go away), *see 18, 22*; **to l. behind, l. for someone** оставля́ть, оста́вить (*22*)
lecture ле́кция (12), докла́д (12); **to give a l.** (про)чита́ть ле́кцию (докла́д) (12)
lecturer докла́дч.ик, *f.* -ица (27)
left ле́вый (11); **on the l.** нале́во (12), сле́ва (26); **to the l.** нале́во (12); **to be l.** остава́ться, оста́ться (*25*)
leg нога́ (10)
lemon лимо́н (11)
to lend одáлживать, одолжи́ть (*22*)
Leningrad Ленингра́д (5)
less ме́ньше (+ *gen.*) (*8*); ме́нее (*25*)
lesson уро́к (3); **at the l.** на уро́ке (5)
let пусть, пуска́й; **l. us** дава́й(те) (*25*); **let's go** идём, пойдём (23); **l. me know** да́й(те) мне́ зна́ть (21)
letter письмо́ (4)
library библиоте́ка (5)
to lie, be lying лежа́ть (imperf.) (*11*); **to l. down** ложи́ться (imperf.) (*21*), лечь (perf.) (*21*)
life жизнь (*f.*) (11)
light (*noun*) свет; (*adj.*) **(bright)** све́тлый (светло́) (7); **(not heavy)** лёгкий (легко́) (6); **lighter (not so heavy)** ле́гче (*25*)
likeable ми́лый (9), симпати́чный (20)
like как (4); **(similar to)** похо́ж на (+ *acc.*) (*23*); **l. this (that)** так; **He looks l ....** О́н похо́ж на (+ *acc.*) (*23*).
to like люби́ть (imperf.) (*11*, *19*); нра́виться, по-; **I l. that.** Э́то мне́ нра́вится (*19*). **I would l. to ....** Я́ бы хоте́л (+ *inf.*) (24).
likely вероя́тно (5)
line (of writing) строка́, стро́чка (25)
linen бельё (24)
to listen (to) слу́шать (5, 8), по- (18)
literary литерату́рный (20)
literature литерату́ра (20)
little ма́ленький (6); **l. (of)** ма́ло (+ *gen.*) (*5*); **a l.** немно́го, немно́жко (+ *gen.*) (*20*)
to live жить (imperf.) (5, *9*)
lively весёлый (ве́село) (16)
livestock скот (*collect.*) (23)
living-room гости́ная (10)
located, to be находи́ться (imperf.) (*22*)
London Ло́ндон (5)
lonely одино́кий (18)
long (*adj.*) дли́нный; **a l. while/time** до́лго (11); **for a l. time** до́лго (11), надо́лго (*22*); **l. ago, l. since** давно́ (*7*, *9*, *11*); **not l. ago** неда́вно (7); **how long? (time)** ско́лько вре́мени? (12); **Have you been here l.?** Вы́ давно́ зде́сь? (7). **I haven't written for so l.** Я́ так давно́ не писа́л (9).
to look смотре́ть, по- (*17*); **to l. at** (по) смотре́ть на (+ *acc.*) (*17*); **He looks like ....** О́н похо́ж на (+ *acc.*) (23). **to l. for** иска́ть (imperf.) (*24*)
to lose теря́ть, по- (22)
lot: a lot (of) мно́го (+ *gen.*) (5)
loud гро́мкий (гро́мко) (19); **louder** гро́мче (*25*)
loudspeaker громкоговори́тель (*m.*) (26)

love любо́вь (*f.*) (*12*)
to love люби́ть (imperf.) (*11, 19*)
low ни́зкий (10); **(quiet)** ти́хий (8); **lower** ни́же (*25*); **(quieter)** ти́ше (*25*)
lunch за́втрак (11); **to have l.** за́втракать, по- (17)

machine маши́на (12)
machinist машини́ст, *f.* -ка (14)
mad (person) сумасше́дший (25)
magazine журна́л (3)
mail по́чта (12)
main гла́вный (13)
to make де́лать (5, 8), с- (14)
mama ма́ма (5)
man (person, human being) челове́к (*8, 13, 16*); **(male)** мужчи́на (*20*)
many мно́го (+ *gen. pl.*) (*16*); мно́гие (*nom. pl.*) (*20*); **how m.** ско́лько (+ *gen. pl.*) (*16, 20*); **so m.** так мно́го (+ *gen. pl.*); сто́лько (+ *gen. pl.*) (*16, 20*); **m. thanks** большо́е спаси́бо (10)
map ка́рта (3)
March март (23)
mark (grade) отме́тка (13)
married (of men) жена́т (*26*); **(of women)** за́мужем (*26*)
marvellous чу́дный (17), чуде́сный (19)
mass, a ма́сса (17)
match спи́чка (24); **(sports)** матч (22)
matter де́ло; **What is the m. with you?** Что́ с ва́ми? (23)
mausoleum мавзоле́й (18)
may мочь (imperf.) (*10*); **one m.** мо́жно (*21*); **one m. not** нельзя́ (*21*); **M. I?** Мо́жно (мне́) (+ *inf.*)? (*21*)
May май (23)
maybe мо́жет быть (10)
mean: What does that m.? Что́ э́то зна́чит? (18). **I m. . . .** Я́ хочу́ сказа́ть (14).
meat мя́со (6)
to meet (encounter) встреча́ть, встре́тить (*16*); **to m. (each other)** встреча́ться, встре́титься (*19*); **(to be introduced to each other)** знако́миться, по- (*20*)
meeting собра́ние (12); съезд (20)
memorial па́мятинк (7)
to memorize запомина́ть, запо́мнить (*18*)
memory па́мять (*f.*) (11)
mention: Don't m. it. Не́ за что (10). Не сто́ит благода́рности (18).
merry весёлый (ве́село) (16)
Mexico Ме́ксика (18)
middle (*noun*) середи́на (18); (*adj.*) сре́дний (22); **in the m. of** посреди́ (+ *gen.*) (27)
midnight по́лночь (*f.*) (19)
milk молоко́ (7)
million миллио́н (*26*)
mind: I don't mind. Мне́ всё равно́ (10).
mine мой (*4, 12, 20*)
minute мину́та (18)
mistake оши́бка (14); **to make a m.** (с)де́лать оши́бку (14)
mistaken, to be ошиба́ться, ошиби́ться (*22*)
modern совреме́нный (20)
Monday понеде́льник (18)
money де́ньги (*pl.*) (15)
month ме́сяц (8); **(in) this m.** в э́том ме́сяце (23)
monument па́мятник (7)
moon ме́сяц (8), луна́ (21)
more бо́льше (+ *gen.*) (*8*); бо́лее (*25*); **(in addition)** ещё (*10*); **one m.** ещё оди́н (10); **no m.** бо́льше не (10); **comparative,** *see 25*
morning у́тро (7); **in the m.** у́тром (11); **from m. to evening** с утра́ до ве́чера (25); **Good m.!** До́брое у́тро! (7). (*adj.*) у́тренний (26)
Moscow Москва́ (5); (*adj.*) моско́вский (12)
most са́мый (+ *adj.*) (13, *25*); **m. of all** бо́льше всего́ (все́х) (*25*)
mother мать (4, *12, 20*)
motion picture фильм (12), карти́на; **m. p. house** кино́ (*12*)
mountain гора́ (13)
mournful гру́стный (17)
mouth рот (2)
movie фильм (12), карти́на; **to go to a m.** идти́/пойти́ в кино́
movie-house кино́ (*12*)
Mr. господи́н (*11*)
Mrs. госпожа́ (*11*)
much мно́го (+ *gen.*) (*5, 20*); **how m.** ско́лько (+ *gen.*) (*7, 20*); **so m.** так мно́го (+ *gen.*), сто́лько (+ *gen.*) (*16*); **(with comparatives)** гора́здо (25); **to like very**

m. о́чень люби́ть; **to want very m.** о́чень хоте́ть (10); **How m. is (are) ...?** Ско́лько сто́ит (сто́ят)? (16)
municipal городско́й (21)
museum музе́й (2)
music му́зыка (8)
musician музыка́нт (7)
must до́лжен (*8*); на́до, ну́жно (*9*)
mutual о́бщий (20)
my мой (*4, 12, 20*)
myself, *see* **self**

name (first n.) и́мя (*n.*) (7, *12, 20*); **(last n.)** фами́лия (4); **(of an object)** назва́ние (7); **What is your n.? (first n.)** Ка́к ва́ше и́мя? (7); **(last n.)** Ка́к ва́ша фами́лия? (4); **What is the n. of (an object, book, etc.)?** Ка́к назва́ние (+ *gen.*) (7), Ка́к называ́ется (+ *nom.*)?
to name называ́ть, назва́ть (*18*); **to be named, called (of an object)** называ́ться, назва́ться
to narrate расска́зывать, рассказа́ть (*15*)
narrow у́зкий (8)
narrower у́же (*25*)
nation наро́д (20)
national наро́дный (21), национа́льный
native родно́й; **one's n. town** родно́й го́род (27)
nature приро́да (16)
near (*adv.*) бли́зко (5), ря́дом (11); **n. (to)** бли́зко от (+ *gen.*) (25), ря́дом с (+ *instr.*) (11); (*prep.*) о́коло (+ *gen.*) (16); (*adj.*) бли́зкий; **in the n. future** в ближа́йшем бу́дущем (25); **nearer** бли́же; **n. to** бли́же к (+ *dat.*) (*25*)
necessary ну́жен (*10*); необходи́мый (27); **It is n. to ...** Ну́жно (на́до) (+ *inf.*) (*9*)
necktie га́лстук (24)
need: I need ... Мне́ ну́жен (+ *nom.*) (*10*)
neighbor сосе́д (*nom. pl.* -и) (10, *20*)
neither ... nor ни ... ни (*8*)
nephew племя́нник (22)
never никогда́ (не) (*8*)
nevertheless всё-таки (19)
new но́вый (6); **What's new (with you)?** Что́ (у ва́с) но́вого?
New York Нью-Йо́рк (5)
news но́вость (*f.*), но́вости (*pl.*) (14); изве́стие (27); **That's n.** Э́то но́вость. (14)
newspaper газе́та (4)
next (*adv.*) пото́м (11); (*adj.*) сле́дующий (27); **(future)** бу́дущий (14); **(in the) n. year** в бу́дущем году́ (15); **What n.?** Что́ да́льше? (14); **n. to, n. door to** ря́дом с (+ *instr.*) (11)
nice хоро́ший (хорошо́) (*6*); **(of persons)** ми́лый (9)
niece племя́нница (22)
night ночь (*f.*) (6); **at n.** но́чью (11); **all n. (long)** всю но́чь (6); (*adj.*) ночно́й; **Good n.!** Споко́йной но́чи! (21)
nine де́вять (*17, 26*)
nineteen девятна́дцать (*17, 26*)
ninety девяно́сто (*21, 26*)
ninth девя́тый (18)
no нет (2); (*adj.*) никако́й (не) (*21*); **There is (are) n.** нет (+ *gen.*) (*10*); **n. more** бо́льше не (не́т) (10); **n. longer** уже́ не (не́т); **n. one** никто́ (не) (*8, 10*)
nobody никто́ (не) (*8, 10*)
noise шум (16); **to make n.** шуме́ть (imperf.) (*25*)
noisy шу́мный (16)
noon по́лдень (*m.*) (19)
nor ни (*8*)
normal норма́льный (6)
north се́вер; **to the n.** на се́вер; **in the n.** на се́вере (22)
northern се́верный (22)
nose нос (2, *12*)
not не (2); нет (*at end of sentence*): **Of course n.** Коне́чно не́т. **Why n.?** Почему́ не́т? **n ... but** не ..., а (*4*); **n. at all** совсе́м не (не́т) (11)
to note down запи́сывать (13), записа́ть (*15*)
notes запи́ски (*f. pl.*) (13)
notebook тетра́дь (*f.*) (13)
nothing ничего́ (не) (*8, 10*)
to notice замеча́ть, заме́тить (*22*)
novel рома́н (6)
November ноя́брь (*m.*) (23)
now тепе́рь (2), сейча́с (14); **to n.** до сих по́р (21); пока́ (14)
nowhere нигде́ (не) (*8*); **(going) n.** никуда́ (не) (*17*)

number число́ (26); но́мер (*nom. pl.* -а́) (12); **a n. of** не́сколько (+ *gen. pl.*) (*16, 20*)
nursery де́тская (22)

to obey (*trans.*) слу́шать (5), по- (18)
to obtain получа́ть (13), получи́ть (*15*)
occupation заня́тие (21)
occupied занято́й (22), за́нят (*23*); **to be o. with** занима́ться, заня́ться (+ *instr.*) (*19*)
to occupy занима́ть, заня́ть (*22*)
to occur случа́ться, случи́ться (*20*); происходи́ть, произойти́ (*21*)
o'clock, *see 16, 26*
October октя́брь (*m.*) (23)
of—*genitive case* (*7*); **(about)** о, об, обо (+ *loc.*) (*5, 12*); **o. course** коне́чно (5); **a friend o. his** оди́н его́ дру́г (15); **one o. his friends** оди́н из его́ друзе́й (20)
off (*prep.*) с (+ *gen.*) (*17*)
office конто́ра (9)
officer офице́р (11)
often ча́сто (9); **more o.** ча́ще (*25*); **less o.** ре́же (*25*)
oil ма́сло (17)
old ста́рый (6); **o. age** ста́рость (*f.*) (18); **o.-fashioned** старомо́дный (16); **o. man** стари́к (22); **o. woman** стару́ха (22); **older** ста́рший (8, *25*), ста́рше (*25*); **oldest** ста́рший (8, *25*), са́мый ста́рый (ста́рший) (*25*)
on на (+ *loc.*) (*5*); **with expressions of time**, *see 17*; **(further)** да́льше; **Read o.** Чита́йте да́льше!; **to go o. (continue)** продолжа́ть (+ *inf.*) (16)
onto на (+ *acc.*) (*17*)
once (one time) (оди́н) ра́з (16); **(in the past)** одна́жды (20), когда́-то (*22*)
one оди́н (*8, 12*); *not translated after adjectives—see 6*; **o . . . another** оди́н . . . друго́й (13); **the o. who (which, that)** то́т, кото́рый (7); **o. = you** (*indefinite*)—*2nd pers. sing. verb* (*20*); **o. can (may)** мо́жно (+ *inf.*) (*21*); **o. cannot (may not)** нельзя́ (+ *inf.*) (*21*); **o. must** на́до (ну́жно) (+ *inf.*) (*9*); **o. must (should) not** нельзя́ (+ *inf.*) (*21*); **o.'s own** свой (*9, 12, 20*); **at o. time** одно́ вре́мя; **o. another** дру́г дру́га (*13*); **o. of my friends** оди́н из мои́х друзе́й (20); **no o.** никто́ (*8, 10*)
oneself, *see* **self**
only то́лько (4); **the o. (one)** еди́нственный (27)
open откры́т/ый
to open (*trans.*) открыва́ть (8), откры́ть (*15*); (*intrans.*) открыва́ться, откры́ться (*19*)
opinion мне́ние (23); **in the o. of** по мне́нию (+ *gen.*) (23); **in my o.** по-мо́ему (14); **in your o.** по-ва́шему
opposite про́тив (+ *gen.*) (21)
or и́ли (2)
order поря́док (24); **in o. to/that** чтобы (*24*)
ordinary обы́чный (9), обыкнове́нный (13)
original (*adj.*) оригна́льный (9)
other друго́й (13); **each o.** дру́г дру́га (*13*); **some . . . others** одни́ . . . други́е (13)
otherwise (or else) а то́; **(differently)** ина́че (22); по-друго́му (21)
ought to до́лжен (+ *inf.*) (*8*); до́лжен был бы (+ *inf.*) (*24*)
our, ours наш (*4, 12, 20*)
ourselves, *see* **self**
out of из (+ *gen.*) (*15*)
outside, out of doors (static) на у́лице (7), на дворе́ (24)
over над (+ *instr.*) (*19*); **o. there** там (2); во́н (та́м)
overcoat пальто́ (*n. indecl.*) (*12*)
own: one's o. свой (*9, 12, 20*); **(related, native)** родно́й (*27*); со́бственный

P.M. дня **(in the afternoon)** (16); ве́чера **(in the evening)** (16)
package паке́т (22), посы́лка (22)
page страни́ца (26)
to pain боле́ть (imperf.) (*23*)
pair па́ра (13)
papa па́па (*20*)
paper бума́га (2); **(newspaper)** газе́та (4)
paragraph абза́ц (18)
parcel посы́лка (22)
to pardon извиня́ть, извини́ть (*18*); **p. me** прости́те (4), извини́те (18)
parents роди́тели (*pl.*) (16)
Paris Пари́ж (5)
park парк (6)

part часть (*f.*) (12); **on your p.** с ва́шей стороны́ (18); **(role)** роль (*f.*) (12); **to take p. in** принима́ть уча́стие в (+ *loc.*) (21)
party (evening) ве́чер (7); вечери́нка (8); **political p.** па́ртия (14)
to pass (go by) проходи́ть, пройти́ ми́мо (+ *gen.*) (*22*); **(time)** проводи́ть, провести́ (*23*)
passenger пассажи́р, *f.* -ка (22)
past (by) ми́мо (+ *gen.*) (*22*); **(former)** про́шлый (12); **the p.** про́шлое (24)
patience терпе́ние (18)
patient (sick person) больно́й (23)
patronymic о́тчество (11); **What is your p.?** Ка́к ва́ше о́тчество? (*20*)
to pay плати́ть, за- (*16*); **to p. for** (за)п. за (+ *acc.*) (16)
peace мир (10)
peasant крестья́н.ин, *f.* -ка (*20*)
pen перо́ (2, *20*)
pencil каранда́ш (3)
people лю́ди (13, *16*); **(nation)** наро́д (20)
pepper пе́рец (21)
per в (+ *acc.*) (*17*)
perhaps мо́жет быть (10)
person челове́к (*pl.*, *see* лю́ди) (*8*, *13*, *16*)
personal ли́чный (27)
pessimist пессими́ст, *f.* -ка
photograph фотогра́фия (16)
physician врач (16)
piano роя́ль (*m.*) (6)
picture карти́на (5); **(photo)** фотогра́фия (16)
piece кусо́к (7)
pillow поду́шка (24)
pink ро́зовый (16)
pipe тру́бка (11)
pity: it's a p. жаль (6). **I p. him.** Мне́ его́ (*acc.*) жа́ль. **What a p.!** Как жа́ль! (6)
place ме́сто (11); **at someone's p. (house, etc.)** у (+ *gen.*) (*10*); **to someone's p.** к (+ *dat.*) (*17*); **from someone's p.** от (+ *gen.*) (*17*); **in the first p.** во-пе́рвых (20); **to its (proper) p.** на ме́сто (24); **in its p.** на ме́сте (24); **in p. of** вме́сто (+ *gen.*) (23)
to place, *see 24*
plan план (14)
plant (factory) заво́д (12); **at the p.** на заво́де (12)
plate таре́лка (13)
play (drama) пье́са (8)
to play игра́ть (6), сыгра́ть (perf. trans.) (*14*); **to p. the piano** игра́ть на роя́ле (6); **to p. chess** игра́ть в ша́хматы (20); **to p. cards** игра́ть в ка́рты (14)
pleasant прия́тный (6)
please пожа́луйста (3)
to please нра́виться, по- (*19*) (+ *dat.*)
pleased дово́лен (*11*, *23*)
pleasure удово́льствие (11)
poet поэ́т (16)
poetry поэ́зия (23)
politics поли́тика
poor бе́дный (13); **(bad)** плохо́й (пло́хо) (5, 6)
population населе́ние (25)
porch вера́нда (16)
portrait портре́т (22)
position положе́ние (18)
possible возмо́жно (18, *21*); **it is p. (one can)** мо́жно (*21*); возмо́жно (18, *21*)
post office по́чта (12); **at the p. o.** на по́чте (12)
potato(es) карто́фель (*m.*, *no pl.*) (*11*)
pound фунт (7)
power си́ла (25)
practical практи́ческий (23)
practice пра́ктика (14)
to predict предска́зывать, предсказа́ть (*27*)
to prefer предпочита́ть, предпоче́сть (*18*)
to prepare гото́вить (*13*), при- (*14*)
present (gift) пода́рок
present (time) настоя́щее; (*adj.*) настоя́щий (9), тепе́решний
to present представля́ть, предста́вить (*27*)
president президе́нт (11)
press (newspapers) пре́сса (6)
pretty краси́вый (6)
price цена́ (7); **What is the p. of . . . ?** Кака́я цена́ (+ *gen.*)? (7)
prince принц (19)
probably вероя́тно (5), наве́рно(е) (18)
produce проду́кты (*pl.*) (19)

production произво́дство (27)
professor профе́ссор (*nom. pl.* -а́) (4)
to promise обеща́ть (imperf.) (*21*)
to pronounce произноси́ть, произнести́ (*19*)
pronunciation произноше́ние (19)
proposition предложе́ние (19)
to prove дока́зывать, доказа́ть (*27*)
punishment наказа́ние (27)
pupil учен.и́к, *f.* -и́ца (10)
purchase поку́пка (22)
purse су́мка (22)
to put (down), *see 24*; **to p. on** надева́ть, наде́ть (*24*)

quarter че́тверть (*f.*) (*26*)
queen короле́ва (18)
question вопро́с (6); **to ask a q.** задава́ть/зада́ть вопро́с (*13*)
to question спра́шивать (6), спроси́ть (*15*)
quick бы́стрый (8)
quiet ти́хий (8); **quieter** ти́ше (*25*)
quite совсе́м (11), дово́льно (10)

radio ра́дио (*9*); **on the r.** по ра́дио
rain дождь (*m*) (17); **It is raining.** Идёт до́ждь (17). **It began to r.** Начался́ до́ждь (22).
rare ре́дкий (16); **rarely** ре́дко (9); **more r.** ре́же (*25*)
rather (fairly) дово́льно (10)
to read чита́ть (imperf.) (5), про- (perf., 14) *or* прочéсть (perf.) (*24*); **Read!** Чита́йте! (3)
reader чита́тель, *f.* -ница (18)
reading чте́ние (8)
ready гото́в/ый (13, *23*)
real настоя́щий (9)
reason: for some r. почему́-то (12)
to recall, recollect вспомина́ть, вспо́мнить (*26*)
to receive получа́ть, получи́ть (*15*); **(receive guests)** принима́ть, приня́ть (*20*)
recently неда́вно (7)
reception приём (20)
to recognize узнава́ть, узна́ть (*21*)
record (phonograph) пласти́нка (8)
red кра́сный (8)
regards приве́т (9); **Give my r. to ....** Переда́йте от меня́ приве́т (+ *dat.*)
relative ро́дствен.ник, *f.* -ница (27)
to relax отдыха́ть (8), отдохну́ть (*21*)
relaxation о́тдых (8)
to rely on наде́яться (imperf.) на (+ *acc.*) (*19*)
to remain остава́ться (*25*)
remarkable замеча́тельный (12)
to remember по́мнить (imperf.) (*16*)
to rent снима́ть, снять (*24*)
to repeat повторя́ть, повтори́ть (*18*); **Repeat!** Повтори́те! (3)
repetition повторе́ние (18)
reply отве́т (9)
to reply отвеча́ть (9), отве́тить (*15*); **to r. to** (+ *dat.* or на + *acc.*—*15*)
report (oral) докла́д (12)
reporter журнали́ст, *f.* -ка (4)
to represent представля́ть, предста́вить (*27*)
to resemble: He resembles .... О́н похо́ж на (+ *acc.*) (23).
to respect уважа́ть (imperf. only) (27)
rest о́тдых (8)
to rest отдыха́ть (8), отдохну́ть (*21*)
restaurant рестора́н (7)
to return (*trans.*, **to give back**) возвраща́ть (imperf.), возврати́ть (perf.) *or* верну́ть (perf.); (*intrans.*, **to go/come back**) возвраща́ться, возврати́ться or верну́ться (*21*)
revolution револю́ция (12)
to rewrite перепи́сывать, переписа́ть (*15*)
rich бога́тый (10); **richer** бога́че (*25*)
to ride, *see 17, 18, 22*
right пра́вый (11, *23*); **on (to) the r.** напра́во (12), спра́ва (26); **(correct)** пра́вильный (18); прав (**of people,** *in pred. only*) (14, *23*); **r. away** сейча́с же (14); **That's r.** Э́то пра́вда (5).
to ring звони́ть (*9*), по- (*14*)
river река́ (3)
road доро́га (17)
role роль (*f.*) (12)
roof кры́ша (7)
room ко́мната (4); **hotel r.** но́мер (*12*)
ruble рубль (*m.*) (18)
rug ковёр (10)
rule пра́вило (9)
rumor слух (27)

Russia Россúя (11)
Russian рýсский (6, *20*); **R. language** рýсский язы́к (12); **in R.** по-рýсски (*5*)

sad грýстный (17), печáльный (22)
to sail, *see 24*
salad салáт (11)
saleslady продавщúца (13)
salesman продавéц (13)
salt соль (*f.*) (18)
salvation спасéние (27)
same тóт же (сáмый) (18); **the s. thing** тó же сáмое (25); **all the s. (nevertheless)** всё-таки (19); **It's all the s. to me.** Мнé всё равнó (11).
satisfied довóлен (10, *11*, *23*); **s. with** (+ *instr.*) (*11*)
Saturday суббóта (18)
sausage (bologna) колбасá (17); **(frankfurter)** сосúска (17)
to say говорúть (imperf.) (5, *8*), сказáть (perf.) (*14*)
saying поговóрка (18)
schedule расписáние (26)
scholar, scholarly учёный (*22*)
scholarship стипéндия (23)
school шкóла (3); (*adj.*) шкóльный (27)
schoolboy ученúк (18), шкóльник (23)
schoolgirl ученúца (18), шкóльница (23)
scientist учёный (*22*)
sea мóре (12)
seashore бéрег мóря (12)
seagull чáйка (26)
season врéмя гóда (13)
seat мéсто (11)
second (*adj.*) вторóй (15); **in the s. place** во-вторы́х (20)
secret секрéт (14)
secretary секретáрша (4)
to see вúдеть (*11*), у- (*21*); **to s. one another** вúдеться, у- (*19*); **go (come) to s. someone** быть у (+ *gen.*) (*10*); ходúть/идтú/пойтú к (+ *dat.*) (*17*), приходúть/прийтú к (+ *dat.*) (*18*)
to seem казáться, по- (+ *instr.*) (*19*)
seldom рéдко (9); **more s.** рéже (*25*)
-self—*see suffix* -ся (*17*); *reflexive pronoun* себя́ (*23*); *intensive pronoun* сам (14, *23*)
selfish person эгоúст, *f.* -ка (14)
to sell продавáть (*9*), продáть (*15*)
to send посылáть (9), послáть (*19*)
sentence предложéние (19)
September сентя́брь (*m.*) (23)
serious серьёзный (6)
to serve служúть (*12*)
service слýжба (14)
to set an alarm clock for . . . (по)стáвить будúльник на (+ *acc.*) (24)
seven семь (*17*, *26*)
seventeen семнáдцать (*17*, *26*)
seventh седьмóй (18)
seventy сéмьдесят (*21*, *26*)
several нéсколько (+ *gen. pl.*) (*16*, *20*)
Shakespeare Шекспúр (14)
sharp: at two o'clock s. рóвно в двá часá (16)
to shave (*trans.*) брить, по-; (*intrans.*) брúться, по- (*24*)
she онá (*2*)
sheet (of paper) лист (13)
shelf пóлка (2)
to shine (*intrans.*) светúть (imperf.) (*26*)
ship парохóд (18)
shirt рубáшка (13)
shoe ботúнок (13, *16*)
shop магазúн (8); **(small)** лáвка (25)
shore бéрег (*nom. pl.* -á) (12); **on the s.** на берегý
short корóткий (кóротко) (13); **(for) a s. time** недóлго
shorter корóче (*25*)
should: he s. . . . . Óн дóлжен (был бы) (+ *inf.*). **He s. have . . . .** Óн дóлжен был (бы) (+ *inf.*) (*8*, *9*, *24*).
to shout кричáть, крúкнуть (*21*)
to show покáзывать (9), показáть (*15*)
shower душ (24)
shut закры́т/ый (*26*)
to shut (*trans.*) закрывáть (8), закры́ть (*15*); (*intrans.*) закрывáться, закры́ться (*19*)
Siberia Сибúрь (*f.*) (12)
sick бóлен (*23*); **a s. person** больнóй (*23*); **to be s. (sometimes, often)** болéть (imperf.) (23); **to fall s.** заболéть (perf.) (*25*)
sickness болéзнь (*f.*) (23)
side сторонá (17); **on all sides** со всéх сторóн (27)

siege оса́да (27)
sight: to catch s. of уви́деть (perf.) (*21*)
sign (mark, symptom) знак (19)
to sign подпи́сывать, подписа́ть (*15*)
silly глу́пый (9)
simple просто́й (12); **simpler** про́ще (*25*)
simply про́сто (10); **more s.** про́ще (*25*)
since (after) по́сле (+ *gen.*) (*10*); **(because)** та́к как (12); **s. the time that** с тех по́р, как (21)
to sing петь, с- (*16*)
singer пев.е́ц, *f.* -и́ца (16)
single: not a s. ни оди́н (ни одного́) (*20*)
sister сестра́ (4, *13*)
to sit, be seated сиде́ть (imperf.) (*11*); **to sit at table** сиде́ть за сто̀ло́м
to sit down сади́ться, сесть (*21*); **to s. d. to table** сади́ться/се́сть за сто́л (21)
situation положе́ние (18)
six шесть (*17*, *26*)
sixteen шестна́дцать (*17*, *26*)
sixth шесто́й (18)
sixty шестьдеся́т (*21*, *26*)
size (measure) разме́р (13)
skirt ю́бка (13)
sky не́бо (16)
Slav славяни́н, *f.* славя́нка (*20*)
sleep сон (*26*)
to sleep спать (imperf.) (7, *11*); **to s. a little** поспа́ть (perf.) (*25*)
slender то́нкий (13)
slowly ме́дленно (8)
small ма́ленький (6); **smaller** ме́ньше (*25*)
smile улы́бка (27)
smoke дым (27)
to smoke кури́ть (imperf.) (*11*)
snow снег (*13*)
snowing: It's s. Идёт сне́г (17).
so так (4); (*with attributive adjs.*) тако́й (*6*); **s. far (till now)** до сих по́р (21); **s. much (many)** сто́лько (+ *gen.*) (*16*, *20*); **s. that** (та́к), чтобы (*with hypothetical mood*) (*24*); **s.-s.** та́к себе (19)
society о́бщество (20)
sock носо́к (24)
sofa дива́н (11)
soft мя́гкий (19); **softer** мя́гче (*25*)
soldier солда́т (*gen. pl.* солда́т) (*16*)
some (several) не́сколько (+ *gen. pl.*) (*16*, *20*); **(certain ones)** не́которые (*19*); **s. of my friends** не́которые из мои́х друзе́й (20); **(a quantity of)**—*partitive gen.* (*10*); **Do you want s. bread?** Вы́ хоти́те хле́ба? (*10*); **s . . . others** одни́ . . . други́е (13)
somehow ка́к-то, почему́-то (12)
someone, something, somewhere, etc., *see 22*
sometimes иногда́ (8)
son сын (4, *20*)
song пе́сня (13, *20*)
soon ско́ро (5); **as s. as** как то́лько (14)
sorry: I feel s. for him. Мне́ его́ (*acc.*) жа́ль (18).
soup суп (17)
south юг; **to the s.** на ю́г; **in the s.** на ю́ге (22)
southern ю́жный (22)
Soviet сове́тский (7); **S. Union** Сове́тский Сою́з (7)
Spaniard испа́н.ец, *f.* -ка (20)
Spanish (*adj.*) испа́нский (20); **in S.** по-испа́нски (20)
to speak говори́ть (5, *8*), по- (*25*)
speaker (public) докла́д.чик, *f.* -чица (27)
speech речь (*f.*) (24); докла́д (12); **to give a s.** произноси́ть/произнести́ ре́чь (24); (про)чита́ть ле́кцию/докла́д (12)
to spell: This word is spelled so. Э́то сло́во пи́шется та́к (19).
to spend (time) проводи́ть, провести́ (*23*); пробы́ть (perf.) (*21*)
spite: in spite of несмотря́ на (+ *acc.*) (27)
spoon ло́жка (16)
spring весна́; **(in s.)** весно́й (11); (*adj.*) весе́нний (19)
square (public) пло́щадь (*f.*) (12)
stamp ма́рка (17)
to stand стоя́ть (imperf.) (5, *11*); **to s. up** встава́ть, встать (*16*); **(to take up a standing position)** станови́ться, стать (*21*); (*trans.*—**to place standing**) ста́вить, по- (*24*)
to start (*trans.*) начина́ть (8), нача́ть (*15*) **to**

(+ *inf.*); (*intrans.*) начина́ться, нача́ться (*19*)
station ста́нция (12); **(terminal)** вокзал (17); **at the s.** на ста́нции, на вокза́ле
to stay (remain) остава́ться, оста́ться (*25*); **(live, dwell)** жить (*9*), по- (*25*) *or* про- (perf.) (*25*); **(spend time)** проводи́ть, провести́ (ча́с, ле́то, *etc.*) (*23*); **to s. at home** сиде́ть до́ма; **to s. in a hotel, etc.** остана́вливаться, останови́ться (*22*)
steak бифште́кс (18)
steppe степь (*f.*) (13)
still ещё (6); **(nevertheless)** всё-таки (19), всё-же (25)
stomach живо́т (23); желу́док
stop (bus) остано́вка (22)
to stop (*trans.*) остана́вливать, останови́ть (*22*); (*intrans.*) остана́вливаться, останови́ться (*22*); **(to cease)** перестава́ть, переста́ть (+ *inf.*) (*22*); **to s. in to see** заходи́ть, зайти́ к (+ *dat.*) (*22*)
store магази́н (8)
story расска́з (10); **(floor)** эта́ж (18)
stout то́лстый (8)
stove плита́ (24)
straight (*adv.*) пря́мо (17)
strange стра́нный (5, 6)
street у́лица (5)
to stroll гуля́ть, по- (16)
strong си́льный (21)
student студе́нт, *f.* -ка (2)
studious приле́жный (10)
study уче́ние (18); **(room)** кабине́т (5)
to study занима́ться (imperf.) (+ *instr.*) (*19*, *23*); учи́ться (imperf.) (+ *dat.*) (*23*); изуча́ть, изучи́ть (+ *acc.*) (12, *23*)
stuffy ду́шный (17)
stupid глу́пый (9)
style (fashion) мо́да (13)
subject те́ма; **on that s.** на э́ту те́му (12)
subway метро́ (*n. indecl.*); **by s.** на метро́ (12)
success успе́х (27)
such (a) тако́й (*6*)
suddenly вдруг (13)
suffering (*noun*) страда́ние (27)
sufficiently доста́точно (25)
sugar са́хар (11, *12*)
suit костю́м (6)
suitcase чемода́н (22)
summer ле́то (6); **in s.** ле́том (11); (*adj.*) ле́тний (6); **s. house** да́ча (12)
sun со́лнце (*16*)
Sunday воскресе́нье (18)
superior (*noun*) нача́льник (9); (*adj.*) ве́рхний (27)
supper у́жин (16); **to (for) s.** к у́жину; **to have s.** у́жинать, по- (16)
sure уве́рен (18, *23*); **s. of** уве́рен в (+ *loc.*) (*23*)
surely наве́рно (18)
surprise удивле́ние (22); **(a) s.** сюрпри́з
surprised удивлён (*23*)
to surround окружа́ть, окружи́ть (*27*)
to swim, *see 24*

table стол (2); **to sit down at t.** сади́ться/се́сть за сто́л (19); **to be at the t.** сиде́ть за столо́м
to take брать (imperf.), взять (perf.) (*14*); **to t. from** бра́ть/взя́ть у (+ *gen.*) (14); **(carry, transport, etc.)**—*see 22*; **to t. off** снима́ть, снять (*24*); **to t. an exam** держа́ть экза́мен (13); **to t. place (occur)** происходи́ть, произойти́ (21); **to t. part in** принима́ть уча́стие в (+ *loc.*) (21); **to t. a train** се́сть на по́езд (21); **to t. a walk** гуля́ть, по- (16)
talented тала́нтливый (9)
to talk говори́ть (5, *8*), по- (*25*); **t. to** (по) говори́ть с (+ *instr.*) (11)
talk, a (conversation) разгово́р (4)
tall высо́кий (10); **taller** вы́ше (*25*)
taste вкус (25)
taxi такси́ (*n. indecl.*) (12); **by t.** на такси́
tea чай (11, *12*)
to teach учи́ть, на- (*23*); преподава́ть (imperf.) (*23*)
teacher учи́тель (*nom. pl.* учителя́), *f.* -ница (3)
teaching преподава́ние (23)
team (sports) кома́нда (22)
telegram телегра́мма (9)
telephone телефо́н (9); **on the t.** по телефо́ну (9)

to telephone звони́ть (*9*), по- (по телефо́ну) (*14*) (+ *dat.*)
television set телеви́зор (9)
to tell (say) говори́ть (imperf.) (5, *8*), сказа́ть (perf.) (*14*); **(narrate, recount)** расска́зывать, рассказа́ть (*15*); **T. me about ....** Расскажи́те мне́ о (+ *loc.*).
temperature температу́ра (23)
ten де́сять (*17*, *26*)
tenth деся́тый (18)
tenant жил.е́ц, *f.* -и́ца (21)
terminal вокза́л; **at the t.** на вокза́ле (17)
terrible ужа́сный (13); **(frightening)** стра́шный (27)
terror у́жас (21)
textbook уче́бник (10)
than чем (or *gen.*) (*25*)
to thank благодари́ть, по- (+ *acc.*) (*18*); **t. you** спаси́бо (3); благодарю́ ва́с (18); **thanks for** спаси́бо за (+ *acc.*) (16); **many thanks** большо́е спаси́бо (10)
thankful благода́рный (18, *23*)
that (*demonstr.*) э́тот; тот (*4, 12, 20*); **T. is ...** Э́то ... (2); (*conj.*) что (*5*, *15*); (*rel. pronoun*) кото́рый (*6*); **t. which** то́, что (13); **in t. way** так (4)
the—*definite article not translated* (*2*); **t. ... t.** чем ... тем (*25*); **t. more t. better** чем бо́льше, тем лу́чше
theater теа́тр (5); **motion-picture t.** кино́ (*n. indecl.*) (12)
their, theirs их (*7*)
theme те́ма (12)
themselves, *see* **self**
then (at that time) тогда́ (10, *11*); **(next)** пото́м (*11*); **if ... t.** е́сли ... то́ (19)
there там (2); **(to) t., thither** туда́ (*17*); **from t.** отту́да (*17*); **t. is/are (pointing)** вот (*2*); **(not pointing)** есть (+ *nom.*) (*10*); **t. is/are not** нет (+ *gen.*) (*10*); **over t.** там, во́н (та́м)
therefore поэ́тому (9)
they они́ (2)
thick то́лстый (8); **thicker** то́лще (*25*)
thin (slender) то́нкий (13); **(lean)** худо́й (20); **thinner** то́ньше (*25*)
thing вещь (*f.*) (13); **(matter)** де́ло (14); **not a t.** ничего́ (не) (*8*); **The t. is that ....** Де́ло в то́м, что ... (14). **How are things?** Ка́к дела́?
to think ду́мать (5, 8), по- (14)
third тре́тий (*18*)
thirteen трина́дцать (*17*, *26*)
thirty три́дцать (*21*, *26*)
this (*demonstr.*) э́тот (*4*, *12*, *20*); **t. is ...** э́то ... (*2*); **in t. way** так (4); **(in) t. year** в э́том году́ (12)
though хотя́ (и) (10)
thought мысль (*f.*) (25)
thousand ты́сяча (*26*)
three три (*10*, *26*)
throat го́рло (23)
to throw броса́ть, бро́сить (*24*)
Thursday четве́рг (18)
thus так (4)
to tick ти́кать (imperf.) (24)
ticket биле́т (17)
till (*prep.*) до (+ *gen.*) (10); (*conj.*) пока́ ... не (*21*); **t. now** до сих по́р (21)
time вре́мя (*12*, *20*); **(occasion)** раз (*gen. pl.* раз) (16); **for the first t.** в пе́рвый ра́з (16); **many times** мно́го ра́з (16); **at that t.** в то́ вре́мя (17); **at one t.** одно́ вре́мя; **on t.** во́время (24); **at times** иногда́ (8); **for a long t.** до́лго (11), надо́лго (22); **for some t.** не́которое вре́мя (14); **a long t. ago** давно́ (7); **at what t.?** в кото́ром часу́? (16); **at any t.** когда́-либо (25); **all the t.** всё вре́мя (17); **I'm having a good t.** Мне́ ве́село (20). **It's t. to ....** Пора́ (+ *dat. and inf.*) (17); **It's high t. to ....** Давно́ пора́ (+ *inf.*). **What t. is it?** Кото́рый ча́с? (16)
timetable (train) расписа́ние поездо́в (26)
tired: to grow t. устава́ть,у ста́ть; **to be t.**—*past tense of* уста́ть (21)
title назва́ние (7); **What is the t. of ...?** Ка́к назва́ние (+ *gen.*) (7)
to—*dative case* (*9*); в (+ *acc.*); на (+ *acc.*); к (+ *dat.*) (*17*, *22*); **t. the house of** к (+ *dat.*) (*17*)
today сего́дня (5); **t.'s** сего́дняшний (6)
together вме́сте (5)
tomorrow за́втра (10); **day after t.** послеза́втра (17)
tongue язы́к (12)

to worry беспоко́иться (imperf.) (*24*)
worse ху́же (23, *25*), ху́дший (*25*); **I feel w.** Мне́ ху́же (23); **worst** (са́мый) ху́дший (*25*); **at the w.** в ху́дшем слу́чае (25)
to worship обожа́ть (imperf.) (23)
worth, to be сто́ить (imperf.) (*16*)
would—*future tense or hypothetical mood* (*15, 24*); **He w. not ....** О́н не хоте́л (+ *inf.*) (10)
to wound ра́нить (imperf. and perf.) (27)
to write писа́ть (5, *9*), на- (*14*); **to w. down** запи́сывать, записа́ть (*15*)
writer писа́тель, *f.* -ница (5)
writing писа́ние (14)
wrong непра́в (**of persons,** *in pred. only*) (14); **(of things)** непра́вильно

yard двор (16)
year год (*12*); **(in) this y.** в э́том году́; **(in) last y.** в про́шлом году́ (12); **(in) next y.** в бу́дущем году́ (15)
yellow жёлтый (11)
yes да (2)
yesterday вчера́ (5); **y.'s** вчера́шний (6); **day before y.** позавчера́ (18), тре́тьего дня́ (21)
yet ещё (6); **not y.** ещё не (*with pred.*); ещё не́т (*final in sentence*) (16)
you ты, вы (*2*); *indefinite* (= *one*), *2nd pers. sing. verb* (*20*)
young молодо́й (6); **younger** мла́дший (8, *25*), мла́дше, моло́же (*25*); **youngest** (са́мый) мла́дший (*25*)
your, yours твой; ваш (*4, 12, 20*)
yourself, *see* **self**
youth мо́лодость (*f.*) (27)

zero ноль (*m.*), нуль (*m.*) (*26*)

INDEX

In general, Russian and English vocabulary listings have not been included in this index; for them the student should consult the vocabularies, which give the relevant unit numbers.

The abbreviation *n.* used below denotes a reference to a footnote.

ABCDEFGHIJ 06987654
PRINTED IN THE UNITED STATES OF AMERICA